HISTORIC HOUSES
CASTLES & GARDENS

THE ORIGINAL GUIDE TO THE TREASURES OF GREAT BRITAIN & IRELAND

Sudeley Castle, Gloucestershire
Winner Christie's / HHA Garden of the Year Award presented in 1997

a
JOHANSENS
publication

1

ARUNDEL CASTLE

Family home of the Dukes of Norfolk
For details see West Sussex Section

Introduction from the Editor

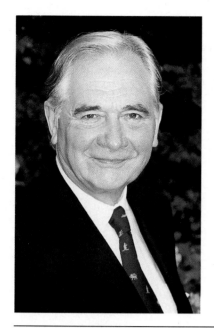

This edition of Historic Houses, Castles and Gardens takes a timely step into the near future – for the first time there are details of over sixty properties in Continental Europe in addition to the traditional array representing the national heritage of Great Britain and Ireland.

Through the ages, the history of Europe has been a chronicle of cultural and material development, albeit often motivated by rivalry. In the realm of architecture especially it is easy to see how international influences have altered fashion and design in buildings and gardens in Great Britain.

Historic Houses, Castles and Gardens 1998 reflects the diversity of our national heritage. As we move towards the next millennium, historic properties are not only places of interest on show. Today, they are offering their visitors a wider range of facilities and activities than ever before. Whether you are organising a special event or wedding, want to attend a concert, or are looking for local accommodation, Historic Houses, Castles and Gardens presents you with a broad and varied selection of what to see, what to do and where to stay.

I do hope that this, the 44th edition of Historic Houses, Castles and Gardens, will lead you to many interesting new discoveries as well as to the familiar landmarks of our heritage.

Rodney Exton

Rodney Exton

NPI

PROVIDING PENSIONS SINCE 1835

Regulated by the Personal Investment Authority

NPI and Johansens

The perfect partnership for preserving Britain's Heritage

In the pages of this Johansens Guide you will find all that is important about this country's heritage, and why it is so vital too, that our heritage is saved for the generations to come.

NPI is one of this country's largest pensions specialists, and it has been helping to secure people's futures for over 160 years now.

So it's no surprise that NPI is just as keen on securing the heritage of Britain, which makes NPI a perfect preferred partner with Johansens, publishing Historic Houses, Castles & Gardens 1998.

NPI is also the power behind the National Heritage Awards, the only awards scheme which allows you to vote for your favourite heritage property. The 1997 overall winner was the magnificent Brodsworth Hall and voting for the 1998 Awards is now starting. For your voting form, just call NPI on 01892 705342 and we'll add your name to our mailing list. It's your chance to reward those properties which, through their efforts to make them more enjoyable and accessible, are making real progress to secure Britain's unique heritage for the future.

And talking about securing futures, you may well find it worthwhile to get in touch with NPI. NPI is the pensions and retirement specialist, and has a vast range of investment products specifically designed with retirement in mind. From this range, you can be sure that between NPI and yourself, you will find the right kind of pension plan for you.

For more information about NPI, have a word with your Financial Adviser. Alternatively, if you would like to talk to someone from NPI about receiving retirement planning advice, please call NPI Membership Services on 0800 174192.

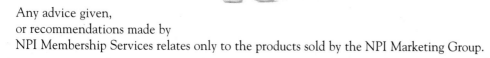

Any advice given, or recommendations made by NPI Membership Services relates only to the products sold by the NPI Marketing Group.

THE GARDENS AT
HATFIELD HOUSE Hertfordshire

"There are nearly 14 acres of formal and informal gardens dating back to the late 15th century. From 1609 to 1611 John Tradescant the Elder laid out and planted the gardens for Robert Cecil, the builder of the House. Today the gardens, much embellished in the last years, contain many of the same plants growing in knot gardens typical of the period, arranged in the court of the 15th century Palace where Queen Elizabeth I spent much of her childhood. There are herb and sweet gardens, a parterre of herbaceous plants and roses, fountains, statuary and a foot maze or labyrinth, the whole enclosed in ancient rose-brick walls, topiaried yews, holly and pleached limes.

A wilderness garden, planted with forest and ornamental trees, blossoms in the spring with crabs, cherries, magnolias and rhododendrons underplanted with many flowers and bulbs, the whole providing colour and interest (for there are many rare and unusual plants) for all seasons."
"Photographs by Mick Hales, Garry Rogers and Jeremy Whitaker."

"I feel at home here as I gaze down and respond to the feeling of total delight which it gives me . . ." Sir Roy Strong

"Hatfield's gardens are the most completely beautiful and fit for their purpose of any great house in England." "Tradescant" of the RHS Journal.

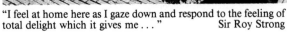

FOR DETAILS SEE HERTFORDSHIRE SECTION

How to use this guide

If you want to identify a historic house, castle or garden, whose name you already know, look for it in the Index of all properties from page 283.

If you want to find a historic house, castle or garden in a particular county or area you can:
• Turn to the maps at the back of the book
• Look through the guide for the county you require
Each county is in alphabetical order. The properties are then listed alphabetically wherever possible. The maps cover the counties of England, Ireland, Scotland and Wales. Each historic house, castle and garden is clearly named and marked on these maps. Properties in Belgium, France and Germany have their approximate positions labelled on the illustrated maps in their introductions.

Starting from page 258 there are a number of properties listed in certain categories: garden specialists, weddings, art collections, teas, open all year, conference facilities and accommodation.

To find somewhere local to stay, a full listing of Johansens recommended hotels, country houses and inns are included in county order on page 272.

Editor:	Rodney Exton
Copy Editor:	Yasmin Razak
Promotions Editor:	Fiona Patrick
Sales Executive:	Juliette Dearlove
Production Manager:	Daniel Barnett
Production Controller:	Kevin Bradbrook
Designer:	Michael Tompsett
Sales & Marketing Manager:	Laurent Martinez
Marketing Executive:	Emma Woods
Marketing–Sales Executive:	Babita Sareen
Map Illustrations:	Linda Clark
Publisher:	Phoebe Hobby
Managing Director:	Andrew Warren

Johansens, 175-179 St John Sreet, London EC1V 4RP
Tel: 0171 490 3090 Fax: 0171 490 2538

Find Johansens on the Internet at : http://www.johansen.com

Copyright © 1998 Johansens Ltd.
a subsidiary of the Daily Mail and General Trust plc
ISBN 1 860 175066
Printed in England by St Ives plc
Colour origination by Catalyst Creative Imaging
Distributed in the UK and Europe by Biblios PDS Ltd, Partridge Green, West Sussex, RH13 8LD (bookstores) and Johnsons International Media Services Ltd (direct sales). In North America by general sales agent: ETL Group, New York, NY (direct sales) and The Cimino Publishing Group, INC. New York (bookstores). In Australia and New Zealand by Bookwise International, Findon, South Australia.

Key to Symbols

❦	The National Trust
♔	The National Trust for Scotland
⌂	Historic Scotland
✠	English Heritage
❀	CADW
⌂	Historic Houses Association
▨	HITHA
♣	Park
✿	Garden
☕	Refreshments
⚠	Childrens Playground
⛺	Accommodation Available
✕	Meals Available
⊓	Picnic Area
♪	Wedding Licence
♿	Disabled Access
👫	Guided Tours
⬦	Gift Shop
❀	Nurseries – Plants for Sale
🎭	Live Entertainment
Ⓐ	House by Appointment Only
👻	Haunted
Ⓒ	Conference Facilities
▣	Privilege Card Accepted

The Duke and Duchess of Northumberland

The 12th Duke and Duchess of Northumberland were interviewed at their family home, Alnwick Castle 'Windsor of the North', by Sarah Tucker. The castle has been in the family since the 14th century, bought by the Bishop of Durham from one of the beneficiaries of the trust of which he was the Executive. The walled gardens are in the process of undergoing extensive renovation.

Alnwick Castle is the principal seat of the Duke of Northumberland and the Percy family. Its early history is almost certainly connected with ancient Romans, Britons and Saxons. It was Yvo de Vesci, the first Norman Baron of Alnwick, who erected the earliest parts of the present castle around 1100. In 1309 Sir Henry de Percy became the owner of the Barony of Alnwick and set about the restoration of the castle with a view to converting it into a stronghold fit to maintain itself in the warfare of the period.

The early Percys maintained Alnwick Castle as a forward base for the centuries of border warfare with Scotland, initiated by Edward I and ending with the Union of the Crowns in 1603. Henry, the 2nd Baron Percy, continued the restoration of the castle which his father had begun.

After the Union, the castle fell into decay and, by the late 17th century, it was almost a ruin although it continued to be the residence of the baronial officials. In the 18th century, the 6th Duke of Somerset repaired and fitted up a portion of the castle for his residence. His son, the 7th Duke of Somerset, frequently stayed at Alnwick during the reign of George II. He was the first of his family to reside there after an absence of over 100 years. His only daughter, Elizabeth, who was heir to the Barony and the Northumberland estates, married Sir Hugh Smithson, a Yorkshire baronet. In 1750 Smithson reorganised the administration of the estates and introduced up to date methods of farming, equipment and management; he also planted large areas with trees. In a few years, by his business capacity, energy and enterprise, he transformed the appearance of the countryside around Alnwick. In 1755, Smithson and his wife commenced the rebuilding of Alnwick Castle. The architect was the celebrated Robert Adam, who adopted the style generally known as 'Gingerbread' or 'Strawberry Hill' Gothic.

Sir Hugh Smithson, who was reputed to be the most handsome man in England at the time, was a close friend and supporter of King George III, serving him in 1763 as Lord Lieutenant of Ireland. George III created Smithson Earl and later Duke of Northumberland (1763). An amusing anecdote of the time relates that the new Duke suggested to the King that he was the only Northumberland never to have received the Order of the Garter, to which the King replied that 'only a Smithson would ask for the Garter', implying that a Percy would not. The Duke's children took the Percy name which has remained with their descendants ever since.

Algernon, 4th Duke of Northumberland, served in the Navy during the Napoleonic wars and retired with the rank of Admiral. He travelled extensively in Africa and the near East and was a liberal patron of the arts and sciences, especially archaeology. He rebuilt most of the farmhouses and cottages on his estate and when this work was finished he set about another complete restoration of Alnwick Castle. The work began in 1855 under the direction of Salvin, whilst the interior decoration was entrusted to a celebrated Italian architect and archaeologist, Canina. Much of what is seen now at Alnwick was done during this restoration. The 4th Duke died in 1865, without enjoying the full splendour of the work he had instigated, which was completed during the lifetime of the 6th Duke.

I asked His Grace why visitors refer to Alnwick as the 'Windsor of the North'. 'The epithet became popularly associated with the building at

about the time of its mid-nineteenth century restoration. It emphasised the scale and magnificence of the restored castle. It was similar in size to Windsor and stood second to it as the largest inhabited castle in the country. The term also seeks to assert that in terms of the splendour of its castle, the north was a match for the south'.

I then asked if His Grace had a favourite room or piece of furniture at Alnwick. 'There are some beautiful pieces in the collection, and it is hard to chose a favourite. I love the Claude Lorraine in the Guard Chamber, which displays the most beautiful sunset scene. I hadn't noticed until recently, that someone (probably one of my aunts as a child) had carefully painted a beard and spectacles over one of the figures in the foreground. You have to look closely to see it, and though it is undoubtedly an act of vandalism, it does demonstrate that Alnwick has always been a family home, never a museum.

Another of my favourite pieces is the Canaletto of Northumberland House in the Strand, which was demolished in the late nineteenth century to make way for Charing Cross Road. The lion on the roof used to face Buckingham Palace, but the then Duke felt he had been slighted by the King, so he turned the lion around as a protest. The Dobson in the Music Room is another favourite. It shows the despair of the painter and two royalist compatriots after the civil war, and is a wonderful character portrait.

His Grace continued 'Without a doubt, my favourite room is the Library, not just because of the wonderful books, but because it is a beautiful and very comfortable room. The oak bookcases, inlaid with maple, the ceiling depicting history, science, painting and poetry, the chimney pieces inlaid in white marble and the busts of Shakespeare, Newton and Bacon are of the finest quality, but when the house is closed to the public, it becomes a real family room and whether there are two or twenty people in it, it still retains a warm and cosy atmosphere.

His Grace was born in one of the bedrooms at Alnwick and brought up there, although he only returned to live in the castle with his wife and four children two years ago. 'As a child you don't really appreciate your surroundings and it's only when you're grown up you fully understand what's going on, that this place actually comes to life. My children are probably in slightly the same boat as me when I was growing up at Alnwick and they're not really appreciative of the contents yet – but that will come. I do know they enjoy it here, they love it.'

Their Graces are also in the process of renovating the gardens at Alnwick and Her Grace, the Duchess of Northumberland, is presently managing the design herself to ensure that the walled garden, which should be complete by the Millennium, acts as a public park for the

Two of the Duke's favourite peices from his collection.
Top: A beautiful sunset scene by Claude Lorraine
Bottom: Northumberland House by Canaletto
Below facing page: The Library at Alnwick Castle

people of Alnwick as well as visitors from further afield.

Her Grace explained to me how the missing link with Alnwick – at the moment – was the gardens. 'Everything at Alnwick is in quite good condition – the castle, the park, the grounds – but work was needed to be done on the gardens when we arrived. You can still see the old framework – all the old walls are there. Beautifully landscaped and wonderful terracing. I am a very keen gardener, although no expert by any means, but I will be co-ordinating the design. I plan to create a modern, new garden for the 21st century, using the very best European designers and architects. When the garden was given to me to develop I had a very definite direction of where the garden was going but I could never have done it by myself. So my job is to find the right people and I stuck with that idea until I found the people I was happy with'.

Whilst the landscape around the castle was designed by Capability Brown, the gardens themselves have evolved over hundreds of years according to the whims of the different generations. Since the war, the formal gardens have dwindled to dereliction, although the old walls and structure remain. The project will be run within a charitable trust and will be open to the public all year round, adding a new and exciting dimension to castle visitors.

Her Grace continued, 'We're starting from scratch. The area is rather wild at the moment but has incredible potential which we want to realise. In every area of the garden we consider different elements which appeal to children, so for example, waterworks musn't be too dangerous and there must be certain areas where children can play and you know its going to be safe'.

Following a visit to Padova in Italy, Her Grace discovered the delights of a 'poison garden'. School groups can be taught about the gruesome side of gardening – how arrows were tipped with poison centuries ago to give the enemy a slow and painful death and how some plants, conversely, are able to cure life threatening diseases.

Her Grace has also considered the blind when co-ordinating the project. 'We're trying to make the garden appeal to everybody so we thought we'd try to make the water work for us here – make the water falls sound unusual and special – introducing different types of water. It's amazing what you can make water do. Jumping over hedges, through hedges, even through hoops – stopping in mid air and jumping through another hoop. We will have signs in Braille and use plants with interesting and contrasting textures which people would be able to touch'.

Employing designers Jacques and Peter Wirtz, to develop the structure of the garden and the overall design, Her Grace says. 'Jacques

take approximately 18 months to complete, bringing in a team of fifty who will help in building a pavilion, installing the waterworks, putting in the pumping, the lighting and the planting, among numerous other tasks.

'I want visitors to the garden – in particular those who live in Alnwick – to think of it as their garden. To use it and spend afternoons sitting around the waterworks, picnicking or reading a book. Not feeling they have to be great gardening experts to appreciate the gardens. I want to create something beautiful for people to come and sit in' Her Grace explains. 'I believe there will be those who visit Alnwick for the castle and are happiest looking round the Staterooms and appreciate the furnishings and history. And there will be those who enjoy the fresh air and would prefer to walk through the gardens and simply enjoy the scenery'.

'I think the gardens will be totally unique to the UK. The project is on such a grand scale, using talents from America and the European continent, using technology to enhance the beauty of nature, with taste. I think this will be a real challenge'.

The Duchess chose designers, planters and landscape artists from the European continent by chance rather

The impressive grounds of Alnwick Castle

and Peter work well with clipped trees and hedging. This is their speciality. And I know the garden will look fantastic for twelve months of the year. I think its such a fantastic setting here, it would have been so easy to make it look special only in the summer by planting fairly ordinary herbaceous borders. But to make it look wonderful in the winter – in the frost, the drizzle, the mist, was the real test and this is the forte of Jacques and Peter Wirtz. They enjoy working with trees which are clipped in an unusual way – using very sharply defined shapes'

Louis Benech from France, is being commissioned as the planter. 'Louis is a great plants man, who plants in drifts from the German style of gardening, so there isn't the uniformity you may find in other gardens in England. It's a sort of sensation more than a structure with the planting. I hope the planting will soften the architecture and enhance it for the five greyest months of the year'.

A water garden is planned in the design of the garden to entertain the children. 'I've seen waterworks where its all done with technology and pressure points and when the children reach this door of water, which looks just like a wall of water, the wall parts and falls into two curtains. I will also have an area with bubbling mud. I've seen it at a butterfly house in Edinburgh and they do it all with pipes underneath which blow hot air through to the surface so the area appears almost like a geyser. My children are fascinated by the idea and I think all children will be'.

The top garden which is also within a wall, through three stone arches will be a working fruit and vegetable garden and Their Graces hope to grow every sort of fruit – resembling a very old pottage.

Her Grace needs £10 million in sponsorship for the project which will

than by intention. 'I did look in England for designers originally but after initial research I didn't ever think I would be able to find a working team here. Plus the garden itself was so Italian in style that it wasn't really suited to traditional English garden design. So by chance I have this European team and I'm told it will be the first truly European garden – so its a great boost for this country and especially the north east to have such a project here'.

Her Grace adds finally, 'One of the criticisms that has been put my way is that I have gone to Europe and haven't used an English team to design the gardens. But I believe we can learn a lot from fresh influences. After all, the local carving school in Alnwick was only formed as a result of Salvin bringing his master craftsmen with him when he redesigned the interiors of the castle in 1850. We have a wonderful opportunity to learn from these European designers, who will perhaps open our eyes to another direction in garden design in this country'.

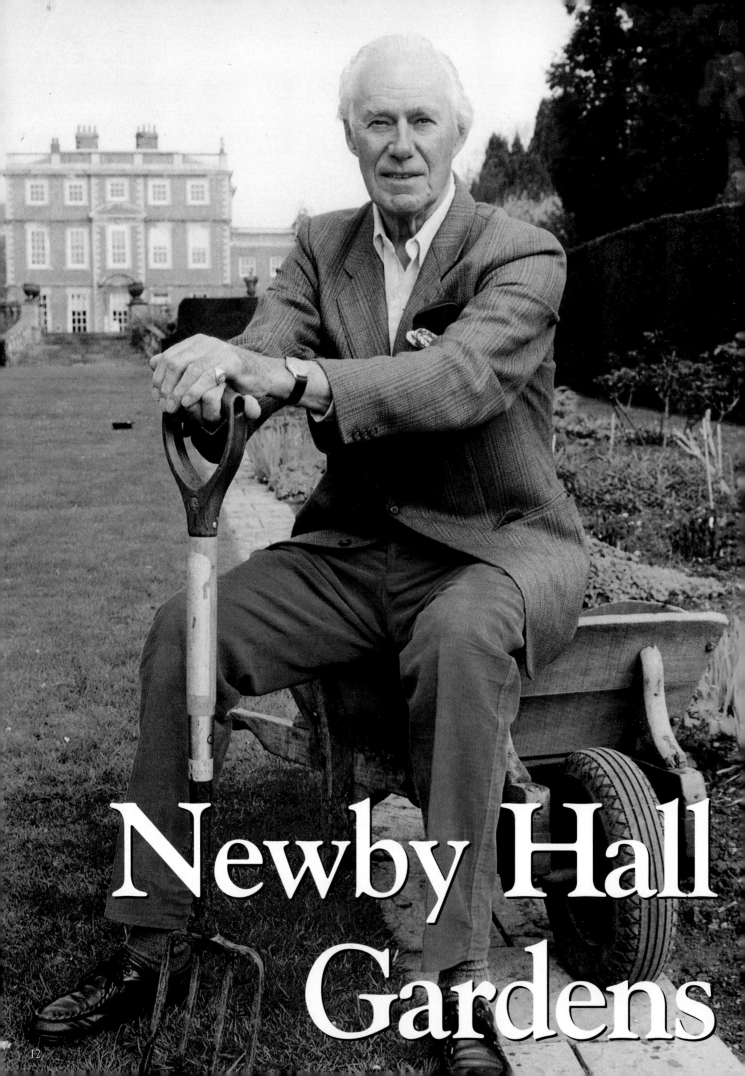

Newby Hall Gardens

'The 45 acre gardens were largely designed by my father between 1921 and 1977 when he died. Before his time there were two Victorian Parterre Gardens to the south and west of the house, an imposing Statue Walk crossing the south front, an impressive Rock Garden designed by Ellen Willmott and a few clumps of large trees. The rest was grass and the wind blew through mainly from the south and west.

Fortunately for Newby my father had an unerring eye for perspective and proportion and he was not in a hurry. Shelter belts had to be planted to keep out the wind and while they were growing he turned the grassy areas into a 9 hole golf course and nearer the river a croquet lawn and tennis court, much to the delight of his family! Meanwhile his plans were taking shape on paper.....

The planting really began circa 1930 with the now famous Herbaceous Borders backed by hedges of yew forming the main axis down to the River Ure. Off this axis he designed a series of formal gardens, each to provide colour and interest for successive periods of the season. In this design he was undoubtedly influenced by Hidcote.

When we arrived at Newby in 1978 the Gardens had deteriorated seriously as gardens rapidly can. Luckily I have studied gardening most of my life and my wife is equally keen with a sensitive eye for colour and form. We proceeded to simplify the planting scheme for ease of maintenance: we also wanted to make the Gardens more romantic by introducing new vistas, glades, fountains and a Water Garden with many other new features. Above all we planted many beautiful trees, shrubs and rare plants. In 1986 we were proud to receive the Christies / HHA Garden of the Year award and in 1988 we were approved to hold the National Collection of Dogwoods. We are prouder still that the gardens now give so much pleasure to over 100,000 visitors each year.'

Written by Robin Compton (left), the owner of Newby Hall

Above: Newby Hall Gardens, a marvellous orgy of colour
Left: Robin Compton, owner of Newby Hall
Below: The Water Garden

False teeth and other curiosities...

Eric Knowles is best known for his appearances on BBC1's Antiques Road show and Going for a Song, where his knowledge and experience have made many an unsuspecting collector aware of the market value of the heirloom which has been passed down through the family, or has been left to collect dust until his judgement. Mr Knowles is also a director of Bonhams, the London auctioneers and is the resident antiques expert on Radio 2's Jimmy Young programme once a month.

He spoke to Sarah Tucker about how he became interested in antiques and where to find some of the most unusual collections in the historic houses of Great Britain.

'I became interested in antiques probably around the age of six or seven when I was taken to our local museum which was this wonderful country house. What made the visit even more exciting for me as a child was that it had battlements – and even more exciting than that, – dungeons. It was a wonderful Tudor building which really used to set my imagination racing.

My parents used to take me to York Castle and Clitheroe –

Eric Knowles is best known for his appearances on BBC1's Antiques Road show and Going for a Song, where his knowledge and experience have made many an unsuspecting collector aware of the market value of the heirloom which has been passed down through the family, or has been left to collect dust until his judgement. Mr Knowles is also a director of Bonhams, the London auctioneers and is the resident antiques expert on Radio 2's Jimmy Young programme once a month.

He spoke to Sarah Tucker about how he became interested in antiques and where to find some of the most unusual collections in the historic houses of Great Britain.

'I became interested in antiques probably around the age of six or seven when I was taken to our local museum which was this wonderful country house. What made the visit even more exciting for me as a child was that it had battlements – and even more exciting than that, – dungeons. It was a wonderful Tudor building which really used to set my imagination racing.

My parents used to take me to York Castle and Clitheroe – both places I loved to visit for the drama of the occasion. I grew up in a part of the north which has its fair share of great houses and castles. But really I think it was my grandmother's passion for junk shops which first ignited my fascination for antiques. Her passion for antiques rubbed off on me. I started watching 'Going for a Song' each Sunday afternoon, where I was joined by the rest of the family. We all used to join in and write down our prices to what we thought the answers were. It wasn't until then that I became aware of the fact that antiques are for everybody – not just the elite minority.

I have also always been a collector. I used to collect anything, but my current interest is reference books. I see a reference book, no matter how obscure and know I will find a use for it. I soak up knowledge and information like a complete sponge, which is extremely useful, if not vital in my position. I recently collected reference books on wild flowers, which have enabled me to talk with more flair and detail about floral decorations on antique vases, or featured in paintings. I've even collected a book on false teeth, which proved invaluable when someone presented me with what were purported to be George Washington's false teeth. I was able to determine that they were not, with help from this book and a local dentistry expert. If they had been the President's false teeth, they would have been very valuable indeed.

To do what I do, I believe you need a 'good eye' which is mainly instinctive and can be only partially learnt. You can tell the difference between good lacquer and bad lacquer on a vase, good ivory and bad ivory.

One of my favourite historic houses is Leighton House in Holland Park, London where you can view wonderful De Morgan, and Standen, the Philip Webb house in Sussex. Both contain wonderful examples of arts and crafts. My specialisms are art nouveau, art deco and the 18th and 19th century and very few big houses contain examples of this period but these two properties do. I'm still looking for more.

Who's been sleeping in my (historic) bed?

Above & Right: Unique Chinese Chippendale Day Beds in the Drawing Room of Stanway, Gloucestershire.

It is the social history and its associations with a house that make a bed such a fascinating subject of interest. While those on display may no longer be slept in they continue to be a focus of attention. Beds are objects with which people can easily identify and almost all visitors are interested to know who slept in them. Discovering the State beds which have literally been 'made' in the anticipation of royalty; marriage beds built for the first night of nuptials, mourning beds, travelling beds and even a bed of nails are among some of the more unexpected surprises found at the historic houses and castles around the British Isles.

The Tower of London even has a bed, possibly dating from the early 17th century, but I presume those invited to the Tower had little use of a bed and invariably were not able to sleep anyway.

Stanway House has magnificent Chinese Chippendale Day Beds, on view in one of Britain's most romantic manor houses. Circa 1755, they were made in the Chinese style for Francis Charteris, later the 7th Earl of Wemyss for Amisfield House, East Lothian and later brought to Stanway. Politicians who have slept here include the Earl of Balfour, Lord Curzon, Sir Henry Cust, and from the world of literature H G Wells, L P Hartley and Sir James Barrie who introduced a parlour game which for some reason has resulted in five postage stamps stuck to the ceiling of the Great Hall. Princess Margaret has also slept here.

At **Sudeley Castle** in Gloucestershire, Richard III, Queen Catherine Parr (who lived at Sudeley), Lady Jane Grey, Elizabeth I and Charles I all slept here. After the Civil War the castle fell into considerable decay and many of the contents were stolen. The bed slept in by Charles I was later found in a farmhouse in a nearby village.

Then there are of course, more scandalous beds. Sir Edward Hulse, Baronet and owner of the beautiful **Breamore House**, who lives there still today tells me a Queen Anne bed situated in The Blue Bedroom has been slept in by none other than HRH Queen Mary, Rudyard Kipling and HRH The Duke of Windsor and Wallis Simpson. HRH The Prince Regent has slept in another at Breamore. And would you be interested to hear about a Cardinal at **Ugbrooke Park**? Hugh Charles, 7th Lord Clifford of Chudleigh, born in 1790, married Mary Lucy Weld in 1819. Mary Lucy was the daughter of Thomas and Lucy Weld of Lulworth Castle, Dorset. Thomas Weld lost his wife in 1815 and when his only child married Hugh Charles Clifford he was at liberty to take holy orders and in due course became first a Bishop and then was admitted to the College of Cardinals in 1830. The Clifford family spent much time in Rome and naturally, Cardinal Weld was a regular visitor to Ugbrooke Park in Chudleigh, Devon, when he came to stay with his daughter and grandchildren. The 'Cardinal's Room' and four poster bed, vestments, travelling case and several paintings may be seen by present day visitors to Ugbrooke.

No beds at **Bramall Hall** are original to the house, however, the one most people seem to always remember and associate with the Hall is the travelling bed. Even though it is called a travelling bed with stories that is may have had wheels attached and been horse drawn to wherever it was needed or that it was taken apart and then put into a cart and re-erected in situ, this cannot be verified. Made in its present form in the Victorian period by somebody who appreciated and collected timber of different periods and had it made into a an interesting item of furniture, more as a curiosity than as a functional piece, it is quite well sprung, so it could have been slept in.

Other historic beds hide dark secrets. The bed at **Traquair Castle**, where Mary Queen of Scots slept, for example, had previously been transformed into a Mourning Bed. It was the custom, when the head of a great family died, to lay his body on a bed hung with black and to hang the walls of the bedchamber with black velvet. Friends and relatives would come to pay their respects to the deceased and his family. After the funeral the widow slept in the bed during the period of mourning. The bed had been transformed into 'mourning' by simply painting over the original yellow hangings with a black water soluble paint. It was still in this sad livery when present owner Mr Francis Maxwell Stuart, the present Laird's father, discovered glimpses of the original yellow underneath and painstakingly restored it to its former glowing colour.

One of the most famous beds in the British Isles is in **Osborne House**, in the Isle of Wight. Queen Victoria slept here until not long before her death in January 1901, but she actually died on a small couch bed situated at the foot of the double one she had shared with Prince Albert.

Sherborne Castle was built by Sir Walter Raleigh in 1594 and his bedchamber is still one of the principal rooms of the house. It remained in use as a bedroom until the second World War. William of Orange stayed three nights at Sherborne in November 1688 and slept in this room. While he was at Sherborne he received the support of the navy and part of the army commanded by John Churchill (later Duke of Marlborough) and he and his wife Mary were jointly offered the crown by parliament in London three months later.

A bed to be found at **Doddington Hall** in Lincoln, has had some very interesting and colourful residents. Dating from 1720, the four poster bed in the Tiger Room, is covered in the original magnificent Spitalfield silk hangings which survive in beautiful condition. This bed was originally made for the house of Seaton Delaval in Northumberland, and brought here by the Delaval family in 1804. While at Seaton Delaval it was slept in by the notorious Butcher Cumberland, Duke of Cumberland brother of the King. Cumberland was at the time on his way north to surpress the 1745 Scottish Rebellion which culminated in the Battle of Culloden. The Duke himself was only five foot high but weighed 23 stone, and the bed steps beside this four poster bed would have been as essential part of equipment.

The Hathaway Bed in one of the bedchambers at **Anne Hathaway's Cottage** at Shottery was purchased by the Trust from a descendent of the Hathaway family, Mary Baker, when the property was purchased by the Shakespearean Trust in 1892. The bed was obviously in the possession of the family for some time, although it is uncertain whether William Shakespeare's wife, Anne Hathaway ever slept in it (at least in its present form). Interestingly in his will

of 1616, William Shakespeare left his wife his 'second best bed' – and it is possible this is the marital bed. It is not known to whom he bestowed his best bed.

For more unusual beds visit **Temple Newsam House** in Leeds. The Duke and Duchess of York slept here in 1894, and Henry Stewart, Lord Darnley, father of James I also slept here 350 years earlier – but it is the type of beds on display which inspire curiosity. There is a footman's bed from Raby Castle with bracketed extension for an extra tall footman. A bed which folds up into a box which appears then to be a blanket chest, c1760 – originating from Nostell Priory, and a Canopy bed with single posts in the centre of the head and footboard c1835–40, from Raby Castle. It is unusual to have two central posts, rather than corner posts. People obviously thought highly of their beds and bedrooms. A bed dating from 1530 which was removed from **Bretton Hall** in Wakefield, together with the panelling and furnishings of the entire bedroom, was allegedly slept in by Henry VIII.

Top left: State Bed, by J-B II Tilliard, Temple Newsam House, Leeds. Above: The Cardinal's Room, Ugbrooke Park, Devon.

Baronet Sir Humphry Wakefield's **Chillingham Castle** in Northumberland has some unexpected surprises for visitors quite apart from its one Royal bed made for King William III in his Kimbolton Castle. Kimbolton Castle is no more but the bed, battered but beautiful with its needlework birds and flowers, soldiers on. In medieval days it was Henry II or Edward I, Hammer of the Scots, who slept in Chillingham's rough set beds resting between battles. Today visitors are invited to sleep in a Russian bed from the palace of a 19th century Prince Warantzov relation. The Torture Chamber, an iron bed of nails, formerly at Nuremberg in Germany, tells of less happy days.

Hatfield House, as we know it today, was built in 1607 by Robert Cecil, Chief Minister to James I, taking four years to complete. Before talking about the gardens, I asked Lady Salisbury what she particularly liked about Hatfield House. 'Apart from its beauty, the house is a very friendly old place. Although it is enormous and many of the rooms are very grand, it is still a cosy house, partly due, I believe, to the characteristics of a Jacobean house. Its rose brick walls without and its wood clad walls within give it a certain intimacy and warmth that perhaps the classical houses of a later century lack. They are very impressive but there is a certain coldness about their classical beauty. To my mind, earlier Stuart houses in general have a more comfortable feeling about them. I've

Harmony at Hatfield House

always been very fond of the early houses, having lived in one all my married life'.

The house has Courts to the north and the south and gardens on the east and west with the Wilderness Gardens beyond the formal gardens. Robert Cecil was a keen gardener and spared no expense to

Above: Lord and Lady Salisbury. Top Right: Old Palace & Knot Garden

create a garden which would complement his new house, employing the Frenchman Salaman de Caux to create formal gardens around it.

Lady Salisbury explained further, 'Since we came to live here after my father-in-law's death in 1972, we have tried to bring the gardens

more into harmony with the house, which itself has so little changed since it was built. The gardens as originally designed, were enclosed by brick walls and filled with statues, garden houses, fountains and pavilions and amongst other things, there was a great water parterre. Alas, there are no plans of this work by Salaman de Caux but I have tried to reconstruct what I felt in my mind the gardens might have looked like by studying plans of early 17th century gardens and doing much research in garden books of the period as well as being able to read a description of part of the gardens written by a Frenchman who visited the house in the 17th century. Of course, one can never recreate exactly nor accurately the same aspect but through these studies, I have tried to get a real feel of what Jacobean gardens might have been like. I hope that a feeling of intimacy between the house and the garden has developed and that there may now be harmony between the two'. The gardens flourished for more than fifty years but towards the end of the 17th century, a decline set in and they withered, decayed and slept for a century. The interests of the Lady Salisbury at that time, wife of the 1st Marquess, were in hunting and gambling and not gardening and she swept away the original gardens and brought the park up to the walls of the house following the prevailing fashion of the day. Her son, the 2nd Marquess, restored the gardens as he thought they would have been in Jacobean days. He altered the terraces on the east and west making them three feet higher and much wider than the originals thus affecting the proportions of those aspects of the house. He heavily Victorianised the gardens creating large areas of gravel and

a typical 19th century formal layout trying to imitate the Jacobean style. 'We have grassed down a lot of extensive areas of gravel and have planted a great deal of yew and topiary and enclosed flower beds with box hedges, planted walks of formal evergreen oaks and created herb and scented gardens, a Knot Garden with a foot maze and we have made a green parterre with fountains and topiary in the outer Court to the south of the house. We have introduced some 17th century statues and I have selected plants of the period for the Knot Garden. I have also introduced many old roses and 17th century fruit trees and some modern English roses which have a feeling of the old roses about them'.

In the Knot Garden, which is laid out on the east side of the Old Palace, we have quite a large selection of early plants particularly those dating from the 16th, 17th and 18th centuries, many of which were brought here from other parts of Europe and America by John Tradescant the Elder and his son, the famous plant hunters and explorers, John Tradescant the Elder being gardener to Robert Cecil. The foot maze is a typical 17th century feature of gardens of this date and they were sometimes thought to symbolise man's passage through a Christian life.

I asked Lady Salisbury if she had a favourite part of the garden. 'I don't think I really have a particular favourite. I think one's temporary favourite part of the garden is that part in which one is working on at the moment - all your interest is concentrated on it. A thing I regret is that I didn't start by planting trees when I arrived in 1972, as they would be fairly mature by now. I focused initially on the flower gardens. But it's really only in the last few years that I've really got round to planting trees. I suppose my desire to plant further trees was triggered by the two great storms we experienced in 1988 in which we lost a great many major trees. 36 in the gardens alone in the first hurricane and about 56 in the second. It was a major disaster and terribly sad to see these great old friends lying on the ground. It took at least two years to clear away the fallen trees and we've done a tremendous amount of replanting since then.'

One of the gardens created by Lady Salisbury is the Scented Garden. Enclosed on three sides by ancient walls and on the other side by a clipped holly hedge, there must have been a garden on this site for at least four hundred years. In May you'll notice the magnolia with scented hanging flowers and in January a huge bush of fragrant honeysuckle. You will also discover violets, double and

single auriculas, narcissi and Guernsey stocks. In its centre, there is a herb garden enclosed by a sweet briar hedge.

Above: The Scented Garden. Below: The West Garden

Lady Salisbury thought perhaps the very best time of year to see the garden would be at the end of June and first week of July. A visit then will find all the roses out and most other summer plants in the parterres should be looking at their very best, but it is very difficult to decide what is the best moment - in February, there are the sheets of snowdrops to be seen (we open for Snowdrop Sunday) and in the spring there are the daffodils followed by the bluebells. I love the autumn too, when the colours in late October or early November are brilliant and with the sun shining out of a blue sky, the garden can look as beautiful as at anytime of the year. I have tried to design the gardens to look splendid throughout the year and with so much that is evergreen in its architecture, with the topiary and hedges of yew, holly and phillyrea, as well as the greys and gre ens of the evergreen and evergrey plants in the beds and borders, the garden looks furnished throughout the seasons.

I asked Lady Salisbury where she found her love of gardening. 'I think I must have inherited it from my mother and Irish grandfather. My mother was a great gardener and loved gardening perhaps as much as anything else. My grandfather also was passionately interested in plants and especially knowledgeable about trees. I learnt a lot from him and would spend time with him walking around the gardens of my father's family home at Adare Manor in Ireland, when he would tell me about the plants and the names of the trees. I also developed a great love for wild flowers as a child. I joined the Wild Flower Society and used to paint them in my wild flower book - this has remained a great interest and passion for me.'

Lady Salisbury has attempted in the last 26 years to redesign the gardens so that they may have something of a manner and style of the Jacobean gardens originally created by Robert Cecil when he built the house, bringing them back into sympathy with the great house. 'It is my dream that one day they will be filled with plants as deliciously fragrant and homely as those of Stuart times, with sweetness and the hum of bees and become again a place of fancies and conceits, surprises and mysteries, where both pleasure and peace may be found.'

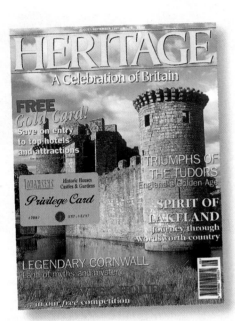

The British Isles

William Blake was right. England is a green and pleasant land. You will also find soaring medieval cathedrals, tributes to the faith of the churchmen and craftsmen who built them, grand country mansions of the aristocracy, filled with treasures, amongst them paintings, furniture and tapestries and set in elegantly landscaped grounds; fortified castles, their grey stone walls still fronting a bygone hostile world; and endless beautiful gardens, rich with lilies, roses and other delights, tended by generations of dedicated gardeners. All these can be visited by everyone, either free or for a small entrance fee. Great Britain and the islands around it are more than one vast historical theme park. Driving or walking through the countryside, during any season of the year, allows you to indulge in the changing landscape.

A short ride, for instance, from York, will take you through long stretches of wild, heather-covered moorland, ablaze with colour in the autumn, or past the steep, sheep covered slopes of the Dales.

Further afield the beauty of the land will impress any traveller. Ireland, for example, has a fine countryside, a seaside of amazing beauty and wonderful golf courses.

The hillside of the Cairngorms in Scotland, covered in bright purple heather, is a place where only game birds and deer are hardy enough to survive. The dramatic mountain peak of Snowdon, the tallest mountain in Wales – is a magnificent backdrop to the Snowdonia National Park –with its wooded valleys, mountain lakes, moors and estuaries, or the country lanes of the Lake District – a combination of peaks, rivers, waterfalls and glistening lakes.

The pages that follow for the British Isles go through the counties of England and the areas of Wales and Scotland, followed by Ireland. Details of all the properties and counties can be found on the maps which begin on page 289.

Bedfordshire

The Globe Inn, Linslade

There is something gracious about the landscape of Bedfordshire, a quality which is apparent in all its four types of scenery – in the chalk hills in the south, in the green sand hills of the centre, in the broad basin of the Ouse, and in the gently undulating countryside of the north.

Contrasts in the landscape of this home county, are in turn echoed to some extent in its town architecture. Bedfordshire plays host to two very different towns: Bedford itself, firstly is a town Anglo-Saxon origins, and has a long standing association with John Bunyan, the rebellious and unconventional author of Pilgrim's Progress. By complete contrast, Milton Keynes, is the largest example of a new town in England.

Bedfordshire's gentle landscapes are easily accessed. A vast network of motorways leads out from the urban sprawl of London to this county of contrasts.

SWISS GARDEN

Old Warden, Biggleswade, Bedfordshire
Tel: 01767 627666 (Bedfordshire County Council)

9 acre landscaped garden, set out in the 1830s, alongside a further 10 acres of native woodland with lakeside picnic area. Garden includes many tiny buildings, footbridges, ironwork features and intertwining ponds. Romantic landscape design highlighted by daffodils, rhododendrons and old rambling roses in season. **Location:** Signposted from A1 and A600. 2 miles W of Biggleswade, next door to the Shuttleworth Collection. **Open:** 3 Mar–end Sept Mon–Sat 1–5pm, Sun 10–5pm. **Admission:** Adults £2.50, concs/children £1.25 (Share to 'Friends of the Swiss Garden®'). Disabled access. Plants available for sale. No dogs except guide dogs.

WOBURN ABBEY

Woburn, Bedfordshire,
Tel: 01525 290666 Fax: 01525 290271
(The Marquess of Tavistock and the Trustees of the Bedford Estates)

Woburn Abbey is the home to the Marquess and Marchioness of Tavistock and their family. The art collection, one of the most important in the country, includes paintings by Van Dyck, Gainsborough, Reynolds and Velasquez. In the Venetian Room there are 21 views of Venice by Canaletto. There is also French and English 18th century furniture, silver and gold and exquisite porcelain. There are 9 species of deer in 3,000 acre deer park including the Pere David deer, saved from extinction here at Woburn. The Flying Duchess Pavilion serves simple lunches, snacks and teas and there are gift shops and an Antiques Centre. Woburn Abbey and Safari Park has been named as the 1998 Good Guide to Britain Family Attraction of the Year.

WREST PARK

Silsoe, Beds
Tel:01525 860152 (English Heritage)

Take a fascinating journey through a century and a half of gardening styles. Enjoy a leisurely stroll by the Long Wate, canals and Leg O'Mutton Lake and explore a charming range of garden buildings, including the baroque Archer Pavilion, Orangery and classical Bath House. Discover bridges and ponds, temples and altars, fountains and statues in over 90 acres of carefully landscaped gardens, laid out before a fabulous French-style Victorian Mansion. There is an informative audio-tour available. Location: 10 miles south of Bedford. **Open:** 1 Apr–1 Nov daily 10–6pm weekends and Bank Holidays only (or dusk if earlier in Oct). **Admission:** Adult £2.95, conc £2.20, child £1.50 (15% discount for groups of 11 or more).

map 4
E2

Berkshire

Berkshire is an unassuming county. Quiet and unpretentious – little concerned with outside approbation and making no effort to popularise its charms or to advertise its beauty and serenity. Whilst it is host to arguably the most famous castle in the kingdom and the school which is presently educating the future king of England and is graced with some of the most charming and unspoilt villages in the Thames Valley, it is reticent about its attractions. To the east of the county is Windsor, which is undoubtedly Berkshire's jewel. The town is dwarfed by the enormous castle on the hill above, which is surrounded by narrow streets, brimming with shops and old buildings.

Crossing over the Thames lies Eton and its famous public school, founded by Henry VI in 1440.

To the west of Berkshire lies Newbury, which was once a centre for the wool trade. Across the rolling Berkshire Downs is the Ridgeway, which was a vital trade route during the Bronze Ages and now offers wonderful walks across some of the highest points in the county.

The Savill Garden

BASILDON PARK

Lower Basildon, Reading RG8 9NR
Tel: 0118 984 3040 Fax: 0118 984 1267 (The National Trust)

Elegant classical 18th century house designed by Carr of York. Overlooking the River Thames is the Octagon drawing room containing fine furniture and pictures. The grounds include formal and terrace gardens, pleasure grounds and woodland walks. **Open:** 1 Apr–1 Nov, Wed–Sun & BH Mon 1–5.30pm. (Closed Good Friday. Park, garden & woodland walks: 11.30–5.30pm. Note: House & grounds close at 5pm on 15 August. **Admission:** House, park & garden: Adult £4, child £2, family ticket £10. Park & Garden only: Adult £1.60, child 80p, family ticket £4.

map 4
C4

ETON COLLEGE

Windsor, Berkshire SL4 6DW, UK
Tel: 01753 671177 Fax: 01753 671266

Founded in 1440 by Henry VI, Eton College is one of the oldest schools in the country. Visitors are invited to experience and share the beauty and traditions of the College. **Open:** Times are governed by both the dates for term and holidays on the school calendar, but the College will be open to visitors from the end of March until the beginning of October. Guided Tours during the season are available for individuals at 2.15 and 3.15pm daily. Guided Tours for groups by prior arrangement with the Visits Manager.

map 4
C4

DORNEY COURT

Dorney, Nr Windsor, Berkshire SL4 6QP
Tel: 01628 604638 Fax: 01628 665772 (Mr & Mrs Peregrine Palmer)

'One of the finest Tudor Manor Houses in England' – Country Life. Built about 1440 and lived in by the present family for over 450 years. The rooms are full of the atmosphere of history: early 15th and 16th century oak, 17th lacquer furniture, 18th and 19th century tables, 400 years of portraits, stained glass and needlework. The 14th century church of St. James is a lovely, cool, cheerful and very English Church. **Location:** 2 miles W of Eton & Windsor in village of Dorney on B3026. From M4 use exit 7. **Open:** May: Bank Hol Mons & Preceding Sun. July & Aug: Mon, Tues, Wed & Thur, 1–4.30pm, Last admin. 4pm. Adults £4.50, children over 9 £2.50, 10% discount for Nat Trust, NADFAS and OAPSs. Parties by arrangement. **Refreshments:** Teas at the Plant Centre. Outstanding collection of plants for sale at Bressingham Plant Centre, PYO fruit from June–September.

map 4
E4

HIGHCLERE CASTLE
Nr Newbury, RG20 9RN
Tel 01635 253210

Designed by Charles Barry in the 1830s at the same time as he was building the Houses of Parliament. This soaring pinnacled mansion provided a perfect setting for the 3rd Earl of Carnarvon one of the great hosts of Queen Victoria's reign. Old master paintings mix with portraits by Van Dyck and 18th century painters. Napoleon's desk and chair rescued from St. Helena sits with other 18th century furniture. The 5th Earl of Carnarvon, discovered the Tomb of Tutankhamun with Howard Carter. The castle houses a unique exhibition of some of his discoveries which were only rediscovered in the castle in 1988. The current Earl is the Queen's Horseracing Manager. In 1993 to celebrate his 50th year as a leading owner and breeder 'The Lord Carnarvon Racing Exhibition' was opened and offers a fascinating insight into a racing history that dates back three generations. The magnificent parkland, with its massive cedars, was designed by Capability Brown. The Secret Garden has a romance of its own with a beautiful curving lawn surrounded by densely planted herbaceous gardens. A place for poets and romantics. Guided tours are often provided, free of charge, to visitors. **Location:** 4.4 miles S of Newbury on A34, Jct 13 of M4 about 2 miles from Newbury. **Open:** 5 Jul–6 Sept, Tues–Sun 11–5pm, last adm. 4pm, Sat last adm. 2.30pm. **Refreshments:** Lunches, teas, ices, soft drinks. **Conferences:** Business conferences, management training courses, film and photographic location. Licensed for civil weddings. Ample car park and picnic area adjacent to Castle. Suitable for disabled persons on ground floor only. One wheelchair available. Visitors can buy original items in Castle Gift Shop. No dogs are permitted in the house or gardens except guide dogs. No photography in the house. Occasionally subject to closure.

map 4
C5

GODDARDS

Abinger Common, Dorking, Surrey, RH5 6TH
Tel: The Landmark Trust: 01628 825920
(Leased to the Landmark Trust by the Lutyens Trust)

Built by Sir Edwin Lutyens in 1989–1900 and enlarged by him in 1910. Garden by Gertrude Jekyll. Managed and maintained by the Landmark Trust, which lets buildings for self-catering holidays. **Open:** By appointment only. Must be booked in advance, including parking, which is very limited. Visits booked for Wed afternoons from the Wed after Easter until last Wed of Oct between 2–6pm. **Admission:** Tickets £3, obtainable from Mrs Baker on 01306 730871, Mon–Fri, 9–6pm. Visitors will have access to part of the garden and house only. **Accommodation:** Available for up to 12 people for self-catering holidays. Tel: 01628 825925 for bookings. Full details of Goddards and 163 other historic buildings are featured in The Landmark Handbook (price £8.50 refundable against a booking) from The Landmark Trust, Shottesbrooke, Maidenhead, Berkshire, SL6 3SW.

ST GEORGE'S CHAPEL WINDSOR

Windsor, Berks SL4 1NJ
Tel: 01753 865538 Fax: 01753 620165 (The Dean & Canons of Windsor)

A fine example of perpendicular architecture. Begun in 1475 by Edward IV and it was completed in the reign of Henry VIII. Choir stalls dedicated to the order of the Knights of the Garter, founded by Edward III. **Location:** OS Ref: SU968 770. In Windsor town, just off the M4. **Open:** Please call visitors office. **Admission:** Free admission on payment of charge into Windsor Castle.

MAPLEDURHAM HOUSE & WATERMILL

Nr. Reading, Oxfordshire, Tel: 01189 723 350, RG4 7TR
Fax: 01189 724 016 (The Mapledurham Trust)

Late 16th century Elizabethan home of the Blount family. Original plaster ceiling, great oak staircase, fine collection of paintings and private chapel in Strawberry Hill Gothic added in 1797. The 15th century Watermill is fully restored and producing flour and bran which are sold in the gift shop. **Location:** 4 miles NW of Reading on North bank of River Thames. Signposted from A40704. **Open:** Easter-end Sept, Sat–Sun & Bank Hols. Midweek parties by arrangement. **Admission:** Please phone for details. **Refreshments:** Tearooms serving cream teas. **Events/ Exhibitions:** By arrangement. **Conferences:** By arrangement. **Accommodation:** 11 self-catering holiday cottages. Wedding receptions by arrangement. Car parking and picnic area.

THE SAVILL GARDEN

Windsor Great Park
Tel: 01753 860222

World renowned woodland garden of 35 acres, situated in the tranquil surroundings of Windsor Great Park. The garden contains a fine range of rhododendrons, azaleas, camellias and magnolias; with adjoining rose gardens and herbaceous borders. Autumn provides a great feast of colour and the whole garden offers much of great interest and beauty at all seasons. Queen Elizabeth Temperate House. **Location:** To be approached from A30 via Wick Road and Wick Lane, Englefield Green. **Station(s):** Egham (3 miles). **Open:** Daily 10–6pm Mar–Oct, 10–4pm Nov–Feb (closed December 25/26). **Admission:** Adults £3.80, senior citizens £3.30, parties 20+ £3.30, accompanied children under 16 free of charge. **Refreshments:** Licensed self-service restaurant. Well stocked plant centre/gift shop. Ample parking.

SWALLOWFIELD PARK

Swallowfield, Berkshire RG7 1TG
Tel: 0118 9883815 Fax: 0118 9883930 (Country Houses Association)

Built by the Second Earl of Clarendon in 1678. **Location:** In the village of Swallowfield 6 miles SE of Reading. **Open:** June–Aug, Mon & Fri 2–5pm. Last entry 4pm. **Admission:** Adults £2.50, children £1. Free car park. No dogs admitted. Groups by arrangement, £2pp.

WELFORD PARK

Welford, Newbury RG20 8HU
Tel: 01488 608203 (J.H.L. Puxley)

Queen Anne house with later additions. Attractive gardens and grounds. **Location:** 6 miles NW of Newbury and 1 mile N of Wickham village off B4000. **Station:** Newbury. **Open:** Spring and Summer Bank Holidays and 1–26 June inclusive from 2.30–5pm. **Admission:** Adults £3, OAPs and under 16 £2. Interior by prior appointment only.

WINDSOR CASTLE

Windsor, Berkshire SL4 1NJ
Tel: Visitor Office 01753 868 286 Fax: 01753 832 290

Buckingham Palace, Windsor Castle and the Palace of Holyroodhouse are the Official Residences of the Sovereign and are used by The Queen as both home and office. The Queen's personal standard flies when Her Majesty is in residence. Furnished with works of art from the Royal Collection, these buildings are used extensively by The Queen for State ceremonies, audiences and official entertaining and are opened to the public as much as these commitments allow. A significant proportion of Windsor Castle is opened to visitors on a regular basis including the Upper and Lower Wards, the North Terrace with its famous view towards Eton, the State Apartments, including newly restored rooms, The Gallery, Queen Mary's Dolls' House and St. George's Chapel. <u>Open:</u> Every day (except 10 Apr, 15 Jun, 25 and 26 Dec) Nov–Feb 10–4pm (last admission 3pm); Mar–Oct 10–5.30pm (last admission 4pm). St. George's Chapel is closed to visitors on Suns as services are held throughout the day. Worshippers are welcome. <u>Admission:</u> Adult £9.50, children (under 17) £5, OAPs (over 60) £7, family (2 adults and 2 children under 17) £21.50. Reduced charges apply if part of the Castle is not open.

map 4
E4

Buckinghamshire

Buckingham, county town has higgeldy-piggledy streets and lively pubs for such a small place, thanks in part to the patronage of the students from the country's only private university. The markets on Tuesdays and Saturdays and the Old Gaol Museum on Market Hill are absorbing, as well as the many stately homes, including Stowe, which are all worth a visit.

Three counties – Oxfordshire, Berkshire and Buckinghamshire – meet at Henley on Thames – although it officially rests in Buckinghamshire. The town is a long established stopping place for travellers between Oxford and London. Its brick and half timbered buildings are elegant and are a fitting backdrop to the annual Royal Regatta.

Hughenden Manor

CHENIES MANOR HOUSE

Chenies, WD3 6ER
Tel: 01494 762888 (Lt Col & Mrs Macleod Matthews)

15/16th century Manor House with fortified tower. Original home of the Earls of Bedford, visited by Henry VIII and Elizabeth I. Home of the Macleod Matthews family. Contains contemporary tapestries and furniture. Surrounded by a beautiful Tudor sunken garden, a white garden, herbaceous borders, a fountain court, a physic garden containing a very wide selection of medical and culinary herbs, a parterre and two mazes. The kitchen garden is in the Victorian style with unusual vegetables and fruit. Plants for sale. **Location:** Off A404 between Amersham & Rickmansworth (M25 – Jct 18). **Station(s):** Chorleywood (1½ miles). **Please telephone for admission times and prices.** Parties throughout the year by prior arrangement – min charge £50. Corporate events welcome. **Events/Exhibitions:** Spectacular tulip display. **Conferences:** Welcome. Free parking. No dogs.

CHILTERN OPEN AIR MUSEUM

Newland Park, Gorelands Lane, Chalfont St. Giles, Buckinghamshire, HP8 4AD. Tel: Information Line: 01494 872 163 Office 01494 871 117 (Chiltern Open Air Museum Ltd)

A museum of historic buildings, rescued from demolition and re-erected in 45 acres of beautiful parkland, reflects the vernacular heritage of the Chilterns. You can explore barns, granaries, cartsheds and stables, a blacksmiths forge, a toll house, a 1940's prefab and more. Special events at weekends and daily in August include demonstrations and displays of traditional skills such as the pole-lathe, spinning and dyeing, spoon making and rag rug making. The working Victorian farm illustrates aspects of our rural past and is home to our animals. **Open:** Please phone 01494 871117 to confirm opening times & prices. **Refreshments:** Tearooms, shop, playground, nature/seat trail.

CLAYDON HOUSE

Middle Claydon, Nr Buckingham, Bucks MK18 2EY
Tel: 01296 730349 (The National Trust)

One of England's most extraordinary houses. In continuous occupation by the Verney family for over 350 years. Claydon was originally a Jacobean manor house, but was remodelled in the 1750s at a time when the craze for Chinoiserie was at its height. The result was the remarkable series of rooms we see today, lavishly decorated in intricately-carved white woodwork covered with motifs based on Oriental birds, pagodas and summerhouses. **Open:** 4 Apr–1 Nov: daily except Thur & Fri, 1–5pm. Closed Good Fri. **Admission:** £4, family ticket £10. Tearoom: open 2–5pm (open at 1pm on Sun & Bank Hol Mon).

 map 4 D3

CLIVEDEN

Taplow, Maidenhead, SL6 0JA, Bucks
Tel: 01628 605069 Fax: 01628 669461 (The National Trust)

Perched on cliffs above the Thames, this estate has magnificent views over the river. The great 19th-century mansion (now let as a hotel) was once the home of Nancy, Lady Astor. There are a series of gardens, each with its own character and featuring roses, topiary, water gardens, statuary, and formal parterre. **Open:** Woodlands only: 1 Mar–1 Nov. Entire Estate: 28 Mar–1 Nov: daily 11–6pm. Nov & Dec: daily 11–4pm. House (three rooms open): Apr–Oct: Thurs & Sun 3–6pm. Entry by timed ticket from information kiosk. **Admission:** Woodland Car Park only £2, family ticket £5. Grounds: £4.80, family ticket £12. House £1 extra. Licensed conservatory restaurant and shop.

map 4 D4

COWPER & NEWTON MUSEUM

Orchard Side, Market Place, Olney, MK46 4AJ
Tel: 01234 711 516 e-mail: museum@olney.co.uk

Once the home of the 18th century poet and letter writer William Cowper and now containing furniture, paintings and belongings of both Cowper and his ex-slave trader friend, Rev. John Newton (author of "Amazing Grace"). Attractions include re-creations of a Victorian country kitchen and wash-house, two peaceful gardens and Cowper's restored summerhouse, costume gallery, important collections of dinosaur bones and bobbin lace and local history displays. **Location:** 6 miles N of Newport Pagnell via A509. (Leave M1 at Junction 14). **Station(s):** Milton Keynes or Bedford. **Open:** 1 Mar–23 Dec, Tue–Sat & Bank Hol Mons, 10am–1pm & 2–5pm. Closed Good Friday. **Admission:** Adults £2, Children/Students (with cards) £1, Concs £1.50, Family £5.

 map 4 D2

HUGHENDEN MANOR

High Wycombe, Bucks HP14 4LA
Tel: 01494 532580 (The National Trust)

The home of Queen Victoria's favourite Prime Minister, Benjamin Disraeli. Much of his furniture, pictures and books remain and there are beautiful walks through the surrounding park and woodland. The garden is a recreation of the colourful designs of his wife, Mary Anne. **Open:** House: 1–30 Mar: Sat & Sun only: 1 Apr–31 Oct: daily except Mon & Tues (closed Good Fri, but open Bank Hol Mon) 1–5pm. Garden: same days as house 12–5pm. Park & Woodland: open all year. **Admission:** House & garden: £4, family ticket £10. Garden only £1, children 50p. Park & Woodland free. Tearoom and shop available.

map 4 D3/4

NETHER WINCHENDON HOUSE

Aylesbury HP18 0DY
Tel: 01844 290199
(Trustees of Will Trust of J.G.C. Spencer Bernard Dec'd)

Medieval and Tudor manor house with 18th century Gothic additions. Home of Sir Francis Bernard, Governor of New Jersey and Massachusetts, 1760. **Location:** 1 mile N of A418 Aylesbury/Thame Road, in village of Lower Winchendon, 6 miles SW Aylesbury. **Stations:** Aylesbury (7 miles). Haddenham and Thame Parkway (2 miles). **Open:** May 1–May 28 and Aug 30/31, 2.30–5.30pm. Last party each day at 4.45pm. Parties at any time of year by written appointment. **Admission:** Adults £3, children (under 12) and OAPs £1.50 (not weekends or bank holidays). **Refreshments:** By arrangement. Correspondence to Administrator, R.V. Spencer Bernard Esq.

map 4
D3

STOWE (STOWE SCHOOL)

Stowe, MK18 5EH
Tel: 01280 813650

Formerly the home of the Dukes of Buckingham it is a house adorned with the traditions of aristocracy and learning. For over one and a half centuries up to the great sale of 1848, the Temples and Grenvilles almost continuously rebuilt and refurbished it in an attempt to match their ever growing ambitions with the latest fashions. Around the mansion is one of Britain's most magnificent landscape gardens now in the ownership of the National Trust. **Location:** 4 miles N of Buckingham town. **Stations:** Milton Keynes. **Open:** 22 Mar–12 Apr, 6 Jul–6 Sept, daily 2–5pm. Sun 12–5pm. The house is closed, at times, for private functions. Please telephone first to check. **Admission:** Adults £2 children £1. Guide books and souvenirs available from Stowe Bookshop situated in the Menagerie on the South Front – open 10–5pm.

map 4
D2

STOWE LANDSCAPE GARDENS

Buckingham, Bucks MK18 5EH
Tel: 01280 822850. Fax: 01280 822437 (The National Trust)

One of the first and finest landscape gardens in Europe. Adorned with buildings by Vanbrugh, Gibbs and Kent, including arches, temples, a Palladian bridge and other monuments, the sheer scale of the garden must make it Britain's largest work of art. **Open:** 20 Mar–12 Apr: daily; 13 Apr–5 Jul: Mon, Wed, Fri, Sun; 6 Jul–6 Sept: daily; 7 Sept–1 Nov: Mon,Wed, Fri, Sun; 27 Dec–5 Jan 1999; daily 10–5pm or dusk if earlier. Last admission one hour before closing. **Admission:** Gardens £4.40. Family £11. Licensed tearoom.

map 4
D2

WINSLOW HALL

Winslow, Buckinghamshire, MK18 3HL
Tel: 01296 712 323 (Sir Edward & Lady Tomkins)

Built 1698–1702. Almost certainly designed by Sir Christopher Wren. Has survived without any major structural alteration and retains most of its original features. Modernised and redecorated by the present owners. Good 18th century furniture, mostly English. Some fine pictures, clocks and carpets. Several examples of Chinese art, notably of the Tang period. Beautiful gardens with many unusual trees and shrubs. **Location:** At entrance to Winslow on A413, the Aylesbury road. **Station(s):** Milton Keynes or Aylesbury (both 10 miles). **Open:** All Bank Hol weekends (except Christmas), 2–5pm. July–Aug, Wed & Thur, 2.30–5.30pm or by appointment throughout the year. **Admission:** Adults £5.00, children free. **Refreshments:** Catering by arrangement.

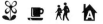

map 4
D2

WADDESDON MANOR

Nr. Aylesbury, Buckinghamshire, HP18 0JW
Tel: 01296 651211 Fax: 01296 651142

Waddesdon Manor was built between 1874 and 1889. Its creator, Baron Ferdinand de Rothschild, intended it as a great house in which to entertain his guests and display his works of art. Today, this French Renaissance-style chateau houses one of the finest collection of French 18th century decorative arts in the world, much with Royal provenance and an important collection of English portraits. The garden includes a fine example of a Victorian parterre, a Rococo-style aviary, shrubberies and woodland. Thousands of bottles of vintage Rothschild wines are found in the wine cellars. There are gift and wine shops and a licensed restaurant serving home-made food. Many events are organised throughout the year including floodlit openings, wine tastings, garden workshops and collection study days. **Location:** A41 between Aylesbury & Bicester. **Open: Grounds (including garden aviary, restaurant and shops)** 1 Mar–20 Dec, Wed–Sun & Bank Hol Mons, 10–5pm. **House (including Wine Cellars)** 2 Apr–1 Nov, Thur–Sun, Bank Hol Mons and Weds in Jul & Aug. 11–4pm. (Recommended last admission 3pm) Bachelors' Wing open Thursday. **Admission: House & Grounds:** Adults £9, child £7.50. **Grounds only:** Adults £3, child £1.50. Bachelors' Wing £1. National Trust Members free. Timed tickets to the House can be purchased on site or reserved in advance by phoning 01296 651226, Mon–Fri 10–4pm. Advance booking fee: £2.50 per transaction.

map
4D3

Cambridgeshire

Wansford

In Cambridge and Ely, this county has two of the most historic cities in England. Cambridge is an idyllic and irresistibly charming city, home to one of the oldest universities in the world. Some of the most ancient of Cambridge's thirty colleges adorn the timeless velvety green banks of the River Cam. Others, such as the ancient college of Gonville & Caius, one of Cambridge's oldest, lie grouped around squares known as courts and line the ancient streets of this busy market city. The bustling student community, and their bicycles, create a wonderfully lively atmosphere in this collegiate city.

The ancient city of Ely is dominated by its wonderful cathedral, which overlooks the flat fens that surround it. Indeed the city is reputed to take its name from the Saxon word "elig", meaning "Eel Island" and was once an island. Today, the drained fens form some of the most fertile agricultural land in England. It is also home, at Wicken Fen, to the oldest nature reserve in Britain.

By Appointment to
Her Majesty Queen Elizabeth
The Queen Mother

J. W. BOYCE

Bush Pasture, Carter Street, Fordham, Ely,
Cambridgeshire, CB7 5JU.
Tel: 01638 721 158 (Roger Morley)

Specialists in garden seeds for over 80 years. Specialising in the production of pansy seed and plants. Also over 1,000 items of seed which includes a wide range of separate colours for cut flowers, bedding and drying. Also old and unusual vegetables. Seed list free on request. (Write or telephone as above).

map 5
G1

ELY CATHEDRAL

The Chapter House, The College, Ely CB7 4DL
Tel: 01353 667735 Fax: 01353 665658

A wonderful example of Romanesque architecture. The Octagon and the Lady Chapel are of particular interest. There are superb medieval domestic buildings around the Cathedral. Stained glass window in the museum. **Location:** 15 miles N of Cambridge city centre via the A10. **Open:** Summer: 7–7pm. Winter: Mon–Sat, 7.30–6pm, Sun and week after Christmas, 7.30–5pm. Sun services: 8.15am, 10.30am and 3.45 pm. Weekday services: 7.40am, 8am & 5.30pm (Thurs only also 11.30am & 12.30pm). Admission charges apply.

 ## ELTON HALL

Elton, Peterborough PE8 6SH
Tel: 01832 280468 Fax: 01832 280584 (Mr & Mrs William Proby)

This romantic house has been the home of the Proby family for over 350 years. Excellent furniture and outstanding paintings by Gainsborough, Reynolds, Constable and other fine artists. There are over 12,000 books, including Henry VIII's prayer book. Wonderful gardens, including restored Rose Garden, knot and sunken gardens and recently planted Arboretum. Stunning new Gothic Orangery. Bressingham Plant Centre and The Essential Gardener Shop in walled Kitchen Garden. **Location:** On A605, 8 miles W of Peterborough. **Open:** 2–5pm Last Bank Hol in May (Sun/Mon 24/25 May) Weds in June, Weds, Thurs and Suns July and Aug and Bank Hol Mon (31). **Admission:** Adults £4.50, children free. Garden only: Adults £2.50, children free. Private parties by appointment with Administrator. **Refreshments:** Home-made teas, lunches by arrangement.

map 9
7F

Cambridgeshire

ISLAND HALL

Post Street, Godmanchester PE18 8BA
Tel: 0171 491 3724 (Mr Christopher & The Hon Mrs Vane Percy)

A mid 18th century mansion of great charm owned and restored by an award winning Interior Designer. This family home has lovely Georgian rooms, with fine period detail and interesting possessions relating to the owners' ancestors since their first occupation of the house in 1800. A tranquil riverside setting with formal gardens and ornamental island forming part of the grounds in an area of Best Landscape. **Location:** Centre of Godmanchester next to car park. 1 m S of Huntingdon. 15 m NW of Cambridge (A14). **Open:** Sundays – July 5, 12, 19, 26, 2.30–5pm. **Admission:** House and Grounds: Adults £3, Children 13–16 £2. Grounds only: Adults £1.50, Children £1. Under 13 grounds only. Group rate (by appt), May–Sept (except Aug) £2.50 per head (when over 40 persons); under 15 persons min charge £45 per group.

KIMBOLTON CASTLE

Kimbolton, Cambs
Tel: 01480 860505, Fax: 01480 861763 (Governors of Kimbolton School)

Tudor manor house associated with Katherine of Aragon, completely remodelled by Vanbrugh (1708–20); courtyard c.1694. Fine murals by Pellegrini in chapel, boudoir and on staircase. Gatehouse by Robert Adam, Parkland. **Location:** 8 miles NW of St Neots on B645; 14 miles N of Bedford. **Station(s):** St Neots (9 miles) **Open:** Easter Sun & Mon, Spring Bank Hol Sun & Mon, Summer Bank Hol Sun, also 22, 23, 26, 29, 30 July, 2, 5, 6, 9, 16, 23, 30 Aug 2–6pm **Admission:** Adults £2, Children & OAPs £1. **Conferences:** By negotiation. Guided tours for groups of 20 or more by arrangement on days other than advertised.

KING'S COLLEGE

King's Parade, Cambridge CB2 1ST
Tel: 01223 331212 (Provost and Fellows)

Visitors are very welcome, but remember that this is a working College. Please respect the privacy of those who work, live and study here at all times. Recorded messages for services, concerts and visiting times: 01223 331155. **Open:** Out of term time – Mon–Sat, 9.30–4.30pm. Sun, 10–5pm. In term: Mon, 9.30–4.30pm, Tue–Fri, 9.30–3.30pm. Sat, 9.30–3.15pm. Sun, 1.15–2.15pm, 5–5.30pm. Admission charges apply. Child under 12 is free if part of a family unit.

THE MANOR

Hemingford Grey, Huntingdon, Cambs PE18 9BN
Tel: 01480 463134 Fax: 01480 465026 (Mr & Mrs Peter Boston)

Built about 1130 and made famous as Green Knowe by the author Lucy Boston this house is reputedly the oldest continuously inhabited house in the country and much of the Norman house remains. It contains the Lucy Boston patchworks. The garden has topiary, one of the best collections of old roses in private hands, large herbaceous borders with many scented plants and a variety of Dykes Medal winner irises. **Open:** House all the year round but only by prior appointment. Garden open daily all year 10–6pm (dusk in winter). **Admission:** House and Garden: Adults £4, children £1.50. Garden only: Adults £1, children 50p.

Cambridgeshire

OLIVER CROMWELL'S HOUSE

29 St. Mary's Street, Ely, Cambridgeshire
Tel: 01353 662062 Fax: 01353 668518 (East Cambridgeshire District Council)

Oliver Cromwell and his family moved here in 1636 and remained in Ely for some ten years. The 13th century house has been beautifully restored and in 1995, the first floor rooms also opened to the public. Period rooms, sets, exhibitions and videos give insight into 17th century domestic life, the fascinating character of Oliver Cromwell and the Fen Drainage story. **Open:** 1st Oct–31 Mar 10–5.15 Mon to Sat. 1 Apr–30 Sept 10–6 daily. **Admission:** Charge of £2.30 per person, £1.80 concessionary rates. Family ticket £5. Group prices on request. Guides can be booked to show parties around the house.

map 4
F1

PETERBOROUGH CATHEDRAL

Peterborough PE1 1XS
Tel: 01733 343342 Fx: 01733 52465

West front unique in Christendom. Painted Nave Ceiling (c.1220), unique in England. Pure Romanesque interior. Exquisite fan vaulting (c.1500) in retro-choir. Burial place of Katherine of Aragon. Former burial place of Mary Queen of Scots. Saxon sculptures and Roman Remains. **Location:** 4 miles E of A1, in City Centre. Open: Mon–Sat 7–6.15pm. Sun 7.30–5pm. Services throughout the week.

PRIOR CRAUDEN'S CHAPEL

The College, Ely Cambridgeshire
Tel: 01353 662837 Fax: 01353 662187 (The Bursar, The King's School)

Built as a private chapel in 1324/1325 for Prior Crauden, the Prior of the Medieval Benedictine Monastery from 1321 to 1341. Recently restored to show glimpses of coloured walls, painted glass and wall paintings. **Location:** In the precincts of Ely Cathedral. **Station(s):** Ely 5 mins walk. **Open:** Mon–Fri 9–5pm excluding statutory and Bank Hols. Key available from Chapter Office in Firmary Lane. **Admission:** Free. Parking in Cathedral Car Park. Not suitable for disabled visitors.

UNIVERSITY BOTANIC GARDEN

Cory Lodge, Bateman Street, CB2 1JF
Tel: 01223 336265 Fax: 01223 336278 (University of Cambridge)

Owned by the University of Cambridge. Laid out by Henslow in 1846. Forty acres of outstanding gardens with lake, glasshouses, winter garden, chronological bed and nine National Collections, including Geranium and Fritillaria. **Location:** 1 mile S of Cambridge centre. Entrance on Bateman Street. **Stations:** Cambridge Railway Station 1/4 mile. **Open:** Open all year except Christmas Day and Boxing Day 10-6 (summer), 10-5 (autumn & spring), 10-4 (winter). **Admission:** Charged weekends and Bank Holidays throughout the year and weekdays Mar 1-Oct 31. All parties must be pre-booked. Pre-booked school parties and disabled people free. No reductions for parties. **Refreshments:** Tearoom and shop in the Gilmour Building; picnic area. No dogs except guide dogs. Guided tours by the Friends of the Garden available by arrangement.

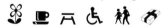

map 4
F1

ANGLESEY ABBEY AND GARDEN

Lode, Cambridge CB5 9EJ Tel: 01223 811200 Fax: 01223 811200

Open: House: 21 March to 11 Oct: daily except Mon & Tues (but open BH Mon) 1–5. Garden: 21 March to 1 Nov: Wed to Sun & BH Mon 11–5.30; also open Mon & Tues 6 July to 13 Sept (but house closed Mon & Tues). Lode Mill: 21 March to 1 Nov: Wed to Sun & BH Mon 1–5. Last admission to house, garden and Lode Mill 4.30. Property closed Good Fri. Note: Timed tickets to the house are issued Sun & BH Mon to ease overcrowding. Visitors are advised that at BH periods the delay in gaining admission to the house may be considerable and very occasionally admission may not be possible. Events: please send s.a.e. for details of musical events, theatre and garden tours.

PECKOVER HOUSE & GARDEN

North Brink, Wisbech PE13 1JR Tel: 01945 583463 Fax: 01945 583463

Open: House & garden: 28 March to 1 Nov: Sat, Sun, Wed & BH Mon 12.30–5.30. Last admission 5. Garden only: Mon, Tues & Thur 12.30–5.30.

Last admission 5. Parties welcome on house open days and at other times by appointment. Events: special programme to celebrate 50th anniversary of the Trust's acquisition of the house; please tel. for details. **Admission:** £3.20 (£2 on garden only days); family discounts available. Parties £2.50. Note: Members may, by written appointment with the tenants, view Nos. 14 and 19 North Brink

WIMPOLE HALL

Arrington, Royston SG8 0BW Tel: 01223 207257 Fax: 01223 207838

Open: Hall: 14 March to 1 Nov: daily except Mon & Fri 1–5 (but open Goo Fri 1–5, BH Sun & BH Mon 11–5). Additional opening every Fri in Aug 1–5. Garden: open as Hall. Park: open daily throughout the year from sunrise to sunset, but closes at 5 on concert nights. Events: 18/19 July, open-air concerts with fireworks; 22/23 Aug, garden concerts with fireworks. For bookings tel. 01223 207001. **Admission:** Hall & garden £5.50, child £2.25. Adult party rate (12+ in group) £4.50, child party rate £1.75. Adult joint ticket with Home Farm £7.50, child £3.50. Garden only £2. Car park 200m

Cheshire

Cheshire

Chester

Known for its cats, its cheese, its excellent roads and surprisingly varied scenery, the county of Cheshire manages brilliantly to retain its rural character.

The county town of Chester comes from the Latin term 'Castra Devana', meaning 'camp on the Dee'. The town lies on an elbow of the River Dee and was founded by Romans during the first century AD. The town is surrounded by a medieval wall, packed with historic buildings, winding streets and a wealthy atmosphere. The picturesque Cheshire Plain is the home for a multitude of pretty villages and lush countryside.

Knutsford, with its black and white houses and winding streets, is typical of the towns clustered in the region. The whole area is a delight for the visitor.

ADLINGTON HALL

Nr Macclesfield, Cheshire SK10 4LF
Tel: 01625 820875 Fax: 01625 828756 (Mrs C Legh)

Adlington Hall is a Cheshire Manor and has been the home of the Leghs since 1315. The Great Hall was built between 1450 and 1505, the Elizabethan 'Black and White' in 1581 and the Georgian South Front in 1757. The Bernard Smith Organ was installed c1670. A 'Shell Cottage', Yew Walk, Lime Avenue, recently planted maze and rose garden. Recently restored follies include a Chinese bridge, Temple to Diana and Tig House. Occasional organ recitals **Location:** 5 miles N of Macclesfield on the Stockport/Macclesfield Road (A523). **Station(s)** Adlington (½m) **Open:** Throughout the year to groups by prior arrangement only. **Admission:** Hall and Gardens Adults £4 Children £1.50 (over 25 people £3.50). **Refreshments:** At the Hall. Car park free.

map 8 B4

ARLEY HALL AND GARDENS

Arley, Northwich Cheshire CW9 6NA
Tel: 01565 777353 Fax: 01565 777465 (Lord & Lady Ashbrook)

Arley Hall, built about 1840, stands at the centre of an estate which has been owned by the same family for over 500 years. An important example of the early Victorian Jacobean style, it has fine plaster work and oak panelling, a magnificent library and interesting pictures, furniture and porcelain. There is a private Chapel designed by Anthony Salvin and a 15th century cruck barn. The gardens overlooking parkland provide great variety of style and design, winning the Christies/HHA Garden of the Year Award in 1987. Features include the Double Herbaceous Border established in 1846, clipped Quercus Ilex avenue, pleached Lime avenue, Topiary, collections of shrub roses, exotic trees and shrubs and over 200 varieties of Rhododendron. **Location:** 5 m N Northwich; 6 m W of Knutsford; 7 m S of Warrington; 5 m off M6 at junctions 19 & 20; 5 m off M56 at junctions 9 & 10. Nearest main roads A49 and A50. **Open:** Easter- Sept inclusive. Gardens & Grounds, Tues-Suns & Bank Hol Mons 11-5. Guided Tours and Parties by arrangement. Hall dates and times may vary. Hall closed Saturdays. **Admission:** Gardens £3.60, Hall £2.50 extra. Concessions and group bookings. **Refreshments:** Lunches and light refreshments in converted Tudor barn. **Events/Exhibitions:** Antique fairs, Garden Festival, Craft Shows, Fireworks & Laser Concert etc., Outdoor Theatre, Christmas Events. **Conferences:** Facilities available. Corporate activities, launches, filming, weddings, themed events, countryside days etc., Private & Corporate Dinners. Shop and Plant Nursery. Woodland Walk. Facilities for disabled. Dogs allowed in gardens on leads. Picnic area. Arley Garden Festival 27–28 June.

map 6 C1

BRAMALL HALL

Bramhall Park, Bramhall, Stockport, Cheshire, SK7 3NX
Tel: 0161 485 3708 Fax: 0161 486 6959 (Stockport Metropolitan Borough Council)

This magical Tudor manor house is set in 70 acres of parkland, with lakes, woods and gardens. The house contains 16th century wall paintings, Elizabethan fine plaster ceilings, Victorian kitchens and servant's quarters. Excellent stables, Tearoom and gift shop. **Location:** 4 miles S of Stockport, off A5102. **Stations:** Cheadle Hulme. **Open:** Good Fri–30 Sept, Mon–Sat, 1–5pm. Sun & B.Hols, 11–5pm. 1 Oct–1 Jan, Tue–Sat, 1–4pm. Sun, 11–4pm. Closed 25–26 Dec. 2 Jan–Easter Sat & Sun & B.Hols, 12–4pm. Parties by arrangement, including out of hours bookings. **Admission:** Adults £3.50, children/OAPs £2. **Refreshments:** Stables, tearooms. **Events/Exhibitions:** Full events programme. **Conferences:** Available for corporate entertaining and civil marriages. Disabled access on ground floor, shop and tearooms.

map 8 B4

CAPESTHORNE HALL

Capesthorne, Siddington, Nr. Macclesfield, Cheshire, SK11 9JY
Tel: 01625 861 221 Caravan Park - 01625 861 779 Fax: 01625 861 619 (Mr & Mrs W. A. Bromley-Davenport)

Capesthorne has been this family's home together with the Capesthornes and Wards since Domesday times. The Davenport family, originally appointed Chief Foresters, was responsible for law and order in the King's forests of Macclesfield and Leek. The Bromley family has produced a Chancellor and Speaker in Parliament and several Bromley-Davenports have been elected Members of Parliament. The original Hall was designed by the Smiths of Warwick, 1719–1732, then altered by Blore and ultimately Salvin rebuilt the centre after a disastrous fire. This home has a fascinating collection of paintings, sculptures, furniture and family muniments and Americana. **Location:** 7 miles south of Wilmslow on A34 (Manchester–London Road). 6.5 miles north of Congleton. M6, Junction 18. **Station(s):**

Chelford (3 miles). Alderley Edge (3.5 miles). Macclesfield (6 miles). **Open:** Please phone for opening times and dates **Admission: Hall & Gardens:** £4.50. **Gardens only:** £2.50. Concessions available. Free coach and car park. **Refreshments:** Light snacks served in the Bromley Rooms. **Events/Exhibitions:** Open air concerts, craft fairs & classic car shows are just some of the attractions held in the park throughout the year. **Conferences:** Capesthorne is an attractive location for corporate entertaining and promotion work. A brochure is available. Whilst Capesthorne is not licensed to hold Civil wedding ceremonies, it is a perfect venue for receptions. Dogs permitted in the park area only. Gift shop, Touring Caravan park and fishing. Enquiries to the Administrator.

map 8 B5

CHOLMONDELEY CASTLE GARDEN

Malpas, Cheshire, SY14 8AH. Tel: 01829 720383/203
(The Marchioness of Cholmondeley)

Extensive pleasure gardens dominated by romantic Gothic Castle, built in 1801 of local sandstone. Imaginatively laid out with fine trees and water gardens, it has been extensively replanted from the 1960's with rhododendrons, azaleas, magnolias, cornus, acer and many other acid loving plants. As well as the beautiful water garden, there is a rose garden and many mixed borders. Lakeside picnic area, rare breeds of farm animals, including llamas. Ancient private chapel in park. **Location:** Off A41 Chester/Whitchurch Road and A49 Whitchurch/Tarporley Road. **Station(s):** Crewe. **Open:** Wed 1 Apr – Wed 30 Sept, every Wed & Thur 12–5pm, Sun and Bank Hols 11.30–5.30pm. Other days by prior arrangement. **Enquiries to:** The secretary, Cholmondeley Castle (House not open to public). **Admission:** Adults £2.50, OAPs £2.00, Children 75p. Other days for coach parties of 25 and over by prior arrangement at reduced rates. Plants for sale.

map 6 C/D1

DORFOLD HALL

Nantwich CW5 8LD
Tel: 01270 625245 Fax: 01270 628723 (Mr Richard Roundell)

Jacobean country house built 1616. Beautiful plaster ceilings and panelling. Interesting furniture and pictures. Attractive gardens including spectacular spring garden and summer herbaceous borders. Guided tours. **Location:** 1 mile W of Nantwich on A534 Nantwich/Wrexham Road. **Stations:** Nantwich (1½ miles). **Open:** Apr–Oct Tues and Bank Holidays Mons 2–5pm. At other times by appointment only. **Admission:** Adults £3, children £1.50.

map 6 D1

DUNHAM MASSEY HALL

Altrincham, Cheshire
Tel: 0161 941 1025 Fax: 0161 929 7508 (The National Trust)

18th century house containing the treasures of the 2nd Earl of Warrington who also laid out the formal parkland. The tranquil garden contains remnants from past layouts such as the moat, Elizabethan mount and Orangery, all set amongst sweeping lawns and waterside plantings. **Admission:** NT members free. House and Garden: Adult £5, child £2.50, family £12, booked parties £4.50 (min 15 paying adults). House only: Adult £3, child £1.50. Garden only: Adult £3, child £1.50. Car entry: £2.80 per car, £5 per coach/minibus (free to booked parties), £1 per motorcycle. **Open:** House and garden open 4 Apr–1 Nov. House, Sat to Wed 12–5pm (last entry 4.30pm, open at 11am Bank Hol Suns and Mons). Garden, Shop and Restaurant daily 11–5pm. Park open daily all year round.

map 6 B1

NT Photographic Library, Nick Meers

GAWSWORTH HALL

Macclesfield, Cheshire
Tel: 01260 223456 Fax: 01260 223469 (Mr and Mrs Timothy Richards)

Tudor half-timbered manor house with tilting ground. Former home of Mary Fitton, Maid of Honour at the Court of Queen Elizabeth 1 and the supposed 'Dark Lady' of Shakespeare's sonnets. Pictures, sculpture and furniture. Open air theatre, fully seated, covered grandstand–Jun/Jul/Aug. Situated half-way between Macclesfield and Congleton in an idyllic setting close to the lovely medieval church. Open Air Theatre: Shakespeare's Henry V–18 Jun–27 Jun–plus musicals, plays, concerts, etc, up to 15 Aug. Major Flower Festival 28–31 May. Telephone for details. **Location:** 3 miles South of Macclesfield on the A536 (Congleton/Macclesfield Road). **Station(s):** Macclesfield. Open: 10 Apr–4 Oct. **Admission:** Adults £3.80, children £1.90. Groups of 20 or more £2.80. **Events/Exhibitions:** Major Flower Festival 29–31 May. Craft Fairs Spring and Aug Bank Hols.

map 8 B5

LITTLE MORETON HALL

Congleton, Cheshire CW12 4SD
Tel: 01260 272018 (The National Trust)

Begun in 1450, Little Moreton is regarded as the finest example of a timber-framed moated manor house in England. The Chapel, Great Hall and Long Gallery, where ghosts still walk, together with the Knot Garden, make Little Moreton an exceptional day out. Location for Granada TV's recent (1996) adaptation of 'Moll Flanders'–costumes on exhibition Apr–Oct. Traditional and local recipes in our restaurant and visit the shop with its extensive range of gifts and crafts. Parties welcome. See the Great Hall decorated for an Elizabethan Yuletide with Christmas Festivities, seasonal refreshments and shopping. **Adult:** £4, child £2, family £10. Open 21 Mar–1 Nov, Wed–Sun 12–5.30pm (Bank Hol Mon 11–5.30) 7 Nov–20 Dec, Sat & Sun 12–4pm. Tel: 01260 272018.

NORTON PRIORY MUSEUM & GARDENS

Tudor Road, Manor Park, Runcorn, Cheshire WA7 1SX
Tel: 01928 569895 (The Norton Priory Museum Trust)

The beautiful 30 acre woodland gardens with an award winning walled garden are the setting for the now demolished mansion of the Brookes, built on the site of a former Augustinian priory. Excavated remains of the priory & the atmospheric 12th century undercroft can be found with displays on the medieval priory, the later houses & gardens in the museum. Contemporary sculpture is situated in the grounds. **Location:** From M56 (junction 11) turn towards Warrington and follow Norton Priory road signs. **Open:** Open daily all year. Apr–Oct, Sat, Sun & Bank Hols 12–6pm; Mon to Fri 12–5pm; Nov–Mar, daily 12–4pm. Walled Garden open Mar–Oct, closed 24/25/26 Dec, 1 Jan. Special arrangements for groups. **Admission:** Adults £3, concs £1.70, family £7.90 (2 adults & up to 3 children under 16).

map 6 C1

RODE HALL

Church Lane, Scholar Green ST7 3QP
Tel: 01270 873237 Fax: 01270 882962
(Sir Richard Baker Wilbraham Bt)

18th century country house with Georgian stable block. Later alterations by L Wyatt and Darcy Braddell. **Location:** 5 miles SW of Congleton between A34 and A 50. **Open:** Easter–end Sept, Wednesdays and Bank Holidays. Garden only Tuesdays and Thursdays 2–5pm. **Admission:** House, garden and kitchen garden £3.50. Garden and kitchen garden £2.00. **Refreshments:** Home-made teas by agreement.

map 8
B5

TABLEY HOUSE

Knutsford, Cheshire, WA16 0HB.
Tel: 01565 750 151 Fax: 01565 653 230
Owners: The Victoria University of Manchester

Fine Palladian mansion designed by John Carr of York for the Leicester family. The staterooms show family memorabilia, furniture by Gillow, Bullock and Chippendale and the first collection of English paintings ever made. **Location:** 2 miles W of Knutsford, entrance on A5033 (M6 Junction 19, A556). **Open:** Apr–end Oct: Thurs, Fri, Sat, Sun and Bank Hols, 2–5pm. (Last entry 4.30pm). Free car park. Main rooms and the Chapel suitable for the disabled. **Admission:** Adults £3.50. Child/Student with card £1. **Refreshments:** Tearoom and shop facilities. ALL ENQUIRIES TO THE ADMINISTRATOR. **Conferences:** Small meetings, civil wedding licence.

map 6
C1

TATTON PARK

Knutsford, Cheshire WA16 6QN
Tel: 01565 654 822 Fax: 01565 650179 (Cheshire County Council)

Large Regency mansion with extravagantly decorated staterooms, family rooms and servants workrooms. A superb collection of Gillow furniture, Baccarat glass and paintings by Italian and Dutch masters. Two exhibition rooms, newly opened in 1997, one of which features personal memorabilia of the Egerton family. 1000 acres of deer park open to visitors with its lakes woods and open vistas, provide the setting for the magnificent mansion and help make Tatton one of England's most complete country estates. The Garden contains many unusual features and rare species of plants shrubs and trees. Considered to be one of the finest and most important gardens within the National Trust. Features include: Conservatory by Wyatt, Fernery by Paxton, Japanese, Italian and Rose gardens. The rare collection of plants including rhododendrons, tree ferns, bamboo and pines are the result of 200 years of collecting by the Egerton family. **Open:** Managed and Financed by Cheshire County Council.

map 6
C1

LITTLE MORETON HALL

Congleton CW12 4SD Tel: 01260 272018

Open: 21 March to 1 Nov: daily except Mon & Tues 12–5.30 or dusk if earlier (open BH Mon 11–5.30 and opens at 11 Wed to Sun 25 July to 6 Sept). Last admission 5. 7 Nov to 20 Dec: Sat & Sun 12–4, access to Great Hall, Parlour, garden, shop and restaurant only. Special openings at other times, for pre-booked parties, including evening tours with buffet supper. Events: 22 March to 1 Nov: Chapel Service every Sun 3.45. Open-air theatre in July.

LYME PARK

Disley, Stockport SK12 2NX Tel: 01663 762023/766492 Fax: 01663 765035

Open: House: 3 April to 31 Oct: daily except Wed & Thur 1–5 (BH Mon 11–5). Last admission 4.30. Garden: 3 April to 31 Oct: Fri to Tues 11–5; also Wed & Thur 1–5; Nov to 20 Dec: Sat & Sun 12–3. Park:

April to Oct: daily 8am–8.30pm; Nov to March: 8–6 daily. Events: details from Estate Office (please send s.a.e.). **Admission:** House & garden £4; family £10. House only £3; garden only £2. Park only £3.30 per car (NT members free)

QUARRY BANK MILL

Wilmslow SK9 4LA Tel: 01625 527468 Fax: 01625 539267

Open: Open all year. April to Sept: Mill: daily 11–6. Last admission 4.30. Also pre-booked specified evenings in May, June & Sept. Apprentice House & garden: (closed Mon except BH Mon) Tues to Fri 2–4.30. Weekends & during Aug: as Mill. Timed entry tickets: to avoid disappointment please reserve timed ticket at reception on arrival. Oct to March: Mill: daily 11–5 except Mon. Last admission 3.30. Pre-booked groups from 9.30 except weekends & BH Mon. Apprentice House and garden: Tues to Fri 2–4.30; weekends: as Mill. Events: details of programme available from property.

Cornwall

*I*t is usual to bracket Devon and Cornwall as if they shared many things in common. They share little except contiguity. Their scenery is vastly dissimilar – their speech and customs entirely different. Their climate is different. Even their cream is not the same.

Cornwall is far more rugged, its inland scenery barer. Devon wears an air of rich comfort. You feel in Cornwall the fierceness of man's struggle against nature. Yet on the south coast especially, man and nature have combined to create some of the most splendid gardens in Britain.

The place names of Cornwall sound foreign. Ventongimps, Trevisquite, Tol-Pedn-Penith, Lostwithiel, Menheniot, Chy-an-Drea, Tregeargate and Egloskerry. Cornwall is not English territory. The enchantment of Cornwall is legendary – Merlin, King Arthur,

Padstow

Tristan and Isolde – the magic lives on! The fortified headland of Tintagel, the picturesque fishing villages of St Ives, Port Gaverne and Port Isaac, the torrents and rock formations of Bodmin Moor and the clenched little harbour of Boscastle – are typical of Cornwall's craggy appeal, but the full elemental power of the ocean can best be appreciated on Cornwall's twin pincers of The Lizard point and Land's End, where the splintered cliffs resound to the constant thunder of the waves.

BOSVIGO

Bosvigo Lane, Truro, Cornwall
Tel: 01872 275774 Fax: 01872 275774 (Michael and Wendy Perry)

Unlike most Cornish Gardens, Bosvigo is a 'summer' garden. Shrubs take second place to herbaceous perennials, carefully planted to give a succession of colour from Jun through 'til Sept. The gardens comprise a series of walled or hedged 'rooms' all around the Georgian house (not open). Each room has its own colour theme. A Victorian conservatory houses a collection of semi-tender climbers and plants–a delightful place to sit and relax. This is a plantsman's garden–the harder you look, the more plants you will see. Featured in many books, magazines and on television. **Open:** Mar–end Sept, Wed–Sat, 11–6pm. **Admission:** Adults £2, children 50p (no commissions). Part suitable for disabled. Sorry, no dogs.

`map 2 C6`

BURNCOOSE NURSERIES & GARDEN

Gwennap, Redruth TR16 6BJ
Tel: 01209 861112 Fax: 01209 860011 (C H Williams)

The Nurseries are set in the 30 acre woodland gardens of Burncoose. Some 12 acres are laid out for nursery stock production of over 3000 varieties of ornamental trees, shrubs and herbaceous plants. Specialities include camellias, azaleas, magnolias, rhododendrons and conservatory plants. The Nurseries are widely known for rarities and for unusual plants. Full mail order catalogue £1 (posted). **Location:** 2 miles southwest of Redruth on the main A393 Redruth to Falmouth road between the villages of Lanner and Ponsanooth. **Open:** Mon–Sat 9–5pm, Sun 11–5pm. Gardens and tearooms open all year (except Christmas Day). **Admission:** Nurseries free, Gardens £2.00.

`map 2 C6`

CAERHAYS CASTLE AND GARDENS

Gorran, St Austell PL26 6LY
Tel: 01872 501310 Fax: 01872 501870

One of the very few Nash built castles still left standing - situated within approximately 60 acres of informal woodland gardens created by J C Williams, who sponsored plant hunting expeditions to China at the turn of the century. Noted for its camellias, magnolias, rhododendrons and oaks. **English Heritage Listing:** Grade One, Outstanding. **Open:** Gardens 16 Mar – 8 May, 11–4pm. House 23 Mar –1 May, 2–4pm. Monday to Friday only. House closed on Bank Holidays. Additional openings (Gardens only) Sat 25 & Sun 26 Apr, 11–4pm. **Admission:** House £3.50, Gardens £3.50, Children £1.50, House/Gardens £6. Guided Tour by head Gardener for groups can be arranged outside normal opening times, £4 each. Please contact for details of charity openings.

`map 2 C6`

 # GODOLPHIN HOUSE

Godolphin Cross, Helston, Cornwall TR13 9RE
Tel: 01736-762409 (Mrs M. Schofield)

Godolphin is of the Tudor and Stuart periods with Tudor stables. The garden retains its early raised walks. Elizabethan carp ponds are awaiting restoration. The Godolphins included Sidney, the Carolean poet and Sidney the 1st Earl, Lord High Treasurer, to Queen Anne. The 2nd Earl, Francis, owned the famous Godolphin Arabian horse, a painting of which hangs in the house. **Open:** Bank Hol Mon 2–5pm, May and Jun: Thurs 2–5pm, Jul and Sept: Tues and Thurs 2–5pm, Aug: Tues 2–5pm, Groups of 20 and over by arrangement: Thur 10–1pm and 2–5pm **Admission:** Adults: £3, children £1, under 5s free. Garden: Adults: 50p, children free, groups £2.

map 2 **B6**

LANHYDROCK HOUSE

Bodmin, Cornwall
Tel: 01208 73320 Fax: 01208 74084 (The National Trust)

Lanhdrock, one of Cornwall's grandest houses, dates back to the 17th century but much was rebuilt after a fire in 1881 destroyed all but the north wing, which includes the magnificent Long Gallery with its extraordinary plaster ceiling. A total of 49 rooms are on show today, including servants' bedrooms, kitchens, the nursery suite and the grandeur of the dining-room. Surrounding the house are formal Victorian gardens, wooded higher gardens where magnolias, rhododendrons and camellias climb the hillside. **Open:** Gardens and Park only: 1 Mar–1 Nov 1998. House: 1 Apr–1 Nov 98 daily 11–5.30pm. Closes 5pm in October. House closed Mons (except Bank Hol Mons). **Admission:** House & Gardens: Adult £6.20, child £3.10. Garden & Grounds only: Adult £3.10, child, £1.55. Group Rate: House, Park and Gardens £5.50. Park and Gardens only: £3.10.

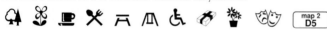

map 2 **D5**

MOUNT EDGCUMBE HOUSE AND COUNTRY PARK

Cremyll, Torpoint PL10 1HZ
Tel: 01752 822236 Fax: 01752 822199
(Cornwall County and Plymouth City Councils)

The Tudor home of the Earls of Mount Edgcumbe set in magnificent 18th century gardens on the dramatic sea-girt Rame Peninsula. Wild fallow deer, follies, forts; the National camellia collection at its best in March. One of the Great Gardens of Cornwall. **Open:** House and Earl's Garden open 8 April to 18 October, 11–5pm, Wednesdays–Sundays, and Bank Holiday Mondays (admission charge). Country Park open free, all year.

map 2 **E6**

ST MAWES CASTLE

St Mawes, Falmouth, Cornwall
Tel: 01326 270526 (English Heritage)

Designed with three huge circular bastions resembling a clover leaf, Henry VIII's picturesque fort stands in delightful sub-tropical gardens. Climb to the battlements and experience the breathtaking views across the bay to Falmouth and take a trip on the ferry across the estuary to Pendennis Castle. **Location:** In St Mawes on A3078 **Open:** 1 Apr–1 Nov: daily, 10am–6pm (or dusk if earlier in Oct). 2 Nov–31 Mar: Fri–Tues, 10am–4pm. (Closed 24–5 Dec) **Admission:** Adult: £2.50, Conc: £1.90, Child: £1.30. (15% discount for groups of 11 or more).

map 2 **C6**

ST MICHAEL'S MOUNT

Marazion, Nr Penzance, Cornwall
Tel: 01736 710507/01736 710 265 (The National Trust)

Home of Lord St Levan. Medieval and early 17th century with considerable alterations and additions in 18th and 19th century. **Location:** 1/2 mile from the shore at Marazion (A394), connected by causeway. 3 miles E Penzance. **Open:** 1 April–31 Oct, Mon–Fri, 10.30–5.30pm (last adm 4.45pm). **Weekends:** The castle and grounds are open most weekends during the season. Nov to end of Mar: Guided tours as tide, weather and circumstances permit. (NB: ferry boats do not operate a regular service during this period. **Admission:** Adults £3.90, children £1.95, pre-booked parties £3.50–for 20 or more paying people. These are special charity open days when National Trust members are asked to pay.

map 2 **B6**

PENCARROW

Washaway, Bodmin PL30 3AG
Tel: 01208 841369 (The Molesworth-St Aubyn Family)

Georgian house and listed gardens, still owned and lived in by the family. A superb collection of 18th century pictures, furniture, and porcelain. Mile long drive and Ancient British Encampment. Marked walks through beautiful woodland gardens, past the great granite Victorian Rockery, Italian and American gardens, Lake and Ice House. Approximately 50 acres in all. Over 700 different rhododendrons, also an internationally known specimen conifer collection. **Open:** Easter–15 Oct, 1.30–5pm (1 June–10 Sept and Bank Hols 11am). **Admission:** Adults – House & Gardens £4, Gardens only £2. Children – House £2, Gardens: children and dogs very welcome and free. Group rate £3.75. NPI National Heritage Award Winner 1997.

map 2 D5

PRIDEAUX PLACE

Padstow PL28 8RP (Peter Prideaux–Brune)
Tel: 01841 532411

Tucked away in the busy port of Padstow, the family home of the Prideauxs for the past 400 years is surrounded by gardens and wooded grounds overlooking a deer park and the Camel estuary to the moors beyond. The house still retains its E shape Elizabethan front and contains fine paintings and furniture. The 16th century plaster ceiling in the great chamber has been uncovered for the first time since 1760. The impressive outbuildings have been restored in recent years. **Location:** 5 miles from A39 Newquay / Wadebridge link road. Signposted. **Open:** Please phone to confirm opening times and prices.

PENDENNIS CASTLE

Falmouth, Cornwall
Tel: 01326 316594 (English Heritage)

Facing the castle of St Mawes, with glorious views over the mile wide mouth of the River Fal, Pendennis Castle has stood in defence of our shores for almost 450 years. Descend through the tunnels to the Second World War Gun Battery. Explore the First World War Guardroom with its cells and see a Tudor gun deck in action complete with the sights and sounds of battle. A trip on the delightful ferry to St Mawes Castle will make your day even more enjoyable. **Location:** On Pendennis Head 1m SE of Falmouth. **Open:** 1 Apr–1 Nov: daily, 10am–6pm (or dusk if earlier in Oct).Open from 9am during July–Aug. 2 Nov–31 Mar daily 10am–4pm, (Closed 24–5 Dec) **Admission:** Adult: £3, Conc £2.30, Child: £1.50. (15% discount for groups of 11 or more).

map 2 C6

TREBAH GARDEN

Mawnan Smith, Nr Falmouth, Cornwall
Tel: 01326 250448. Fax: 01326 250781 (Trebah Garden Trust)

The steep wooded 25 acre wild ravine gardens run down to a sheltered beach on the Helford. A stream, cascading over waterfalls, winds through water gardens and ponds with koi carp and trout, past glades of large sub-tropical tree ferns, palms and towering Gunnera manicata, under an over-arching canopy of 100 year old rhododendrons and through 2 acres of massed blue and white hydrangeas then spilling on to the beach. A paradise for plantsmen, artists and families. **Location:** 4 miles SW of Falmouth. Follow brown and white tourism signs from Junction of A399 & A394. **Open:** Every day of the year 10.30–5pm (last admission). **Admission:** Adults £3.20, OAPs £3, children (5–15) £1; under 5 Free. Reduced rates for groups and winter months. RHS members free.

map 2 C6

TREGREHAN HOUSE

Par PL24 25J
Tel: 01726 814389 (Mr T C Hudson)

Woodland garden created since early 19th century by Carlyon family concentrating on species from warm-temperate regions. Fine glasshouse range in walled garden. Small nursery, also open by appointment, specialising in wild source material, and camellias bred by the late owner. **Location:** 2 m E of St Austell on A390. 1 m W of St Blazey on A390. **Stations:** Par. **Open:** Mid Mar-end of June and Sept 10.30–5pm closed Easter Sun. Guided tours for parties by prior arrangement. **Refreshments:** Teas available. **Accommodation:** Self catering cottages available. Parking for cars and coaches. Access for disabled to half garden only. No dogs.

TRELISSICK GARDEN

Feock, Truro, Cornwall TR3 6QL
Tel: 01872 862090 (The National Trust)

A garden and estate of rare tranquil beauty with glorious maritime views over Carrick Roads to Falmouth Harbour. The tender and exotic shrubs make this garden attractive in all seasons. Extensive park and woodland walks beside the river. There is an Art and Craft Gallery. **Location:** OS Ref. SW837 396. 6 miles S Truro by road, on both sides of B3289 above King Harry Ferry. **Open:** 1 Mar–1 Nov, Mon–Sat, 10.30–5.30pm, Sun 12.30–5.30pm (restaurant open noon). Closes 5pm Mar & Oct. Nov & Dec: Shop, gallery and restaurant open 10.30–4.30pm. Sun 12.30–4.pm. Woodland walks open all year. **Admission:** £4. Pre-arranged group £3.20. Family ticket £10. £1.50 car park fee refundable on admission.

map 2 C6

TRELOWARREN HOUSE & CHAPEL

Mawgan-in-Meneage, Helston, Cornwall, TR12 6AD
Tel: 01326 221 366 (Sir Ferrers Vyvyan, Bt.)

Home of the Vyvyan family since 1427. Part of the house dates from early Tudor times. The Chapel, part of which is pre-Reformation and the 17th century part of the house are leased to the Trelowarren Fellowship, an ecumenical charity, for use by them as a Christian residential healing and retreat centre. (Phone for details). The Chapel and main rooms containing family portraits are open to the public at certain times. Sunday services are held in the Chapel during the holiday season. **Location:** 6 miles S of Helston, off B3293 to St. Keverne. **Open: House & Chapel:** 31 Mar–24 Sept, Wed & Bank Hol Mons, 2.15–5pm. **Admission:** Adults £1.50, children 50p (under 12 free), including entry to various exhibitions of paintings. **Events/Exhibitions:** Exhibitions of paintings. Only the ground floor is suitable for disabled.

WETHERHAM

St Tudy, Cornwall PL30 3NJ
Tel: 01208 851492 (The Amor Family)

Beautiful secluded Manor House overlooking a lake, contained and encircled by its own land of 40 acres, approached through Cornish lanes. These forbidden gardens date from the restoration period (c. 1660) and are now under restoration and restructuring. Mill pond, bog, box hedged potager, herb garden, chess garden, hexagonal walled rose garden and other special features including a dovecote. Mature trees and new plantings. Bluebell strewn woodland walks. Children most welcome. Lots of animals and a nature trail. **Location:** OS Ref. SX058 757. 2m E of A39 midway between Camelford and Wadebridge. Entrance 1m S of St Tudy on the St Mabyn Road. **Open:** Garden only: daily, 10.30–5pm or dusk if earlier in winter. Please check for winter opening times. **Admission:** Adult £2.50, Child £1.50. Groups by appointment. Rates on request.

map 2 D5

ANTONY

Torpoint, Plymouth PL11 2QA Tel: 01752 812191

Open: 1 April to 29 Oct: Tues, Wed, Thur & BH Mon (also Sun in June, July & Aug) 1.30–5.30, car park opens 12.30. Last admission 4.45. Bath Pond House can be seen by prior written application to Custodian and only when house is open. Woodland Garden (not NT – Carew Pole Garden Trust) open 1 March to 31 October, daily 11–5.30. **Admission:** £4. Pre-arranged parties £3. £2.50 for access to Woodland Garden (NT members free on days when house open). Combined gardens-only ticket for Antony garden and adjoining woodland garden £3. Pre-arranged parties £2.40 per person

COTEHELE

St Dominick, nr Saltash, PL12 6TA Tel: 01579 351346

Open: House: 1 April to 1 Nov: daily except Fri (open Good Fri) 11–5 (11–4.30 in Oct). Last admission 30min before closing or dusk if earlier (tel. 01579 350434) Mill: 1 April to 1 Nov: daily except Fri (open Good Fri and Fri in July & Aug) 1.30–5.30 (1.30–6 in July & Aug, 1.30–4.30 in Oct). Last admission 30min before closing or dusk if earlier (tel. 01579 350606). Garden: open daily 11 to dusk (tel. 01579 350909). Events: Please contact the Property Manager for details (tel. 01579 351346). **Admission:** House, garden & mill £5.60; family ticket £14. Garden & mill only £2.80; family ticket £7. Pre-arranged parties £4.50 by prior written arrangement only with the Property Manager. Coach party organisers must book and obtain a copy of the route from the Property Manager. No parties Sun or BH weekends

GLENDURGAN GARDEN

Mawnan Smith, nr Falmouth TR11 5JZ

Tel: 01326 250906 (opening hours only) or 01208 74281

Open: 3 March to 31 Oct: Tues to Sat & BH Mon (closed Good Fri) 10.30–5.30. Last admission 4.30. **Admission:** £3.20. Family ticket £8. Pre-arranged parties £2.70 per person

LANHYDROCK

Bodmin PL30 5AD Tel: 01208 73320 Fax: 01208 74084

Open: House: 1 April to 1 Nov: daily except Mon, but open BH Mon, 11–5.30 (closes 5 in Oct). Last admission to house 30min before closing. Garden: 1 March to 1 Nov: daily 11–5.30 (closes 5 in March & Oct); Nov to end Feb: daily during daylight hours. Events: 11 July, open-air jazz concert; programme details available from the Property Manager. **Admission:** House, garden & grounds £6.20; family ticket £15.50. Garden & grounds only £3.10. Pre-arranged parties £5.50

TERICE

nr Newquay TR8 4PG Tel: 01637 875404 Fax: 01637 879300

Open: 1 April to 1 Nov: daily except Tues & Sat (but open daily 27 July to 6 Sept), 11–5.30 (closes 5 in Oct). Last admission 30min before closing. Events: programme available from the Property Manager (s.a.e. please). **Admission:** £4; family ticket £10. Pre-arranged parties £3.40

Cumbria

Through the middle ages, successive kings and rulers fought over this territory. This has left the area with a multitude of Celtic monuments, Roman remains, stately homes and monastic ruins.

The Lake District dominate Cumbria, despite the attractions of other places of interest in the county. Windermere, Grasmere, Bowness, Ambleside, Kendal and Keswick are all best visited on foot. The lakes vary in character considerably, from the sombre Wastwater to the bright and breezy Windermere, the centre of most of the activities. The number of fells and lakes in the area is astonishing.

Carlisle, the county town set in the north of Cumbria, is a fine cathedral city which is steeped in the history of battle.

Loweswater

ABBOT HALL ART GALLERY

Kendal, Cumbria LA9 5AL
Tel: 01539 722464 Fax: 01539 722494 (Lake District Art Gallery & Museum Trust)

This elegant Georgian building provides a superb setting for its collection of fine art. Paintings by George Romney fill the walls of rooms furnished by Gillows of Lancaster. Touring exhibitions complement the permanent collection of 18th, 19th and 20th century British art. The gallery is situated by the banks of the River Kent overlooking Kendal castle. The adjacent Museum of Lakeland Life looks at 300 years of local history. Exhibits include a Victorian street scene, reconstructed farmhouse rooms and a re-creation of Arthur Ransome's study. Also situated nearby is Kendal Museum of Natural History and Archaeology. **Open:** 7 days a week 12 Feb–24 Dec. 1998 10.30–5pm (reduced hours in winter). **Admission:** Concessions, family tickets and season tickets available. Guided tours by appointment. **Directions:** 10 minutes drive from junctions 36 of the M6. Follow brown Museum signs to South Kendal.

map 11 F6

ACORN BANK GARDEN & WATERMILL

Temple Sowerby, Nr Penrith CA10 ISP
Tel: 017683 61893 (The National Trust)

A walled garden renowned for its impressive herb collection of culinary and medicinal plants. There are also mixed herbaceous and rose borders and orchards containing a wide range of northern varieties of fruit tree. There are circular walks on the estate, including a circular woodland route along the Crowdundle Beck to Acorn Bank Watermill which is open to the public. Light refreshments are available, together with a shop and plant sales. **Open:** 28 Mar–1 Nov: daily 10–5.30pm, last admission 5.00. **Admission:** Adults £2.20, children £1.10, family ticket £5.80, pre-arranged parties £1.60 per person. Car parking. **Events:** 28 May, newt-watching, 18 Oct Apple Day.

map 11 F5

THE BEATRIX POTTER GALLERY

The Square, Hawkshead, Ambleside, Cumbria
Tel: 015394 36355 Fax: 015394 36118 (The National Trust)

An annually changing exhibition of original illustrations from Beatrix Potter's story books for children. One of many historic buildings in this picturesque village. This was once the office of the author's husband, the solicitor William Heelis and the interior remains largely unaltered since his day. **Open:** 1 Apr–1 Nov Sun–Thur (closed Fri & Sat except Good Friday) 10.30–4.30pm. Last admission 4pm. **Admission:** By timed ticket (including NT members) Adults £2.80, children £1.40, no reduction for parties. Car & coach parking in village car park, 200m.

map 10 E6

BRANTWOOD

Coniston, Cumbria
Tel: 015394 41396 Fax: 015394 41263 (The Brantwood Trust)

Brantwood is the most beautifully situated house in the Lake District and was the home of John Ruskin from 1872 until his death in 1900. It is a constant memorial to his life and work, with continual displays of his drawings, watercolours and personal memorabilia, video programme and bookshop, glorious woodland walks, full seasonal programme of activities, events and theatre evenings, Jumping Jenny's restaurant and tearooms, coach house craft gallery, regular sailings by Coniston Launch and Steamyacht Gondola. **Location:** 2 miles from Coniston Village, on opposite side of Coniston Water. **Open:** Open all year–daily mid Mar–mid Nov 11–5.30pm. Winter season Wed to Sun 11–4pm. **Admission:** (1998 prices) Adults £3.90, students £2.10, children £1 (5–15 yrs), family £9.50. Gardens only £1.50.

APPLEBY CASTLE
Appleby–In–Westmorland, Cumbria CA16 6XH
Tel: 017683 51402 Fax: 017683 51082 (Appleby Castle Limited)

Dominated by its impressive Norman Keep, the castle was a major stronghold of the powerful Clifford family, who helped to hold the northern Marches during medieval times and fought (and sometimes died) in most of the famous medieval battles, Bannockburn, Crecy, the Wars of the Roses and Flodden. Later the Castle was a favourite home of Lady Anne Clifford, the last in her line, who stubbornly held out for her heritage in the troubled years of the civil war and left an enduring legacy at the castle, which was further enhanced by her descendants, the Tufton family. Today visitors may enjoy a castle which has something to offer from each period of history. The Norman Keep has five floors and a dramatic view from the top. The curtain wall and defensive earthworks are amongst the most impressive in northern England. The Great Hall of the castle contains the famous Great Painting of Lady Anne and her family, together with other period pieces. In the grounds, the castle has a variety of birds and animals, both domestic and foreign, including rare breeds, with special gentle areas for children. The castle's stable block, built in the outer bailey is also of interest as is Lady Anne's 'Beehouse', actually a small oratory. **Open:** Daily, 4 Apr–31 Oct 1998. 10–5pm (last admissions) (closes 4pm October). **Admission:** Grounds, Keep & Great Hall: Adults £4, children under 5 years free, children 5-15 years £2, senior citizens £2, family tickets 2A + 2C £10. Parties of 20 or more: Adults: £3, children £1.50, senior citizens £1.50, bus driver: Free plus free tea. School parties *NB excluding Great Hall* Adults & teachers £2.50, children £1.25, one teacher free per 15 pupils. Worksheets: History Worksheets 10p, Castle Challenge Quiz 10p, Nature Trail 10p, Triptych Information 10p.

map 11
F5

DALEMAIN

Nr Penrith, Cumbria CA11 0HB
Tel: 017684 86450   Fax: 017684 86223 (Robert Hasell-McCosh)

Medieval Tudor and Georgian House and Gardens. Behind the impressive Georgian façade lies the real surprise of Dalemain–its sheer variety. There has been a settlement on this site since Saxon times. The House has evolved as dictated sometimes by domestic or agricultural demands or sometimes by the fashion of the day. As a result, parts of the house are a glorious confusion of winding passages, quaint stairways, unexpected rooms–the sort of house that children love to play in. Indeed, part of the charm of Dalemain is that it remains very much a family home still occupied by the same family who have lived here since 1679. The variety, extent and richness of the furniture portraits and contents at Dalemain is quite exceptional for a house of its size. Museums: Westmorland and Cumberland Yeomanry, Countryside, Agricultural and Fell Pony Museums. The delightful gardens have many rare plants and a collection of over 100 old-fashioned roses. Enjoy delicious home-made meals and teas beside the log fire in the medieval old hall. Dalemain was featured as Lowood Institution (Jane Eyre's School) in LWT's recent production. **Open:** Sun 5 Apr–Sun 4 Oct. 1998 inclusive. Sun to Thur. Hours: 10.30–5pm. Gardens, tearooms, shop and agricultural and countryside museums. Hours: 11.15–5pm House. **Admission:** House & Gardens: Adult £5 child £3, family £13. Gardens: Adult £3, child free when accompanied. For furthur information or to discuss events, party visits and conferences please contact Bryan McDonald the Administrator. **Location:** A592 Penrith to Ullswater, M6 J40 2 miles.

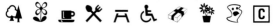

map 10
E5

CASTLETOWN HOUSE

Rockcliffe, Carlisle, Cumbria CA6 4BN
Tel: 01228 74792 Fax: 01228 74464 (Gilee Mounsey-Heysham, Esq)

Period House set in attractive gardens and grounds. **Location:** 5 miles NW of Carlisle on Solway coast, 1 mile W of Rockcliffe village and 2 miles W of A74. **Open:** House Only by appointment only.

map 10
E4

HERON CORN MILL & MUSEUM OF PAPERMAKING

Waterhouse Mills, Beetham, Milnthorpe, Cumbria
Tel: 01 5395 65027 Fax: 01 5395 65033 (Heron Corn Mill–Beetham Trust)

Open: 11–5pm Tue–Sun. Easter/ 1 Apr–30 Sept. Open Bank Hols. Heron Corn Mill is a water driven lowder type corn mill now run as a working museum. The mill celebrated its 900 years of milling on the site in 1996. An exhibition mounted for this celebration now forms part of the permanent exhibitions. All the machinery in the mill is driven by a 14ft high breast shot wheel. Milling demonstrations are given and cereal products are on sale. The Museum of Papermaking is housed in the renovated "Carter's Barn " on the same site. Both buildings are basically 18th century. The museum attempts to show the making of paper by both ancient and modern methods, with displays, artefacts and exhibitions. Occasional demonstrations of "Hand making of paper" are given to pre-booked groups and on special open days. **Admission:** Adults £1.50, OAPs £1, children £1, group 20+ 10% discount.

map 10
E6

HOLKER HALL AND GARDENS

Cark-in-Cartmel, nr Grange-over-Sands LA11 7PL
Tel: 015395 58328 Fax: 015395 58776 (Lord and Lady Cavendish)

Cumbria's premier Stately home has 25 acres of National Award winning gardens with water features, rare plants and shrubs, 'World Class ... not to be missed by foreign visitors' (Good Gardens Guide '97). Also exhibitions, Deer Park, Adventure Playground, Motor Museum. Home of the spectacular Holker Garden Festival 29–31 May '98. (Show Office 015395 58838). **Location:** N of Cark-in-Cartmel on B5278 from Haverthwaite; 4 miles W Grange-over-Sands. **Stations:** Cark-in-Cartmel. **Open:** Apr 1–Oct 30 everyday excluding Sat, 10–6 last admission 4.30pm. **Admission:** From £3.35, reduction for groups of 20 or more. **Refreshments:** Home-made cakes, sandwiches, salads in the Coach House Cafe. Free car parking.

map 10
E6

HUTTON-IN-THE-FOREST
Penrith
Tel: 017684 84449 Fax: 017684 84571 (Lord and Lady Inglewood)

The home of Lord Inglewood's family since 1605. Built around a medieval pele tower with 17th, 18th and 19th century additions. Fine English furniture and pictures, ceramics and tapestries. The lovely walled garden established in 1730 has an increasing collection of herbaceous plants, wall trained fruit trees and topiary. Also dovecote and woodland walk through magnificent specimen trees, identifiable from leaflet. **Location:** 6 miles NW of Penrith on B5305 Wigton Road (3 miles from M6 exit 41). **Stations:** Penrith. **Open:** House 1–4pm 1 May–4 Oct, Thur, Fri and Sun, also Easter Fri, Sun, Mon and Bank Hols. Gardens 11–5pm everyday except Sat. Groups by arrangement from Apr–Oct. **Admission:** House and Gardens: adult £4, child £2, family £10. Gardens only: adult £2.50, children free. **Refreshments:** Home-made light lunches & teas in Cloisters when house is open, 12–4.30pm.

map 10 E4

ISEL HALL
Cockermouth, Cumbria CA13 0QG
(The Administrator)

Pele Tower with domestic range and gardens set on north bank of River Derwent. The house is small, so groups limited to 30. **Location:** 3 1/2 miles N.E. of Cockermouth. **Station(s):** Aspatria 9 miles; Penrith 32 miles. **Open:** Mondays, 13 April – 12 October, 2–4pm. Other times by written arrangement. **Admission:** £3. No dogs. No photography inside. It is regretted there is no disabled access upstairs.

map 10 D4

LEVENS HALL
Kendal LA8 0PD
Tel: 015395 60321 Fax: 015395 60669 (C H Bagot Esq)

Elizabethan house and home of the Bagot family containing fine furniture and the earliest English patchwork (c.1708). The world famous Topiary Gardens (c.1694) are past winners of the HHA/Christies Garden of the Year Award. In addition there is a collection of working model steam engines. **Location:** 5 minutes drive from Exit 36 of the M6. 5 miles S of Kendal on the A6. **Station:** Oxenholme. **Open:** 1 Apr–15 Oct, Sun–Thur (including Bank Hols). Garden & Tearoom 10–5pm. House Noon–5pm. Last Admissions 4.30pm. Closed Fri & Sat. **Admission:** House and Garden: Adults £5.20, children £2.80. Gardens only: Adults £3.80, children £2.10. **Refreshments:** Home-made light lunches & teas. We regret the house is not suitable for wheelchairs.

map 10 E6

MIREHOUSE
Mirehouse, Keswick CA12 4QE
Tel: 01768 772287 Fax: 01768 772287 (Mr & Mrs Spedding)

In a spectacular setting this old family home offers a relaxed welcome and unique, wide ranging literary connections. Our visitors particularly appreciate the varied sheltered gardens and walks, the natural adventure playgrounds, the live classical music in the house and the personal attention of members of the family. **Location:** 3½ miles N of Keswick on 591. Regular Stagecoach bus service. **Open:** April–October inclusive. **Grounds and tearoom:** Daily 10–5.30pm. **House:** Sunday, Wednesdays (also Fridays in August) 2.00pm, last entries 4.30pm. Group visits welcome at other times by appointment. Please telephone for Winter opening times. **Refreshments:** The Old Sawmill Tearoom is known for generous Cumbrian cooking. Catering for events and groups is also available in the licensed Garden Hall.

map 10 E5

MUNCASTER CASTLE
Ravenglass, Cumbria CA18 1RQ
Tel: 01229 717 614 Fax: 01229 717 010 (Mrs P. Gordon-Duff-Pennington)

Home of the Pennington family from 1208 to the present day. The Pele Tower stands on Roman foundations. Set in superb gardens with magnificent views of the Lakeland Fells. Owl Centre with daily talk and flying display. **Open:** Castle 29 Mar–1 Nov daily except Sat, 12.30–4pm (last entry). Gardens & Owl Centre 11–5pm daily all year. **Admission:** Castle, Gardens & Owls: Adults £5.20, children £3.50, family £14.50. Gardens & Owls: Adults £3.50, children £2, family £9.50. **Refreshments:** Stable Buttery serves light refreshments to full meals 11–5pm and is licensed. Gift shops, plant centre, children's play area, nature trail, orienteering, free parking.

map 9 D6

SIZERGH CASTLE & GARDEN
Kendal, Cumbria, LA8 8AE
Tel: 015395 60070 (The National Trust)

The 14th century Pele Tower rises to 60ft, containing original windows, floors and fireplaces; 16th century wings; fine panelling ceilings; French and English Furniture, china and family portraits. Extensive garden includes the largest limestone gardens owned by the Trust with Japanese maples, dwarf conifers, hardy ferns, perennials and bulbs; water garden; herbaceous borders, wild flower banks; fine autumn colour. **Location:** 3½ miles S of Kendal NW of A590/A591 Interchange. **Open:** Castle and Garden 1 Apr–29 Oct, Sun–Thur, 1.30–5.30pm. Garden & Shop 12.30–5.30pm. **Admission:** House and Garden £4, Garden only £2. Children half price. Parties by prior arrangement. No dogs. Wheelchairs available for use in garden only.

map 10 E6

WORDSWORTH HOUSE
Main Street, Cockermouth CA13 9RX
Tel : 01900 824805 (The National Trust)

Birthplace of William Wordsworth in 1770. Seven rooms furnished in the Regency style, with some personal effects of the poet. Walled Georgian garden with terrace walk (Wordsworth's "The Prelude"). "Wordsworths Lake District" video showing in the stables. Kitchen restaurant (home baking). Shop. Events during the season. Parking in town. **Open:** 1 Apr–30 Oct, Mon–Fri 11–4.30pm. Also Sats 11 Apr, 2 & 23 May. All Sats 27 Jun–5 Sep & Sat 24 Oct. Closed remaining Sat and Sun. **Admission:** Adults £2.80, children £1.40, family ticket (2 adults and 2 children) £7.50. Group rate, adults £2, children £1 each – pre-booked, minimum 15.

map 10 D5

NAWORTH CASTLE

Naworth Castle, Brampton, Cumbria
Tel: 016977 3229 Fax: 016977 3679 (Philip Howard)

Naworth Castle is a romantic Border Castle dating back to 1335. Owned by Philip Howard it is now Cumbria's premier historic function venue and offers exclusive use and outstanding personal service. In 1997 over 40 weddings took place. Corporate clients include British Telecom, Thorn Security, Ford U.K., Iveco, Kleinwort Benson and Jaguar Cars. 1997 filming included Border Television, Granada T.V.'s "Love Me Do". The castle was Thornfield in LWT's Jane Eyre and used in Catherine Cookson's "Black Candle". Horse riding stables, clay pigeon shooting, river & lake fishing, game shooting. Conference and corporate breaks, team building days, product launches, fashion shows, concerts, charity events, exhibits. High quality retained caterers available for all events and overnight parties. Own wine list and wine company 'Naworth Castle Wines'. Accommodation available with special functions. 13 double bedrooms with en suite shower/bath rooms. Separate 2 bedroomed apartment. Civil Wedding Licence. Other facilities: 17th century Walled Garden, 400 acres of woodlands. **Open:** All year by appointment only. All tours must be pre-booked, minimum 15 people, maximum 100. Lunches, teas and dinners available. Most guided tours by owner. Tours can be conducted throughout the year depending upon availability. We also can accommodate small specialist parties during the week and the owner can arrange to accompany them on tours of the region. **1998 Special Events:** Fri 27–Sun 29th Mar: Galloway Antiques Fair. Sun 19th Apr, Open Day organised by the Rotary. Thur 25 Jun, Thomson Roddick & Laurie Fine Pictures & Furniture Auction (viewing day Wed 24 Jun.) Fri 28 Aug–Mon 31 Aug Galloway Antique Fair. 22 Oct Thomson Roddick & Laurie Fine Art and Furniture Sale (viewing day on Wed 21 Oct).

map 11
F4

Derbyshire

Of all the English counties, this is probably the most traditional. Within its borders England passes from the plain country to the hill country, from the newer and softer rocks to the old and harder. As the Lake District dominates Cumbria, so the Peak District dominates Derbyshire.

The Peak District became Britain's first National Park in 1951. This vast rolling landscape stretches for an area of over five hundred square miles and is a favourite with walkers, climbers and pot-holers who congregate on the Pennine Way. The Tissington Trail is equally popular with walkers as it winds its spectacular way around this charming old village. Tissington was responsible for reviving the custom of well-dressing in the seventeenth century, as an act of thanksgiving for its deliverance from the deadly plague. Well-dressing continues to be a popular event in this area to this day.

At the Northern extremity of Derbyshire, lies the former spa town of Buxton. This town is a rare gem where elegant sweeping terraces echo those found at Bath. To the southwest, the modern city of Derby, is famed for its Crown Derby porcelain. Either of these towns would provide a welcome stopover point for energetic walkers to rest their weary feet.

Viaduct in Monsdale

Matlock is another fine Spa town, developed in the eighteenth century and home to some impressive buildings including the former hydrotherapy centre, perched on a hill above the town. Matlock is also an ideal base from which to venture out on the A6 as it makes its way through the stunning Derwent Gorge. Those travelling to the north of the county will be rewarded by the beauty of two great historic houses, Chatsworth and Haddon Hall.

BOLSOVER CASTLE

Bolsover, Derbyshire
Tel: 01246 823349 (English Heritage)

Winner of the 1995/6 NPI National Heritage Award, having been voted by the public as one of Britain's favourite national treasures, Bolsover has the air of a romantic story book castle. Visitors can explore the enchanting 17th century mansion and 'Little Castle' with its elaborate Jacobean fireplaces, panelling and wall paintings. Discover the mock-medieval fortifications, battlements, ruined staterooms and indoor riding school, one of the oldest in Europe. An inclusive audio tour and exhibition brings this magical castle to life. **Location:** Off M1 at junction 29, 6m from Mansfield. In Bolsover 6m E of Chesterfield on A632. **Open:** 1 Apr–1 Nov: daily, 10–6pm (or dusk if earlier in Oct). 2 Nov–31 Mar: Wed-Sun, 10am–4pm. (Closed 24–26 Dec) **Admission:** Adult: £2.95, Conc: £2.20, Child: £1.50. (15% discount for groups of 11 or more).

map 8
D5

CALKE ABBEY

Ticknall, Derby DE73 1LE
Tel: 01332 863822 Fax: 01332 865272

The house that time forgot; a baroque mansion built 1701–3 for Sir John Harpur and set in a landscaped park. Little restored, Calke is preserved by a conservation programme as a graphic illustration of the English country house in decline; containing the family's collection of natural history, a fine 18C state bed and interiors that are virtually unchanged since the 1880s. Walled garden, pleasure grounds and newly restored Orangery. Early 19C church. Historic parkland with Portland sheep and deer. **Open:** 1 Apr–1 Nov, Sats–Weds 12.45–5.30pm. Last entries 4.45pm. House & church: 1–5.30pm. Garden: 11–5.30pm. Last entries 5pm. House, church & garden closed 15 Aug. Park: open every day, all year £2. Shop & restaurant: as house. Christmas shop & restaurant Nov & Dec weekends 12–4pm. **Admission:** £4.90, child £2.45, farm ticket £12.25, gardens only £2.20. NT members free.

map 8
C6

CHATSWORTH

Chatsworth, Bakewell, Derbyshire, DE45 1PP
Tel: 01246 582 204 Fax: 01246 583 536 (Chatsworth House Trust)

Chatsworth, one of the Treasure Houses of England, is set in the heart of the Peak District National Park. The 26 richly decorated rooms on view contain one of the most important private art collections in the world, including famous displays of paintings and sculpture, gold and silver plate, porcelain and curiosities and a magnificent library. The 100 acre garden contains many notable features; the Cascade, spectacular fountains and rockeries, a maze, rose and kitchen gardens and 5 miles of walks among rare shrubs and forest trees. **Location:** 16 miles from M1, Junction 29. **Station(s):** Chesterfield (30 mins). **Open:** Daily 18 Mar–1 Nov, 11–4.30pm.

map 8
C5

CARNFIELD HALL

S. Normanton, Alfreton, Derbyshire, DE55 22BE.
Tel: 01773 520084 (J B Cartland)

Unspoilt Elizabethan "Mansion House" with 1698 E. Grant. Atmospheric interior with panelled rooms, two 17th Century staircases, great parlour, Georgian drawing room. Three centuries of portraits, furniture, porcelain, glass, costumes, needlework, royal relics and manorial documents. Collections of 18th century fans, snuff boxes, toys and lace by arrangements. Interesting guided tours by the owner. **Location:** 1.5m west of M1/J28 on 136019 adjoining garden centre and restaurant. Alfreton station 5 mins walk. **Open:** Bank Hols including Good Fri and Mons 11–5.30pm. Jul & Aug: Most Tues and Thurs 2–5.30pm. By appointment for groups (numbers 4–25) throughout year and evenings. Candlelit tours in winter. **Admission:** Adults: £3.50, Child £2, OAPs and students £2.50.

map 8 C/D5

ELVASTON CASTLE COUNTRY PARK & ESTATE MUSEUM

Borrowash Road, Elvaston, Derby, Derbyshire
Tel: 01332 571342 Fax: 01332 758751 (Derbyshire County Council)

Step back in time and enjoy the gardens of Elvaston Castle. Stroll in the Old English Garden, linger in the Italianate and Parterre gardens. Stay for a while for lunch or afternoon tea, overlooking the parterre. The Estate Museum allows you to explore workshops from a time gone by. For the more adventurous, visit the Elvaston Riding Centre, hire a bicycle and ask for our Events leaflet.

map 8 C6

HARDWICK OLD HALL

Doe Lea, Nr Chesterfield S44 5QJ
Tel: 01246 850431 (English Heritage)

This large ruined house, finished in 1591, still displays Bess of Hardwick's innovative planning and interesting decorative plasterwork. The views from the top floor over the country park and 'New' Hall are spectacular. **Location:** 9½ miles SE of Chesterfield, off A6175, from Jct 29 / M1. **Open:** 1 Apr–1 Nov, Wed–Sun 10–6pm (or dusk if earlier in October).

EYAM HALL

Eyam, Hope Valley, Derbyshire, S32 5QW
Tel: 01433 631976 Fax: 01433 631603 (Mr R H V Wright)

Built by the Wright family in 1671 in the famous "plague village" of Eyam and still their family home, Eyam Hall is a cosy and intimate house offering family portraits, costumes, tapestries and other fascinating artefacts collected over 3 centuries. **Location:** Approx. 10 miles from Sheffield, Chesterfield and Buxton and off the A623, Eyam Hall is in the centre of the village. **Open:** 1 Apr–1 Nov: Wed, Thur, Sun & Bank Hol: 11–4.30pm. Schools Programme: phone for details. **Admission:** Adult £3.50, child £2.50, conc. £3. Family £10.50. Party rates available with advance booking. Craft Centre & Shops in converted farm buildings with crafts people at work and a selection of unusual products for sale. Licensed Buttery with delicious lunches, light snacks and home-made cakes. **Open:** 28 Feb–24 Dec daily except Mons 10.30am–5.30pm. Victorian Christmas Tours in December – pre-booking essential. Events, concerts and private tours – please enquire.

map 8 C4

KEDLESTON HALL AND PARK

Kedleston Hall, Derby DE22 5JH
Tel: 01332 842191 Fax: 01332 841972 (The National Trust)

Experience the age of elegance in this neoclassical house built between 1759 and 1765 for the Curzon Family. Set in 800 acres of parkland with an 18 C pleasure ground, garden and woodland walks. Parties welcome. Introductory talks can be arranged. **Location:** 5m NW of Derby, signposted from roundabout where A38 crosses A52. **Open:** House: 28 Mar–1 Nov daily except Thurs & Fri (closed Good Fri) 1–5.30pm (11–5.30pm on BH weekends) last admissions 5pm (4pm from 18 Oct). Garden: same days as house 11–6pm. Park: 28 Mar–1 Nov: daily 11–6pm; Nov–20 Dec: Sat & Sun only 12–4pm. Events: concerts and theatre. Aug BH, Working Crafts Show: details from Property Manager. **Admission:** Adults £4.70, child £2.40, family £11.50. £1 reduction for pre-booked parties of 15+. Park & Garden only:Adults £2, child £1 (refundable against tickets for house); Thur & Fri vehicle charge of £2 for park only.

map 8 C6

HADDON HALL

Bakewell, Derbyshire
Tel: 01629 812855 Fax: 01629 814379 (The Duke of Rutland)

William the Conqueror's illegitimate son, Peverel and his descendants held Haddon for a hundred years before it passed into the hands of the Vernons. The following four centuries saw the development of the existing medieval and Tudor manor house from its Norman origins. In the late 16th century, it passed through marriage to the Manners family, later to become Dukes of Rutland, in whose possession it has remained ever since. Little has been added since the reign of Henry VIII, whose elder brother was a frequent guest and despite its time-worn steps, no other medieval house has so triumphantly withstood the passage of time. The terraced gardens, one of the chief glories of Haddon, were added during the 16th century. Now with roses, clematis and delphiniums in abundance, it is perhaps the most romantic garden in all England. A popular choice with film producers, Haddon Hall has in just the past two years appeared in: Elizabeth 1 (1997); Jane Eyre (1996); The Prince and The Pauper (1996); Moll Flanders (1996). **Location:** On the A6, 2 miles S of Bakewell. Open: 1 Apr–30 Sept, 1998. **Admission:** Adult £5.50, OAP £4.75, child £3, family (2+3) £14.75. **Refreshments:** Licensed restaurant serving home-made food.

map 8
C5

Derbyshire

MELBOURNE HALL & GARDENS

Melbourne, DE73 1EN
Tel: 01332 862502 Fax: 01332 862263

This beautiful house of history is the home of Lord and Lady Ralph Kerr. In its picturesque pool-side setting, Melbourne Hall was once the Home of Victorian Prime Minister William Lamb who, as 2nd Viscount Melbourne, gave his name to the famous city in Australia. One of the most famous formal gardens in Britain featuring Robert Bakewell's wrought iron 'Birdcage'. **Location:** 7 m S of Derby off the A453 in village of Melbourne. **Open:** House open every day of Aug only (except first 3 Mons) 2–5pm. Garden open Apr to Sept Weds, Sats and Suns, Bank Hols Mons 2–6pm. Please phone for details of prices. **Refreshments:** Melbourne Hall Tearooms – open throughout the year Tel: (01332) 864224/863469. Visitor centre and shops open at various times throughout the year. Car parking limited – none reserved. Suitable for disabled persons.

map 8 C6

LEA GARDENS

Lea, Matlock, Derbys DE4 5GH
Tel: 01629 534380 Fax: 01629 534260 (Mr & Mrs Jonathan Tye)

Visit Lea Gardens where you can see our highly acclaimed unique collection of rhododendrons, azaleas, kalmias and other plants of interest introduced from the far corners of the world. The gardens are sited on the remains of a medieval millstone quarry and cover an area of approximately four acres amidst a wooded hillside. The excellent rock gardens contain a huge variety of alpines with acers, dwarf conifers, heathers and spring bulbs. The teashop on site offers light lunches and home baking. A plant sales area reflects the contents of the garden offering up to 200 varieties of rhododendrons and azaleas. **Admission:** Adults £3, children 50p, season ticket £4.

map 8 C6

RENISHAW HALL

Near Sheffield, Derbyshire S31 9WB
Tel: 01246 432310 (Sir Reresby Sitwell)

Home of Sir Reresby and Lady Sitwell. Seven acres of Italian style formal gardens stand in 300 acres of mature parkland, encompassing statues, shaped yew hedges, a water garden and lakes. The Sitwell museum and art gallery (display of Fiori de Henriques sculptures) are located in the Georgian stables alongside craft workshops and café, furnished with contemporary art. Located three miles from Exit 30 of the M1, equidistant from Sheffield and Chesterfield. An entirely new exhibition of 20th century artists' paintings opens in June 1998. Tours of house and gardens can be arranged. Telephone for details. Open Easter to mid September Fridays, weekends and Bank Holidays 10.30–4.30pm. Free car parking.

CALKE ABBEY

Ticknall, Derby DE73 1LE Tel: 01332 863822 Fax: 01332 865272

Open: House, garden & church: 1 April to 1 Nov: daily except Thur & Fri, incl. BH Mon (closed Good Fri). House & church: 12.45–5.30; last admission 4.45. Garden: 11–5.30; last admission 5. Ticket office: 11–5. Last admission 5. Admission to house for all visitors (incl. NT members) is by timed ticket, obtained on arrival. This gives the time of entry to the house, but does not restrict the time visitors may spend on their tour. Park: open during daylight hours all year; April to Oct closed 9pm (or dusk if earlier); Nov to March closes at dusk.

HARWICK HALL

Doe Lea, Chesterfield S44 5QJ Tel: 01246 850430 Fax: 01246 854200

Open: Hall: 1 April to 1 Nov: Wed, Thur, Sat, Sun & BH Mon 12.30–5 (closed Good Fri). Last admission to hall 4.30. Garden: 1 April to 1 Nov: daily 12–5.30. No picnics in garden; only in car park & parkland. Car park gates close 6. Parkland open daily throughout the year, 7am to 7pm. Old Hall (EH): 1 April to 1 Nov: Wed to Sun & BH Mon (but closed Good Fri) 10–6. Events: details from Property Manager.

THE OLD MANOR

Norbury, Ashbourne DE6 2ED

Open: Medieval hall by written appointment only with the tenant, Mr C. Wright. 1 April to end Sept: Tues, Wed & Sat

PACKWOOD HOUSE

Lapworth, Solihull B94 6AT Tel: 01564 782024

Open: 1 March to 22 March: car park only, Sat & Sun 12–4; 25 March to end Sept: daily except Mon & Tues (but closed Good Fri and open BH Mon) car park opens 12, garden 1.30–6, house 2–6. Oct & 1 Nov: daily except Mon & Tues 12.30–4.30, car park opens 12. Last admission 30min before closing. Events: 7 June, Teddy Bears' Picnic; July, 1920s Summer Follies; tel. bookings from 1 April. For full summer events leaflet please send s.a.e. to Property Manager

Devon

There is beauty in Devon, whether inland or seaward. The colour of the soil is most unusual. Nowhere else will you find earth of quite such a rich hue. Nowhere else are the hedges of the fields quite so high or quite so thick.

Devon is a land of infinite variety - in its contours as well as in its colours. Level spaces are so uncommon, cricket pitches are hard to find. It is no place for cyclists, as the hills are ominous and well spread through the whole county. To see the region properly, you should travel on foot.

The varied scenery makes Devon the perfect holiday county. The climate is almost tropical for England – the sun shines warmly, and then the rain appears! This produces lush green beauty, and stunning gardens.

Romantic moorland covers vast areas of inland Devon. Dartmoor covers 365 square miles in the south. This is the land of 'The Hound of the Baskervilles'. There are many rare birds that can be seen on the moor, as well as flocks of sheep who keep the undergrowth down and small groups of wild ponies.

The coast line is truly beautiful, with long stretches of sandy beaches. There is a constant reminder of Devon's seafaring history along both coasts. Exeter, Dartmouth and Torbay all offer excellent bases for touring the south of Devon. The varied attractions and beautiful scenery allow you to relax and unwind in this slow moving county.

Barnstaple, on the north coast, is steeped in history. In the centre of the town, on the Strand is a wonderful arcade topped with a statue of Queen Anne.

Don't miss the teas!

South Pool

ARLINGTON COURT
Arlington, Nr Barnstaple, Devon
Tel: 01271 850296 Fax: 01271 850711 (National Trust)

The house, built for the Chichesters in 1822 and given to the National Trust by Miss Rosalie Chichester, maintains the atmosphere of a Victorian household, with much original furniture. It is full of collections for every taste, including model ships, costume, pewter, shells and personal belongings. The house is set in mainly informal gardens which have been planned and sculptured throughout the 1800s along with additional woodland where many rare plants and wildlife are to be seen. The tranquil gardens include the terraced Victoria garden with herbaceous borders, conservatory and pond. The National Trust's extensive carriage collection and Carriage Driving School are housed in the stables and carriage rides are available around the gardens. Miles of walks through woods and the parks, grazed by Shetland ponies and Jacob sheep, which are descendants of those owned by Miss Chichester. **Open:** House, Victorian garden & park: 1 Apr–1 Nov, daily except Sat, open BH Sat 11–5.30pm. Park: daily Nov–Mar. **Admission:** £5.10, family £12.80, garden only £2.80. Special pre-arranged party rate.

map 2 E3

BICKLEIGH CASTLE

Bickleigh, Nr. Tiverton, EX16 8RP, Devon.
Tel: 01884 855363 (M.J. Boxall)

A Royalist Stronghold with 900 years of history and still lived in. The 11th century detached Chapel, Armoury Guard Room with Tudor furniture and pictures, the Great Hall, Elizabethan bedroom, 17th century farmhouse. Museum of 19th century domestic and agricultural objects and toys. Picturesque moated garden, 'spooky' tower. **Location:** 4 miles south of Tiverton, A396. **Open:** Easter Week (Good Fri–Fri), then Wed, Sun, Bank Hol Mons to late Spring Bank Hol; then to early Oct daily (except Sat) 2–5pm. (Last admission 4.30pm). Parties of 20 or more by prior appointment. **Admission:** Adults £4, Children (5–15) £2. Popular for wedding receptions, civil wedding licence etc. For further details please telephone the Administrator.

 map 3 F4

CASTLE DROGO

Drewsteignton, Exeter, Devon, EX6 6PB
Tel: 01647 433306 Fax: 01647 433186 (The National Trust)

This granite castle, built between 1910 and 1930, is one of the most remarkable works of Lutyens. It stands at over 900 feet overlooking the wooded gorge of the river Teign with beautiful views of Dartmoor. Spectacular walks through surrounding 600 acre estate. Formal garden with roses, flowering shrubs and herbaceous borders. **Open:** 1st Apr–1st Nov daily except Fri (open good Fri). Garden, shop, tearoom open daily, 11–5pm. **Admission:** Adults £5.20, children £2.60. National Trust members free.

map 3 F5

BUCKFAST ABBEY

Buckfastleigh, Devon, TQ11 OEE
Tel: 01364 642519 Fax: 01364 643891 (Buckfast Abbey Trust)

The monks of Buckfast welcome visitors to their famous Abbey–England's only medieval monastery to have been put back to its original use. The magnificent church was rebuilt by just four of the monks; today's activities include bee-keeping and making stained glass and tonic wine. **Location:** ½ mile from the A38 Plymouth to Exeter road at Buckfastleigh. **Open:** Daily all year, church and precinct 5.30–9.30pm; amenities 9–5.30pm (summer), 10–4pm (winter). **Admission:** Free except exhibition (75p). **Parking:** Free **Refreshments:** Grange Restaurant serves refreshments and meals (all home-made) all day. Facilities: Exhibition, video, herb gardens, gift shop, bookshop and unique Monastic Shop selling products from Buckfast and many other European abbeys.

map 3 F5

CADHAY

Ottery St Mary, EX11 1QT
Tel: 01404 812432 (Mr O William-Powlett)

Cadhay is approached by an avenue of lime-trees and stands in a pleasant listed garden, with herbaceous borders and excellent views over the original medieval fish ponds. Cadhay is first mentioned in the reign of Edward I. The main part of the house was built about 1550 by John Haydon who had married the de Cadhay heiress. He retained the Great Hall of an earlier house, the fine timber roof (about 1420) can be seen. An Elizabethan Long Gallery was added by John's successor in 1617, thereby forming a unique and lovely courtyard. Georgian alterations were made in the mid 18th century. **Location:** 1 mile NW of Ottery St Mary on B3176. **Open:** Late Spring & Summer Bank Hol Suns & Mons, also Tues, Weds, Thurs in July and Aug 2–6 (last adm. 5.30pm) **Admission:** Adults £3, children £1.50. Groups by arrangement only.

map 3 F5

ENDSLEIGH HOUSE

Milton Abbot, Tavistock PL19 0PQ
Tel: 01822 870248 Fax: 01822 870502 (Endsleigh Fishing Club Ltd)

Arboretum, Shell House, flowering shrubs, rock garden. **Location:** 8 miles W of Tavistock on B3362. **Open:** House and Gardens Apr–Sept weekends 12–4pm, Tues and Fri by appointment 12–4pm, Bank Hols 12–4pm. **Admission:** Honesty Box in Aid of Trust. **Refreshments:** Lunches and teas at Endsleigh House by appointment. No dogs. Limited car parking. No coaches. Not suitable for the disabled. No wheelchairs.

 map 2 E5

FLETE

Ermington, Ivybridge, Plymouth, Devon, PL21 9NZ.
Tel: 01752 830 308 Fax: 01752 830 309
(Country Houses Association)

Built around an Elizabethan manor, with alterations in 1879 by Norman Shaw. Wonderful II drop waterfall garden, designed by Russell Page ably assisted by Laurance of Arabia in the 1920's. **Location:** 11 miles E of Plymouth, at junction of A379 and B3121. **Station(s):** Plymouth (12 miles), Totnes (14 miles). **Bus Route:** No. 93, Plymouth–Dartmouth. **Open:** May–Sept, Wed & Thurs, 2–5pm. (Latest admission time 4.30pm). **Admission:** Adults £3, children free. Free car park. No dogs admitted.

  map 2 E6

KINGSTON HOUSE

Staverton, Totnes, Devon, TQ9 6AR

Tel: +44(0)1803 762 235 Fax: +44(0)1803 762 444 E-mail: kingston.estate.devon.co.uk (Michael, Elizabeth & Piers Corfield)

Kingston House, which was begun in 1726, was built for the wealthy wool merchant John Rowe, whose family had owned the Kingston Estate since 1502. John Rowe, nephew of William Rowe, appointed Lord High Sheriff of Devon by the ill-fated James II during his brief reign of 1685–1688, had a 'fine moderne built mansion' created to the north of the previous house, the ruins of which still survive in the gardens. Kingston House, now the home of the Corfield family, represents one of the finest surviving examples of early 18th century architecture in Britain today, possessing the finest marquetry staircase in England and a wealth of 18th century wall paintings. The Gardens at Kingston, following years of restoration, are approaching maturity and perfectly reflect the style of the period in a number of formal gardens as individual as the rooms of the house itself. **Open:** Gardens & Grounds: 22 June, 29 June & 13 July, in aid of NGS and The National Rose Society and by prior written agreement. **Refreshments:** The Kitchens specialise in English haute cuisine with vegetables, fruit and herbs from the walled gardens, to match an extensive cellar. **Accommodation:** Within the Kingston Estate grounds lie a variety of listed buildings built between 1650 and 1830 now sympathetically converted to provide period cottages for guests to stay on the estate. Each cottage has a four poster bed in the master bedroom, is furnished in keeping and is equipped to an unusually high standard. Three exceptional period suites within the house are also available for visitors wishing to stay in this historic house.

map 3
F5

FURSDON

Cadbury, Thorverton, Exeter EX5 JS
Tel: 01392 860860 (E D Fursdon, Esq)

Fursdon is set in a beautiful rural landscape and the Fursdons have lived here for over 700 years. It remains primarily a family home. There is a Regency library, oak screen from the medieval hall, family portraits and annual displays from the family costume collection including some fine 18th century examples. Attractive developing garden. **Location:** 9 miles N of Exeter, 6 miles SW of Tiverton; 3/4 miles off A3072. **Open:** Easter Mon–end Sept Thurs and Bank Hol Mon. Tours at 2.30 and 3.30. Parties over 20 by arrangement please. **Admission:** House & Gardens £3.50, children £1.75, under 10 years free. £3.25pp for parties of twenty or more. **Refreshments:** Home-made teas in Coach Hall on open days. **Internet:** www.eclipse.co.uk/fursdon/

POWDERHAM CASTLE

Exeter, EX6 8JQ, Devon
Tel: 01626 890 243 Fax: 01626 890 729 (Lord & Lady Courtenay)

Originally built as a medieval castle by Sir Philip Courtenay (1390), the Castle is still lived in by his descendants. A guided tour of the Staterooms brings alive the history of this lived-in family home. **Location:** 8 miles S of Exeter, off A379 in Kenton Village. **Station(s):** Starcross (1.5 miles). **Open:** 5 Apr–1 Nov. Every day except Sat. **Admission:** Please contact General Manager for details of 1998 prices. **Refreshments:** Licensed restaurant open all day. **Events/Exhibitions:** Special events include Classic Car Rallies, Open Air Concerts and Country Fairs. Ring for details. **Conferences:** The Castle is fully and exclusively available for corporate meetings entertainment, private parties, civil weddings and receptions, filming and product launches.

SAND

Sand, Sidbury, Sidmouth EX10 0QN
Tel: 01395 597230 (Lt Col P V Huyshe)

Lived in Manor house owned by Huyshe family since 1560, rebuilt 1592-4, situated in unspoilt valley. Screens passage, panelling, family documents, heraldry. Also Sand Lodge roof structure of late 15th century Hall House. **Location:** 3/4 mile NE of Sidbury; 400 yards from A375. Grid ref 146925. **Open:** Easter, Mayday, late Spring and August Bank Hols Sun & Mon 2–6pm. Last tour 4.45pm. Also 16 & 17 Aug. **Admission:** Adults £3, children/students 60p. Sand Lodge and outside of Sand by written appointment £1. **Refreshments:** Light teas in house.

RHS GARDEN ROSEMOOR

Great Torrington EX38 8PH
Tel: 01805 624067 Fax: 01805 624717 (Royal Horticultural Society)

A garden for all seasons. Lying in the wooded valley of the River Torridge, it includes an informal woodland area, mixed borders and intimate gardens close to the 18th century house. Within its original 8 acres, visitors will see a wide range of plants in a variety of beautiful settings and the Society is in the process of expanding the garden from 8 acres to 40. **Location:** 1 mile SE of Great Torrington on B3220 to Exeter. **Open:** Garden open all year from 10–6pm Apr–Sept and 10–5pm Oct–Mar. **Admission:** Adults £4, children under 6 yrs free, children 6–16 £1. Groups of more than 10 £2.75. One person accompanying a blind visitor or wheelchair user free. **Refreshments:** A restaurant provides home-made lunches and Devon Cream teas. Coaches welcome by appointment. Dogs are not admitted (except guide dogs).

TIVERTON CASTLE

Tiverton, Devon, Ex16 6RP. Tel: 01884 253 200/255 200
Fax: 01884 253200 (Mr & Mrs A. K. Gordon)

Few buildings evoke such an immediate feeling of history as Tiverton Castle. Originally built in 1106 by Richard de Redvers, Earl of Devon, on the orders of Henry I, it was then rebuilt in stone in 1293. Now many styles of architecture down the ages, from medieval to the present day can be seen. The magnificent medieval gatehouse and tower contain important Civil War armoury. Furnishings and exhibits reflect the colourful history of the Castle and with continuing restoration there is always something new and interesting to see. **Open:** Easter to end of June and Sept. Sun, Thur & Bank Hol Mon. July & Aug, Sun–Thurs. 2.30–5.30pm. Open at other times to parties of 12+ by prior arrangement. **Admission:** Adults £3, children (7–16) £2, (under 7) free. **Conferences:** Available for hire. **Accommodation:** 4 superb self-catering holiday apartments. 4 keys, highly commended.

TORRE ABBEY

The Kings Drive, Torquay TQ2 5JX
Tel: 01803 293593 Fax: 01803 215948 (Torbay Council)

For 800 years, Torre Abbey has been the home of Torquay's leading citizens. Founded as a monastery in 1196, the Abbey later became a country house and the Cary family's residence for nearly 300 years. As well as important monastic remains, you can see over twenty historic rooms, including the beautiful family chapel, a splendid collection of paintings and Torquay terracotta, colourful gardens, and mementoes of crime writer Agatha Christie. Teas are served in the Victorian kitchen. **Open:** Daily, Easter to 1 Nov, 9.30–6pm. Last admission 5pm.

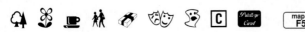

UGBROOKE PARK

Chudleigh, Devon, TQ13 OAD
Tel: 01626 852 179 Fax: 01626 853 322 (Lord Clifford)

Beautiful scenery and quiet parkland in the heart of Devon. Original House and Church built about 1200, redesigned by Robert Adam. Home of the Cliffords of Chudleigh. Ugbrooke contains fine furniture, paintings, beautiful embroideries, porcelain, rare family military collection. Capability Brown Park with lakes, majestic trees, views to Dartmoor. Guided tours relate stories of Clifford Castles, Shakespeare's 'Black Clifford', Henry II's 'Fair Rosamund, Lady Anne Clifford who defied Cromwell, The Secret Treaty, the Cardinal's daughter, Clifford of the CABAL and tales of intrigue, espionage and bravery. **Location:** Chudleigh, Devon. **Open:** 12 July–3 Sept, Sun, Tue, Wed & Thurs. Grounds open 1–5.30pm. Guided tours of House 2pm and 3.45pm. **Admission:** Adults £4.20. Children (5–16) £2. Groups (over 20) £3.80. Private party tours/functions by arrangement.

map 3
F5

TOTNES CASTLE

Castle Street, Totnes TQ9 5NU
Tel: 01803 864406 (English Heritage)

By the North Gate of the hill town of Totnes you will find a superb motte and bailey castle, with splendid views across the roof tops and down to the River Dart. It is a symbol of lordly feudal life and a fine example of Norman fortification. **Location:** In Totnes, on the hill overlooking the town. Access in Castle Street off west end of High Street. **Open:** 1 Apr–1 Nov, daily, 10–6pm (or dusk if earlier in October) 2 Nov–31 Mar '99, Wed–Sun 10–4pm. Closed 1–2pm in winter. **Admission:** £1.60, £1.20, 80p.

YARDE

Yarde Farm, Malborough, Kingsbridge, Devon TQ7 3BY
Tel: 01548 842367 (John and Marilyn Ayre)

Grade I listed. An outstanding example of the Devon farmstead with a Tudor Bakehouse, Elizabethan farmhouse and Queen Anne mansion under restoration. Still a family farm. **Location:** On A381 ½ mile E of Malborough. 4 miles S of Kingsbridge. **Open:** Easter–31 Sept, Sun, Wed, & Fri 2–5pm. **Admission:** Adults £2. Children 50p. Under 5s Free.

map 3
F6

A LA RONDE
Summer Lane, Exmouth EX8 5BD Tel: 01395 265514

Open: 1 April to 1 Nov: daily except Fri & Sat 11–5.30. Last admission 30min before closing. Timed tickets may be in operation during busy periods. **Admission:** £3.20, children £1.60. No party reduction; unsuitable for coaches or large groups except by prior arrangement with the Custodian.

BRADLEY
Newton Abbot TQ12 6BN Tel: 01626 54513

Open: 1 April to 30 Sept: Wed 2–5; also Thur 2 & 9 April, 17 & 24 Sept. Last admission 4.30. **Admission:** £2.60. No party reduction; organised parties by appointment with Secretary. Lodge gates are too narrow for coaches. No refreshments. No WC

BUCKLAND ABBEY
Yelverton PL20 6EY Tel: 01822 853607 Fax: 01822 855448

Open: 1 April to 1 Nov: daily except Thur 10.30–5.30; also 7 Nov to end March 1999: Sat & Sun 2-5 (weekdays for pre-arranged parties only). Last admission 45min before closing. Closed 4–22 Jan 1999. Note: Some rooms in the Abbey may be closed or access restricted during the early part of the year for refurbishment - please ring to check. Events: 27/28 June, Summer Craft Fair; 10/11 Oct, Tudor Experience; first three weekends in Dec, Christmas decorations. Please ask for events leaflet. **Admission:** £4.30; family ticket £10.70. Grounds only £2.20. Pre-arranged parties of 15 or more £3.50. Winter admission (2 Nov to March): reduced price for house; grounds and workshops only at no charge. NB: Additional charge (incl. NT members) on 27/28 June Craft Fair days. Car park 150m, occasional charge of £1 refundable on admission

COLETON FISHACRE GARDEN
Coleton, Kingswear, Dartmouth TQ6 0EQ Tel: 01803 752466

Open: March: Sun only 2–5; also 1 April to 1 Nov: Wed, Thur, Fri, Sun & BH Mon 10.30–5.30 or dusk if earlier. Last admissions 30min before closing. Events: for details please send s.a.e or telephone the property **Admission:** £3.50. Pre-booked parties £2.80

COMPTON CASTLE
Marldon, Paignton TQ3 1TA Tel: 01803 872112

Open: 1 April to 29 Oct: Mon, Wed & Thur 10–12.15 and 2–5, when the courtyard, restored Great Hall, solar, chapel, rose garden and old kitchen are shown. Last admission 30min before closing. **Admission:** £2.80. Pre-booked parties £2.20; organisers should notify Secretary. Additional parking and refreshments at Castle Barton opposite entrance

KILLERTON
Broadclyst, Exeter EX5 3LE Tel: 01392 881345

Open: House: 14 March to 1 Nov: daily except Tues 11–5.30. Special pre-Christmas opening from 12 Dec. Last admission 5. Park & garden: open all year from 10.30 to dusk. Events: costume exhibitions: from mid June, "Glamour" (dress for special occasions) plus "Portrait of a Collector" featuring Paulise de Bush collection; 18/19 July, Exeter Festival open-air concerts. Full events programme from Property Manager, s.a.e. please. Note: on 18/19 July, only ticket holders to the Exeter Festival Concerts will be admitted to the garden after 4.30; house will close at 4.30. **Admission:** £4.50; family ticket £12.50. Garden and park only £3.50. Garden and park reduced winter rate (Nov to Feb). Pre-booked parties £4

KNIGHTHAYES COURT
Bolham, Tiverton EX16 7RQ Tel: 01884 254665 Fax: 01884 243050

Open: 1 April to 1 Nov: House open daily except Fri (but open Good Fri) 11–5.30; please note that some items normally on view may not be displayed due to conservation work. Garden open daily 11–5.30. Last admission 5. Nov & Dec: Sun 2–4 for pre-booked parties only. Events: for details please tel. 01884 254665 **Admission:** £5.10. Garden & grounds only £3.50. Pre-booked parties £4.40. Parking 400m. Visitor reception: (tel. 01884 257381)

Dorset

The countryside of Dorset is bewitching. From dawn till dusk, through each season, the changing light reveals a new slant to the landscape. Black country lanes score the fields like tiny veins pumping the visitors through its picturesque villages. You could not descibe the countryside as wild or grand, just charming and a little quaint, the home to beautiful thatched flint-and-chalk cottages.

Around Lyme Regis, which is at Dorset's western point, the cliffs are forebearing. The Purbeck Hills once linked the headlands of Brittany with the white cliffs of Dover.

The county town, Dorchester, is still recognized as the

backdrop for Thomas Hardy's novel 'The Mayor of Casterbridge'. The high street is lined with 17th century and Georgian houses. The town has a wonderful feel to it, with many small and friendly places to eat.

North of Poole stands Wimbourne Minster, which was Thomas Hardy's home for many years. Cranborne, to the north of Wimbourne Minster, is a beautiful village on the edge of what used to be a royal forest and is now a stunning woodland.

The county holds a vast number of historic properties and some of the most beautiful gardens in England; they are well worth a visit.

Hardy's Cottage

ATHELHAMPTON HOUSE & GARDENS

Athelhampton, Dorchester
Tel: 01305 848363, Fax: 01305 848135 (Patrick Cooke)

Athelhampton is one of the finest 15th century manor houses and is surrounded by one of the great architectural gardens of England. The house contains many finely furnished rooms including The Great Hall, Great Chamber, Wine Cellar and the Library & Billiard Room. The glorious Grade I garden, dating from 1891, is full of vistas and gains much from the fountains and River Piddle flowing through. The walled gardens include the world famous topiary pyramids and collections of tulips, magnolias, roses, clematis and lilies in season. Also 15th century Dovecote. **Location:** on the A35, 5 miles E of Dorchester. **Open:** 1 Mar – 1 Nov 1998 daily (except Saturday) 10.30–5pm. Also open on Sundays in winter. New restaurant serving lunches, cream teas and refreshments. Gift shop and free car park.

CHIFFCHAFFS

Chaffeymoor, Bourton, Gillingham, SP8 5BY, Dorset.
Tel: 01747 840 841(Mr & Mrs K. R. Potts)

The garden surrounds a typical 400 year old stone Dorset cottage, which contains a very wide range of bulbs, alpines, herbaceous trees and shrubs, many of them unusual. It is planted for long periods of interest and divided into small individual gardens with many surprise views. In addition, we have a 1.5 acre woodland garden filled with azaleas, camellias, rhododendrons, bog primulas and daffodils, etc, and a host of unusual trees and shrubs. The bluebells are particularly beautiful in the spring. **Location:** 3 miles E of Wincanton, just off A303. **Open:** 5 Apr–30 Sept. Every Wed & Thurs and 1st & 3rd Sun each month and Bank Hol Weekends, 2–5.30pm. Also by appointment. Groups Welcome. **Admission:** £2.

map 3
J3

CHRISTCHURCH PRIORY

Quay Road, Christchurch, Dorset BH23 1BU
Tel: 01202 485804 Fax: 01202 488645

A medieval monastic church begun in 1094. Famous for the "Miraculous Beam" Norman nave and turret, monks' quire with Jesse reredos to high altar, Lady Chapel, chantries, 15th century bell tower and St Michael's Loft, a former school but now a museum. Guided tours can be arranged. **Admission:** No charge but donations invited of £1 per adult and £0.20 per student. Charge to ascend tower: adult £0.50, child/student £0.30 and to visit museum; adult £0.50, child/student £0.30. **Open:** Every day except 25 Dec subject to church services: weekdays 9.30–5pm, Suns 2.15 to 5pm. Church Services; Suns; 8am Holy Communion, 9.45am Sung Eucharist, 11.15am Choral Matins with sermon, 6.30pm Choral Evensong with sermon. Weekdays: 7.30am morning prayer, 8am Holy Communion. Thurs 11 Holy Communion, 5.30 daily, evening prayer.

map 3
K4

COMPTON ACRES GARDENS

Canford Cliffs Road, Poole, Dorset
Tel: 01202 700778 Fax: 01202 707537 (Mr L. Green)

Compton Acres is set in a delightful area of Canford Cliffs in Poole, overlooking Poole Harbour and the Purbeck Hills beyond. Covering nearly ten acres, the nine gardens include an Italian Garden, an authentic Japanese Garden, a Rock and Water Garden and a Woodland Walk. The Tea Rooms and Terrace Brasserie serve a variety of food throughout the day, with our gift shop, ice cream parlour and well stocked Garden Centre. Compton Acres is one of the south's top attractions. **Location:** Off the B3065 onto Canford Cliffs Road. **Open:** 1 Mar–End Oct. **Admission:** Adult £4.75, OAP £3.70, child £1. Group rates 20 +, adult £4, OAP £3, child 90p.

map 3
K5

CRANBORNE MANOR GARDEN

Cranborne, BH21 5PP
Tel: 01725 517248, Fax: 01725 517862
(The Viscount and Viscountess Cranborne)

Walled gardens, yew hedges and lawns; wild garden with spring bulbs, herb garden, Jacobean mount garden, flowering cherries and collection of old-fashioned and specie roses. Beautiful and historic garden laid out in the 17th century by John Tradescant and much embellished in the 20th century. **Location:** 18 miles N of Bournemouth B3078; 16 miles S of Salisbury A354, B3081. **Open:** Garden Centre open Mon–Sat 9–5pm, Sun 10–5pm. Something for every gardener, but specialising in old-fashioned and specie roses, herbs, ornamental pots and garden furniture. Garden only Mar–Sept, Wed 9–5pm. South Court occasionally closed. Free car park.

map 3
K5

DEANS COURT GARDEN

Deans Court, Wimborne, BH21 1EE, Dorset.
(Sir Michael & Lady Hanham)

Garden–Partly wild with specimen trees, peacocks, monastery fishpond, herb garden with over 200 species. Kitchen Garden with 18th c. Long serpentine wall. House–Mainly early Georgian but with medieval origins and some 19th century and later work. Free parking. Wholefood and home-made teas. Chemical-free plants and produce usually available. Open: Garden:12 Apr; 24 May; 30 Aug; 20 Sept. 2–6pm Mons 13 Apr; 25 May; 31 Aug. 10–6pm. Other dates may be arranged. Contact T.I.C. 01202 886116 for details. Adults £2; OAPs £1.50; children 50p. House: By written appointment–rates on application. Group visits to both house and garden welcomed by prior written application.

map 3
K4

FORDE ABBEY AND GARDENS

Forde Abbey, Chard, Somerset TA20 4LU
Tel: 01460 221290, Fax: 01460 220296 (Mr M Roper)

Forde Abbey is the finest example of a Cistercian monastery still used as a family home today. The House contains a collection of magnificent Mortlake tapestries. The Abbey is surrounded by 30 acres of gardens with many unusual plants and shrubs. In the Spring, the garden is awash with spring bulbs and throughout the season there is always something of interest, including azaleas, magnolias, herbaceous borders, rock garden and bog garden. **Location:** 1 mile E of Chard Junction, 4 miles SE of Chard signposted off A30. **Open:** Gardens open daily throughout the year 10–4.30. House open April 1– end Oct Sun Wed & Bank Hols 1–4.30pm. **Admission:** House and Gardens: Please Telephone for details. **Refreshments:** Undercroft open for light lunches and teas 11–4.30 daily Easter – end Oct.

map 3
H4

HORN PARK GARDENS

Horn Park, Beaminster, Dorset
Tel: 01308 862 212 (Mr & Mrs John Kirkpatrick)

Large and beautiful garden. House built 1910 by a pupil of Lutyens – unique position, magnificent view to sea. Plantsman's garden, unusual trees, shrubs and plants in rock, water gardens terraces and herbaceous borders. Woodland Garden, Bluebell Woods, Wild flower meadow with over 160 species including orchids. Plants for sale. In RHS "Twelve Beautiful Gardens" calendar for 1998. Wedding receptions. **Location:** 1.5 miles N of Beaminster on A3066. **Station(s):** Crewkerne. **Open:** 1 Apr–31 Oct. Every Sun–Thur incl., 2–6pm & Bank Hol Mons. **Admission:** Adults £3. (Under 16 and wheelchair users free). Groups welcome any day or time, by prior arrangement, with teas if booked. Dogs on leads.

map 3
H4

EDMONDSHAM HOUSE & GARDENS

Edmondsham House, Edmondsham, Wimborne, BH21 5RE
Tel: 01725 517207 (Mrs Julia E Smith)

A family home since the 16th century and a fine blend of Tudor and Georgian architecture, with a Victorian stable block and dairy, interesting furniture, lace and other exhibits. The Gardens include an old-fashioned walled garden, cultivated organically with an excellent display of spring bulbs, shrubs, lawns and herbaceous border. **Location:** Between Cranborne and Verwood, off the B3081. **Open:** House & Gardens – Easter Sun, all Bank Hol Mons, all Weds in Apr and 2–5 Oct. Groups by arrangement at other times. Gardens – Open at all times when the House is open and on all Wed and Suns in Apr to 2–5 Oct. **Admission:** Charges apply.

KNOLL GARDENS AND NURSERY

Stapehill Road, Hampreston, Nr Wimborne, Dorset BH21 7ND
Tel: 01202 873931 Fax: 01202 870842

Award-winning 6 acre gardens with 5000+ named plants from the world over. Wide range of trees, shrubs and colourful hardy plants in an informal English setting. Beautiful water gardens, tumbling waterfalls and ponds with exotic fish. New Gravel garden; 'dragon' garden. 2 National Collections: Ceanothus & Phygelius. Spacious all-weather visitor centre with video presentations. **Truly a Gardener's Garden!** **Location:** OS Ref SU059 001. Between Wimborne & Ferndown. Exit A31 Canford Bottom roundabout. B3073 Hampreston. Signposted 1½m. **Open:** Mar: Wed–Sun 10–4pm. 1 Apr–31 Oct: daily 10–5.30pm, Oct: 4.30pm. **Admission:** Adult £3.40, child (5–15) £1.70, OAP £2.90, student £2.40. Groups: Adult £2.95, child £1.50, OAP £2.60, student £2.10. Family (2 +2) £8.20.

map 3
K4

LULWORTH CASTLE

The Lulworth Estate, East Lulworth, Wareham, Dorset BH20 5QS
Tel: 01929 400352

Lulworth Castle has been the home of the Weld family since 1641. Tragically the Castle endured a serious fire in 1929 but has just been restored by English Heritage. This is the first year that the Castle will be fully opened to the public. In the castle visitors can learn about the history of the castle and the whole Estate. Young and old can attempt to solve the 'Lulworth Riddles' and win prizes! The Children's Summer Farm gives the opportunity to meet a variety of animals and learn about rare breeds. The Lulworth Shop stocks a wide range of quality gifts and the Stable Cafe serves home cooked meals all day with most of the produce supplied from Mrs Weld's kitchen garden. **Open:** Summer 10–6pm, Winter 10–4pm.

map 3
J5

MAPPERTON

Mapperton, Beaminster, Dorset DT8 3NR
Tel: 01308 862645, Fax: 01308 863348 (Earl & Countess of Sandwich)

Terraced valley gardens surround charming Tudor/Jacobean manor house, stable blocks, dovecote and All Saints' Church. Pevsner's Dorset guide says, "There can hardly be anywhere a more enchanting manorial group than Mapperton". Above, the Orangery and Italianate formal garden with fountain court and topiary. Below, a 17th century summer house and fishponds. Lower garden with specimen shrubs and trees. Magnificent walks and views. Shop with plants, pots and gift items. Featured in Country Life, Country Living, Daily Telegraph and used as location in films, 'Emma', 'Restoration' and the BBC's 'Tom Jones'. **Location:** 1 mile off B3163, 2 miles off B3066. **Station:** Crewkerne. **Open:** Mar–Oct daily 2–6pm. **Admission:** Adults £3, under 18s £1.50, under 5s free. House open to group tours by appointment, adults £3.

map 3
H4

MINTERNE GARDENS

Minterne Magna, Nr Dorchester, Dorset, DT2 7AU
Tel: 01300 341 370 (The Lord Digby)

Important rhododendron garden. The home of the Churchill and Digby families for 330 years. The valley was landscaped after the manner of Capability Brown in the 18th century. Over 1 mile of wild woodland walks with rhododendrons and magnolias, towering over small lakes, cascades and streams. Brilliant Autumn colouring. **Location:** On A352 Dorchester/Sherborne Rd 2 miles N of Cerne Abbas **Open:** Daily, 28 March–10 November 10–7pm. **Admission:** Adults £3 (Acc. children free).

map 3
J4

MILTON ABBEY CHURCH

Milton Abbas, Nr. Blandford, Dorset, DT11 0BP
Tel: 01258 880489 (Organising Secretary)

A Church has stood here for over 1000 years. The present Abbey dates from the 14/15th century. The 18th century Gothic style house was built to compliment the Abbey & ancient Abbots Hall. Exterior by Sir William Chambers, interior in classic style by James Wyatt. Idyllic tranquil setting in the heart of Dorset, 1/2 mile from 200 year old 'new' village of Milton Abbas with its identical cottages. The Abbey is situated in grounds of Milton Abbey School and owned by diocese of Salisbury. **Location:** 3 1/2 from A354 (Puddletown to Blandford road). **Open:** Abbey Church throughout the year. House and grounds: Easter, Mid-July – End August, 10–6pm. **Admission:** Adults £1.75, Children free. when house and grounds are open. At other times donations are invited.

THE OLD RECTORY

Litton Cheney, Dorset
Tel: 01308 482 383 (Mr & Mrs Hugh Lindsay)

Greatly varied garden with small walled garden, partly paved with a prolific quince tree. A steep path leads to 4 acres of beautiful natural woodland on steep slope with springs, streams and ponds, primulas, native plants, wild flower lawn. (Stout shoes recommended). **Location:** 1 mile S of A35. 10 miles from Dorchester. 6 miles from Bridport. **Open:** For NGS. Also open with Little Cheney Gardens. Private visits also welcome by appointment, Apr–June. **Admission:** Charges apply. Please phone for details. Limited parking for infirm and elderly, otherwise park in village and follow signs. Plants available for sale.

PARNHAM HOUSE & GARDENS

Parnham, Beaminster, Dorset
Tel: 01308 862 204 Fax: 01308 863 494 (John & Jennie Makepeace)

Tudor manor house built in 1540, enlarged by John Nash in 1810. Inspiring 20th century craftsmanship in the home of John and Jennie Makepeace, who have restored and enlivened this fascinating historic house and beautiful gardens into a world-renowned centre of excellence. Surrounded by 14 acres of formal and informal gardens, extensively restored and replanted by Jennie Makepeace. Parnham lies in a hidden valley, deep in the beautiful countryside of West Dorset. Furniture commissioned for public and private collections is designed by John Makepeace and can be seen in his studio. Pieces are available for sale or can be commissioned during your visit. **Location:** Take exit 25 from M5. From London take M3/A303 Crewkerne-Beaminster Road. Follow A3066. Parnham is ½ mile S of Beaminster. 5 miles N of Bridport. **Open:** 1 Apr–31 Oct, Sun, Tues, Weds, Thurs and Bank Holidays 10–5pm. **Admission:** Adults £5, children (10–15) £2, Children (under 10) free, Students £2. **Refreshments:** Licensed Buttery with delicious home-made food, tea and coffee. **John Makepeace Furniture Studio:** unique furniture in the making. **Shop:** books and exciting work by British craftsmen and women in textiles, ceramics and wood. Available for weddings, film location and events.

PURSE CAUNDLE MANOR

Purse Caundle, Nr. Sherborne, Dorset, DT9 5DY
Tel: 01963 250400 (Michael de Pelet Esq)

Interesting 15th/16th century Manor House. Lived in as a family home. Great Hall with minstrel gallery; Winter Parlour; Solar with oriel; bedchambers; garden. Not commercialised! Come and visit us. **Location:** 4 miles E of Sherborne; 1/4 mile S of A30. **Open:** Easter Mon and May–Sept. Thurs, Sun & Bank Hol Mon 2–5pm showing every half hour. Coaches welcomed by appointment. **Admission:** £2.50. Children free. Free car park. **Refreshments:** Home-made cream teas by prior arrangement at £2 each for coach parties.

SANDFORD ORCAS MANOR HOUSE

The Manor House, Sandford Orcas, Sherborne, Dorset DT9 4SB.
Tel: 01963 220206 (Sir Mervyn Medlycott, Bt.)

Tudor Manor House in remarkable original state of preservation, with gatehouse, spiral staircases and Tudor and Jacobean panelling. Fine collection of 14th–17th century stained glass, Queen Anne and Chippendale furniture, Elizabethan and Georgian needlework and 17th century Dutch paintings. Terraced gardens, with fine mature trees, topiary and herb garden. **Location:** 2 miles N or Sherborne, entrance next to church. **Open:** Easter Mon 10–6pm then May–Sept: Suns 2–6pm & Mons 10–6pm. **Admission:** £2.50, children £1. Pre-booked parties (of 10 or more) at reduced rates on other days if preferred.

SHERBORNE CASTLE

Sherborne DT9 3PY
Tel: 01935 813182, Fax: 01935 816727 (Sherborne Castle Estates)

Built by Sir Walter Raleigh in 1594. Home of the Digby family since 1617. The House contains fine furniture, porcelain and pictures. Set in 20 acres of lawns and pleasure grounds planned by 'Capability' Brown around the 50 acre lake. **Location:** 5 miles E of Yeovil off A30 to S, Station Sherborne. **Open:** Easter Sat–end Sept, Thurs, Sat, Sun and Bank Hol Mons. House 1.30–4.30pm. Grounds and tearoom 12.30. **Admission:** Charges on request, parties by arrangement. **Refreshments:** Tearoom. **Events/Exhibitions:** Various, telephone for details. Gift shop. Car parking on site.

SMEDMORE HOUSE

Kimmeridge, Wareham, Dorset BH20 5PG
Tel: 01929 480719 Fax: 01929 480702 (Mr Gargett)

The home of the Mansel family for nearly 400 years nestling at the foot of the Purbeck hills looking across Kimmeridge Bay to Portland Bill. Originally built in 1620 by the present owner's ancestor William Clavell, the imposing Georgian front was added in the 1760s. Beautiful walled garden which contains many special and interesting plants. Available for Holiday lets, Weddings, Business & Private functions. **Open:** House & Gardens open to the public on 17 May and 13 Sept 1998 from 2–5pm: £3.50. Groups by arrangement at other times. Contact Mr T Gargett.

ST CATHERINE'S CHAPEL

Abbotsbury
Tel: 01179 750700 (English Heritage)

A small stone chapel, set on a hilltop, with an unusual roof and small turret used as a lighthouse. **Location:** ½ mile S of Abbotsbury by pedestrian track to the hilltop. **Open:** Any reasonable times.

SHERBORNE OLD CASTLE

Castleton, Sherborne DT9 3SA
Tel: 01935 812730 (English Heritage)

The ruins of this 12th century castle are a testament to the 16 days it took Cromwell to capture it during the Civil War, after which it was abandoned. A gatehouse, some graceful arcading and decorative windows survive. **Location:** 1/2 m E of Sherborne off B3145. 1/2m N of the 1594 castle. **Open:** 1 Apr–1 Nov, daily, 10–6pm (or dusk if earlier in October). 2 Nov–31 March '99, Wed–Sun, 10–4pm. Closed 1–2pm in winter. **Admission:** £1.60, £1.20, 80p

WOLFETON HOUSE

Dorchester, Dorset DT2 9QN
Tel: 01305 263 500 Fax: 01305 265090 (Capt. NTLL Thimbleby)

A fine medieval and Elizabethan Manor House lying in the water-meadows near the confluence of the Rivers Cerne and Frome. It was much embellished around 1580 and has splendid plaster ceilings, fireplaces and panelling of that date. See the Great Hall, stairs and chamber; parlour, dining room, chapel and cyder house. The medieval gatehouse has two unmatched and older towers. There are many fine works of art. **Location:** 1.5 miles form Dorchester on Yeovil road (A37); indicated by Historic House signs. **Station(s):** Dorchester South and West, 1.75 miles. **Open:** 1 May–30 Sept. Sun, Tue, Thurs & BHols. At other times throughout the year parties by arrangement. **Admission:** Charges not available at time of going to press. **Refreshments:** Ploughman's lunches, teas, evening meals for parties, by arrangement. Cyder for sale.

CLOUDS HILL

Wareham, Dorset BH20 7NQ Tel: 01929 405616

Open: 5 April to 1 Nov: Wed, Thur, Fri, Sun & BH Mon 12–5 or dusk if earlier; no electric light. Party viewing outside these times by prior arrangement with the Custodian (tel. 01929 405616). **Admission:** £2.30. No reduction for parties or children. Unsuitable for coaches or trailer caravans. No WC

CORFE CASTLE

Corfe Castle, Wareham BH20 5EZ Tel/fax: 01929 481294

Open: 1 March to 1 Nov: daily 10–5.30 (4.30 in early March/late Oct); 3 Nov to 1 March 1999: daily 11–3.30 (closed 25/26 Dec and for 2 days at end Jan for training). Events: medieval and civil war events, archaeology days, evening opening and tours; please tel. for details. **Admission:** £3.80, children £2; family tickets £9.60/£5.80. Parties £3.50, children £1.80. Car- & coach-parking available at Castle View off A351; also at Norden park & ride and West St (not NT)

HARDY'S COTTAGE

Higher Bockhampton, nr Dorchester DT2 8QJ Tel: 01305 262366

Open: 5 April to 1 Nov: daily except Fri & Sat (but open Good Fri) 11–5 (or dusk if earlier). Approach only by 10min walk from car park through woods. **Admission:** £2.60. No reduction for children or parties. School parties and coaches by prior arrangement only. No WC. Hardy's works on sale

KINGSTON LACY

Coleton, Kingswear, Dartmouth TQ6 0EQ Tel: 01803 752466

Open: House: 28 March to 1 Nov: daily except Thur & Fri, 12–5.30; last admission 4.30. Park and garden: 28 March to 1 Nov: daily 11–6. 2 Nov to 21 Dec: house closed, but park, garden, shop and restaurant open Fri, Sat & Sun 11–4. Special snowdrop days and spring flower opening in early 1999; for details tel. Infoline 01202 880413. Events: 17 July, Bournemouth Sinfonietta; 31 July, jazz; 14 Aug, Palm Court (all with fireworks); to book tel. 01985 843601.

County Durham

A county of moors and rivers, County Durham is beautifully dramatic. One of the most famous of its vistas can be seen in the town of Durham itself, where the mighty towers of the cathedral stand silhouetted over the River Wear. Durham Cathedral has huge dimensions with 900 year old columns, piers and ribbed vaults. The city was built in its entirety, in the year 995 on 'Dunholm' or Island Hill, a rocky peninsula quite unique to Durham. To this day, the ancient centre of Durham is reached by a series of bridges that connect the older buildings with the modern town that has developed over the centuries.

Moving westwards from this historic city, the beautiful moorland scenery features a series of stunning Pennine valleys and spectacular waterfalls. Visit Teesdale's high force waterfall for a particularly splendid example of Durham's rugged beauty.

Barnard Castle, locally known as 'Barney', is a pretty little town, littered with cobble stone roads and a market place. The town is overlooked by the ruins of a Norman castle, hence its namesake.

The crumbly 'Cotherstone' sheep's cheese is a speciality of the dales surrounding Middleton-in-Teesdale.

Low Force Waterfall

DURHAM CASTLE
Durham, DH1 3RW
Tel: 01913 743 863 Fax: 01913 747 470 (The University of Durham)

Durham Castle, the former home of the Prince Bishop of Durham, was founded in the 1070s. Since 1832 it has been the foundation College of the University of Durham. With the Cathedral it is a World Heritage Site. Important features include the Norman Chapel (1072), the Great Hall (1284), the Norman Doorway (1540s). With its 14th century style Keep it is a fine example of a Motte and Bailey Castle. In vacations the Castle is a conference and holiday centre and prestige venue for banquets etc. **Location:** In the centre of the city (adjoining Cathedral).

Station(s): Durham (Ω m) **Open:** Guided tours only Mar–Sept 10–12 noon and 2–5pm. Oct–Mar 2–4pm. **Admission:** £2.75 Children £1.50, Family ticket £6. Guide book £2.50. **Events/ Exhibitions:** Contact conference and accommodation secretary 0191 374 3863 **Accommodation:** Contact conference and accommodation secretary 0191 374 3863. **Conferences:** Contact conference and accommodation secretary 0191 374 3863 Fax 0191 374 7470.

✗ 🛏 🚶 C

map 11
H4

AUCKLAND CASTLE

Bishop Auckland, Co Durham, DL14 7NR
Tel: 01388 601627

Principal country residence of the Bishops of Durham since Norman times and now the official residence of the present day Bishops. State Rooms, Chapel and Exhibition area available to visitors. Also access to the adjacent Bishop's park and 18th century Deerhouse. **Open:** 2–5pm May, June & September – Friday and Sunday; July – Thursday, Friday and Sunday; August – Thursday, Friday, Saturday and Sunday. Also the same hours on Bank Holiday Mondays. **Admission:** Adults £3, Children over 12 and over 60's £2, Children under 12 free. Excellent venues for concerts, exhibitions, conferences and meetings.

⊞ AUCKLAND CASTLE DEER HOUSE

Bishop Auckland, Durham
Tel: 01912 611585 (English Heritage)

A charming building erected in 1760 in the park of the Bishops of Durham so that the deer could shelter and find food. Location: In Bishops Auckland Park, just north of town centre on A689. About 500 yards N of the castle. **Open:** Daily, May–Sept, 7am–sunset. **Admission:** Free.

⊞ BARNARD CASTLE

Castle House, Durham DL12 9AT
Tel: 01833 638212 (English Heritage)

The substantial remains of this large Castle stand on a rugged escarpment overlooking the River Tees. Parts of the 14th century Great Hall and the cylindrical 12th century tower, built by the Baliol family can still be seen. **Location:** In Barnard Castle. No Parking. **Open:** 1 Apr–1 Nov, daily 10–6pm (or dusk if earlier in October) 2 Nov–31 Mar '99, Wed–Sun 10–4pm. Closed 1–2pm all year.

RABY CASTLE

Staindrop, Darlington, Co. Durham, DL2 3AY
Tel: 01833 660 202. Fax: 01833 660169 (The Lord Barnard, T.D.).

Principally 14th century, alterations made in 1765 and mid-19th century. The Castle is one of the largest 14th century castles in Britain and was built by the Nevills, although one of the towers probably dates back to the 11th century. Interior mainly 18th and 19th century; medieval kitchen and Servants' Hall. Fine pictures of the English, Dutch and Flemish Schools and good period furniture. Collection of horse-drawn carriages and fire-engines. Large walled gardens. **Location:** 1 mile N of Staindrop village, on the Barnard Castle-Bishop Auckland Road (A688). **Station(s):** Bishop Auckland & Darlington. **Open:** Easter Weekend (Sat–Wed). 1 May–30 June, Wed & Sun. 1 July–30 Sept, daily (except Sat). May & Spring & Summer Bank Hols, Sat–Wed. Castle: 1–5pm. Park & Gardens: 11–5.30pm. **Admission: Castle, Park & Gardens:** Adults £4.00, children £1,50, OAPs £3.00, Family (2 adults & 3 children) £10.00. **Park & Gardens only:** Adults £1.50, children/OAPs £1.00. Separate admission charge for Bulmer's Tower when open. Rates may vary when charity events are held. Special terms for parties of 25+ on above days by arrangement. (Tel. the Curator). **Refreshments:** Tea at the Stables. Picnic area. **e-mail:** D.Hall@RabyCastle.onyxnet.co.uk

Essex

Dedham

Essex is the most generous and least ambitious of the Home Counties. Rumour suggests that it is monotonous – and although it boasts no mountains nor hills, the chalk uplands of the north-west are compensation for the lack of sterner beauty.

True, the county is pancake flat in comparison to the neighbouring hump of Suffolk and hop fields of Kent. Yet this unwrinkled landscape favours Essex as a far more accessible and pleasurable place to explore on foot or bike. Visitors are able to truly appreciate its gentle patchwork countryside and experience its wider, soft-hued horizon.

Dotted between nature's mosaic, the inland towns of Essex, such as Coggeshall, Dedham and Ingatstone, wait patiently for visitors. Like old gentlemen bursting with incredible stories of battle, war and witchcraft to tell, they sit silently, anxious to be asked.

The towns on the coast have well defined characters of their own. The quayside of Maldon, locally known as the Hythe, is an ideal place to view the Thames sailing barges. Travel to Burnham-On-Crouch, which is the sailing home of Essex. The last week in August is Burnham Sailing Week, when the whole place heaves with sailors and nautical groupies.

AUDLEY END HOUSE

Saffron Waldon, Essex
Tel: 01799 522399 (English Heritage)

"Too large for a King but might do for a Lord Treasurer", was how King James I described Audley End, built by his own Lord Treasurer Thomas Howard. Come and see its wonderful palatial interiors containing a famous picture collection and an intriguing display of over 1,000 stuffed animals and birds. As you explore the 31 rooms on view your guide will enlighten you with Audley End's celebrated history. Then, stroll in 'Capability' Brown's fine landscaped parkland with its enchanting follies and see the colourful Parterre Garden. **Location:** 1m W of Saffron Walden on B1383 (M11 exits 8, 9 Northbound only & 10) **Open:** 1 Apr–30 Sept: Wed–Sun and Bank Holidays, 11–6pm. Last admissions 5pm. 1 Oct–1 Nov Wed–Sun 10am–3pm. (Closed 24–26 Dec) **Admission:** Hse & Grounds: Adult: £5.75, Conc: £4.30, Child: £2.90. Grounds only: Adult: £3.60, Conc: £2.70, Child: £1.80 (15% discount for groups of 11 or more).

map 5
F2

CHELMSFORD CATHEDRAL

New Street, Chelmsford, Essex CM1 1AT
Tel: 01245 263660

15th century building became a Cathedral in 1914. Extended in 1920s, major refurbishment in 1980's with contemporary works of distinction and a splendid new organ in 1994. **Location:** In Chelmsford. **Open:** Daily: 8–5.30pm. Sun services: 8am, 9.30am, 11.15am, 11.15am and 6pm. Weekday services: 8.15am and 5.15pm.

GOSFIELD HALL

Halstead, Essex, CO9 1SF
Tel: 01787 472 914 Fax: 01787 479551(Country Houses Association)

Very fine Tudor gallery. **Location:** 2^1/$_2$ miles SW of Halstead on Braintree/Haverhill Road (A1017). **Stations(s):** Braintree. Bus route 310 Braintree-Halstead. **Open:** May–Sept Weds & Thurs 2–5pm. House tours 2.30 and 3.15. Latest admission time 3.15pm. **Admission:** Adults £2.50, children 50p, groups £2.50 per head. Free car park. **Conferences:** By arrangement. No dogs admitted.

map 5
G2

HEDINGHAM CASTLE

Castle Hedingham, Nr. Halstead, Essex
Tel: 01787 460261 Fax: 01787 461473 (The Hon. Thomas Lindsay)

Splendid Norman keep built in 1140 by the famous de Veres, Earls of Oxford, Visited Kings Henry VIII and Queen Elizabeth I and besieged by King John. Magnificent Banqueting Hall with Minstrel's Gallery and finest Norman arch in England. Beautiful grounds, peaceful woodland and lakeside walks. Beside medieval village with fine Norman Church. Ivanhoe was filmed here. **Location:** On B1058, 1 mile off A604 between Colchester & Cambridge, close to Constable country, easy reach of London and M11. **Open:** Week before Easter to End of Oct 10–5pm daily. **Admission:** Adults £3, children £2 (5–15), family £9 (2 adults & 5 children). **Events:** For 1998 include Special Viewing of Snowdrops in Feb (please telephone to confirm opening times), A Medieval Weekend at Easter presented by The White Company, to include archery, cooking, music and dancing.

map 5
G2

LAYER MARNEY TOWER

Nr Colchester, Essex CO5 9US
Tel & Fax: 01206 330 784 (Mr Nicholas Charrington)

Lord Marney's 1520 masterpiece is the tallest Tudor gate house in the country. Visitors may climb the tower for excellent views of the Essex countryside. Explore the formal gardens and visit the Long Gallery, Corsellis Room and church. The Medieval Barn has rare breed farm animals and the deer are on the farm walk. Guided Tours are available by arrangement (minimum of 25 people). The Long Gallery and Corsellis Rooms may be hired for corporate days, weddings, receptions, banquets or concerts. **Location:** 6 miles S of Colchester, signpost off the B1022 Colchester–Maldon Road. **Open:** 1 Apr–4 Oct 98 everyday except Saturday 12pm–5pm. Bank Holiday Sundays and Mondays 11am–6pm. Groups anytime by arrangement. **Admission:** Adults £3.25, Children £1.75, Family Ticket £9.00. **Refreshments:** Stable Tearoom.

C
map 5
H3

INGATESTONE HALL

Hall Lane, Ingatestone, Essex CM4 9NR
Tel: 01277 353010, Fax: 01245 248979 (Lord Petre)

Tudor mansion in 11 acres of grounds, built by Sir William Petre, Secretary of State to four monarchs. The house continues to be the home of his descendants and contains furniture, pictures and memorabilia accumulated over the centuries. The house retains its original form and appearance including two priests' hiding places. **Location:** From London, end of Ingatestone High Street, take Station Lane. House is half a mile beyond the level crossing. **Open:** Easter to end Sept. Sat, Sun and Bank Holidays. 1–6pm Plus school hols only, Wed, Thurs and Fri 1–6pm. **Admission:** Adults £3.50 OAPs/students £3, children 5–16 £2 (under 5s free) parties 20 or more 50p per head reduction. **Refreshments:** Tearoom. Car park adjacent to gates. 200m walk to house. Gift shop. No dogs (except guide dogs). The upper floor and some rooms downstairs are inaccessible to wheelchairs.

map 5
G3

THE SIR ALFRED MUNNINGS
ART MUSEUM

Castle House, Dedham, CO7 6AZ, Essex.
Tel: 01206 322127 Fax: 01206 322127 (Castle House Trust)

Large collection of paintings and other works by the late Sir Alfred Munnings, KCVO PRA 1944-1949. **Special Exhibition for 1998:** 'Military Munnings' 29 World War I pictures on loan from Canadian War Museum. **Location:** Three quarters of a mile from Dedham Village, 7 miles NE of Colchester, 2 miles E of Ipswich Road (A12). **Station(s):** Colchester, Manningtree, Ipswich. **Open:** May 3 – Oct 4, Wed, Sun and Bank Holiday Mons. Also Thurs and Sats in August, 2–5pm. **Admission:** Adult £3.00, concessions £2.00, child £0.50. Private parties by arrangement. Free car park.

map 5
H2

RHS GARDEN HYDE HALL

Rettendon, Chelmsford, Essex CM3 8ET
Tel: 01245 400256 (Royal Horticultural Society)

A charming hilltop garden which extends to over 24 acres. Highlights include the spring bulbs, the modern all and intermediate bearded irises in late May and the rope walk of climbing roses and large beds ablaze with floribunda and hybrid tea roses in midsummer. There is also a small plant centre and delightful hot and cold meals are available in the Essex thatched barn when the garden is open.

map 5
G3

PAYCOCKE'S

West Street, Coggeshall, Colchester CO6 1NS Tel: 01376 561305

A merchant's house, dating from c.1500 and containing unusually rich panelling and wood carving. Coggeshall was famous for its lace, examples of which are displayed inside the house, and there is also a pleasant garden. **Open:** 29 March to 11 Oct: Tues, Thur, Sun & BH Mon 2–5.30. Last admission 5. **Admission:** £2. Parties of 10 or more must book in advance with the tenant. No reduction for parties. Children must be accompanied by an adult. Joint ticket with Coggeshall Grange Barn £3. Parking at Grange Barn (10min walk) until 5

Gloucestershire

The picturesque honey coloured cottages of the Cotswolds are quite charming. It is easy to see why Gloucestershire attracts thousands of visitors every year, with its quaint blend of meandering lanes and fine chuches. Many Cotswold villages were established as early as the twelfth century, with money from the medieval wool trade.

The cities of Gloucester and Cheltenham are well worth exporing. Gloucester, on the River Severn, houses a magnificent

Bibury

cathedral, the scene of the coronation of Henry III and famous for its wonderful early fan vaulting.

Cheltenham is a city of elegance which becomes the centre of the horse racing world during Gold Cup week. In the 18th century the high society flocked to the spa town to "take the waters".

To the south east is the picturesque town of Cirencester, known as the capital of the Cotswolds.

BARNSLEY HOUSE GARDEN

The Close, Barnsley, Nr. Cirencester, Glos GL7 5EE
Tel & Fax: 01285 740 281 (Rosemary Verey)
01285 740 561 (Charles & Denzil Verey)

Old garden re-planned since 1960 inside 1770 wall. 4¹/2 acres. **Special features:** Spring bulbs & blossom, laburnum walk (in flower early June), mixed borders, autumn colour and berries, knot garden, decorative potager & winter interest. Tuscan Temple & Gothick Summer house (both 1770's). House 1697 – not open. Plants, garden furniture & antiques for sale. **Location:** 4 miles northeast of Cirencester, on B4425. **Open:** All the year, Mon, Wed, Thur & Sat 10am–6pm (or dusk). Sat 9 May Barnsley Festival. Several gardens in village open, including Barnsley Park, 10–5pm. **Admission:** £3.50, OAPs £2.50. Guided tour by R Verey £100.

 map 4 B3

CHAVENAGE

Tetbury, Gloucestershire GL8 8XP
Tel: 01666 502329 Fax: 01453 836778 (David Lowsley-Williams, Esq.)

Elizabethan House (1576) set in the tranquil Cotswold countryside with Cromwellian associations. 16th and 17th century furniture and tapestries. Personally conducted tours, by the owner or his family. **Location:** 2 miles N of Tetbury, signposted off A46 (Bath–Stroud) or B4014. **Open:** Thurs, Sun and Bank Hols, 2–5pm. May – end Sept plus Easter Sun and Mon. **Admission:** Adults £3, children half-price. Parties by appointment as shown or other dates and times to suit. **Refreshments:** Catering for parties by arrangement. **Conferences:** Wedding receptions, dinners, corporate hospitality, also available for film and photographic location.

 map 4 A3

BERKELEY CASTLE

Gloucestershire, GL13 9BQ
Tel: 01453 810332 (Mr R J G Berkeley)

England's most Historic Home and Oldest Inhabited Castle. Completed in 1153 by Lord Maurice Berkeley at the command of Henry II and for nearly 850 years the home of the Berkeley family. 24 generations have gradually transformed a savage Norman fortress into a truly stately home. The castle is a home and not a museum. Enjoy the castle at leisure or join one of the regular one-hour guided tours covering the dungeon, the cell where Edward II was murdered, the medieval kitchens , the magnificent Great Hall and the State Apartments with their fine collections of pictures by primarily English and Dutch masters, tapestries, furniture of an interesting diversity, silver and porcelain. Splendid Elizabethan Terraced Gardens and sweeping lawns surround the castle, Tropical Butterfly House with hundreds of exotic butterflies

in free flight – an oasis of colour and tranquillity. Facilities include free coach and parks, picnic lawn and two gift shops. Tea rooms for refreshments, light lunches and afternoon teas. **Location:** Midway between Bristol and Gloucester, just off A38, M5 junctions 13 or 14. **Open:** April & May, Tues–Sun 1–5pm; June & Sept, Tues–Sat 11–5pm, Sun 1–5pm; Jul & Aug, Mon–Sat 11–5pm, Sun 1–5pm; Oct, Sun only 1–5pm; Bank Holiday Mondays 11–5pm. **Admission:** Adult £4.95 Child £2.60 Sen. Citz £3.95. Pre-booked parties 25 or more: Adult £4.45 Child £2.30 Sen. Citz £3.65 Family Ticket £13.50 (2 adults & 2 children). Gardens only: Adult £1.75 Child 90p. Butterfly Farm: Adult £1.75 Child/OAP 85p School Groups 50p.

 map 3 J1

CHEDWORTH ROMAN VILLA

Yanworth, Cheltenham
Tel: 01242 890256 Fax: 01242 840 544 (The National Trust)

Chedworth Roman Villa is one of the finest Roman-period sites in Britain. Nestling in a wooded combe in the Cotswolds, it contains the ruins of a large, opulent country house of the 4th century. There are some very special features surviving–fine mosaics, a water shrine with running spring, two bath-houses, several hypocaust systems (Roman central heating) and many artefacts in the site museum. There is a ten minute video introduction to the site and a new audio tour which guides the visitor around the villa. There are various events and open days during the year and archaeological work continues. Visit Chedworth for a flavour of life in 4th century Britain. **Open:** Mar–Nov, Tues–Sun and BHols, 10–5pm (closes at 4pm after 25 Oct). **Admission:** Adult £3.50, child £1.60, family £8.00 (2 adults & 4 children). **Location:** 20 mins from Cirencester.

map 4
B3

FRAMPTON COURT

Frampton-on-Severn, Gloucester
Tel: 01452 740698 (Mr & Mrs P.R.H. Clifford)

Listed Grade I, by Vanburgh. 1732. Stately family home of the Cliffords who have lived at Frampton since granted land by William the Conquerer, 1066. Fine collection of the original period furniture, tapestries, needle work and porcelain. Panelled throughout. Fine views over well kept parkland to extensive lake. A famous Gothic orangery stands in the garden reflected in a long Dutch ornamental canal similar to Westbury. The original well known floral water colours by the gifted 19th century great Aunts hang in the house. These inspired the book "The Frampton Flora". **Open:** All year by appointment £4. Tel: 01452 740267. Near jct. 13 of M5 motorway.

map 4
A3

HARDWICKE COURT

Nr Gloucester, Glos
Tel: 01452 720212 (C G M Lloyd-Baker)

Late Georgian house designed by Robert Smirke, built in 1816–1817. Entrance Hall, Drawing Room, Library and Dining Room open. **Location:** 5 miles S of Gloucester on A38 (between M5 access 12 S only and 13). **Open:** Easter Mon-end Sept, Mon only 2–4pm other times by prior written agreement. **Admission:** £1, parking for cars only. Not suitable for disabled.

map 4
A3

HODGES BARN GARDENS

Shipton Moyne, Tetbury, Gloucestershire GL8 8PR
Tel: 01666 880202 Fax: 01666 880373 (Mrs Amanda Hornby)

One of the finest private gardens in England. Spring bulbs, magnolias and flowering trees are followed by a superb collection of old fashioned and climbing roses and many mixed shrub and herbaceous beds. **Open:** 1 Apr–19 Aug Mon, Tues, Fri 2–5pm. **Admission:** Adults £2.50, children free. Dogs on leads.

map 4
A4

KELMSCOTT MANOR

Kelmscott, Nr. Lechlade, Oxfordshire, GL7 3HJ.
Tel: 01367 252 486 Fax: 01367 253 754 (Society of Antiquaries)

Kelmscott Manor was the country home of William Morris – poet, craftsman and socialist – from 1871 until his death in 1896. It is the most evocative of all his houses and continues to delight with the charm of its architecture, the fascination of its contents and the charm of its garden, which has recently undergone extensive restoration and now contains many fine examples of plants and flowers which would have been an inspiration to Morris. **Location:** 2 miles SE of Lechlade, on the Lechlade/Faringdon Road. **Open:** Apr-Sept, Wed 11am–1pm, 2–5pm; the 3rd Sat in each month, 2-5pm; Thurs & Fri by appointment only. **Admission:** Adults £6, Children £3, Students £3. **Events/Exhibitions:** Centenary exhibition "William Morris at Kelmscott". Gift shop and bookshop.

map 4
B3

KIFTSGATE COURT GARDENS

Chipping Campden, Gloucestershire, GL55 6LW
Tel: 01386 438 777 Fax: 01386 438 777 (Mr & Mrs J G. Chambers)

Garden with many unusual shrubs and plants including tree peonies, abutilons, etc, specie and old-fashioned roses. **Location:** 3 miles NE of Chipping Campden. **Open:** Apr–May & Aug–Sept; Wed, Thurs and Sun, 2–6pm. June-July; Wed, Thurs, Sat and Sun, 12noon-6pm. Bank Hols Mon 2-6pm. **Admission:** Adults £3.50, children £1. **Refreshments:** Whitsun – 1 Sept. Light lunches in June and July. Coaches by appointment only. Unusual plants for sale on open days.

map 4
B2

LITTLEDEAN HALL

Littledean, The Royal Forest of Dean, Gloucs GL14 3NR
Tel: 01594 824213 Tel/Fax: 01594 827337 (Sheila Christopher)

Littledean Hall is reputedly England's oldest inhabited house (Guinness Book of Records). The house has Saxon and Celtic remains in the cellars dated to before the 11C and is believed to have originated in the 5 or 6C. Two officers were put to the sword in the dining room when the house became a royalist garrison during the civil war. Exhibits include a packaging collection and ballooning memorabilia. Virgin balloon flights launch from the grounds. Ancient chestnut trees, a Victorian walled garden and a Roman temple site are in this wonderful setting. It is hoped that a café will be opened and B&B available in 1998. **Location:** 12m SW of Gloucester, 2m E of Cinderford, 400yds from A4151 on Littledean/Newnham-on-Severn road, turn at Kings Head or follow brown signs. **Open:** Apr 1–31 Oct, every day, 11–5pm. Other times by appointment. **Admission:** Adult £3, senior citizens £2.50, child £1.50.

map 3
J1

LYDNEY PARK SPRING GARDENS

Lydney, Gloucestershire GL15 6BU
Tel: 01594 842844 Fax: 01594 842027 (Viscount Bledisloe)

Magnificent Woodland Garden in secluded valley with lakes and a wide selection of rhododendrons and azaleas, fine shrubs and trees. Museums and Roman Temple Site. Deer Park. Plants for sale. **Location:** 1/2 mile W of Lydney on A48 (Gloucester to Chepstow) **Open:** 11–6pm, Suns, Wed and Bank Hol from Easter to 14 June. Every day 25–31 May. Parties by appointment. **Admission:** Adults £2.40, Wed £1.40. Accompanied children and car park free. **Refreshments:** Morning coffee and teas in Dining Room (House not otherwise open). Picnics in deer park. Dogs on lead. Taurus Café/Restaurant. Craft shop and Pottery at Old Park. Open all year (separate entrance when gardens closed). Free car park.

MISARDEN PARK GARDENS

Miserden, Stroud, Gloucestershire
Tel: 01285 821303, Fax: 01825 821530 (Major M T N H Wills)

Spring flowers, shrubs, fine topiary (some designed by Sir Edwin Lutyens) and herbaceous borders within a walled garden, roses and specimen trees. 17th century manor house (not open), stunning position overlooking Golden Valley. **Location:** Miserden 7 miles from Gloucester, Cheltenham, Stroud & Cirencester; 3 miles off A417 (signed). **Open:** Every Tues, Wed & Thurs from 1 Apr–30 Sept, 9.30–4.30pm. Nurseries adjacent to garden open daily except Mons. **Admission:** Adults £3, (guided tour extra). Children (accompanied) free. Reductions for parties (of 20 or more) by appointment.

map 4
A3

OWLPEN MANOR

Owlpen, Nr Uley, Gloucestershire, GL11 5BZ
Tel: 01453 860261, Fax: 01453 860819 (Mr & Mrs C N Mander)

Romantic Tudor manor house (1450-1616), home of the Mander family. Magnificent Great Hall, Jacobean solar wing, unique painted textiles in a room haunted by Queen Margaret of Anjou (in 1471), and family and Cotswold Arts and Crafts collections. The formal terraced garden (1723) has fine yew topiary, parterres and mill pond walk. Medieval outbuildings include the Cyder House Restaurant (open daily), the Grist Mill and Court House (now holiday cottages) and a richly-detailed Victorian church. The house lies at the bottom of a picturesque wooded valley under the edge of the Cotswolds, with miles of walks. **House Open:** 2–5pm, April 1–October 30, every day except Mondays (but open on Bank Holiday Mondays). "*Owlpen in Gloucestershire - ah what a dream is there!*" – Vita Sackville-West.

map 4
A3

PAINSWICK ROCOCO GARDENS

The Stables, Painswick House, Painswick, Gloucestershire GL6 6TH
Tel & Fax: 01452 813204 (Painswick Rococo Garden Trust)

Painswick Rococo Garden is a unique survivor from a brief period of 18th century garden design. It is set in a hidden Cotswold valley near the picturesque, historic wool town of Painswick. The garden boasts many charming contemporary buildings, a large kitchen garden, herbaceous borders, woodland walks and wonderful views of the surrounding countryside. One of its most noted features is the magnificent carpet of snowdrops during late winter, early spring. **Open:** Gardens from 15 Jan–30 Nov, Wed–Sun, plus Bank Hol Mons 11–5pm; daily in July and Aug. **Admission:** Adult £3, senior £2.70, child £1.60. The Old Coach House containing the restaurant/tearooms and gift shop are open Wednesday to Sunday. Ample car parking. The garden is a registered charity. **E-Mail:** painsgard@aol.com **Internet:** www.beta.co.uk/painswick

map 4
A3

SEZINCOTE

Moreton-in-Marsh, Gloucestershire GL56 9AW
(Mr & Mrs D Peake)

Oriental water garden by Repton and Daniell with trees of unusual size. House in Indian style, inspiration of Royal Pavilion, Brighton. **Location:** 1 mile W of Moreton-in-Marsh on A44 to Evesham; turn left by lodge before Bourton-on-the-Hill. **Station(s):** Moreton-in-Marsh **Open:** Garden Thurs, Fri & Bank Hol Mons 2–6pm (or dusk if earlier) throughout the year, except Dec. House May, June, July & Sept Thurs & Fri 2.30–6pm parties by appointment. Open in aid of National Gardens Scheme Sun July 5th 2–6pm. **Admission:** House and Garden £4.50; Garden only £3, children £1, under 5s free. **Refreshments:** Hotels and restaurant in Moreton-in-Marsh. No dogs.

map 4
B2

SUDELEY CASTLE

Winchcombe, Gloucestershire GL54 5JD
Tel: 01242 602 308 (Lord & Lady Ashcombe)

Sudeley Castle, Winner of the 1996 HHA/Christie's Garden of the Year Award and the home of Lord and Lady Ashcombe, is one of England's great historic houses with royal connections stretching back 1000 years. Sudeley was the magnificent palace of Queen Katherine Parr, Henry VIII's sixth wife, who is buried in the Castle Church. Henry VIII, Elizabeth I and Charles I, amongst others, have all stayed here. A programme of reconstruction during the Victorian era enhanced Sudeley's earlier magnificence amongst the wealth of history on show, there is an impressive collection of masterpieces by Turner, Van Dyck and Ruebens. Visitors can enjoy the eight award-winning gardens surrounding the Castle. These enchanting gardens include the Queen's Garden, with its fine collection of old roses and the Victorian Kitchen Garden. **Open:** 1–31 Mar: Tue–Sun. Gardens, Plant Centre & Shop:

11–4.30pm. 1 Apr–31 May: Tue–Sun. Open Bank Hol Mons. Castle and Gardens Closed 9 & 10 May. Castle Apartments and Church: 11–5pm. Gardens, Exhibition Centre, Shop, Plant Centre, Refreshments: 10.30–5.30pm. 1 Jun–13 Sept: Every day. Times as above. 14 Sept–31 Oct: Tues–Sun. Times as above. **Admission:** Castle & Gardens: Individual: Weekdays: Adults £5.50, OAPs £4.80, children (5–15 yrs) £3. Sat/Sun & Bank Hols: Adults: £5.95, OAP's £4.95, children £3.45. Family ticket (2 Adults & 2 Children): £16, family season ticket £32. Groups (min 20) Weekdays: Adults: £4.50, OAP's £3.95, children (5–15 yrs) £3, Sat/Sun & Bank Hols: Adults: £4.95, OAP's £3.95, children (5–15 yrs) £3.45, adult season ticket £16. Gardens & Exhibition Only. Individual. Weekdays: Adults £4, OAP's £3.20, children (5–15 yrs) £1.80. Sat/Sun & Bank Hols: Adults: £4.45, OAP's £3.45, children £1.95.

map 4 B2

RODMARTON MANOR

Cirencester, Gloucestershire GL7 6PF
Tel: 01285 841253 Fax 01285 841298 (Mr & Mrs Simon Biddulph)

The house is a unique example of the Cotswold Arts and Crafts and was built and furnished with local materials entirely by hand. The garden consists of a series of outdoor rooms. There are hedges, topiary, a troughery, a rockery, lawns, magnificent herbaceous borders and kitchen garden all in a romantic setting. **Location:** Off A433 6m west of Cirencester. **Open:** The house is open to groups for conducted tours only by written appointment. It is not possible to arrange a tour of the house on Wed afternoons or Sat afternoons when the garden is open. The garden is open Weds 15 Apr–26 Aug 2–5pm and Sats 16 May–29 Aug 2–5pm. Groups are very welcome to visit the garden at other times by appointment. **Admission:** Conducted tour of the house with unconducted tour of the garden. £5 (children under 16 £2.50). Min. group charge £35. Garden only £2.50 (accompanied children under 16 free).

map 4
A3

STANWAY HOUSE

Cheltenham, Gloucestershire GL54 5PQ
Tel: 01386 584469 (Lord Neidpath)

The jewel of Cotswold Manor houses is very much a home rather than a museum and the centre of a working landed estate, which has changed hands once in 1275 years. The mellow Jacobean architecture, the typical squire's family portraits, the exquisite Gatehouse, the old Brewery, medieval Tithe Barn, the extensive gardens, arboretum pleasure grounds and formal landscape contribute to the timeless charm of what Arthur Negus considered one of the most beautiful and romantic houses in England. **Location:** 1 mile off B4632 Chelteham/Broadway road; on B4077 Toddington/Stow-on-the-Wold road: M5 junction 9. **Open:** June–Sept: Tues and Thurs 2–5pm **Admission:** Please phone for details. **Refreshments:** Teas in Old Bakehouse in the village (01386 584204).

map 4
B2

WOODCHESTER MANSION

Nymspfield. (Visitor information) Tel: 01453 860661
Tel: 01453 750455 (Woodchester Mansion Trust Office)

Hidden in a wooded valley (NT owned) near Stroud is one of the most intriguing houses in the country. Woodchester Mansion was started in 1856 but abandoned, incomplete, in 1870. It offers a unique insight into traditional building techniques. It is now leased by the Woodchester Mansion Trust, whose repair programme includes training courses in stone masonry and building conservation. **Location:** By Coaley Peak Picnic Site on B4066 Stroud-Dursley, ½ mile from Nympsfield village. **Station(s):** Stroud 3m **Open:** First weekend in each month from Easter–Oct (Sat/Sun) and Bank Holiday weekends (Sat/Sun/Mon). Gates open 11–4pm. Regular guided tours. Free minibus service (if available) or walk down ¾m wooded track. Gift shop. Private group visits Tel: 01453 860531. **Refreshments:** Teas and snacks. No dogs, please.

map 4
A3

WHITTINGTON COURT

Whittington, Nr Cheltenham, Gloucestershire GL54 4HF
Tel: 01242 820556 (Mrs J L Stringer)

Small Elizabethan stone-built manor house with family possessions. **Location:** 4 miles E of Cheltenham on A40. **Open:** Sat 11 Apr–Sun 26 Apr and Sat 15 Aug–Bank Hol Mon 31 Aug inclusive. **Admission:** Adults £2.50, OAPs £2, children £1. Open to parties by arrangement.

map 4
B3

DYRHAM PARK

nr Chippenham SN14 8ER

Tel: Property Office 0117 937 2501; Warden's Office 01225 891364

HIDCOTE MANOR GARDEN

Hidcote Bartrim, nr Chipping Campden GL55 6LR

Tel: 01386 438333 Restaurant 01386 438703 Fax: 01386 438817

SNOWSHILL MANOR

Snowshill, nr Broadway WR12 7JU Tel: 01386 852410

Hampshire

Curled in the semi circle formed by the Western Downs, the Hampshire Downs and the South Downs and sheltered from the Channel winds by the pearl and emerald hills of the Isle of Wight, the county of Hampshire basks in as mellow a climate as any part of the British Isles.

This is a land overflowing with incredible landscapes, charming villages, world-famous stately homes, forests, castles and manor houses. Its unassuming county town, Winchester, was the one time capital of England, and is home to a beautiful cathedral and many points of historic interest.

Hampshire's new forest – 145 square miles of heath and woodland – is the largest area of unenclosed land in Southern Britain. William the Conqueror's 'new'

New Forest Ponies

Chawton Church

forest, despite its name, is one of the few primeval oak woods in England. The New Forest was a popular hunting ground for Norman kings and is the home of the Rufus Stone, where William II was shot dead. The forest is home to numerous shaggy New Forest ponies and over 1,500 fallow deer.

Once a vital naval port, Portsmouth today is a much quieter town, with a fascinating naval history from the 16th century to the Falklands war. The harbour is very busy and a mecca for day sailors with endless pubs and fish and chip bars.

AVINGTON PARK

Winchester, Hampshire SO21 1DD
Tel: 01962 779260 Fax: 01962 779864 (Mrs A M Hickson)

Avington Park is a Palladian mansion, where both Charles II and George IV stayed at various times. It was enlarged in 1670 with the addition of two wings and a classical portico surmounted by three statues. The State Rooms on view include the magnificent silk and gilded Ballroom, hand painted Drawing Room, Library and Hall. In a delightful parkland and lakeside setting, it adjoins an exquisite Georgian church, which may be visited. **Open:** May to September 2.30 to 5pm, Sundays and Bank Hol. Monday. Last tour 5pm. **Admission:** Adults £3, Children £1.50. Coaches welcome by appointment all year.

map 4 D5

BASING HOUSE RUINS

Redbridge Lane, Basing, Basingstoke, Hants
Tel: 01256 467294 Fax: 01256 326283 (Hampshire County Council)

Basing House Ruins were once the country's largest private house, the palace of William Paulet, Lord Treasurer of England. The Civil War brought disaster to Basing which fell to Oliver Cromwell in person after 2½ years of siege in 1645. The ruins, which cover about 10 acres, contain Norman earthworks, the remains of Tudor kitchens, cellars, towers, a 300 foot long tunnel, a spectacular barn, Civil War defences designed by Inigo Jones and a re-created 16/17th century formal garden. **Location:** 2m from Basingstoke Town Centre & 2m from Jct. 6 of M3. **Open:** 1 Apr–30 Sept, Wed–Sun and Bank Hols 2–6pm. Parties any time by prior arrangement. **Admission:** £1.50. Children and OAPs 70p. Refreshments: Meals can be obtained at two public houses near main entrance. Car parking. (For disabled persons–please telephone on advance for easier parking).

map 4 D5

BREAMORE HOUSE

Nr. Fordingbridge, Hampshire SP6 2DF
Tel: 01725 512468 (Sir Edward Hulse)

Elizabethan Manor House (1583) with fine collections of paintings, tapestries, furniture. Countryside Museum takes the visitor back to when a village was self-sufficient. Exhibition of Rural Arts and Agricultural machinery. **Location:** 3 miles N of Fordingbridge off the main Bournemouth Road (A338) 8 miles S of Salisbury. **Open:** 1 Apr–30 Sept 1998. House 2–5.30pm Countryside Museum 1–5.30pm. Other times by appointment. **Admission:** Combined ticket adults £5 children £3.50, reduced rate for parties and OAPs. **Refreshments:** Home-made snacks and teas available from midday.

map 4 C5

BEAULIEU

Beaulieu, Brockenhurst Hampshire SO42 7ZN
Tel: 01590 612345 Fax: 01590 612624 Internet: www.beaulieu.co.uk

Set in the heart of the New Forest, Beaulieu is a unique day out where you can enjoy 800 years of history and heritage in one day. Overlooking the Beaulieu River, Palace House has been Lord Montagu's family home since 1538. The House was once the Great Gatehouse of Beaulieu Abbey and its monastic origins are reflected in such features as the fan vaulted ceilings. Many treasures, which are reminders of travels all round the world by past generations of the Montagu family, can also be seen. Walks amongst the gardens and by the Beaulieu River can also be enjoyed. Beaulieu Abbey was founded in 1204 and although most of the buildings have been destroyed, much of beauty and interest remains. The former monks' Refectory is now the local Parish Church. The Domus, which houses an exhibition of monastic life, is home to beautiful wall hangings. Beaulieu is also home of the world famous National Motor museum which traces the story of motoring from 1894 to the present day. 250 vehicles are on display including legendary World Record breakers such as Bluebird and Golden Arrow plus Veteran, Vintage and Classic cars. In addition, there are various rides and drives on a transportation theme to be enjoyed by everyone including a monorail and replica 1912 London open topped bus **Open:** daily 10–5pm except Easter–Sept 10–6pm. Closed Christmas Day. **Location:** By car take the M27 to junction 2 then follow the Brown Tourist Signs. **Admission:** Please phone for details on 01590 612345.

map 4
C6

BROADLANDS

Romsey, Hampshire SO51 9ZD
Tel: 01794 517888

Fine example of Palladian architecture set in Capability Brown parkland on the banks of the River Test. Well known country residence of the late Lord Mountbatten. Visitors may view the house, enjoy views from Riverside lawns or relive Lord Mountbatten's life and times in the Mountbatten Exhibition and spectacular Mountbatten AV Presentation. **Open:** 13 June–6 Sept incl. 12 noon–5.30pm (last admission 4pm) **Admission:** Adults £5, Senior Citizens £4.25, Students £4.25, Disabled £4.25, Children 12–16 £3.50 and children under 12 free. For group admission rate please call the number detailed above.

EXBURY GARDENS

Nr Southampton SO45 1AZ, Tel: 01703 891203
Fax: 01703 243380 (E.L. de Rothschild, Esq.)

Described as 'Heaven with the gates open', this 200 acres garden, created by Lionel de Rothschild, contains magnificent displays of rhododendrons, azaleas and other woodland shrubs. Free 'Trail Guides' in Spring, Summer and Autumn to encourage the visitor to see newly planted areas, making this a beautiful day out any time. **Location:** Exbury village, south drive from Jct.2 M27 west of Southampton. Turn W off A326 at Didben Purlieu towards Beaulieu. **Open:** Daily 10–5.30pm (dusk if earlier). Free entry to Gift shop and Plant Centre.

map 4 C6

BRAMDEAN HOUSE

Bramdean, nr Alresford
Tel: 01962 771214

Carpets of spring bulbs. Walled garden with famous herbaceous borders. 1 acre working kitchen garden, large collection of unusual plants. **Location:** In Bramdean village on A272 midway between Winchester and Petersfield. **Open:** By appointment, as well as various dates. Please call for times and dates.

map 4 C6

GILBERT WHITE'S HOUSE & GARDEN & THE OATES MUSEUM

'The Wakes', Selborne, Nr. Alton, Hampshire, GU34 3JH
Tel: 01420 511275

Historic 18th century house and glorious garden, home of famous naturalist Rev. Gilbert White. Furnished rooms and original manuscript. Also fascinating museum depicting Capt. Lawrence Oates, hero of Scott's ill-fated Antarctic Expedition. Tea Parlour. Excellent shop. Plant sales. **Open:** 11–5 daily mid March – Christmas, then weekends only during winter. Groups welcome all year and summer evenings. **Admission:** Adults £3.50, OAPs £3, Children £1, Group Rates also. **Events:** Unusual Plants Fair 20/21 June '98. Picnic to 'Jazz in June' 20 June '98. Mulled Wine & Christmas Shopping Day 29 November '98.

map 4 D5

HIGHCLERE CASTLE

Newbury RG20 9RN
Tel: 01635 253210

Designed by Charles Barry in the 1830s at the same time as he was building the Houses of Parliament. This soaring pinnacled mansion provided a perfect setting for the 3rd Earl of Carnarvon, one of the great hosts of Queen Victoria's reign. Old master paintings mix with portraits by Van Dyck and 18th century painters. The 5th Earl of Carnarvon, discovered the Tomb of Tutankhamun with Howard Carter.
FURTHER INFORMATION, OPENING TIMES AND DATES WITH PHOTOGRAPHY CAN BE SEEN UNDER THE COUNTY OF BERKSHIRE.

map 4 C5

HOLLYCOMBE STEAM FAIR

Iron Hill, Midhurst Road, Liphook, Hants
Tel: 01428 724900 (Hollycombe Steam & Woodland Garden Society)

Do you remember the thrills and smells of the old steam-driven fairground rides? You do? Then a trip to the Hollycombe Steam Fair on the West Sussex/Hampshire border should be a must, for Hollycombe boasts the country's biggest working Edwardian steam fairground, as well as three railways, traction, engine-hauled rides, working agricultural machinery, all set in acres of woodland gardens established early in the 1800s. **Open:** 1–6pm Suns and Bank Hols from Good Fri to 11 Oct. Daily from 26–31 Jul and 16–31 Aug. **Admission:** Adults £5.50, children/OAPs £4.50. Saver Ticket £17 (2 adults + 2 children). Many special events. Tel: 01428 724900 for details.

map 4 D3

HOUGHTON LODGE GARDENS

Stockbridge, Hampshire SO20 6LQ
Tel: 01264 810177 Fax: 01794 388072 (Capt & Mrs M W Busk)

Landscaped pleasure grounds and fine trees surround unique 18th C 'Cottage Ornee' beside the River Test with lovely views over the tranquil and unspoilt valley. Featured in "The Buccaneers" (BBC TV) and the film "Wilde". Chalkcob walls shelter the 1 acre kitchen garden with ancient espaliered fruit trees, glasshouses and newly established herb garden. (Fuchsias a speciality). THE HYDROPONICUM IS A LIVING EXHIBITION OF SOILLESS HORTICULTURE WITH BIOLOGICAL CONTROL OF GREENHOUSE PESTS. <u>Location:</u> 1$\frac{1}{2}$ miles S of A30 at Stockbridge on minor road to Houghton village. <u>Station(s):</u> Winchester, Andover. <u>Open:</u> Mar–Sept, Sat, Sun & Bank Holidays 10–5pm, Mon, Tues, Thurs and Fri 2–5pm. <u>Admission:</u> £3.50 per person. Discount for groups. House open for groups by appointment only.

map 4 C5

LANGLEY BOXWOOD NURSERY

Rake, Nr Liss, Hampshire GU33 7JL
Tel: 01730 894467 Fax: 01730 894703 (Elizabeth Braimbridge)

This small nursery, in a beautiful setting, specialises in box-growing, offering a chance to see together a unique range of old and new varieties, hedging, topiary, specimens and rarities. Some taxus also. Descriptive list available (4 x 1st class stamps). <u>Location:</u> On B2070 (old A3) 3 miles S of Liphook. <u>Open:</u> Mon–Fri 9–4.30pm, Sat – enquire by telephone first. National Collection – Buxus.

map 4 D6

MOTTISFONT ABBEY

Mottisfont, Nr Romsey, Hants, SO51 OLP
Tel: 01794 340757 Fax: 01794 341492 (The National Trust)

The abbey and garden form the central point of an 809 hectare estate which includes most of the village of Mottisfont, farmland and woods. It is possible to walk along a tributary of the River Test which flows through the garden, forming a superb and tranquil setting for a 12th century Augustinian priory, which, after the Dissolution, became a house. It contains the spring or 'font' from which the place-name is derived. The magnificent trees, walled garden and the national collection of old-fashioned roses combine to provide interest throughout the seasons. The abbey contains a drawing room decorated by Rex Whistler and the cellarium of the old priory. In 1996 the Trust acquired Derek Hill's 20th-century picture collection.

C map 4 C6

SPINNERS GARDEN

Boldre, Lymington, Hants, SO41 5QE
Tel: 01590 673347 (P.G.G. Chappell)

A woodland garden on a slope overlooking the River Lymington Valley with rhododendrons, magnolias, Japanese maples, hydrangea species etc interplanted with a diversity of choice woodland and groundcover plants. Amongst a large collection of bog and woodland plants a NCCPG collection of Trilliums. Press mentions in '97 include a Roy Lancaster article in the July issue of 'The Garden'. The nursery contains as wide a selection of less common hardy plants, shrubs and trees as you will find anywhere. <u>Open:</u> 1 Apr–14 Sept Tues to Sat 10–5pm. <u>Admission:</u> £1.50. After 14 Sept part of garden and nursery still open. No charge.

map 4 C7

JANE AUSTEN'S HOUSE

Chawton, Alton GU34 1SD
Tel/Fax: 01420 83262 (Jane Austin Memorial Fund)

17th century house where Jane Austen wrote or revised her six great novels. The house contains many items associated with her and her family, documents and letters, first editions of the novels, pictures, portraits and furniture. Pleasant garden, suitable for picnics, bakehouse with brick oven and wash tub, houses Jane's donkey carriage. <u>Location:</u> Just S of A31, 1 mile SW of Alton, signposted Chawton. <u>Open:</u> 1 Mar–1 Jan daily. Jan & Feb, Sat & Sun. Admission charges apply.

STRATFIELD SAYE HOUSE

Stratfield Saye,m Reading, Hampshire RE7 2BT
Tel: 01256 882882 (The Duke of Wellington)

Home of the Dukes of Wellington since 1817. The house and exhibition pay tribute to Arthur Wellesley, the first and great Duke – soldier, statesman and victor of the Napoleonic wars. <u>House:</u> Contains a unique collection of paintings, furniture and personal effects of the Great Duke. <u>Wellington Exhibition:</u> Depicts the life and times of the Great Duke and features his magnificent funeral carriage. <u>Grounds:</u> Include gardens and the grave of Copenhagen, the Duke's favourite charger that carried him throughout the battle of Waterloo. <u>Location:</u> 1 mile W of A33 between Reading & Basingstoke (turn off at Wellington Arms Hotel); signposted. <u>Open:</u> House & Gardens May: Sat, Sun & Bank Hol Mon. Jun–Aug: daily except Fri. Sept: Sat & Sun. Grounds & Exhibition 11.30–6pm Last admission 4pm. House 12–4pm. <u>Admission:</u> Please telephone for charges.

C map 4 D5

WEST GREEN HOUSE & GARDEN

Thackhams Lane, West Green, Nr. Hartley Wintney, Hampshire
Tel: 01252 845 582 Fax: 01252 844 611 (National Trust)

Hidden in a quiet corner of Hampshire is the manor house of West Green built in the 1740s. For the past 7 years this 8 acre garden has been hidden from view but now its herbaceous borders are being replanted, the fruit cages restocked and rebuilt and its parterres restored. The neo-classical park that surrounds West Green House is unique, a series of follies, birdcages and monuments along sylvan allees in a newly planted lake field. This reclamation is the inspiration of an Australian gardener, gardening on both sides of the world trying out different colour and plant combinations in one of the most romantic of English gardens, as well as in Australia's acclaimed Kennerton Green. **Directions:** From A30 at Hartley Wintney: B3304 at Mattingley **Open:** 21 May-3 Aug, Wed-Sun. **Admission:** £3.00.

 # THE VYNE

Vyne Road, Sherborne St John, Basingstoke, Hampshire RG24 9HL
Tel: 01256 881337 Fax: 01256 881720 (The National Trust)

House re-opens 3 June 1998 following two years of repair. New areas of the house open for the first time to visitors. Built in the early 16th century in beautiful diaper brickwork by William Sandys, Lord Chamberlain to Henry VIII. Passed to the Chute family in the mid-17th century resulting in extensive alterations. Tudor chapel contains extremely fine renaissance glass and majolica floor tiles. A wealth of tudor panelling and collections of furniture, ceramics and textiles. Herbaceous borders, lawns sloping down to lake and surrounded by parkland. Woodland walks. Refreshments. **Open:** Wed-Sun, Bank Hol Mons. Grounds: 25 Mar-end Oct 12.30-5.30pm. House: 3 Jun-end Oct 1.30-5.30pm. Last admission 1/2 hr before closing. **Admission:** House & Grounds £4.50. Grounds only £2.50.

map 4
D5

UPPARK

South Harting, Petersfield, Hampshire GU31 5QR
Tel: 01730 825415 Fax: 01730 825873 (The National Trust)

Elegant 18th century interior, restored after 1989 fire, including grand tour paintings, fine ceramics, textiles and furniture. Interesting servants' rooms. Garden restored to Repton's design. **Location:** 5 miles SE of Petersfield on B2146. **Open:** 1 Apr-29 Oct: Car Park, tickets, garden, shop, tearoom 11.30-5.30pm. House: 1-5pm. **Admission:** House, Garden & Exhibition: £5.50; family £13.75. Parties (no reduction) must be pre-booked-weekdays only. Timed tickets-some available for booking a week ahead on 01730 825415.

map 4
D6

WINCHESTER CATHEDRAL

Winchester SO23 9LS
Tel: 01962 853137 Fax: 01962 841519

The cathedral was founded in 1079 on a site where Christian worship had already been offered for over 400 years. Among its treasures are the 12th century illuminated Winchester Bible, the font, medieval wall paintings and six chantry chapels. **Location:** Winchester city centre. **Open:** 7.15-6.30pm. East end closes 5pm. Access may be restricted during services. **Admission:** Donations recommended. Group tours, £3, should be booked through the education centre. (Tel: 01962 866854 between 9-1pm).

WINCHESTER COLLEGE

77 Kingsgate Street, Winchester S023 9PE
Tel: 01962 868778   Fax: 01962 840207

This is one of the oldest public schools in the country. The college was founded by Bishop William of Wykeham in 1382. **Location:** In Winchester city centre, south of the Cathedral. **Open:** Apr-Sept, Mon-Sat, 10-1pm and 2-5pm. Oct-Mar, Mon-Sat, 10-1pm & 2-4pm. Closed on Sunday mornings. **Admission:** Charges apply. Guided tours may be booked for groups of 10+.

HINTON AMPNER GARDEN

Bramdean, nr Alresford SO24 0LA Tel: 01962 771305 Fax: 01962 771305

Scented plants, unexpected vistas and glorious countryside combine to provide year-round interest in this splendid 20th-century shrub garden. The garden achieves the vision of tranquility of its creator, Ralph Dutton, by uniting a formal design with various informal plantings in pastel shades. The house, restored after a fire in 1960, displays his fine collection of Regency furniture and Italian paintings. **Open:** Garden: 15 & 22 March, then 28 March to end Sept: Tues, Wed, Sat, Sun & BH Mon 1.30-5.30; last admission 5. House: 28 March to end Sept: Tues & Wed only, plus Sat & Sun in Aug 1.30-5.30. No access to grounds before 1.15. Events: 17 May, Spring Plant Fair 11-5; details on application. **Admission:** House & garden £4, garden only £3. Special entrance for coaches; please book in advance. No group bookings in Aug. Party rate on application

SANDHAM MEMORIAL CHAPEL

Burghclere, nr Newbury RG15 9JT Tel: 01635 278394 Fax: 01635 278394

This red-brick chapel was built in the 1920s, specially to house the remarkable murals inside. Painted by Stanley Spencer, they cover the chapel walls in a touching and sensitive account of the everyday life of soldiers in the First World War. The chapel sits amidst beautiful and tranquil scenery, with views across to Watership Down. **Open:** March & Nov: Sat & Sun only 11.30-4; Apr to end Oct: Wed to Sun & BH Mon 11.30-5; (closed Wed following BH Mon); Dec to Feb by appointment only. **Admission:** £2. No reduction for pre-booked groups. Road verge parking. Picnics on front lawn

Hereford & Worcester

Right against the Welsh border lies the old county of Herefordshire. The River Wye winds its way across this rugged land of pastoral landscapes, offering excellent salmon fishing. Situated along its meandering route lies the city of Hereford which is graced with a beautiful Norman cathedral that towers above the River Wye. The spectacular Black Mountains lie to the South West along the Welsh borders, where trickling streams run through fertile valleys.

Worcester is famous for its fine timber buildings and its porcelain, particularly in Friar Street and New Street which houses the best examples of such architecture. Greyfriars and the Commandery are particularly worthy of a mention. Like Hereford, Worcester is dominated by a beautiful cathedral with an especially fine crypt. This wonderous place is also renowned for hosting a wide variety of musical events.

Ross-on-Wye

AVONCROFT MUSEUM OF HISTORIC BUILDINGS

Stoke Heath, Bromsgrove, Worcestershire B60 4JR
Tel: 01527 831363/831886 Fax: 01527 876934 (Council of Management)

25 buildings of historic, architectural and social value authentically restored and re-erected on 15-acre rural site. Covering 7 centuries, it ranges from the magnificently carved timber roof of the Priory of Worcester Cathedral, now gracing a fine new Guesten Hall, to a 1946 Pre-Fab, authentically furnished. English life over the centuries is illustrated – early agriculture by a range of timber-framed buildings, including a working windmill; the local 19th century industries of nail and chainmaking; and many aspects of domestic social life. We also house the national Telephone Kiosk Collection. **Location:** At Stoke heath 2 miles south of Bromsgrove. **Open:** March–Nov from 10.30am. Some days closed. **Admission:** Adult £4.25 Senior Citizen £3.50 Child £2.15. Group Rates: Adult £3.50 Senior Citizen £2.75 Child £1.60

map 4
A1

BROBURY HOUSE & GARDEN

Brobury, Nr. Hereford, Herefordshire, HR3 6BS
Tel: 01981 500 229 (Mrs Leonora Weaver)

Brobury House is a magnificent Victorian Gentleman's country house which overlooks the beautiful Wye Valley at Bredwardine, famous for its Francis Kilvert connection. Brobury House is a private home open to the public only by appointment for functions and B&B. The 8 acres of beautifully landscaped grounds are a gardener's delight, since the owners have lavished 25 years of love and care into them! The internationally known art gallery has over 100,000 antique maps and prints for sale. All of Great Britain's counties, all the countries of the world and most subject matter are represented in our stock. So if you are looking for that unusual gift we could be of help. **Open:** Mon – Sat 9–4.30pm, all year. Closed Sundays. B&B by appointment only.

map 7
G2

BURTON COURT

Eardisland, Nr Leominster, Herefordshire HR6 9DN
Tel: 01544 388231 (Lt. Cmdr. & Mrs. R. M. Simpson)

A typical squire's house, built around the surprising survival of a 14th century hall. The East Front re-designed by Sir Clough Williams-Ellis in 1912. Some European and Oriental costume, natural history specimens and models including a childrens working model fairground. Pick your soft fruit in season. **Location:** 5 miles W of Leominster signposted on A44. **Open:** Spring Bank Holiday to end September, only for organised party visits. **Admission:** Adults £2.50, children £2. **Refreshments:** Only coach parties catered for. **Conferences:** Subject to availability.

map 7
F2

DINMORE MANOR & GARDENS

Nr Hereford HR4 8EE
Tel: 01432 830322 (Mr R G Murray, Dinmore Manor Estate Limited)

Spectacular hillside location. A range of impressive architecture dating from 14th to 20th century. Chapel, Cloisters, Great Hall, (Music Room) and extensive roof walk giving panoramic views of the countryside and beautiful gardens below. Large collection of stained glass. Interesting and unusual plants for sale in plant centre. **Location:** 6 miles N of Hereford on A49. **Open:** All the year daily 9.30–5.30pm. **Admission:** Adults £3, Children (under 14) free when accompanied. **Refreshments:** Available in the Plant Centre most afternoons.

HOPTON COURT

Hopton Court, Cleobury Mortimer, Kidderminister, DY14 OEF
Tel: 01299 270734 Fax: 01299 271132 (C. R. D Woodward)

Substantial changes were made to the house and grounds from 1798 to 1803. The works were supervised by John Nash and Humphrey Repton. Around 1820, a conservatory (graded II* in 1995) of cast-iron and glass was built. To the north east of the house lies the stable block incorporating the Coach House. Both the Conservatory and the Coach House were renovated in 1997. Three rooms in the house and the Conservatory are licensed for civil ceremonies. The Conservatory is open four days a year without appointment, at other times by prior appointment. The Coach House is available for receptions.

EASTNOR CASTLE

Eastnor, Ledbury, Herefordshire HR8 1RL
Tel: 01531 633160 Fax: 01531 631776 (Mr J. Hervey–Bathurst)

Home of the Hervey-Bathurst family, this magnificent Georgian Castle was built in 1812 and is dramatically situated in a 5000 acre estate in The Malvern Hills. Lavish Italianate and Gothic interiors recently restored to critical acclaim. Unique collection of armour, tapestries, furniture and pictures by Van Dyck, Kneller, Romney & Watts. Castellated terraces descend to a beautiful lake and the castle is surrounded by a famous arboretum and 300 acre Deer Park which can be used for large outdoor events. **Location:** 5 miles from junction 2 of M50. 2 miles east of Ledbury on A438 Tewkesbury Road. **Open:** 12 Apr–4 Oct on Sun and Bank Holiday Mon plus every day in Jul and Aug, except Sat. **Admission:** Castle and Grounds: Adults: £4.50, children £2. Reduced rates for groups, families and grounds only. Eastnor Castle is also available for exclusive corporate and private entertainment, activity and teambuilding days, wedding ceremonies and receptions and luxury accommodation for small groups.

HARTLEBURY CASTLE

Nr Kidderminster, Worcester, Hereford & Worcester DT11 7XX
Tel: 01299 250410 (Bishop's office); 01299 250416 (Museum)

Home of the Bishops of Worcester for over 1,000 years. Fortified in 13th century, rebuilt after sacking in Civil War and gothicised in 18th century. State Rooms include medieval Great Hall, Hurd Library and Saloon. Fine plaster work and collection of episcopal portraits. Also County Museum in North Wing. **Location:** In village of Hartlebury, 5 mile S of Kidderminster, 10 miles N of Worcester off A449. **Station:** Kidderminster 4 miles. **Open:** State Rooms: Easter Mon–Sept 6, first Sun every month. Bank Hols and following Tues 2–5pm. Also every Wed during this period 2–4pm. Country Museum: Mar–Nov, Mon–Thurs 10–5pm, Fri & Sun 2–5pm. Closed Good Friday. **Admission:** State rooms: Adults 75p children 25p OAPs 50p guided tours for parties of 30 or more on weekdays by arrangement. County Museum £1.90 Concessions 90p Family tickets £5.

HARVINGTON HALL

Harvington, Kidderminster, Hereford & Worcester DY10 4LR
Tel: 01562 777846 (the Roman Catholic Archdiocese of Birmingham)

Moated medieval and Elizabethan manor house containing secret hiding places and rare wall paintings. Georgian Chapel in garden with 18th century altar, rails and organ. **Location:** 3 miles SE of Kidderminster, ½ mile from the junction of A448 and A450 at Mustow Green. **Station(s):** Nearest Kidderminster. **Open:** 2 Mar–31 Oct, Suns, Tues, Weds and Thurs from 11.30–5.30pm. Closed at other times except by appointment. **Admission:** Adults £3.50, OAPs £2.50,

children £2, admission to gardens £1, private tours, wedding receptions etc. by arrangement. Free car parking. Refreshments: The licensed restaurant is open when the Hall is open, for both lunches and light refreshments. Bookings can be made for Sunday lunch, evening functions and wedding and other receptions. **Events/Exhibitions:** Sealed Knot – mid May. Harvington Festival (including outdoor play) – mid July. Wassail – mid December.

map 4 A1

HELLENS

Much Marcle, Ledbury, Herefordshire HR8 2LY
Tel: 01531 660 668 (The Pennington Mellor Charity Trust)

Built first as a monastery and then as a stone fortress in 1292 by Mortimer, Earl of March, with Tudor, Jacobean and Stuart additions, this manorial house has been lived in ever since by descendants of the original builder. Visited by the Black Prince, Bloody Mary and the family ghost (a priest murdered during the Civil War). Interesting family paintings relics and heirlooms from the Civil War and possessions of the Audleys, Walwyns and Whartons as well as Anne Boleyn. Also beautiful 17th century woodwork carved by the 'King's

Carpenter' John Abel. All these historical stories incorporated into guided tours, revealing the loves and lives of those who lived and died here. Goods and chattels virtually unchanged and certainly not modernised. **Open:** Good Friday–2 Oct, Wed, Sat, Sun and Bank Hol Mons. Guided tours only on the hour 2–5pm (last tour 5pm). Other times by written appointment with the custodian. **Admission:** Adults £3.50, children £1.50 (must be accompanied by an adult).

map 7 G1

HERGEST CROFT GARDENS

Kington, Herefordshire HR5 3EG
Tel: 01544 230160 Fax: 01544 230160 (W.L. Banks, Esq.)

Spring bulbs to autumn colour, this is a garden for all seasons. Old-fashioned kitchen garden; spring and summer borders, roses. Over 59 champion trees and shrubs in one of the finest collections in the British Isles. National Collections of birches, maples and zelkovas. Rhododendrons up to 30ft. **Location:** On outskirts W of Kington off Rhayader Road (A44) (signposted to Hergest at W end of bypass). **Station(s):** Leominster – 14 miles. **Open:** 10 Apr–1 Nov 1.30–6pm. **Admission:** Adult £2.75, children under 16 free. Groups of 20+ by appointment anytime £2.25. Season tickets £10, access Apr–Mar. **Refreshments:** Home-made light lunches and teas. **Events:** Mon 4 May Flower Fair: plant stalls, special events. (£5 admission). Gift shop: Attractive gifts. Plant sales: Rare, unusual trees and shrubs. **Internet:** www.kc3.co.uk/local/herintro/html (W L Banks)

map 7
G2

HOW CAPLE COURT GARDEN

How Caple, HR1 4SX, Hereford & Worcester.
Tel: 01989 740 612 Fax: 01989 740 611 (Mr R. & Mrs H. M. Lee)

11 acres overlooking the River Wye. Formal Edwardian gardens; extensive plantings of mature trees and shrubs, water features and a sunken Florentine garden undergoing restoration. Norman church with 16th century Diptych. Specialist nursery plants and old variety roses for sale. **Location:** B4224, Ross-on-Wye (4.5 miles), Hereford (9 miles). **Open:** Mon–Fri, 9–5pm, all year. Sun 10–5pm, all year. Sat 9–5pm Apr/Oct. **Admission:** Adults £2.50, children £1.25. Parties welcome by appointment. **Refreshments:** Teas and light snacks, Apr–Oct. **Events/Exhibitions:** Sat June 13 – open air opera. Plant centre, dried flower outlet, gift shop. Car parking. Toilets.

map 7
G1

KENTCHURCH COURT

Nr. Pontrilas, Hereford, Herefordshire, HR2 0DB
Tel: 01981 240 228 (Mr & Mrs John Lucas-Scudamore)

Fortified border manor house altered by Nash and Gateway. Part of the original 14th century house still survives. Pictures and Grinling Gibbons carving. Owen Glendower's tower. **Location:** Off B4347, 3 miles SE of Pontrilas. Monmouth (12 miles). Hereford (14 miles). Abergavenny (14 miles). On left bank of River Monnow. **Open:** May–Sept. All visitors by appointment only. **Admission:** Adults £3.00, Children £1.50. **Refreshments:** At Kentchurch Court by appointment. **Accommodation:** By appointment.

map 7
G2

KINNERSLEY CASTLE

Kinnersley, Herefordshire HR3 6QF
Tel: 01544 327407 Fax: 01544 327663 (Katherina Henning)

Welsh Border castle, remodelled by Roger Vaughan in 1580's. Home of De Kinnardsleys and De le Beres and parliamentary general Sir Thomas Morgan. Still a family home. Fine plaster work and panelling. Specimen trees include one of the largest Ginkgo trees in UK, yew hedges and walled gardens, restoration programme under way, organic plant sales. Guided lectures on organic gardening by arrangement. **Location:** 4 miles W of Weobley on A4112. **Station(s):** Hereford or Leominster. **Open:** Times and dates will be available from local Tourist Information Offices from Easter 1998 (Hereford, Leominster, Hay-on-Wye) or phone as above. Coach parties by arrangement throughout the year. **Admission:** £2.50, Children £1, OAPs Student/UB40 & Groups £1.75. **Events:** Traditional music events and summer outside Shakespeare performance.

map 7
G2

LANGSTONE COURT

Llangarron, Ross on Wye, Herefordshire
Tel: 01989 770254 (R M C Jones Esq.)

Mostly late 17th century house with older parts. Interesting staircases, panelling and ceilings. **Location:** Ross on Wye 5 miles, Llangarron 1 miles. **Open:** Wednesdays & Thursdays 11–3pm between May 20 and August 31.

map 7
H1

LITTLE MALVERN COURT

Nr Malvern, Hereford & Worcester, WR14 4JN
Tel: 01684 892966 Fax: 01684 893057 (Mrs Berington)

14th century Prior's Hall once attached to 12th century Benedictine Priory, with Victorian addition by Hansom. Family and European paintings and furniture. Collection of 18th and 19th century needlework. Home of the Berington family by descent since the Dissolution. 10 acres of former monastic grounds. Magnificent views, lake, garden rooms, terrace. Wide variety of spring bulbs, old fashioned roses, shrubs and trees. **Location:** 3 m S of Great Malvern on Upton-on-Severn Road (A4104). **Open:** April 15–July 16 Wed and Thur 2.15–5pm parties by prior arrangement. Guided tours – last admission 4.30pm. **Admission:** Adults: House and Garden £4; House or Garden only £3.00. Children: House & Garden £2; House or Garden only £1. **Refreshments:** Home-made teas only available for parties by arrangement. Unsuitable for wheelchairs.

map 4
A2

MAWLEY HALL

Cleobury Mortimer, Nr. Kidderminster, Worcestershire, DY14 8PN

18th century house attributed to Francis Smith. Fine plaster work and panelling. **Location:** 1 mile S of Cleobury Mortimer (A4117). 7 miles W of Bewdley. **Open:** 13 Apr–16 July, Mon & Thur, 2.30–5pm. Visitors are requested to give advanced notice to Mrs R Sharp, Bennet House, 54 St. James's Street, London SW1A 1JT. Tel: 0171 495 6702 **Admission:** £3.

map 4 A1

MOCCAS COURT

Moccas, Herefordshire, HR2 9LH
Tel: 01981 500 381 (Trustees of Baunton Trust)

Built by Anthony Keck in 1775 overlooking the River Wye, decoration including the round room and oval stair by Robert Adam. Scene of famous 17th century romance and destination of epic night ride from London. Set in 'Capability' Brown parkland with an attractive walk to The Scar Rapids. **Location:** 10 miles E of Hay on Wye. 13 miles W of Hereford on the River Wye. 1 mile off B4352. **Station(s):** Hereford. **Open:** House & Gardens: Apr–Sept, Thur, 2–6pm. **Admission:** £2.00. **Refreshments:** Food and drink available at the Red Lion Hotel, Bredwardine, by pre-booking only. **Accommodation:** Available at the Red Lion Hotel, Bredwardine. Disabled access in the garden only.

map 7 G2

PERHILL PLANTS

Perhill Nurseries, Worcester Road, Great Witley, Worcestershire
Tel: 01299 896 329 Fax: 01299 896 990 (Perhill Plants)

Specialist growers of 2,500 varieties of alpines, herbs and border perennials. Many rare and unusual. Specialties include penstemons, salvias, osteospermums, dianthus, alpine, phlox, alliums, campanulas, thymes, helianthemums, diascias, lavenders, artemesias, digitals and scented geraniums. **Location:** 10 miles NW of Worcester, on main Tenbury Wells Road (A443). **Open:** 1 Feb–15 Oct, daily, 9–5pm. Sun 10.30–4.30pm. Closed 16 Oct–31 Jan except by appointment.

map 4 A1

WORCESTER CATHEDRAL

College Green, Worcester, Worcestershire, WR1 2LA
Tel: 01905 28854 Fax: 01905 611 139 (Dean & Chapter)

Beside the River Severn, facing the Malvern Hills. Built between 1084 and 1375. Norman Crypt and Chapter House. Early English Quire, Perpendicular Tower. Monastic buildings include the refectory (now College Hall and open on request during August), cloisters, remains of guesten hall and dormatories. Tombs of King John and Prince Arthur. Elgar memorial window. Misericords. **Location:** Centre of Worcester. Main roads Oxford and Stratford to Wales. 3 miles M5, Junction 7. **Station(s):** Foregate Street (easier). Shrub Hill (taxi). **Open:** Every day, 7.30–6pm. Choral Evensong daily (except Thur and school hols). **Admission:** Suggested donation £2. **Guided** **tours:** Visits Officer 01905 28854.

map 4 A2

 # SPETCHLEY PARK GARDEN

Spetchley Park, Worcester, Hereford & Worcester WR5 1RS
Tel: 01905 345224 (Spetchley Gardens Charitable Trust)

This lovely 30 acre garden is a plantsman's delight, with a large collection of trees, shrubs and plants, many of which are rare or unusual. There is colour and interest throughout the months that the garden is open to visitors. The park contains red and fallow deer. **Location:** 3 miles E of Worcester on Stratford-upon-Avon Road (A422). **Open:** Gardens: 1 Apr–30 Sept. Tues–Fri, Suns and Bank Hols. Closed all Sats & all other Mons. **Admission:** Adults £2.90, children £1.40, concessions for pre-booked parties. **Refreshments:** Tea in the garden. Regret no dogs. House not open.

map 4 A2

 ## BERRINGTON HALL

Summer Lane, Exmouth EX8 5BD Tel: 01395 265514

Open: April: Fri, Sat & Sun (open BH Mon but closed Good Fri) 1.30–5.30. May, June & Sept: daily except Mon & Tues (but open BH Mon) 1.30–5.30. July & Aug: daily 1.30–5.30. Oct to 1 Nov: Fri, Sat & Sun 1.30–4.30. Last admission 30min before closing. Garden from 12.30–6 (Oct 5.30). Park walk open July, Aug, Sept & Oct same days and times as house. Events: August horse trials; for details of this and other events please contact the Property Manager.

CROFT CASTLE

nr Leominster HR6 9PW Tel: 01568 780246

Open: April & Oct to 1 Nov: Sat & Sun 1.30–4.30 (closed Good Fri). May to end Sept: daily except Mon & Tues (but open BH Mon) 1.30–5.30. Last admission to house 30min before closing. Car park, parkland and Croft Ambrey open all year.

 ## THE GREYFRIARS

Friar Street, Worcester WR1 2LZ Tel: 01905 23571

Open: 13 April to end Oct: Wed, Thur & BH Mon 2–5. Events: 3,4 & 5 Dec, Street Fayre. **Admission:** £2.40; family ticket £6. Parties of 15 or more by written appointment. No reductions. Not suitable for large parties of children. Public car park in Friar Street. No WC

HANBURY HALL

Droitwich WR9 7EA Tel: 01527 821214 Fax: 01527 821251

Open: 29 March to 28 Oct: Sun to Wed 2–6. Last admission 5.30 (dusk if earlier). Events: varied programme through the year: for details and inclusion on mailing list please send s.a.e. to the property. **Admission:** House & garden £4.30; family ticket £10.50. Garden only £2.50. House is available for private and commercial functions and civil wedding ceremonies; please contact Property Manager. Free car- and coach-parking.

Hertfordshire

Aland of woods and streams and cornfields – a gracious countryside, undulating, varied, typically English, strangely remote and rich in historic monuments – Hertfordshire is a county which retains its ancient character in the midst of rapid development.

St Albans is a well blended medley of medieval and modern features grafted onto the site of Verulamium, the town founded by the Romans soon after the invasion of 43 AD. It was here in 209 AD, that a Roman soldier became the country's first Christian martyr when he was beheaded for giving shelter to a priest. Pilgrims later flocked to the town that bears his name, where the place of execution was marked by a hilltop cathedral, once one of the largest churches in the Christian world. Not just a religious centre, St Albans flourished as a staging post on the route to London from the north, and has an air of affluence best appreciated on foot.

Aldbury, Tring

Walk along St. Michael's Street – over one of the prettiest stretches of the River Ver, past a sixteenth century century mill and up gently curving Fishpool Street, a quiet road lined with medieval inns and handsome Georgian houses.

Just outside St Albans, the tiny villages of Ayot St Lawrence, hiding among gentle hills in one of the prettiest corners of Hertforshire, boasts the romantic ruins of a Gothic church and a fine pub, but its fame stems from its association with George Bernard Shaw, who lived in the house known as Shaw's Corner from 1906 until his death in 1950.

ASHRIDGE

Berkhamsted, Hertfordshire HP4 1NS
Tel: 01442 843491, Fax: 01442 841209
(Governors of Ashridge Management College)

150 acres of both parkland and intimate smaller gardens. The landscape influenced by Humphry Repton. Mature trees combined with unique features e.g. Beech Houses with windows and doors in a Pink and Grey Garden, Grotto – Ferns planted between Herts Pudding Stone. **Location:** 3½ miles N of Berkhamsted (A4251), 1 miles S of Little Gaddesden. **Station(s):** Berkhamsted. **Open:** Gardens open Apr–Sept Sat & Sun & B/Holidays 2–6pm. **Admission:** Gardens: Adults £2 Children/OAP £1. **Conferences:** For information please contact Carol Johnston, Conference Manager (01442 841027).

map 4 E3

AYLETT NURSERIES LTD

North Orbital Road, St. Albans, Herts
Tel: 01727 822255. Fax: 01727 823024 (Mr and Mrs R S Aylett)

Aylett Nurseries of St Albans is a well-known family business with a reputation of high quality plants and service. Famous for dahlias– having been awarded a Gold Medal by the Royal Horticultural Society every year since 1961. In the spring our greenhouses are full of all popular bedding plants. Facilities also include spacious planteria, garden shop, coffee and gift shop, houseplants, florist, garden furniture. From the middle of October do not miss our Christmas Wonderland. **Location:** 2 miles out of St Albans, 1 mile from M10, M1, M25 & A1. **Open:** Daily (excl. Christmas). Mon–Sat 8.30–5 Sun 10–4. **Admission:** Free. Events: Dahlia Festival–end Sept.

map 4 E3

BENINGTON LORDSHIP

Benington
Tel: 01438 869668 (Mr & Mrs C.H.A Bott)

Hilldrop garden on castle ruins overlooking lakes. Amazing April display of Scillas, scented rose garden, hidden rock/water garden, spectacular borders, ornamental kitchen garden, nursery. **Location:** 5m E of Stevenage, in Benington Village. **Open:** Please phone to confirm times, dates and prices.

COCKHAMSTED

Braughing
(Mr & Mrs David Marques)

2 acres of informal gardens. Shrub roses surrounded by open country. Island with trees surrounded by water filled 14th century moat. Teas in aid of Leukaemia Research. **Location:** 2m E of village towards Braughing Friars. **Open:** Please phone to confirm times, dates and prices.

CATHEDRAL AND ABBEY CHURCH OF SAINT ALBAN

St Albans, Hertfordshire AL1 1BY.
Tel: 01727 860780 Fax: 01727 850944 (Dean and Cathedral Council of St Albans)

Standing in the centre of the historic city of St Albans, the Cathedral is the imposing and beautiful abbey church of a Benedictine monastery founded by King Offa in 793 on the site of execution of St Alban, first British martyr (died c.209). The present church was built in 1077 using Roman brick from nearby Verulamium. Became the parish church of St Albans in 1539 and a cathedral in 1877. **Admission:** Free. Spectacular multi image audiovisual show 'The martyr's Cathedral' (£1.50 adults/£1 children). Shop and Refectory Restaurant. Guided Tours available. All enquiries 01727 860780. **E-mail:** cathedra@alban.u-net.com. **Internet:** www.stalbans.gov.uk/diocese/abbey.htm.

map 4
E3

GORHAMBURY

St Albans, Hertfordshire AL3 6AH
Tel: 01727 854051 Fax: 01727 843675 (The Earl of Verulam)

Mansion built 1777-84 in classical style by Sir Robert Taylor, 16th century enamelled glass and historic portraits. **Location:** 2 miles W of St Albans, entrance off A4147 at Roman Theatre. **Station(s):** St Albans **Open:** May–Sept, Thurs 2–5. Gardens open with the house. **Admission:** Adults £4, Children £2.50, OAPs £2. Guided tours only. Parties by prior arrangement, Thurs £3.50, other days £5.

map 4
E3

THE GARDENS OF THE ROSE

Chiswell Green, St Albans, Herts AL2 3NR
Tel: 01727 850461, Fax: 01727 850360 (The Royal National Rose Society)

The Royal National Rose Society's Gardens provide a wonderful display of one of the best and most important collections of roses in the world. There are some 30,000 roses in 1800 different varieties. The Society has introduced many companion plants which harmonise with the roses including over 100 varieties of clematis. The garden, named for the Society's Patron HM The Queen Mother, contains a fascinating collection of old garden roses. Here can be seen the red rose of Lancaster and the White Rose of York and the Gallica 'Rosa Mundi', said to have been named for Fair Rosamund, the mistress of Henry II! Various cultivation trials show just how easy roses are to grow and new roses can be viewed in the International Trial Ground. **Open:** 13 Jun–11 Oct, Mon–Sat 9–5pm, Sun & Aug Bank Hols 10–6pm. **e-mail:** mail@rnrs.org.uk **internet:** roses.co.uk

C map 4
E3

HATFIELD HOUSE

Hatfield, Hertfordshire AL9 5NQ
Tel: 01707 262823, Fax: 01707 275719 (The Curator)

This celebrated Jacobean house, which stands in its own great park was built between 1607 and 1611 by Robert Cecil, 1st Earl of Salisbury and Prime Minister to King James I. It has been the family home of the Cecils ever since. The Staterooms are rich in world-famous paintings, fine furniture, rare tapestries and historic armour. The beautiful stained glass in the chapel is original. Within the delightful gardens stands the surviving wing of the Royal Palace of Hatfield (1497) where Elizabeth I spent much of her girlhood and held her first Council of State in November 1558. She appointed William Cecil, Lord Burghley as her Chief Minister. Some of her relics can be seen in the house. **Location:** In Hatfield, Junction 4 A1(M); 7 m M25. **Station(s):** Hatfield 25 minutes by regular fast train service from Kings Cross to Hatfield (station faces Park gates). **Open:** 25 Mar–4 Oct 1998(closed Good Fri). House: Tue–Fri 12–4 & Sat 12–4.30 (guided tours only). Sun 1–4.30pm & Bank Hols 11–4.30pm. Park: Daily 10.30–8pm. Gardens: Daily 11–6pm. **Admission:** House, park and gardens: Adult £5.70, OAP £4.80 and child £3.40. (Groups 20+ adult £4.80 and child £2.90). Park and gardens: Adult £3.10, OAP £2.90 and child £2.30. (Groups 20+ adult £2.90 and child £2.10). **Refreshments:** Licensed restaurant and tearooms. **Events/Exhibitions:** Living crafts 7–10 May, Festival of Gardening 20–21 June. A Tudor Revel 18–19 July, The Hatfield Park Prom 1 Aug, Art in Clay 7–9 Aug, Lesley Garrett & Fireworks 22 Aug and Country Lifestyle Fair 11–13 Sep. **Conferences:** Licensed for Civil Weddings, Old Palace and Riding School 01707 262055.

C map 4
E/F3

CAPEL MANOR

Bullsmoor Lane, Nr Enfield, Hertfordshire EN1 4RQ
Tel: 0181 366 4442 Fax: 01992 717544 (Capel Manor Charitable Corporation)

Capel Manor is Greater London's only specialist College of Horticulture and Countryside studies with the 30 acres of richly planted and diverse gardens, which surround the Georgian manor, fully open to the public. A comprehensive self-guided tour starts from the new visitor's centre with information boards and free leaflets to help visitors get the most from their visit at all times of the year. **Location:** 3 mins from M25 junction M25/A10 S and turn right at traffic lights. Nearest station Turkey Street/Liverpool Street line. (Not Sun). **Admission:** Charges apply. Special rates for coaches and garden tours.

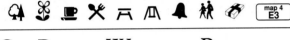

CROMER WINDMILL

Ardeley, Stevenage SG2 7QA
Tel: 01438 861662 (Hertfordshire Building Preservation Trust)

Hertfordshire's last surviving Post Mill now fully restored, with grants from English Heritage and Heritage Lottery Fund. Short video for visitors showing method of working. 1/2 hour video available on loan, with brochure giving history of Mill. Disabled wheelchairs, adequate parking, no lavatories, literature and tea towels on sale. **Open:** Sundays, Bank Holidays, 2 and 4 Saturday 2.30–5pm mid May–end Aug. Special parties by arrangement. Simon Bennett 01438 861662. **Admission:** Adults £1.20, children 25p. **Location:** OSS TL304287. On the B1037 between Stevenage and Cottered.

 # KNEBWORTH HOUSE

Knebworth, Hertfordshire
Tel: 01438 812661 (The Lord Cobbold)

Spectacular stately home with High Gothic decoration. Contains beautiful rooms with important paintings and furniture. Knebworth was the home of Constance Lytton the Suffragette and Robert Lytton, Viceroy of India. Charles Dickens and Winston Churchill were frequent visitors. Gracious parkland includes large children's adventure playground. Beautiful formal gardens feature Knebworth Maze. **Location:** Knebworth 28 miles N of Central London. Own direct access off the A1(M) junction 7 (Stevenage South A602) 12 miles N of M25. **Open:** Park, gardens & playground 4 April–20 April and 23 May–7 Sept. Plus weekends and bank holidays 25 April–17 May; weekends only from 12–27 Sept. 11am–5.30pm. House as above except closed Mondays but open Bank Holiday Mondays noon–5pm.

 map 4 E3

ST. PAULS WALDEN BURY

Hitchin, Herts. SG4 8BP
Tel: 01438 871218/871229. Fax: As telephone. (Bowes Lyon)

Formal landscape garden, laid out around 1730, covering about 40 acres. Listed Grade I. Avenues and rides span woodland gardens leading to temples, statues, lake and ponds. There are also more recent flower gardens, best from Apr–Jul. This is the childhood home of Queen Elizabeth, the Queen Mother. **Open:** Suns, 19 Apr, 10 May, 7 Jun 2–7pm. £2 adults, 50p children. Home-made teas. Lakeside Concert Jul to be announced. Also by appointment, £5 entry. Proceeds go to charity.

 map 4 E2

SHAW'S CORNER

Ayot St Lawrence, Nr Welwyn, Herts AL6 9BX
Tel: 01438 820307 (The National Trust)

The home of George Bernard Shaw from 1906 until his death in 1950. The rooms remain much as he left them, with many literary and personal effects evoking the individuality and genius of this great dramatist. The garden has richly planted borders and views over the Hertfordshire countryside. **Open:** 1 Apr–1 Nov: daily except Mon & Tues (but closed Good Fri and open Bank Hol Mon) 1–5pm. **Admission:** £3.20, family ticket £8. **Location:** At SW end of village, 2 miles NE of Wheathampstead: approx. 2 miles from B653.

 map 4 E3

SCOTT'S GROTTO

Scott's Road, Ware, Herts SG12 9SQ
Tel: 01920 464131, 01992 584322 (East Hertfordshire District Council)

Grotto, summerhouse and garden built 1760–73 by Quaker poet John Scott. Described by English Heritage as 'one of the finest grottos in England.' Now extensively restored by The Ware Society. **Location:** Scott's Road, Ware (off A119 Hertford Road). **Station:** Ware/Liverpool Street line. **Open:** Every Sat beginning of Apr–Sept and Easter, Spring and Summer Bank Hol Mons 2–4.30pm. **Admission:** Free but donation of £1 requested. Please park in Amwell End car park by level crossing (300 yards away) and walk up Scott's Road. Advisable to wear flat shoes and bring a torch. Parties by prior arrangement.

 map 5 F3

Isle of Wight

Freshwater Bay

The Isle of Wight is an extremely popular holiday destination. Its magnificent landscape is complemented by some unique scenery, such as the stunning Needles. The old capital of Carisbrooke is home to the 11th century Norman castle where Charles I was imprisoned in 1647.

Visitors will be fascinated by the history and splendour of Osborne House, designed by Prince Albert.

The Isle of Wight's popular resorts are Sandown, Shanklin and Newport, renowned for their golden beaches.

The island is a famous base for sailing, the big highlight of the sailing calendar being Cowes Week.

CARISBROOKE CASTLE

Newport, Isle of Wight
Tel: 01983 522107 (English Heritage)

Royal fortress and prison to King Charles I, Carisbrooke is set dramatically on a sweeping ridge at the very heart of the Isle of Wight. One of the most popular attractions are the famous Carisbrooke donkeys. See them tread the huge wheel in the medieval well house, much as donkeys would have done in the 18th century. Discover the popular interactive exhibitions and museum, which trace the history of the castle. The island's World War I Memorial chapel offers a moment of contemplation before admiring the breathtaking views from the castle walls. **Location:** 1¼ m SW of Newport. **Open:** 1 Apr–1 Nov daily 10–6pm (or dusk if earlier in Oct), 2 Nov–31 Mar 10–4pm. (Closed 24–5 Dec) **Admission:** Adults £4, concs. £3, children £2. Family £10. (15% discount for groups of 11 or more).

map 4 C7

DEACONS NURSERY (H.H)

Moor View, Godshill, PO38 3HW, Isle of Wight
Tel: 01983 840 750 Fax: 01983 523 575 (G. D. Deacon & B. H. Deacon)

Specialist national fruit tree growers. Trees and bushes sent anywhere so send NOW for a FREE catalogue. Over 250 varieties of apples on various types of root stocks from M27 (4ft), M26 (8ft) to M25 (18ft). Plus pears, peaches, nectarines, plums, gages, cherries, soft fruits and an unusual selection of family trees. Many special offers. Catalogue always available (stamp appreciated). Many varieties of grapes; dessert and wine, plus hybrid hops and nuts of all types. **Location:** The picturesque village of Godshill. Deacons Nursery is in Moor View off School Crescent (behind the only school). **Open:** Winter – Mon–Fri, 8–4pm. Summer – Mon–Fri, 8–5pm. Sat, 8–1pm.

map 4 C7

NUNWELL HOUSE & GARDENS

Coach Lane, Brading, Isle of Wight
Tel: 01983 407240 (Col. & Mrs J A Aylmer)

Nunwell House has been a family home for 5 centuries and reflects much island and architectural history. Finely furnished with Jacobean and Georgian wings. Lovely setting with Channel views and 5 acres of tranquil gardens. Special family military collections. **Location:** 1 mile from Brading turning off A3055 signed; 3 mile S of Ryde. **Station:** Brading. **Open:** 13 Jul–23 Sep, Mon, Tues & Weds 1–5pm with House tours at 1.30, 2.30 and 3.30pm. **Admission:** £4 (includes guide book) – reductions for senior citizens, children and parties. Gardens only £2.50. **Refreshments:** Picnic areas: large parties may book catering in advance. Parties welcome out of season if booked. Large car park. Regret no dogs.

map 4 C7

OSBORNE HOUSE

East Cowes, Isle of Wight
Tel: 01983 200022 (English Heritage)

Visit the magnificent Osborne House, the beloved seaside retreat of Queen Victoria and gain insight into the private family life of Britain's longest reigning monarch. The Royal Apartments, full of treasured mementoes, have been preserved almost unaltered since Victoria died here in 1901. The Swiss Cottage, a chalet built in the grounds for the children gives a fascinating insight into their lives. **Location:** 1m SE of East Cowes. **Open:** 1 Apr–1 Nov daily, 10–5pm (last admission 4.30pm). For winter and spring guided tours, please phone for details. **Admission:** Hse & Grounds: Adult: £6.50, Conc: £4.90, Child: £3.30 Grounds only: Adult: £3.50, Conc: £2.60, Child: £1.80. (15% discount for groups of 11 or more).

map 4 C7

Kent

The fruitful fields of the lowlands and the inspiring contours of the downland ridges present a typical picture of England, as the idealist would have it.

This garden of England has an unfair share of splendid castles, beautiful gardens, historic houses and estates. The county boasts gorgeous countryside, picturesque villages, an elegant spa town, the definitive white cliffs and a county town which is one of the most venerable in England.

With numerous links with France, it is not surprising that Kent remains one of the most popular and accessible destinations in the country.

Canterbury, on the River Stour, is the centre of the Anglican church and seat of the Archbishop of Canterbury. The cathedral houses a

Matfield Village Green

magnificent collection of twelfth and thirteenth century stained glass and the tomb of the Black Prince.

Kent's seaside towns of Whitstable, Margate and Broadstairs are an odd combination of the nostalgic and frivolous. Viking Bay is just one of several sandy coves that dent Thanet's eastern shore. Between Broadstairs and Margate you'll find Stone, Joss, Kingsgate and Botany Bay, with Louisa Bay to the south – all quiet and undeveloped gems.

This is where Julius Caesar landed all those years ago. The modern voyager is more likely to land at Dover.

BELMONT

Belmont Park, Throwley, Faversham, Kent ME13 0HH
Tel: 01795 890202 (Harris (Belmont) Charity)

Charming late 18th century mansion by Samuel Wyatt set in fine parkland. Seat of the Harris family since 1801 when it was acquired by General George Harris, the victor of Seringapatam. The delightfully furnished house contains interesting mementoes of the family's connections with India and colonies, plus the fifth Lord Harris's fine clock collection. Tearoom and gifts. **Location:** 4¹/₂ miles south-southwest of Faversham, off A251 (signed from Badlesmere). **Open:** 13 Apr–27 Sept 1998, Sat, Sun & Bank Hols from 2–5pm. (Last admission 4.30pm) Groups on Tue & Thur by appointment. **Admission:** House & Garden: Adult £5.00, OAP £4.50, Child (2–16 yrs) £2.50; Garden: Adult £2.75, OAP £2.75, Child £1.

map 5
H5

BLACK CHARLES

Underriver, Nr Sevenoaks, Kent TN15 0RY
Tel: 01732 833036 (Mr & Mrs Hugh Gamon)

Charming 15th century home of John de Blakecherl and his family. A hall house with beautiful panelling, fireplaces and many other interesting features. **Location:** 3 m S of Sevenoaks off A21; 1 m E in the village of Underriver. **Open:** Open to groups by appointment (minimum of 10). **Admission:** £3.50.

map 5
F5

THE NEW COLLEGE OF COBHAM

Cobham, Nr Gravesend, Kent DA12 3BX
Tel: 01474 812503 (The New College of Cobham Trust)

Almshouses based on medieval chantry built 1362, part rebuilt 1598. Originally endowed by Sir John de Cobham and descendants. **Location:** 4 miles W of Rochester; 4 miles SE of Gravesend; 1¹/₂ miles from junction Shorne-Cobham (A2). In Cobham rear of Church of Mary Magdelene. **Station(s):** Sole St (1 mile). **Open:** Apr–Sept, daily 10–7pm. Oct–Mar, daily 10–4pm. **Refreshments:** Afternoon teas by prior arrangement. Guided tours by prior arrangement.

map 5
G4

COBHAM HALL

Cobham, Nr Gravesend, Kent DA12 3BL
Tel: 01474 823371/824319 Fax: 01474 822995/824171

Cobham Hall is an outstandingly beautiful, red brick mansion in Elizabethan, Jacobean, Carolian and 18th century styles. Former home of the Earls of Darnley, set in 150 acres of parkland. Charles Dickens used to walk through the grounds from his house to the Leather Bottle in Cobham Village. There are many fine 17th century marble fireplaces and an 18th century historic snetzler organ in the magnificent Gilt Hall. Cobham Hall is now an independent, international school for girls. **Location:** By A2/M2, between Gravesend & Rochester, 8 miles from Jct 2 on the M25. Open April, July & August most Wednesday, Thurs & Sun and Easter Weekend, 2–5pm each day. All tours guided. Please call to check dates & times. **Admission:** £3/£2.50. **Events/Exhibitions:** Many through year, please phone details. **Excellent venue for conferences.**

map 5 G4

DODDINGTON PLACE GARDENS

Sittingbourne, Kent ME9 0BB
Tel/Fax: 01795 886101 (Mr and Mrs Richard Oldfield)

10 acres of landscaped gardens in an area of outstanding natural beauty. Woodland garden (spectacular in May/June), an Edwardian rock garden, formal terraces with mixed borders, impressive clipped yew hedges, a new folly, fine trees and lawns. **Location:** 4 miles from A2 and A20. 5 miles from Faversham. 6 miles from Sittingbourne, 9 miles from Canterbury. **Station(s):** Sittingbourne, Faversham. **Open:** May–Sept: Suns 2–6pm Weds and Bank Hol Mons 11–6pm. Groups also on other days by prior arrangement. **Admission:** Adults £2.50, children £0.25p, group rate £2 coaches by prior arrangement. Restaurant serving morning coffee, lunches, afternoon teas. Gift shop.

map 5 H5

DOVER CASTLE

Dover, Kent
Tel: 01304 201628 (English Heritage)

The special highlight of a visit to Dover Castle is the network of secret wartime tunnels which functioned as the nerve centre for the evacuation of Dunkirk. There is even an underground hospital where visitors can experience the sights, sounds and smells of life underground. However, there is as much to see above ground as there is below. Visitors will unlock over 2,000 years of history when they explore Henry II's Keep, the new and exciting seize exhibition, the Royal Regiment Museum, Saxon Church and Roman lighthouse – the tallest Roman structure still standing in Europe. **Location:** On East side of Dover. **Open:** 1 Apr–1 Nov daily 10–6pm (or dusk if earlier in Oct), 2 Nov – 31 Mar, 10–4pm. (closed 24–5 Dec) **Admission:** Adult £6.60, concs £5, child £3.30, family £16.50. (15% discount for groups of 11 or more).

map 5 J5

DOWN HOUSE

Downe, Kent, BR6 7JT
Tel: 01689 859119 (English Heritage)

Explore the home of one of the world's greatest scientists, Charles Darwin. Down House was his family home for 40 years where he developed his theories that scandalised and revolutionised the world culminating the publication of the 19th century book 'On the Origin of Species'. View the enthralling Darwin exhibitions and see thousands of personal effects from his epic voyage of discovery on HMS Beagle. Visitors can walk along the 'Sandwalk', as Darwin did every morning to compose his thoughts. **Location:** In Luxted Road, Downe off A21 near Biggin Hill. Open 10 Apr–31 Oct, Wed–Sun 10–6pm (or dusk if earlier in Oct), 1 Nov–31 Jan, Wed–Sun 10–4pm. 1–31 Mar 10–4pm (Closed 24–26 Dec & 1–28 Feb). **Admission:** Adult £5, conc £3.80, child £2.50 (15% discount for groups of 11+). Visits to the house to be made in advance by phoning: 0870 603 0145.

FINCHCOCKS

Goudhurst, Kent TN17 1HH
Tel: 01580 211702, Fax: 01580 211007 (Mr & Mrs Richard Burnett)

Georgian manor in beautiful garden, housing a magnificent collection of ninety historical keyboard instruments. Many of these are fully restored and played whenever the house is open in entertaining musical tours. Pictures, prints and exhibition 'The Lost Pleasure Gardens'. **Location:** Off A262 1½ west of Goudhurst, 10 miles from Tunbridge Wells. **Open:** Easter–end of Sept, Suns & BH Mons & Wed & Thur in Aug: 2–6pm. **Admission:** Adult £5.50, Children £4, Family Ticket £13. **Garden only** £2. Free parking. **Refreshments:** Teas. **Reserved Visits:** Groups & Individuals most days April to October. **Events:** Finchocks Festival: weekends in September. Craft & Garden Fairs: end of May and October. **Civil Marriages & Receptions:** Available for functions.

GAD'S HILL PLACE

Rochester, Kent ME3 7PA
Tel: 01474 822366 (Gad's Hill School Ltd)

Grade 1 listed building, built in 1780. Home of Charles Dickens from 1857 to 1870. **Location:** On A226; 3 miles from Rochester, 4 miles from Gravesend. **Station:** Higham (1½ m) **Open:** 1st Sun in Month Apr–Oct and Bank Hol Sun (incl. Easter) 2–5pm. During Rochester Dickens Festivals (June and Dec) 11–4pm. At other times by arrangement. Parties welcome. Rooms, including newly restored conservatory, can be hired for weddings/parties (wedding licence). Free coach/car parking. **Admission:** £2.50, child £1.50 parties by arrangement. Proceeds to restoration fund. **Refreshments:** Sundays, cream teas; Dickens Weekends, Dickensian refreshments; other catering by arrangement.

GREAT MAYTHAM HALL

Rolvenden, Cranbrook, Kent, TN17 4NE.
Tel: 01580 241 346 Fax: 01580 241 038
(Country Houses Association)

Built in 1910 by Sir Edwin Lutyens. **Location:** Half a mile S of Rolvenden Village, on road to Rolvenden Layne. **Station(s):** Headcorn (10 miles), Staplehurst (10 miles). **Open:** May–Sept, Wed & Thurs, 2–5pm. (Last entry 4.30pm). **Admission:** Adults £3.50, children £1.75. Free car park. No dogs admitted. Groups by arrangement. Up to 20 £3.50pp, over 20 £4pp, including tea & biscuits.

GREAT COMP GARDEN

Comp Lane, St. Mary's Platt, Borough Green, Sevenoaks, Kent TN15 8QS.
Tel: 01732 886 154/882 669 (Great Comp Charitable Trust)

Skillfully designed 7 acre garden of exceptional beauty, surrounding a fine early 17th century manor house. Sweeping lawns, romantic ruins and tranquil woodland walks guide the visitor through areas of different character. The extensive collection of trees, shrubs and perennials offer inspiration and pleasure and include many which are rarely seen. The Italian Garden, completed in 1994 offers shelter to the more tender species of plants including Salvias, Bottlebrushes and Cordelines and is at its most colourful during the summer months. The nursery offers a wide and unusual range of plants, most of which can be seen growing in the garden. **Open:** Apr–Oct, daily, 11–6pm. **Admission:** Adults £3, children £1. Refreshments: Teas at weekends and Bank Hols. **Special Events:** 26 Apr – Spring Plant Fair with Special Guest Roy Lancaster. 21–23 Aug. Celebrating the 80th Birthday of Roderick Cameron, owner and creator of Great Comp Garden. Includes: Hardy Plant Society Annual Show, Plant stalls from leading specialist nurseries, concerts, lectures by Roderick Cameron and Chris Brickell, former director of the Royal Horticultural Society. Disabled access.

HEVER CASTLE

Nr Edenbridge, Kent TN8 7NG
Tel: 01732 865224 Fax: 01732 866796 (Hever Castle Ltd)

Hever Castle is a romantic 13th century moated castle, once the childhood home of Anne Boleyn. In 1903, William Waldorf Astor bought the castle and created beautiful gardens. He filled the castle with wonderful furniture, paintings and tapestries which visitors can enjoy today. The spectacular award-winning gardens include topiary, Italian and Tudor gardens, a 110 metre herbaceous border and a lake. A yew maze (open May–Oct) and a new water maze (open April–Oct) are also in the gardens. The Miniature Model Houses Exhibition must also be seen. **Location:** Hever Castle is 30 miles from London, 3 miles SE of Edenbridge. Exit M25 junctions 5 or 6. Stations: Edenbridge Town 3 miles (taxis available), Hever 1 mile (no taxis). **Open:** Daily 1 Mar–30 Nov. Gardens open 11am. Castle opens 12 noon. Last admission 5pm. Final exit 6pm. Mar & Nov 11–4pm. **Admission:** Castle & Garden ticket, Gardens only ticket and Family ticket. Group discounts also available (minimum 15). Pre-booked guided tours of the castle available for groups. **Refreshments:** Two licensed self-service restaurants serving hot and cold food throughout the day. Picnics welcome. **Events:** Special events includes May Day Music and Dance 2–4 May, Merrie England Weekend (23–25 May) and the Patchwork & Quilting exhibition (11–13 Sept). **Conferences:** Exclusive luxury conference facilities available in the Tudor Village.

map 5
F5

GROOMBRIDGE PLACE GARDENS

Groombridge Place, Groombridge, Nr. Royal Tunbridge Wells, TN3 9QG
Tel: 01892 863 999 Fax: 01892 863 996 (Blenheim Asset Management Ltd)

Surrounded by acres of breathtaking parkland, Groombridge Place has an intriguing history stretching back to medieval times. Flanked by a medieval moat, with a classical 17th century manor as its backdrop, the beautiful formal gardens boast a rich variety of "rooms", together with extensive herbaceous borders. High above the walled gardens and estate vineyard, hidden from view, lies The Enchanted Forest, where magic and fantasy await discovery. Here are secret mysterious gardens to challenge and delight your imagination and reward your mind's ingenuity. Winner of SE England Tourist Board Visitor attraction of the year 1997 **Location:** On B2110, (off A264), 4 miles SW of Tunbridge Wells, 9 miles E of East Grinstead. **Open & Admission:** 4 Apr–1 Nov daily 9–6pm. Adult £5.50, child £3.50, OAPs & students £4.50.

HALL PLACE

Bourne Road, Bexley, DA5 1PQ, Kent
Tel: 01322 526 574 Fax: 01322 522 921
(Bexley Council)

Historic house built in 1540, with additions c.1650. Museum and other exhibitions. (There is no disabled access to the first floor). Outstanding rose, rock and herb gardens and floral bedding displays. Conservatories, parkland and topiary. **Location:** Near the junction of A2 and A223. **Station(s):** Bexley (half a mile). **Open:** House: Mon–Sat, 10am–5pm (4.15 in winter). British Summer Time only – Suns, 2–6pm. Park & Grounds: Daily during the daylight during the year. **Admission:** Free. **Refreshments:** At café & restaurant.

LADHAM HOUSE

Goudhurst, Kent
Tel: 01580 211203 Fax: 01580 212596
(Mr and Mrs Alastair Jessel)

10 acres of rolling lawns, fine specimen trees, rhododendrons, azaleas, camellias, shrubs and magnolias. Newly planted arboretum. Spectacular twin mixed borders. Fountain garden and bog garden. Fine view. Restored old rock garden with waterfall. **Open:** Sun 3 May, Sun 17 May, Sun 4 Oct 1998, 2–5.30pm – in aid of NGS. Every Wed 2–5pm from May–Sept. **Admission:** Adults £3, children 50p. **Refreshments:** Teas available on these days.

LULLINGSTONE CASTLE

Eynsford, Kent DA14 0JA
Tel: 01322 862114 (Guy Hart Dyke, Esq) Fax: 01322 862115

Family portraits, armour, Henry VII gatehouse, church, herb garden. **Location:** In the Darenth valley via Eynsford on A225. **Station:** Eynsford (1/2 m) **Open:** Castle and grounds Apr–June, Sun & Bank Hols only. July–Sept Sat, Sun & Bank Hols. Wed, Thur and Fri by arrangement (2–6pm). Telephone for enquiries or bookings. **Admission:** Adults £3.75, children £1.50, OAPs £3. Free car parking. **Refreshments:** In the gatehouse tearooms. **Events/Exhibitions:** July 25/26 open air concerts.

LYMPNE CASTLE

Nr Hythe, Kent CT21 4LQ
Tel: 01303 267571 (Harry Margary, Esq)

This romantic medieval castle with an earlier Roman, Saxon and Norman history was once owned by the Archdeacons of Canterbury. It was rebuilt about 1360 and restored in 1905, 300 feet above the well known Roman Shore Fort – Stutfall Castle. Four miles from the ancient Cinque Port of Hythe, it commands a tremendous view across Romney Marshes to Fairlight over the great sweep of the coast from Dover to Dungeness and across the sea to France. Terraced gardens with magnificent views out to sea. **Location:** 3 miles NW of Hythe off B2067, 8 miles W of Folkestone. **Open:** Mon–Thur and occasionally on Suns 25 May–17 Sept, 10.30–5.30pm. **Admission:** Adults £2, children 50p. **Conferences:** Conferences, licensed for civil weddings. Reception facilities.

LEEDS CASTLE

Maidstone, Kent ME17 1PL.
Tel: 01622 765400 Fax: 01622 735616 (Leeds Castle Foundation)

Leeds Castle is built on two islands surrounded by a lake. The building has been on the site since the Doomsday Book, but it was during the Medieval times that the castle became a royal palace ending its royal ownership in the hands of King Henry VIII. The Castle now boasts a fine collection of arts, tapestries and furnishings. The medieval Gate Tower is home to the unique Dog Collar Museum. The Garden and Park contain surprises all year round. Spring sees the Wood Garden at its best with new life in the Duckery; Summer sees the English cottage Culpeper Garden full of flowers and fragrance whilst the majestic trees in the park take on a golden hue in Autumn. There is also a fascinating maze with its intriguing underground grotto, a range of greenhouses, a vineyard and an enchanting exotic bird aviary and breeding centre. Now owned by the Leeds Castle Foundation, a private charitable trust, the Castle is also used as a high level residential conference centre. **Location:** 4 miles east of Maidstone, M20/A20 junction 8 midway between London and the Channel ports. **Open:** All year (except 27 Jun, 4 Jul and 25 Dec 1998). **Admission:** Please phone for details. **1998 Special Events:** New Year's Day Treasure Trail 1 Jan, A Celebration of Easter 11–13 Apr, Festival of English Food & Wine 16–17 May, Balloon & Vintage Car Fiesta 6–7 Jun, Leeds Castle Open Air Concerts 27 Jun and 4 Jul, Flower Festival 16–19 Sept, Grand Firework Spectacular 7 Nov, Christmas at the Castle 14–24 Dec.

map 5
G5

OWL HOUSE GARDENS

Lamberhurst, Kent

Tel: 01892 890963 (Maureen, Marchioness of Dufferin & Ava)

13 acres of romantic gardens surround this 16th century timber framed wool smuggler's cottage. Spring flowers, roses, rare flowering shrubs and ornamental fruit trees. Expansive lawns lead to leafy woodland walks graced by English and Turkish oaks, elm, birch and beech trees. Rhododendrons, azaleas, and camellias encircle peaceful informal sunken water gardens. **Location:** 8 miles SE of Tunbridge Wells; 1 mile from Lamberhurst off A21. **Station(s):** Tunbridge Wells or Wadhurst. **Open:** GARDENS ONLY. All the year – daily and weekends including all Bank Hol weekends 11–6pm. **Admission:** £4, children £1 (proceeds towards Lady Dufferin's charity, Maureen's Oast House for Arthritics). Free parking. Dogs on lead. Coach parties welcome.

map 5
G5

PATTYNDENNE MANOR

Goudhurst, Kent TN17 2QU

Tel: 01580 211361 (Mr & Mrs D C Spearing)

Manor house built of oak trees before Columbus discovered America. Special architectural features include banqueting hall, dragon beams, upturned oak trees, enormous fireplaces, 13c prison, pleasant gardens. Connected with Henry VIII. Lived in as a family house, furnished, lecture tour by owner. **Location:** 1 miles S of Goudhurst on W side of B2079. **Open:** Open to groups by appointment (minimum approx. 20). Connoisseur's tour also possible. **Admission:** £4.50 **Refreshments:** Light refreshments available.

map 5
G5

PENSHURST PLACE AND GARDENS

Penshurst, Nr Tonbridge, Kent TN11 8DG

Tel: 01892 870307 Fax: 01892 870866 (Viscount & Viscountess De L'Isle)

The Ancestral home of the Sidney Family since 1552, with a history going back six and a half centuries, Penshurst Place has been described as "the grandest and most perfectly preserved example of an unfortified manor house in all England". See the awe-inspiring medieval Barons Hall with its 60ft high chestnut beamed roof, where Kings, Queens, noblemen, poets and great soldiers have all dined. The Staterooms contain fine collections of tapestries, furniture, portraits, porcelain and armour from the 15th, 16th, 17th and 18th centuries. The Gardens, first laid out in the 16th century have remarkably remained virtually unaltered during 400 years. A network of trimmed yew hedges and flower terraces make up the 10 acre patchwork of individual garden rooms designed to give colour all year round. Other features include a toy museum, adventure playground, shop, restaurant, 200 acre park with lakes and a nature trail. Penshurst Place offers an exquisite arena for corporate and private entertainment amidst beautiful Kent countryside. **Open:** Weekends from 28 Feb, daily from 28 Mar–1 Nov. **Admission:** House & Gardens: Adults £5.70 students/OAPs £5.30 children (5–16) £3.20 Family ticket £15. Adult party (20+) £5.10. Gardens only: Adults £4.20, students/OAPs £3.70, children (5–16) £2.80, family ticket £12. Garden season ticket £20.

map 5
F5

PORT LYMPNE WILD ANIMAL PARK, MANSION & GARDENS

Lympne, Hythe CT21 4PD
Tel: 01303 264647 Fax: 01303 264944 (John Aspinall, Esq)

Location: 3 m W of Hythe; 6 m W of Folkestone; 7 m SE of Ashford exit 11 off M20.

map 5 H5

TONBRIDGE CASTLE

Tonbridge, Kent TN9 1BG
Tel: 01732 770929, Fax: 01732 770449 (Tonbridge & Malling Borough Council)

A fine example of the layout of a Norman Motte and Bailey Castle set in landscaped gardens overlooking the River Medway. The site is clearly interpreted and the exhibition in the Castle Gatehouse depicts life as it was 700 years ago. Tours are available from the Tourist Information Centre. **Location:** In town centre off High Street. **Station(s):** Tonbridge (Main line Charing Cross). **Location:** Apr–Sept Mon–Sat 9–5pm, Sun and BH 10.30–5pm; Oct–Mar, Mon–Fri 9–5pm, Sat 9–4pm, Sun 10.30–4pm. Last tours leave 1 hr before closing time. Self guided headset tours, guided tours by arrangement. Please ring to confirm times after Sept 1998 **Admission:** Adults £3.25, child, snr citizens £1.60, family £7.75 **Refreshments:** Nearby. **Accomodation:** Nearby. **Conferences:** Room for hire. Approved for civil marriages.

map 5 G5

RIVERHILL HOUSE GARDENS

Riverhill, Sevenoaks, Kent TN15 0RR
Tel 01732 458802 (The Rogers Family)

A lived in family home. Panelled rooms, portraits and interesting memorabilia. Historic hillside garden with sheltered terraces. Rhododendrons, azaleas and bluebells in woodland setting. **Location:** 2 miles S of Sevenoaks on road to Tonbridge (A225). **Station(s):** Sevenoaks. **Open:** Gardens: April, May and June only. Every Wed, Sun and all Bank Holiday weekends during this period. 12–6pm. The House is also open for Party Bookings of 20 upwards, (adults only) in above period. **Admission:** Gardens: Adults £2.50, children 50p. House and Garden: £3.50. **Refreshments:** Home-made teas in the Old Stable. Catering for booked parties. Ploughmans lunches, teas etc by arrangement. Unsuitable for wheelchairs. No dogs. All enquiries to Mrs Rogers (01732 458802/452557).

map 5 F5

SQUERRYES COURT

Westerham, Kent TN16 1SJ
Tel: 01959 562345, Fax: 01959 565949 (Mr J St. A Warde)

Squerryes Court is a beautiful, privately owned Manor House built in 1681 in a parkland setting. The house was acquired by the Warde family in 1731 and is lived in by the same family today. The Old Master paintings, furniture, porcelain and tapestries were collected by the Wardes in the 18th century. The lovely gardens, landscaped in the 18th century, are interesting throughout the year with a lake, spring bulbs, borders, recently restored formal garden, topiary and 18th century dovecote. **Location:** Western outskirts of Westerham signposted from A25. Junctions 5 & 6 M25 10 mins. **Station(s):** Oxted or Sevenoaks. **Open:** 1 Apr–30 Sept. Wed, Sat, Sun & BH Mon. Garden: 12–5.30pm. House 1.30–5.30pm (last entry 5pm). **Admission:** House/Grounds:

Adults £3.90, OAPs £3.50, children (14 and under) £2.20. Grounds only: Adults £2.40, OAPs £2.10, children (14 and under) £1.40. Parties over 20 (any day) by arrangement. House & Garden £3.30. Garden only £2.10. Guided (small extra charge). Pre-booked lunches/teas. Restaurant Licence. **Refreshments:** Home-made teas served in Old Library from 2–5pm on open days. **Conferences:** House and Grounds are available for private hire all year e.g. Marquee Wedding Receptions, Corporate Conferences, Luncheons, Dinners, Promotions, Launches, Clay Pigeon Shoots. Dogs on leads in grounds only. Free parking at house.

map 5 F5

THE THEATRE ROYAL

102 High Street, Chatham, Kent ME4 4BY
Tel: 01634 831028 (Chatham Theatre Royal Trust Ltd)

The Theatre Royal, built in 1899 to accommodate 3000 people, is Kent's finest surviving Victorian Theatre. No expense was spared in its construction or furnishing and it played host to many top stars of their day. In 1955 the curtain finally fell and the building converted to shops and warehousing. Threatened with demolition in the early 1990s the near derelict building was listed and purchased by a charitable trust who are working to reopen it as a first class venue. This gives the public an ideal opportunity to see restoration work in progress. The theatre is open for guided tours most weekdays and groups are welcome any day or time by appointment. Admission is by donation.

map 5 G4

WALMER CASTLE & GARDENS

Kingsdam Road, Walmer, Deal, Kent
Tel: 01304 364288 (English Heritage)

Walmer Castle was originally built by Henry VIII to defend the south coast but has since been transformed into an elegant stately home. As the residence of the Lords Warden of the Cinque Ports, Walmer was used by the Duke of Wellington, (don't miss the Duke's famous Wellington boots) and is still used today by HM the Queen Mother. Many of her rooms are open to view. Recently opened is the Queen Mother's Gardens that commemorate her 95th birthday. The gardens are stunning in summer and the herbaceous borders are exceptional. **Location:** On coast S of Walmer on A258 **Open:** 1 Apr–1 Nov daily 10–6pm (or dusk if earlier in Oct), 2 Nov–31 Mar Wed–Sun 10–4pm. Closed Jan & Feb weekends only. **Admission:** Adult: £4, Conc: £3, Child: £2. (15% discount for groups of 11 or more).

map 5 J5

CHARTWELL

Westerham TN16 1PS Tel: Information 01732 866368

Open: House, garden & studio: 1 April to 1 Nov: daily 11–5 (except Mon & Tues, but open BH Mon and see What's new above); last admission 4.30.

EMMETTS GARDEN

Ide Hill, Sevenoaks TN14 6AY Tel: 01732 750367 Enquiries 01732 868381

Open: 1 April to 1 Nov: Sat, Sun & Wed, plus BH Mon & Good Fri 11–5.30. Last admission 4.30. Events: for details of concerts and other events tel. 01892 891001.

IGHTHAM NOTE

Ivy Hatch, Sevenoaks TN15 0NT Tel: 01732 810378 Fax: 01732 811029

Open: 1 April to 1 Nov: daily except Tues & Sat 11–5.30. Last admission 5. Car park open dawn to dusk throughout the year. Estate walks leaflet available. Events: for details tel. 01892 891001

KNOLE

Sevenoaks TN15 0RP Tel: 01732 462100 Infoline: 01732 450608

Open: House: 1 April to 1 Nov: Wed, Thur, Fri & Sat 12–4; last admission 3.30 (but 1hr recommended for visit); Sun, Good Fri & BH Mon 11–5; last admission 4.30. Pre-booked groups on Wed, Thur, Fri & Sat 12–3. Park: open daily to pedestrians by courtesy of Lord Sackville. Garden: May to Sept: first Wed in each month only, by courtesy of Lord Sackville, 11–4; last admission 3. Events: programme of concerts and lectures; for details tel. 01892 891001.

OWLETTS

The Street, Cobham, Gravesend DA12 3AP Tel: 01892 890651

Open: 1 April to 30 Sept: Wed & Thur only, 2–5. Last admission 4.30 **Admission:** £2, children £1.10. Parties by arrangement; please write to tenant. No WC

QUEBEC HOUSE

Westerham TN16 1TD Tel: (Regional Office) 01892 890651

Open: 5 April to 27 Oct: Tues & Sun only 2–6. Last admission 5.30. Parties by arrangement; please write to tenant.

SCOTNEY CASTLE GARDEN

Lamberhurst, Tunbridge Wells TN3 8JN Tel: 01892 891081

Open: Garden: 1 April to 1 Nov: (Old Castle: May to 13 Sept) Wed to Fri 11–6; Sat & Sun 2–6, or sunset if earlier; BH Sun & BH Mon 12–6 (closed Good Fri). Last admission 1hr before closing. Events: tel. 01892 891001 for details.

SISSINGHURST CASTLE GARDEN

Sissinghurst, nr Cranbrook TN17 2AB Tel: 01580 715330

Open: 1 April to 15 Oct: Tues to Fri 1–6.30; Sat, Sun & Good Fri 10–5.30. Closed Mon, incl. BH. Last admission 30min before closing. Ticket office & exhibition open at 12 on weekdays. (The garden is less crowded in April, Sept & Oct, also Wed to Fri after 4 and on Sat)

SMALLHYTHE PLACE

Smallhythe, Tenterden TN30 7NG Tel: 01580 762334

Open: 1 April to 28 Oct: daily except Thur & Fri (but open Good Fri) 1–5.30, or dusk if earlier. Last admission 30min before closing. (The Barn Theatre may be closed some days at short notice)

SPRIVERS GARDEN

Horsmonden TN12 8DR Tel: (Regional Office) 01892 890651

Open: 23 & 30 May, 13 June: 2–5.30. Last admission 5

STONEACRE

Otham, Maidstone ME15 8RS Tel: 01622 862871

Open: 1 April to 31 Oct: Wed & Sat 2–6. Last admission 5

Lancashire

Ribble Valley

Lancashire is well endowed with beauty, charm and even grandeur – and much maligned by its image of dreary industrial mines, mills, ugly towns and smoke blackened countryside. There is farming land with great expanses of cornfields, meadows, pleasant vales and bare moorlands, whilst in the north it shares some of the finest mountain and lake scenery in Britain. Inland some of the best scenery is the Forest of Bowland and the Ribble Valley, both offering fantastic views.

Southport, a beautiful seaside resort, is famous for its annual international flower show. It is a lively and cosmopolitan town.

The historic county town of Lancaster is tiny when compared to Liverpool and Manchester, but it boasts a long history. The Romans named it after their camp over the River Lune . Today, its university and cultural life still thrive and the Norman castle, Georgian streets, Lune Aqueduct and a smattering of museums will fascinate the traveller.

BROWSHOLME HALL

Nr Clitheroe, Lancashire BB7 3DE
Tel: 01254 826719 Fax: 01254 826739 (Robert Redmayne Parker)

Built in 1507 and set in a landscaped park, the Ancestral home of the Parker family, with an Elizabethan facade and Regency West Wing recast by Sir Jeffrey Wyatville. Portraits (incl. Devis & Romney) a major collection of furniture, arms, stained glass and other strange antiquities from stone age axes to fragment of a zepellin. **Location:** 5 miles NW of Clitheroe: off B6243; Bashall Eaves–Whitewell signposted; **Open:** 2–4pm Good Fri, Easter Weekend and Spring Bank Hol Weekend. Fri, Sat and Sun in Aug and Aug Bank Hol Mon. **Admission:** £3 adults, £1 children. **Coach parties particularly welcome by appointment.**

map 11 F7

GAWTHORPE HALL

Padiham, Nr Burnley, Lancashire BB12 8UA
Tel & Fax: 01282 770353 (Lancashire County Council)

Built between 1600–1605, former Shuttleworth family home. 1850's restoration by Sir Charles Barry. The Rachel Kay-Shuttleworth textile collections exhibited. Portrait collection loaned by National Portrait Gallery. Events and exhibitions during high season. **Open:** Hall 1 Apr–31 Oct: daily except Mon and Fri, open Good Fri & BH Mon. 1–5pm. Last admission 4.15pm. Garden: all year, daily 10–6pm. Tearoom open as Hall 12.30–4.30pm. **Admission:** Hall £2.90 adults; £1.30 children; £8 family ticket; £1.45 concessions. Garden: free. Parties by prior arrangement. Free parking 150m. Hall not suitable for baby-packs or pushchairs. **Location:** ¾ mile out of Padiham on A671 to Burnley. Bus services from Burnley (Barracks & Manchester Road Tel: 01282 423125.) Railway station 2m (Rose Grove). Managed by Lancashire Council. Free to NT members.

map 8 B3

HOGHTON TOWER

Nr Preston PR5 OSH
Tel: 01254 852986 Fax: 01254 852109

Hoghton Tower is the home of the 14th Baronet Sir Bernard de Hoghton. It is one of the most dramatic looking houses in Lancashire. There have been 3 houses on the present site stretching back to 1100 AD whilst the estates have remained in unbroken succession since the Norman conquest. The grounds are sited on the hill commanding extensive views of the sea, the Lakes and north Wales. There are also some walled gardens. Location: M6 Jct 28, 10 mins. 6 miles SE of Preston, E of A675. **Open:** July, Aug & Sept, Mon–Thur, 11–4pm & Sun, 1–5pm. Group visits may be arranged all year around. **Admission:** Charges apply. Please phone confirming times and prices.

LEIGHTON HALL

Carnforth LA5 9ST
Tel: 01524 734474 Fax: 01524 720357

The Hall's neo–Gothic façade was superimposed on an 18th century house, which in turn, had been built on the ruins of the original medieval house. Leighton Hall is situated in a bowl of parkland, with a panoramic view of the Lakeland fells rising behind it. Connoisseurs of furniture will enjoy the 18th century pieces by Gillow of Lancaster. The main garden has a continuous herbaceous border and rose covered walls. **Location:** 3 miles N of Carnforth. 1½ mile W of A6. **Open:** May–September, Tue–Fri & Sun 2–5pm and BH Mons. Groups 25+ may be pre–booked at any time. **Admission:** Charges apply.

BLACKBURN CATHEDRAL

Blackburn BB7 3DG
Tel:01254 514491 Fax: 01254 667309

Blackburn Cathedral is set on a historic Saxon site in the town centre. Built as the Parish Church in 1826, subsequent extensions give a uniqueness to both interior and exterior. Features including the lantern tower, central altar with corona above, fine Walker organ, stained glass from medieval period onwards. Recent restoration work gives a new magnificence. **Location:** 9 miles E of M6 / Jct 31, via A59 and A677, city centre. **Open:** Mon–Fri 9–5.30pm. Sat 9.30–4pm. Sun 8–5pm. **Admission:** Donations.

ASTLEY HALL

Off Hallgate, Astley Park, Chorley PR7 1NP
Tel: 01257 262166 Fax: 01257 232441

The Hall dates back to Elizabethan times with major additions in the 1660s and 1820s. Interiors contain elaborate plaster ceilings and fine furniture. **Location:** 5 mins SW from J8 off M61, 10 mins SE of J28 off M6. Follow signs for Chorley and brown tourist signs. 10 mins walk through park from town centre. **Open:** April–October Tue–Sun 12–5pm open Bank Hol Mons, Nov–Mar Fri–Sun 12–4pm. **Refreshments:** Adjacent Cafe in Park. **Conferences:** Licensed for Civil Weddings.

RUFFORD OLD HALL

Rufford, Nr Ormskirk, L40 1SS
Tel: 01704 821254 Fax: 01704 821254 (The National Trust)

Come and enjoy the former ancestral home of the Lords of the Manor of Rufford, one of Lancashire's finest 16th century buildings. There's a glorious garden, kitchen restaurant and shop and within the House, a wide variety of tapestries, arms, armour and paintings. The Great Hall has an intricately carved movable wooden screen and dramatic hammerbeam roof. **Location:** 7 miles N of Ormiskirk, in the village of Rufford on E side of A59. **Open:** 1 Apr–1 Nov, Sat–Wed 1–5pm. Also open Thurs 16 April, 28 May, 23 July–27 Aug & 29 Oct. Garden: same days 12–5.30pm. **Admission:** House & Garden £3.50, children £1.70, family ticket £9.50. Garden only: £1.80 (children free during school holiday). Gift shop, wheelchair, food, picnic site.

map 6
B2

SAMLESBURY HALL

Preston, New Road, Preston PR5 OUP
Tel: 01254 812010 Fax: 01254 812174 (Samlesbury Hall Trust)

Built in 1325, the hall is an attractive black and white timbered manor house set in extensive grounds. Relax in pleasant surroundings and enjoy a superb selection of antiques, collectors items, crafts and exhibitions. **Location:** N side of A677, 4m WNW of Blackburn. **Open:** All year everyday except Mon: 11–4.30pm. Closed over Christmas and New Year. **Admission:** Adult £2.50, Child £1. Parking for 70 cars.

STONYHURST COLLEGE

Stonyhurst, Clitheroe. Lancashire BB7 9PZ
Tel: 01254 826345, Fax: 01254 826732

The original house (situated close to the picturesque village of Hurst Green in the beautiful Ribble Valley) dates from the late 16th century. Set in extensive grounds which include ornamental gardens. The College is a Catholic boarding & day school, founded by the Society of Jesus in 1593. **Location:** Just off the B6243 (Longridge–Clitheroe) on the outskirts of Hurst Green. 10 miles from junction 31 on M6. **Station(s):** Preston. **Open:** House weekly 20 July–24 Aug, daily except Fri (incl. Aug Bank Hol Mon) 1–5pm. Grounds and Gardens weekly 1 July–24 Aug, daily except Fri (incl. Aug Bank Hol Mon) 1–5pm. **Admission:** House and Grounds £4, children (4–14) £3 (under 4 free), senior citizens £3. Grounds only £1. **Refreshments:** Refreshments/Gift shop: Limited facilities for disabled. Coach parties by prior arrangement. No dogs permitted.

map 8
A3

TOWNELEY HALL ART GALLERY & MUSEUMS

Burnley, Lancashire, BB11 3RQ
Tel: 01282 424213, Fax: 01282 436138 (Burnley Borough Council)

The former home of the Towneley family, dating originally from the 14th century, has been an Art Gallery and Museum since 1903. Collections include oak furniture, 18th and 19th century paintings and decorative arts. Major summer exhibitions and temporary loan exhibitions. There is a Natural History Centre with aquarium and nature trails in the grounds. A separate museum of Local Crafts and Industries is housed in the former brew-house. **Location:** 1/2 mile SE of Burnley on the Burnley/Todmorden Road (A671). Station(s): Burnley Central (1¹/2 miles). **Open:** All the year Mon–Fri 10–5pm, Sun 12–5pm, closed Sat throughout year and Christmas–New Year. **Admission:** Free. **Refreshments:** At cafe on grounds.

map 8
B3

TURTON TOWER

Chapeltown Road, Turton, Bolton, Lancashire, BL7 0HG
Tel: 01204 852 203 Fax: 01204 853 759
(Lancashire County Council)

Originally a medieval tower, but extended into a country house through a series of developments in Tudor, Stuart and Victorian times. Furnished throughout in period style, there are collections which include a major loan from the Victoria & Albert Museum. Displays are complemented by an exhibitions programme and related activities. There are 9 acres of woodland gardens, a tearoom, a shop, a picnic site and car park. Also disabled toilets. **Open:** Feb–Nov.

map 6
A1

Leicestershire

Within its borders, the Midland plain falters and dies and the level stretches of East Anglia merge into gentle, undulating countryside. This is the charm of Leicestershire – simplicity of landscape, a green and pleasant land with few industrial blots to mar its peaceful expanse.

Of the many picturesque and interesting corners of Leicestershire, two are frequently overlooked. The first is linked with a date almost as well known as 1066. Every school child knows that in 1485 Richard III was defeated and slain by Henry of Richmond at Bosworth Field. The actual site of the battle is not the little town of Market Bosworth – but between Shenton and Sutton Cheney.

The other is Charnwood Forest. Compared with the mountains of Cumbria, these hills are insignificant, but the eyes delight at the scraggy rocks jutting out abruptly through the fern clad miniature mountains. Picturesque

Town Hall Square, Leicestershire

villages nestle into the countryside, such as Woodhouse Eaves, Newtown Linford and Swithland, with its world famous quarry of blue slate.

Leicester, one of England's cleanest cities, is home to great antiquity. The Old Town Hall is one of Britain's oldest buildings. Here, under the magnificent oak beamed roof, Shakespeare recited his verses to Queen Elizabeth. Traditionally the home of King Lear, with the old Roman walls still standing, the city during Saxon times was the seat of East Mercian Bishops and during the reign of the House of Lancaster, possessed a royal castle. But of Leicester's greatest pride, only the outer walls remain of the abbey where Wolsey came to lay his bones.

If you like to walk, the wolds around Melton Mowbray offer wonderful opportunities. Melton Mowbray is a very pretty market town, offering many interesting little shops and cosy places to eat.

BELVOIR CASTLE
Nr Grantham, Lincolnshire NG32 1PD
Tel: 01476 870262 (Duke of Rutland)

Seat of the Dukes of Rutland since Henry VIII's time and rebuilt by Wyatt in 1816. A castle in the grand style, commanding magnificent views over the Vale of Belvoir. The name dates back to the famous Norman Castle that stood on this site. Many notable art treasures, and interesting military relics. The Statue gardens contain many beautiful 17th century sculptures. Flowers in bloom throughout most of the season. Medieval Jousting Tournaments. Conference and filming facilities. Banquets, school visits, private parties. **Location:** 7 m WSW of Grantham, between A607 (to Melton Mowbray) and A52 (to Nottingham). **Open:** 31 Mar – 1 Oct, Tues, Wed, Thurs Sat 11–5 Sun and Bank Hols 11–6. Suns only in Oct 11–5. Other times for groups by appointment. **Admission:** Adults £5, Children £3, Seniors £4. Parties 20+ Adults £4, Seniors £3.60. School parties £2.50. Privilege Card holders – party rate. On Jousting Tournament days an extra charge of 50p per person will apply. Ticket office and catering facilities in the Castle close approximately 30 mins before the Castle. Books are on sale at the ticket office or inside the Castle, or by post £3.50 include. post and packing. We regret that dogs are not permitted (except Guide dogs).

map 8 E6

95

KAYES GARDEN NURSERY

1700 Melton Road, Rearsby, Leicester, Leicestershire LE7 4YR
Tel: 01664 424578 (Mrs Hazel Kaye)

Hardy herbaceous perennials and good selection of climbers and shrubs. The garden and nursery are in Rearsby, in the lovely Wreake valley. Once an orchard, the one acre garden houses an extensive selection of hardy herbaceous plants. Mixed borders and fine pergola, informal herb garden and a new water garden provide year-round interest, while the nursery offers an excellent range of interesting plants. Location: Just inside Rearsby village, N of Leicester on A607, on L.H. side approaching from Leicester. **Open:** Mar–Oct inclusive Tues–Sat 10–5pm Sun 10am–Noon. Nov–Feb inclusive Fri and Sat 10–4.30. Closed Dec 25–Jan 31 inclusive.

map 8
D6

LYDDINGTON BEDE HOUSE

Blue Coat Lane, Lyddington, Uppingham LE15 9LZ
Tel:01572 822438 (English Heritage)

Set among golden–stone cottages, the Bede House was originally a medieval palace of the Bishop of Lincoln. It was later converted into an alms house. **Location:** In Lyddington, 6 miles N of Corby, 1 mile E of A6003. **Open:** 1 Apr–1 Nov, daily 10–6pm (or dusk if earlier in October). Closed 1–2pm.

THE MANOR HOUSE

Donington-Le Heath
Tel: 01530 831259 (Leicestershire Museums, Arts and Records Service)

Fine medieval manor house circa 1280 with 16th to 17th century alterations. Free entry to house. Guide Book. Special events. Car and coach parking. **Open:** Wed before Easter–30 Sept incl. Wed–Sun 2–6pm & Bank Hols 2–6pm.**Admission:** Free.

map 8
C/D7

STANFORD HALL

Lutterworth, Leicestershire, LE17 6DH
Tel: 01788 860250, Fax: 01788 860870 (The Lady Braye)

William and Mary house, fine pictures (including the Stuart collection), furniture and family costumes. Replica 1898 flying machine, motorcycle museum, rose garden, nature trail. Craft centre (most Sundays). **Location:** M1 Exit 18, M1 Exit 19 (from/to North only); M6 exit at A14/M1(N) junction. **Open:** Easter–end Sept, Sats, Suns, Bank Hol Mons & Tues following 2.30–5.30pm (last admission 5pm). On Bank Hols and Event Days open 12 noon (House 2.30pm). **Admission:** House and Grounds: Adult £3.80, child £1.90. Grounds Only: Adult £2.10, child £1. Prices subject to increase on some Event Days. Parties (min 20) Adult £3.50, OAP £3.30, child £1.70. Museum: Adult £1, child 35p. **Refreshments:** Home-made teas. Light lunches most Sundays. Suppers, teas, lunches for pre-booked parties any day during season.

map 4
C1

WARTNABY

Wartnaby, Leicestershire
Tel: 01664 822 296 (Lord & Lady King)

Medium sized garden, shrubs, herbaceous borders, newly laid out rose garden with good collection of old-fashioned roses and others. Small arboretum. Formal vegetable garden. **Location:** 4 miles NW of Melton Mowbray. From A606, turn W in Ab Kettley. From A46 at Six Hills Hotel, turn E on A676. **Open:** For NGS: **Admission:** Charges apply. (Share to Wartnaby Church®). Disabled access. Plants available for sale.

map 8
D6

Lincolnshire

In this county the fens and the great stretches of southern waterways come into their own, revealing a land where field upon field extends over unending acres of plain, to a distant skyline tinged to deepest red by the setting sun. The Spalding Fens, where the endless acres of red, white, blue and variegated yellow tulips wave majestically under the

The view from Bluestone Heath Road

power of stiff breezes and the mixed holdings of daffodils, narcissi and hyacinths have an intoxicating effect, mingle like an eastern carpet at your feet.

The windmills of England are fast disappearing but many are still to be found in the Lincolnshire fens. A visit to the old town of Boston, with its magnificent parish church and a well rounded climb to the top of the 272 foot high lantern tower, reveals the splendour of the fens and the array of ancient windmills dotting a landscape which is forever divided into long straight fields of varying colours.

During the middle ages profits from the wool industry

enabled the development of towns such as Lincoln, the county town, which still houses many fine, historic buildings. Lincoln sits on a cliff above the River Witham. The whole city seems to rise out of the flat fens, with the towers of Lincoln Cathedral being visible for many miles around. The Romans first settled here in AD48 and the historic flavour of the city still remains.

There are many pretty towns in Lincolnshire: Grantham is the site of a wonderful medieval church and an alternative shrine is to the place where Margaret Thatcher was born! Stamford, in the very southern point, is a beautiful little town, with spires, antique shops, splendid churches and a quarry of little lanes and cobbled alleys.

Lincolnshire is also home to a large coastline. It shares The Wash with Norfolk and houses the popular seaside resort of Skegness, which attracts many holidaymakers in the height of the season.

AUBOURN HALL
Aubourn, Nr. Lincoln, Lincolnshire, LN5 9DZ
Tel: 01522 788 270 (Lady Nevile)

Late 16th century house attributed to J. Smythson (Jnr). Important carved staircase and panelled rooms. New rose garden and pond. **Location:** Aubourn village, 7 miles S of Lincoln. **Open:** July–Aug, Wed, 2–5pm. Also by appointment. **Admission:** Adults £2.50, OAPs £2.00.

 map 9 E5

BURGHLEY HOUSE
Stamford
Tel: 01780 752451 Fax: 01780 480125 (Burghley House Trustees)

The finest example of later Elizabethan architecture in England, built (1565–1587) by William Cecil, the most able and trusted adviser to Queen Elizabeth I. Eighteen magnificent staterooms are open to visitors. Those painted by Antonio Verrio in the late 17th century form one of the greatest decorated suites in England. Burghley is a sumptuous Treasure House and contains one of the finest private collections of 17th century Italian paintings in the world. **Location:** 1 m SE of Stamford, clearly signposted from the A1 and all approaches. Station(s): Stamford (1 mile) Peterborough (10 miles). **Open:** 1 Apr–4 Oct daily, 11–4.30pm except 5 Sept. **Admission:** Adults £5.85, OAPs £5.55. Party rates available.

DODDINGTON HALL
Doddington, Lincoln LN6 4RU
Tel: 01522 694308 (A Jarvis)

Doddington Hall is a superb Elizabethan Mansion surrounded by walled gardens and courtyards and entered through a Tudor Gate House. It stands today as it was built, and its fascinating contents reflect 400 years of unbroken family occupation with fine china, textiles, furniture and family portraits. The gardens contain magnificent box-edged parterres, sumptuous borders and a wonderful succession of spring flowering bulbs that give colour in all seasons. **Open:** Gardens only: Sundays 2-6pm March and April. House and Gardens: Weds, Suns and Bank Hol Mons 2-6pm May to Sept. Parties and school parties at other times by appointment. **Admission:** Adults: House & Gardens £4, Gardens only £2; Children: House & Gardens £2, Gardens only £1; Family ticket: £11.

  map 8 E5

ELSHAM HALL COUNTRY AND WILDLIFE PARK AND ELSHAM HALL BARN THEATRE

Brigg, Humberside DN20 OQZ
Tel: 01652 688698 Fax: 01652 688240 (Capt Jeremy Elwes and Robert Elwes)

Beautiful lakes and gardens; miniature zoo; giant carp; falconry centre; wild butterfly walkway; adventure playground; garden and working craft centre: Granary tearooms and restaurant; animal farm, museum and art gallery; caravan site; ten National Awards. Also excellent new theatre with indoor winter and new outdoor summer programme. **Location:** Near Brigg M180 Jct 5, near Humberside Airport. **Station(s):** Barnetby. **Open:** Times and prices on application. Contact Manager. **Refreshments:** Granary Tearooms, ice cream shop, restaurant, banqueting. **Conferences:** Conference facility. Licensed for civil weddings, medieval banquets and corporate entertainments/paintballing.

map 8
E3

GAINSBOROUGH OLD HALL

Parnell Street, Gainsborough DN21 2NB
Tel: 01427 612669 (English Heritage)

A large medieval house with a magnificent Great Hall and suite of rooms. A collection of historic furniture and re-created medieval kitchen are on display. **Location:** In the centre of Gainsborough, opposite library.

GRIMSTHORPE CASTLE

Grimsthorpe, Bourne, Lincolnshire PE10 0NB. Tel: 01778 591205, Fax: 01778 591259 (Grimsthorpe & Drummond Castle Trust)

The home of the Willoughby de Eresby family since 1516. Examples of early 13th century architecture, the Tudor period of the reign of Henry VIII and work by Sir John Vanburgh. State Rooms and Picture Galleries open to the Public. **Location:** 4 miles NW of Bourne on A151. **Open:** Sun, Thur and Bank Hols from Easter Sun until 27 Sept. Also daily in Aug except Fri and Sat. Park and Gardens open 11–6. Castle open 2pm (last admission 5pm). **Admission:** Adults £3, Concession £2, Child £1.50. Additional separate charge for Castle – Adults £5, Concession £4, Combined Ticket Adults £6 Concession £4.50. **Refreshments:** The Coach House serves light lunches, teas and refreshments 11.15, last orders 5.30 – licensed. **Events/Exhibitions:** For special major events alternative charges may operate. Conference room. Nature trail. Adventure playground. Red deer herd. Cycle trail. Ornamental vegetable garden.

map 8
E6

LINCOLN CASTLE

Castle Hill, Tel: 01522 511068
(Recreational Services Dept., Lincolnshire County Council)

Built by William the Conqueror in 1608, the Castle with its towers, walls and gatehouses, dominates the bail, alongside Lincoln's great Cathedral. The 1215 Magna Carta, sealed by King John at Runnymeade, is set in an informative exhibition. The administration of law and order is well established here with a history stretching back over 900 years. Visitors may attend Crown Court sittings on most weekdays. Encompassed within the walls is a unique Victorian prison chapel where incarceration can be 'experienced'. Events throughout the year. **Location:** Opposite west front of Lincoln Cathedral in the centre of Historic Lincoln. **Open:** BST: Sat 9.30–5.30pm, Sun 11–5.30pm. **GMT:** Mon–Sat 9.30–4pm, Sun 11–4pm. Closed Christmas Day, Boxing Day and New Year's Day.

map 8
E5

MARSTON HALL

Grantham
Tel: 01400 250225 (The Rev Henry Thorold, FSA)

Tudor manor house with Georgian interiors, held by Thorold family since 14th century. Interesting pictures and furniture. Romantic garden with long walks and avenues, high hedges enclosing herbaceous borders and vegetables. Gothick gazebo and ancient trees. **Open:** Suns, 14 & 21 June, 26 July and 9 Aug, 2–6pm and by appointment. **Admission:** House & Garden £2.50. **Refreshments:** Home-made cream teas. In aid of local causes. **Location:** 6 miles NW of Grantham.

map 8
E6

 # BELTON HOUSE

Grantham NG32 2LS Tel: 01476 566116 Fax: 01476 579071

Open: 1 April to 1 Nov: daily except Mon & Tues (but closed Good Fri and open BH Mon) House: 1–5.30; please note that there is much to see and at least one hour is recommended to take full advantage. Garden & park (incl. adventure playground): 11–5.30 (27 June 11–4.30; July & Aug 10–5.30); last admissions 5 (4 on 27 June).

GUNBY HALL

Gunby, nr Spilsby PE23 5SS Tel: Regional Office 01909 486411

Open: Ground floor & basement of house & garden: 1 April to end Sept: Wed 2–6. Last admission 5.30. Closed BHols. Garden also open Thur 2–6. House & garden also open Tues, Thur and Fri by written appointment only with J. D. Wrisdale at above address.

GRANTHAM HOUSE

Castlegate, Grantham NG31 6SS Tel: (Regional Office) 01909 486411

Open: Ground floor only: 1 April to end Sept: Wed 2–5 by written appointment only with the tenant, Major-General Sir Brian Wyldbore-Smith

TATTERSHALL CASTLE

Tattershall, Lincoln LN4 4LR Tel: 01526 342543

Open: House: 1 April to 1 Nov: Wed, Thur, Fri & Sat 12–4; last admission 3.30 (but 1hr recommended for visit); Sun, Good Fri & BH Mon 11–5; last admission 4.30. Pre-booked groups on Wed, Thur, Fri & Sat 12–3. Park: open daily to pedestrians by courtesy of Lord Sackville. Garden: May to Sept: first Wed in each month only, by courtesy of Lord Sackville, 11–4; last admission 3.

WOOLSTHORPE MANOR

23 Newton Way, Woolsthorpe-by-Colsterworth, nr Grantham Tel: 01476 860338

Open: 1 April to 1 Nov: Wed to Sun plus BH Mon (closed Good Fri) 1–5.30. Last admission 5.

London

London is beautiful even if the sky is grey. Westminster Abbey in the glow of sunset is majestic, offering the promise of permanence in a world of change. St Paul's, rising above the drabness of Victorian warehouses and offices, adorns a city where Wren churches tucked away in odd corners and the halls of city companies are exquisite gems of craftsmanship.

London is one of the most exciting cities in the world. Johnson declared that someone who is tired of London must be tired of life. Indeed London is awash with endless possibilities: the social and cultural heart of the city has long been the bustling West End, where the contagious lively atmosphere lasts long into the night in the street cafés and restaurants.

Regents Park and Lake

It is also possible to escape from London's hectic streets and snatch a moment's reflection in one of London's great parks. Hyde Park, Regents Park or Richmond Park are mere examples of London's leafy heritage. It is sometimes easy to forget that these verdant glades are just a stones throw from the bustle of a capital city.

London's many street markets are an alternative to the chic department stores of Knightsbridge: Petticoat Lane, Camden Lock, Portobello Road, all harbour a unique vibrancy.

Today more than ever, London whets the appetite for living.

BANQUETING HOUSE
Whitehall Palace, London
Tel: 0171 930 4179

From the days of Henry VIII until its destruction by fire in 1698, the Palace of Westminster was the Sovereign's main London residence. The only part to survive that fire was the Banqueting House. It is also the only building in Whitehall that is open to the public and it offers an oasis of peace and tranquillity amidst the bustle of Westminster. The Banqueting House was built in 1622 from a design by Inigo Jones, the leading architect of the time. The beautiful vaults beneath are known as the Undercroft—a favourite haunt of James I. When Charles I came to the throne, he further enhanced the building's interior by commissioning the Flemish painter, Rubens, to paint the ceiling. In 1635 Ruben's nine canvasses, including two measured 28x20 feet and two measuring 40x10 feet, were finally put in place. These exquisite paintings are still intact and provide a spectacular sight for today's visitors. Just as the Banqueting House featured in his early career as King, so it was to feature at the end of Charles I's reign. On 30 January 1649 on a high platform outside the north end of the building, Charles was beheaded, the only British Monarch ever to suffer such a fate. **Location:** London underground–Westminster (District/Circle line) Embankment (District/Circle, Northern & Bakerloo lines), Charing Cross (Northern, Bakerloo & Jubliee lines). BR–Charing Cross. **Open:** Mon–Sat 10–5pm. Closed Suns, 24–26 Dec, 1 Jan, Good Friday & other public holidays & at short notice for Government Functions. **Admission:** Adults £3.55, senior citizens £2.50, child under 16 yrs £2.15, under 5s free.

map 5
J6

APSLEY HOUSE, THE WELLINGTON MUSEUM

149 Piccadilly, Hyde Park Corner, London, W1V 9FA
Tel: 0171 499 5676 Fax: 0171 493 6576

Apsley house was designed by Robert Adam and built between 1771 and 1778 for Baron Apsley. It was the first house to be encountered after passing a toll gate from the West, hence its name 'No. 1 London'. In 1817, Apsley House was bought by the first Duke of Wellington. The palatial interiors provide a magnificent setting for the Duke's outstanding collection of paintings, including works by Velasquez, Goya, Rubens, Wilkie, Dutch and Flemish masters; porcelain, silver, sculpture, furniture, swords, medals and memorabilia. **Open:** Tue–Sun 11–5pm. **Admission:** Adults £4.50, concessions £3, pre-booked groups £2.50, children under 12 free.

BOSTON MANOR HOUSE

Boston Manor Road, Brentford, Middlesex, TW8 9JX
Tel: 0181 560 5441 Fax: 0181 862 7602(London Borough of Hounslow)

Boston Manor House is a fine Jacobean Manor built in 1623, extended in 1670 when the Clitherow family bought the house. It was their family home until 1924. Boston Manor is renowned for its fine English Renaissance plaster ceilings in the State Rooms on the first floor. These rooms are furnished with items on loan from Gunnersbury Park Museum. The ground floor rooms date from the early 19th century and house part of the local collection of paintings. **Station(s):** Underground Boston Manor, Piccadilly Line 200 yards north of House. **Open:** Sat, Sun, Bank Hol Mons and from the first Sat in April to the last Sun in October, 2.30-5pm. Children must be accompanied by an adult. **Admission:** Free. Parking in Boston Manor Road.

BURGH HOUSE

New End Square, Hampstead, London, NW3 1LT
Tel: 0171 431 0144 Fax: 0171 435 8817 (London Borough of Camden)

A Grade I listed building erected in 1703, in the heart of old Hampstead. Home to many notable professional people before the war. Re-opened in 1979, it houses the Hampstead Museum, an Art Gallery with regularly changing exhibitions, and a panelled Music Room popular for weddings, (the house is now licensed), wedding receptions, seminars and conferences. Also used for recitals, talks, local society meetings, book fairs and other events. Licensed basement Buttery and award-winning Gertrude Jekyll-inspired terrace garden. Buttery reservations on 0171 431 2516. **Station(s):** Underground, Hampstead. Rail, Hampstead Heath. **Buses:** 24, 46, 168, 210, 268, C11, C12. **Open:** Wed–Sun, 12noon–5pm. Bank Hols & Good Friday, 2–5pm. Buttery: 11–5.30pm. Closed Christmas/New Year. **Admission:** Free to House/Museum. **Refreshments:** The Buttery.

CARLYLE'S HOUSE

24 Cheyne Row, Chelsea, London SW3 5HL
Tel: 0171 352 7087 (The National Trust)

Part of a terrace in a quiet backwater of Chelsea, this Queen Anne house was the home of writer and historian Thomas Carlyle from 1834 until his death. The house, which contains the original furniture and many books, portraits and relics of his day, was visited by many illustrious Victorians, including Chopin, Dickens, Tennyson and George Eliot. The restored Victorian walled garden also reflects the Carlyle's life here. **Open:** 1 Apr–1 Nov: Wed to Sun (but open Bank Hol Mon) 11–5pm. Last admission 4.30pm. Closed Good Fri. Price: £3.20; child £1.60.

BUCKINGHAM PALACE
London, SW1A 1AA
Tel: The Visitor Office 0171 839 1377 Fax: 0171 930 9625

Buckingham Palace is one of the official residences of the Sovereign and is used by The Queen as both home and office. The Queen's personal standard flies when Her Majesty is in residence. Furnished with works of art from the Royal Collection, this building is used extensively by The Queen for State ceremonies, audiences and official entertaining and is opened to the public as much as these commitments allow. **THE STATE ROOMS:** During each August and September these rooms are opened to visitors. **Open:** 10 August–30 September (provisional) every day 9.30–4.30 pm. Tickets available each day from Ticket Office in Green Park. Pre-booking for individuals or groups, telephone Visitor Office. Disabled access. **Admission:** Adult £9.50, children (under 17) £5, OAPs (over 60) £7. **THE QUEEN'S GALLERY:** A diverse programme of exhibitions from the Royal Collection is mounted each year. **Exhibitions:** Michelangelo and his Influence 23 Jan–19 Apr; The Quest for Albion 15 May–11 Oct; Mark Catesby's Natural History of America The Watercolours from the Royal Library, Windsor Castle 30 Oct–10 Jan '99. **Open:** Every day during exhibitions (except 10 Apr, 25 and 26 Dec) 9.30–4.30pm (last admission 4pm). Gallery shop open every day (except 10 Apr, 25 and 26 Dec) 9.30–5pm. **Admission:** Adult £4, children (under 17) £2, OAPs (over 60) £3. **Entrance:** Buckingham Palace Road. **THE ROYAL MEWS:** As one of the finest working stables in existence, the Royal Mews provides a unique opportunity for visitors to see a working department of the Royal Household. Disabled access. Open 1 Jan–23 Mar Wed, 24 Mar–2 Aug Tue–Thurs, 3 Aug–1 Oct Mon–Thurs, 2 Oct–31 Dec Wed; 12–4pm, 10.30–4.30pm (last admission half an hour before closing). **Admission:** Adults £4, children (under 17) £2, OAPs (over 60) £3.

map 5
J6

CHELSEA PHYSIC GARDEN

66 Royal Hospital Road, London, SW3 4HS
Tel: 0171 352 5646 (The Chelsea Physic Garden Company)

The second oldest botanic garden in the country, founded in 1673 including notable collection of medicinal plants, comprises 4 acres densely packed with c. 6,500 plants, many rare and unusual. **Location:** Swan Walk, off Royal Hospital Road, Chelsea; nr. junction of Royal Hospital Road and Chelsea Embankment. **Station(s):** Sloane Square – underground. **Open:** Apr–end Oct, Suns, 2–6pm, Wed 12–5pm. Also 12–5pm in Chelsea Flower Show Week and Chelsea Festival Week. Open at other times for subscribing. Friends and groups by appointment. **Admission:** Adults £3.50, Children/Students/Unemployed £1.80. Garden accessible for disabled and wheelchairs via 66 Royal Hospital Road. Parking in street on Sun and on other days across Albert Bridge in Battersea Park. **Refreshments:** Home-made teas. No dogs (except guide dogs).

CHISWICK HOUSE

Burlington Lane, Chiswick, London, W4
Tel: 0181 995 0508 (English Heritage)

Lord Burlington's internationally celebrated villa never fails to inspire a sense of awe in all who visit. An exhibition on the ground floor reveals why this villa and its gardens are so important to the history of British architecture and an audio-tour will escort you through the fine interiors, including the lavish Blue Velvet Room. The Italianate grounds are equally impressive and have, at every turn, something to surprise and delight – including statues, temples, obelisks and urns. **Location:** Burlington Lane, W4. **Open:** 1 Apr–30 Sept daily 10–6pm, 1–21 Oct daily 10–5pm, 22 Oct–31 Mar Wed–Sun 10–4pm. Closed 24–25 Dec & 4–17 Jan 1999. From Spring 1998 Chiswick House will be available for exclusive private occasions. Tel: 0171 973 3494. **Admission:** Adults £3, concs £2.30, child £1.50. (15% discount for groups of 11 or more).

COLLEGE OF ARMS

Queen Victoria Street, London, EC4V 4BT
Tel: 0171 248 2762 Fax: 248 6448 (College of Arms)

Mansion built in 1670s to house English Officers of Arms and panelled Earl Marshal's Court. Official repository of Armorial Bearings and Pedigrees of English, Welsh, Northern Ireland and Commonwealth families, with records covering 500 years. **Location:** S of St. Paul's Cathedral **Station(s):** Blackfriars or St Pauls **Open:** Earl Marshal's Court: All year (except public holidays and State and special occasions), Mon–Fri, 10–4pm. Record Room: Open for tours (Groups of up to 20) by special arrangement in advance with Officer in Waiting. (Fee by negotiation). **Admission:** Free. Officer in Waiting available to take enquiries concerning grants of Arms and genealogy.

CROYDON PALACE

Old Palace School, Old Palace Road, Croydon, Surrey, CR0 1AX
Tel: 0181 688 2027 / 01243 532717 Fax: 0181 680 5877
(The Whitgift Foundation)

Seat of the Archbishops of Canterbury since 871 AD. 15th century Banqueting Hall and Guardroom. Tudor Chapel. Norman Undercroft. **Location:** In Croydon Old Town, adjacent to the Parish Church. **Station(s):** East Croydon or West Croydon. **Open:** Conducted Tours only. Doors open 2pm. Last tour begins 2.30pm. 14 Apr–18 Apr & 25–29 May & 13–18 July & 20–25 July. **Admission:** Adults £4.00, children/OAPs £3, family £10. Includes tea served in the Undercroft. Parties catered for by prior arrangement (Tel: 01243 532717). Souvenir shop. Unsuitable for wheelchairs.

THE DE MORGAN FOUNDATION

Old Battersea House, 30 Vicarage Crescent, Battersea, SW11 3LD

A substantial part of The De Morgan Foundation collection of ceramics by William De Morgan and paintings and drawings by Evelyn De Morgan (née Pickering), her uncle Roddam Spencer Stanhope, J. M. Strudwick and Cadogan Cowper are displayed on the ground floor. Old Battersea House – a Wren-style building which is privately occupied. **Location:** 30 Vicarage Crescent, Battersea. **Open:** Admission by appointment only, usually Wed afternoons. All visits are guided. **Admission:** £2 (optional catalogue £1.50). Parties – max. 30 (split into two groups of 15). Admission by writing in advance to The De Morgan Foundation, 15 Cotman Close, London, SW15 6RG.

THE DICKENS HOUSE

48 Doughty Street, London, WC1N 2LF
Tel: 0171 405 2127 Fax: 0171 831 5175 (Dr. David Parker)

House occupied by Charles Dickens and his family from 1837-1839, where he produced Pickwick Papers, Oliver Twist, Nicholas Nickleby and Barnaby Rudge. Contains the most comprehensive Dickens library in the world, as well as numerous portraits, illustrations and signed letters. **Location:** Near Greys Inn Road/Guildford St. **Station(s):** London Underground – Russell Square. **Open:** Mon–Sat, 10–5pm. **Admission:** Adults £3.50, Students £2.50, Children/OAP £1.50, Family £7.

map 5
J6

FENTON HOUSE

Windmill Hill, Hampstead, London NW3 6RT.
Tel: 0171 435 3471 (The National Trust)

A late 17th century house with an outstanding collection of porcelain and early keyboard instruments, most of which are in working order. The delightful walled garden includes fine displays of roses, an orchard and vegetable garden. **Open:** 1 to 22 Mar: Sat & Sun only 2–5pm. 1 Apr–1 Nov: Sat, Sun & Bank Hol Mon 11–5pm; Wed, Thurs & Fri 2–5pm; last admission 30 minutes before closing. **Admission:** £4; family ticket £10. **Location:** Visitor's entrance on W side of Hampstead Grove.

map 4
E4

FULHAM PALACE (MUSEUM OF FULHAM PALACE)

Bishops Avenue, Fulham, London SW6 6EA
Tel: 0171 736 3233 (Museum & Tours)
0181 748 3020 x4930 (Hire of Rooms)
(L. B. of Hammersmith & Fulham and Fulham Palace Trust)

Former home of the Bishop of London (Tudor with Georgian additions and Victorian chapel). Three rooms available for functions. The museum in part of the Palace tells the story of this ancient site; the displays include paintings, archaeology and garden history. The gardens, famous in the 17th century, now contain specimen trees and a knot garden of herbs. **Open:** Gardens open daylight hours. Museum open Mar–Oct: Wed–Sun 2–5pm; Nov–Feb: Thu–Sun 1–4pm. **Admission:** Gardens free. Museum: Adults 50p, concs 25p. Tour of 4 rooms & garden every 2nd Sun all year at 2pm (£2). Private tours by appointment (£4 per head incl. tea). Ring for details of current events.

   [C]

map 12
U22

GREENWICH – OBSERVATORY

National Maritime Museum, Romney Road, Greenwich, SE10 9NF
Tel: 0181 858 4422 Fax: 0181 312 6632 (National Maritime Museum)

Three historic buildings, the Old Royal Observatory (Wren), Queen's House (Inigo Jones) and the National Maritime Museum in the Royal Park at Greenwich contain Britain's historic maritime records, exhibition on Nelson, Harrison's famous marine timekeepers and location of Greenwich Meridian, Longitude 0 degrees. There is also a fine art collection. Please note: During 1998, work continues on rebuilding the Maritime Museum (fully open Spring 1999). **Location:** Off A2. River boats from central London. **Station(s):** Maze Hill. **Open:** Daily (except 24–26 Dec) 10–5pm. **Admission:** Adults £5, children £2.50, concessions £4, family £15. **Internet:** www.nmm.ac.uk

[C] Privilege Card

map 5
J6

HOGARTH'S HOUSE

Hogarth Lane, Great West Road, Chiswick, London, W4 2QN
Tel: 0181 994 6757 Fax: 0181 862 7602(Hogarth House Foundation)

Just 50 yards away from the busy Hogarth Roundabout lies this charming early 18th century house, which was the country home of William Hogarth, the famous painter and engraver. He lived here from 1749 until 1764, the year of his death. The house is now a gallery, describing the life and works of Hogarth and his various interests, as well as showing his famous engravings. **Location:** 50 yards W of Hogarth Roundabout, on A4 Great West Road. **Station(s):** BR Chiswick (from Waterloo) – 1/2 mile. Turnham Green Underground, District Line – 1 mile. **Open:** Tue-Fri: Apr–Oct, 1–5pm. Nov–Mar, 1–4pm. Sat & Sun: Apr–Oct, 1–6pm. Nov–Mar, 1–5pm. Closed Mondays (excluding Bank Hols), Good Friday and the month of January. **Admission:** Free. Parties by arrangement. Parking as for Chiswick House Grounds – signed and also named spaces in Axis Business Centre behind house.

map 5
H7

HAMPTON COURT PALACE

East Molesey, Surrey KT8 9AU
Tel: 0181 781 9500

With its 500 years of royal history Hampton Court has been home to some of Britain's most famous kings and queens and also the setting for many great historical events. When viewed from the west, Hampton Court is still the red brick Tudor palace of Henry VIII, yet from the east it represents the stately Baroque façade designed by Sir Christopher Wren for William III. The sumptuous interiors reflect the different tastes of its royal residents and are furnished with great works of art, many still in the positions for which they were originally intended. Discover the delights that this marvellous palace has to offer – the recently restored Privy Garden, the 16th century Tudor kitchens and the Mantegna's, a series of nine paintings that represent some of the most important Italian Renaissance works of art in the world.

Costumed guides give lively and informative tours of the stunning interiors of the King's Apartments, giving a unique insight into the daily lives of the kings and their courtiers. Location: Take Exit 12 & A308 from M25 or Exit 10 onto the A307. **Station:** Hampton Court 32 minutes from London Waterloo via Clapham Junction. **Open:** Mid Mar–Mid Oct, Tue–Sun 9.30–4.30pm, Mon 10.15–4.30pm. Closed 24–26 Dec. **Admission:** Adults £9.25, senior citizens/students: £7, child under 16yrs £6.10, child under 5yrs free, family ticket (up to 2 adults & 3 children): £27.65. **Events/Exhibitions:** Half-term activities include storytelling for children, young and old and at Christmas time, the palace is a hive of activity with preparations for a banquet fit for Henry VIII along with a myriad of 16th century entertainments.

map 4
E4

KEATS HOUSE

Keats Grove, Hampstead, London, NW3 2RR
Tel: 0171 435 2062 Fax: 0171 431 9293 (Corporation of London)

Keats House was built in 1815-1816. John Keats, the poet, lived here from 1818 to 1820; here he wrote 'Ode to a Nightingale' and met Fanny Brawne, to whom he became engaged. It houses letters, books and other personal relics of the poet and his fiancée. **Location:** S end of Hampstead Heath, near South End Green. **Station(s):** BR – Hampstead Heath. Underground – Belsize Park or Hampstead. Bus: 24, 46, C11, C12 (alight South End Green), 268 (alight Downshire Hill). **Open:** Keats House will be closed to the public from 1 Dec until further notice for urgent major repairs. **Admission:** Free.

KENSINGTON PALACE STATE APARTMENTS

Kensington, London
Tel: 0171 376 2452

The history of Kensington Palace goes back to 1689 when the newly crowned William III and Mary II commissioned Sir Christopher Wren to convert the then Nottingham House into a Royal Palace. The palace was again altered when George I had the artist William Kent paint the magnificent and elaborate trompe l'oeil ceilings and staircases which can still be enjoyed at this most private of Royal Palaces. While the palace remains a busy Royal residence, the State Apartments have been unoccupied since 1837 and 1998 marks one hundred years since they were first opened to the public by Queen Victoria. 1998 also sees the unveiling of an exciting new representation of the Royal Ceremonial Dress Collection which comprises of Royal, Ceremonial and Court dress. Items on display range from individual buttons to full outfits, dating from the 18th century to the present day. Guided tours take visitors around the Dress Collection and audio guides are available for the State Apartments. **Location:** On the edge of Hyde Park, just off Kensington High Street. **Open:** Please phone for details of opening hours & admission prices. **Refreshments:** Available all day in the Orangery.

KENWOOD HOUSE

Hampstead, London
Tel: 0181 348 1286 (English Heritage)

Discover a true hidden gem amongst the multitude of attractions in London and visit Kenwood, a neoclassical house containing the finest private collection of paintings ever given to the nation, all set in 112 acres of landscaped parkland. With important works by many world-famous artists, including Rembrandt, Vermeer, Turner, Reynolds and Gainsborough, a visit to Kenwood is a must for art lovers. In the 1760s the house was re-modelled by Robert Adam and the breathtaking library is one of his finest achievements. Outside, the sloping lawns and ornamental lake form a wonderfully atmospheric backdrop for our programme of hugely popular lakeside concerts with their dramatic firework finales. **Location:** Hampstead Lane NW3 **Open:** 1 Apr–30 Sept daily 10–6pm, 1 Oct–31 Oct daily 10–5pm. 1 Nov–31 Mar daily 10–4pm (closed 24–25 Dec). **Admission:** Free. Guided tours by appointment.

KEW GARDENS, ROYAL BOTANIC GARDENS

Kew, Richmond, Surrey, TW9 3AB
Tel: 0181 940 1171 Fax: 0181 332 5197 (Royal Botanic Gardens)

At any time of the year, Kew's 300 acres offer many special attractions: bluebells in the spring; colourful displays in the summer; beautiful autumn tints. Whatever the weather, there are exciting tropical vistas in the 65 ft high Palm House and in the Princess of Wales Conservatory with its 10 climatic zones – ranging from wet tropics to the desert. For blooms from the Caribbean and South Africa try the Temperate House. The smaller greenhouses, such as the Waterlily and Alpine houses, contain much to fascinate and delight. The new Evolution House takes visitors on a 3,500 million year journey and under the Palm House is the Marine Display with plants of the swamp and the seashore. Kew also has two art galleries, one devoted to the Victorian traveller, Marianne North and the other with changing exhibitions on botanical themes. Guided tours and trails are available to enable visitors to enjoy the gardens to the full. There are also catering facilities, a visitor centre and two shops. **Station(s):** Kew & Kew Bridge (British Rail). **Open:** Kew: Daily (except Christmas Day & New Year's Day), 9.30am. Further info. on 0181 940 1171. Wakehurst Place: Daily (except Christmas Day & New Year's Day), 10.00am. Further info. on 0181 332 5066. Closing times for both properties varies according to season; ring for details. **Admission:** Please contact for 1998 admission charges.

map 4
E4

LEIGHTON HOUSE MUSEUM & ART GALLERY

12 Holland Park Road, London, W14 8LZ
Tel: 0171 602 3316 Fax: 0171 371 2467

Leighton House was the first of the magnificent Studio Houses to have been built in the Holland Park area and today is open to the public as a museum of High Victorian Art. The home of the great classical painter and President of the Royal Academy, Frederic Lord Leighton, was designed by George Aitchison. The Arab Hall, is the centrepiece of Leighton House with dazzling gilt mosaics and authentic Isnik tiles. Temporary exhibitions are held throughout the year. **Nearest Underground:** High Street Kensington. **Buses:** 9, 9a, 10, 27, 28, 49. **Open:** All year, Mon–Sat, 11–5pm. Closed Sun & Bank Hols. **Admission:** Free. Private functions and concerts by arrangement with the curator.

map 5
J6

LINLEY SAMBOURNE HOUSE

18 Stafford Terrace, London, W8 7BH
Tel: 0171 937 0663 Fax: 0181 995 4895
(The Royal Borough of Kensington & Chelsea)

The home of Linley Sambourne (1844-1910), chief political cartoonist at 'Punch' Magazine. A unique survival of a late Victorian town house. The original decoration and furnishings have been preserved together with many of Sambourne's own cartoons and photographs, as well as works by other artists of the period. **Location:** 18 Stafford Terrace. **Station(s):** London Underground – Kensington High St. **Buses:** 9, 10, 27, 28, 31, 49, 52, 70. **Open:** 1 Mar–31 Oct. Wed, 10am–4pm. Sun, 2–5pm. Parties at other times by prior arrangement. Apply to The Victorian Society, 1 Priory Gardens, London, W4. Tel: 0181 994 1019. **Admission:** Adults £3.00, Children (under 16) £1.50, OAPs £2.50.

map 5
J7

MARBLE HILL HOUSE

Twickenham, London
Tel: 0181 892 5115 (English Heritage)

Explore this magnificent Palladian Thames-side villa with its 66 acres of parkland. Admire the Great Room with its lavishly gilded decoration and architectural paintings by Panini. See the important collection of early Georgian paintings and furniture and the Lazenby Bequest Chinoiserie display. The inclusive audio tour, exhibition and film will reveal the history of this beautiful house and its residents. Marble Hill House was originally built for the Countess of Suffolk, mistress to King George II. Today it offers a wonderful riverside backdrop for a programme of spectacular open-air concerts. **Location:** Richmond Road, Twickenham **Open:** 1 Apr–30 Sept daily, 10–6pm. 1–21 Oct daily, 10–5pm. 22 Oct–31 Mar Wed–Sun, 10–4pm. (Closed 24–5 Dec & 4–17 Jan 1999) **Admission:** Adult £3, conc £2.30, child £1.50. (15% discount for groups of 11).

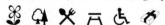

map 4
E4

MUSEUM OF GARDEN HISTORY

Lambeth Palace Road, London SE1 7LB
Tel: 0171 401 8865 Fax: 0171 401 8869 (The Tradescant Trust)

Fascinating permanent exhibition of the history of gardens, collection of ancient tools and re-created 17th century garden displaying flowers and shrubs of the period – seeds of which may be purchased in the Garden Shop. Plus knowledgeable staff, gift shop, cafe and tombs of the Tradescants and Captain Bligh of the Bounty. Lectures, courses, concerts and art exhibitions held regularly throughout the year. **Location:** Lambeth Palace Road. **Station(s):** Waterloo or Victoria, then 507 Red Arrow bus, alight Lambeth Palace. **Open:** Mon–Fri, 10.30–4pm. Sun 10.30–5pm. Closed Sat. Closed 2nd Sun in Dec to 1st Sun in Mar. **Admission:** Free. Donations appreciated **Refreshments:** Tea, coffee, light lunches. Parties catered for but prior booking essential. Literature sent on request with SAE.

OSTERLEY PARK

Isleworth, Middlesex, London TW7 4RB
Tel: 0181 560 3918 (The National Trust)
Recorded Visitor Information 0181 568 3164.

Although originally a Tudor house, Osterley was transformed into what we see today by Robert Adam in 1761. The spectacular interiors contain one of Britain's most complete examples of his work and include exceptional plasterwork, carpets and furniture. The house also has an interesting kitchen. The house is set in extensive park and farmlands. **Open:** House: 1 Apr–1 Nov; Wed to Sat 2–5pm but open Bank Hol Mon and every Sun 1–5pm. Closed Good Fri. Last admission 4.30. Park and Pleasure grounds open all year 9–7.30pm or sunset if earlier. **Admission:** £4; family ticket £10. Tearoom and shop available. Recorded Visitor Information 0181 568 3164.

map 4
E4

SIR JOHN SOANE'S MUSEUM

13 Lincoln's Inn Fields, London WC2A 3BP
Tel: 0171 430 0175 Fax: 0171 831 3957
(Trustees of Sir John Soane's Museum)

Built by the leading architect Sir John Soane, RA, in 1812–1813, as his private residence. Contains his collection of antiquities and works of art. **Stations(s):** london Underground – Holborn. **Open:** Tue–Sat, 10–5pm. Lecture tours, Sat 2.30pm, Max. 22 people. Tickets £2, on a first come, first served basis from 2pm, no groups (Tel: 0171 405 2107). Groups welcome at other times by prior arrangement. Late evening opening on first Tue of each month, 6–9pm. Also library and architectural drawings collection by appointment. Closed Bank Hols. **Admission:** Free but donations welcome. **Events/Exhibitions:** Changing exhibitions of drawings in the 'Soane Gallery'. Oct 97–Feb 98 'The Soanes at Home: A Day in the Life of Regency London'. Museum available for hire, private tours, etc.

map 5
J6

PITSHANGER MANOR & GALLERY

Mattock Lane, Ealing, London W5 5EQ
Tel: 0181 567 1227 Fax: 0181 567 0595

Pitshanger Manor and Gallery is set in the beautiful surroundings of Walpole Park, Ealing in West London. The Manor's most illustrious owner was the architect Sir John Soane (1753–1837), 'Architect and Surveyor' to the Bank of England. He rebuilt most of the house to create a Regency villa using highly individual ideas in design and decoration. The house is continually being restored and refurbished to its early 19th century style. A Victorian wing houses a large collection of Martinware pottery. Pitshanger Manor and Gallery is open to the public as a historic house and cultural centre. **Open:** Tue–Sat 10–5pm. Closed Sun and Mon. Also closed Christmas, Easter and New Year. **Admission:** FREE Parties by arrangement.

ST. JOHN'S GATE
(MUSEUM OF THE ORDER OF ST. JOHN)

St. John's Lane, Clerkenwell, London, EC1M 4DA
Tel: 0171 253 6644 Fax: 0171 336 0587(The Order of St. John)

Tudor Gatehouse, Grand Priory Church, 12th century Crypt and Museum. Fascinating insight into religious, medical and military history of the Order of St. John, from the crusades to present day. Includes rare 16th century wooden spiral staircase, Maltese silver and furniture, armour, pharmacy jars, prints, drawings and paintings relating to the history of the Hospitaller Knights of St. John. St. John's gate also has historic associations with Shakespeare, Hogarth, Cave and Dr. Johnson. Collections also include Order's modern work – St. John Ambulance and St. John Ophthalmic Hospital in Jerusalem. **Location:** St. John's Lane. **Station(s):** London Underground – Farringdon, Barbican. **Open:** Museum: Mon–Fri, 10–5pm. Sat, 10–4pm. Tours of Gate, Church & Crypt: 11am & 2.30pm, Tue Fri & Sat. **Admission:** Free. (Donations requested).

map 5
J6

SOUTHSIDE HOUSE
Woodhayes Road, Wimbledon, SW19 4RJ
Tel 0181 946 7643 (The Pennington Mellor Charity Trust)

Built by Robert Pennington in 1665 after the death of his first born in the Plague. The family befriended or were related to many distinguished names through the centuries; amongst others Ann Boleyn's descendants, Nelson and the Hamiltons, the infamous "Hell-fire Duke of Wharton" and Natalie, the widowed Queen of Serbia. Family portraits and possessions of theirs are on show. Bedroom prepared for Prince of Wales in 1750 and gifts to John Pennington–family 'Scarlet Pimpernel'. In 1907 the heiress, Hilda Pennington Mellor married Axel Munthe the Swedish doctor and philanthropist. After the Second World War Hilda and her sons Viking and Malcolm restored the house. Haunted by his vision of a bombed out Europe, Malcolm who had lived extraordinary adventures during the war, determined to make a cultural ark of the family inheritance, and with minimal resources but fine aesthetical sense made good the war damage. Guided tours give reality and excitement to the old family histories. **Location:** On S. Side of Wimbledon Common (B281) Opposite Crooked Billet Inn. **Open:** 2 Jan–Jun 24, Tue, Thur, Sat & Bank Holiday Mons. Guided tours only on the hour 2–5pm (last tour 5pm). Also open for private parties by special arrangement only with the Administrator from 1 Dec–24 Jun. **Admissions:** Adults £5, (child accompanied by adult £2).

 map 5 **F4**

SPENCER HOUSE
27 St James's Place, London, SW1A 1NR
Tel: 0171 514 1964 Fax: 0171 409 2952

Spencer House, built 1756–1766, for the first Earl Spencer, an ancestor of Diana, Princess of Wales (1961–97) is London's finest surviving 18th century town house. This magnificent private palace, overlooking Green Park, has regained the full splendour of its 18th century appearance after a painstaking ten year restoration. Eight staterooms are open to the public on Sundays and are available for private and corporate entertaining during the rest of the week. **Station(s):** Green Park. **Open:** Every Sun, except during Jan & Aug, 10.30–5.30pm. Tours last approx. 1 hour (Last tour 4.45pm). Tickets available at door from 10.30 on day. Enquiry Line: 0171 499 8620. **Admission:** Adults £6, concessions £5 (students/Friends of the Royal Academy, Tate and V&A, all with cards/children 10–16; under 10 not admitted). Prices valid until end 1998.

 map 5 **J6**

THE TOWER BRIDGE EXPERIENCE
Tower Bridge, London SE1 2UP
Tel: 0891 600 210 Fax: 0171 357 7935 (Corporation of London)

One of London's most unusual and exciting exhibitions is situated inside the world's most famous bridge – Tower Bridge. Animatronic characters from the bridge's past guide you through a series of audio visual presentations explaining to you why and how this spectacular bridge was built. Walk across the high-level walkways, which link the two towers, to experience one of the most breathtaking views of London. Finally visit the magnificent, original Victorian Engine Rooms. Location: Adjacent to Tower of London. **Nearest Tube:** Tower Hill. **Open:** 10–6.30pm (Apr–Oct), 9.30–6pm (Nov–Mar). **Closed:** 24–26 Dec, 1 & 28 Jan 1988. **Admission:** Adult: £5.95, OAP/student/child: £3.95, family: (1/2A+3/2C) £14.95

  map 5 **K6**

THE TRAVELLERS CLUB
106 Pall Mall, London, SW1Y 5EP
Tel: 0171 930 8688 Fax: 0171 930 2019

The Club House was designed by 34 yr. old Charles Barry. His design broke architectural precedent, the Pall Mall façade being derived from the Palazzo Pandolfino in Florence, causing considerable comment in its day. Barry went on to design the Houses of Parliament. **Location:** 106 Pall Mall. **Station(s):** London Underground: Piccadilly Circus, Charing Cross. **Open:** By prior appointment only, Mon–Fri, 10–12noon. Closed Bank Hols, August and Christmas. **Admission:** Adults £8 by prior appointment. **Refreshments:** Included.

  map 5 **J6**

SYON PARK

Syon Park, Brentford, Middlesex TW8 8JF
Tel: 0181 560 0881 Fax: 0181 568 0936 (Syon Park Ltd)

Sir John Betjeman described Syon House as "The Grand Architectural Walk". Syon House is the London home of the Duke of Northumberland, whose family have lived here since the late 16th century. The present house is Tudor in origin, having been built by Lord Protector Somerset on the site of a Medieval Abbey. It was in the Long Gallery that Lady Jane Grey was offered the Crown and at Syon where some of Charles 1st's children were imprisoned during the Civil War. The first Duke of Northumberland commissioned Robert Adam to remodel the interior into the magnificent suite of staterooms on view today. The parkland was landscaped by Capability Brown. Within it there are 30 acres of gardens which incorporate 'The Great Conservatory', (shown below) designed by Charles Fowler in the 1820s, a Rose Garden and over 200 species of rare trees. Housed in the former stables is one of the country's best known garden centres. Patio Cafeteria, National Trust Gift Shop. <u>Open:</u> House 11–5pm, Wed–Suns and Bank Hols, Fri & Sat closes 3.30pm, Apr–Oct. Gardens open daily 10–6pm or dusk except 25–26 Dec. Party Rates, Guide service if required.

map 4
E4

STRAWBERRY HILL HOUSE

Waldegrave Road, Strawberry Hill, Twickenham, Middlesex.
Tel: 0181 240 4114 Fax: 0181 255 6174 (St. Mary's University College)

Horace Walpole converted a modest house into a fantasy villa. It is widely regarded as the first substantial building of the Gothic Revival and as such internationally known and admired. A century later Lady Waldegrave added a magnificent wing to Walpole's original structure. Guided tours take approximately 75 minutes and it is worth coming to see this unique house. These magnificent rooms can also be hired for corporate events, wedding receptions and conferences both day and residential. **Open:** Advance group bookings by appointment only are taken throughout the year and the House is open to the general public on Suns from Easter to Mid October, between 2pm and 3.30pm. This information was correct at the time of going to print, please phone 0181 240 4224 for up to the minute information. **Admission:** £4.50 concessions for OAP's, a maximum of 20 people per tour, the house is not suitable for disabled or children under 14 years of age. For information regarding advance groups bookings or functions, please call the conference office on 0181 240 4114, 0181 240 4311 or 0181 240 4044.

map 4 E4

THE WALLACE COLLECTION

Hertford House, Manchester Square, London
Tel: 0171 935 0687 Fax: 0171 224 2155

The Wallace Collection is a national museum located in Hertford House, which was built in 1776. Within the superb range of fine and decorative arts are magnificent 18th century French paintings, furniture and porcelain, paintings by Titian, Rembrandt and Rubens and opulent displays of gold boxes, sculpture, miniatures and Renaissance works of art. Formed by three generations of one family, the collection is displayed in sumptuous rooms, which are available for private and corporate entertaining. **Location:** Manchester Square (behind Selfridges). **Station(s):** London Underground Bond Street. **Open:** Mon–Fri, 10–5pm. Sun, 2–5pm. Extended Suns, Apr–Sept, 11–5pm. Free lectures on the collection, daily. **Admission:** Free (donations).

 # 2 WILLOW ROAD

2 Willow Road, Hampstead, London NW3 1TH
Tel: 0171 435 6166 (The National Trust)

The former home of Erno Goldfinger, designed and built by him in 1939. One of Britain's most important examples of modernist architecture, the house is filled with furniture also designed by Goldfinger. The interesting art collection includes work by Henry Moore and Max Ernst. **Open:** 2 Apr–31 Oct: Thurs, Fri & Sat 12–5pm. Last admission 4pm. Guided tours every 45 minutes. **Admission:** £4. No parking at house. Limited on-street parking.

WESTMINSTER CATHEDRAL

Victoria SW1P 1QW
Tel:0171 798 9055 Fax: 0171 798 9090

The Roman Catholic Cathedral of the Archbishop of Westminster. Spectacular building in the Byzantine style, designed by Johansens F Bentley, opened in 1903, famous for its mosaics, marble and music. Westminster Cathedral celebrated the Centenary of its foundation in 1995. **Location:** On Victoria Street, between Victoria station and Westminster Abbey. **Open:** All year, 7–7pm. Please telephone for times over Christmas and Easter. **Admission:** Free, but there is a lift charge.

map 4 E4

map 5 J6

TOWER OF LONDON

Tower Hill, London
Tel: 0171 709 0765

The Tower of London was first built by William the Conqueror, for the purpose of protecting the King and controlling the city. Over the ensuing 900 years, The Tower of London has served as a Royal Palace, armoury, fortress, Royal Mint and more infamously a prison and place of execution. The Tower remains home to the magnificent Crown Jewels. The Imperial State Crown is still worn by H.M. The Queen at the annual State Opening of Parliament. The Crown Jewels also boast the largest cut diamond in the world at 530 carats, the 'First Star of Africa', which is set in the Sovereign's Sceptre. Once inside The Tower, the famous Yeoman Warders give free guided tours providing an unrivalled insight into the dark secrets of The Tower's history. Visitors to The Tower can stand on Tower Green where two of Henry VIII's wives lost their heads, enter the Bloody Tower where Sir Walter Raleigh was imprisoned and look down upon Traitor's Gate through which many, including Guy Fawkes, made their last journey. Costumed guides give special presentations in Edward I's Medieval Palace, where the restored rooms evoke life in 1280s. A stroll along the Wall Walk takes you from Salt Tower to the Martin Tower with its fascinating crowns and diamonds exhibition, not to mention the breathtaking view across the Thames. **Location:** London Underground – Tower Hill (District/Circle Line). BR – Fenchurch Street & London Bridge stations. **Open:** Mar–Oct: Mon–Sat 9.00–6.00pm, Sun 10.00–6.00pm. Nov–Feb: Tue–Sat 9.00–5.00pm, Sun–Mon 10.00–5.00pm. Closed 24–26 Dec & 1 Jan. Last ticket sold one hour before closing. **Admission:** Please phone for details.

map 5
J7

Greater Manchester

Canal Street

Manchester houses a buzzing cultural scene. Museums, classical concerts, ballet, theatre, ethnic festivals and clubs famous for footballers, test cricketers and other sportsmen are all part of its legend.

With the approach to the millennium, historic edifaces are being spruced up, architects are transforming the old mills, exciting new buildings are springing up, the canals have been cleared and are attracting the colourful barges and small boats again, while the inner city estates are improving beyond recognition.

In 1830, the railway to Liverpool was opened and carried the first passenger trains in the world. Over a century later, the imposing Victorian Gothic Architecture still proudly dominates the city as it approaches the millennium.

BOLTON'S HISTORIC HOUSES

Halli'th'wood: Greenway, off Crompton Way. Smithhills Hall: Off Smithhills Dean Road. Bolton
(Bolton Metropolitan Borough Museum and Art Gallery)

HALLI'TH'WOOD: Dating from latter half of the 15th century and furnished throughout in the appropriate period. The Hall, built in the post and plaster style, dates from 1483, a further extension was added in 1591, the last addition being made in 1648. Home of Samuel Crompton in 1779 when he invented the Spinning Mule. House contains Crompton relics. **Location:** In Green Way, off Crompton Way; 01204 301159 2miles NE of town centre off A58 (Crompton Way) signposted Halli'th'Wood (1/2 mile). **Open:** Apr–Sept Tues–Sat 11–5pm Sun 2–5pm closed Mons, except Bank Hols Oct–Mar closed to general public. Open to pre-booked parties and evening party tours. **Admission:** Adults £2, concessions £1, groups £1.50. Concessionary double ticket with Smithills Hall.

SMITHILLS HALL: One of the oldest manor houses in Lancashire, a house has stood on this site since the 14th century. The oldest part of Smithills, the Great Hall, has an open timber roof. Smithills has grown piece by piece over the centuries and such irregularly planned buildings, give the hall its present day picturesque effect. Furnished in the styles of the 16th and 17th centuries. Withdrawing room contains linenfold panelling. **Location:** Off Smithills Dean Road 01204-841265. 1½m NW of town centre off A58 (Moss Bank Way); signposted. Station(s) Bolton. **Open:** Apr–Sept Tues–Sat 11–5pm, Sun 2–5pm. Closed Mons except BHs. Oct–Mar Closed to general public. Open to pre-booked educational parties and to evening party tours. **Admission:** Adults £2, Concs. £1, groups £1.50. Concessionary double ticket with Halli'th'wood Hall.

map 6
B1

HEATON HALL

Heaton Park, Prestwich, Manchester, Lancashire, M25 2SW
Tel: 0161 773 1231/236 5244 Fax: 0161 236 7369
(Manchester City Art Galleries)

Set in 650 acres of rolling parkland, Heaton Hall is a magnificent Grade I listed building described as 'the finest house of its period in Lancashire and one of the finest in the country'. Designed by James Wyatt in 1772, the building's beautifully restored 18th century interiors are furnished with fine paintings and furniture of the period. The unique circular Pompeiian Room and elegant Music Room are particularly noteworthy. **Open:** May–Sept.

map 8
B4

MANCHESTER CATHEDRAL

Manchester M3 1SX
Tel: 0161 833 2220 Fax:0161 839 6226

In addition to regular worship and daily offices, there are frequent professional concerts, day schools, organ recitals, guided tours and brass-rubbing. The Cathedral contains a wealth of beautiful carvings and has the widest medieval nave in Britain. **Location:** Manchester city centre. **Open:** Daily. **Admission:** Donations.

Merseyside

Liverpool

L iverpool stands majestically on the estuary of the River Mersey and used to be England's second greatest port. The city today still tells the story of its great maritime past with an impressive museum and many other edifices. Many of the old docks have been renovated, such as the Albert Dock, designed by Jesse Hartley in 1846, which has been transformed into shops and cafés and houses an offshoot of the London Tate Gallery, 'The Beatles Story' and the sight and sound show.

Liverpool, not only famous for The Beatles, is a must for football fans. Anfield, home of Liverpool Football Club displays a fascinating collection of memorabilia and trophies. This famous city houses two cathedrals which face each other across the urban sprawl.

Merseyside also has an expanse of coastline, facing the Irish Sea. To the north is Southport which overlooks this often rough stretch of water. Situated close to Liverpool, is the appealing seaside resort of Wallasey, which sits on the peninsular of the Wirral, with fantastic sandy beaches.

The Wirral used to be a royal game reserve; it is now a wonderful haven for waders and waterfowl. The salt marshes of the Dee estuary produce an area that attracts these feathered delights, perfect for bird-watchers.

CROXTETH HALL & COUNTRY PARK
Tel: 0151 228 5311 Fax: 0151 228 2817
(Liverpool City Council)

500 acre Country Park centred on the ancestral home of the Molyneux family, Earls of Sefton. Hall rooms with character figures on the theme of an Edwardian house party. Victorian Home Farm and Walled Garden both with quality interpretive displays: superb collection of farm animals (Approved Rare Breeds Centre). Miniature Railway. Special events and attractions most weekends. Picnic areas and adventure playground. **Location:** 5 miles NE of Liverpool City Centre: Signposted from A580 & A5088 (ring road). **Open:** Parkland daily throughout year, admission free. Hall, Farm & garden 11–5pm daily in main season. Telephone for exact dates. Free car parking. **Refreshments:** 'The Old Riding School' café during season.

 map 6 C2

LIVERPOOL CATHEDRAL
Liverpool L1 7AZ
Tel: 0151 709 6271 Fax: 0151 709 1112

Sir Giles Gilbert Scott's greatest creation. Built this century from local sandstone with superb glass, stonework and major works of art, it is the largest Cathedral in Britain with a fine musical tradition, a tower offering panoramic views and award-winning refectory. There is a unique collection of church embroidery, a full range of souvenirs, cards and religious books. **Location:** Central Liverpool, 1/2 mile south of Lime Street station. Open: 8–6pm. **Admission:** Donations please.

MEOLS HALL

Southport PR9 7LZ
Tel: 01704 29826 Fax: 01704 29826 (R Hesketeh Esq.)

A 17th century manor house, with subsequent additions, containing an interesting collection of pictures, furniture, china etc. **Location:** 1 mile N of Southport: 16 miles SW of Preston: 20 miles N of Liverpool; near A565 & A570. **Station(s):** Southport. **Open:** 14 Aug to 14 Sept 2–5pm. **Admission:** Adults £3, children £1, those under 10 accompanied by adult free. **Refreshments:** Available in local village 200 yards. Afternoon teas available for group bookings. Tithe Barn available for weddings and corporate hospitality. **Events:** For 1998 include Vintage Vehicle Rally, Classical Concert, Jazz Festival and Bonfire Night.

 map 6 B2

SPEKE HALL

The Walk, Liverpool L24 1XD
Tel:0151 427 7231 Fax: 0151 427 9860 (The National Trust)

One of the most famous half–timber houses in the country, set in varied gardens and attractive wooded estate. Tudor Great Hall, Victorian interiors, William Morris wallpapers. There is a Rose and Stream Gardens. Woodland walks and stunning views of the Mersey estuary. **Location:** North bank of the Mersey, 6m SE of city centre. Follow signs for Liverpool airport.

 map 6 C2

Norfolk

Norfolk is one of Englands most peaceful counties. This flat county, boasts some of the most glorious, unspoilt, coastline which has a unique network of inland waterways, tranquil heaths, woodland and hedgerows.

Norfolk remains unspoilt by man or time. This reflects in the county town, Norwich, which to this day is one of the best preserved towns in England. In the 9th century, Norwich was fortified by the Saxons, and the medieval street plan remains.

The Norfolk Broads National Park attracts birdwatchers and boaters from around the country. The Broads to the east, best seen on a boat, contain many slow moving shallow rivers which meander through the countryside, until they join the coast around the popular holiday resort of Great Yarmouth.

Kings Lynn

THE FAIRHAVEN GARDEN TRUST

South Walsham, Nr Norwich, Norfolk NR13 6EA
Tel & Fax: 01603 270449 (G.E. Debbage)

A delightful natural woodland and water garden in the heart of broad land. Primroses, bluebells, candelabra primulas, azaleas, rhododendrons, giant lilies, rare shrubs and plants, native wild flowers, 900 year old King oak, private inner broad, separate bird sanctuary for bird watching. Boat trips. **Location:** 9 miles NE Norwich on B1140. **Open:** 1 April–31 Oct, Tues–Sun 11–5.30pm. Closed Mondays except bank holidays. Primrose Weeks 12–26 Apr; Candelabra Primula Weeks 17–31 May. **Admission:** Adults £3, OAPs £2.70, Children £1, Under 5s free. Season Ticket £10, Family Season £25. Parties by arrangement. Group discount. Free guided walks. **Refreshments:** Morning coffee, light lunches, afternoon teas. Free parking. Plants for sale. Charity No. 265686.

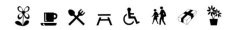
map 9
K6

HOLKHAM HALL

Wells-next-the-Sea, Norfolk NR23 1AB
Tel: 01328 710227, Fax: 01328 711707 (The Earl of Leicester)

One of Britain's most majestic stately homes, situated in a 3,000 acre deer park, on the beautiful north Norfolk coast. This celebrated Palladian style mansion, based on designs by William Kent, was built between 1734 and 1762 by Thomas Coke, 1st Earl of Leicester. The magnificent alabaster entrance hall rises the full height of the building and in the richly and splendidly decorated Staterooms are Greek and Roman statues, brought back by the 1st Earl from his Grand Tour of Europe, fine furniture by William Kent and paintings by Rubens, Van Dyck, Claude, Poussin and Gainsborough. In addition to the Hall there is a Bygones Museum in the original stable block, History of Farming

Exhibition in the porters' lodge and Holkham Nursery Gardens in the 18th century walled kitchen garden. **Location:** 2 miles W of Wells-next-the-Sea. S off the A149. **Open:** Suns–Thurs (incl.) 24 May–30 Sept 1–5pm. Plus Easter, May, Spring & Summer Bank Hols. Sun & Mon 11.30–5pm. (last admission 4.45pm). **Admission:** Hall: Adults £4, children £2. Bygones: Adults £4, children £2. Combined ticket: Adults £6, children £3. Reduction on parties of 20 or more. **Refreshments**: Tearoom. **Events:** Stately Car Boot Sale in aid of Norfolk Churches Trust, Sat 23 May. Gift shop and pottery.

map 9
H6

HOUGHTON HALL
Kings Lynn
Tel: 01485 528569 (The Marquess of Cholmondeley)

The Home of the Marquess of Cholmondeley, Houghton Hall was built in the 18th century for Sir Robert Walpole by Colen Campbell and Thomas Ripley, with interior decoration by William Kent and is regarded as one of the finest examples of Palladian architecture in England. Houghton was later inherited by the 1st Marquess of Cholmondeley through his grandmother, Sir Robert's daughter. Situated in beautiful parkland, the house contains magnificent furniture, pictures and china. Pleasure grounds. A private collection of 20,000 model soldiers and militaria. Newly restored walled garden. Location: 13 miles E of King's Lynn; 10 miles W of Fakenham off A148. **Open:** 12 April-27 September 2pm-5:30pm, last admission 5pm. **Admission:** House, park and grounds: (include soldier museum, walled garden, tearoom and gift shop) Please telephone for details.

map 9
H6

 ## HOVETON HALL GARDENS
Hoveton Hall, Norwich, Norfolk.
Tel: 01603 782798 Fax. 01603 784 564 (Andrew & Barbara Buxton)

Hoveton Hall Gardens—15 acres of rhododendron and azalea filled woodland, laced with streams leading to a lake. Daffodils galore in Spring. Formal walled herbaceous and vegetable gardens. Morning coffee, light lunches and delicious home-made teas. **Open:** Easter Sun to mid Sept, Wed, Fri, Sun and Bank Hol Mons—11-5.30pm. Coaches welcome by appointment.

MANNINGTON HALL
Saxthorpe, Norfolk
Tel: 01263 584175, Fax: 01263 761214 (Lord and Lady Walpole)

15th century moated house and Saxon church ruins set in attractive gardens. Outstanding rose gardens. Extensive walks and trails around the estate. **Location:** 2 miles N of Saxthorpe, near B1149; 18 miles NW of Norwich; 9 miles from coast. **Open:** Walks daily all year; Garden May–Sept Sun 12–5pm. Also June–Aug Wed, Thurs and Fri 11–5. **Admission:** Adults £3, children (accompanied children under 16) free OAPs/students £2.50. House open by prior appointment only. **Refreshments:** Coffee, salad lunches and home-made teas.

map 9
J6

NORWICH CASTLE MUSEUM
Norwich, Norfolk NR1 3JU
Tel: 01603 493648 Fax: 01603 765651

The ancient Norman Keep of Norwich Castle dominates the city and is one of the most important buildings of its kind in Europe. Once a royal castle, it now houses one of England's finest regional collections of natural history, archaeology and art including the Norwich School of Painters. Also on display is the world's largest collection of teapots. Guided tours of the battlements and dungeons offer the chance to discover the darker secrets of this 900 year old castle. A lively programme of special events, children's activities and exhibitions, including an annual display from the Tate Gallery collection are offered throughout the year. Open all year Mon–Sat 10–5pm, Sun 2–5pm. Cafeteria & shop available. **Admission:** Jul–Sept: Adult £3.20, concs £2.20, child £1.60, family £8. Oct–Jun: Adult £2.40, concs £1.60, child £1.10, family £5.90.

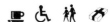

map 9
J7

RAVENINGHAM HALL GARDENS

Raveningham, Norwich NR14 6NS
(Sir Nicholas Bacon Bt)

Gardens laid out approximately 100 years ago around a red brick Georgian house which is not open to the public. **Location:** Between Beccles and Loddon off B1136 / B1140. **Open:** May, June, July. Sun & BH Mondays, 2–5pm. **Admission:** Adult charges apply. Groups by prior arrangement please.

SANDRINGHAM HOUSE

Estate Office, Sandringham, Norfolk PE35 6EN
Tel: 01553 772675 (Her Majesty The Queen)

Sandringham is the charming country retreat of Her Majesty The Queen hidden in the heart of sixty acres of beautiful wooded grounds. All the main ground floor rooms used by The Royal Family, full of their treasured ornaments, portraits and furniture, are open to the public. More Royal possessions dating back more than a century are displayed in the Museum housed in the old stable and coach houses. Glades, dells, lakes and lawns are surrounded by magnificent trees and bordered by colourful shrubs and flowers. **Location:** 8 miles NE of King's Lynn (off A148). **Open:** April 9th–21st July daily 11–4.45pm (26th July, Grounds & Museum) and 6th August–4th October 11–5pm. **Admission:** House, Grounds & Museum: Adults £4.50, seniors/students £3.50, children (5–15) £2.50. Grounds & Museum: Adults £3.50, seniors/students £3.00, children (5–15) £2.00.

map 9 G6

 WALSINGHAM ABBEY GROUNDS

Walsingham, Norfolk NR22 6BP
Tel: 01328 820 259 Fax: 01328 820 098 (Walsingham Estate Co.)

Set in Walsingham, a picturesque medieval village, the grounds contain the remains of an Augustinian Priory founded in 1153 on a site next to the Holy House and provide pleasant river and woodland walks. Snowdrop walks during Feb/Mar. Open to the public from 10–4pm every day from Good Fri to end of October and during the snowdrop season. Entry through museum or estate office when main gate closed. Access through estate office end of Oct–Good Fri–normal office hours. **Admission:** Adults £2 (Combined Grounds/Museum) children and senior citizens £1. Adults £1.50 (Grounds only) children and senior citizens 75 pence. **Refreshments/ Accommodation:** Wide range available in the village. Car park: Pay and display 50 years.

map 9 H6

WOLTERTON PARK

Erpingham, Norfolk
Tel: 01263 584175, Fax: 01263 761214 (Lord and Lady Walpole)

Extensive historic park with lake and 18th century Mansion house. **Location:** Near Erpingham, signposted from A140 Norwich to Cromer Road. **Station(s):** Gunton. **Open:** Park open all year, daily 9–5pm or dusk if earlier. **Admission:** Park £2 per car. Hall for 1998 opening hours see local press. See local press for details of special events and garden and Hall tours. **Refreshments:** Pub at drive gate. **Events/Exhibitions:** Yes. **Accommodation:** Limited. **Conferences:** Yes.

map 9 J6

NORFOLK WINDMILL'S TRUST

Tel: 01603 222705

Why not visit some of Norfolk's more unusual Historic Buildings in 1998? The county is famous for its windmills and many are open to the public on specified days, courtesy of Norfolk Windmill's Trust. Old Buckingham Mill, reputedly the largest mill in Great Britain, was opened for the first time in 1996. Extensive restoration of Denver Mill continues to restore it to full working order. For full details of opening times and location or leaflet 'Mill Open days 1998', contact the trust on the above telephone number.

BLICKLING HALL, GARDEN & PARK

Blickling, Norwich NR11 6NF Tel: 01263 733084 Fax: 01263 734924

Open: House: 4 April to end July: Wed to Sun & BH Mons 1–4.30; Aug: Tues to Sun & BH Mon 1–4.30 (guided tours on Mon 3, 10, 17 & 24 Aug); Sept to Nov: Wed to Sun 1–4.30. Last admission 4.30. Garden: same days as house 10.30–5.30 (gates close at 6), and open daily 1–30 Aug; 2 Nov to 31 March 1999: Sun only 11–4. Park and woods: daily all year dawn to dusk. Events: wide-ranging programme; details from Property Manager. **Admission:** House & garden £6. Garden only £3.30. Family and group discounts available. Groups please book with s.a.e. to Property Manager. Coarse fishing in lake; permits available from Warden at 1 Park Gate (tel. 01263 734181). Free access to South Front, shop, restaurant and plant centre

FELBRIGG HALL, GARDEN & PARK

Felbrigg, Roughton, Norwich NR11 8PR Tel: 01263 837444

Open: House: 28 March to 1 Nov: daily except Thur & Fri 1–5 (but open Good Fri); BH Mon & Sun preceding BH Mon 11–5; last admission 4.30. Garden: same days 11–5.30. Woodland, lakeside walks and parkland: daily all year, dawn to dusk (closed Christmas Day). Events: for details of full programme please send s.a.e. to Property Manager or contact Events Box Office (tel. 01263 838297). **Admission:** House & garden £5.40; family discounts available. Parties £4.40; please book with s.a.e. to Property Manager. Garden only £2.20

OXBURGH HALL, GARDEN & ESTATE

Oxborough, King's Lynn PE33 9PS Tel: 01366 328258 Fax: 01366 328066

Open: House: 28 March to 1 Nov: daily except Thur & Fri 1–5; BH Mon 11–5. Garden: 7–22 March: Sat & Sun 11–4, then same days as house 11–5.30 but garden open daily in Aug. Events: programme of brass band concerts and garden open days; s.a.e. to Administrator for details. **Admission:** House, garden & estate £4.80; family discounts available. Pre-arranged parties £3.80 per person; please book with s.a.e. to Administrator. Garden & estate only £2.40

Northamptonshire

Cottesbrooke Hall

Northamptonshire is a gently undulating county where church spires and grand estates nestle amongst rolling hills rising to a lofty height of seven hundred feet above sea level in places. The impressive town of Northampton is the setting for one of only four surviving round Norman churches in England. This wonderful old building contains works of art by Henry Moore and Graham Sutherland. As you walk around this town, it is easy to appreciate the spacious, ordered layout of this town, created after Northampton was destroyed by a huge fire in the seventeenth century.

Oundle

BOUGHTON HOUSE

Boughton House, Kettering, Northamptonshire.
Tel: 01536 515731 Fax: 01536 417225 (Duke of Buccleuch)

Northamptonshire home of the Duke of Buccleuch and his Montagu ancestors since 1528. A 500 year old Tudor Monastic building, gradually enlarged until French style addition of 1695 led the sobriquet "The English Versailles". Outstanding Collection of 17th, 18th century French and English Fine Arts. **Internet:** Information, including 'virtual' tour, see *www. boughtonhouse.org.uk.* **Open:** Daily (including Fri) 1 Aug–1 Sept. Park from 1pm, House 2pm, last entry 4.30pm. Staterooms strictly by pre-booked appointment – telephone for details. Park: Daily, except Fri, 1 May–15 Sept, 1–5pm Plant Centre, Adventure Play area, Tearoom open daily in Aug and weekends during Park opening. Educational groups throughout the year, by prior appointment. **Admission:** House and Park: Adults £4, OAP/child £3. Park only: Adults £1.50, OAP/child £1. Wheelchairs visitors free.

map 4
D1

COTTESBROOKE HALL AND GARDENS

Nr Northampton, Northants NN6 8PF
Tel: 01604 505808, Fax: 01604 505619 (Captain & Mrs John Macdonald-Buchanan)

Architecturally magnificent Queen Anne house commenced in 1702. Renowned picture collection, particularly of sporting and equestrian subjects. Fine English and Continental furniture and porcelain. Main vista aligned on celebrated 7th century Saxon church at Brixworth. House reputed to be the pattern for Jane Austen's 'Mansfield Park'. Celebrated gardens of great variety including herbaceous borders, water and wild gardens, fine old cedars and specimen trees. The magnolia, cherry and acer collections are notable, as also are the several fine vistas across the park. **Location:** 10 miles N of Northampton (A14–A1/M1 Link Road), near Creaton on A5199, near Brixworth on A508. **Open:** Easter to end Sept. **House and Gardens:** Thurs and Bank

Hol Mon afternoons, plus all Sun afternoons in Sept 2–5.30pm. Last admission 5pm. **Gardens Only:** Tues, Wed and Fri afternoons 2–5.30pm. Last admission 5pm. **Admission: House and Gardens:** Adults £4, **Gardens Only:** £2.50; Children half price. **Refreshments:** Tearoom open 2.30–5pm. Gardens, but not House, suitable for disabled. Car park. Plants for sale. No dogs. **PRIVATE BOOKINGS:** Available for group visits to the House and Gardens, or Gardens only, on any other day during the season, except weekends, by prior appointment. **Lunches/refreshments** for groups available by prior arrangement. Please telephone for information.

map 4
D1

ALTHORP

FIVE HUNDRED YEARS

Althorp has been the home of the Spencer family since 1508. The Park became the focal point for the World's attention on 6th September 1997, when Diana, Princess of Wales was laid to rest there after her tragically early death. She now lies on the island in the Round Oval, an ornamental lake, surrounded by her Family's ancestral heritage.

Next to the mansion at Althorp, lies the honey-stoned Stable Block; a truly breathtaking building that is perhaps of greater external beauty than the House itself. This is the setting for the Visitor Centre, which houses an exhibition celebrating the former Lady Diana Spencer's life and honouring her memory after her death. The displays will include childhood personal effects as well as family photographs and cine film taken by her father, the 8th Earl Spencer. The freshness and modernity of the facilities will be a unique tribute to a woman who captivated the World in her all-too-brief existence.

All visitors are invited to view the House and grounds as well as the island in the Round Oval where Diana, Princess of Wales is laid to rest. There is no public access to the island itself, but for those wishing to pay their respects, the 'temple' at the edge of the lake has been dedicated to Diana's memory.

Althorp is clearly signed from junction 15A of the M1. The Park is located 5 miles west of Northampton off the A428 heading from Northampton to Rugby.

Open daily, 1st July to 30th August 1998, 10am to 5pm. Last admission 4pm.

All visitors are requested to apply in advance for an invitation to visit Althorp. This is necessary in order to avoid overcrowding and thus preserve the dignity and tranquillity of every visit. Visitors arriving without an invitation will not be admitted.

Adults £9.50
Senior Citizens £7
Children (5–17) £5

Coach parties will not be admitted to Althorp in 1998. The necessary facilities are under construction but will not be complete until 1999 when group visits will be welcome.

Please contact our dedicated booking line (24 hour service)*:

01604 592020

*maximum 6 admissions per household.

Althorp, Northampton NN7 4HQ Tel: 01604 770107 Fax: 01604 770042

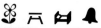

CASTLE ASHBY

Castle Ashby House
Castle Ashby, Northampton NN7 1LQ

The lands at Castle Ashby were given to the Compton family in 1512 by Henry VIII. In 1574 Queen Elizabeth 1 gave William, Lord Compton, permission to demolish the derelict 13th century castle and build the present House on this site. The original plan of the House was in the shape of an 'E' in honour of Queen Elizabeth and in 1625 the courtyard was enclosed by a screen designed by Inigo Jones. Castle Ashby is still the home of the Compton family, the 7th Marquess of Northampton being the 27th generation. The Castle and the Compton family have a fascinating history; related by marriage to most of the aristocratic families in this country. These liaisons are still remembered in the names given to each of the bedrooms. Castle Ashby stands at the heart of a 10,000 acre working estate, surrounded by 200 acres of beautiful parkland. **It is not open to the public and is the only Stately**

Home available on an exclusive basis with 26 exquisitely refurbished bedrooms, in addition to the recently restored State Suite which is absolutely unique in the country. Despite its seclusion and tranquillity, Ashby is capable of hosting the most sophisticated event, whilst clients are cared for by experienced professionals. Our aim is to provide discreet service with a touch of informality to allow guests to experience the enjoyment of using the house as if it were their own. Located 55 miles from London the Capability Brown landscape contains many superb walks and lakes for fishing. Horse riding, clay shooting and carriage driving are also accessible. The vast gardens incorporate a Triumphal Arch, Orangery, Italian Gardens and Camellia Houses.

map 4
D2

DEENE PARK

Corby, Northants
Tel: 01780 450278 / 450223 Fax: 01780 450282

A very interesting house which developed over six centuries from a typical medieval manor round a courtyard into a Tudor and Georgian mansion. Many rooms of different periods are seen by visitors, who enjoy the impressive yet intimate ambience of the family home of the Brudenells, seven of whom were Earls of Cardigan. The most flamboyant of them was the 7th Earl, who led the Light Brigade charge at Balaklava and of whom there are some historic relics and pictures. The present owner is Mr Edmund Brudenell, who has carefully restored the house from its dilapidated condition at the end of the last war and also added considerably to the furniture and picture collection.The gardens have been made over the last thirty years, with long, mixed borders of shrubs, old-fashioned roses and flowers, a recent parterre designed by David

Hicks and long walks under fine, old trees by the water. The car park beside the big lake is a good place for picnics. **Location:** 8 miles NW of Oundle; 6 miles NE of Corby on Kettering/Stamford Road (A43). **Open:** Easter, May, Spring & Summer Bank Hol Sun & Mons, also every Sun in Jun, Jul & Aug 2–5pm. Special guided tours to parties of twenty or more may be arranged throughout the year on application to the House Keeper. **Admission:** House & Gardens: Adult £4.50, child (10–14) £2. Child (under 10) free with accompanying adult. Gardens only: Adult £2.50, child (10–14) £1.25. Child (under 10) free with accompanying adult. **Refreshments:** Home-made teas are served in the Old Kitchen on open days. Luncheons, cream teas and suppers are available for pre-booked parties, by arrangement. There is a gift shop within the courtyard.

map 8 / E7

COTON MANOR GARDEN

Nr Guilsborough, Northampton, Northamptonshire NN6 8RQ
Tel: 01604 740219, Fax: 01604 740838 (Mr & Mrs I Pasley-Tyler)

Traditional old English garden set in Northamptonshire countryside, with yew and holly hedges, extensive herbaceous borders, rose garden, water garden, herb garden, woodland garden, famous bluebell wood (early May) and wild fowl collection. Recently featured in Channel 4's Garden Party and Country Living. **Location:** 10 miles N of Northampton and 11 miles SE of Rugby. Follow tourist signs on A428 and A5119. **Station(s):** Northampton, Long Buckby. **Open:** 1 Apr–4 Oct daily Weds-Sun and Bank Hol Mons 12–5.30pm. **Admission:** Adults £3, Senior Citizens £2.50, Children £1.50. **Refreshments:** Restaurant serving home-made lunches and teas. **Events/Exhibitions:** Spring and Autumn Plant Sale. Unusual plants propagated from the garden for sale during season.

map 4 / D1

HADDONSTONE SHOW GARDEN

The Forge House, Church Lane, East Haddon, Northampton, NN6 8DB
Tel: 01604 770711 Fax: 01604 770027 (Haddonstone Limited)

See Haddonstone's classic garden ornaments in the beautiful setting of the walled manor gardens – including urns, troughs, fountains, statuary, bird baths, sundials and balustrading. Featured on BBC Gardeners' World, the garden is on different levels with shrub roses, ground cover plants, conifers, clematis and climbers. As part of Haddonstone's Silver Jubilee Celebrations, the garden was substantially expanded to allow a temple and pavilion to be displayed. **Location:** 7 miles NW of Northampton off A428. **Open:** Mon–Fri 9–5.30pm closed weekends, Bank Hols and Christmas period. **Admission:** Free. Groups must apply in writing for permission to visit.

map 4 / D1

KELMARSH HALL

Kelmarsh, Northampton, Northants NN6 9LU
Tel & Fax: 01604 686543 (Kelmarsh Hall Estate Preservation Trust)

1732 Palladian house by Gibbs. Chinese Room with wallpaper from 1740s. Entrance lodges by Wyatt. Interesting gardens with lake and woodland walks. Herd of British White Cattle. **Location:** 12 miles N of Northampton; 5 miles S of Market Harborough on A508/A14 (J2). **Open:** Suns and Bank Hols between 12 April and 31 August 2.30–5pm. **Admission:** Adults £3.50, OAPs £3, children/garden only £2. Group bookings by arrangement. **Refreshments:** Home-made teas. Private functions, wedding receptions.

map 4 / D1

⌂ HOLDENBY HOUSE GARDENS & FALCONRY CENTRE

Holdenby, Northampton, Northants NN6 8DJ
Tel: 01604 770074 Fax: 01604 770962 (Mr & Mrs James Lowther. Administrator: Sarah Maughan)

Situated just two miles across the fields from Althorp, few places have played such a pivotal role in our history as Holdenby House. Built by Queen Elizabeth's Chancellor as a place in which to entertain the Queen, it became by an ironic twist of fate first the Palace and then the prison of her successor, Charles I, after his defeat in the Civil War. Today, Holdenby, though no longer the largest House in England, provides a splendid backdrop to beautiful grounds, with many features designed to evoke Holdenby's historic past. There is a Falconry Centre, where you can see this traditionally royal pursuit demonstrated and even try it yourself. Rosemary Verey's Elizabethan Garden is a reconstruction in small scale of Sir Christopher Hatton's magnificent garden while Rupert Golby has recently replanted the Fragrant Border.

There is a full working Armoury, where suits of armour are still made using traditional methods, a 'bodgers' stall, as well as makers of historic costumes and pine furniture. Our 17th century Farmstead powerfully evokes the sights and smells of 17th century life. For the children there are lakeside train rides, a play area and children's farm. **Location:** 7 miles NW of Northampton, off A428 & A50. M1 exit 15a or 18. **Station:** Northampton. **Open:** Easter Sun–end Sept. Gardens and Falconry, daily (excluding Saturday) 2–6pm. Bank Hol Sun and Mon 1–6pm. House open 12 Apr, 25 May, 31 Aug or by appointment. **Admission:** Gardens & Falconry Centre: Adults £2.75, children £1.75. House, Garden & Falconry Centre: Adults £4, children £2. Refreshments, teas and shop.

map 4 D1

LAMPORT HALL & GARDENS

Lamport, Northamptonshire, NN6 9HD
Tel: 01604 686 272 Fax: 01604 686 224

Built for the Isham family. The South West front is a rare example of John Webb, pupil of Inigo Jones and was built in 1655 with wings added in 1732 and 1740. The Hall contains a wealth of outstanding books, paintings, furniture and china. Set in spacious wooded parkland with tranquil gardens including a remarkable rock garden. **Location:** 8 miles N of Northampton on A508. **Open:** Easter–4 Oct, Sun & Bank Hol Mons, 2.15–5.15pm. 24–25 Oct, 2.15–5.15pm. Last tour/admission 4.00pm. Aug, Mon-Sat one tour at 4.30pm. **Group Visits:** Welcome at anytime by prior arrangement. **Admission:** Adults £3.80, senior citizens £3.30, children £2. **Refreshments:** Home-made teas in the Victorian Dining Room. **Events:** Telephone for a free brochure. **Conferences:** Available for conferences/corporate hospitality.

 map 4 D1

THE MENAGERIE, HORTON

Horton, Northampton, NN7 2BX, Northamptonshire.
Tel: 01604 870 957 (The Executors of the late G. Jackson-Stops)

A garden of the 1990s, designed by the late Ian Kirby and surrounding a folly built by Thomas Wright of Durham for the 2nd Earl of Halifax, c.1754-1757. Spiral mount, hornbeam alleys, formal ponds with fountains and exotic and native bog gardens, thatched arbours in the classical and gothic styles. Plant sales. Teas. **Location:** 6 miles S of Northampton, 1 mile S of Horton, on B526. Turn left immediately after lay-by. **Open:** Apr–end Sept. Garden only, Thurs 10am–4pm, last Sun each month 2–6pm. House, Garden and Shell Grotto open to groups of 20 or more by appointment at other times. **Admission:** Garden: Adults £3, children £1.50.

 map 4 D1

SOUTHWICK HALL

(Christopher Capron)
Southwick, Peterborough, Northants PE8 5BL
Tel: 01832 274064 (W.J. Richardson)Manager

A family home since 1300, retaining medieval building dating from 1300, with Tudor rebuilding and 18th century additions. Exhibitions: Victorian and Edwardian life; collections of agricultural and carpentry tools, named bricks and local archeological finds and fossils. **Location:** 3 miles N of Oundle; 4 miles E of Bulwick. **Open:** Bank Holidays, 30 Mar–31, May 4–5, 25–26, Aug 24–25, and Wed May 7–Aug 27, 2–5pm. Parties at other times (Easter–Aug) by arrangement with the Manager. **Admission:** Adults £3, OAPs £2.50, children £1.50. **Refreshments:** Teas available.

 map 8 E7

THE PREBENDAL MANOR HOUSE

Nassington, Nr. Peterborough, Northamptonshire, PE8 0QG
Tel: 01780 782 575 (Mrs J. Baile)

Grade 1 listed and dating from the early 13th century the Prebendal Manor is the oldest house in Northamptonshire, steeped in history and still retaining many architectural features. Unique to the region are the 14th century re-created medieval gardens which include a rose arbour, herber, flowery mead, and medieval fish ponds. Also included are the 15th century dovecote and tithe barn museum. Home-made teas. Lunches to order. **Location:** 6 miles N of Oundle, 7 miles S of Stamford, 8 miles W of Peterborough. **Open:** May, June & Sept, Wed & Sun 2–5.30pm. July and Aug, Sun, Wed & Thurs, 2–6pm. All Bank Hol Mon, 2–5.30pm. Closed Christmas. **Admission:** Adults £3.50, children £1.00.

 map 8 E7

CANONS ASHBY HOUSE

Canons Ashby, Daventry NN11 3SD Tel: 01327 860044

Open: House: 11 April to 1 Nov: Sat to Wed incl. BH Mon (closed Good Fri) 1–5.30 or dusk if earlier. Last admission 5. Park, gardens & church: same days as house 12–5.30, access through garden. Events: details from Property Manager (s.a.e. please). **Admission:** £3.60; children £1.80; family ticket £8.90. Discount for parties; contact Property Manager. Donation box for church. Parking 200m; coaches and parties should pre-book in writing with the Property Manager.

THE GREAT HOUSES OF NORTHAMPTONSHIRE

Northamptonshire Chamber of Commerce, Training & Enterprise, Tourism & Conference Bureau, Royal Pavilion, Moulton Park, Northampton, NN3 6BJ. Tel: 01604 671 200 Fax: 01604 670 362

Private View: You are cordially invited to visit a selection of Northamptonshire's magnificent historic homes & gardens. This is a unique opportunity to enter apartments, rooms, galleries and other areas within these historic family residences not normally open to the public; to view furniture, paintings and other objets d'art–many of them prized possessions passed from generation to generation–and stroll through the gardens and parkland of great beauty. This exclusive privilege is brought to you by the Northamptonshire Tourism & Conference Bureau who have gained the kind permission of the families involved to gather interested people together to form appropriate groups to take part in guided tours on specific dates during 1998.

Group Travel Northamptonshire: For those organisers wishing to bring groups to visit the stately homes and attractions of the Rose of the Shires, Group Travel Northamptonshire offers a Free Central Booking Service to make life as easy as possible for planning your tour. One call to outline your initial requirements and we will provide detailed itineraries, suggestions for lunch & tea stops, information on Blue Badge Guides and negotiate rates at our local accommodation establishments. With our central location and superb communications network, your group will have the maximum time to explore the County of Spires and Squires.

For further details on Northamptonshire or to request a full pack of information, please contact the Northamptonshire Tourism & Conference Bureau.

Northumberland

Northumberland is steeped in the past; with its boundaries on two sides – the River Tweed and the Cheviot Hills separating it from Scotland, it was the scene of many fierce battles as armies came along the original route of today's A1.

Parts of Hadrian's Wall, built by the Roman emperor of that name still straddle the wild, undulating moorland. Romans would have difficulty in recognising some of the terrain today, modern man having planted large pine forests and built a huge artificial lake.

Northumberland has glorious scenery – The National Park is famous for its unspoilt rugged beauty, and its stark, dramatic coastline is spectacular. Viking invasions drove the monks from Holy Island (Lindisfarne). The Farne Islands are now a nature reserve for seals and seabirds. Villages with fascinating names cluster round ancient crosses, runic inscriptions still visible; water mills and old

Lindisfarnde Castle

smithies are reminders of past trades. But every century is represented – the Norman Churches, Saxon towers, Hexham Abbey, Alnwick Castle and the magnificent manor houses, still with topiary and knotted herb gardens, through to the traditional fishing quays and 19th century corn mills. Newcastle -Upon- Tyne, the county's metropolis, now in the county of Tyne and Wear) once a giant in the ship building industry and home of the first railway, has always been the hub of Northumberland's commerce and today its cultural activities span the arts.

BAMBURGH CASTLE

Bamburgh ME69 7DF
TEL: 01669 620314

Bamburgh Castle is the home of Lady Armstrong and her family. The earliest reference to Bamburgh shows the craggy citadel to have been a royal centre by AD 547. The public rooms contain many exhibits, including the collections of armoury on loan from HM Tower of London. Porcelain, china , jade, furniture from many periods, oils, water – colours and a host of interesting items are all contained within one of the most important buildings of Britain's national heritage. **Location:** 42m N of Newcastle–upon–Tyne. 6m E of Belford by B1342 from A1 at Belford. **Open:** April–October daily 11–5pm. Last entry 4.30pm. **Admission:** Charges apply.

map 11
H1

⊞BELSAY HALL, CASTLE & GARDENS

Northumberland
Tel: 01661 881636 (English Heritage)

Explore a ruined castle, manor house and neoclassical hall all set amidst 30 acres of magnificent landscaped grounds – a great and varied day out for all who visit. The beautiful honey-coloured stone from which the Belsay Hall is built came from its own quarries which have since become the unusual setting for one of the series of spectacular gardens, deservedly listed Grade I in the Register of Gardens. Enjoy the mix of formal and informal; rhododendrons, magnolias, ornate terraces and even a winter garden are among Belsay's special features. **Location:** In Belsay, 14m NW of Newcastle on A696. **Open:** 1 Apr-1 Nov daily 10am-6pm, (or dusk if earlier in Oct), 2 Nov-31 Mar daily 10am-4pm. (Closed 24-5 Dec). **Admission:** Adult: £3.60, Conc: £2.70, Child: £1.80 (15% discount for groups of 11 or more).

 map 11
G3

ALNWICK CASTLE

Alnwick, Northumberland NE66 1NQ
Tel: 01665 510777 Fax: 01665 510876 (His Grace the Duke of Northumberland)

Described by the Victorians as 'The Windsor of the North', Alnwick Castle is the home of the Duke of Northumberland whose family, the Percys, have lived here since 1309. This border stronghold has survived many battles, but now peacefully dominates the picturesque market town of Alnwick, overlooking landscape designed by Capability Brown. The stern, medieval exterior belies the treasure house within, furnished in palatial Renaissance style, with paintings by Titian, Van Dyck and Canaletto, fine furniture and a exquisite collection of Meissen china. Other attractions include the Regimental Museum of Royal Northumberland Fusiliers, museum of early British and Roman relics as well as the Museum of PercyTenantry volunteers, Coach House, Dungeon, Gun Terrace and Grounds, which offer peaceful walks and superb views over the surrounding countryside. Children's playground. Gift shop. **Location:** Just off the town centre on the northern side of Alnwick. **Station:** Alnmouth (5m) **Open:** Daily (except Fridays), Easter to end of September, 11am to 5pm (last admission 4.15pm). Open all Bank Holidays, including Good Friday. Address: Estate Office, Alnwick Castle, Alnwick, Northumberland NE66 1NQ. Free parking for cars and coaches. **Refreshments:** Tearoom serving home-made fare. **Events/Exhibitions:** For details, contact the Castle Administrator, Alnwick Castle, Alnwick, Northumberland, NE66 1NQ. Tel: 01665 510777. Mon-Fri and weekends during season only (01665 603942). Disabled please enquire.

map 11
H2

CHILLINGHAM CASTLE & GARDENS

Chillingham, Nr Alnwick NE66 5NJ
Tel: 01668 215359 Fax: 01668 215463 (Sir Humprey Wakefield BT)

This medieval family fortress remains home since the 1200's to the Earls Grey and their relations. Complete with jousting course, alarming dungeon and even a torture chamber, the castle displays many remarkable restoration techniques in action alongside antique furnishings, paintings, tapestries, arms and armour. Wrapped in the nation's history it occupied a strategic position as fortress during Northumberland's bloody border feuds, often besieged and at many times enjoying the patronage of royal visitors. The Italian ornamental garden, landscaped avenues and gate lodges were created by Sir Jeffrey Wyatville, fresh from his triumphs at Windsor Castle. The castle grounds command breathtaking views of the surrounding countryside. As you walk to the lake you will see, according to the season, drifts of snowdrops, daffodils or bluebells and an astonishing display of rhododendrons. **Location:** 12 miles N of Alnwick, signposted from A1 and A697. **Open:** Good Fri–Easter Mon & 1 May–30 Sept, 12–5pm. Open 7 days a week July & Aug. Closed Tue–May, Jun–Sept. **Admission:** Adults £3.90, OAPs £3.75. Children free when accompanied. Parties (10 +) £3.30. Coaches welcome. **Refreshments:** Tearoom within the castle. Restaurant facilities available to groups by prior arrangement. Events/Exhibitions: Musical and Theatrical events regularly planned. Fishing and clay pigeon shooting–by prior arrangement. **Accommodation:** Private family suites of rooms available at times within the castle. Coaching rooms available for let in original stable buildings. **Conferences:** Facilities with original theatre for presentations. Access for disabled may be difficult due to number of stairs.

map 11 G2

CHIPCHASE CASTLE & GARDENS

Wark on Tyne, Hexham, Northumberland
Tel: 01434 230203, Fax: 01434 230740 (Mrs P J Torday)

An imposing 17th and 18th century Castle with 14th century Pele Tower set in formal and informal gardens. A chapel stands in the park. One walled Garden is now a Nursery specialising in unusual perennials. **Location:** 2 miles S of Wark on the Barrasford Road **Open:** Castle: 1-28 June, daily 2-5pm. Tours by arrangement at other times. Gardens and Nursery: Easter-31 July, Thurs to Sun and Bank Hols 10-5. **Admission:** Castle £3, Gardens £1.50, Nursery Free.

map 11 G3

HOWICK HALL GARDENS

Alnwick NE66 3LB
Tel/Fax: 01665 577285 (Howick Trustees Ltd)

Extensive grounds including a natural woodland garden in addition to the formal gardens surrounding the Hall. **Location:** 6 m NE of Alnwick, nr Howick village. **Open:** Apr–Oct daily 1–6pm. **Admission:** Charges apply. Season tickets are available.

LINDISFARNE PRIORY

Holy Island, Berwick–upon–Tweed TD15 2RX
Tel: 01289 389200 (English Heritage)

The site of one of the most popular early centres of Christianity in Anglo–Saxon England. St Cuthbert converted pagan Northumbria and miracles occurring at his shrine established this 11th century priory as a major pilgrimage centre. The evocative ruins, with the decorated 'rainbow' arch curving dramatically across the nave of the church, are still the destination of pilgrims today. **Location:** On Holy Island, check tide times. **Open:** 1 April–1 Nov: daily, 10–6pm. 2 Nov–31 March: daily 10–4pm. **Admission:** £2.70, £2, £1.40.

MELDON PARK

Morpeth, NE61 3SW
Tel: 01670 772661 (M Cookson)

Isaac Cookson III purchased the Meldon land in 1832. John Dobson, the famous architect, was commissioned to build the house. The entrance is through an Ionic porch having two rows of columns to the front door. Once inside, there is an enormous staircase lit by an outstanding window facing the north. Between the two wars Edwin Lutyens was employed to enrich the Hall, which included mahogany balustrades and 18th century decorations. The garden has a wonderful collection of rhododendrons best seen in early June, an old fashioned Kitchen gardens and many greenhouses. **Location:** 7m west of Morpeth on the B6343. 5m north of Belsay. **Open:** Last week in May– end of 3rd week in June and August BH weekend. 2–5pm.

PRUDHOE CASTLE

Prudhoe NE42 6NA
Tel: 01661 833459 (English Heritage)

Set on a wooded hillside overlooking the River Tyne are the extensive remains of this 12th century castle including a gatehouse, curtain wall and keep. There is a small exhibition and video presentation. **Location:** In Prudhoe, on a minor road north from A695. **Open:** 1 April–1 Nov, daily, 10–6pm (or dusk if earlier in October) **Admission:** £1.70, £1.30, 90p.

SEATON DELAVAL HALL

Seaton Sluice, Whitley Bay, Northumberland NE26 4QR
Tel: 0191 237 3040, 0191 237 1493 (The Lord Hastings)

A splendid English Baroque house regarded by many as Sir John Vanbrugh's masterpiece. The playwright who turned so successfully to architecture began the house in 1718 for Admiral George Delaval. The wings, which are arcaded and pedimented, include the East Wing containing the magnificent stables. In the grounds are extensive and beautiful gardens. There is also a unique Norman church, a Coach House with an interesting collection of vehicles and a restored Ice House. **Open:** May, Bank Hol Suns and Mons. June, Weds and Suns, July & Aug Weds, Thurs, Suns and Bank Hols. **Admission:** £3, children £1, OAPs £2.50. **Refreshments:** Tearoom. Free car park.

map 11 H3

CHERRYBURN

Station Bank, Mickley, Nr Stocksfield NE43 7DB Tel: 01661 843276

Open: 2 April to 1 Nov: daily except Tues and Wed 1–5.30. Last admission 5. Events: First May BHol, May Day celebration with maypole dancing and children's entertainment; 28 June, Scottish country dancing; plant sales throughout summer season; engraving, bookbinding and printing demonstrations on most days; please send s.a.e to Administrator for details.

LINDISFARNE CASTLE

Holy Island, Berwick-upon-Tweed TD15 2SH Tel: 01289 389244

Open: 1 April to 29 Oct: daily except Fri (but open Good Fri) 1–5.30. Last admission 5. Castle may open at the earlier time of 11–5, tide and staff permitting; please tel. to check. Admission to garden only when gardener is in attendance (usually Fri but please check with Administrator before making a special journey).

CRAGSIDE HOUSE, GARDEN & GROUNDS

Rothbury, Morpeth NE65 7PX Tel: 01669 620150/620333

Open: House: 1 April to 1 Nov: daily except Mon but open BH Mon, 1–5.30. Last admission 4.45. Grounds: same days as house 10.30–7. Last admission 5. Also selected days in Nov & Dec. Events: for details please send s.a.e. to Property Manager

WALLINGTON

Cambo, Morpeth NE61 4AR Tel: 01670 774283

Open: House: 1 April to 30 Sept: daily except Tues 1–5.30. Last admission 5. 1 Oct to 1 Nov: daily except Tues 1–4.30. Last admission 4. Walled garden: 1 April to end Sept: daily 10–7; Oct: daily 10–6; Nov to March 1999: daily 10–4 (or dusk if earlier). Grounds: all year during daylight hours. Events: Easter egg hunt, open air-concerts, Family Fun Day, Shakespeare on the lawn; for details send s.a.e to House Manager. Wallington is available for weddings, corporate bookings and special events.

Nottinghamshire

The river Trent and its tributaries are the determining factors to the scenery of Nottinghamshire. The county is shaped like an elongated oval, through the eastern half of which the broad sleepy Trent flows without haste in a placid pastoral landscape- a county fertile in crops and fields of thousands of head of cattle.

Nottinghamshire is perhaps most famous for the traditions surrounding Robin Hood and Sherwood forest. Indeed the entire county was once swathed in this dense forest which is now confined to an area of some twenty miles. The tree alleged to have been frequented by Robin Hood and his merry men, still stands (albeit on crutches!) in Sherwood Forest Country Park. This part of the forest has survived almost untouched for centuries and it is easy to conjurer up images of this thirteenth century rogue astride his trustworthy stead.

To the South of Sherwood Forest lies the city of Nottingham, which once commanded a ford over the river. Famous for centuries for its lace and textiles, Nottingham today is a lively and thriving city where life congregates at Market Square or at the annual Goose Fair held each October. Nottingham also has one of the most successful of the new universities established after World War II.

Nottingham

HODSOCK PRIORY GARDENS

Blyth, nr Worksop
Tel: 01909 591204 Fx: 01909 591578 (Lady Buchanan)

We invite you to share the beauty and peace of a romantic traditional 5 acre private garden on the historic Doomsday site bounded by a dry moat and Grade 1 listed brick gatehouse C 1500. Sensational snowdrops and woodland walk. Massed daffodils, bluebell wood, fine trees , summer borders, roses and lilies. **Location:** Less than 2m from A1 at Blyth, off B6045 Blyth to Worksop road. **Open:** Please call for dates times and prices. **Refreshments:** Winter – Hot refreshments & light lunches daily. Summer – Teas in Priory conservatory, Suns – At farmhouse, weekdays. No dogs in garden or wood.

NEWARK TOWN HALL

Market Place, Newark, Nottinghamshire. Tel: 01636 640 100
Fax: 01636 640 967 (Newark Town Council)

One of the finest Georgian Town Halls in the country, the building has recently been refurbished in sympathy with John Carr's original concept. On display is the Town's collection of Civic Plate, silver dating generally from the 17th and 18th century, including the 'Newark Monteith' and the Newark 'Siege Pieces'. Other items of interest are some early historical records and various paintings including a collection by the artist Joseph Paul. **Location:** Market Place, Newark. Located on A1 and A46. **Station(s):** Newark Castle. Northgate (½ mile). **Open:** All year, Mon–Fri, 10–12noon & 2–4pm. Open at other times for groups by appointment. Closed: Sat, Sun, Bank Hol Mons & Tue following and Christmas week.

NORWOOD PARK

Norwood Park, Southwell, Nottinghamshire NG25 OPF
Tel/Fax: 01636 815649 (Sir John and Lady Starkey)

Norwood Park is a delightful Georgian hunting lodge, set in beautiful medieval oaked parkland, on the edge of the Minster town of Southwell. It lends itself perfectly to both business and social occasions, ranging from conferences, training sessions and corporate activity days to fairytale wedding receptions and themed dinner parties. This venue offers a good combination of facilities, excellent services and is easily accessible locality-wise.

PAPPLEWICK HALL

Nr. Nottingham, NG15 8FE, Nottinghamshire
Tel: 0115 963 3491 Fax: 0115 964 2767 (Dr R. Godwin-Austen)

Fine Adam house built 1784 with lovely plasterwork ceilings. Park and woodland garden, particularly known for its rhododendrons. **Location:** 6 miles N of Nottingham, off A69. 2 miles from Junction 27, M1. **Open:** By appointment only, all year. **Refreshments:** By arrangement. **Events/Exhibitions:** 3rd Sat in June – annual fête and maypole dancing. **Conferences:** Up to 30 people. **Admission:** £3.50.

map 8
D6

Oxfordshire

Oxfordshire will appeal to the lover of noble architecture. The churches stand out as the most consistently handsome of any county of England. The manor houses which represent every period of architecture, cry out to be discovered. And then there is Oxford – the city of dreaming spires which still maintain a medieval character.

Oxford's architectural beauty is best appreciated on foot. Some of the best examples of college architecture are to be found around Radcliffe Square and the Bodelian Library, crowned by its famous domed Baroque rotunda.

Oxford's college buildings are quite unique, and many of them have retained their original features over many centuries. Oxford is a wonderful place in which to spend a few relaxing hours. Once you have taken your fill of wondrous architecture, why not take a riverside walk, or, if the sun shines, go punting on the river.

Around Oxford, the Vale of the White Horse, White Horse Hill and Uffington are all worth visiting. Standing in the heart of the Vale, the village of Uffington provides a good vantage point, overlooking this great prehistoric horse.

Oxford Botanic Garden

AYNHOE PARK

Suite 10, Aynho, Banbury, Oxfordshire, OX17 3BQ
Tel: 01869 810 636 Fax: 01869 811 054
(Country Houses Association)

17th century mansion. Alteration by Soane. **Location:** Junction 10 M40, then 3 miles W on B4100. **Station(s):** Banbury (7.5 miles), Bichester (8 miles). **Open:** May–Sept, Wed & Thurs, 2–5pm. (Last entry 4.45pm). **Admission:** Adults £2.50, children £1. Free car park. No dogs admitted. Groups by arrangement.

 map 4 C2

BROUGHTON CASTLE

Banbury, Oxfordshire OX15 5EB
Tel: 01295 262624 (the Lord Saye and Sele)

The home of the family of Lord and Lady Saye & Sele for 600 years. Surrounded by a moat, it was built in 1300 and greatly enlarged in 1550. It contains fine panelling and fireplaces, splendid plaster ceilings and good period furniture. Civil War Parliamentarian connections. Beautiful walled gardens, with old roses, shrubs and herbaceous borders. **Location:** 2 miles W of Banbury on the B4035 Shipston-on-Stour Road. **Open:** Weds and Suns 18 May–14 Sept. Also Thurs in July and August. Bank Hol Suns and Mons (including Easter) 2–5pm. Groups welcome on any day and at any time during the year, by appointment. Telephone 01295 262624 or 01689 337126. **Admission:** Adult £3.90, Senior Citizens £3.40, Students £3.40, Children £2. Groups reduced rates. Tearoom and Shop.

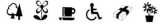 map 4 C2

DITCHLEY PARK

Enstone, Chipping Norton, Oxfordshire OX7 4ER
Tel: 01608 677346, Fax: 01608 677399 (Ditchley Foundation)

Third in size and date of the great 18th century houses of Oxfordshire, Ditchley is famous for its splendid interior decorations (William Kent and Henry Flitcroft). For three and a half centuries the home of the Lee family and their descendants - Ditchley was frequently visited at weekends by Sir Winston Churchill during World War II. It has now been restored, furnished and equipped as a conference centre devoted to the study of issues of concern to the people on both sides of the Atlantic. **Location:** 1 1/2 miles W of A44 at Kiddington; 2 miles from Charlbury (B4437). **Station(s):** Charlbury (2 miles) **Open:** Group visits by prior arrangement with the Bursar, Mon, Tues and Thurs afternoons only. Closed July-mid Sept. **Admission:** House opening fee £30. Entry fee £4 per person.

 map 4 C3

FAWLEY COURT

Henley-on-Thames, Oxon RG9 3AE
Tel: 01491 574917 Fax: 01491 411587 (Congregation of Marian Fathers)

Designed by Sir Christopher Wren, Fawley Court was built in 1684 for Colonel William Freeman as a family residence. The Mansion House, decorated by Grinling Gibbons and later by James Wyatt, is situated in a beautiful park designed by Lancelot 'Capability' Brown. The Museum consists of a library, various documents of the Polish kings, a very rare and well preserved collection of historical sabres and many memorable military objects of the Polish Army. **Location:** 1 m N of Henley-on-Thames via A4155 to Marlow. **Station(s):** Henley-on-Thames (1 1/2 m). **Open:** Mar–Oct Wed Thurs Sun 2–5pm closed Easter and Whitsuntide weeks. Nov and Feb open to groups by pre-booked appointment. **Admission:** Charges apply. **Refreshments:** Tea, coffee and home-made cakes available. Car park. No dogs.

BLENHEIM PALACE

Woodstock, OX20 1PX
Tel: 01993 811325 (24hrs information) Fax: 01993 813527 (His Grace the Duke of Marlborough)

Blenheim Palace, home of the 11th Duke of Marlborough and birthplace of Sir Winston Churchill, was built for John Churchill, 1st Duke of Marlborough in recognition of his great victory over the French at the Battle of Blenheim, 1704. The Palace, designed by Sir John Vanbrugh, is set in 2,100 acres of parkland landscaped by "Capability" Brown and is one of the finest examples of English Baroque. The collection comprises tapestries, paintings, sculpture and fine furniture set in magnificent gilded staterooms. The Gardens are renowned for their beauty and include the formal Water Terraces, Italian Garden, Rose Garden and Arboretum. In the Pleasure Gardens are the Butterfly House, Adventure Play Area, Cafeteria and a Shop, as well as the Marlborough Maze, the world's largest symbolic hedge maze.

An inclusive ticket covers the Palace Tour, Park, Gardens, Launch, Train, Nature Trail and car parking. Close to Oxford and next to the historic town of Woodstock, the Palace is easily accessible by car, train and coach. In 1998 events include Craft Fairs at the May Day and August Bank Holiday Weekends, Firework Concerts, and the Blenheim International Horse Trials (10–13 Sept). **Open:** 16 March – 1 Nov 10.30–5.30pm (last admission 4.45pm) Licensed Restaurant and self-service Cafeterias. **Conferences:** The Orangery and Spencer Churchill Rooms offer luxurious Conferences and Corporate Hospitality facilities overlooking the Italian Garden, throughout the year. **Education:** A Sandford Award holder since 1982. **Admission:** Please phone for details.

map 4
C3

KELMSCOTT MANOR

Kelmscott, Nr. Lechlade, Oxfordshire, GL7 3HJ.
Tel: 01367 252 486 Fax: 01367 253 754 (Society of Antiquaries)

Kelmscott Manor was the country home of William Morris – poet, craftsman and socialist – from 1871 until his death in 1896. It is the most evocative of all his houses and continues to delight with the charm of its architecture, the fascination of its contents and the charm of its garden, which has recently undergone extensive restoration and now contains many fine examples of plants and flowers which would have been an inspiration to Morris. **Location:** 2 miles SE of Lechlade, on the Lechlade/Faringdon Road. **Open:** Apr-Sept, Wed 11am–1pm, 2–5pm; the 3rd Sat in each month, 2-5pm; Thurs & Fri by appointment only. **Admission:** Adults £6, Children £3, Students £3. **Events/Exhibitions:** Centenary exhibition "William Morris at Kelmscott". Gift shop and bookshop.

map 4 B3

KINGSTON BAGPUIZE HOUSE

Nr Abingdon, Oxfordshire OX13 5AX
Tel: 01865 820259, Fax: 01865 821659 (Mr and Mrs Francis Grant)

Beautiful 1660's manor house remodelled in early 1700's in red brick with stone facings. Cantilevered staircase and finely proportioned panelled rooms. Set in mature parkland, the gardens contain a notable collection of plants including rare trees, shrubs, perennials and bulbs. Available for functions. **Location:** In Kingston Bagpuize village, S of A420/A415 intersection. Abingdon 5 miles, Oxford 9 miles. **Station(s):** Oxford or Didcot. **Open:** Mar 8 ; Apr 5, 11, 12, 13, 25, 26; May 2, 3, 4, 23, 24, 25; Jun 13, 14; Jul 15 ,18 , 19; Aug 5, 8, 9, 29, 30, 31; Sept 9, 12, 13, 23, 26, 27; Oct 11. 2.30–5.30pm. Garden: Last entry 5pm. House: Guided tours only, last tour 4.45pm. **Admission:** House & Garden: Adult £3.50, OAP £3, child £2.50. Garden only £1.50 (children under 5 not admitted to house but free to garden). Groups welcome by appointment. Wheelchairs garden only. No dogs. **Refreshments:** Home-made teas.

NUFFIELD PLACE

Huntercombe, Henley-on-Thames, Oxon RG9 5RY
Tel: 01491 641224 (Nuffield College/Friends of Nuffield Place)

Home from 1933–63 of William Morris, Lord Nuffield, car manufacturer and benefactor. A rare survival of a complete upper-middle class home of the 1930's, retaining majority of furniture and contents acquired on taking up residence. Fine quality rugs, clocks, tapestries and custom-made furniture. Four acre gardens, laid out around 1914 when house was built, contain mature trees, yew hedges, rose pergola, rockery and pond. **Location:** Approximately 7 miles Henley-on-Thames just off A4130 to Oxford. Coach service X39 Oxford/ Heathrow. **Open:** May–Sept every 2nd and 4th Sun 2–5pm. **Admission:** Adults £3, concession £2, children 50p. Garden only £1. Parties by arrangement. **Refreshments:** Home-made teas. Ground floor and gardens suitable for disabled. No disabled lavatory.

map 4 D4

MAPLEDURHAM HOUSE & WATERMILL

Nr. Reading, Oxfordshire, Tel: 01189 723 350, RG4 7TR
Fax: 01189 724 016 (The Mapledurham Trust)

Late 16th century Elizabethan home of the Blount family. Original plaster ceiling, great oak staircase, fine collection of paintings and private chapel in Strawberry Hill Gothic added in 1797. The 15th century Watermill is fully restored and producing flour and bran which are sold in the gift shop. **Location:** 4 miles NW of Reading on North bank of River Thames. Signposted from A40704. **Open:** Easter-end Sept, Sat–Sun & Bank Hols. Midweek parties by arrangement. **Admission:** Please phone for details. **Refreshments:** Tearooms serving cream teas. **Events/ Exhibitions:** By arrangement. **Conferences:** By arrangement. **Accommodation:** 11 self-catering holiday cottages. Wedding receptions by arrangement. Car parking and picnic area.

map 4 D4

MILTON MANOR HOUSE

Abingdon OX14 4EN
Tel: 01235 831871 Fax: 01235 831287 (A Mockler–Barrett)

Extraordinarily beautiful family house, traditionally designed by Inigo Jones, with a celebrated Gothick library and a beautiful Catholic chapel. The park has old fine trees, attractive walled garden, two lakes, stables, shire horse cart–rides, rare breed pigs, llamas and other animals. Woodland Wigwam walk. **Location:** Just off A34, village and house signposted. 3 miles from Abingdon and Didcot. **Open:** Daily 11–5pm. **Admission:** Charges apply.

UNIVERSITY OF OXFORD BOTANIC GARDEN

Rose Lane, Oxford, Oxfordshire
01865 276920 Fax: 01865 276920 (University of Oxford)

The University of Oxford Botanic Garden is the oldest botanic garden in Britain. For more than 375 years this Walled Garden, built before the English Civil War, has stood on the bank of the River Cherwell in the centre of Oxford. It has evolved from a seventeenth century collection of medical herbs to the most compact yet diverse collection of plants in the world. In addition to the botanical family beds there is a range of glasshouses including a Tropical Lily House, Palm House and Arid House. Outside the original Walled Garden there are herbaceous borders, a newly restored bog garden and a rock garden. **Open:** Open all year (Except Good Fri and Christmas Day). Apr–Sept 9–5pm. Oct–Mar 9–4.30pm. **Admission:** £2: Apr–Beg. Sept

map 4 C3

ROUSHAM HOUSE

Rousham, Steeple Aston, Oxfordshire OX6 3QX
Tel: 01869 347110 or 0860 360407 (C Cottrell-Dormer Esq.)

Rousham House was built by Sir Robert Dormer in 1635 and the shooting holes were put in the doors while it was a Royalist garrison in the Civil War. Sir Robert's successors were Masters of Ceremonies at Court during eight reigns and employed Court artists and architects to embellish Rousham. The house stands above the River Cherwell one mile from Hopcrofts Holt, near the road from Chipping Norton to Bicester. It contains 150 portraits and other pictures and much fine contemporary furniture. Rooms were decorated by William Kent (1738) and Roberts of Oxford (1765). The garden is Kent's only surviving landscape design with classic buildings, cascades, statues and vistas in thirty acres of hanging woods above the Cherwell. Wonderful herbaceous borders, pigeon house and small parterre. Fine herd of rare Long-Horn cattle in the park. Wear sensible shoes and bring a picnic and Rousham is yours for the day. **Location:** 12 miles N of Oxford; E of A4260; S of B4030. **Station:** Heyford (1 mile). **Open:** Apr–Sept inclusive Wed Sun & Bank Hols 2–4.30pm. Gardens Only every day all year 10–4.30pm. No children under 15. No dogs. Groups by arrangement on other days. **Admission:** House: Adults £3. Garden £3.

STONOR PARK

Nr Henley-on-Thames, Oxfordshire RG9 6HF
Tel: 01491 638587, Fax: 01491 638587 (Lord and Lady Camoys)

Ancient home of Lord and Lady Camoys and the Stonor family for over 800 years and centre of Catholicism throughout the Recusancy Period, with its own medieval Chapel where mass is still celebrated today. Sanctuary for St. Edmund Campion in 1581. An exhibition features his life and work. The house is of considerable architectural interest, built over many centuries from c.1190 and the site of prehistoric stone circle, now recreated within the grounds. A family home containing fine family portraits and rare items of furniture, paintings, drawings, tapestries, sculptures and bronzes from Britain, Europe and America. Peaceful hillside gardens with magnificent roses and ornamental ponds. Souvenir gift shop and afternoon tearoom serving home-made cakes. Parties welcome, lunches available by prior arrangement. **Location:** On B480; 5 miles N of Henley-on-Thames, 5 miles S of Watlington. **Station(s):** Henley-on-Thames. **Open:** April: Suns & Bank Hol Mons. May: Weds, Suns & Bank Hol Mons. June: Wed & Suns. July: Weds, Thurs & Suns. Aug: Weds Thurs, Suns & Bank Hol Mon & Sat 29th Aug. Sept: Weds & Suns. 2–5.30pm on each occasion, last admissions 5pm. Parties by prior arrangement in addition to the above times on Weds and Thurs mornings throughout the season and Weds & Thurs afternoons on those occasions the house is not open to the public. Min. number 12 persons on public days, 20 for private visits. **Admission:** House & Gardens: Adults £4.50, child (under 14 with adult) free. Adults (Group) £4 subject to group payment on arrival. Private tours £5 per person subject to group payment. Gardens only: Adults £2.50. **Refreshments:** Tearoom. Group lunches and suppers by arrangement.

🏛 STANTON HARCOURT MANOR

Stanton Harcourt
Tel: 01865 881928 (Mr Crispin & The Hon Mrs Gascoigne)

Unique medieval buildings in tranquil surroundings – Old Kitchen, (Alexander) Pope's Tower and Domestic Chapel. House maintained as family home, containing a fine collection of pictures, silver, furniture and porcelain. 12 acres of garden with great fish pond and stew ponds. **Location:** 9 m W of Oxford, 5 m SE of Witney; off B4449, between Eynsham & Standlake. **Open:** Please phone for details of 1998 opening times. **Admission:** Charges apply. **Contact:** The Hon Mrs Gascoigne, Tel: 01865 881928

⊞ WALLINGFORD CASTLE GARDENS

Castle Street, Wallingford, Oxfordshire.
Tel: 01491 835 373 Fax: 01491 826 550
(Wallingford Town Council)

These gardens are situated on part of the site of Wallingford Castle, which was built by William the Conqueror and demolished by Oliver Cromwell in 1652. The remains of St. Nicholas Priory are a feature of the Gardens, which is a haven of beauty and tranquillity and has a well-established wildlife area. **Location:** Bear Lane, Castle Street, Wallingford, Oxfordshire. **Open:** Apr–Oct, 10–6pm. Nov–Mar, 10–3pm. **Admission:** Free. **Events/Exhibitions:** Band concerts some Sundays in summer. Telephone for details. 'Britain in Bloom' winner 1993, 1996 and 1997. Car parking in the town. **Tourist Information Office:** 01491 826 972.

map 4
C4

⊞ MINSTER LOVELL

Witney
Tel:01179 750700 (English Heritage)

The ruins of Lord Lovell's 15th century manor house stands in a lovely setting on the banks of the River Windrush. **Location:** Adjacent to Minster Lovell church, ½ a mile north east of the village. 3 miles west of Witney. **Open:** At all times. **Admission:** Free.

⊞ RYECOTE CHAPEL

Rycote
Tel: 01844 339346 / 0117 9750700 (English Heritage)

A 15th century chapel with exquisitely carved and painted woodwork. It has many intriguing features, including two roofed pews and a musicians' gallery. **Location:** 3 miles south west of Thame, off A329. 1½ mile north east of M40 Jcn 7.

ASHDOWN HOUSE

Lambourn, Newbury RG16 7RE Tel: 01488 72584

Open: Hall, stairway, roof and grounds only: April to end Oct: Wed & Sat 2–5. Guided tours only; at 2.15, 3.15 & 4.15 from front door. Closed Easter weekend & every BHol. Last admission to house 4.15. Woodland: all year: Sat to Thur, dawn to dusk.

BUSCOT PARK

Faringdon SN7 8BU Tel: 01367 240786 Fax: 01367 241794

Open: House & grounds: 1 April to end Sept: Wed to Fri 2–6 (incl. Good Fri and also open Easter Sat & Sun). Also open every second & fourth Sat and immediately following Sun 2–6 (i.e. April 11 & 12, 25 & 26; May 9 & 10, 23 & 24; June 13 & 14, 27 & 28; July 11 & 12, 25 & 26; Aug 8 & 9, 22 & 23; Sept 12 & 13, 26 & 27). Timed entry to house may be imposed if crowding occurs. Last admission to house 5.30. Grounds only: 1 April to end Sept: open as house but also Mon (but not BH Mon) & Tues 2–6.

CHASTLETON HOUSE

Chastleton, Moreton-in-Marsh GL56 0SU Tel: 01608 674355

Open: 1 April to end Oct: Wed to Sat 12–4. Last admission 3.30 or dusk if earlier. Admission for all visitors (incl. NT members) by pre-booked timed ticket only; bookings can be made by letter (do not include payment) to the ticket office or tel. 01608 674284, Mon to Fri 2–5 from 3 Feb 1998.

GREYS COURT

Rotherfield Greys, Henley-on-Thames RG9 4PG Tel: 01491 628529

Open: House (part of ground floor only): 1 April to end Sept: Mon, Wed & Fri 2–6. (closed Good Fri). Garden: daily except Thur & Sun 2–6 (closed Good Fri). Last admission 5.30. Events: for details please send s.a.e. to the Box Office, PO Box 180, High Wycombe, Bucks HP14 4XT. **Admission:** House & garden £4.40; family ticket £11. Garden only £3.20; family ticket £8. Parking 220m.

WATERPERRY GARDENS

Nr Wheatley, Oxfordshire OX33 1JZ
Tel: 01844 339226/254 Fax:01844 339883

The peaceful gardens at Waterperry feature a magnificent herbaceous border, shrub and heather borders, alpine and rock gardens, a formal garden and a new rose garden. Together with stately trees, a river to walk by and a quiet Saxon Church to visit – all set in 83 acres of unspoilt Oxfordshire. The long established herbaceous and alpine nurseries provide year round interest. For the experienced gardener, the novice, or those who have no garden of their own, here is a chance to share, enjoy and admire the order and beauty of careful cultivation. Garden Shop and Plant Centre with exceptionally wide range of plants, shrubs etc produced in the nurseries for sale. Main agents for Haddonstone, Pots and Pithoi and Whichford Pottery. The Pear Tree Teashop provides a delicious selection of freshly prepared food made on the premises. Serving hot and cold light lunches, morning coffee, cream teas etc. Wine licence. The Art in Action Gallery, exhibits and sells quality ceramics, wood, glass, paintings, jewellery, textiles, etchings and engravings. **Location:** 9 miles from Oxford, 50 miles from London, 42 miles from Birmingham, M40 Junction 8. Well signposted locally with Tourist Board symbol. **Station(s):** Oxford & Thame Parkway. **Open:** Gardens & Shop: Apr–Oct 9–5.30pm, Nov–Mar 9–5pm. Pear Tree Teashop: Apr–Oct 10–5pm, Nov–Mar 10–4pm. Art in Action Gallery: Apr–Oct 9–5pm, Nov–Mar 9–4.30pm. **Admission:** Apr–Oct 9–5pm, Nov–Mar 9–4.30pm. Open daily except Christmas and New Year Holidays. Open only to Art in Action visitors (enquiries 0171 381 3192) 16–19 July. The Pear Tree Teashop will close from 15 July–20 July incl. **Admission:** Apr–Oct Adults £3, Senior Citizens £2.50, Parties (20+) £2.50. Nov–Mar £1.25 all categories. Coaches by appointment only.

map 4
D3

Shropshire

This county is a hidden treasure, a real gem for visitors although it remains off the main tourist routes. The popularity of Ellis Peter's televised Brother Cadfael stories – Shropshire based tales of medieval monastic sleuthing – has encouraged fans to visit the county, and Shrewsbury in particular.

The hills and mountains to the west separate Shropshire and Wales. The north of the county is home to seven beautiful lakes, which are wonderful for walking and a home to a large number of birds.

Shrewsbury, sits in a large loop of the River Severn. This made an excellent defence system during the frontier battles between England and Wales. Within the town is a

Left: Cardington Mill Valley. Above: Old Market Hall, Shrewsbury

wealth of medieval buildings and monuments. There are many timber framed buildings, narrow streets and a beautiful old market square. East of Shrewsbury the Romans built a garrison in AD60 which has developed into Wroxeter.

Ludlow retains a huge amount of geological interest, with many fossils having been found around there, that are now on display in the museum. The town is also home to lots of pretty little shops and half-timbered Tudor buildings.

ADCOTE SCHOOL

Little Ness, Nr Shrewsbury, Shropshire SY4 2JY
Tel: 01939 260202, Fax: 01939 261300
(Adcote School Educational Trust Ltd)

'Adcote is the most controlled, coherent and masterly of the big country houses designed by Norman Shaw' (Mark Girouard, "Country Life" Oct 1970). Adcote stands in 27 acres of parkland. The Main House, a Grade 1 Listed Building, was built in 1879 to a Tudor design. It contains William Morris windows and De Morgan tiles. Adcote participates in the National Garden Scheme with beautiful landscape gardens, a small lake and fine specimen trees. **Location:** 7 miles NW of Shrewsbury off A5. **Open:** 30 Mar–3 April, 13 July–28 Aug. Please ring Bursar on 01939 261392. All other times by appointment. **Admission:** Free but Governors reserve right to make a charge. **Refreshments:** For large parties by prior booking only.

map 6
E2

⊞ BOSCOBEL HOUSE & THE ROYAL OAK

Shifnal, Shropshire
Tel: 01902 850244 (English Heritage)

Discover the fascinating history of the fully restored and refurbished lodge and famous 'Royal Oak' tree where the future King Charles II hid from Cromwell's troops in 1651. The panelled rooms, secret hiding places and pretty gardens lend a truly romantic character. A fascinating guided tour and an award winning exhibition also cover the later additions to the site – a Victorian farmhouse, dairy, smithy and farmyard complete with resident ducks and geese. <u>Location:</u> On minor road between A41 and A5, 8m NW of Wolverhampton. <u>Open:</u> 1 Apr–1 Nov: daily, 10–6pm (or dusk if earlier in Oct), last admission 5.30pm. 2 Nov–31 Mar: Wed–Sun, 10am–4pm, last admission 3.30pm. House will be closed 24–26 Dec & 1–31 Jan. <u>Admission:</u> Adult: £3.95, Conc: £3, Child: £2. (15% discount for groups of 11 or more).

map 8
B7

BURFORD HOUSE GARDENS

Tenbury Wells, Worcestershire, WR15, 8HQ
Tel: 01584 810 777 Fax: 01584 810 673 (C. Chesshire)

Four-acre garden and early Georgian House in beautiful riverside setting. Home to National Clematis Collection, with over 200 varieties and 2,000 kinds of other plants, in serpentine borders of harmonised colour schemes, set around sweeping lawns along the banks of the River Teme. (Visitors should allow a minimum of 40 minutes in the Gardens). Also on site is Treasures Plant Centre/Nursery, specialising in Clematis – over 200 varieties; herbaceous shrubs, climbers; quality selection of plants, pots and tools at competitive prices; friendly practical advice; Burford House Gallery: exhibiting contemporary artists and one botanical art show annually; Abode Gift Shop: decorative and functional gifts, books, cards and stationery; Woodturning Centre; Burford Conservatories; Mulu Exotic Plants and Jungle Giants. **Location:** 8 miles from Ludlow, 1 mile west of Tenbury Wells on A456. **Open:** All year, 7 days a week, 10am – 5pm (evenings by arrangement). **Admission:** Adults £2.50, Children £1.00; Groups of 10+ £2.00 (booked in advance). Car Parking: Free parking for cars (approx. 120); coaches (approx. 10). **Refreshments:** Burford Buttery, serving home-cooked hot and cold dishes, cakes and pastries, teas and coffees. Seating 55 inside, 40 outside. Disabled toilet/baby changing facilities; 2 wheelchairs for loan on site. No access for dogs in Gardens. Dogs allowed on lead around Plant Centre. **E-mail:** treasures@ burford.co.uk

map 7
F1

THE DOROTHY CLIVE GARDEN

Willoughbridge, Market Drayton, Shropshire, TF9 4EU
Tel: 01630 647 237 (Willoughbridge Garden Trust)

The garden is known for its woodland plantings, established in a disused gravel quarry. A spectacular waterfall cascades between mature rhododendrons, azaleas and choice woodland plants. A south facing hillside garden provides views of surrounding countryside. A scree garden, water features and colourful summer borders are among the many delights. Location: A51, midway between Nantwich and Stone, 3 miles S of Bridgemere Garden World. **Open:** Garden only: 28 Mar–31 Oct, daily 10– 5.30pm. **Admission:** Adults £2.80, senior citizens £2.40, children up to 11 yrs free, 11–16 yrs £1. Free car park. **Refreshments:** Tearoom open daily. Beverages, home baking and light snacks.

map 8
A6

HAWKSTONE HALL & GARDENS

Marchamley, Shrewsbury, Shropshire, SY4 5LG
Tel: 01630 685 242 Fax: 01630 685 565 (The Redemptorists)

Grade I Georgian mansion and gardens set in spacious parkland. From 1556-1906, Hawkstone was the seat of the distinguished Hill family of Shropshire. The principal rooms include the Venetian Saloon, the Ballroom, the Refectory Gallery, the Billiard Room, the Drawing Room and the Winter Garden. The gardens, which have been fully restored over the past 8 years, comprise terraces and lawns, a rose garden, a lily pool and woodland with a magnificent collection of trees. **Location:** Entrance at Marchamley on A442, 2 miles N of Hodnet. **Open:** 5–31 Aug, 2–5pm. **Admission:** £2.50.

map 6
D1

HAWKSTONE HISTORIC PARK & FOLLIES

Weston-under-Redcastle, Shrewsbury, Shropshire, SY4 5UY
Tel: 01939 200 611 Fax: 01939 200 311 (Hawkstone Park Leisure Ltd.)

Few places in the world can claim to be truly unique. However, Hawkstone Park with its well hidden pathways, concealed grottoes, secret tunnels and magical collection of follies earns that right. It is an ideal day out for both the young and old. A giant theatre in landscape - it was originally one of the most visited landscapes in Britain and is the only Grade I landscape in Shropshire. Work to restore the Park to its former glory began in April 1991. After a 100 year closure, visitors are once more privileged to enter the Hawkstone Labyrinth. Folly buildings, it has been said 'indulge a natural urge to express eccentricity with the resources of wealth and imagination". It is a description which sits perfectly on the shoulders of the hills of Hawkstone. Sir Roland Hill started it all in the 18th century with his son Richard "The Great Hill", not only taking over but also increasing the tempo and arranged for some 15 miles of paths and some of the best collections of follies in the world to be constructed in the grounds of their ancestral home. At the turn of the 19th century the Hills could no longer accommodate the growing number of sightseers to the Hall. As a result an inn, now the Hawkstone Park Hotel, was opened and guided tours were organised. Hawkstone, according to one top writer, became "the inspiration for Longleat, Wombourne and other stately homes which attract visitors". Little has changed since then. The Park is full of attractions, surprises and features. You can, for example, tread the timeless stone steps, see the dramatic cliffs and rocks, towers, monuments, towers, tunnels, passageways, precipice rocks, paths, rustic sofas and romantic secret valleys. Deer have now been reintroduced into the Park after a 100 year absence. It takes about 3 hours to complete the whole tour of the Park. <u>Location:</u> 8 miles N of Shrewsbury, off A49. <u>Open:</u> 1 Apr–1 Nov, daily from 10am, and Sat & Sun Nov–28 Feb. <u>Admission:</u> Adults £4.50, child £2.50, senior citizen £3.50. Family £12. Additional charges apply on Bank Holidays and special events. Special reduced rates for coaches. Gift shop, tearoom and hotel & golf course adjacent. Please wear sensible shoes. Dogs admitted on leads.

map 6
D1

HODNET HALL GARDENS

Hodnet, Market Drayton, Shropshire, TF9 3NN
Tel: 01630 685 202 Fax: 01630 685 853
(Mr & the Hon. Mrs. A. Heber-Percy)

The 60 acres of Hodnet Hall Gardens are amongst the finest in the country. Forest trees, ornamental shrubs and flowers have been carefully planted to give interest and colour from early spring to late autumn. The walled Kitchen Garden continues to grow a wide range of flowers and produce and here, plants and vegetables can be purchased. Light lunches and afternoon teas are available in the 17th century half-timbered tearooms, which houses Big Game trophies. Adjacent is a gift shop. We welcome disabled visitors for whom large parts of the Gardens are accessible, especially if they are accompanied. **Location:** A53 (Shrewsbury–Market Drayton); A442 (Telford–Whitchurch): M6 exits 12 & 15: M54 exit 3. **Open:** 1 April–30 Sept. Tues–Sat (closed Mon) 12–5pm: Suns & Bank Hol. Mons 12–5.30pm. **Admission:** Adult £3, OAPs £2.50, Child £1.20. Special rates for parties.

map 6
D1

LUDLOW CASTLE

Castle Square, Ludlow, Shropshire
Tel: Custodian: 01584 873 947. Ticket Office: 01584 873 355 (Trustees of the Powis Castle Estate)

Originally a Norman Castle of which the remains include a round nave of a Chapel with fine Norman doorways. Then a fortified Royal Palace and headquarters of the Council of the Marches. An unusually complete range of medieval buildings still stands. Visitors can enjoy the large open space of the outer bailey, an audio tape guided tour and gift shop/gallery. The **Holodeck** hologram exhibition open daily. **Location:** Castle Square, Ludlow. **Station(s):** Ludlow. **Open:** 7 days a week except Christmas Day and weekdays in Jan. May–Sept 10–5pm. Rest of the year 10–4pm. **Castle Admission:** Adults £2.50, children £1.50, OAPs £2, family £7.50. Schools by arrangement. Discount available by contacting the Custodian. Holodeck Admission: Adults £1.50, children 50p. **Events/Exhibitions:** May – Craft Fair. June–July – Ludlow Festival. September – Food and Drink Fair.

map 7
F1

LUDFORD HOUSE

Ludlow, Shropshire, SY8 1PJ
Tel: 01584 872542 Fax: 01584 875662 (D. F. A. Nicholson)

A historic house, in part dating back to the 11th century, with later additions. Standing in 6 acres of well-maintained gardens and grounds. **Location:** ½ mile S of Ludlow, B4361. **Station(s):** Ludlow. **Open:** Spring & summer by written appointment only, with limited inspection of the interior. **Admission:** £3.00. **Refreshments:** Hotels and restaurants in Ludlow. Unsuitable for disabled.

  map 7 F1

ROWLEY'S HOUSE MUSEUM

Barker Street, Shrewsbury, Shropshire
Tel: 01743 361196 Fax: 01743 358411 (Shrewsbury and Atcham Borough Council)

Major regional museum displaying varied collections in timber-framed 16th century warehouse and adjoining 17th century brick mansion. Archaeology, including Roman Wroxeter; geology; costume; natural and local history; temporary exhibitions including contemporary arts and crafts. **Open:** Tue–Sat 10–5pm; Summer Suns and Bank Hol Mons 10–4pm. Closed Christmas/New Year period. **Admission:** Adults £3, concessions £1, children £1 (1998 prices).

SHIPTON HALL

Much Wenlock, Shropshire, TF13 6JZ.
Tel: 01746 785 225 Fax: 01746 785 125 (J. N. R. N. Bishop)

Delightful Elizabethan stone manor house c.1587 with Georgian additions. Interesting Rococo and Gothic plaster work by T. F. Pritchard. Stone walled garden, medieval dovecote and parish church dating from late Saxon period. Family home. **Location:** In Shipton, 6 miles SW of Much Wenlock near junction B4378 & B4368. **Station(s):** Craven Arms (10 miles), Telford (14 miles), Ludlow (14 miles). **Open:** Easter–end Sept, Thurs, Suns & Bank Hol Suns & Mons (except Christmas & New Year) 2.30–5.30pm. Also by appointment at all other times for parties of 20+. **Admission:** House & Garden: Adults £3, children £1.50, parties of 20+ less 10%. **Refreshments:** Teas/buffets by prior arrangement.

map 6 E1

SHREWSBURY CASTLE & SHROPSHIRE REGIMENTAL MUSEUM

Castle Street, Shrewsbury, Shropshire
Tel: 01743 358516 Fax:01743 358411

Norman castle with substantial alterations by Thomas Telford in the eighteenth century. The Great Hall now houses the collections of the Shropshire Regimental Museums plus graphic displays on the history of the castle. **Open:** Museum, Tue–Sat & summer Suns, 10–4.30pm. **Admission:** Adults £3, concs £1, children £1. Closed Dec–mid Jan. Free admission to the grounds Mon–Sat (and summer Suns).

STOKESAY CASTLE

Craven Arms, Salop
Tel: 01588 672544 (English Heritage)

A visit to Stokesay guarantees a day out to remember. Take a trip back in time with our free audio tour or relax in the charming 'cottage' style garden framed by the tranquil Welsh borders scenery. Historically the castle represents the country's finest example of a fortified manor house built in a style that owes more to fashion than to fortification. The solid walls and crenellated battlements form part of an ostentatious building programme begun by the wool merchant. Lawrence of Ludlow in 1281. The majority of features familiar to the original owner can still be seen including the Great Hall that once echoed to the sounds of feasts and banquets. **Location:** 7m NW of Ludlow off A49. **Open:** 1 April–1 Nov: daily, 10am–6pm (or dusk if earlier in Oct). 2 Nov–31 Mar: Wed–Sun, 10am–4pm. (Closed 24–26 Dec). **Admission:** Adult: £2.95, Conc: £2.20, Child: £1.50. (15% discount for groups of 11 or more).

map 7 F2

PREEN MANOR

Church Preen, Nr. Church Stretton
Tel: 01694 771 207 (Mr & Mrs P Trevor-Jones)

6 acre garden on site of Cluniac monastery and Norman Shaw mansion. Kitchen, chess, water and wild gardens. Fine trees in park and woodland walks. Featured in NGS video 1. Replanning still in progress. **Location:** Wenlock-Church Stretton road. **Open:** Please phone for details. Private visits of 15+ groups and coach parties by appointment, June & July only. **Admission:** Adults £2, Children 50p. **Refreshments:** Tea and home-made cakes available. (Oct – tea only). Not suitable for wheelchairs. Plants available for sale. No dogs except guide dogs.

WALCOT HALL

Lydbury North, Nr. Bishops Castle, SY7 8AZ, Shropshire.
Tel: 0171 581 2782 Fax 0171 589 0195 (C. R. W. Parish)

Built by Sir William Chambers for Lord Clive of India, this Georgian House possesses a free-standing ballroom; stable yard with clock towers; extensive walled garden and fine arboretum noted for its rhododendrons, azaleas and specimen trees. **Location:** 3 miles E of Bishops Castle, on B4385, half a mile outside Lydbury North. **Station(s):** Craven Arms. **Open:** Bank Hols, Sun & Mon (Except Christmas and New Year) 2.15–4.30pm. All other times by appointment. **Admission:** Adults £2.50, children (under 15) free. **Refreshments:** Powis Arms. Teas when available. **Accommodation:** All year holiday flats. Estate suitable for film and photographic locations, conferences etc.

map 7 F2

WESTON PARK

Weston-U-Lizard, Nr Shifnal, Shropshire
Tel: 01952 850207 Fax: 01952 850430 (Weston Park Foundation)

Nestled in 1,000 acres of "Capability" Brown Parkland and formal gardens this superb Stately Home, built in 1671 and designed by Lady Wilbraham, contains a magnificent collection of treasures, including work by Van Dyck, Lely and Gainsborough. The house has 28 historic bedrooms, available on an exclusive basis for conferences & private parties. An extensive event programme available during the summer, including a balloon festival, outdoor symphony firework concert and a game & country sports fair. The Parkland includes a deer park, woodland adventure playground, pets corner, and miniature railway. The Old Stables, now renovated into a tearoom and licensed bar, serves lunch and afternoon tea. **Location:** Situated on A5, 8 miles M6 Junction 12 and 3 miles M54 Junction 3. **Open:** Apr 11,12,13 & 14. Apr 15–Jun 14 weekends, Bank Hols & Whit Week (23–31 May). Jun 15–Jul 26 daily (except Mons & Fri & Sat Jul 18). Jul 27, Sept 6 daily (except Sat 15 & Sun 16 Aug). Sept 7–20 weekends only. Park 11–7pm last admission 5pm. House 1–5pm last admission 4.30pm. **Admission:** House, Park & Gardens £5, Adults, OAP's £3.75, children £3. Park & Gardens only £3.50. Adults OAP's £2.50. Adults OAP's £2.50, children £2. Group rates available. Dogs (on leads) welcome.

map 8
B7

BENTHALL HALL

Broseley TF12 5RX Tel: 01952 882159

Situated on a plateau above the gorge of the Severn, this 16th-century stone house has mullioned and transomed windows and a stunning interior with carved oak staircase, decorated plaster ceilings and oak panelling. There is an intimate and carefully restored plantsman's garden, old kitchen garden and interesting Restoration church. **Open:** 5 April to 30 Sept: Wed, Sun & BH Mon 1.30–5.30. Last admission 5. House and/or garden for parties at other times by arrangement: Tues & Wed am. Events: church services most Suns 3.15; visitors welcome. **Admission:** £3, children £1. Reduced rates for booked parties. Garden only £2. Parking 150m. Coaches by appointment. **Location:** 1ml NW of Broseley (B4375), 4ml NE of Much Wenlock, 1ml SW of Ironbridge [127: SJ658025] Bus: Midland Red 9 & 99 Telford/Wellington–Bridgnorth, alight Broseley, 1ml (pass close B Telford Central) (tel. 0345 056785) Station: Telford Central 7ml

DUDMASTON

Quatt, nr Bridgnorth WV15 6QN Tel: 01746 780866 Fax: 01746 780744

A late 17th-century house with intimate family rooms containing fine furniture and Dutch flower paintings, as well as interesting contemporary paintings and sculpture. The delightful gardens are a mass of colour in spring and include a walk in the Dingle, a wooded valley. There are also estate walks starting from Hampton Loade. **Open:** 1 April to 30 Sept: Wed & Sun only 2–5.30. Last admission 5. Special opening for pre-booked parties only, Thur 2–5.30. Events: please send s.a.e. to Administrator. **Admission:** House & garden £3.50, children £2; family ticket £8. Garden only £2.50. Parking 100m **Location:** 4ml SE of Bridgnorth on A442 [138: SO746887] Bus: Shropshire Bus 297 Bridgnorth–Kidderminster (passing close B Kidderminster) (tel. 0345 056785) Station: Hampton Loade (Severn Valley Rly) 1ml; Kidderminster 10ml

ATTINGHAM PARK

Shrewsbury SY4 4TP Tel: 01743 709203 Fax: 01743 709352

One of the jewels of the Midlands. An elegant mansion of the late 18th century, with magnificent Regency interiors and exceptional collections of silver, neo-classical furniture and paintings. The park was landscaped by Repton and there are attractive walks along the river. **Open:** House: 28 March to 1 Nov: Sat to Wed (and Good Fri)1.30–5; BH Mon 11–5. Last admission to house 4.30. Deer park & grounds: March to Oct: daily 8–9; Nov to Feb 1999 daily 8–5 (closed Christmas Day). Events: please send s.a.e. to Property Manager. **Admission:** House & park £4; family ticket £10. Park & grounds only £1.50. Pre-booked parties £3. **Location:** 4ml SE of Shrewsbury, on N side of B4380 in Atcham village [126: SJ550099] Bus: Williamsons 96, X96, Midland Red 81/2/4, 481 Shrewsbury–Telford/Wellington (all passing close B Shrewsbury & Telford Central (tel. 0345 056785) Station: Shrewsbury 5ml

Somerset

Glastonbury Tor

Bristol

caverns – notably Cheddar Gorge and Wookey Hole – while in the neighbouring Quantock Hills – where you cross clear streams and silently watch red deer graze, you enter the heartlands of Somerset. This is a region of verdant glens, thatched pubs and village greens.

The mood changes dramatically at Exmoor, a protected

With the county border changes, Somerset now includes Bath and the old county of Avon.

Somerset is an underrated county. There is more scenic variety in Somerset than in any other part of the West Country – impressive moorland, verdant hills, romantic coastal reaches, combes, woodlands and flats. This county also contains the birthplace of Christianity in this land – Glastonbury, a place of unrivalled mystique and legend.

Two other towns in Somerset – Taunton and Wells – dominate the county. Both are set in a time lock which tourists and developers thankfully fail to crack.

The nearby Mendip Hills are characterised by chasms and

wilderness which extends as far as the coast, where the cliffs and sea create a perfect setting.

Bath was transformed by the Romans. It was the first spa town in the 18th century. Today it remains ever popular.

THE BISHOP'S PALACE
Wells, Somerset, BA5 2PD
Tel: 01749 678 691 (The Church Commissioners)

The fortified and moated medieval palace unites the early 13th century first floor hall (known as The Henderson Rooms), the late 13th century Chapel and the now ruined Great Hall, also the 15th century wing which is today the private residence of the Bishop of Bath and Wells. The extensive grounds, where rise the springs that give Wells its name, are a beautiful setting for borders of herbaceous plants, roses, shrubs, mature trees and the Jubilee Arboretum. The Moat is home to a collection of waterfowl and swans. **Location:** City of Wells: enter from the Market Place through the Bishop's Eye or from the Cathedral Cloisters, over the Drawbridge. **Station(s):** Bath and Bristol. **Open:**

The Henderson Rooms, Bishop's Chapel and Grounds: Easter Sat – 31 Oct, Tues, Wed, Thur, Fri 11–6pm and Sun 2–6pm and daily in Aug, 10am-6pm. Also for exhibitions as advertised. As this is a private house, the Trustees reserve the right to alter these times on rare occasions. **Admission:** As advertised – guided and educational tours by arrangement with the Manager. **Refreshments:** A limited restaurant service is available in the Undercroft, unless prior bookings made. **Events/Exhibitions:** Wedding receptions. Open air theatre. **Conferences:** Conferences and special events by arrangement with the manager.

Somerset

⊞ JOHN BARSTAPLE ALMSHOUSE

Old Market St, Bristol, BS2 0EU
Tel: 01179 265 777 (Bristol Municipal Charities)

Victorian almshouse with garden courtyard. Location: Half a mile from Bristol city centre, on A4. **Station(s):** Bristol Temple Meads. **Open:** Garden & Exterior buildings only (now extensively renovated): Weekdays all year, 10am–1pm. By appointment only telephone 0117 9265777. **Admission:** Free. The almshouses are occupied mainly by elderly residents and their rights for privacy should be respected.

COMBE SYDENHAM COUNTRY PARK

Monksilver, Taunton, Somerset, TA4 4JG
Tel: 01984 656 284 Fax: 01984 656 273

Built in 1580 on the site of the monastic settlement, home of Elizabeth Sydenham, wife of Sir Francis Drake. Beautifully restored Courtroom and Cornmill. National Museum of Baking display. Elizabethan style gardens. Deer park. Play area. Woodland walks with the 'Alice' Trail and the 'Ancient' Trail of Trees. Fish farm – coarse fishing available. Picnic area. **Open:** Country Park Walks, Play area & Woods: Mar, Apr, May, June & Sept, Sun–Fri. July, Aug everyday. All other attractions open only by guided tour from May Spring Bank Hol-end Sept, Mon, Thur & Fri, 2pm. Evening tours of private rooms & supper by arrangement. **Admission:** Car park £2.00 per vehicle, refunded when guided tour taken. Adults £4.00, Children £2.00.

map 3 G3

CROWE HALL

Widcombe Hill, Bath, Somerset, BA2 6AR
Tel: 01225 310322 (John Barratt)

Elegant George V classical Bath villa, retaining grandiose mid-Victorian portico and great hall. Fine 18th century and Regency furniture: interesting old paintings and china. 10 acres of romantic gardens cascading down hillside. Terraces, Victorian grotto, ancient trees. **Location:** Approx. 1/4 mile on right up Widcombe Hill, 1 mile from Guildhall. **Open:** 22 March, 19 April, 10 & 24 May, 14 June, 12 July and groups by appointment. **Admission:** Adults £2, Children £1. **Refreshments:** Teas on opening days and by appointment. Dogs welcome.

map 3 V16

DODINGTON HALL

Nr. Nether Stowey, Bridgwater, Somerset, TA5 1PU
Tel: 01278 741 400
(Lady Gass, Occupiers Mr & Mrs P.Quinn)

Small Tudor manor house on the lower slopes of the Quantock Hills. Great hall with oak roof. Carved stone fireplace. Semi-formal garden with roses and shrubs. **Location:** 1/2 mile from A39, 11 miles from Bridgwater. 7 miles from Williton. **Open:** 5–6, 12–13, 19–20, 26–27 June, 4–5 July 2–5pm. **Admission:** Donations for charity. Parking for 15 cars. Regret unsuitable for disabled.

map 3 G3

EAST LAMBROOK MANOR GARDEN

South Petherton, Somerset Tel: 01460 240 328
Fax: 01460 242 344 (Mr & Mrs Andrew Norton)

This Grade I listed garden is one of the best loved in Britain. It was the home of the late Margery Fish. It is also the subject of many books, articles and television and radio programmes. The 17th century malthouse has been developed to provide modern facilities for visitors retaining its unique character. During the summer months there are exhibitions of paintings by local artists. The Margery Fish Plant Nursery offers an extensive range of plants propagated from the garden. The garden also contains the National Collection of Geraniums. **Location:** Off A303. 2 miles N of South Petherton. **Open:** 1 Mar–31 Oct, Mon–Sat, 10–5pm. **Admission:** Adults £2.50, Students/Children 50p, OAPs £2.

map 3 H4

FAIRFIELD

Stogursey, Bridgwater, Somerset
Tel: 01278 732251 Fax: 01278 732277 (Lady Gass)

Elizabethan House of medieval origin, undergoing extensive repairs. Woodland garden. Location: 11 miles W of Bridgwater, 8 miles E of Williton. From A39 Bridgwater/Minehead turn N; house 1 mile W of Stogursey. **Open:** House open in summer (when repairs allow) for groups by appointment only. Garden open for NGS and other charities on dates advertised in spring. **Admission:** Donations for charity. Disabled access. No dogs, except guide dogs.

map 3 G3

GAULDEN MANOR

Tolland, Lydeard St Lawrence, Nr Taunton, Somerset TA4 3PN
Tel: 01984 667213 (James Le Gendre Starkie)

Small historic red sandstone Manor House of great charm. A real home lived in and shown by the owners. Past seat of the Turberville family immortalised by Thomas Hardy. Great Hall has magnificent plaster ceiling and oak screen to room known as the chapel. Fine antique furniture and many hand embroideries worked by the wife of owner. Interesting grounds include rose gardens, bog garden with primulas and moisture loving plants, butterfly and herb garden. Visitors return year after year to enjoy this oasis of peace and quiet set amid superb countryside. **Location:** 9 miles NW of Taunton signposted from A358 and B3224. **Open:** May 24–Aug 30 on Thur, Sun & Summer Bank Hols, 2–5pm. Parties on other days by prior arrangement. **Admission:** Adults House and Garden £3.80. Garden only £1.80, children £1.80.

map 3 G3

142

HATCH COURT

Hatch Beauchamp, Taunton, Somerset, TA3 6AA
Tel: 01823 480 120 Fax: 01823 480 058 (Dr & Mrs Robin Odgers)

A most attractive and unusual Grade I listed Bath stone Palladian mansion, surrounded by extensive gardens, beautiful parkland with a herd of fallow deer and stunning views over the Somerset countryside. A much loved and lived-in family home, shown by present members of the family (youngest aged 10), containing fine furniture, paintings and a unique semicircular china room and a small private military museum. **Location:** 6 miles SE Taunton, off A358. **Open: House:** 11 June–12 Sept, Thur, 2.30–5.30pm. Home-made teas. **Garden:** 13 Apr–30 Sept daily 10am–5.30pm. Plant sales. **Admission:** House: £3.50, Groups £2.75. Garden: £2.50, Groups £2. Groups welcome anytime, by prior arrangement. **Refreshments:** Full catering available. **Conferences:** Functions, promotions, etc. Full facilities and experienced staff. Entire gardens – wheelchair accessible.

map 3
H4

MILTON LODGE GARDENS

Old Bristol Road, Wells, Somerset
Tel: 01749 672168 (Mr D C Tudway Quilter)

Grade II listed terraced garden dating from 1906, with outstanding views of Wells Cathedral and Vale of Avalon. Mixed borders, roses, fine trees. Separate 8 acre early XIX century arboretum. **Location:** 1/2m N of Wells. From A39 Bristol-Wells turn N up Old Bristol Road; free car park first gate on left. **Open:** Garden and arboretum only Easter–end Oct daily (except Sat) 2–6pm. Parties and coaches by prior arrangement. **Admission:** Adults £2, children (under 14) free. Open on certain Suns in aid of National Gardens Scheme. **Refreshments:** Teas available Suns and Bank Hols Apr-Sept. No dogs.

map 3
H3

HESTERCOMBE GARDENS

Hestercombe, Cheddon Fitzpaine, Taunton, Somerset TA2 8LG
Tel: 01823 413923 Fax: 01823 413747

Over three centuries of garden history are encompassed in Hestercombe's fifty acres of formal gardens and parkland near Cheddon Fitzpaine, Taunton. The unique Edwardian gardens, designed by Sir Edwin Lutyens and planted by Gertrude Jekyll, were completed in 1906. With terraces, pools and an orangery, they are the supreme example of their famous partnership. These gardens are now reunited with Hestercombe's secret Landscape Garden, which opened in Spring '97 for the first time in 125 years. Created by Coplestone Warre Bampfyide in 1750s, these Georgian pleasure grounds comprise forty acres of lakes, temples and delightful woodland walks. **Location:** 4m NE of Taunton off A361. **Open:** Daily 10–last admission 5pm. **Admission:** Adults £3.25, children (5–15) £1. Groups and coaches by prior arrangement only.

map 3
G3

MAUNSEL HOUSE

North Newton, Nr Bridgwater, Somerset TA7 O8U
Tel: 01278 663413 / 661076 (Sir Benjamin Slade)

Imposing 13th century manor house, partly built before the Norman Conquest but mostly built around a Great Hall erected in 1420. Geoffrey Chaucer wrote part of The Canterbury Tales whilst staying at the house. Maunsel House is the ancestral seat of the Slade family and is now the home of the 7th baronet, Sir Benjamin Slade. Wedding receptions, private and garden parties, conferences, functions, filming, fashion shows, archery, clay pigeon shooting, equestrian events. **Location:** OS Ref: ST302 303, Bridgwater 4m, Bristol 20 miles, Taunton 7 m, M5/J24, turn left North Petherton 2½ m SE of A38 at North Petherton. Gardens only 1 Apr–1 Oct (to include Easter). £3 (Honesty Box) Mons 2–5.30pm. **Open:** Coach and group parties welcomed by appointment. **Admission:** For further info tell: 0181 573 0005 (office hrs) or 0171 352 4573.

map 3
G3

NUMBER ONE, ROYAL CRESCENT

Bath, Avon.
Tel: 01225 428 126 Fax: 01225 481 850 (Bath Preservation Trust)

Number One was the first house built in the Royal Crescent in 1767 and is a fine example of John Wood the Younger's Palladian architecture. Visitors can see a grand town house of the late 18th century with authentic furniture, paintings and carpets. There is a study, dining room, lady's bedroom, drawing room, kitchen and museum shop. **Location:** Bath, upper town, close to the Assembly Rooms. **Open:** 10 Feb–25 Oct, Tue-Sun, 10.30–5pm. 27 Oct–29 Nov, Tue–Sun, 10.30–4pm. Last admission 30 mins before closing. Private tours out of hours if required by arrangement with the Administrator. Open Bank Hols and Bath Festival Mon. Closed Good Fri. **Admission:** Adults £3.80, children/students/OAPs £3, all groups £2.50, family ticket £8.

map 4
A4

KENTSFORD HOUSE
Washford, Watchet, Somerset.
(Mrs Wyndham)

House open only by written appointment with Mr R. Dibble. **Open:** Gardens Tues and Bank Hols. 10 Mar–31 Aug. **Admission:** Donations towards renovation of fabric.

ORCHARD WYNDHAM
Williton, Taunton, Somerset TA4 4HH
Tel: 01984 632309 Fax: 01984 633526 (Wyndham Est Office)

English Manor House. Family home for 700 years encapsulating continuous building and alteration from 14th to 20th centuries. **Location:** 1 mile from A39 at Williton. **Open:** House and Gardens Thurs, Fri and Bank Hol 31 Jul–31 Aug 2–5pm. Guided Tours only, last tour 4pm. Limited showing space within the house. To avoid disappointment please advance book places on tour by telephone or fax. House unsuitable for wheelchairs. Narrow road suitable for light vehicles only. **Admission:** Adults £4. Children under 12 £1.

map 3
G3

SHERBORNE GARDEN (PEAR TREE HOUSE)
Litton, Bath BA3 4PP
Tel: 01761 241220 (Mr & Mrs J Southwell)

4 acre garden of considerable horticultural interest. Collections of hollies (150), ferns (250), hostas, hemerocallis, rose species, giant and small grasses, all well labelled. Ponds and bridges, small pinetum, plantation with young collection of oak trees. T.V. Gardeners' World and Garden Club. Location: Litton, 7 miles N of Wells, Somerset, on B3114 off A39. 15 miles from Bath & Bristol. **Open:** Suns & Mons, Jun–Oct. Other times by appointment. **Admission:** £1.50. Children free. Tea/coffee available. Suitable for disabled. Dogs on leads. Parties by arrangement. Picnic area. Free car parking.

map 3
H3

BARRINGTON COURT
Barrington, nr Ilminster TA19 0NQ Tel: 01460 241938

Open: 1 April to 31 Oct: daily except Fri 11–5.30. Last admission 5. Coach parties by appointment only (tel. 01460 241938). Events: 12 April, Easter Egg Hunt; for details tel. 01985 843601. **Admission:** £4.20, children £2.10. Parties £3.70, children £1.90

BATH ASSEMBLY ROOMS
Bennett Street, Bath BA1 2QH Tel: 01225 477789 Fax: 01225 428184

Open: The Rooms are open to the public all year daily (Mon to Sat 10–5, Sun 11–5; closed 25 & 26 Dec), when not in use for pre-booked functions. Access is guaranteed during Aug, but otherwise visitors are advised to check in advance. Events: available for wedding functions; please tel. for details. **Admission:** No admission charge to Rooms; admission charge to Museum of Costume (incl. NT members)

BLAISE HAMLET
Henbury, near Bristol Tel: (Regional Office) 01985 843600

Open: 1 April to 30 Sept: Wed 2–5; also Thur 2 & 9 April, 17 & 24 Sept. Last admission 4.30. **Admission:** £2.60. No party reduction; organised parties by appointment with Secretary. Lodge gates are too narrow for coaches. No refreshments. No WC

COLERIDGE COTTAGE
35 Lime Street, Nether Stowey, Bridgwater TA5 1NQ Tel: 01278 732662

Open: Parlour and reading room only shown: 1 April to 1 Oct: Tues to Thur & Sun 2–5. In winter by written application to the Custodian. Parties please book. **Admission:** £1.70, children 80p. No reduction for parties which must book

DUNSTER CASTLE
Dunster, nr Minehead TA24 6SL Tel: 01643 821314

Open: Castle: 30 March to 30 Sept: daily except Thur & Fri (closed Good Fri) 11–5; also 3 Oct to 1 Nov: daily except Thur & Fri 11–4. Garden and park: Jan to March, Oct to Dec: daily 11–4 (closed 25 Dec); April to Sept 10–5 (open Good Fri). Last admission in all cases 30min before closing. Events: outdoor theatre and family activity days; ghost tours and Christmas activities; for full events programme tel. 01985 843601. **Admission:** Castle, garden & park: £5.20, children (under 16) £2.70; family ticket £13.40 (2 adults & up to 3 children). Pre-booked parties £4.60. Garden & park only £2.80, children (under 16) £1.30; family ticket £6.70. A 10min steep climb to castle from car park, but electrically powered vehicle available to give lifts when necessary. Car park in grounds

LYTES CARY MANOR
Nr Charlton Mackrell, Somerton TA11 7HU Tel: Regional Office 01985 843600

Open: 1 April to 31 Oct: Mon, Wed & Sat 2–6 or dusk if earlier; last admission 5.30. **Admission:** £4, children £2. No reduction for parties. Large coaches cannot pass the gate piers so must stop in narrow road, √ml walk. Coaches strictly by appointment only

MONTACUTE HOUSE
Montacute TA15 6XP Tel: 01935 823289

Open: House: 1 April to 1 Nov: daily except Tues 12–5.30. Last admission 5. Garden & park: 1 April to 1 Nov: daily except Tues 11–5.30 (dusk if earlier); also open 4 Nov to March 1999: Wed to Sun 11.30–4. Events: 19 June, open-air theatre; 11/12 July, horse trials; for further details of all events tel. 01985 843601. **Admission:** House, garden & park: £5.20, children £2.60; family ticket (2 adults & 2 children) £13. Pre-booked parties (15+) £4.80, children £2.30. Limited parking for coaches which must be booked in advance. Garden and park only, 1 April to 1 Nov: £2.90, children £1.30; from 4 Nov to March 1999: £1.50.

PRIOR PARK LANDSCAPE GARDEN
Ralph Allen Drive, Bath BA2 5AH Tel: 01225 833422

Open: Daily, except Tues 12–5.30 (or dusk if earlier). Closed 25/26 Dec & 1 Jan 1999. **Admission:** £3.80, children £1.90. To thank visitors for using public transport, all those who produce a valid bus or train ticket will receive £1 off admission; NT members will receive a £1 voucher (to be used towards the cost of a guidebook, cream tea or a purchase of £1 or more at the NT shops in either Bath centre or Dyrham Park). There is a bus and coach drop-off point outside the gates to the garden. Coach parties should book in advance on tel. 01225 833422; every passenger qualifies for a discount

Staffordshire

If there is a Cinderella of the shires with beauty undiscovered, it is Staffordshire. Large numbers of people still cherish an utterly wrong impression of the county because of its famous "potteries" and industrial towns. It contains some of Britain's fairest treasures.

The Dove flows beside a string of market towns and hamlets; gems of lovely unspoiled England. Picturesque Ellastone, which lies below the lofty limestone ridge of the Weaver Hills, was George Eliot's scene for 'Adam Bede' – high above is quaint Wooton with its great park.

The capital of North Staffordshire is the town of Stoke-on-Trent, immortalised in the work of Arnold Bennett. Some of the finest porcelain in the world originates from this area and there are plenty of museums devoted to the development of this craft. For those interested in more energetic pastimes, the theme park at Alton Towers lies just fifteen miles to the east.

Lichfield, the birth place of Dr Samuel Johnson, is famous for its distinctive, three-spired cathedral, built in the thirteenth century and housing some magnificent Belgian stained glass.

ANCIENT HIGH HOUSE

Greengate Street, Stafford, Staffordshire, ST16 2HS
Tel: 01785 223 181 (Stafford Borough Council)

The Ancient High House is the largest timber-framed townhouse in England. It was built in 1595 by the Dorrington family. Its most famous visitor was King Charles 1, who stayed here in 1642. Now a registered museum, the fascinating history of the house is described in a series of displays. The top floor contains the Museum of the Staffordshire Yeomanry. Stafford's Tourist Information Centre is on the ground floor. An attractive gift shop is on the first floor, adjacent to the temporary exhibition area. **Location:** Town centre. **Admission:** Free.

  map 8 B6

BARLASTON HALL

Barlaston, Staffs ST12 9AT
Fax: 01782 372391 (Mr and Mrs James Hall)

Barlaston Hall is a mid-eighteenth century palladian villa, attributed to the architect Sir Robert Taylor, extensively restored during the 1990s with the support of English Heritage. The four public rooms, open to visitors, contain some fine examples of eighteenth century plaster work. **Open:** By appointment to groups of 10–30. £3.50 per head including refreshments. If you wish to visit the hall, please write or fax giving details of your group including numbers, range or possible dates and a telephone contact.

DUNWOOD HALL

Longsdon, Nr Leek, Staffordshire ST9 9AR
Tel: 01538 385071

Dunwood Hall is a private lived-in country house on the Staffordshire, Cheshire, Derbyshire borders near the Peak District. It is a listed building, recorded in Pevsner and is an unspoiled example of the Victorian neo-Gothic period, both the interior and the exterior influenced by Pugin. The unique stone architecture, period décor, secluded gardens, plus the listed stables, all make a venue with authentic mid-Victorian ambience. Interested societies or groups are welcome by arrangement for private visits. Dunwood Hall is in Longsdon, 3 miles west of Leek on the A53 to Stoke-on-Trent. Accommodation available. Open all year.

 map 8 B5

CHILLINGTON HALL

Nr Wolverhampton, Staffordshire WV8 1RE
Tel: 01902 850236 (Mr & Mrs Peter Giffard)

Georgian house. Part 1724 (Francis Smith); part 1785 (Sir John Soane). Fine saloon. The lake in the park was created by 'Capability' Brown. The bridges by Brown and Paine and the Grecian and Roman Temples, together with the eye-catching Sham House, as well as many fine trees add great interest to the four mile walk around the lake. Dogs welcome in grounds if kept on lead. **Location:** 4 miles SW of A5 at Gailey; 2 miles Brewood. Best approach is from A449 (Jct 12, M6 Jct 2, M54) through Coven (no entry at Codsall Wood). **Open:** June–Sept 14 Thurs (also Suns in Aug) 2.30–5.30pm open Easter Sun & Suns preceding May and late Spring Bank Holidays 2.30–5.30pm. Parties of at least 15 other days by arrangement. **Admission:** Adults £3 (Grounds only £1.50) Children half-price.

  map 8 B7

FORD GREEN HALL

Ford Green Road, Smallthorne, Stoke-on-Trent, Staffordshire.
Tel: 01782 233 195 Fax: 01782 233 194
(Stoke-on-Trent City Council)

A timber-framed farmhouse built for the Ford family in 1624, with eighteenth century brick additions. The house is furnished according to inventories of the 17th and 18th century to give a flavour of the domestic life of the Ford family. Regular performances of Early Music and other events; guided tours available. **Location:** Smallthorne on B5051 Burslem-Endon Road. **Station(s):** Nearest Stoke-on-Trent. **Open:** Sunday–Thursday 1–5pm. Closed 25 Dec–1 Jan. **Admission:** Adult £1.50 Concessions £1.00. Group/Coach parties by appointment. **Refreshments:** Small tearoom. Events/Exhibitions: Wide variety of events held throughout the year. Small parties by prior arrangement.

IZAAK WALTON'S COTTAGE

Worston Lane, Shallowfield, Nr. Great Bridgeford,
Stafford, Staffordshire, ST15 0PA
Tel: 01785 760 278 (Stafford Borough Council)

Izaak Walton's Cottage was bequeathed to Stafford by this famous author of the 'Compleat Angler'. It is a delightful timber-framed, thatched cottage and registered museum. It has a series of angling displays showing how the equipment for this sport developed over the years. The events programme takes place each summer, both in the cottage and within its' beautiful garden. It has facilities for disabled visitors, although gravel paths can make access difficult. There are refreshment facilities. **Open:** Apr – Oct.

THE WOMBOURNE WODEHOUSE

Staffordshire, West Midlands
Tel: 01902 892202 (Mr & Mrs J. Phillips)

There was a house on this site in 1240. The present house dates from 1350. In 1708, Sam Hellier started work on the garden, putting in the main landscape features, including the lake and terracing the lawns. Succeeding generations have extended and altered the garden which today is an informal area of lawn, herbaceous borders, water garden with azaleas and rhododendrons leading to a woodland walk. Also an enormous Victorian walled garden with over 100 different varieties of tall bearded irises (not open on NGS days). **Location:** 4 miles S of Wolverhampton, just of A449 on A463 to Sedgley. **Open:** Please phone for details. Private visits welcome May–July, by appointment. **Admission:** Adults £2, Children free. **Refreshments:** Teas. Disabled access. Plants available for sale. No dogs except guide dogs.

SANDON HALL

Sandon, Stafford, Staffordshire
Tel: 01889 508004, Fax: 01889 508586 (The Earl of Harrowby)

Situated in the heart of Staffordshire and surrounded by 400 acres of parkland, this elegant neo-Jacobean house is a superb venue for a wide range of functions and for visits. Sandon Hall, ancestral home of the Earl of Harrowby, is steeped in history and contains many letters, clothes and furnishings of national importance which can be viewed in the museum. The 50 acre garden is landscaped and is especially beautiful in May/June, while the rolling parkland, laid out in the mid-18th century, is a visual delight throughout the seasons. **Location:** 5 miles NE of Stafford on A51, 10 mins from Jct 14, M6. **Open:** Throughout the year in booked groups only. **Admission:** Guided Tour £3.50 (concessions £3). Gardens £1.50 (concessions £1). **Refreshments:** Tea and cakes or Ploughman's Lunch – advance booking essential.

THE SHUGBOROUGH ESTATE

Milford, Nr. Stafford, ST17 0XB, Staffordshire.
Tel: 01889 881 388 (Staffordshire County Council)

Seat of the Earls of Lichfield. Architecture by James Stuart and Samuel Wyatt. Rococo plaster work by Vassalli. Extensive parkland with neo classical monuments. Beautiful formal garden with Edwardian terrace and rose garden. Working rare breeds farm with restored mill. County museum with Victorian working kitchens and laundry. **Location:** 6 miles E of Stafford on A513, entrance Milford Common. 10 mins from M6, Junction 13. **Station(s):** Stafford. **Open:** Daily 28 Mar–27 Sept, 11–5pm, Oct – Suns only. All year to booked parties. A superb range of tours and packages for schools and adult groups. For further information, please contact the Bookings Officer. **Admission:** Adults £3.50, concs £2.50. All-in-Ticket (House, farm & museum) Adults £8, concs £6. Site entry £1.50 per vehicle. **Conferences:** Facilities available. Please contact Mrs Anne Wood.

Staffordshire

STAFFORD CASTLE & VISITOR CENTRE

Newport Road, Stafford, Staffordshire, ST16 1DJ
Tel: 01785 257 698 (Stafford Borough Council)

Stafford Castle is the impressive site of a Norman motte and bailey fortress. A later stone castle was destroyed during the Civil War, after being defended by Lady Isabel Stafford. It was partly rebuilt in the early 19th century and although now a ruin, is an important example of Gothic Revival architecture. A series of trail boards tell the story of the site. The Visitor Centre displays artifacts from a series of archeological excavations. An audio-visual presentation narrated by Robert Hardy sets the scene. A collection of chain mail and other objects are fun to try on. A herb garden and attractive gift shop complete this interesting corner of Staffordshire. Picnic area, disabled access and guided tours available.

 map 8 B6

TAMWORTH CASTLE

The Holloway, Tamworth, Staffordshire B79 7LR
Tel: 01827 63563, Fax: 01827 56567 (Tamworth Borough Council)

A Norman motte and bailey shell-keep castle. The oldest parts date from the late 12th century. Period rooms cover 800 years. Popular features include the speaking 'Living Images' in the permanent Norman and 'Tamworth Story' exhibitions and in the Haunted Bedroom. **Location:** Town centre, in Castle Pleasure Grounds; 15 miles NE of Birmingham. **Station:** Tamworth. **Open:** All year Mon–Sat 10–5.30pm and Sun 2–5.30pm (last admission 4.30pm). Open Bank Hols, closed Christmas Eve, Christmas Day, Boxing Day. **Admission:** Adults £3.40, concs £1.75, family ticket £8.55. **Events:** Approx 12 special events are held annually. Many are on Bank Holidays. **Internet:** www.zipmail.co.uk/tbc

map 8 C7

WHITMORE HALL

Whitmore, Nr Newcastle-under-Lyme, Staffordshire ST5 5HW.
Tel: 01782 680478 Fax: 01782 680906 (Guy Cavenagh-Mainwaring Esq)

Attractive Carolinian House, owners' family home for over 900 years. Continuous family portraits dating back to 1624. Outstanding Tudor Stable block. **Location:** 4 miles from Newcastle-under-Lyme, on A53 to Market Drayton. **Open:** 1 May–31 August, Tues, Wed and Bank Hols inclusive 2–5.30pm. Last tour 5pm.

 map 8 A6

BIDDULPH GRANGE GARDEN

Biddulph Grange, Biddulph, Stoke-on-Trent ST8 7SD Tel: 01782 517999

Open: 1 April to 1 Nov: Wed to Fri 12–6, Sat, Sun & BH Mon 11–6 (closed Good Fri). Last admission 5.30 or dusk if earlier. Also open 7 Nov to 20 Dec: Sat & Sun 12–4 or dusk if earlier. Events: for details please send s.a.e. to Property Manager. **Admission:** 1 April to 1 Nov: £4; family ticket £10. Pre-booked parties £3 per person. Joint ticket with Little Moreton Hall £6; family ticket £15. 7 Nov to 20 Dec: Sat & Sun, £2; family £5. Free car park 50m. Coach party organisers must book in advance

ILAM PARK

Ilam, Ashbourne DE6 2AZ Tel: 01335 350245

Open: Grounds and Park: all year, daily. Hall is let to YHA and is not open. Note: small caravan site run by NT (basic facilities) open to Caravan Club/NT members; Easter to Oct (tel. 01335 350310). **Admission:** Free. Pay-and-display car park (NT members free)

MOSELEY OLD HALL

Moseley Old Hall Lane, Fordhouses, Wolverhampton Tel: 01902 782808

Open: 28 March to 13 Dec; March to May: Sat & Sun, BH Mon and following Tues (except Tues 5 May) 1.30–5.30 (BH Mon 11–5); June to Oct: Wed, Sat, Sun, BH Mon and following Tues; also Tues in July & Aug 1.30–5.30 (BH Mon 11–5); Nov & Dec: Sun 1.30–4.30 (guided tours only, last tour at 4). Pre-booked parties at other times incl. evening tours. Events: summer events and concerts; for programme please send s.a.e. to Property Manager. **Admission:** £3.60; family ticket £9

WALL ROMAN SITE (LETOCETUM BATHS & MUSEUM)

Watling Street, Wall, nr Lichfield WS14 0AW Tel: 01543 480768

Open: 1 April to 31 Oct: daily 10–6 or dusk if earlier (closed for lunch 1–2). Closed in winter. Events: send s.a.e. to property for details **Admission:** Museum & site £1.75, children 90p. OAPs and UB40 holders £1.30 (all prices provisional). Parties of 11 or more 15% discount. School bookings (tel. 01604 730325)

Suffolk

Those who delight in wide open spaces, blowing winds and delicate, shifting colour will find their paradise in Suffolk. There is a lyrical, quirky quality to the names of streets, villages and towns in Suffolk. The charmed villages and seaside towns of Orford, Somerleyton, Walberswick, Southwold and Aldeburgh remain resolutely unspoilt and almost Dickensian in appearance, despite their seasonal popularity. Aldeburgh wakes up for three weeks in June to play host to East Anglia's most compelling cultural gathering, the Aldeburgh Festival, and then promptly falls back to sleep again.

Southwold, lying in the middle of this aptly named " heritage coast" retains all the charm of a bygone age. There is an impression that the whole of East Anglia is a flat and unrelieved landscape, but in fact it is alive with undulating hills, completely gold with corn in the summer, interspersed with dark, dense copses of

Snape Maltings

trees and sprinkled all over of this, the large pink Suffolk farmhouses.

The county has suffered changing fortunes, but a testament to former immense wealth can be seen in the huge churches, which dwarf all that now surrounds them. The town of Dunwich used to have thirteen of these mini-cathedrals, but due to fierce erosion they, along with the entire town and its once great port, have been lost.... to the sea!

CHRISTCHURCH MANSION

Christchurch Park, Ipswich, Suffolk
Tel: 01473 253 246 Fax: 01473 281 274(Ipswich Borough Council)

A fine tudor house set in beautiful parkland. Period rooms furnished in styles from 16th to 19th centuries. Outstanding collections of china, clocks and furniture. Paintings by Gainsborough, Constable and other Suffolk artists. Attached, the Wolsey Art Gallery shows a lively temporary exhibition programme. **Location:** Christchurch Park, near centre of Ipswich. **Station(s):** Ispwich (1.25 miles). **Open:** All year, Tue-Sat, 10am-5pm (dusk in winter). Sun 2.30-4.30pm (dusk in winter). Also open Bank Hol Mons. Closed 24-26 Dec, 1-2 Jan & Good Fri. **Admission:** Free.

map 5
H2

EUSTON HALL

(Nr.Thetford), Suffolk
Tel: 01842 766366 (The Duke and Duchess of Grafton)

Euston Hall – Home of the Duke and Duchess of Grafton. The 18th century country house contains a famous collection of paintings including works by Stubbs, Van Dyck, Lely and Kneller. The pleasure grounds were laid out by John Evelyn and William Kent, lakes by Capability Brown. 17th century parish church in Wren style. Watermill, craft shop, picnic area. **Location:** A1088; 3 miles S Thetford. **Open:** June 4–Sept 24 Thurs only 2.30-5pm, also Sun June 28 and Sept 6, 2.30–5pm. **Admission:** Adults £3, Children 50p, OAPs £2.50. Parties of 12 or more £2.50 per head. **Refreshments:** Teas in Old Kitchen.

`map 5 H1`

GAINSBOROUGH'S HOUSE

46 Gainsborough Street, Sudbury, Suffolk CO10 6EU
Tel: 01787 372958, Fax: 01787 376991 (Gainsborough's House Society)

Gainsborough's house is the birthplace of Thomas Gainsborough RA (1727-88). The Georgian fronted town house, with an attractive walled garden, displays more of the artist's work than any other Gallery. The collection is shown together with 18th century furniture and memorabilia. Commitment to contemporary art is reflected in a varied programme of exhibitions throughout the year. These include fine art, craft, photography, print making, sculpture and highlights in particular the work of East Anglian artists. **Location:** 46 Gainsborough Street, Sudbury. **Station(s):** Sudbury (1/2 mile). **Open:** All year Tues-Sat 10-5, Sun 2-5pm. Closes 4pm 1 Nov-31 Mar. Closed Mondays, Good Friday and between Christmas and the New Year. **Admission:** Adults £2.80, OAP £2.20, Children and Students £1.50.

`map 5 G2`

HAUGHLEY PARK

Nr Stowmarket, Suffolk IP14 3JY
Tel: 01359 240205 (Mr & Mrs R J Williams)

Imposing red-brick Jacobean manor house of 1620, set in gardens, park and woodland. Unaltered three storey east front with five gables topped with crow steps and finials. North end rebuilt in Georgian style, 1820. Six acres of well tended gardens including walled kitchen garden. Nearby 17th century brick and timber barn restored as meeting rooms. Three woodland walks (1.5 to 2.5 miles) through old broadleaf and pine woodland with bluebells and lily of the valley (May) and rhododendron, azaleas, camellias (June). **Location:** 4 miles W of Stowmarket signed off A14 (Haughley Park, not Haughley). **Open:** Gardens: May–Sept, Tues and first two Sundays in May 2–5.30pm. House: by appointment (01359 240205) May–Sept, Tues 2–5.30pm. **Admission:** Adults £2, Children £1.

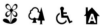

`map 5 H1`

HENGRAVE HALL CENTRE

Hengrave Hall, Bury St Edmunds, Suffolk
Tel: 01284 701561 Fax: 01284 702950 (Religious of the Assumption)

Hengrave Hall is a Tudor mansion of stone and brick built between 1525 and 1538. Former home to the Kytson and Gage families, it was visited by Elizabeth I on her Suffolk Progress. Set in 45 acres of cultivated grounds, the Hall is now run as a Conference and Retreat Centre by the Hengrave Community of Reconciliation. The ancient church with Saxon tower adjoins the Hall and continues to be used for daily prayer. **Location:** 3.5 miles NW of Bury St Edmunds on the A1101. Enquire: The Warden for: Tours (by appointment); Conference facilities (Day/ Residential); Retreats, Programme of Events; School's Programme.

`map 5 G1`

IPSWICH MUSEUM

Ipswich, Suffolk, IP1 3QH.
Tel: 01473 213 761 (Ipswich Borough Council)

Geology and natural history of Suffolk; Mankind galleries covering Africa, Asia, America and the Pacific. 'Romans in Suffolk' and 'Anglo-Saxons in Ipswich' exhibitions. Temporary exhibitions in attached gallery. **Location:** High Street in Ipswich town centre. **Station(s):** Ipswich. **Open:** Tue–Sat, 10am–5pm. Closed Dec 24, 25 & 26, Jan 1 & 2. Closed Bank Holidays. Temporary exhibition programme. **Admission:** Free.

`map 5 H2`

EAST BERGHOLT PLACE GARDEN

East Bergholt
Tel: 01206 299 224 (Mr & Mrs R. L. C. Eley)

15 acres of garden and arboretum, originally laid out at the beginning of the century by the present owner's great grandfather. A wonderful collection of fine trees and shrubs, many of which are rarely seen growing in East Anglia and originate from the famous plant hunter George Forrest. Particularly beautifully in the spring when the rhododendrons, magnolias and camellias, are in bloom. A specialist plant centre has been set up in the Victorian Walled Garden, **Location:** 2 miles E of A12, on B1070 Manningtree Road, on the edge of East Bergholt. **Open:** Mar–Sept, Tue–Sun & Bank Hols, 10–5pm. Also open on extra dates for the NGS. Please phone for details. **Admission:** Adults £2, Children free. **Refreshments:** Teas on NGS days and on other days by application. No dogs.

`map 5 H2`

KENTWELL HALL

Long Melford, Suffolk, CO10 9BA,
Tel:01787 310207. Fax: 01787 379318 (Mr and Mrs J.P.M. Phillips)

Kentwell Hall is a mellow redbrick Tudor Mansion surrounded by a broad Moat. A family home with a tranquil atmosphere, described by Country Life as "The epitome of many people's image of an Elizabethan house". The House is set amidst peaceful gardens, within parkland and pasture, a mile from the nearest road. The present Hall was started in about 1520 and substantially completed by about 1560. The exterior has changed little. Kentwell has been the home of Patrick and Judith Phillips and their children since 1971, when it was in a much neglected state. Since then, building works have proceeded almost without interruption. Each summer, Kentwell turns the clock back to the Tudor age. For the Great Annual Re-Creation, over 300 volunteers re-create, as authentically as possible, the domestic activities of a given year

during the sixteenth century at this great Tudor manor. The manor is peopled by members of the Clopton Family, their servants and retainers. Those taking part dress, talk and follow activities of the Tudor age and visitors feel they are meeting figures from the past. **Open:** House, Gardens and Farm open selected days from March to October – please call for days and times. Award–Winning Tudor Re-Creations – Bank Holiday weekends and other selected weekends. Great Annual Re-Creation mid June–mid July – please call for days and times. Kentwell Hall, Long Melford, Suffolk, CO10 9BA. Tel: 01787 310207. Fax: 01787 379318. **Location:** By road–off the A134, 4 miles north of Sudbury, 10 miles south of Bury St Edmunds. By rail–Stations Sudbury (4 m); Bury St Edmunds (10 m).

map 5 G2

OTLEY HALL

Otley, Nr Ipswich IP6 9PA, Tel: 01473 890264
Fax: 01473 890803 (Mr Nicholas & Mrs Ann Hagger)

A stunning medieval Moated Hall, grade I listed and a family home. Rich in history and architectural detail: ornately carved beams, superb linenfold and 16 C wall paintings. Home of the Gosnold family for 250 years from 1454. Bartholomew Gosnold voyaged to the New World in 1602 and named Cape Cod and Martha's Vineyard: he returned in 1606/7 to found the Jamestown settlement, the first English-speaking settlement in the US, 13 years before the Mayflower landed. Also linked to Shakespeare. The 10 acre gardens include a historically accurate medieval knot and herb garden. **Location:** 7 miles north of Ipswich, off the B1079. **Open:** Bank Hol Suns and Mons, 12.30–6pm; Gardens only Weds from 15 Apr–23 Sept, 2–5pm. **Admission:** Adult £4, child £2.50. Garden Days: Adult £2.50, child £1. Coach parties by appointment for private guided tours. Receptions and corporate entertaining.

map 5 H2

SOMERLEYTON HALL & GARDENS

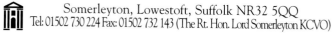

Somerleyton, Lowestoft, Suffolk NR32 5QQ
Tel: 01502 730 224 Fax: 01502 732 143 (The Rt. Hon. Lord Somerleyton KCVO)

Home of Lord and Lady Somerleyton, Somerleyton Hall is a splendid early Victorian mansion built in Anglo-Italian style with lavish architectural features, magnificent carved stonework and fine state rooms. Paintings by Landseer, Wright of Derby and Stanfield, wood carvings by Willcox of Warwick and Grinling Gibbons. The justly renowned 12 acre gardens feature an 1846 yew hedge maze, glasshouses by Paxton, fine statuary, pergola, walled garden, Vulliamy tower clock, magnificent specimen trees and beautiful borders. Also Loggia Tea Rooms and miniature railway. **Location:** 5 miles NW Lowestoft B1074. **Open:** Easter Sunday to end September, Thursdays, Sundays and Bank Holidays plus Tuesdays and Wednesdays during July and August. Gardens 12.30–5.30pm, Hall 1.30–5pm. Coach parties welcome, private tours and functions by arrangement.

map 9 K7

SHRUBLAND PARK GARDENS

Shrubland Park, Coddenham, Ipswich, Suffolk
Tel: 01473 830221 Fax: 01473 832202 (Lord De Saumarez)

The extensive formal garden of Shrubland Park is one of the finest examples of an Italianate garden in England. Much use is made of evergreens clipped into architectural shapes to complement the hard landscaping of the masonry. Pines, cedars, holly and holm oak soften this formal structure and add to the Italian flavour. Sir Charles Barry exploited the chalk escarpment overlooking the Gipping Valley to create one of his famous achievements, the magnificent 'Grand Descent' which links the Hall to the lower gardens through a series of terraces. **Location:** 6 miles north of Ipswich to the east of A14/A140 Beacon Hill junction. **Open:** Suns 2–5pm from 5 Apr–13 Sept inclusive, plus Bank Hol Mons. **Admission:** £2.50 adults, £1.50 children and seniors. Guided tours by arrangement. Toilet facilities but no refreshments. Limited suitability for wheelchairs.

map 5 H2

WINGFIELD OLD COLLEGE & GARDENS

Wingfield, Nr Stradbroke, Suffolk IP21 5RA
Tel: 01379 384888 Fax: 01379 384034 (Ian Chance Esq)

This delightful medieval house with walled gardens offers a unique Arts and Heritage experience. Like Charleston in Sussex, this is a house where art and life are inextricably mixed. Exhibitions of contemporary art plus permanent collections of textiles, ceramics and garden sculpture. Discover the exploits of history's colourful characters associated with it – the Black Prince – William de la Pole – and Mary Tudor. Spectacular Medieval Great Hall. Walled Gardens, Old Roses and Topiary. **Location:** Signposted off B1118 (Off the A140 Ipswich/Norwich trunk road) and the B1116 (Harleston–Fressingfield). **Open:** Easter Sat–end Sept Sats, Suns, Bank Hol Mons 2–6pm. **Admission:** Adults £2.80, Seniors £2.20, Children/Students £1, Family ticket £6.50. **Refreshments:** Cream teas and cakes.

map 5 H1

WYKEN HALL

Stanton, Bury St.Edmunds, Suffolk IP31 2DW
Tel: 01359 250287 Fax: 01359 252256

The garden, vineyard, country store and vineyard restaurant at Wyken are at the heart of an old Suffolk manor that dates back to Domesday. The garden, set among old flint walls and fine trees embraces herb and knot gardens, an old-fashioned rose garden, maze, nuttery and gazebo set in a wild garden with spring bulbs. The Leaping Hare Vineyard Restaurant in the 400 year old barn serves Wyken's award-winning wines and is the 1998 Good Food Guide's 'Vineyard Restaurant of the Year'. The Country Store offers a unique collection of textiles, pottery and baskets from the Suffolk Craft Society. A walk through ancient woodland leads to the vineyard.

map 5 H1

ICKWORTH HOUSE, PARK & GARDEN

Ickworth, The Rotunda, Horringer, Bury St Edmunds IP29 5QE

Tel: Property Office 01284 735270/735151

LAVENHAM: THE GUILDHALL OF CORPUS CHRISTI

Market Place, Lavenham, Sudbury CO10 9QZ Tel: 01787 247646

MELFORD HALL

Long Melford, Sudbury CO10 9AH Tel: 01787 880286

Surrey

A county of sandy heaths and spacious commons. Surrey commands wide views of the chequered Weald where oak and Elm thrive.

Leafy lanes, steep and twisted, are an attractive feature of Surrey towns. The town planners seem to have determinedly built roads around both natural resources and old buildings, giving each town an intricate cobweb of infrastructure and genuine charm.

Surrey's verdant beauty was appreciated amongst some of the most prestigious literary figures of the past. Jane Austen, Sheridan, Keats and EM Forster gained inspiration from this county. Explore the cobbled charm of Surrey's Georgian capital, Guildford, or the tiny streets of hidden villages, and you will feel equally as inspired.

River Wey, Guildford

ALBURY PARK

Albury, Guildford, Surrey, GU5 9BB.
Tel: 01483 202 964 Fax: 01483 205 013
(Country Houses Association)

Country mansion by Pugin. **Location:** 1.5 miles E of Albury, off A25 Guildford–Dorking Road. **Station(s):** Chilworth (2 miles), Gomshall (2 miles), Clandon (3 miles). **Bus Route:** Tillingbourne No. 25, Guildford–Cranleigh. **Open:** May–Sept, Wed & Thurs, 2–5pm. (Last entry 4.30pm). **Admission:** Adults £2.50, Children free. Free car park. No dogs admitted. Groups by arrangement.

map 4
E5

GREATHED MANOR

Dormansland, Lingfield, Surrey, RH7 6PA.
Tel: 01342 832 577 Fax: 01342 836 207
(Country Houses Association)

Victorian manor house. **Location:** 2.5 miles SE of Lingfield on B2028 Edenbridge road. Take Ford Manor road beside Plough Inn, Dormansland, for final one mile. **Station(s):** Dormans (1.5 miles), Lingfield (1.5 miles). **Bus Route:** No 429 to Plough Inn, Dormansland. Open: May–Sept, Wed & Thurs, 2–5pm. (Last entry 4.30pm). **Admission:** Adults £2.50, children free. Free car park. No dogs admitted. Groups by arrangement.

map 5
F5

CLANDON PARK

West Clandon, Guildford, Surrey, GU4 7RQ
Tel: 01483 222482 Fax: 01483 223479 (The National Trust)

An outstanding Palladian country house of dramatic contrasts; from the magnificent neo-classical marble hall to the Maori Meeting House in the garden; the opulent saloon to the old kitchen, complete with old range, below stairs. All this adds up to a fascinating insight into the different lifestyles of the ruling and serving classes in the 18th century. The house is rightly acclaimed for housing the famous Gubbay Collection of porcelain, furniture and needlework, as well as Onslow family pictures and furniture, the Mortlake tapestries and the Ivo Forde collection of Meissen Italian comedy figures. The garden has a grotto and parterre and there is a gift shop and licensed restaurant. **Location:** At West Clandon on the A247, 3 miles E of Guildford. B Rail Clandon 1 mile. **Open:** 1 Apr–29 Oct, Tue, Wed, Thur, Sun plus Bank Hols 11.30–4.30pm.

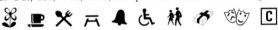

CLAREMONT

Claremont Drive, Esher, Surrey, KT10 9LY
Tel: 01372 467 841 Fax: 01372 471 109
(The Claremont Fan Court Foundation Limited)

Excellent example of Palladian style. Built in 1772 by 'Capability' Brown for Clive of India. Henry Holland and John Soane were responsible for the interior decoration. It is now a co-educational school run by Christian Scientists. **Location:** 1/2 mile SW of Esher on A307, Esher-Cobham Road. **Open:** Feb-Nov, first complete weekend (Sat-Sun) in each month (except first Sat in July), 2–5pm. Last tour 4.30 pm. **Admission:** Adults £3, Children/OAPs £2. Reduced rates for parties. Guided tours and souvenirs.

map 4
E5

GODDARDS

Abinger Common, Dorking, Surrey, RH5 6TH
Tel: The Landmark Trust: 01628 825920
(Leased to the Landmark Trust by the Lutyens Trust)

Built by Sir Edwin Lutyens in 1989–1900 and enlarged by him in 1910. Garden by Gertrude Jekyll. Managed and maintained by the Landmark Trust, which lets buildings for self-catering holidays. **Open:** By appointment only. Must be booked in advance, including parking, which is very limited. Visits booked for Wed afternoons from the Wed after Easter until last Wed of Oct between 2–6pm. **Admission:** Tickets £3, obtainable from Mrs Baker on 01306 730871, Mon–Fri, 9–6pm. Visitors will have access to part of the garden and house only. **Accommodation:** Available for up to 12 people for self-catering holidays. Tel: 01628 825925 for bookings. Full details of Goddards and 163 other historic buildings are featured in The Landmark Handbook (price £8.50 refundable against a booking) from The Landmark Trust, Shottesbrooke, Maidenhead, Berkshire, SL6 3SW.

map 4
E5

Surrey

CLAREMONT LANDSCAPE GARDEN

Portsmouth Road, Esher, Surrey
Tel: 01372 469421 (The National Trust)

One of the earliest surviving English landscape gardens, restored to its former glory. Features include a lake, island, grotto and extraordinary turf ampitheatre. Dogs: Not admitted Apr–October, admitted on leads Nov–Mar. Coach parties must pre-book. **Open:** All year, Nov–end Mar, Tue–Sun 10–5pm, or sunset if sooner. Apr–end Oct, Mon–Fri 10–6pm. Sat, Sun & Bank Hol Mons 10–7pm. Closed all day 25 Dec, 1 Jan, 14 Jul. Closed at 2pm 15–19 Jul. **Admission:** Adults £3, children £1.50, family ticket £8, pre-booked parties 15+ £2.50, pre-booked guided tours 15+ £1. Wheelchairs can be booked. Telephone for further details 01372 469421.

FARNHAM CASTLE

Farnham, Surrey GU7 0AG
Tel: 01252 721194, Fax: 01252 711283 (Church Commissioners)

Bishop's Palace built in Norman times by Henry of Blois, with Tudor and Jacobean additions. Formerly the seat of the Bishops of Winchester. Fine Great Hall re-modelled at the Restoration. Features include the Renaissance brickwork of Wayneflete's tower and the 17th century chapel. **Location:** 1/2 miles N of Town Centre on A287. **Station(s):** Farnham. **Open:** All year round, Weds 2–4pm; parties at other times by arrrangement. All visitors given guided tours. Centrally heated in winter. **Admission:** Adults £1.20, OAPs/children/students 60p, reductions for parties. **Conferences:** Please contact Conference Organiser. Centrally heated in winter. Not readily accessible by wheelchair.

GUILDFORD HOUSE GALLERY

155 High Street, Guildford, Surrey, GU1 3AJ
Tel: 01483 444740, Fax: 01483 444742 (Guildford Borough Council)

A restored 17th century town house with some original features including finely carved staircase, panelled rooms and decorative plaster ceilings. Throughout the year, selections from the Borough's Collection are displayed including pastel portraits by Guildford-born artist John Russell, RA (1745-1806), contemporary craft work, historical and modern paintings, drawings and prints. There is also a varied temporary exhibition programme including paintings of local and national importance, photography and craft work. Free exhibition and events leaflet available. **Location:** Central Guildford on High Street. Public car parks nearby off pedestrianised High Street. **Open:** Tues-Sat 10-4.45. **Admission:** Free. **Refreshments:** Old kitchen Tea-room. **Gallery Shop** with attractive selection of cards, craftwork and other publications.

HATCHLANDS PARK

East Clandon, Guildford, Surrey GU4 7RT
Tel: 01483 222482 Fax: 01483 223479

Built in 1758 for Admiral Boscawen and set in a beautiful Repton park offering a variety of park and woodland walks, Hatchlands contains splendid interiors by Robert Adam, his first commission in a country house in England, decorated in appropriately nautical style. It houses the Cobbe Collection, the world's largest group of early keyboard instruments associated with famous composers, e.g. Purcell, JC Bach, Mozart, Chopin, Mahler and Elgar. There is also a small garden by Gertrude Jekyll flowering from late May to early July, plus a gift shop and licensed restaurant. Audio Guide available in the House. **Location:** 5 miles E of Guildford, on A246 Guildford–Leatherhead Road. **Open:** 1 Apr–29 Oct, walks daily 11.30–6pm. House: Tue, Wed, Thur, Sun plus BH Mons and all Fris in Aug 2–5.30pm. Last admission half hour before closing. **Events:** 3–5 July 1998 Hatchlands Hat Trick Open Air Concerts Tel: 01372 451596.

153

LOSELEY PARK

Guildford, Surrey, GU3 1HS
Tel: 01483 304 440 Fax: 01483 302 036 (Mr & Mrs More-Molyneux)

Loseley is a home lived in by three generations and was built by a direct ancestor, Sir William More, over four hundred years ago. The House was originally built from stone brought from the ruins of Waverley Abbey. It is a fine example of Elizabethan architecture, dignified and beautiful, set amid magnificent parkland. Inside are many fine works of art, including panelling from Henry VIII's Nonsuch Palace. In 1993, the Walled Garden changed from being a Vegetable Garden to becoming a Formal Garden. It commenced with the planting of over 1,000 old-fashioned rose bushes, rich in both colour and scent. The following year the Herb Garden was started, illustrating the use of herbs for culinary, medicinal, dyeing and cosmetic purposes, as well as

ornamental. The third phase was the Flower Garden, which provides interest and colour throughout each season. New for 1998 will be the Fountain Garden. **Location:** 2.5 miles SW of Guildford. (Take B3000 off A3 through Compton). 1.5 miles N of Godalming (off A3100). **Station(s):** Farncombe (2 miles). Guildford (3 miles). **Admission:** House & Gardens: Adult £4.50, child £2.75, OAP/disabled £3.75. Gardens only: Adult £2.25, child £1.25, OAP/disabled £1.75. Trailer ride: Adult £2.75, child £1.25, OAP/disabled £2.25. Special group rates. **Refreshments:** Courtyard Tearoom open for light lunches and teas. **Conferences:** The Tithe Barn is available for weddings – conferences – company days, fun days and product launches-etc.

map 4
E5

PAINSHILL LANDSCAPE GARDEN

Portsmouth Road, Cobham, Surrey KT11 1JE
Tel: 01932 868113 Fax: 01932 868001 (Painshill Park Trust)

One of Europe's finest eighteenth century landscape gardens. Designed to surprise and mystify, leaving visitors spellbound at every turn. Walk around the huge lake. A Gothic temple, Chinese bridge, crystal grotto, Turkish tent, replanted shrubberies all disappear and reappear as the walk proceeds. **Location:** W of Cobham of A245; 200 miles E of A307 roundabout. Visitor entrance: Between Streets, Cobham. **Open:** April–Oct daily except Mon (open Bank Hols). 10.30–6.00 (last entry 4.30). Nov–Mar daily except Mon & Fri, Christmas Day & Boxing Day. 11–4pm dusk if earlier. **Admission:** Adults £3.80, concessions £3.30, children 5–16 £1.50. School groups must arrange with Education Trust 01932 886743, prices vary. Adult groups of 20+ £3 (**must pre-book phone 01932 868113**). No dogs please.

map 4
E5

RHS GARDEN WISLEY

Wisley, Woking, Surrey GU23 6QB
Tel: 01483 224234 (Royal Horticultural Society)

A world famous garden which extends to 240 acres and provides a unique chance to glean new ideas and inspiration. The Alpine Meadow, carpeted with wild daffodils in spring, Battleston Hill, brilliant with rhododendrons in early summer, the heathers and autumnal tints together with the glasshouses, trials and model gardens are all features for which the garden is renowned. But what makes Wisley unique is that it is not just beautiful to look at. As the showpiece of the Royal Horticultural Society, the Garden is a source of not only practical advice but also over 9,000 plants available in the Plant Centre. **Location:** Wisley is just off M25 Jct 10, on the A3. **Open:** Every day of the year (except Christmas Day) though please note, Sundays is for Members only. **Further Information phone 01482 224234.**

map 4
E5

MILLAIS RHODODENDRONS

Crosswater Farm, Crosswater Lane, Churt, Farnham, GU10 2JN
Tel: 01252 792698, Fax: 01252 792526 (The Millais Family)

Six acre woodland garden and specialist nursery growing over 650 varieties of rhododendrons and azaleas. The nursery grows a selection of the best hybrids from around the world and also rare species collected in the Himalayas and available for the first time. Mail order catalogue 5 x 2nd class stamps. The gardens feature a plantsman's collection of rhododendrons and azaleas, with ponds, a stream and companion plantings. Trial garden displays hundreds of new varieties. **Location:** From Churt, take A287 1/2 mile towards Farnham. Turn right into Jumps Road and after 1/2 mile left into Crosswater Lane. **Open:** Nursery: Mon–Fri 10–1, 2–5pm. Plus Saturdays in Spring and Autumn. Garden and nursery open daily in May. Teas available on National Gardens Scheme Charity Days 4 & 25 May '98.

WHITEHALL

1 Malden Road, Cheam SM3 8QD
Tel: 0181 643 1236 Fax: 0181 770 4666 (London Borough of Sutton)

A Tudor, timber–framed house c.1500 with later additions, in the heart of Cheam village conservation area. Twelve rooms open to view with displays on Nonsuch Palace, timber–framed buildings, Cheam pottery, Cheam school and William Gilpin. Changing exhibition programme and special events run throughout the year. There is an attractive rear garden featuring a medieval well from c.1400. **Location:** 2 miles south of A3 on A2043 just north of junction with A332. **Open:** All year around, please phone for dates and times. **Admission:** Charge.

TITSEY PLACE AND GARDENS

Titsey Hill, Oxted, Surrey RH8 0SD
Tel: 01273 475411 (The Trustees of the Titsey Foundation)

Stunning 17th century Mansion House. Situated outside Limpsfield, Surrey. Extensive formal and informal gardens containing Victorian Walled Garden, lakes, fountains and rose gardens. Outstanding features of this House include important paintings and object d'art. Home of the Gresham and Leveson Gower Family since the 15th century. **Location:** A25 Oxted to Westerham, at main traffic lights in Limpsfield turn left and then at the bottom of Limpsfield High Street on sharp bend, turn left in to Bluehouse Lane and then first right in to Water Lane. Under motorway and turn right in to Titsey Park. **Open:** Between 20 May–20 Sept on Weds and Suns. 1–5pm. Guided Tours of the House at 2pm, 3pm and 4pm. Private parties by prior arrangement. **Admission:** £4 House and Garden, £2 Garden Only. Contact: Kate Moisson.

POLESDEN LACEY

Great Bookham, nr Dorking RH5 6BD Tel: Infoline: 01372 458203

Open: House: 1 April to 1 Nov: daily except Mon & Tues 1.30–5.30; also open BH Mon (starting with Easter) 11–5.30; last admission to house 30min before closing. Grounds: daily all year: 11–6 (or dusk if earlier). Events: 20 June to 5 July open-air theatre: send s.a.e. for booking form to Theatre Box Office, P.O. Box 10, Dorking, Surrey RH5 6FH; tel. 01372 451596. 5 July, Polesden Fair; additional charge for all visitors, incl. NT members. Variety of winter events, please tel. for details. Estate includes a YHA hostel (tel. 01372 452528). **Admission:** Garden, grounds & landscape walks open all year round: £3; family ticket £7.50. House: £3 extra; family ticket £7.50 extra. Pre-booked groups £5. Parking 200m. Croquet lawn available; equipment for hire from the house. Picnics welcome outside formal garden

SHALFORD MILL

Shalford, nr Guildford GU4 8BS Tel: 01483 561617

Open: Daily 10–5. **Admission:** Free but donations in the box (emptied daily) most welcome. No parking at property. Children must be accompanied by an adult

WINKWORTH ARBORETUM

Hascombe Road, Godalming GU8 4AD Tel: 01483 208477

Open: All year: daily during daylight hours, but may be closed during bad weather (esp. high winds). **Admission:** £2.70; family ticket £6.75 (2 adults, 2 children, additional family member £1.25). No reduction for groups. Coach parties must book in writing with Head of Arboretum to ensure parking space

Sussex

Lewes

O f all the counties Sussex is the easiest to visualise. Sussex lies in four parallel strips – the northern boundary being forest, the next strip the clay Weald, then the smooth green line of the downs and lastly, the coastline of chalk-cliff and low lying plain-each sublime in its own way.

The scenery of East Sussex is dramatically beautiful. Inland, the rolling Downs provide a chalky background to the mysterious figure of the Long Man of Wilmington, and the River Cuckmere carves its way down towards the beach at Cuckmere Haven. On the coast lies Brighton which has been described as "London By The Sea" and is an intensely lively, vibrant place. Shades of Brighton's regency past are equally as apparent, seen most ostentatiously in Nash's oriental Royal Pavilion.

West Sussex plays host to the historic town of Chichester where four atmospheric bustling streets meet at a central sixteenth century market cross. Chichester's cathedral is also worth a visit and its majestic spire dominates the countryside around it.

Sussex, in the Season, hosts Glyndebourne and Goodwood. "Glorious Goodwood" as it is known, attracts thousands of race-goers who delight in a days racing at one of the most attractive racing venues in Britain. The vast stands are silhouetted against the South Downs skyline and can be seen for miles around.

ANNE OF CLEVES HOUSE

52 Southover High Street, Lewes, Sussex BN7 1JA
Tel: 01273 474 610 Fax: 01273 486 990 (Sussex Past)

This beautiful 16th century timber-framed Wealden hall-house contains wide-ranging collections of Sussex interest. Furnished rooms give an impression of life in the 17th and 18th centuries. Exhibits include artefacts from nearby Lewes Priory, Sussex pottery, Wealden ironwork and kitchen equipment. **Station(s):** Lewes (10 mins walk). **Bus route:** Adjacent. Bus station 15 mins walk away. **Open:** 1 Jan–24 Mar & 10 Nov–31 Dec, Tue, Thurs & Sat 10–5pm. 25 Mar–9 Nov, Mon–Sat, 10–5.30pm; Sun 12noon–5.30pm. **Admission:** Adults £2.20, children £1.10. Family (2+2) £6; combined ticket with Lewes Castle available. 50% discount to EH members. No dogs. **Email:** sussexpast@pavilion.co.uk

map 5
F6

APULDRAM ROSES

Apuldram Lane, Dell Quay, Chichester, West Sussex
Tel: 01243 785 769 Fax: 01243 536 973 (Mrs D. R. Sawday)

Specialist Rose Nursery growing over 300 varieties of Hybrid Teas, Floribundas, Climbers, Ramblers, Ground Cover, Miniature and Patio Roses. Also a large selection of shrub roses, both old and new. Mature Rose Garden to view. Field open during summer months. Suitable for disabled, but no special toilet. **Location:** 1 mile SW of Chichester. A286 Birdham–Wittering Road from Chichester. Turn right into Dell Quay Road and then right again into Apuldram Lane. **Open:** 8 Jan–22 Dec, daily. Mon–Sat, 9am–5pm. Sun & Bank Hols, 10.30am–4.30pm. Parties can be taken around by prior arrangement with guided tour of roses, June–Sept. **Refreshments:** Ice creams. **Events/Exhibitions:** Open evenings, 25 June & 1 July. Ample car parking.

map 4
D6

BAYHAM OLD ABBEY

Lamberhurst, Sussex
Tel / Fax: 01892 890381 (English Heritage)

These riverside ruins are of a house of 'white' canons, founded c.1208 and preserved in the 18th century, when its surroundings were landscaped to create the delightful setting in which you will find the ruins today. **Location:** 1¼ miles west of Lamberhurst off B2169.

ARUNDEL CASTLE

Arundel, West Sussex, BN18 9AB.
Tel: 01903 883136 Fax: 01903 884581 (Arundel Castle Trustees Ltd)

Situated on high ground, a castle has overlooked the picturesque town of Arundel and the meandering River Arun for almost 1000 years. The castle is set in beautiful, spacious grounds, which include a fully restored Victorian kitchen garden. The original castle suffered some destruction by Cromwell's troops during the Civil War. With restoration and later additions, the Arundel Castle of today is quite magnificent and houses a very fine collection of furniture dating from the 16th century, tapestries, clocks and paintings by Canaletto, Gainsborough, Van Dyck and many other masters. The Library with its spectacular carved and vaulted ceiling, the Victoria Room with the sumptuous gilt state bed made for Queen Victoria, the Barons' Hall, the Grand Staircase, there really is so much to see and enjoy. **<u>Open:</u>** 1 Apr–30 Oct, 12–5pm, the last admission on any day is at 4pm. The Castle is closed on Saturdays. Delicious home-made food for lunch and afternoon tea is served daily in the restaurant. Pre-booked parties are welcome, menus are available on request. Gifts and mementoes, chosen especially by the Countess of Arundel, can be purchased in the shop which is open at the same time as the Castle. For further information please contact: The Comptroller, Arundel Castle, West Sussex BN18 9AB. Tel: 01903 883136/882173. Fax: 01903 884581.

map 4
E6

BATTLE ABBEY

Battle, East Sussex
Tel: 01424 773792 (English Heritage)

Battle Abbey stands at one of the turning points in history, 1066 and the Battle of Hastings. Through unique and exciting displays and exhibitions you can experience the battle at its fiercest. A free interactive audio tour will lead you around the battlefield itself and you can even stand on the exact spot where King Harold fell. Explore the impressive abbey ruins then walk the abbey walls to the Great Gatehouse and see an exhibition on abbey life in the Middle Ages. **Location:** At S end of Battle High Street. Battle is reached by road by turning off A21 onto the A2100. **Open:** 1 Apr–1 Nov: daily 10–6pm (or dusk if earlier in Oct), 2 Nov–31 Mar :10–4pm. (Closed 24–5 Dec) **Admission:** Adult: £4, Conc: £3, Child: £2. (15% discount for groups of 11 or more).

map 5
G6

BENTLEY HOUSE & GARDENS

Halland, Nr. Lewes, East Sussex, BN8 5AF
Tel: 01825 840573 (East Sussex County Council) Fax: 01825 841322

Bentley House dates back to early 18th century times and was built on land granted to James Gage by the Archbishop of Canterbury, with the permission of Henry VIII. The family of Lord Gage was linked with Bentley from that time until 1904. The estate was purchased by Gerald Askew in 1937 and during the 1960s he and his wife, Mary, added two, large, double height Palladian rooms to the original farmhouse. The architect who advised them was Raymond Erith, who had previously worked on 10 Downing Street. The drawing room in the East Wing contains mid 18th century Chinese wallpaper and gilt furniture. The Bird Room in the West Wing contains a collection of wildfowl paintings by Philip Rickman. The gardens at Bentley have been created as a series of 'rooms' divided by Yew hedges, one room leading into the next, specialising in many old-fashioned roses including the Bourbons, the Gallicas and the Damask. Nearby 6 stone sphinxes stand along a broad grass walk where daffodils bloom in spring. **Location:** 7 miles northeast of Lewes, signposted on A22, A26 & B2192. **Open:** 16 Mar–31 Oct, daily 10.30–4.30pm (last admissions). House opens 12noon daily 1 Apr–31 Oct. **Admission:** 1998 prices: Adults £4.20, OAP/Student £3.20, Child (4–15) £2.50, Family (2A+4C) £12.50, 10% discount for groups 11+. Special rates for disabled (wheelchairs available). Admission price allows entry to House, Gardens, Grounds, Wildfowl Reserve, Motor Museum, Woodland Walk, Children's Adventure Play Area. Picnic area, Gift shop and Education Centre with audio-visual. **Refreshments:** Licensed tearooms. **Conferences:** Civil wedding ceremonies. Ample free parking. Dogs allowed in this area only. Please phone 01825 840 573 for group visits outside normal hours.

map 5
F6

BORDE HILL GARDEN

Balcombe Road, Haywards Heath, West Sussex RH16 1XP
Tel: 01444 450326, (Borde Hill Garden Ltd) www.bordehill.co.uk

Borde Hill is Britain's best private collection of champion trees. Peaceful gardens with rich variety of all season colour set in 200 acres of parkland and woods. Extensive new planting with new rose & herbaceous garden; Children's trout fishing; "Pirates" adventure playground; Woodland walks and lakes with picnic area. **Location:** 1 1/2 miles N of Haywards Heath on Balcombe Road. Brighton 17 miles; Gatwick 10 miles. **Station(s):** Haywards Heath 1 1/2m. **Open:** All year 10–6pm. **Admission:** Adults £3, Children £1.50. Groups 20+ £2.50 Family day ticket £8. **Refreshments:** Tearoom, Restaurant. New Bressingham plant centre & gift shop. Wheelchair access and dogs on lead.

map 5
F6

BRICKWALL HOUSE & GARDENS

Northiam, Rye, East Sussex, TN31 6NL
Tel: 01797 253388
Fax: 01797 252 567 (The Frewen Educational Trust)

Home of the Frewen family since 1666. 17th century drawing room, superb plaster ceilings and family portraits. Grand staircase. The grounds contain a formal wall garden, topiary and arboretum. **Location:** 7 miles NW of Rye, on B2088. **Open:** By appointment only. **e-mail:** post@frewcoll.demon.co.uk **Internet:** www.frewcoll.co.uk

map 5
G6

CHARLESTON

Firle, Nr Lewes, East Sussex
Tel: 01323 811265 (Visitor Information) Fax: 01323 811628

Charleston was the home of Vanessa Bell, the sister of Virginia Woolf, and Duncan Grant from 1916 until Grant's death in 1978. The house became a 'Bloomsbury' outpost, full of intellectuals, artists and writers; walls, furniture and ceramics were decorated by the artists with their own designs, strongly influenced by post impressionism and interior decoration styles in France and Italy. The walled garden displays a vivid collection of contrasting plants and flowers **Location:** Signposted off the A27, 6 miles E of Lewes, between the villages of Firle and Selmeston. **Open:** 1 Apr–31 Oct, Weds–Sun & Bank Holiday Mons 2–5pm. Jul & Aug Wed–Sat 11.30–5pm, Sun & Bank Holiday Mons 2–5pm. Guided tours Weds–Sats; unguided Suns & Bank Holiday

Mons. Connoisseur Fridays; in-depth tour of the house including Vanessa Bell's studio and the kitchen, not July and Aug. **Admission:** House/Garden: Adult £5, children £3.50, Connoisseur Fridays £6.50, Concessions £3.50 Wed & Thurs only. Organised groups should telephone 01323 811626 for rates and information. **Refreshments:** Tea and cakes available most afternoons. **Events/Exhibitions:** The Charleston Festival 21–25 May. Literature, art and theatre. The Charleston Gallery; explores Charleston's history and influence on contemporary art. The shop is Craft's Council selected; applied art and books. No disabled access beyond ground floor. Disabled toilet. No dogs. No film, video or photography in the house.

map 5
F6

CHICHESTER CATHEDRAL

West Street, Chichester, West Sussex, PO19 1PX
Tel: 01243 782595, Fax: 01243 536190 (The Dean and Chapter of Chichester)

In the heart of the city, this fine Cathedral has been a centre of Christian worship and community life for 900 years and is the site of the Shrine of St Richard of Chichester. Its treasures range from Romanesque stone carvings to 20th century works of art by Sutherland, Feibusch, Procktor, Chagall, Skelton, Piper and Ursula Benker-Schirmer. Treasury. **Location:** Centre of city, British Rail, A27, A286. **Open:** Summer 7.30–7pm; Winter 7.30–5pm. Choral Evensong daily (except Wed) during term time. **Admission:** Free; suggested donations adults £2, children 50p. **Conferences:** Medieval Vicars' Hall (for 100 people max). Loop system during Cathedral services; touch and hearing centre and braille guide for the blind. Guide dogs only. Parking in city car and coach parks.

map 4
D6

DANNY

Hurstpierpoint, Hassocks, Sussex, BN6 9BB.
Tel: 01273 833 000 Fax: 01273 832 436
(Country Houses Association)

Elizabethan E-shaped house, dating from 1593. **Location:** Between Hassocks and Hurstpierpoint (B2116) – off New Way Lane. **Station(s):** Hassocks (1 mile). **Open:** May–Sept, Wed & Thurs, 2–5pm. (Last entry 4.30pm). **Admission:** Adults £2.50, children £1, groups £3.50 – including tea. Free car park. No dogs admitted.

DENMANS GARDEN

Denmans Lane, Fontwell, Nr Arundel, West Sussex BN18 0SU
Tel: 01243 542808, Fax: 01243 544064 (Mr John Brookes)

Unique 20th century Garden artistically planted forming vistas with emphasis on colours, shapes and textures for all year interest; glass areas for tender and rare species. John Brookes school of garden design in the Clock House where seminars are available. **Location:** Between Arundel and Chichester, turn off A27 into Denmans Lane (W of Fontwell racecourse). **Station(s):** Barnham (2 miles). **Open:** Daily from 1 March–31 October including all Bank Hols 9–5pm. Coaches by appointment. **Admission:** Adults £2.50, Children £1.50, OAPs £2.25. Groups of 15 or more £1.95 (1997 prices). **Refreshments:** Restaurant open 11–5pm. Plant centre. No dogs. National Gardens Scheme.

FIRLE PLACE

Nr Lewes, East Sussex BN8 6LP
Tel (Recorded Information): 01273 858335 Telephone/Fax: 01273 858188 Contact: Mrs Brig Davies, (Viscount Gage)

Discover the civilised atmosphere of Firle Place, the beautiful home of the Gage family for over 500 years. Admire and enjoy the magnificent collections of Old Master Paintings, the fine English and European Furniture; plus the notable collection of Sèvres Porcelain. Learn fascinating facts about the Gage family. This welcoming house which connoisseurs will appreciate is set in parkland in an area of outstanding natural beauty at the foot of the South Downs. There is a delightful Tea Terrace and Restaurant for Lunch and Cream Teas. **Location:** 5 miles SE of Lewes on A27 Brighton/Eastbourne Road. **Station:** Lewes.

Open: 24 May–end Sept 1988 plus Bank Hols except Christmas. Wed, Thur, Sun 11.30am–last tickets at 4.30pm. House closes 5.30pm. Group Tours: Apr–end Sept by pre-arrangement with Events Secretary. **Admission:** £4 Adult, £2 Child, £2.95 Disabled. Connoisseur's Day first Wed June–Sept, £4.85. Car park adjacent to House. Restaurant. Shop. Wheelchair access to ground floor. General Information: 01273 858 335. Events Secretary: Tel/Fax: 01273 858 188. Firle Place, Nr Lewes, East Sussex BN8 6LP.

FISHBOURNE ROMAN PALACE

Salthill Road, Fishbourne, Chichester, Sussex PO19 3QR
Tel: 01243 785 859 Fax: 01243 539 266 (Sussex Past)

First occupied as a military base in AD43, Fishbourne's sumptuous palace was built around AD75. Remains include 20 spectacular mosaics and its story is told in the museum and by an audio-visual programme. The Roman garden has been replanted to its original plan and now features a Roman gardening museum. There is also an Education Centre and shop. **Station(s):** Fishbourne (5 mins walk). **Bus route:** 5 mins walk away. **Open:** 1 Jan–7 Feb & 14–31 Dec, Suns only 10–4pm. 8 Feb–13 Dec daily 10–5pm (Mar–Jul & Sep–Oct) 10–6pm (Aug) 10–4pm (Feb, Nov–Dec) **Admission:** Adults £4, children £2.20. Students/OAP £3.40, disabled £3.30, family (2+2) £10.50. 50% discount to EH members. **Refreshments:** Cafeteria. Picnic area. Suitable for disabled. Parking and toilets. No dogs. **E-mail:** sussexpast@pavilion.co.uk

GLYNDE PLACE

Glynde, Lewes, East Sussex, BN8 6SX
Tel: 01273 858 224 Fax: 01273 858 224 (Viscount & Viscountess Hampden)

Set below the ancient hill fort of Mount Caburn, Glynde Place is a magnificent example of Elizabethan architecture and is the manor house of an estate which has been in the same family since the 12th century. Built in 1569 of Sussex flint and Caen stone round a courtyard, the house commands exceptionally fine views of the South Downs. Amongst the collections of 17th and 18th century portraits of the Trevor family, a collection of Italian old masters brought back by Thomas Brand on his Grand Tour and a room dedicated to Sir Henry Brand, Speaker of the House of Commons 1872-1884. The house is still the family home of the Brands and can be enjoyed as such. **Location:** In Glynde village, 4 miles SE of Lewes, on A27. **Station(s):** Within easy walking distance of Glynde station, with hourly services to Lewes, Brighton and Eastbourne. **Open: Gardens only:** Easter Day & Easter Mon and Sun in April. **House and Gardens:** May, Sun and Bank Hols only; Jun-Sept, Wed, Sun & Aug Bank Hol only. Guided tours for parties (25 or more) can be booked on a regular open day (£2.50 per person) or on a non-open day (£5 per person). Contact Lord Hampden on 01273 858 224. House open 2pm. Last admission 4.45pm. **Admission:** Adults £4, Children £2. Free parking. **Refreshments:** Sussex cream teas in Georgian Stable block. Parties to book in advance as above. Exhibition of watercolours and prints by local artists and shop. **Exhibitions:** 'Harbert Morley and the Great Rebellion 1638–1660', the story of the part played by the owner of Glynde Place during the Civil War. **Weddings:** Glynde Place can be hired for a civil wedding.

map 5
F6

GOODWOOD HOUSE

Goodwood, Chichester, West Sussex PO18 0PX
Tel: 01243 755040 Fax: 01243 755005 (The Duke of Richmond)

The family home of the Dukes of Richmond has been dramatically restored and reinvigorated. The magnificent art collection of paintings, furniture, porcelain and tapestries is displayed in rich, glowing rooms. Location: 3 1/2 miles north east of Chichester. **Open:** 1–5pm on Suns and Mons from Easter (12 Apr) to 28 Sept, Suns through to Thurs in Aug. (Closed: 19,20 Apr, 10 May, 7,14,15 June, 20 Sept). Groups welcome on these open days. Special guided tours for groups on Mon mornings by arrangement and on Connoisseurs Days: 5 & 12 May, 1 Jul, 10 Nov. All groups must book in advance. **Admission:** Adult £5.50, child (12–18) £2, groups (min. 25) £4.50. Connoisseurs Days group rate £7.50. **Refreshments:** Light lunches and Goodwood teas. Free coach/car park.

map 4
D6

GREAT DIXTER HOUSE AND GARDENS

Northiam, Nr Rye, East Sussex TN 31 6PH.
Tel: 01797 252 878 Fax. 01797 252 879 (Mr Christopher Lloyd)

Great Dixter is a beautiful example of a half-timbered manor house, including one of the largest surviving timber-framed great halls in the country. The principal medieval features of the hall remain relatively intact and the combination of both tie and hammer beams is unique. The house forms a splendid backdrop to Christopher Lloyd's acclaimed gardens where an exciting combination of mixed borders, meadows, ponds, yew hedges, topiary and the unforgettable exotic garden can all be seen to reflect Christopher's bold style. **Location:** Signposted off the A28 in Northiam. **Open:** 1 Apr–25 Oct; Tues–Sun 2–5pm (last admission); open Bank Hol Mons. **Admission:** House and Gardens: Adult £4, child £1. Gardens: Adult £3, child 50p.

 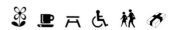

map 5
G6

HAMMERWOOD PARK

East Grinstead, Sussex, RH19 3QE. Tel: 01342 850 594
Fax: 01342 850 864 (Mr & Mrs David Pinnegar)

Hammerwood Park is said by visitors to be the most interesting house in Sussex. Built in 1792 as a temple of Apollo, the house was the first work of Latrobe, the architect who designed both The White House and The Capitol in Washington, D.C., USA. Set in Reptonesque parkland on the edge of Ashdown Forest, the house is an early example of Greek Revival. Award winning restoration works have been completed including a trompe l'oeil decoration scheme in the staircase hall. Restoration of the gardens is now under way. Guided tours by the owner and his family, luscious cream teas. **Location:** 3.5m E of East Grinstead on A264 to Tunbridge Wells. 1m W of Holtye. **Station(s):** East Grinstead **Open:** Easter Mon-end Sept, Wed, Sat & Bank Hol Mons 2–5.30pm. Guided tour starts just after 2pm. Coaches (21+) by appointment. **Admission:** Adults £3.50, Children £1.50. Privilege card: 3 for 2, Apr–28 Jun (except B Hol weekends). **Accommodation:** B&B in an idyllically peaceful location only 20 mins from Gatwick.

map 5 F5

HIGH BEECHES GARDENS

Handcross, West Sussex RH17 6HQ
Tel: 01444 400589 (High Beeches Gardens Conservation Trust. Reg. non profit making Charity No. 299134)

Help us to preserve these twenty acres of enchanting landscaped woodland and water gardens, with magnolias, rhododendrons, and azaleas in Spring. In Autumn, one of the most brilliant gardens for leaf colour. Gentians and primulas are naturalised. Many rare plants. Tree trail. Four acres of natural wildflower meadows. Recommended by Christopher Lloyd. **Location:** 1 mile E of A23 at Handcross, on B2110. **Open:** Gardens only: 1–5pm Apr 1–June 30, Sept 1–Oct 31 daily except Weds 1–5pm. July 1–Aug 31 Mon and Tues only 1–5pm. **Admission:** £3.50. Privilege Card admits 2 adults for the price of 1. Accompanied children free. **Refreshments:** Hot and cold drinks, ice cream and biscuits in Gate Lodge. Sadly, gardens not suitable for wheelchairs. Regret no dogs.

map 5 F6

LEWES CASTLE

Barbican House, 169 High Street, Lewes, Sussex, BN7 1YE
Tel: 01273 486 290 Fax: 01273 486 990 (Sussex Past)

Lewes' imposing Norman castle provides an invigorating climb rewarded by magnificent views. Adjacent Barbican House Museum follows the progress of Sussex people from their earliest beginnings. The Lewes Living History Model is a superb scale model of Victorian Lewes and an audio-visual presentation. There is also an Education Centre and shop. **Station(s):** Lewes (7 mins walk). **Bus route:** Adjacent. Bus station 10 mins walk away. **Open:** Daily (except Christmas & Boxing Day), 10–5.30pm. (Sun & Bank Hols 11–5.30pm). **Admission:** (**1998 Prices**) Adults £3.40, children £1.80. 50% discount to EH members. Joint ticket with 'Anne of Cleves House': Adult £4.50, children £2.50. 50% discount to EH members. Audio tours 50p + deposit. No dogs. **E-mail:** sussexpast@pavilion.co.uk

map 5 F6

MARLIPINS MUSEUM

High Street, Shoreham-by-Sea, Sussex BN43 5DA
Tel: 01273 462994

Shoreham's local and especially its maritime history are explored at Marlipins, itself an important historic Norman building believed to have once been used as a Customs House. It has a beautiful chequer-work facade of Caen Stone and inside, much of the original timberwork of the building is open to view. The maritime gallery contains many superb nautical models and fine paintings, while the rest of the museum houses exhibits dating back to Man's earliest occupation of the area. The development of Shoreham's airport and life in the town during the war years feature prominently in the displays. **Open:** 1 May–30 Sept, Tues–Sat, 10–1pm & 2–4.30pm, Sun 2–4.30 pm. **Admission:** Adults £1.50, children 75p, senior citizen/student £1.00.

THE PRIEST HOUSE

North Lane, West Hoathly, Sussex RH19 4PP
Tel: 01342 810479

The Priest House nestles in the picturesque village of West Hoathly, on the edge of Ashdown Forest. Originally a 15th century timber-framed farmhouse with central open hall, it was modernised in Elizabethan times with stone chimneys and a ceiling in the hall. Later additions created a substantial yeoman's dwelling. Standing in the beautiful surroundings of a traditional cottage garden, the house has a dramatic roof of Horsham stone. Its furnished rooms, including a kitchen, contain a fascinating array of 17th and 18th century domestic furniture, needlework and household items. In the formal herb garden, there are over 150 herbs used in medicine and folklore. **Open:** 1 March–31 Oct, Mon–Sat, 11–5.30pm, Sun 2–5.30pm. **Admission:** Adults £2.20, children £1.

LEONARDSLEE GARDENS

Lower Beeding, Nr Horsham RH13 6PP
Tel: 01403 891212 Fax: 01403 891305 (Mr Robin Loder)

Leonardslee Gardens, created and maintained by the Loder family since 1889, are set in a peaceful 240-acre valley. There are delightful walks around seven beautiful lakes, giving rise to glorious views and reflections. Camellias, magnolias and the early rhododendrons provide colour in April, while in May it becomes a veritable paradise, with banks of sumptuous rhododendrons and azaleas overhanging the paths which are fringed with bluebells. Also in May, the Rock Garden becomes a Kaleidoscope of colour with Japanese evergreen azaleas and ancient dwarf conifers. Superb flowering trees and interesting wild-flowers enhance the tranquillity of summer and the mellow seasonal tints of autumn complete the season. The fascinating Bonsai collection shows this oriental living art-form to perfection. Many visitors are surprised to see the wallabies, which have been used as environmentally–friendly mowing machines for over 100 years! Axis Fallow and Sika Deer roam in the parks and wildfowl are seen on the lakes. The Loder family collection of Victorian Motor Cars (1895–1900) has some fine examples–all in running order–from the dawn of motoring! There is a licensed restaurant and a café for refreshments, as well as a gift shop and a wide selection of plants for sale. **<u>Open:</u>** Daily 1 Apr–31 Oct, 9.30–6pm. **<u>Admission:</u>** May £4.50, all other times £3.50. Children (age 5–15) £2.

map 4
E6

MICHELHAM PRIORY

Upper Dicker, Hailsham, Sussex, BN27 3QS
Tel: 01323 844 224 Fax: 01323 844 030 (Sussex Past)

Enclosed by a medieval moat, the remains of this beautiful Augustinian Priory are incorporated into a splendid Tudor mansion featuring a fascinating array of exhibits. Superb gardens are enhanced by a 14th century gatehouse, water mill, physic herb and cloister gardens, smithy, rope museum and dramatic Elizabethan Great Barn. **Location:** O.S. map ref: OS 198 TQ 558093. **Station(s):** Polegate (3 miles). Berwick (2 miles). **Buses:** Bus route (1.5 miles). **Open:** Wed–Sun. 15 Mar–31 Oct. Mar & Oct, 11–4pm. Apr–July & Sept, 10.30–5pm. Daily in Aug, 10.30–5.30pm. **Admission:** (1998 prices) Adults £4, children £2.20. (50% discount to English Heritage members). **Refreshments:** Tearoom/restaurant. Picnic area. Museum, education centre and shop. Dogs are admitted in car park. **E-mail:** sussexpast@pavilion.co.uk

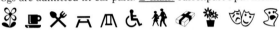

map 5
F6

PALLANT HOUSE

9, North Pallant, Chichester, West Sussex, PO19 1TY
Tel: 01243 774557

Meticulously restored Queen Anne Townhouse with eight rooms decorated and furnished in styles from early Georgian to late Victorian. Also Georgian style gardens and important displays of Bow Porcelain (1747–1775) and Modern British Art (1920–1980). **Location:** Chichester City centre. Open: All year Tues–Sat 10–5.15 (last admission 4.45) **Admission:** Adults £2.80, over 60s £2.20, students/UB40 £1.50. **Refreshments:** Available nearby. Events/Exhibitions: Call for details.

map 4
D6

PERRYHILL NURSERIES

Hartfield, East Sussex, TN7 4JP
Tel: 01892 770 377 Fax: 01892 770 929 (Mrs S. M. Gemmell)

The Plant Centre for the discerning gardener, with the widest range of plants in the south east of England. Old-fashioned and shrub roses a speciality, also herbaceous plants. Trees, shrubs, alpines, fruit trees and bushes, bedding plants in season. No mail order. Catalogues £1.65 incl. postage. **Location:** 1 mile N of Hartfield on B2026. **Open:** Mar–Oct, 9–5pm. Nov–Feb, 9–4.30pm. Seven days a week.

map 5
F5

PARHAM HOUSE & GARDENS

Parham Park, near Pulborough, West Sussex. Tel: 01903 742021
Info Line: 01903 744888 Fax: 01903 746557(Parham Park Ltd)

On a sunny plateau, beneath the South Downs, nestled between Church and gardens, this Elizabethan family home contains an important collection of early paintings, furniture and 17th century needlework. Celebrating their Golden Jubilee in 1998 – Parham House was one of the very first historic houses to open to visitors. The gardens include a four-acre walled garden (with plant sales). Built into a corner of this walled garden is a beautiful stone 'Wendy House'. The 18th century Pleasure Grounds are the setting for a Garden Weekend (18/19 Jul 1998) with a Steam Rally, Craft Fair and Country Show taking place in the Park (various dates). **Open:** 1st Apr–29 Oct: Wed, Thur, Sun and Bank Hol afternoons, with private guided tours arranged for groups on any weekday.

map 4
E6

PASHLEY MANOR GARDENS

Pashley Manor, Ticehurst, E. Sussex
Tel: 01580 200692 Fax: 01580 200102 (Mr and Mrs J. Sellick)

Pashley Manor is a Grade I Tudor house standing in a well timbered park with magnificent views across to Brightling Beacon. The 9 acres of formal garden dating from the 18 century, created in true English romantic style, have many ancient trees and fine shrubs. New plantings add interest and subtle colouring throughout the year. Water features, a classical temple, walled rose gardens and new herbaceous borders. Home-made lunches and teas. Wine licence. **Admission:** £4.50, OAP's £4. **Open:** Tues, Wed, Thurs, Sat & Bank Hol Mons. 11 Apr–26 Sept 1998. Closed from Wed 2 Sept–Mon 7 Sept. **Location:** On the B2099, 1.5 miles southeast of Ticehurst, East Sussex. Tel: 01580 200692 for details.

map 5
G6

PRESTON MANOR

Preston Drove, Brighton BN1 6SD
Tel: 01273 292770 Fax: 01273 292871 (Brighton & Hove Council)

Experience the charms of this delightful Manor House which powerfully evokes the atmosphere of an Edwardian gentry home both 'Upstairs' and 'Downstairs'. There are more than twenty rooms to explore over four floors, from the superbly renovated servants' quarters and butler's pantry in the basement to the day nursery and attic bedrooms on the top floor. Situated adjacent to Preston Park, the Manor also comprises picturesque walled gardens and a pets' cemetery. **Location:** 2 miles north of Brighton on the A23 London Road. **Open:** Daily Tues–Sat 10–5pm, Sun 2–5pm, Mon 1–5pm (Bank Holidays 10–5pm). Closed 25 & 26 Dec and Good Friday. **Admission:** Adults £3, children £1.85, conc. £2.50. Please call for details of family and group tickets.

map 5 F6

SACKVILLE COLLEGE

East Grinstead, West Sussex RH19 3AZ
Tel: 01342 321930/326561 (The Trustees, Patron Earl De La Warr)

Jacobean almshouses founded in 1609 by Robert Sackville 2nd Earl of Dorset and still in use. A personal guided tour is given of the common room, hall, chapel and study (where the carol Good King Wenceslas was written). A piece of living social history. **Location:** High Street, East Grinstead off A22. **Station(s):** East Grinstead. **Open:** June, July & Aug, Wed–Sun 2–5pm. Parties by arrangement Apr–Oct. **Admission:** Adults £2, children £1. **Refreshments:** Teas to order for parties.

ROYAL BOTANIC GARDENS, KEW AT WAKEHURST PLACE

Ardingly, Nr Haywards Heath, West Sussex RH17 6TN
Tel: 01444 894066 (Royal Botanic Gardens)

Managed by the Royal Botanic Gardens, Kew, **Wakehurst Place** near Ardingly is a garden for all seasons, set in over 180 acres dating back to the 12th century. Today, vibrant ornamental plantings, providing year round colour and interest, blend into the beautiful natural landscape. Footpaths and trails lead through sweeping woodlands of native and exotic trees, bright with spring and summer wild flowers. Set around a striking Elizabethan mansion containing a gift shop and a nearby restaurant, Wakehurst Place is open daily from 10am except Christmas Day and New Year's Day. Closing time varies. **Admission:** Please phone for details of 1998 admission prices.

map 5 F5

THE ROYAL PAVILION

Brighton, East Sussex BN1 1EE
01273 290900, Fax: 01273 292871 (Brighton & Hove Council)

The Royal Pavilion, the famous seaside palace of King George IV, is one of the most dazzling and exotically beautiful buildings in the British Isles. Originally a simple farmhouse, in 1787 architect Henry Holland created a neo-classical villa on the site. From 1815–1823, the Pavilion was transformed by John Nash into its current distinctive Indian style complete with Chinese-inspired interiors. Magnificent decorations and fantastic furnishings have been re-created in an extensive restoration programme. Throughout the building the main staterooms, apartments and suites have been returned to their original splendour revealing spectacular colours, superb craftsmanship and

many items on loan from HM The Queen. The Royal Pavilion is an ideal location for filming and photography and rooms are also available for corporate entertaining, private hire and wedding ceremonies. **Location:** In centre of Brighton (Old Steine). **Station(s):** Brighton (1/2 mile). **Open:** Daily (except 25 & 26 Dec) June–Sept 10–6pm, Oct–May 10–5pm. **Admission:** Adults £4.50, children £2.75 students/OAPs £3.25. **Refreshments:** Regency teas and refreshments in Queen Adelaide tearooms with balcony providing sweeping views over the restored gardens. **Events/Exhibitions:** A popular winter programme of events.

map 5 F6

St Mary's House & Gardens

Bramber, West Sussex Tel/Fax: 01903 816 205
(P. F. Thorogood)

Magnificent historic house built in 1470 by Waynflete, Bishop of Winchester, founder of Magdalen College, Oxford. Fine panelled rooms. Unique trompe l'oeil 'Painted Room'. English costume-doll collection, family memorabilia and other exhibitions. Still a lived-in family home. "Warmest Welcome" Commendation. Charming gardens with amusing topiary. **Location:** Off A283, 10 miles NW of Brighton. **Station(s):** Shoreham-by-Sea from London (Victoria). **Open:** Easter Sun-last Sun in Sept, Sun & Thur & Bank Hol Mons, 2–6pm. **Group bookings:** Other days by prior arrangement from Apr–Oct. **Admission:** Adults £3.80, children £2.00, OAPs £3.50. Group rate £3.50, (groups of 25+). Parking in grounds. **Refreshments:** Teas in Music Room.

map 4 E6

The Weald & Downland Open Air Museum

Singleton, Nr Chichester, West Sussex
Tel: 01243 811348

The Museum is rescuing and re-erecting historic buildings from South-East England. The collection illustrates the history of vernacular architecture in the Weald and Downland area. Exhibits include a Medieval farmstead, garden and history of farming exhibition centred on Bayleaf Farmhouse (right), timber framed houses, a Tudor market hall, a 16th century treadwheel, farm buildings a blacksmith's forge, plumber's and carpenter's eorkshops and a village school. A 'Hands On' gallery explores building materials and techniques. **Location:** 6 miles N of Chichester on A286 just S of Singleton. **Open:** 1 Mar–31 Oct daily 10.30–5pm, 1 Nov–28 Feb, Wed, Sat and Sun only 10.30–4pm, 26 Dec–1 Jan daily 10.30–4pm. **Admission:** Charged. Parties by arrangement (group rates available). **Refreshments:** Light refreshments during main season.

map 4 D6

West Dean Gardens

The Edward James Foundation, Estate Office, West Dean, Chichester, West Sussex PO18 0QZ
Tel: 01243 818210 Fax: 01243 811342

Extensive downland garden with 300ft pergola, herbaceous borders and bedding displays. Victorian Walled Kitchen Garden with unusual vegetables, cut flowers, fruit collection and 13 original glasshouses (vineries, fig, peach, fern, orchid and tropical houses). Park Walk (2¼ miles) through landscaped parkland and the 45 acre St Roche's Arboretum. New Visitor Centre overlooking West Dean Park, opened by The Prince of Wales, with high quality restaurant, garden shop and plant sales. **Location:** 6 miles N of Chichester on A286. **Open:** Mar–Oct inclusive, daily 11–5pm. Last admission 4.30pm. Parties by arrangement. **Admission:** Adults £3.50, over 60's £3, children £1.50, pre-booked parties 20+ £3 each. **Refreshments:** Restaurant. **Events:** Chilli Fiesta 15–16 August, Apple Day 18 October. Coach/car parking. No dogs.

map 4 D6

BATEMAN'S

Burwash, Etchingham TN19 7DS Tel: 01435 882302 Fax: 01435 882811

Open: House, mill and garden: 4 April to 1 Nov: daily except Thur & Fri 11–5.30 (but open Good Fri). Last admission 4.30. The mill grinds corn every Sat at 2 in the open season.

BODIAM CASTLE

Bodiam, nr Robertsbridge TN32 5UA Tel: 01580 830436

Open: 14 Feb to 1 Nov: daily 10–6 or dusk if earlier; 3 Nov to 3 Jan: Tues to Sun 10–4 or dusk if earlier (closed 24/25/26 Dec, open New Year's Day). Last admission 1hr before closing.

NYMANS GARDEN

Handcross, nr Haywards Heath RH17 6EB Tel: 01444 400321/400777

Open: Garden: 1 March to 1 Nov: daily except Mon & Tues (but open BH Mon) 11–6 or sunset if earlier; last admission 5.30. During June & July the garden only will be open on Sun till 9 – picnics welcome. Winter 1998/9: Sat & Sun, including restaurant & shop, 12–4 (last admission 3.30), but restricted according to ground conditions; tel.

01444 400321 for information. House: Lady Rosse's library, drawing room and forecourt garden will be open free of charge (as part of garden visit) 1 March to 1 Nov: same days as garden 12–4.

PETWORTH HOUSE AND PARK

Petworth GU28 0AE Tel: 01798 342207; Infoline: 01798 343929

Open: House: 28 March to 1 Nov: daily except Thur & Fri (but open Good Fri) 1–5.30. Last admission to house 4.30; kitchens 5. Additional rooms shown weekdays (not BH Mon). Pleasure grounds and car park 12–6 (opens 11 on BH Mon and July & Aug) for walks, picnics and access to tea-room, shop and Petworth town. Park: all year, daily 8 to sunset (closed 26–28 June from 12).

STANDEN

East Grinstead RH19 4NE Tel: 01342 323029 Fax: 01342 316424

Open: 25 March to 1 Nov: daily except Mon & Tues (but open BH Mon). Garden: 12.30–6. House: 12.30–4 (last admission 4). Property may close on Sun & BHols for limited periods to avoid overcrowding. 6 Nov to 20 Dec: garden only, Fri, Sat & Sun 1–4.

SAINT HILL MANOR

Saint Hill Road, East Grinstead, West Sussex RH19 4JY
Tel: 01342 326711 (contact Liz Nyegaard)

Fine Sussex sandstone house built in 1792 and situated near the breathtaking Ashdown Forest. Saint Hill Manor's final owner, acclaimed author and humanitarian, L. Ron Hubbard, lived here for many years with his family. Under his direction extensive renovations were carried out uncovering exquisite period features hidden for over a century. Fine wood panelling, marble fireplaces, Georgian windows and plasterwork ceilings have been expertly restored to their original beauty. Outstanding features of this lovely house include a complete library of Mr. Hubbard's work, the elegant Winter Garden and the delightful Monkey Room, housing John Spencer Churchill's 100ft mural depicting many famous characters as monkeys, including his uncle Sir Winston Churchill. 59 acres of landscaped gardens, lake and woodlands. **Location:** Off A22, N of East Grinstead, down Imberhorne Lane. Straight into Saint Hill Road, 300 yds on right. Stations: East Grinstead. Owner: Church of Scientology. **Open:** All year. Daily, 2–5pm. Tours on the hour or by appointment. Group parties welcome. Parking for coaches and cars. **Admission:** Free. **Events/Exhibitions:** Summer concerts on the terrace, musical evenings throughout the year. Conference and wedding reception facilities available in Saint Hill Castle. Seats up to 600 theatre style and 300 for dinner.

map 5
F5

Warwickshire

Of mountains, valleys and other natural beauties, Warwickshire has few. However, from a historical aspect, Warwickshire is the most fortunate of counties. The names of Warwickshire towns read like chapters in a history book: Stratford Upon Avon, Warwick, Kenilworth, Rugby and Coventry. Towns that, with a few exceptions, boast great beauty as well as great history.

The town of Warwick retains some superb examples of medieval architecture, despite being partly destroyed by a huge fire in the late seventeenth century. Some of the finest buildings are to be found around the High Street and in Northgate Street.

The springs of Royal Leamington Spa, to the East of Warwick, were frequented by royalty when Queen Victoria visited the fashionable town in 1838. Nearby Kenilworth Castle was constructed during Norman times and vastly altered by Elizabeth I's favourite, the Earl of Leicester. It then became renowned as a place of fine music and pageantry.

But it is for its association with William Shakespeare that Warwickshire is invariably best known. The town of Stratford-Upon-Avon stands central to "Shakespeare Country", with its many examples of Shakespearean heritage.

Kenilworth Castle

ARBURY HALL
Nuneaton, Warwickshire, CV10 7PT
Tel: 01203 382804, Fax: 01203 641147 (The Rt. Hon. The Viscount Daventry)

16th century Elizabethan House, Gothicised late 18th century, pictures, period furniture etc. Park and landscape gardens. Arbury has been the home of the Newdegate family since the 16th century. For a country house the Gothic architecture is unique, the original Elizabethan house being Gothicised by Sir Roger Newdigate between 1750 and 1800, under the direction of Sanderson Miller, Henry Keene and Couchman of Warwick. Beautiful plaster ceilings, pictures and fine specimens of period furniture, china and glass. Fine stable block with central doorway by Wren. Arbury Hall is situated in very large grounds and is about 1¹/₂ miles from any main road. Excellent carriage drives lined with trees. George Eliot's 'Cheveral Manor'. **Location:** 2 miles

SW of Nuneaton off B4102. **Station(s):** Nuneaton. **Open:** Sun & B.H. Mon. Easter to end of September. 2–5.30pm (last admission 5pm). **Admission:** Hall & Gardens: Adults £4.50 Children £2.50. Gardens only: Adults £3, Children £2. Organised parties most days (25 or over) special terms by prior arrangement with Administrator. School parties also welcome. **Conferences:** Arbury is an ideal venue for Corporate hospitality functions, promotions and as a film location etc. The Dining Room is also available for exclusive luncheons and dinners. **Events:** June 7 Arbury Motor Transport Spectacular. June 13/14 Rainbow Craft Fair. Aug 22/23 Rainbow Craft Fair. Wheelchair access ground floor only. Gravel paths. Free car park.

map 8 C7

CHARLECOTE PARK
Warwick CV35 9ER
Tel: 01789 470 277, Fax: 01789 470 544

Home of the Lucy family since 1247. Present house built in 1550's. Queen Elizabeth I visited. Victorian interiors; objects from Fonthill Abbey. Park landscaped by Capability Brown. Jacob sheep. Red and fallow deer, reputedly poached by Shakespeare. **Open:** 3 Apr–1 Nov, Fri–Tue, 12–6pm. House open 12–5pm. Shop and restaurant 12–5.30pm. **Admission:** Adult £4.80, child (5–16) £2.40. Family ticket £12. Special group rate £3.80 (weekdays only for parties 15+). Evening guided tours for pre-booked parties £5.50 (including NT members; minimum charge £115 for party). Wheelchair Facilities: All ground floor rooms accessible including Orangery and shop. Parking. Lavatories. **Refreshments:** Morning coffee, lunches, afternoon teas in restaurant (licensed). Picnic in deer park only. Changing and feeding room. No dogs allowed.

 map 4 B2

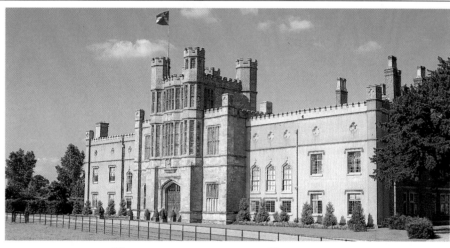

COUGHTON COURT
Alcester, B49 5JA, Warwickshire
Tel: 01789 400 777 Fax: 01789 765 544 Tel: 01789 762435(Visitor Information)

Coughton Court has been the home of the Throckmorton family since the 15th century. The house contains one of the best collections of portraits and memorabilia of one family from Tudor times to the present day. There are two churches in the grounds to visit and magnificent 1½ acre flower garden together with a lake and riverside walks, an orchard and bog garden. Gunpowder Plot Exhibition. **Location:** 2 miles north of Alcester, on A435. **Open:** Mid Mar– Mid Oct. Please contact Visitor Information Line for 1998 opening times & admission prices.

  map 4 B2

THE HILLER GARDEN
Dunnington Heath Farm, Nr. Alcester,
Warwickshire, B49 5PD. Tel: 01789 490 991
Fax: 01789 490 439 (A. H. Hiller & Son Ltd)

Among gravelled walks, large beds display an extensive range of unusual herbaceous perennials providing colour and interest throughout the year in this two acre garden near Ragley Hall. The Rose Gardens, at the peak of their beauty from the end of June, hold a collection of some 200 old-fashioned, species, modern shrub, rugosa and English roses in settings appropriate to their characters. There is a well-stocked plant sales area, a garden gift shop, farm shop and licensed tea rooms. **Location:** 3 miles S of Alcester on B4088 (formerly A435/A441 junction). **Open:** Daily (except Christmas and New Year), 10am–5pm. **Admission:** Free. **Refreshments:** Morning coffee, light lunches, afternoon teas in the Gardens Tea Rooms (licensed).

HONINGTON HALL
Shipston-on-Stour, Warwickshire CV36 5AA
Tel: 01608 661434, Fax: 01608 663717 (Benjamin Wiggin Esq)

This fine Caroline manor house was built in the early 1680s for the Parker family. It was modified in the mid 18th century with the introduction within of exceptional and lavish plaster work and the insertion of an octagonal saloon. It is set in 15 acres of grounds. Location: 10 miles S of Stratford-on-Avon; ½ mile E of A3400. Open: June, July, Aug, Weds & Bank Hol Mons 2.30–5pm. Parties at other times by appointment. Admission: Adults £2.75, Children £1.

  map 4 B2

KENILWORTH CASTLE

Kenilworth, Warks CU8 1NE
Tel 01926 852078 (English Heritage)

Explore England's finest and most extensive castle ruins. Wander through rooms used to lavishly entertain Queen Elizabeth I. You can learn of the great building's links with Henry V, who retired here after his return from his victorious expedition to Agincourt. Today you can view the marvellous Norman keep and John of Gaunt's Great Hall, once rivalling London's Westminister Hall in palatial grandeur, as well as the beautiful reconstructed Tudor gardens. An audio–tour will guide you on a revealing journey around Kenilworth Castle. **Location:** Off A46. Follow A452 to Kenilworth town centre as signposted. **Open:** 1 Apr–1 Nov daily 10–6pm (or dusk if earlier in Oct), 2 Nov–31 Mar 10–4pm daily (closed 24/25 Dec). **Admission:** Adult £3.10, Conc. £2.30, child £1.60 (15% discount for groups of 11 or more).

map 4 B1

LORD LEYCESTER HOSPITAL

High Street, Warwick, Warwickshire, CV34 4BH
Tel: 01926 491 422 Fax: 01926 491 422

In 1571, Robert Dudley, Earl of Leycester, founded his hospital for twelve 'poor' persons in the buildings of the Guilds, which had been dispersed in 1546. The buildings have been restored to their original condition: the Great Hall of King James, the Guildhall (museum), the Chaplain's Hall (Queen's Own Hussars Regimental Museum) and the Brethren's Kitchen. The recently restored historic Master's Garden is now open to the public (Easter–31 Sept £1 donation please). The Hospital, with its medieval galleried courtyard, featured in the TV serials 'Pride and Prejudice', 'Tom Jones', 'Moll Flanders'. **Location:** West Gate of Warwick (A429). **Station(s):** Warwick (¾m). **Open:** All year, Tue–Sun, 10–5pm (Summer) and 10–4pm (Winter). Open BH Mons, Good Fri and Christmas Day. **Admission:** Adult £2.75, children (under 14) £1.50, OAP/Student £2.50. Free car park.

 C map 4 B1

WARWICK CASTLE

Warwick, Warwickshire, CV34 4QU
Tel: 01926 406 600 (The Tussauds Group)

Warwick Castle, the finest medieval castle in England, with its magnificent Towers and Ramparts, offers visitors a thousand years of history. The chilling Dungeon and gruesome Torture Chamber contrast with the elegant splendour of the Great Hall, Staterooms and the 'Royal Weekend Party, 1898'. Visitors can experience the sights, sounds, touch and smell of the medieval household in 1471 in 'Kingmaker – a preparation for battle'. Throughout the year there is an exciting series of special events which bring this medieval world even more to life, from the clash of knights to the soothing sounds of minstrels.

map 4 B1

BADDESLEY CLINTON

Rising Lane, Baddesley Clinton Village, Solihull B93 0DQ Tel: 01564 783294

Open: 4 March to 1 Nov: daily except Mon & Tues (but closed Good Fri and open BH Mon); March, April, Oct & 1 Nov 1.30–5; May to end Sept 1.30–5.30 (grounds, shop and restaurant open from 12). March 1999: daily except Mon & Tues 1.30–5. Last admission to house 30min before closing. Events: for details please send s.a.e to Property Manager or tel. 01564 783294

PACKWOOD HOUSE

Lapworth, Solihull B94 6AT Tel: 01564 782024

Open: 1 March to 22 March: car park only, Sat & Sun 12–4; 25 March to end Sept: daily except Mon & Tues (but closed Good Fri and open BH Mon) car park opens 12, garden 1.30–6, house 2–6. Oct & 1 Nov: daily except Mon & Tues 12.30–4.30, car park opens 12. Last admission 30min before closing. Events: 7 June, Teddy Bears' Picnic; July, 1920s Summer Follies; tel. bookings from 1 April. For full summer events leaflet please send s.a.e. to Property Manager

BENTHALL HALL

Broseley TF12 5RX Tel: 01952 882159

Open: 5 April to 30 Sept: Wed, Sun & BH Mon 1.30–5.30. Last admission 5. House and/or garden for parties at other times by arrangement: Tues & Wed am. Events: church services most Suns 3.15; visitors welcome

FARNBOROUGH HALL

Banbury OX17 1DU Tel: 01295 690002

Open: House, grounds & terrace walk: April to end Sept: Wed & Sat 2–6: also 3 & 4 May 2–6. Terrace walk only: Thur & Fri 2–6. Last admission to the house 5.30

UPTON HOUSE

Banbury OX15 6HT Tel: 01295 670266

Open: 4 April to 1 Nov: daily except Thur & Fri (incl. BH Mon) 2–6. Closed Good Fri. Last admission 5.30 (5 after 25 Oct). Events: fine arts study tours, jazz concert and other events; please send s.a.e. or tel. for details

Mary Arden's House

THE SHAKESPEARE HOUSES IN AND AROUND STRATFORD-UPON-AVON

The Shakespere Centre, Henley Street, Stratford-upon-Avon, Warks CV37 6QW.
Tel: 01789 204016 Fax: 01789 296083

Five beautifully preserved Tudor houses, all associated with William Shakespeare and his family. In Town: **Shakespeare's Birthplace**, Henley Street. Half-timbered house where William Shakespeare was born in 1564. Visitor's centre showing highly acclaimed exhibition **William Shakespeare, His Life and Background. Nash's House and New Place**, Chapel Street. Nash's House was the home of Shakespeare's grand-daughter, Elizabeth Hall and contains exceptional furnishings. Upstairs there are displays about the history of Stratford. Also site and gardens of **New Place** (including Elizabethan style Knott Garden and Shakespeare's Great Garden), where Shakespeare lived in retirement. Discover why the house was demolished and see the foundations and grounds of his final Stratford home. **Hall's Croft**, Old Town. Impressive 16th century house and garden, with Jacobean additions. Owned by Dr John Hall who married Shakespeare's eldest daughter, Susanna. Includes exhibitions about medicine in Shakespeare's time and beautiful walled garden with mulberry tree and herb garden. Out of Town: **Anne Hathaway's Cottage**, Shottery. Picturesque thatched farmhouse cottage which belonged to the family of Shakespere's wife. Contains the famous Hathaway bed and the other original furniture. Outside lies a beautiful English cottage garden, orchard and the Shakespeare Tree Garden. **Mary Arden's House** and **Shakespeare's Countryside Museum**, Wilmcote. This striking farmhouse was Shakespeare's mother's family home and offers a fascinating insight into rural farm life in the Tudor period. See also, falconry displays, working blacksmith, prize-winning livestock and Glebe Farm's kitchen of 1900. **Open:** Daily all year round except 23–26 Dec. Inclusive tickets available to three in-town, or all five houses. The Shakespeare Birthplace Trust is a Registered Charity, No. 209302.

map 4
B2

Anne Hathaway's Cottage

Shakespeare's Birthplace

West Midlands

The West Midlands are famously known as having been at the heart of The Industrial Revolution in the nineteenth century. The city of Birmingham was the base for a wide range of manufacturing trades and oversaw the vast growth in factories and associated housing for its workers.

Today, Birmingham has established itself as a

Meriden

city of culture, with a thriving arts scene: The City of Birmingham Symphony Orchestra has a worldwide reputation for excellence and in recent times, The Royal Sadler's Wells have relocated their Ballet Company to Birmingham, in order to benefit from their excellent facilities. For lovers of Pre-Raphaelite art, the City Museum and Art Gallery offers the perfect opportunity to indulge in the works of, among others, Ford Madox Brown and Sir Edward Burne-Jones.

On the outskirts of the city, the National Exhibition Centre is the venue for many of today's popular events. Indeed, in the last year it has hosted a wide variety of shows ranging from fashion exhibitions to car conventions. It is also a renowned music venue: various popular and classical artists have performed concerts at the Centre.

Britain's first completely modern cathedral, at Coventry, arose out of the ruins of the bombed city centre after the Second World War. Sir Basil Spence's fine building is adorned with superb sculptures by Jacob Epstein and Graham Sutherland.

ASTON HALL

Trinity Road, Aston, Birmingham, West Midlands, B6 6JD
Tel: 0121 327 0062 (Birmingham Museums and Arts)

A magnificent Jacobean mansion built by Sir Thomas Holte between 1618–1635, Aston Hall has over 20 period rooms containing fine furniture, paintings, textiles and metalwork. Decorative highlights include the ceiling and frieze of the Great Dining Room, the carved oak Great chimney-piece. Sharp-eyed visitors can spot the marks of Roundhead cannon shot upon the staircase balustrade. **Open:** Daily, Apr–Oct, 2–5pm. **Guided Tours:** By appointment only. **Admission:** Free. Please quote Ref no. HHCG98.

map 8
B7

BIRMINGHAM BOTANICAL GARDENS & GLASSHOUSES

Westbourne Road, Edgbaston, Birmingham, West Midlands B15 3TR
Tel: 0121 454 1860, Fax: 0121 454 7835 (Birmingham Botanical & Horticultural Society)

The Gardens are a 15 acre 'Oasis of Delight' with the finest collection of plants in the Midlands. The Tropical House, full of rainforest vegetation, includes many economic plants. Palms, tree ferns and orchids are displayed in the Palm House. The Orangery features citrus fruits and conservatory plants while the Cactus House conveys a desert scene. There is colourful bedding on the Terrace plus Rhododendron, Rose, Rock, Herb and Cottage Gardens, Trials Ground, Historic Gardens and the National Bonsai Collection. Children's Playgrounds and Aviaries. Gallery. The 'Shop at the Gardens' has a wide range of gifts, souvenirs and plants. Refreshments in the Pavilion. Bands play summer Sunday afternoons. **Open daily.**

 C map 4 B1

BLAKESLEY HALL

Blakesley Road, Yardley, Birmingham, West Midlands, B25 8RN.
Tel: 0121 783 2193 (Birmingham Museums and Arts)

A timber framed farmhouse in old Yardley village. Step over the threshold and back into time to meet staff in period costume. The hall itself was built in 1590 by Richard Smallbroke; today's furnishings date from an old inventory of 1684. All twelve rooms, from the Painted Chamber to Boulting House, tell their own story. **Open:** Apr–Oct. **Times:** Daily 2–5pm. **Admission:** Free. Please quote Ref no. HHCG98.

CASTLE BROMWICH HALL GARDENS

Chester Road, Castle Bromwich, Birmingham, West Midlands
Tel: 0121 749 4100

The gardens are a cultural gem and a unique example of early 18th century garden design. Succeeding generations developed and enhanced the gardens, including 'An Elegant Kitchen and Fruit Garden after a New and Grand Manor' in the style of Batty Langley (1727); a 'Ladies Border' with plants of the period; a 'Wilderness' of mature trees underplanted with interesting specimen plants to provide a woodland atmosphere, plus a 'Holly Maze' of 19th century design. Major restoration of the original Orangery and Music Room, at either end of the long Holly Walk, together with the classic surrounding walls, enhance the beauty of the gardens. Guided tours, gift shop, refreshments and disabled access.

COVENTRY CATHEDRAL

Coventry

The remains of the blackened medieval Cathedral, bombed in 1940, stand beside the new Cathedral designed by Basil Spence, consecrated in 1962. Modern works of art include a huge tapestry by Graham Sutherland, a stained glass window by John Piper and a bronze sculpture by Epstein. **Location:** Coventry city centre. **Admission:** Donations for the Cathedral.

SOHO HOUSE

Soho Avenue, Handsworth, Birmingham B18 5LB, West Midlands. Tel: 0121 554 9122 (Birmingham Museums & Arts)

The elegant home of industrial pioneer Matthew Boulton, who lived at Soho House from 1766 to 1809. Meeting place of the Lunar Society, some of the most important scientists, engineers and thinkers of the time. Possibly the first centrally heated house in England since Roman times, Soho House has been carefully restored to its 18th century glory and contains some of Boulton's own furniture. **Open:** All year. **Times:** Tue–Sat, 10am–5pm. Sun, 12 noon–5pm. Closed Mon except Bank Holidays. Please quote Ref no. HHCG98. **Admission:** Adults £2, Concessions £1.50, Family ticket £5. 10% discount for groups of 10 or more.

 # HAGLEY HALL

Stourbridge, West Midlands, DY9 9LG
Tel: 01562 882408 Fax: 01562 882632 (The Viscount Cobham)

The last of the great Palladian Houses, designed by Sanderson Miller and completed in 1760. The house contains the finest example of Rococo plasterwork by Francesco Vassali and a unique collection of 18th century furniture and family portraits including works by Van Dyck, Reynolds and Lely. **Location:** Just off A456 Birmingham to Kidderminster, 12 m from Birmingham within easy reach M5 (exit 3 or 4), M6 or M42. **Station(s):** Hagley (1 m) (not Suns); Stourbridge Junction (2 m). **Open:** Please phone for details. **Admission:** Charges apply. **Refreshments:** Tea available in the house. **Conferences:** Specialists in corporate entertaining and conferences throughout the year.

BANTOCK HOUSE MUSEUM

Bantock Park, Bradmore Road, Wolverhampton WV3 9LQ Tel: 01902 312132

Open: Jan to May: Tues to Sat 10–5; Sun 2–5 (closed daily between 1–2). Closed Mon. Closed for major alterations between June 1998 and Easter 1999.

WIGHTWICK MANOR

Wightwick Bank, Wolverhampton WV6 8EE Tel: 01902 761108

Open: House: 1 March to 31 Dec and March 1999: Thur & Sat 2.30–5.30. Also open BH Sat, Sun & Mon 2.30–5.30 (ground floor only, no guided tours). Open for pre-booked parties Wed & Thur and special evening tours. Admission to house by timed ticket, issued from 2 at front door. Owing to the fragile nature of contents and the requirements of conservation, some rooms cannot always be shown; tours will therefore vary during the year. School visits on Wed & Thur, contact Property Manager for details. Garden: Wed & Thur 11–6; Sat, BH Sun & BH Mon 1–6. Other days by appointment.

Wiltshire

Castle Combe

Wiltshire covers a vast and varied area. It remains largely unknown as a county and few visitors are intimate with its great bare sweeps of downland and the smooth lines of the uplands, where bygone tribes first trod the straight tracks and left their camps, dykes and burial mounds. Its gentle and limpid streams flow through the little hamlets and the scores of picturesque villages.

In 1220, Salisbury was founded. This tranquil city is the home to Salisbury Cathedral; a wonderful example of Gothic architecture which has the tallest spire in England. This majestic building dwarfs the charming streets that are strewn haphazardly at its foot and overlooks one of this country's most beautiful closes.

The open countryside of the Salisbury Plain made this area an important centre of prehistoric settlement and today there are many historic sites and relics to show its history. The most famous of these is Stonehenge, a monumental example of prehistoric enterprise that remains something of an enigma to this day.

Further afield, picturesque villages lie waiting to be discovered, including charming Castle Combe, immortalised on television in the Doctor Doolittle stories.

BOWOOD HOUSE & GARDENS

Calne, Wiltshire SN11 0LZ
Tel: 01249 812102 (The Earl and Countess of Shelburne)

Superb 18th century family home. Magnificent Diocletian wing contains Robert Adam's library, the Laboratory where Joseph Priestley discovered oxygen gas in 1774, the Orangery, the Chapel and a Sculpture Gallery. Family treasures include Victoriana, Indiana and a superb collection of watercolours and jewellery. The House is set in parkland landscaped by 'Capability' Brown. The grounds include a Doric Temple, cascade, arboretum and one of the country's finest adventure playgrounds. **Location:** Off the A4 in Derry Hill Village, midway between Calne and Chippenham. **Open:** 1 Apr – 1 November. The Rhododendron Gardens (a separate attraction) open six weeks during May and June.

map 3
K2

CHARLTON PARK HOUSE

Malmesbury, Wiltshire SN16 9DG
(The Earl of Suffolk and Berkshire)

Jacobean/Georgian mansion, built for the Earls of Suffolk, 1607, altered by Matthew Brettingham the Younger, c.1770. **Location:** $1\frac{1}{2}$ miles NE Malmsbury. Entry only by signed entrance on A429, Malmesbury/Cirencester road. No access from Charlton village. **Open:** May-Oct Mon & Thurs 2-4pm Viewing of Great Hall. Staircase and saloon. **Admission:** Adults £1, Children/OAP 50p. Car parking limited. Unsuitable for wheelchairs. No dogs. No picnicking.

map 3
K1

CORSHAM COURT

Corsham, Wiltshire SN13 0BZ
Tel: 01249 701610/701611, Fax: c/o 01249 444556 (J Methuen-Campbell Esq)

Home of the Methuen family since 1745, Corsham Court displays one of the most distinguished collections of Old Master paintings in the country. The surviving collection includes works by Van Dyck and Carlo Dolci which hang alongside family portraits by Reynolds. Georgian State Rooms furnished by Thomas Chippendale and others during late 19th century. **Location:** Signposted 4 miles W of Chippenham from the A4 Bath Road. **Open:** Open throughout the year to groups of 15 or more persons by appointment. Otherwise, open 20 Mar – 30 Oct daily except Mondays (but including Bank Hols) from 11.00–5.30pm. 1 Oct – 19 Mar open weekends from 2.00pm until 4.30pm. Closed December. Last entry 30 minutes before close. **Admission:** Adults £4.50, OAP's £3.50, Child £1.00, Group rates £3.50. **Refreshments:** Available at Johnsons Bakery nearby.

map 3
J2

HAMPTWORTH LODGE

Landford, Nr Salisbury, Wiltshire SP5 2EA
Tel: 01794 390215 (Mr N Anderson)

Rebuilt Jacobean Manor, with period furniture. **Location:** 10 miles SE of Salisbury on the C44 road linking Downton on A338, Salisbury-Bournemouth to Landford on A36, Salisbury-Southampton. **Open:** House and Garden daily, Monday March 30 to Thursday April 30 1998 (inclusive). Conducted parties only 2.30 and 3.45. Coaches by appointment only Apr 1–Sept 30. By appointment all year, 18 hole golf course 01794 390155. **Admission:** £3.50, under 11s free. No special arrangement for parties, but about 15 is the maximum. **Refreshments:** Downtown, Salisbury; nil in house. Car parking; disabled ground floor only.

HEALE GARDEN

Woodford, Salisbury SP4 6NT
Tel: 01722 782504

Grade I Carolean Manor House where King Charles II hid during his escape in 1651. The garden provides a wonderfully varied collection of plants, shrubs, musk and other roses, growing in the formal setting of clipped hedges and mellow stonework. Particularly lovely in the spring and autumn is the water garden. **Location:** 4m north of Salisbury on Woodford valley road between A345 and A360. **Open:** Garden, shop & plant centre, all year 10–5pm. Charges apply.

LONGLEAT

Warminster, Wiltshire, BA12 7NW
Tel: 01985 844400 Fax: 01985 844885 (The Marquess of Bath)

Longleat House lies in a sheltered valley amidst rolling parkland. The magnificent Elizabethan property, built by Sir John Thynne and completed in 1580, has been the home of the same family ever since that time. The House contains many treasures including paintings by Tintoretto and Wootton, exquisite French and Flemish tapestries and fine ceilings from the 'School of Titian'. Lovers of books will revel in the splendid collections which are to be found in Longleat's seven libraries. The Murals in the family apartments in the West Wing were painted by Alexander Thynn, the present Marquess and are fascinating and remarkable additions to the collections. Apart from the ancestral home, Longleat is probably best known for its Safari Park. Here, visitors have the rare opportunity to see animals in a natural setting. The East African Reserve is home to giraffe, zebra and camels and is the only place in Europe where you can walk freely amongst these exotic animals. Rhinos, Rhesus monkeys, gorillas, tigers and the ever popular Longleat lions are also to be found in the park. Other attractions include the 'World's Longest Maze', children's Adventure Castle, Victorian Kitchens, Tropical Butterfly Garden, Doctor Who exhibition, needlecraft centre, boat and train rides – enough variety to keep anyone occupied, whatever their age and interest. Longleat House is open every day except Christmas Day. Telephone 01985 844400 for opening times and prices.

IFORD MANOR GARDEN

Bradford-on-Avon, Wiltshire, BA15 2BA
Tel: 01225 863 146 Fax: 01225 862 364 (Mrs Cartwright-Hignett)

Britannia guards the bridge over the River Frome and the entrance to Harold Peto's internationally influential garden. Mediterranean ideas and plants are grafted onto an English landscape and remnants of classical and renaissance periods complete the scene. **Location:** 7 miles S of Bath via A36. **Open:** Apr & Oct, Sun only. May–Sept, Sat–Sun & Tue–Thur, 2–5pm. **Admission:** Adults £2.50, children (10+) and OAPs £1.90. **Refreshments:** Saturdays and Sundays, May–Sept only.

CANOCK MANOR

Devizes
Tel: 01380 840 227 (Mr & Mrs Bonar Sykes)

Grade II listed house and stables with historic garden. Described by Pevsner as a "Georgian house of great charm', clad in Bath stone ashlar with gothicised windows facing 18th century stable block with copper cupola. Estate cottages. Shrub walk with curved bays matched by tall beech and hornbeam hedges. Magnolia, sorbus, malus and prunus specimens in lawn flanking walled kitchen and garden. Small 'Persian' water garden with geometric patterned paved areas. New small arboretum. Views south to Salisbury Plain and north to Marlborough Downs. Woodland walk. **Location:** 5 miles SE of Devizes, off A342. **Open:** Please phone for details. Also opened for NGS. **Admission:** Adults £1.50, children (under16) free. (Share to 'St. John the Baptist Church'). **Refreshments:** Cream teas. Disabled access. Plants available for sale. No dogs except guide dogs.

Wiltshire

LUCKINGTON COURT

Luckington, Chippenham, Wiltshire SN14 6PQ
Tel: 01666 840205 (The Hon Mrs Trevor Horn)

Mainly Queen Anne with magnificent group of ancient buildings. Beautiful mainly formal garden with fine collection of ornamental trees and shrubs. Home of the Bennet family in the BBC TV adaptation 'Pride and Prejudice'. **Location:** 6 miles W of Malmesbury on B4040 Bristol Road. **Open:** All through the year Weds 2–5pm, garden only. Open Sun 10th May, 2.30–5pm. Collection box for National Gardens' Scheme. Inside view by appointment 3 weeks in advance. **Admission:** Outside gardens only £1, house £2. **Refreshments:** Teas in garden or house (in aid of Luckington Parish Church) on Sun 11 May only.

LYDIARD PARK

Lydiard Tregove, Swindon, Wiltshire SN5 9PA
Tel: 01793 770401 (Swindon Borough Council)

Fully restored ancestral home of the St. John family, remodelled in the Georgian classical style in 1743. The fascinating 17th century painted window and the Lady Diana Spencer room are just some of the delights in store in this friendly house. Adjacent is the church with a glittering array of monuments. There are exciting adventure playgrounds, enjoyment for all the family. **Location:** 4 miles west of Swindon, 1 1/2 miles north of M4 Jcn 16. **Open:** Mon–Sat, 10–1pm, 1pm–5pm. Sun 2pm–5.30pm. Winter closing Nov–Feb at 4pm.

MALMESBURY HOUSE

The Close, Salisbury, Wiltshire, SP1 2EB
Tel: 01722 327 027 Fax: 01722 334 414(J. H. Cordle Esq.)

Malmesbury House was originally a 13 C canonry. It was enlarged in the 14 C and leased to the Harris family in 1660, whose descendant became the first Earl of Malmesbury. The west façade was added by Sir Christopher Wren to accommodate rooms displaying superb rococo plasterwork. Among the many illustrious visitors were King Charles I and the composer Handel, who used the chapel above the St Ann gate for recitals. Francis Webb, a direct ancestor of Queen Elizabeth II lived here in the 1770s. Family in residence. **Location:** City of Salisbury, Cathedral Close, East end of North Walk by St Ann Gate. Coaches to St John's Street. **Open:** Groups by appointment only, lunches served in Music Room. Open Maundy Thur for Easter weekend and all Bank Hols and Tues–Thurs following. 10.30–5.30pm, throughout the year. **Admission:** Adult: £5, students: £3. Price includes entrance to garden.

PYTHOUSE

Tisbury, Salisbury, Wiltshire, SP3 6PB.
Tel: 01747 870 210 Fax: 01747 871 786
(Country Houses Association)

Palladian style Georgian mansion. **Location:** 2.5 miles W of Tisbury, 4.5 miles N of Shaftsbury. **Station(s):** Tisbury (2.5 miles). **Open:** May–Sept, Wed & Thurs, 2–5pm. (Last entry 4pm). **Admission:** Adults £2.50, children £1. Free car park. No dogs admitted. Groups by arrangement.

SALISBURY CATHEDRAL

The Close, Salisbury SP1 2EF
Tel: 01722 328726 Fax: 01722 323569

Surrounded by ancient stone walls, peaceful lawns and historic houses including Malmesbury House (see above), stands Salisbury Cathedral. Built between 1220 and 1258 it is a supreme example of medieval architecture and its spire, at 40ft, is the tallest in England. Treasures include an original Magna Carta and Europe's oldest working clock. There are regular tours of the Cathedral and Tower. All visitors are welcome to attend daily services. **Location:** In the close, just south of the city centre.

STONEHENGE

Amesbury SP4 7DE
Tel:01980 624715 (Information line) (English Heritage)

The mystical and awe–inspiring stone circle at Stonehenge is one of the most famous prehistoric monuments in the world, designated by UNESCO as a World Heritage Site. Stonehenge's orientation on the rising and setting sun has always been one of its most remarkable features. Visitors to Stonehenge can discover the history and legends which surround this unique stone circle, which began over 5,000 years ago. **Location:** 2 miles west of Amesbury on junction of A303 and A344/A360. **Open:** 16 March–31 May daily: 9.30–6pm, 1 June–31 August daily, 9–7pm. 1 September–15 October daily 9.30–6pm. 16 October–15 March, daily 9.30–4pm. **Admission:** £3.90, £2.90, £2.00.

map 3 K3

map 3 J3

STOURHEAD

Stourton, Warminster, BA12 6QD, Wiltshire.
Tel: 01747 841 152 Fax: 01747 841 152 (The National Trust)

Stourhead combines Britain's foremost landscape garden with a fine Palladian mansion. Stourhead Garden is one of the most famous examples of the early 18th century English landscape movement. Planned in the belief that it was "Tiresome for the foot to travel, to where the eye had already been", the garden continually surprises the visitor with fresh glimpses of its' enchanting lakes and temples. The House was designed in 1721 for Henry Hoare by Colen Campbell. Its' contents include a collection of furniture designed by the younger Chippendale and many fine works of art. Interesting features include two Iron Age hill forts and King Alfred's Tower, a 160 ft high red brick folly. This tower offers magnificent views across the three counties of Wiltshire, Somerset and Dorset. Stourhead is owned by the National Trust, an independent charity. **Location:** Stourton, off B3092, 3 miles

N of A303 (Mere). 2hrs from London, 1.5 hrs from Exeter. **Open:** Garden: All Year Daily, 9–7pm (or dusk if earlier), except 23–25 July (Fête Champêtre), when gardens close at 5pm (last admission 4pm). House: 28 Mar–1 Nov, Sat–Wed, 12–5.30pm or dusk if earlier (last admission 5pm). Plant Centre: Open Mar–Sept, 12–6pm (12noon–4pm in Mar). 01747 840 894 **Admission:** Garden or House: Adult £4.40, children £2.40, group (15 or more) £3.80, family £10.30. (2 Adults & up to 3 children). Combined Garden and House: Adult £7.90, children £3.70, family £20.60. Large coach and car park. Guided Tours: Pre-booked garden tours are available on request throughout the year. Please phone 01747 841152 to confirm opening times & prices. **Events:** Held throughout June to October. Please phone for enquiries.

map 3 J3

SHELDON MANOR
Chippenham, Wiltshire, SN14 0RG
Tel: 01249 653 120   Fax: 01249 461 097(Antony Gibbs)

Sheldon Manor has been opened to the public for the past 21 years. Unfortunately during 1998, this splendid manor house, the sole survivor of a deserted medieval village, has had to close. This closure is due to the doctor's advice on the owner's health. Apologies are passed on to any disappointed potential visitors.

map 3
J2

WILTON HOUSE
The Estate Office, Wilton, Salisbury SP2 OBJ
Tel: 01722 746720 Fax: 01722 744447

From 9th century nunnery to the present home of the 17th Earl of Pembroke, Wilton House provides a fascinating insight on British history. Marvel at Inigo Jones' magnificent staterooms, including the Double Cube Room. Admire the world famous art collection. Relax in 21 acres of landscaped parkland, water and rose gardens beside the River Nadder and Palladian Bridge. The modern interpretative displays, including the award winning introductory film Tudor Kitchen and Victorian Laundry bring history to life. Enjoy the 'Wareham Bears' – a unique display of some 200 miniature dressed teddies with their own House and stables. **Open:** 4 Apr–25 Oct 1998, 11–6pm. (Last admission 5pm).

map 4
B5

AVEBURY MANOR AND GARDEN
nr Marlborough SN8 1RF Tel: 01672 539250

Open: Garden: 1 April to 1 Nov: daily except Mon & Thur (open BH Mon) 11–5.30. Last admission 5 or dusk if earlier. House: 1 April to 28 Oct: Tues, Wed, Sun & BH Mon 2–5.30. Last admission as garden.

GREAT CHALFIELD MANOR
nr Melksham SN12 8NJ Tel: 01225 782239 Fax: 01225 783379

Open: 1 April to 29 Oct: Tues, Wed, Thur by guided tours only, starting 12.15, 2.15, 3, 3.45 & 4.30. Guided tours of the manor take 45min and numbers are limited to 25. It is suggested that visitors arriving when a tour is in progress visit the adjoining parish church and garden first. Closed on public holidays. Note: Groups are welcome to visit the Manor in organised parties on Fri & Sat, by prior written arrangement with Mrs Robert Floyd. Organisers of coach parties should plan to allow 2hrs because of limits on numbers in house.

LACOCK ABBEY
Lacock, nr Chippenham SN15 2LG Tel: Abbey 01249 730227

Open: Museum, cloisters & grounds: 1 March to 1 Nov: daily (closed Good Fri) 11–5.30. Abbey: 1 April to 1 Nov: daily, except Tues, 1–5.30; last admission 5. Museum open some winter weekends; tel. for details. Events: leaflet available on request.

MOMPESSON HOUSE
The Close, Salisbury SP1 2EL Tel: 01722 335659

Open: 1 April to 1 Nov: daily except Thur & Fri 12–5.30. Last admission 5.

WESTWOOD MANOR
Bradford-on-Avon BA15 2AF Tel: 01225 863374

Open: 1 April to 30 Sept: Sun, Tues & Wed 2–5. At other times parties of up to 20 by written application with s.a.e. to the tenant. **Admission:** £3.50. No reduction for parties or children. No WC

Yorkshire

Yorkshire nowadays is sub-divided into various administrative areas. Pleasure-seekers can happily forget this contemporary arrangement.

North Yorkshire hosts two national parks, an excellent spa town in Harrogate, the oldest town mentioned in the Doomsday book – Knaresborough and enchanting small cities such as Ripon.

Between the Lake District and the North York Moors lie the Yorkshire Dales which has a farming landscape, with stunning limestone walls, highlands and steep falling valleys.

The capital of the whole region, York, has retained so

Mount Grace Priory, English Heritage

much of its medieval structure that walking into its centre is like entering into a museum. Home to England's largest medieval church, the wonderfully gothic York Minster houses the largest collection of medieval stained glass in Britain and embodies history, with its 18 medieval churches, 2 mile long medieval city walls, elegant Jacobean and Georgian

architecture and fine museums. The town and country landscapes of West and South Yorkshire are striking. The powerful landscape of the Moors and the Pennine Moors which inspired the Brontë family have withstood all attempts to tarnish their glory.

Leeds is the third largest of Britain's provincial cities. Productions at The Grand by Opera North and the impressive collection of British 20th century art at the City Gallery have helped to give Leeds a thriving and prosperous cultural scene.

In the 16th century, neighbouring Bradford was a market town and the opening of its canal in 1774 boosted trade. By 1850, it was the world's capital for the manufacture of wool. Today Bradford and the entire area east of the Pennines have found new ways to achieve prosperity.

Yorkshire traditionally is England's greatest county and home to a huge variety of historic houses and monuments.

Aske Hall

Aske, Richmond, North Yorkshire DL10 5HJ
Tel: 01748 850391 Fax: 01748 823252 (The Marquess of Zetland)

The Hall – a Georgian gem – nestles in Capability Brown parkland with lake, follies, meadows, woods and a new terraced garden, the visionary creation of Lady Zetland described as the most ambitious gardening scheme of the day! It has been the family seat of the Dundas family for over 200 years and boasts an impressive collection of 18th century furniture, paintings and porcelain. **Location:** 2 m from A1 on the Richmond/Gilling West Road (B6274) **Stations:** Darlington 13 m away. **Admission:** £4 – for groups of 15+ by appointment only. "A Taste of Gentility", a tour followed by Yorkshire afternoon tea in the Regency dining room on Weds in July & Aug £12pp. Booking essential Tel 01748 850391 for further details. **Events/Exhibitions:** Telephone for programme. **Conferences:** Suitable for up to a capacity of 100.

map 11 H5

The Bar Convent

17 Blossom Street, York YO2 2AH
Tel: 01904 643238 Fax: 01904 631792

The Bar Convent is an elegant Georgian building (1787) located on the corner of Blossom St and Nunnery Lane. It houses a beautiful neo-classical chapel (1769); both were designed by Thomas Atkinson. The Bar Convent Museum outlines the early history of Christianity in the North of England and also tells the story of Mary Ward, the foundress of the Institute of the Blessed Virgin Mary (IBVM). There are guided museum tours on Mon-Fri at 10.30am and 2.30pm. There is a cafe which serves coffee, tea and wine as well as hot meals (9.30–5.00). There is a small souvenir and gift shop. Conference and residential facilities are available to groups; please contact the Business manager on 01904-643238.

map 8 D2

Bolton Abbey

Skipton, North Yorkshire, BD23 6EX. Tel: 01756 710 227
Fax 01756 710 535 (Trustees of the Chatsworth Settlement)

The Yorkshire Estate of the Duke and Duchess of Devonshire. The Augustine Bolton Priory was founded in 1154 and is now partly parish church. Other historic buildings include the 13th century Barden Tower – formerly owned by the Cliffords of Skipton. The Estate offers spectacular walks in some of the most beautiful countryside in England – along the riverside, on the heather moors and Nature Trails in Strid Wood (S.S.S.I.) renowned for its bird life and rare plants. **Location:** On B6160, N from the roundabout junction with the A59 Skipton-Harrogate Road, 23 miles from Leeds. **Station(s):** Skipton & Ilkley. **Open:** All year. **Admission:** £3.00 car park charge. £1.50 car park charge for disabled. No charge for coaches. Motorised chairs available. **Refreshments:** Restaurant and 2 tearooms. Accommodation: Farmhouse B&B, self-catering cottage, hotel.

map 8 B2

BOLTON CASTLE

Leyburn, North Yorkshire, DL8 4ET
Tel: 01969 623 981 Fax: 01969 623 332
(Hon. Mr & Mrs Harry Orde-Powlett)

Completed in 1399, Bolton Castle was the stronghold of the Scrope family. The Castle has a wealth of history including connections with the "Pilgrimage of Grace" and Richard III. Mary, Queen of Scots was imprisoned here for 6 months. Tableaux displays recreate the idea of everyday life in a medieval castle. Major conservation work was completed in 1995. A medieval garden and vineyard have been redeveloped on the site of the original gardens. Tearoom and gift shop. **Location:** Just off A684, 6 miles W of Leyburn. **Open:** Daily, Mar–Nov. (Mar–Apr, 10–4pm; May–Nov, 10–5pm). **Admission:** Guided tour by arrangement for groups of 15+. Adults £3, OAP/Children £2. **Refreshments:** Tearoom – meals available, picnic area. Wedding licence.

map 8 B1

BRAMHAM PARK

Wetherby, West Yorkshire, LS23 6ND
Tel: 01937 844 265 Fax: 01937 845 923 (G. F. Lane Fox)

The house was created at the end of the 17th century and affords an opportunity to enjoy a beautiful Queen Anne mansion containing fine furniture, pictures and porcelain – set in magnificent grounds with ornamental ponds, cascades and tall beech hedges – unique in the British Isles for its grand vista design stretching into woodlands. **Location:** 5 miles S of Wetherby, on A1. **Open:** Grounds Only: Easter Weekend, May Day Weekend, Spring Bank Hol Weekend. House & Grounds: 21 Jun–6 Sept, Tues, Wed, Thurs, Sun 1.15–5.30pm. Last admission 5pm. Also Bank Hol Mon. **Admission:** The Estate Office, Bramham Park, Wetherby, LS23 6ND, West Yorkshire. Tel: 01937 844 265. **Refreshments:** Picnics in grounds permitted.

map 11 H7

BROCKFIELD HALL

Warthill, York, North Yorkshire YO3 9XJ
Tel: 01904 489298 (Lord and Lady Martin Fitzalan Howard)

A fine late Georgian house designed by Peter Atkinson, whose father had been assistant to John Carr of York, for Benjamin Agar Esq. Begun in 1804, its outstanding feature is an oval entrance hall with a fine cantilevered stone staircase curving past an impressive Venetian window. It is the happy family home of Lord and Lady Martin Fitzalan Howard. He is the brother of the 17th Duke of Norfolk and son of the late Baroness Beaumont of Carlton Towers, Selby. There are some interesting portraits of her old Roman catholic family, the Stapletons, and some good furniture. **Location:** 5 miles east of York, off A166 or A64 **Open:** August 1–31st 1998, 1pm–4pm except Mondays, other times by appointment. **Admission:** Adults £2.50, children £1.

map 11 J7

BRONTË PARSONAGE MUSEUM

Haworth, Keighley, West Yorkshire, BD22 8DR
Tel: 01535 642 323 Fax: 01535 647 131 (The Brontë Society)

Once the home of the remarkable Brontë family, it is now an intimate museum cared for by the Brontë Society. This small Georgian parsonage has rooms furnished as in the Brontës' day, with displays of their personal treasures, their pictures, books and manuscripts. See where the writers of 'Jane Eyre' and 'Wuthering Heights' lived. **Open:** Every day, except 24–27 December 1997 and 12 January – 6 February 1998. Please phone for admission prices and opening times.

map 8 B3

BRODSWORTH HALL

Brodsworth, Nr. Doncaster, South Yorkshire
Tel: 01302 722598 Fax: 01302 337165 (English Heritage)

Brodsworth Hall is an outstanding example of a Victorian country house. Within its grand Italianate exterior, visitors can glimpse a vanished way of life as they progress through over 30 rooms ranging from the sumptuous family reception rooms to the plain but functional servants' wing. A pervasive sense of faded grandeur and of time past adds an element of enchantment to the Hall. The restored Victorian gardens form the ideal setting. **Location:** 5 miles NW of Doncaster, A635 from Junction 37, A1(M). **Open:** 1 Apr– 1 Nov, Tue–Sun & Bank Hols, 1–6pm. Last admission 5pm. Gardens and tearooms open noon. Guided tours mornings by appointment. Gardens, shop and tearooms only winter weekends. **Admission:** Adults £4.50, Children £2.30, Concs £3.40. Garden only tickets available. No dogs.

map 8 B3

BROUGHTON HALL

Skipton, North Yorkshire BD23 3AE
Tel: 01756 792267 Fax: 01756 792362 (H. R. Tempest)

Broughton Hall was built in 1597 and remains the home of the Tempest family. It has since been enlarged on three occasions. The gardens were laid out by **Nesfield** in 1854 and are a fine example of his work. The house was largely refurbished in the 19th century and contains much documented **Gillow** furniture. There is also a fine 18th century **Catholic chapel**, still in regular use. <u>Open:</u> The house is open to the public on the summer bank holidays (except Easter Monday) and for guided groups **by appointment**. Individuals wanting to see the house should contact the Estate office (Tel: 01756 799608). <u>Admission:</u> £5 per person with no concessions. The house and grounds are also available for **Events and Corporate entertainment** by arrangement..

map 8 B2

CANNON HALL

Cawthorne, Barnsley, South Yorkshire, S75 4AT
Tel: 01226 790 270
(Barnsley Metropolitan Borough Council)

18th century house by Carr of York. Collections of fine furniture, paintings, glassware, art nouveau pewter and pottery. Also the Regimental Museum of the 13th/18th Royal Hussars. 70 acres of parkland. Walled garden with historic fruit trees. Gift shop. **Location:** 5 miles W of Barnsley, off A635. 1 mile N of Cawthorne. **House Open:** Apr–Oct. Tue–Sat: 10.30–5pm. Sun: 12 noon–5pm. Closed Mon, except Bank Hol Mons. Winter opening subject to change. Please confirm before your visit. Small admission charge. Park open all year round. **Refreshments:** Victorian kitchen cafe open Summer and Sun pm. Limited disabled access.

BURTON AGNES HALL

Burton Agnes, Diffield, East Yorks YO25 0ND
Tel: 01262 490 324 Fax: 01262 490 513 (Burton Agnes Hall Preservation Trust Ltd).

The Hall is a magnificent example of late Elizabethan architecture - still lived in by descendants of the family who built it in 1598. There are wonderful carvings, lovely furniture and a fine collection of modern French and English paintings of the Impressionist Schools. The walled garden contains a potager, maze, herbaceous borders, campanula collection, jungle garden and giant games set in coloured gardens. Also woodland gardens and walk, children's corner, Norman manor house, donkey wheel and gift shop. **Location:** 6 miles SW of Bridlington on Driffield/Bridlington Rd (A166). **Open:** Apr 1–Oct 31 daily 11–5pm. **Admission:** Adults £4, OAPs £3.50, Children £2. **Gardens Only:** Adults £2, OAPs £1.75, Children £1. **Refreshments:** Licensed cafeteria. Teas, light lunches & refreshments.

map 9 F2

CASTLE HOWARD

Nr York, North Yorkshire YO6 7DA
Tel: 01653 648444 Fax: 01653 648462 (The Hon. Simon Howard)

Magnificent palace designed by Vanbrugh in 1699. One of The Treasure Houses of England and one of Britain's most spectacular stately homes. Impressive Great Hall and beautiful rooms are filled with fine furniture, paintings and objets d'art. Extensive grounds with lakes and colourful woodland. Rose Garden, Plant Centre, Adventure Playground. **Location:** 15 miles NE of York; 3 miles off A64; 6 miles W of Malton; 22 miles Scarborough. **Open:** Daily 14 March – 2 November. Grounds from 10am, House from 11am. Last admission 4.30pm **Admission:** Adult £6.50, Child £3.50, OAP £5.50. Groups (min. 12 people): Adult £5.50, Child £3, OAP £5. Garden only: Adult £4, Child £2 **Refreshments:** Licensed cafeteria in House, Lakeside Cafe. Cafe and Shops facilities in Stable Courtyard.

THE GRAND ASSEMBLY ROOMS

Blake Street, York, North Yorkshire
Tel: 01904 637 257

Georgian Ballroom, fully restored, scheduled monument status. Operates as cafe/restaurant/function room. Available for hire in part or as a whole for weddings, dinner dances, functions etc. Refreshments, light meals, disabled access. Live entertainment.

CONSTABLE BURTON HALL

Constable Burton, Leyburn, North Yorkshire DL8 5LJ
Tel: 01677 450428 Fax: 01677 450622 (Mr Charles Wyvill)

Situated 3 miles east of Leyburn on the A684 and 6 miles west of the A1. A large romantic garden surrounded by 18th century parkland with a superb John Carr house (not open). Fine trees, woodland walks, garden trails and nature trails, rockery with an interesting collection of alpines and extensive shrubs and roses. Set in beautiful countryside at the entrance to Wensleydale. **Open:** Gardens Mar 25–Oct 25 daily 9–6pm. **Admission:** Please phone for details. Group Tours of the house and gardens available by Phil Robinson, The Dales Plantsman. Tel: 01677 460225.

map 8 G1

DUNCOMBE PARK

Helmsley, Ryedale, York, North Yorks YO6 5EB
Tel: 01439 770213 Fax: 01439 771114

Lord and Lady Feversham invite you to join them in exploring and experiencing the delights of Duncombe Park; the mansion is set within sweeping terraces and temples and stands above the Rye valley. It offers dramatic views over the Nature Reserve and surrounding countryside. View the Mansion's restored principal rooms, typical of a late 19th century grand interior. End a perfect day with a visit to our Yorkshire Tearoom and Shop. Family season ticket only £30 includes admission into Duncombe Park Events (except musical) in any one year. **1998 Events:** Country Fair, Antiques Fairs, Steam Fair and Craft Festivals, Point to Point. **Open:** House & Garden: 11–5pm (Last admission 4.30pm) 29 Mar–3 Nov 1998. Apr/Oct: Sun to Thur (Closed Fri and Sats, except Easter Weekend). May–Sept: Sun to Fri (Closed Sats). Parkland Centre Tearoom/Shop, National Nature Reserve (Open to non-visitors to the house) 10.30–5.30pm 29 Mar–3 Nov 1998: Daily. **Admission:** House & Garden: £5.50–adult; £4.50–concession, £4–group, £2.50–child (10-16); £12.50–family (2+2) Garden: £3.50–adult; £1.50–child (10-16). Disabled access to the House, Grounds & Parkland. Free car park and play area. For further information please contact Sally at The Estate Office, Helmsley, York. YO6 5EB Tel: 01439 770213; Fax: 01439 771114.

map 8 D1

HAREWOOD HOUSE

The Harewood Estate, Leeds, West Yorkshire, LS17 9LQ
Tel: 0113 288 6331 Fax: 0113 288 6467 (Earl & Countess of Harewood)

Award-winning Harewood is renowned for its stunning architecture, exquisite interiors and outstanding collections; beautiful gardens and 'Capability Brown' landscape, fascinating Bird Garden and wide variety of special events throughout the year. Winner of 'Visitor Attraction of the Year, 1995' and 'Best Museum of Fine & Applied Arts 1996'. **Location:** A61, between Leeds and Harrogate. **Open:** 17 Mar–1 Nov, daily (except 5 June). Grounds & Bird Garden: 10am. House: 11am. Last admissions 4.30pm. **Admission:** Adult £6.75, OAP £6, children £4.50, family £21. **Events/Exhibitions:** The Watercolour Rooms and contemporary Terrace Gallery reflect the 1998 Year of Photography theme. Below stairs Victorian life explored in a range of events in the Old Kitchen and through Off the Shelf fascinating facts from the three libraries are revealed. Telephone for details.

map 8 C2

HARLOW CARR BOTANICAL GARDENS

Crag Lane, Harrogate, North Yorkshire HG3 1QB
Tel: 01423 565418 Fax: 01423 530663 (Northern Horticultural Society)

Sixty-eight acre headquarters of the Northern Horticultural Society. Vegetable, fruit and flower trials. Rock, foliage, scented, winter and heather gardens. Alpines, herbaceous beds, display houses, fern house, streamside, woodland and arboretum. National collections, Museum of Gardening, Model Village, library, childrens' play area. Fully licensed restaurant, plant and gift centre. Picnic area. Courses, exhibitions, displays, walks and talks held on a regular basis throughout the year. Ample free coach parking, shelters, seating and hard surface pathways. Driver facilities vouchers. **Location:** 1½ miles W of town centre on B6162 Otley road. **Open:** Daily from 9.30am. Last admission 6pm or dusk if earlier. **Admission:** Adults £3.50, OAPs and groups of 20+ £2.60.

map 8 C2

FAIRFAX HOUSE

Castlegate, York, YO1 1RN, North Yorkshire
Tel: 01904 655 543 Fax: 01904 652 262 (York Civic Trust)

An 18th century house designed by John Carr of York, and described as a class architectural masterpiece of its age. Certainly one of the finest town houses in England and saved from near collapse by the York Civic Trust who restored it to its former glory during 1982/84. In addition to the superbly decorated plaster work, wood and wrought iron, the house is now home for an outstanding collection of 18th century furniture and clocks, formed by the late Noel Terry. Described by Christies as one of the finest private collections of this century, it enhances and complements the house and helps to create a very special 'lived in' feeling. The gift of the entire collection by Noel Terry's Trustees to the Civic Trust has enabled it to fill the house with appropriate pieces of the period and has provided the basis for what can now be considered a fully furnished Georgian Town house.

Location: Centre of York, follow signs for Castle Area and Jorvik Centre. **Station(s):** York (10 mins walk). **Open:** 21 Feb–6 Jan, Mon–Thurs & Sat, 11am–5pm, Sun 1.30–5pm. Last admission 4.30pm. Closed Fri, except during Aug. Special evening tours, connoisseur visits and private dinners welcomed by arrangement with the Director. **Admission:** Adults £3.50, children £1.50, OAPs/students £3.00. Adult parties (pre-booked 15+) £2.50, children £1.25. **Events/Exhibitions:** 'The Pleasures of the Table' exhibition, 1 Sept–20 Nov 1998. **Conferences:** By arrangement with the Director. Public car park within 50 yards. Suitable for disabled persons only with assistance (by telephoning beforehand, staff can be available to help). A small gift shop offers selected antiques, publications and gifts. Opening times are the same as the house.

map 8
D2

Yorkshire

HELMSLEY WALLED GARDEN RESTORATION PROJECT

Cleveland Park, Helmsley, York, North Yorkshire, YO6 5AH
Tel: 01439 771 427 Fax: 01439 771 427 (Lord Feversham)

With Helmsley Castle as a backdrop, this fully walled 5 acre garden built for Duncombe Park in 1780, growing fruit, vegetables and flowers. In 1919 it became a market garden until 1981. The glasshouses were derelict, the pond buried and the walls covered in ivy. An ambitious project began in 1994 to restore the gardens to their former glory. Walls refruited, pond and old paths restored and produce growing. Pending charitable status will assist restoration of the glasshouses. Visit and enjoy the progress with exciting projects. **Open:** Easter– 31 Oct. Afternoons Fri–Sun in winter. For further information contact Mrs Alison Ticehurst on 01439 771 427. **Admission:** Adult £2, OAP £1, student £1, child free. Discount for groups.

HOVINGHAM HALL

Hovingham, North Yorkshire YO6 4LU
Tel: 01653 628206 Fax: 01653 628668 (Sir Marcus Worsley)

Palladian House designed c.1760 by Thomas Worsley to his own design. Unique entry by huge riding school. Visitors see family portraits and rooms in everyday use; also the extensive garden with magnificent yew hedges and dove-cot and the private cricket ground, said to be the oldest in England. **Location:** 20 miles N of York on Malton/Helmsley Road (B1257). **Open:** Open for parties of 15 or more *by written appointment* only Apr to end Sept 1998. Tues, Wed & Thurs 11am–7pm. **Admission:** £3.50, Children £1.50. **Refreshments:** At the Hall by arrangement. Meals at the Worsley Arms Hotel, Hovingham. **Conferences:** Facilities for up to 140.

LEDSTON HALL

Hall Lane, Ledston, Castleford, WF10 2BB, West Yorkshire
Tel: 01423 523 423 Fax: 01423 521 373 (G. H. H. Wheler)

17th century mansion with some earlier work. **Location:** 2 miles N of Castleford, off A656. **Station(s):** Castleford (2 3/4 miles). **Open:** Exterior only: May–Aug, Mon–Fri, 9–4pm. Other days by appointment. **Refreshments:** Chequers Inn, Ledsham (1 mile).

LINDLEY MURRAY SUMMERHOUSE

The Mount School, Dalton Terrace, York
Tel: 01904 667500 Fax: 01904 667524

The Summerhouse dated from 1774 and was situated in the grounds of Holgate House, York (now the Collingwood Hotel). Holgate House was the home of Lindley Murray (1795–1826). When the house was sold to the North Eastern Railway Company in 1901, William Wilberforce Morrell, the owner, presented the Summerhouse to the Mount School. Originally positioned adjacent to the boundary wall of the school grounds, it was moved to its present position in 1966. The building is listed Grade II*. A major refurbishment was carried out during 1997. Grants towards the cost of the work undertaken were received from – English Heritage, Mount Old Scholars' Association, York Civic Trust and York Georgian Society. The Grant from the Noel G Terry Charitable Trust was made in memory of the Terry Family, Scholars of The Mount School from 1901–1909. Architect: Clive Sheridan BA (hons), B Arch, RIBA, Gilling East, York.

LOTHERTON HALL

Aberford, Yorkshire, LS25 3EB
Tel: 0113 281 3259 Fax: 0113 281 2100 (Leeds City Council)

Modest late Victorian and Edwardian country house of great charm and character, formerly the home of the Gascoigne family. Fine collections of furniture, silver, pottery and porcelain, paintings, sculpture and costume, including many family heirlooms. Famous period gardens with a deer park and bird garden. **Location:** 1mile E of A1 at Aberford, on the Towton Road (B1217). **Open:** 1 Apr–31 Oct, Tue–Sat 10–5pm, Sun 1–5pm. 1 Nov–31 Mar, Tue–Sat 10–4pm, Sun 12–4pm Closed Jan & Feb, closed Mons. **Admission:** Please contact for details of admission prices. **Refreshments:** Cafe in stable block.

184

MARKENFIELD HALL

Ripon, North Yorkshire HG4 3AD
Tel: 01609 780306 Agent (The Lady Grantley)

Fine example of English manor house 14th, 15th & 16th century buildings surrounded by moat. **Location:** 3 miles S of Ripon off the Ripon/Harrogate (A61). Access is up a road marked Public Bridleway Hell Wath Lane. **Open:** Apr–Oct, Mon 10–12.30pm and 2.15–5pm. **Admission:** Adults £3. Children £1.50 (under 5 free).

map 8
C2

MOUNT GRACE PRIORY

Saddle Bridge DL6 3JG
Tel: 01609 883494 (English Heritage)

Hidden in tranquil wooded countryside at the foot of the Cleveland Hills, this is one of the loveliest settings of any English priory, and it is also the best preserved Carthusian monastery in England. Monks lived like hermits in their cells and one cell, recently restored, is furnished to give a clear picture of their austere routine of work and prayer. Visitors enter through the manor built by Thomas Lascelles in 1654 on the site of the monastery guest house. **Location:** 12 miles north of Thirsk, 7 miles north east of Northallerton on A19. **Open:** 1 April–1 Nov, daily, 10–6pm (or dusk if earlier in October), 2 Nov–31 March: Wed–Sun, 10–4pm. Closed 1–2pm in winter. **Admission:** £2.70, £2, £1.40.

NEWBURGH PRIORY

Coxwold, York, North Yorkshire, YO6 4AS
Tel: 01347 868 435 (Sir George Wombwell, Bt.)

One of the North's most interesting historic houses. Originally built in 1145 with alterations in 1568 and 1720-1760, the Priory has been the home of one family and its descendants since 1538. The house contains the tomb of Oliver Cromwell (his third daughter, Mary, was married to Viscount Fauconberg, the owner from 1647-1700). In the grounds there is a really beautiful water garden full of rare alpines, other plants and rhododendrons. **Location:** 5 miles from Easingwold, off A19, 9 miles from Thirsk. **Open: House & Grounds:** 1 Apr–28 June, Sun & Wed & Bank Hol Mons Easter and Aug. House open 2.30–4.45pm. Grounds open 2–6pm. Open at other times for parties of 25+ by appointment with the Administrator. **Admission: House & Grounds:** Adults £3.50, children £1. Grounds only: Adults £2, children free. **Refreshments:** Afternoon tea is served in the original Old Priory Kitchens.

map 8
D1

NORTON CONYERS

Ripon, North Yorkshire, HG4 5EQ
Tel: 01765 640333 Fax: 01765 692772 (Sir James and Lady Graham)

Visited by Charlotte Brontë, Norton Conyers is an original of 'Thornfield Hall' in 'Jane Eyre' and a family legend was an inspiration for the mad Mrs Rochester. Another visitor was James II when Duke of York, in 1679. The room and the bed he and his wife traditionally used are still to be seen. Over 370 years of occupation by the Grahams (they bought it in 1624) have given the house a noticeably friendly atmosphere. Family portraits, furniture, ceramics and costumes. The paintings in the Great Hall include a celebrated John Ferneley, 'The Quorn Hunt', painted in 1822. The 18th century walled garden, with Orangery and herbaceous borders, includes a plant sales area, specialising in unusual hardy plants. Pick your own fruit in season; please check beforehand. **Location:** Near Wath, 4 miles N of Ripon, 3 miles from A1. **Open:** (House) Bank Hol Suns & Mons, Suns 7 Jun–13 Sept, daily 20–25 Jul, 2–5pm. (Garden) Suns & Bank Hol Mons, 12 Apr – 13 Sep, 11.30–5pm; daily 20–25 Jul, 2–5pm. **Admission:** Adults £2.95, children (10–16) £2.50, OAPs £2. Prices for parties on application. Garden is free (donations welcome); a charge is, however, made at charity openings. **Refreshments:** Teas and light refreshments for booked parties. Teas are available at garden charity openings. Dogs (except guide dogs) in grounds and garden only and must be on a lead. Photography by owners' written permission only. No high-heeled shoes in house, please. Wheelchair access ground floor only.

map 8
C1

NEWBY HALL & GARDENS

Ripon, North Yorkshire, HG4 5AE
Tel: 01423 322 583 Fax: 01423 324 452 (R. E. J. Compton)

The family home of Mr and Mrs Robin Compton is one of Yorkshire's renowned Adam houses. It is set amidst 25 acres of award-winning gardens full of rare and beautiful plants. Famous double herbaceous borders with formal compartmented gardens, including a species rose garden, water and rock garden, the Autumn Garden and the tranquillity of Sylvia's Garden – truly a 'Garden for all Seasons'. Also holds National Collection of genus Cornus. The contents of the house are superb and include a unique Gobelins Tapestry Room, a gallery of classical statuary and some of Chippendale's finest furniture. Other attractions include railway rides beside the river, an adventure garden for children and a woodland discovery walk. There is a shop and plant stall and a picnic area. **Location:** 4 miles SE of Ripon on Boroughbridge Road (B6265). 3 miles W of A1. Harrogate (14 miles). York (20 miles). Leeds (35 miles). Skipton (32 miles). **Station(s):** Harrogate or York. **Open:** House & Garden: 1 Apr– 30 Sept, Tues–Sun and Bank Hol Mons. Garden only open Suns in Oct and school half-term. **Admission: House & Garden:** Adults £6, children/disabled £3.60, OAPs £5. **Garden Only:** Adult £4.30, children/disabled £2.90, OAPs £3.70. **Refreshments:** Lunches and teas in the licensed Garden Restaurant. **Events/Exhibitions:** 10 May – Spring Plant Fair; 6–7 Jun & 5–6 Sept – Rainbow Craft Fair; 19 Jul – Historic Vehicle Rally; 20 Sept – Autumn Plant Fair. **Conferences:** Function room for about 100.

map 8
C2

OAKWELL HALL

Birstall, Nr. Batley, West Yorkshire, WF19 9LG
Tel: 01924 326 240 (Kirklees Metropolitan Council)

This beautiful Elizabethan manor house, set in period gardens, has delighted visitors for centuries. Charlotte Brontë visited it in the 19th century and used it as a model for Fieldhead – the home of the heroine in Shirley. Built in 1583, the hall is now set out as it would have been in the 1690s and is surrounded by 100 acres of the original estate – now a country park. The site boasts excellent visitor facilities including a café, a well-stocked shop and an adventure playground. In addition, the innovative and unique 'Discover Oakwell' exhibition introduces children to the environment of a country park. Events range from period candlelight evenings to lively family activities. **Open:** 11–5pm, Mon–Fri, 12–5pm Sat & Sun.

 map 8 C3

RED HOUSE

Oxford Road, Gomersal, Cleckheaton, West Yorkshire
Tel: 01274 335 100 (Kirklees Metropolitan Council)

Built in 1660 by the Taylor family, Red House gets its name from its unusual red brick construction which sets it apart from the surrounding houses of local stone. Mary Taylor, daughter of the House in the early 19th century, was a close and life-long friend of Charlotte Brontë who stayed there often and featured the House as Briarmains in Shirley. The House now looks very much as it would have done in Charlotte's time; with a mixture of original and reproduction furniture, each room brings you closer to the 1830s. Permanent exhibitions unfold the story of the Taylor family and the museum shop sells an unusual range of period crafts, gifts and books. **Open:** Mon–Fri 11–5pm, Sat–Sun 12–5pm. **Admission:** Free.

 map 8 C3

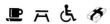

RIEVAULX ABBEY

Helmsley, North Yorks
Tel: 01439 798228 (English Heritage)

Visit the spectacular remains of the first Cistercian monastery in Northern England and experience the unrivalled peace and serenity of its setting in the beautiful wooded valley of the River Rye. Imaginations will be fired as you listen to our audio tour while exploring the extensive remains; the soaring graceful arches silhouetted against the sky will take the breath away. **Location:** In Rievaulx , 2 1/4 m W of Helmsley on minor road off B1257. **Open:** 1 Apr–1 Nov daily 10am–6pm (or dusk if earlier in Oct), Open 9.30am–7pm July–Aug. 2 Nov–31 Mar daily 10am–4pm. (Closed 24–5 Dec). **Admission:** Adult: £2.90, Conc: £2.20, Child: £1.50. (15% discount for groups of 11 or more).

 map 8 D1

SEWERBY HALL & GARDENS

Church Lane, Sewerby, Bridlington, YO15 1EA
Tel: Estate Office:01262 673 769 Hall: 01262 677 874
(East Riding of Yorkshire Council)

Sewerby Hall and Gardens, set in 50 acres of parkland overlooking Bridlington Bay, dates back to 1715. The Georgian House, with its 19th C Orangery, is now the Museum of East Yorkshire and contains history/archaeology displays, art galleries and an Amy Johnson Room with a collection of her trophies and mementos. The grounds include the magnificent walled Old English and Rose gardens and host many events all year round. Activities for all the family include a children's zoo and play areas, golf, putting, bowls, plus woodland and clifftop walks. **Location:** Bridlington, 2m NE. **Station:** Bridlington (2.5 miles). **Open:** Hall: 10 Apr–1 Nov, 10–6pm daily. Off peak 7 Mar–7 Apr and 2 Nov–10 Jan 1999, Sat–Tue (closed Christmas week Mon–Fri). Gardens open throughout the year. **Refreshments:** Traditional tearooms.

 C map 9 F2

RIPLEY CASTLE

Ripley Castle Estate, Harrogate, North Yorkshire.
Tel: 01423 770152   Fax: 01423 771745 (Sir Thomas and Lady Ingilby)

For almost 700 years, Ripley has been the domain of the Ingilby family. The Castle Gatehouse was built to keep the Scots out in 1450, the Old Tower in 1555 and the remainder in 1780. After his victory at Marston Moor, Oliver Cromwell sought shelter at this Royalist stronghold and was rather surprised to find himself held at gunpoint by 'Trooper' Jane Ingilby who, along with her brother, had fought against him at the battle. The Knight's Chamber contains a Priest's Hiding Hole, a relic of the days when Francis and David Ingilby were described as the most dangerous Papists in the North and the family's associations with the Gunpowder Plot. Guided tours take approx. 75 mins and are full of humour and historical anecdote. The Walled Gardens contain two massive Herbaceous Borders, the National Hyacinth Collection and rare vegetables from the HDRA; the hothouses display a collection of tropical plants and ferns. A walk around the lake and deer park, a stroll to the many interesting shops in the adjacent village of Ripley, or a cup of tea or meal at Cromwells (or something stronger at the Boar's Head) complete a lovely day for the family. **Open:** Apr–Jun, Sept–Oct; Thurs–Sun; Jul–Aug daily; Mon–Fri, 10.30–3.30pm; Sat–Sun, 10.30–3pm. Jan–Mar, Nov–Dec, Tues–Thurs, Sat & Sun 10.30–12.30pm. Groups any day by arrangement. Gardens open daily. **Admission:** £4.50 Adults, £2 children. Family ticket £1 (2 adults & 2 children). Gardens: £2.25 adults, £1 children. OAPs and groups £3.50 castle and gardens, £1.75 gardens only. £1 extra garden conducted tour (min 10 persons)

map 8 C2

SHANDY HALL

Coxwold, York, North Yorkshire, YO6 4AD
Tel: 01347 868 465 (The Laurence Sterne Trust)

Here in 1760–1767 the witty and eccentric parson Laurence Sterne wrote 'Tristram Shandy' and 'A Sentimental Journey'. Shandy Hall was built as a timber-framed open-hall in the mid-15th century and added to by Sterne in the 18th century. Not a museum but a lived-in house where you are sure of a personal welcome. Surrounded by a walled garden full of old-fashioned roses and cottage-garden plants. Also one acre of wild garden in an old quarry. **Location:** 20 miles north of York. **Open:** June–Sept. Wed 2–4.30pm. Sun 2.30–4.30pm. Other times by appointment. Gardens open every day May–Sept, except Sat, 11–4.30pm. **Admission:** Adults £3.00, children half price. Garden only £2. **Refreshments:** In village. **Exhibitions:** June–Sept, paintings by local artists. Unusual plants for sale.

map 8
D1

SHEFFIELD BOTANICAL GARDENS

Clarkhouse Road, Sheffield, S10 2LN. Contact: Sheffield City Council, Meersbrook Park. Tel: 0114 250 0500 Fax: 0114 255 2375

Designed in 1833 by Robert Marnock, the original curator, the Gardens (listed Grade II by English Heritage) are a fine example of the Victorian 'Gardenseque' style. Particularly impressive is the straight promenade up to the 'Paxton Pavilions', an important example of early metal and glass curvilinear structure. Occupying 7.6 hectares in the south-west of the city, the Gardens contain around 5,000 species of plants, including the national collections of Weigela and Diervilla. In addition to the Pavilions, the Gardens contain the highest concentration of listed structures in Sheffield. **Open:** Daily, except Christmas, Boxing & New Year's Days. **Admission:** Free. **Refreshments:** For pre-arranged guided tours. **Events/Exhibitions:** Frequently, held by the Friends of the Botanic Gardens and specialist horticultural societies. **Conferences:** Facilities for 80 people.

map 8
C4

SION HILL HALL

Kirby Wiske, Nr Thirsk, North Yorkshire YO7 4EU
Tel: 01845 587206 Fax: 01845 587486 (H.W. Mawer Trust)

Charming Edwardian Country Mansion by Brierley of York – the 'Lutyens of the North'. The last country house built before the Great War and of outstanding architectural merit. This award winning mansion now houses the Mawer Collection of period furniture, porcelain, paintings, clocks & memorabilia–probably the most eclectic collection in the North. 20 rooms open with 'Members of the Household' in Period Costume. Collection of dolls & costume displays. Birds of Prey & Conservation Centre in the Victorian walled garden with over 90 birds of 35 species including many varieties of owls, falcons, hawks, buzzard, vulture & eagle. Resident Falconer gives flying demonstrations 3 times daily. Disabled access to the House, Grounds & Birds of Prey. Free parking. Gift & Bygones Shop. Plant Centre. Granary Tearoom. **Location:** Off A167; 6 miles S of Northallerton: 4 miles W of Thirsk, 8 miles E of A1 via A61. **Open:** Hall: 22 Mar–31 Oct. Wed to Sun & Bank Hol. Mons 12.30–5pm. Groups by arrangement any time Feb–Nov. Birds: Open all day Mar–Oct. H.H.C. &G. Privilege Card. 50p off normal adult entry to hall only.

SHIBDEN HALL

Lister's Road, Halifax, HX3 6XG, West Yorkshire
Tel: 01422 352 246 Fax: 01422 348 440(Calderdale M.B.C. Leisure Services)

Allow yourself to drift into 600 years of history ... a world without electricity ... where craftsmen worked in wood and iron ... a house where you sense the family has just gone out ... allowing you to enjoy a sense of the past at Shibden Hall, Halifax's Historic Home. Set in 90 acres of park, Shibden Hall provides a whole day of entertainment. **Location:** 2 km outside Halifax, on A58 Leeds Road. **Buses:** 548/549 Brighouse, 508 Leeds, 681/682 Bradford. **Open:** Mar–Nov, Mon–Sat, 10–5pm. Sun, 12–5pm. Last admission 4.30pm. Closed December, January and February. **Admission:** Adults £1.60, children 75p, OAPs 80p, family £4.50. Group rate for pre-booked party. **Refreshments:** Tearoom. Shop, amusements, toilets, car park, disabled access.

map 8 B3

SCARBOROUGH CASTLE

Castle Road, Scarborough YO11 1HY
Tel: 01723 372451 (English Heritage)

Spectacular coastal views from the walls of this enormous 12th century castle. The buttressed castle walls stretch out along the cliff edge and the remains of the great rectangular stone keep, still stand to over three storeys high. There is also the site of a 4th century Roman signal station. The castle was frequently attacked, but despite being blasted by cannons of the Civil War and bombarded from the sea during World War 1, it is still a spectacular place to visit. **Location:** Castle road, east of town centre. **Open:** 1 April –1 Nov, daily, 10–6pm (or dusk if earlier in October). 2 Nov–31 March: Wed to Sun 10–4pm. Closed 1–2pm in winter. **Admission:** £2.20, £1.70, £1.10.

SKIPTON CASTLE

Skipton, BD23 1AQ, North Yorkshire
Tel: 01756 792442 Fax 01756 796100

Keeper of the southern gateway to the Yorkshire Dales for over 900 years, this is one of the best-preserved castles in England. A stronghold of the Lancastrian Cliffords inside Yorkshire, – besieged for three years in the Civil War, the last Royalist bastion in the North – every age left marks visible to the attentive visitor today. Yet the Castle is still fully roofed, so that a visit is enjoyable at any season. Within the precincts is a delightful walled picnic area and a shop selling light refreshments and a range of gifts. **Location:** Skipton is an unspoilt, bustling town, with four market days a week. The Castle gateway stands at the head of the High Street. **Open:** Daily, 10am (Sun 12pm). Last admission at 6pm (Oct–Feb, 4pm). Closed Christmas Day. **Admission:** Adults £3.80, children (5–17) £1.90, children (under 5) free, OAPs £3.20. Family ticket, 2 adults and up to 3 children, £10.40. All under 18s receive a free Castle Explorer's badge. Free tour sheets available in 8 languages. Guides are provided for pre-booked parties at no extra charge. Large car & coach park off nearby High Street. **Internet:** www.yorkshirenet.co.uk/skiptoncastle

map 8 B2

STOCKELD PARK

Wetherby, West Yorkshire, LS22 4AH. Tel: 01937 586 101
Fax: 01937 580 084 (Mr & Mrs P. G. F. Grant)

Stockeld is a beautifully proportioned Palladian villa designed by James Paine in 1763, featuring a magnificent cantilevered staircase in the central oval hall. Stockeld is still very much a family home, with a fine collection of 18th and 19th century furniture and paintings. The house is surrounded by lovely gardens of lawns, large herbaceous and shrub borders, fringed by woodland and set in 100 acres of fine parkland in the midst of an extensive farming estate. **Location:** 2 miles N of Wetherby; 7 miles SE of Harrogate on A661. **Open:** 2 Apr–8 Oct, Thurs only, 2–5pm. **Admission:** Adults £3, children £1.50, OAPs £2. Groups bookings by prior appointment with the Estate Office (tel: 01937 586 101); prices on application.

map 8 C2

SUTTON PARK

Sutton–on–the–Forest, York YO6 1DP
Tel: 01347 810249 Fax: 01347 811251 (Mrs Sheffield)

A charming example of early Georgian architecture with a rich collection of furniture and paintings put together with great style. **Location:** 8 miles N of York on B1363, Helmsley Road. **Open:** Gardens, Easter–end Sept, daily 11–5.30pm. **Admission:** Charges apply. Special rates for groups over 25. There are guided tours by arrangement. Disabled access to the grounds only.

WHITBY ABBEY

Whitby YO22 4JT
Tel: 01947 603568 (English Heritage)

An ancient holy place, once a burial place of Kings and an inspiration for Saints. A religious community was first established at Whitby in 657 by Abbess Hilda and was the home of Cadmon, the first English poet. The remains we can see today are of a Benedictine church built in the 13th and 14th centuries, and include a magnificent three–tiered choir and north transept. It is perched high above the picturesque harbour town of Whitby. **Location:** On cliff top east of Whitby. **Open:** 1 April–1 Nov, daily, 10–6pm (or dusk if earlier in October), 2 Nov–31 March: Wed–Sun, 10–4pm. **Admission:** £1.70, £1.30, £0.90.

TEMPLE NEWSAM HOUSE

Leeds, West Yorkshire, LS15 0AE
Tel: 0113 264 7321 Fax: 0113 260 2285 (Leeds City Council)

The magnificent Tudor-Jacobean house was the birthplace of Lord Darnley, husband of Mary, Queen of Scots and later became the home of the Ingham family, Viscounts Irwin. There are over 30 historic interiors (many newly restored), including a spectacular Picture Gallery, with superlative paintings, furniture (including the Chippendale Society collection), silver and ceramics. The thousand acre Capability Brown park (free) contains a home farm with rare breeds of animals, sensational displays of rhododendrons and azaleas (May & June), national collections of delphiniums and phlox (July & Aug), chrysanthemums (Sept) and roses (all summer). Guided tours available. Gift shop. There is limited disabled access. **Open:** Please contact for details of 1998 opening times & admission charges.

map 8 C3

THORP PERROW ARBORETUM

Bedale, North Yorkshire, DL8 2PR
Tel: 01677 425 323 Fax: 01677 425 323 (Sir John Ropner, Bt.)

Thorp Perrow, the country home of Sir John and Lady Ropner, contains the finest arboretum in the north of England. A collection of over 1,000 varieties of trees and shrubs including some of the largest and rarest in the country. It is also the home of three National Collections – ash. lime and walnut – and is becoming a popular attraction for all the family. The arboretum comprises 85 acres of landscaped grounds with a lake, grassy glades, tree trails and woodland walks. Thousands of daffodils carpet the ground in spring, while the summer is noted for bold drifts of wild flowers and the autumn brings glorious and vibrant colour. Nature trail. Children's trail. Tearoom and information centre. Plant centre. Electric wheelchair available. **Location:** Well–Ripon Road, S of Bedale. O.S. map ref: SE258851. 4 miles from Leeming Bar on A1. **Open:** All year, dawn-dusk. Guided tours available. Tel: 01677 425 323. **Admission:** Please contact the Arboretum Office for admission prices. Free car and coach park. **Refreshments:** Tearoom. Picnic area. Dogs permitted on a lead.

map 8 C1

WILBERFORCE HOUSE

25 High Street, Kingston-upon-Hull, East Yorkshire, HU1 1EP
Tel: 01482 613 902 Fax: 01482 613 710 (Kingston-upon-Hull City Council)
Internet: www.hulcc.gov.uk/museums/index.htm

Hull's oldest and most famous museum is a brick-built 17th century merchant's house in the centre of the old town. The birthplace of William Wilberforce (1759–1833), known worldwide for his fight to abolish slavery. The main displays within the museum tell the horrific story of slavery and Wilberforce's fight to abolish it. Wilberforce House is much more than just a reminder of slavery. The building contains survivals of every stage in its history: the oak-panelled 17th century rooms on the first floor; the 18th century staircase with elaborate rococo plasterwork ceilings and the Victorian parlour. The famous collection of Hull silver is displayed in the adjoining Georgian house. **Location:** In the centre of Hull's Old Town. **Open:** All year. Mon–Sat, 10–5pm. Sun, 1.30–4.30pm. **Admission:** Telephone for details and group rates.

map 9 F3

GREAT DAYS OUT IN YORKSHIRE

The National Trust owns and protects all these places for you to enjoy

Treasures…

1.

Interesting buildings…

2.

Lovely gardens…

4.   3.

5.

Curious things…

6.

Special places…

7.

8.

1. & 3. Fountains Abbey & Studley Royal
2. Rievaulx Terrace & 4. Beningbrough Hall
5. Nostell Priory
6. Nunnington Hall
7. Treasurer's House
8. East Riddlesden Hall

The National Trust

Registered charity no. 205846

To find out more about these places pick up a 1998 'Places to visit guide' leaflet at a Tourist Information Centre or ring 01904 702021

TREASURER'S HOUSE

Chapter House Street, York YO1 2JD Tel: 01904 624247

Open: 28 March to 1 Nov: daily except Fri 10.30–5. Last admission 4.30. Events: contact Property Manager for details of function hire and full calendar of special events.

RIEVAULX TERRACE & TEMPLES

Rievaulx, Helmsley, York YO6 5LJ Tel: 01439 798340 Fax: 01439 748284

Open: 1 April to 1 Nov: daily 10.30–6 (closes at 5 in April & Oct). Last admission 1hr before closing. Ionic Temple closed 1–2. Events: contact the Visitor Manager at Nunnington Hall for information (tel. 01439 748283).

MOUNT GRACE PRIORY

Osmotherley, Northallerton DL6 3JG Tel: 01609 883494

Open: 1 April to 31 October: daily 10–6 (closes 4 in Oct). 1 Nov to 31 March: Wed to Sun 10–4; closed 1–2. Events: diary of events available in shop free of charge, or tel. 0191 261 1585.

NOSTELL PRIORY

Doncaster Road, Nostell, nr Wakefield WF4 1QE
Tel: 01924 863892 Fax: 01924 865282

Open: 4 April to 1 Nov: April to June & 5 Sept to 1 Nov: Sat & Sun 12–5 (closed Good Fri); 1 July to 3 Sept: daily except Fri 12–5, BH Mon 12–5. Last admission 4.30. Events: Easter Sat, Sun & Mon, Living Heritage Craft Fair; 24/25 May, Craft, Garden & Flower Show; 19 July, Country Fair (charge for admission to grounds, incl. NT members); 12/13 Sept, Living Heritage Craft Fair

NUNNINGTON HALL

Nunnington, York YO6 5UY Tel: 01439 748283 Fax: 01439 748284

Open: 1 April to 1 Nov: daily except Mon & Tues (but open BH Mon & every Tues during June, July & Aug) 1.30–6 (1.30–5.30 April & Oct); last admission 1hr before house closes. Events: 20 June, outdoor concert; other exhibitions and events through the year; contact Visitor Manager for details

FOUNTAINS ABBEY & STUDLEY ROYAL WATER GARDEN

Fountains, Ripon HG4 3DY Estate Office tel: 01765 608888

Open: Abbey & water garden: open all year daily except Fri in Nov, Dec, Jan and 24/25 Dec. April to Sept: 10–7 (closes at 4 on 10/11 July & 8 Aug); Oct to March 1998: 10–5 (dusk if earlier). Last admission 1hr before closing. Deer park: open all year daily during daylight hours. Floodlighting: Abbey is floodlit on Fri & Sat evenings until 10pm, 28 Aug to 17 Oct. Fountains Hall & St Mary's Church: restoration in progress, apply to Estate Office for opening times. Charge may be reduced on and around event days (10/11 July) due to restricted access to parts of estate. Events: extensive programme of concerts, plays, walks & talks available all year, incl. 18 to 20 June, Shakespeare theatre; 10/11 July, Music by Moonlight; 26 to 18 July, theatre; 8 Aug, outdoor promenade entertainment. Details from Box Office (tel. 01765 609999). All outside events wheelchair-accessible.

DUNSTANBURGH CASTLE

Craster, Alnwick Tel: 01665 576231

Open: 1 April to 1 Nov: daily 10–6 (or dusk if earlier); 2 Nov to 31 March 1999: Wed to Sun 10–4 (closed 24 to 26 Dec & 1 Jan)

EAST RIDDLESDEN HALL

Bradford Road, Keighley BD20 5EL Tel: 01535 607075 Fax: 01535 691462

Open: 1 April to 1 Nov: daily except Thur & Fri (but open Good Fri, & Thur in July & Aug) 12–5, but 1–5 on Sat. Last admission 4.30. Events: 18/19 July, Viking Saga; July & Aug, costumed interpretation; for details of this and of full events programme send s.a.e. marked 'Events'

BENINGBROUGH HALL & GARDENS

Shipton-by-Beningbrough, York YO6 1DD Tel: 01904 470666

Open: 4 April to 1 Nov: Sat to Wed, Good Fri & Fri in July and Aug. House: 11–5. Last admission 4.30. Grounds: 11–5.30. Last admission 5. Events: 17 May, Spring Plant Fair; 13 Sept, Autumn Plant Fair. Licensed for wedding ceremonies and receptions; please contact Assistant Property Manager for details

Great Houses & Gardens of Yorkshire

The Great Houses & Gardens of Yorkshire are a group of over 30 fine houses and gardens, situated throughout the Yorkshire and Humberside region and open to visitors.

Discover the wonderfully rich and varied heritage of this rewarding area. Grand stately homes, elegant country houses and fascinating museums all of which lie waiting to be explored with their unrivalled collections of art and furniture. Many of their treasures were gathered during the Grand Tour of Europe, a cultural mecca and part of every nobleman's education during the eighteenth and nineteenth centuries. These enchanting objects are still a source of wonder for the modern day visitor and will continue to delight for generations to come.

The architectural splendour of these great houses is complimented further by the beauty of Yorkshire's famous gardens and landscapes. Those seeking peace and tranquility will surely find it here.

This is a selection of the Great Houses and Gardens of Yorkshire that are featured in this guide

Brodsworth Hall (ET): *Map Index 1*
Nostell Priory (NT): *Map Index 2*
Temple Newsam: *Map Index 3*
Lotherton Hall: *Map Index 4*
Oakwell Hall: *Map Index 5*
Skipton Castle: *Map Index 6*
East Riddleston Hall (NT): *Map Index 7*
Harewood House: *Map Index 8*
Harlow Carr Gardens: *Map Index 9*
Ripley Castle: *Map Index 10*
Fountains Abbey (NT): *Map Index 11*
Bolton Castle: *Map Index 13*

Constable Burton Hall Gardens: *Map Index 14*
Sion Hill Hall & Falconry UK: *Map Index 16*
Mount Grace Priory (EH): *Map Index 17*
Nunnington Hall (NT): *Map Index 21*
Helmsly Castle (EH): *Map Index 22*
Helmsly Walled Gardens: *Map Index 22*
Rievaulx Abbey (EH): *Map Index 23*
Rievaulx Terrace & Temples (NT): *Map Index 23*
Sewerby Hall: *Map Index 27*
Beningbrough Hall (NT): *Map Index 28*
The Treasurers House (NT): *Map Index 29*
Wilberforce Hall: *Map Index 30*

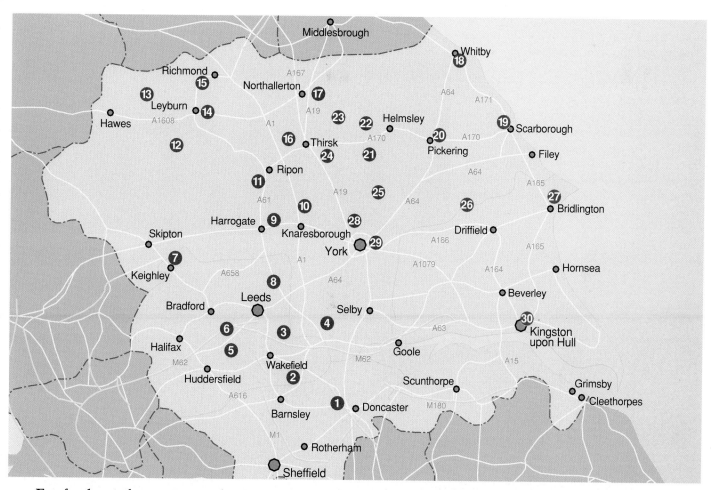

For further information on the Great Houses and Gardens of Yorkshire, please call 01423 770152

Wales

The North West landscape has a dramatic quality reflected in its history. In prehistoric times, Anglesey was a stronghold of the religious elite known as the Druids. Roman and Norman invasions concentrated on the coast, leaving the mountains to the Welsh. These wild areas are the centre of the Welsh language and culture.

The dominant feature of North Wales is Snowdon, the highest mountains in Wales. Snowdonia National Park extends dramatically from the Snowdonia massif south beyond Dolgellau, with thickly wooded valleys, mountain lakes, moors and estuaries. To the east are the softer Clywdian Hills and unspoilt coastlines can be enjoyed on Anglesey and the beautiful Llyn Peninsula, where the Welsh language is still spoken.

Above: Marloes. Right: Harlech Castle. Bottom: Nant Gwynant

South and mid Wales are less homogenous regions than North Wales. Most of the population lives in the southeast corner. To the west is Pembrokeshire, the loveliest stretch of Welsh coastline. To the north the industrial valleys give way to the wide hills of the Brecon Beacons and the rural heartlands of Central Wales.

Magnificent coastal scenery marks the Pembrokeshire Coast National Park and cliff backed Gower Peninsula, while Cardigan Bay and Carmarten Bay offer quieter beaches. Walkers can enjoy grassy uplands in the Brecon Beacons and gentler country in the leafy Wye Valley. Urban life is concentrated in the southeast of Wales, where old mining towns line the valley north of Cardiff, the capital.

CAERPHILLY CASTLE
Caerphilly, Mid Glamorgan, CF83 1JD
Enquiries Tel: 01222 883143
(Cadw: Welsh Historic Monuments)

The largest castle in Wales, with extensive water defences and a famous leaning tower, was built by the De Clare family to defend their territory against the armies of Llewelyn, the last Welsh Prince of Wales. The effectiveness of the finished work is proved by the fact that throughout its long and colourful history, the castle has never been taken by attackers. Due to conservation work in 1776, a large amount of the castle remains undamaged, giving visitors a fascinating insight into medieval life. During the summer reconstructions of warfare, including working replica siege engines, provide an exhilarating and entertaining day out for all the family.

    map 7 J3

CAREW CASTLE & TIDAL MILL
Carew, Nr. Tenby, Pembrokeshire, Wales
Tel/Fax: 01646 651 782
(Pembrokeshire Coast National Park)

A magnificent Norman castle and later an Elizabethan residence. Royal links with Henry Tudor, setting for Great Tournament of 1507. The Mill is the only restored tidal mill in Wales. Automatic talking points explaining milling process. Special exhibition 'The Story of Milling'. **Location:** 4 miles E of Pembroke. **Station(s):** Pembroke. **Bus:** Haverfordwest. **Open:** Easter-end Oct, daily. **Admission:** Please phone for details.

   map 7 H6

CARDIFF CASTLE
Cardiff Castle, Castle Street, Cardiff CF1 2RB
Tel: 01222 878100 Fax: 01222 231417

Set in eight acres of superb grounds in the heart of the Welsh capital, Cardiff Castle has over 2,000 years of history on show within its Roman and Medieval walls. The Castle boasts some of the most exquisite interiors on view anywhere in the UK. A collection of highly individual rooms with the most sumptuous examples of the work of the Victorian architect William Burges, each decorated to illustrate its own fascinating theme and story with lavish mosaics, marquetry, ceramics, stained glass, gilding and wood-carving. In addition to the Roman Wall and Norman Keep, the Castle houses The Welsh Regiment and The Queen's Dragoon Guards museums. Visitors can also enjoy the tearooms for a taste of Wales and a visit to our quality gift shop. Guided tours are available daily all year except Christmas Day, Boxing Day and New Year's Day. The city's superb shopping facilities sit right on the door step where ample parking is available. NB. Occasionally tours are restricted to the Clock Tower, at a reduced rate – please telephone to avoid disappointment.

    map 7 J2

 # CARREG CENNEN CASTLE
Trapp, Dyfed, SA19 6TS
Enquiries Tel: 01558 822291
(Cadw: Welsh Historic Monuments)

Spectacularly situated on a remote crag 300 feet above the River Cennen, this castle has for centuries been sought out by visitors who enjoy mystery and the dramatically picturesque. The site's origins are lost in ancient obscurity, but in the cave under the castle, which can be explored with torches, prehistoric human remains have been discovered. Other finds at the castle include Roman coins and it is believed that the existing castle is built on top of an Iron Age hill fort. The stone fortress we see today was started by a Norman knight, on top of a Welsh castle constructed by The Lord Rhys, the most famous Prince of South Wales.

    map 7 H4

CASTELL COCH
Tongwynlais, Nr Cardiff, South Glamorgan, CF4 7JS
Enquiries Tel: 01222 810101
(Cadw: Welsh Historic Monuments)

One of the most distinctive and memorable castles in Wales, this spectacular building peeks out from the treetops of a cliff towering over the Taff valley near Cardiff. The original medieval castle was rebuilt by the third Lord Bute, who spared no expense on its reconstruction and decoration. From the exterior's re-creation of a medieval fortress complete with conical-roofed towers, the amazed visitor enters the breathtaking apartments of Lord and Lady Bute. Although the castle was intended only for occasional use as a country retreat, the interior is richly and exquisitely carved and painted with scenes from fables and fantasies, all of which are immaculately preserved.

    map 7 J3

CHEPSTOW CASTLE

Chepstow, Gwent NP6 5EZ
Enquiries Tel: 01291 624065
(Cadw: Welsh Historic Monuments)

It comes as quite a surprise to find a great castle in the pretty border town of Chepstow. But on a cliff overlooking the river Wye stands the earliest datable stone fortification in Britain; the great stone keep built by William the Conqueror's most trusted general. Since guarding the border was always an important task, Chepstow castle was developed and enlarged over the centuries in a series of modernisations and gives visitors the opportunity to trace centuries of history in its imposing stones. It was in use up to the Civil War and afterwards was used to keep Henry Marten under house arrest for signing the death warrant of Charles I.

map 7 **J4**

THE CASTLE HOUSE

The Castle House, Usk, Monmouthshire
Tel: 01291 672563 (J.H.L. Humphreys)

Medieval Gatehouse with 19th century interior and 13th century ruins set in a series of gardens providing seasonal interest (Donations to N.G.S.). Location: OS Ref SO 376 011, off Monmouth Road in Usk, opposite Fire Station. **Open:** Castle on request and Gardens by appointment, throughout the year. House: Second Wed every month 2–5pm and Bank Hols. Guided tours only, numbers limited to 5 – prior booking recommended. **Admission:** House & Garden: Adult: £3.50, family £8. Castle & Garden: £2. Children free.

map 7 **H2**

CILGERRAN CASTLE

Cilgerran, Dyfed SA13 2SF
Enquiries Tel: 01239 615007 (Cadw: Welsh Historic Monuments)

Sitting on a high, rocky crag above the meeting-point of two rivers, Cilgerran Castle has the perfect defensive position and is so spectacular that it became a popular subject for romantic artists such as Turner. The earliest castle on this site was built by a Norman lord who married Princess Nest, a famous Welsh beauty. When raiders came to assassinate her husband in his bed, Nest helped him to escape, although she and her children were kidnapped. The castle has had a long and chequered history, passing from English to Welsh hands and back again many times during the long wars for the conquest of Wales. The Castle we see today was the work of the English Marshal family, who extended and strengthened the fortress over a period of two hundred years.

map 7 **G5**

DYFFRYN GARDENS

St. Nicholas, Cardiff, SF5 6SU, The Vale of Glamorgan, Wales
Tel: 01222 593328 Fax: 01222 591966

'A Garden for all Seasons' describes Dyffryn, one of Wales' finest landscaped gardens. The beautifully laid out grounds offer an endless variety of colour and form with many small theme gardens, heather bank, glasshouse ranges and arboretum. Dyffryn Gardens offer a different visual treat at every turn, with easy access, plentiful free parking and calendar of special events. It's always a convenient, colourful and uniquely pleasurable day out – anytime of the year. **Location:** Just off Junction 33, M4. **Privilege Card:** 1 child free to one full paying adult. **Open:** 10–6pm. **Admission:** Please phone for details of 1998 prices.

map 7 **G5**

COLBY WOODLAND GARDENS

Stepaside, Narberth, Pembrokeshire.
Tel: 01834 811885 (National Trust)

Open: Colby Woodland Gardens open daily 10–5pm from 27 Mar–31 Oct. Walled garden 1 Apr 11–5pm. Daffodils and bluebells carpet this tranquil woodland valley in spring. Rhododendrons, azaleas, magnolias and camellias flower from Mar til the end of Jun followed by hydrangeas and eucryphias. A fine collection of rare trees and shrubs offers splendid autumn colour. Children's trail and regular guided walks. Events programme details, please telephone 01834 811885. **Admission:** Adult £2.80. Child £1.40. Family 2 + 2 £7, group rate £2.20. Coaches welcome group rate by appointment.

map 7 **H6**

KIDWELLY CASTLE

Kidwelly, Dyfed SA17 5BQ
Enquiries Tel: 01554 890104
(Cadw: Welsh Historic Monuments)

Perched high above the river Gwendraeth, looking out towards Laugharne across the Taf estuary, Kidwelly's early Norman earth and timber castle could be reached by boat, making it difficult to besiege. However, The Lord Rhys, Prince of South Wales, captured and burned the castle, which did not return to Norman hands until 1244 when the construction of a stone fortress was started. Over the following centuries, the castle and its walled town passed into different hands and was added to and modernised by the Dukes of Lancaster and then by the most powerful man in early Tudor Wales, Sir Rhys ap Thomas.

map 7 **H5**

LAUGHARNE CASTLE
Laugharne, Dyfed
Enquiries Tel: 01994 427906 (Cadw: Welsh Historic Monuments)

Looking out over the estuary that Dylan Thomas was to make famous for its beauty, is Laugharne's "castle, brown as owls". Like its neighbours at Kidwelly and Llansteffan, Laugharne is built on the site of an early Norman earth and timber fort, and was rebuilt in stone during the Middle Ages by the local Lord, Guy de Brian. As the castle passed down through succeeding generations of the family, it was added to and strengthened. By the reign of Elizabeth I, the castle had fallen into disrepair, and it was modernised in the Tudor style by Sir John Perrot, who was tried for treason. In this century, the castle was rented out to author Richard Hughes who wrote his novel "In Hazard" in the castle's gazebo, where Dylan Thomas later wrote "Portrait of the Artist as a Young Dog."

LLANVIHANGEL COURT
Nr Abergavenny, Monmouthshire, NP7 8DH
Tel: 01873 890 217 (Mrs Julia Johnson)

A Grade 1 listed Tudor Manor of 15th century origins. Beautiful early 17th century plaster ceilings and panelling and magnificent yew staircase, leading to a bedroom where Charles I is reputed to have stayed during the Civil War. Remodelled during the 1650s by John Arnold. The main entrance overlooks 17th century terraces and steps. Unusual stables from the same period with turned wood pillars. **Location:** 4 miles north of Abergavenny on A465. **Open:** 8 Aug–1 Sept inclusive, or by appointment. **Admission:** Adults £4, children (5–15) and OAPs £2.50.

map 7
H2

LLAWHADEN CASTLE
Llawhaden, Dyfed
Enquiries Tel: 01222 500200
(Cadw: Welsh Historic Monuments)

The parish and ancient church of Llawhaden have been part of the estates of the Bishops of St Davids since before the Norman conquest. The first Norman Bishop erected an earth and timber fort as part of the local defences of the border with the Welsh Princes to the north and east. At the end of the thirteenth century, Bishop Bek decided to build a new hall at Llawhaden, using the existing earthworks and stone wall to create a splendid, moated manor-house where he could entertain in style. Later bishops added the chapel, towers, gatehouse and additional guest chambers.

map 7
H6

OXWICH CASTLE
Oxwich, Nr Swansea, West Glamorgan
Enquiries Tel: 01792 390359 (Cadw: Welsh Historic Monuments)

On a headland overlooking Oxwich Bay in the beautiful Gower peninsula, stands Oxwich Castle. A Tudor mansion, rather than a medieval fortress, its impressive gatehouse emblazoned with the Mansel family's coat of arms was added more as a show of pride than for military purposes. Like many successful gentlemen, Sir Rice Mansel remodelled his ancestral home in the modern Tudor style, with his son continuing the building programme by adding a stupendous multistory wing during Queen Elizabeth's reign. During conservation work on the castle, a magnificent gold and jewelled brooch was discovered, which may once have been part of King Edward II's lost royal treasure. How it came to be at Oxwich remains an intriguing mystery.

PENHOW CASTLE
Nr. Newport, NP6 3AD South Wales
Tel: 01633 400 800 Fax: 01633 400 990 (Stephen Weeks)

Wales' Oldest Lived-in Castle proudly holds 8 awards for its fine restoration and imaginative interpretation. Originally the first home in Britain of the illustrious Seymour family (ancestors of the Tudor Queen Jane Seymour) this most enchanting Knight's Border Castle has been lovingly restored by the present owner. Cross the drawbridge to explore eight centuries of changing castle life, guided by the acclaimed 'Time Machine' Walkman audio tours included free; there are special children's tours too, also French & German. A charming ensemble of varied stone buildings around its central courtyard, visitors can discover at their own pace, the Norman bedchamber, stunning views from atop the Keep Towers battlements, 15th century Great Hall with minstrels' gallery and more. The robust elegance of the Charles II wing is a perfect contrast to the earlier medieval rooms. **Location:** A48, midway b/w Chepstow and Newport. M4 Jct 24. **Open:** Good Fri-end Sept, Wed–Sun incl. & Bank Hols, 10–5.15pm (last admission). Aug–open daily. Winter, Wed only 10–4pm and selected Sun pm's 1–4pm. Open all year for groups, Evening Candlelit Tours and school visits. Special Christmas Tours 15 Nov–5 Jan: Traditional festive decorations, carols & customs, pies & punch. **Admission:** Adult £3.35, child (5-16) £2.05, family (2+2) £8.75. Price includes Walkman tour. Group discount 10% for 20+. **Accommodation:** B&B by arrangement; the only place in Wales one can stay in a real castle!

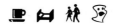

map 7
J2

PICTON CASTLE & WOODLAND GARDENS

Haverfordwest, Pembrokeshire, Wales, SA62 4AS
Tel: 01437 751 326 Fax: 01437 751 326 (Picton Castle Trust)

Built around 1300, Picton Castle has gradually changed over the centuries into a magnificent stately home occupied by the descendants of the Philipps family throughout it's history. The Woodland Gardens extend to 40 acres. There are mature trees and shrubs, a well stocked Walled Garden, a recently planted maze and a picnic area. **Other attractions:** A garden shop: gift shop: art gallery: restaurant. **Location:** 4 miles east of Haverfordwest, off A40. **Open:** Woodland Gardens are open daily (except Mons) from Apr–Oct, 10.30–5pm. Dogs are allowed on leads. The Castle is open July–end Sept, Thurs & Sun pm. Also Easter & Bank Hol Suns & Mons pm. **Admission:** Woodland Gardens: Adults £2.50, children £1, OAPs £2. Castle & Woodland Gardens: Adults £4, children £1, OAPs £3.

map 7
H6

RAGLAN CASTLE

Raglan, Gwent, NP5 2BT
Enquiries Tel: 01291 690228
(Cadw: Welsh Historic Monuments)

A monument to medieval family pride, this imposing fortress-palace was built by the Herbert family. The water-moated Great Yellow Tower was built by Sir William, "The Blue Knight of Gwent", a veteran of Agincourt. His son, William Herbert continued the construction of the majority of the existing castle, using profits he made by importing French wine. William was one of the leading Yorkist supporters in the Wars of the Roses and was so well trusted by King Edward IV that he was given custody of young Henry Tudor, later King Henry VII, who was brought up at Raglan. William's loyalty as the King's right-hand-man in Wales brought a string of titles and estates, but Raglan remained the family's stronghold.

map 7
H2

TREDEGAR HOUSE & PARK

Newport, South Wales, Tel: 01633 815 880, NP1 9YW
Fax: 01633 815 895. (Newport County Borough Council)

South Wales' finest country house, ancestral home of the Morgan dynasty for over 500 years. Visitors have a lively and entertaining tour through 30 rooms in a variety of historical styles. The 90 acre park includes gardens, a lake, carriage rides and craft workshops. Special Events/Family Days throughout the year. **Location:** SW of Newport, signposted from M4, Junction 28, A48. **Open:** Park open daily, 10.30am–sunset. House and attractions open from Good Friday–Sept, Wed–Sun. Also public holidays, daily in Aug and weekends in Oct. House open for guided tours 11.30am (last admission 4pm). **Admission** Please phone for details. **Refreshments:** Available in the Brewhouse Tearoom. Coach and school parties welcome. Conference and meeting facilities. Wedding ceremonies and receptions.

map 7
J2

ST. DAVIDS CATHEDRAL

The Deanery, The Close, St. Davids, Pembrokeshire, Wales
Tel: 01437 720 202 Fax: 01437 721 885 (The Dean and Chapter)

This cathedral, begun in 1181, is at least the fourth church to have been built on a site reputed to be that on which St. David himself founded a monastic settlement in the 6th century. The outstanding features of the building are the magnificent ceilings – oak in the Nave, painted in the Choir and Presbytery – and the sloping floor. The stalls of the Chapter of the cathedral contain medieval misericords and the Chapter is unique in having the reigning Sovereign as a member. The cathedral has been an important place of pilgrimage for nearly fourteen centuries. In 1124, Pope Calixtus II declared that two pilgrimages to St. Davids were equal to one to Rome and that three were equal to one to Jerusalem itself.

map 7
G7

WEOBLEY CASTLE

Llanrhidian, Nr Swansea, West Glamorgan SA3 1HB
Enquiries Tel: 01792 390012
(Cadw: Welsh Historic Monuments)

This fortified manor house perches above the wild northern coast of the beautiful Gower peninsula, looking over the marshes towards the Loughor estuary. It dates from the medieval thirteenth and fourteenth centuries, a rare survivor from those wild and often troubled times. Weobley was designed to be a comfortable home for the knightly de la Bere family, but its defensive tower and turrets provided a safe shelter in times of trouble. In Tudor times, Sir Rhys ap Thomas, the most powerful man in Wales added the two-storey porch block, providing a more stately entrance to the hall and private apartments.

map 7
J5

WHITE CASTLE

Llantilio Crossenny, Gwent NP7 8UD
Enquiries Tel: 01600 780380
(Cadw: Welsh Historic Monuments)

One of a trio of castles built by the Normans to protect the route into Wales from Hereford, White Castle is the classic medieval castle. Standing on a low hill, its six towers and curtain wall are surrounded by a water-filled moat with drawbridge. It was built to house a garrison which, along with troops from Grosmont and Skenfrith castles, was responsible for the defence of the border against the rebellious Welsh. During Llewelyn the Last's attacks into the established Marcher lands of South Wales, the Three Castles were repaired and readied for war, but never saw action. After Henry Bolingbroke became King Henry IV, the castles, which were part of his Duchy of Lancaster, became the property of the Crown.

map 7
H2

GROSMONT CASTLE

Grosmont, Nr Abergavenny, Gwent.
Enquiries Tel: 01222 500200
(Cadw: Welsh Historic Monuments)

To protect the vulnerable area between Wales and Hereford, the Normans built a triangle of castles with Grosmont at its northern tip. Although all three castles were demolished and re-built during the 13th century, their defensive purpose remained the same and troops were garrisoned here to guard against the rebellious Welsh. Later, they were owned by the Dukes of Lancaster and eventually the Crown, when Henry Bolingbroke became King Henry IV. Grosmont was then remodelled to provide accommodation suitable for a royal household which came to enjoy the tranquillity of the rolling Welsh hills and the castle's fine deer park.

SKENFRITH CASTLE

Skenfrith, Nr Abergavenny, Gwent.
Enquiries Tel: 01222 500200
(Cadw: Welsh Historic Monuments)

Nestling in the rolling, green hills of the Welsh Marches is the pretty village of Skenfrith, with its castle tranquil and sleepy now, lulled by the river Monnow which winds around its ancient walls. But things were not always so peaceful. Skenfrith is the easternmost of the triangle of castles forming the Norman defence of the border between Wales and Herefordshire. The castle that exists today was built on the Norman foundations by Hubert de Burgh, a Marcher lord who was influential in the 1220s and 1230s in the court of the child-king Henry III. Sir Hubert's apartments with their fine fireplace, can still be seen in the upper floor of the round keep.

TRETOWER COURT AND CASTLE

Crickhowell, Powys NP8 2RF
Enquiries Tel: 01874 730279 (Cadw: Welsh Historic Monuments)

In the quiet foothills of the Black Mountains stands a unique example of a family's building through the centuries. Alongside the castle which had protected them for 300 years, the Vaughan family built a manor house which was later extended and enlarged into a medieval mansion with elaborately timbered roofs and a galleried courtyard. During the Wars of the Roses, the house was fortified to enable the family to live there in safety. They continued to do so until the seventeenth century, when the great poet Henry Vaughan drew inspiration from his wonderfully well-preserved family home and its beautiful surroundings. Now visitors can also enjoy the re-created medieval garden that was featured in the television programme "Geoff Hamilton's Paradise Gardens."

map 7
H2

BEAUMARIS CASTLE

Beaumaris, Anglesey, Gwynedd, LL58 8AP
Enquiries Tel: 01248 810361
(Cadw: Welsh Historic Monuments)

This lovely castle overlooks the Menai Straits between Anglesey and the North Wales mainland, guarding an important medieval trade route. It was built by Edward I to complete his chain of coastal fortresses and served as Anglesey's garrison, protecting the island and its precious grain stores against invaders. The castle was ingeniously designed to use the straits' tides to both fill the defensive moat and to enable large ships to sail right up to the castle gate at high tide. The castle's picturesque setting and unusual design have drawn visitors for centuries, including Princess Victoria, later to be Queen, who visited for a Royal Eisteddfodd in 1832.

map 6
C4

CRESSELLY

Kilgetty, Pembrokeshire SA68 0SP, Wales
Fax: 01646 687045 (HDR Harrison-Allen Esq.)

Home of the Allen family for 250 years. The house dates to 1770 with matching wings from 1869 and contains good plasterwork and fittings of both periods. The Allens are of particular interest for their close association to the Wedgwood family. **Location:** In the Pembrokeshire National Park, off the A4075. OS Ref SN0 606. **Open:** 28 days between May and September. Please write or fax 01646 687045 for details. **Admission:** Adults £3.50. No children under 12. Wedding receptions and functions in house or marquee for 20 to 300 persons. Dinners, private or corporate events in historic dining room. Guided tours only. Ample parking for cars (coaches by arrangement only). No dogs. Bed and Breakfast and dinner by arrangement. 2 double en suite, single, twin and children by arrangement.

BODELWYDDAN CASTLE

Bodelwyddan, Denbighshire, Wales
Tel: 01745 584 060 Fax: 01745 584 563 (Bodelwyddan Castle Trust)

Set against the magnificent background of the Clwydian Hills, this imposing Victorian mansion has been authentically restored and houses a major collection of 19th century portraits and photography from the National Portrait Gallery, furniture from the Victoria & Albert Museum and sculpture from the Royal Academy. Fascinating 'hands-on' galleries of Victorian amusements and inventions feature parlour games, puzzles and optical illusions – an extravaganza of Victorian fun. Amid the Castle's grounds, gardens and parkland are picnic areas, a woodland trail and children's play facilities. The Castle is a winner of the 'Museum of the Year' Award. **Open:** All year. **Events/Exhibitions:** There is an exciting programme of outdoor events and temporary exhibitions.

map 6
C3

BODNANT GARDEN

Tal Y Cafn, Nr Colwyn Bay, Conwy LL28 5RE
Tel: 01492 650460 Fax: 01492 650448 (The National Trust)

Eighty acres of magnificent garden in the beautiful Conwy Valley. Rhododendrons, camellias and magnolias in Spring, with the famous Laburnum Arch and azaleas flowering mid May-mid Jun. The summer months give a show of herbaceous plants, water lilies, hydrangeas and roses, followed by superb autumn colour. **Open:** 14 Mar–31 Oct, daily 10–5pm. Adult £4.60, child £2.30. **Refreshments:** Pavilion. Ample parking.

map 6
C4

CAERNARFON CASTLE

Caernarfon, Gwynedd, LL55 2AY
Enquiries Tel: 01286 677617
(Cadw: Welsh Historic Monuments)

This most impressive of Edward I's Welsh defences was built near the Roman fort of Segontium, mentioned in the ancient tales of the Mabinogion. Its unique polygonal towers with decorative coloured stone bands echo the walls of the great city of Constantinople and marked the castle as a special place. Indeed, it was intended to be the official residence of the King's chief representative in the Principality and is inextricably linked with the Princes of Wales since it is the birthplace of Edward's heir, Edward Caernarfon, first English Prince of Wales. The twentieth century has seen it rise again to prominence as the site of the Investiture of both this century's Princes of Wales.

map 6
C5

CONWY CASTLE

Conwy, Gwynedd, LL32 8AY
Enquiries Tel: 01492 592358
(Cadw: Welsh Historic Monuments)

This finest and most complete example of a fortified town and castle was constructed after the second Welsh war of independence by Edward I, whose apartments are in the castle's Inner Ward. Edward believed in building walled towns alongside his castles to create small pockets of English dominance in Wales. The town not only housed the community needed to supply the castle, but increased local prosperity and acted as the focal point of local government. Conwy is a classic example of this philosophy, cleverly designed to have 21 "circuit-breaker" towers along the town walls which enabled defenders to isolate an attacking force and ward them off effectively.

map 6
C4

CRICCIETH CASTLE

Criccieth, Gwynedd LL52 0DP
Enquiries Tel: 01766 522227
(Cadw: Welsh Historic Monuments)

Set high on a rocky headland overlooking Cardigan Bay, this is the most striking of the castles built by the native Welsh Princes. Llewelyn the Great built the first castle here, during his long campaign against the English annexation of Wales. When his grandson, Llewelyn the Last continued the struggle, he extended and strengthened Criccieth's defences. Over a century later, during the revolt of Owain Glyndwr, the rebel army was besieged in the castle, but were able to hold out due to the castle's position overlooking the sea, since provisions could be brought in by boat.

map 6
D5

DENBIGH CASTLE

Denbigh, Clwyd
Enquiries Tel: 01222 500200
(Cadw: Welsh Historic Monuments)

Encircling a rocky outcrop overlooking the Vale of Clwyd, Denbigh Castle is built on the site of a traditional Welsh court. At the end of Llewelyn the Last's wars of Welsh independence against Edward I, the English king gave Denbigh to his campaign commander, Henry de Lacy. Together they planned a castle and walled town similar to Edward's own fortresses along the north Welsh coast. Sadly, Henry never finished building the finely decorated gatehouse, the castle's final crowning glory, due to the death of his son in the castle well. In later years, as Denbigh passed into the hands of several powerful owners, the castle saw many famous visitors, including King Charles I.

DOLWYDDELAN CASTLE

Dolwyddelan, Gwynedd
Enquiries Tel: 01690 750366
(Cadw: Welsh Historic Monuments)

Tradition claims Dolwyddelan as the birthplace of Llewelyn ap Iorwerth, Llewelyn the Great; the Prince who united Wales. However, the stone keep that now stands was probably re-built by Llewelyn to guard the road into the heart of the stronghold of Snowdonia and Gwynedd through the strategically important Lledyr Valley. The castle would also have watched over Llewelyn's precious cattle pastures, since this was a time of war when cattle were essential battle supplies that were easily moved to support hungry armies. When Edward 1st took the castle during the Welsh wars for independence under Llewelyn the Last, he outfitted the garrison in white snow camouflage and made some additions to the existing structure.

DINEFWR PARK

Llandeilo, Carmarthenshire
Tel: 01558 823902 Fax: 01558 822036 (The National Trust)

A fine country residence built in 1660, Newton House is set in over 450 acres of landscaped park in the outstanding Upper Towy Valley. Dinefwr Park is home to the ancient herd of Dienfwr White Park Cattle and fallow deer who roam the medieval Deer Park. Outstanding views of the Towy Valley can be seen from many vantage points. A Boardwalk through the Bog Wood and Mill Pond area of the Park allows access to all, to experience the many species of plant and pond life in this virtually undisturbed corner of Dinefwr. A specially constructed Hide with views over the Ox Box lakes provides an ideal location to see many rare and unusual birds. **Open:** Open Daily (except Tue & Wed) 11–5pm. **Admission:** £2.80 adult, £1.40 child, group rates available. Special offers during school summer holiday period.

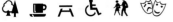

map 7
H4

DOLBADARN CASTLE

Llanberis, Gwynedd
Enquiries Tel: 01222 500200
(Cadw: Welsh Historic Monuments)

This Welsh fortress is so picturesque that artists have come from far and wide to try and capture its lonely majesty. The castle was built by Llewelyn the Great to guard the Llanberis Pass that leads into the heart of Snowdonia, the traditional Welsh stronghold. A mighty round keep with a cunning spiral staircase which reverses direction halfway, to confuse invaders; it stands between two lakes, with the mountains of Snowdonia at its back. Yet the haunting beauty of the castle is only one of the reasons for a visit. For it was here that Llewelyn the Last imprisoned his brother Owain Goch for 22 years as a punishment for attempting to overthrow him.

EWLOE CASTLE

Nr Hawarden, Clwyd
Enquiries Tel: 01222 500200
(Cadw: Welsh Historic Monuments)

After generations of warfare between the Welsh and the invading Saxons, Normans and English, Llewelyn ap Gruffydd, the last Welsh Prince of Wales followed in the footsteps of his grandfather, Llewelyn the Great by making a stand in an attempt to establish an independent Wales. Ewloe, with its strong tower, was built to defend Llewelyn's borders with England. However, Edward I was not prepared to give up land that had been bought with generations of bloodshed and when Llewelyn refused to pay homage to him, the English King mounted a massive attack on North Wales. Ewloe fell to the English and Edward constructed his new fortified beachhead on the seashore at Flint.

map 6
C2

FLINT CASTLE

Flint, Clwyd
Enquiries Tel: 01352 733078
(Cadw: Welsh Historic Monuments)

There is a symbolic element to the naming of the castle of Flint. Perhaps King Edward I was warning Llewelyn the Last that he intended to spark a fire which could consume all that stood in its path. Over five years, Edward blazed a trail along the North Wales coast, constructing a chain of coastal castles based on the design of Flint and its attached walled town, to keep a firm grip on the rebellious Welsh. Flint's next great moment in history came in 1399, when troubled King Richard II said Mass in the castle chapel before going out to meet Henry Bolingbroke and his army on the seashore, to hand over the Crown of England.

GWYDIR CASTLE

Gwydir Castle, Llanrwst, Gwynedd.
Tel: 01492 641687. Fax: 01492 641687 (Mr and Mrs Welford)

Gwydir Castle is situated in the beautiful Conwy Valley and is set within a romantic 10 acre garden. Built by the illustrious Wynn family c.1500, Gwydir is a fine example of a Tudor courtyard house, incorporating re-used medieval material from the dissolved Abbey of Maenan. Further additions date from c.1600 and c.1826. Both house and gardens are undergoing a phased programme of restoration most notably the re-installation of the important 1640's dining room panelling, recently repatriated from the New York Metropolitan Museum. Location: ½ mile W Of Llanrwst on A5106. **Open:** 1 Apr–31 Oct, daily 10–5pm. Limited opening at other times. **Admission:** Adults £3, children £1.50. Group discount 10%.

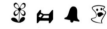

map 6
C4

HARLECH CASTLE

Harlech, Gwynedd LL46 2YH
Enquiries Tel: 01766 780552
(Cadw: Welsh Historic Monuments)

Famed in song and story, Harlech is enshrined in the history of Wales. This is the "castle of lost causes" where a handful of defenders could hold off an army; a fortress which has been the last refuge for defiant, valiant men and women who have refused to compromise their principles. Built by Edward I, it had a clever channel connecting it to the sea, with a water gate and protected walkway to the castle allowing supplies to be brought in by boat. The castle was besieged in the 15th century when it was the headquarters and court of rebel leader, Owain Glyndwr; and again during the Wars of the Roses when it was the last Lancastrian stronghold in Wales to fall to the Yorkists.

map 6
D4

PENNARTH FAWR MEDIEVAL HALL-HOUSE

Chwilog, Pwllheli, Gwynedd.
Enquiries Tel: 01222 500200
(Cadw: Welsh Historic Monuments)

Near Criccieth stands this fascinating example of the home of a medieval gentleman. From outside, the modest building gives few clues to the glorious interior which was lovingly restored earlier this century. Incredibly, this house remained in a single family for over 400 years after it was built in the mid-fourteenth century by a local Welsh gentleman. One member of the family, Hugh Gwyn, was High Sheriff of Caernarvonshire at the end of Queen Elizabeth I's reign, and it was he who modernised the house by adding the large fireplace in the east wall which bears his coat of arms.

PLAS BRONDANW GARDENS

Llanfrothen, Nr. Penrhyndeudraeth, Gwynedd, Wales.
Tel: 01766 771 136 (The Second Portmeirion Foundation)

Created by Sir Clough Williams-Ellis, architect of Portmeirion, below his ancestral home. Italian inspired gardens with spectacular mountain views, topiary and folly tower. **Location:** 2 miles north of Penrhyndeudraeth. ¼ mile off the A4085 on Croesor Road. **Open:** All year, daily, 9–5pm. **Admission:** Adults £1.50, children 25p.

map 6
D4

PORTMEIRION VILLAGE

Portmeirion, Gwynned, Wales LL48 6ET
Tel: 01766 770228 Fax: 01766 771331

Sir Clough Williams-Ellis aimed to show at Porteirion that one could "...*develop even a very beautiful place without defiling it.*" Located on the shores of Cardigan Bay in North Wales, Portmeirion has seven shops inlcuding one selling Portmeirion Pottery seconds, plus restuarants, gardens and miles of beaches. Surrounding the village are the Gwyllt woodland and gardens containing rare Himalayan flowering treees. All the houses in the village are let as part of the Portmeirion Hotel. **Open:** The village is open every day all year round. **Location:** It is located off the A487 at Minffordd between Penrhyndeudracth and Porthmadog. **Admission:** Charges apply.

PLAS MAWR, CONWY

Conwy, Gwynedd LL32 8DE
Tel: 01492 580167 (Cadw: Welsh Historic Monuments)

Within the town of Conwy, best-known for its great medieval fortifications of castle and walls, hides a perfect Elizabethan jewel. Plas Mawr is the best-preserved Elizabethan town house in Britain, famous for the quality and quantity of its plasterwork decoration. Plas Mawr is a fascinating and unique place which gives visitors a chance to peek into the lives of the Tudor gentry and their servants. This was the fast moving time, when the creation of increased wealth among merchants and the gentry meant that private homes such as Plas Mawr could be decorated and furnished lavishly. Cadw gives visitors the opportunity to enjoy all of this through an audio tour which also explains the amazing process of restoration the house has been through.

RHUDDLAN CASTLE

Rhuddlan, Clwyd
Tel: 01745 590777
(Cadw: Welsh Historic Monuments)

One of the first castles built by Edward I in his programme to fortify the North Wales coast, a man-made channel three miles long linked Rhuddlan to the sea, giving supply ships access to the castle. This was reputed to be Queen Eleanor's favourite castle and indeed, it seems that she and King Edward spent a large amount of time here. It was in Rhuddlan that Edward made a treaty with the Welsh Lords and persuaded them to accept his baby son, recently born in Caernarfon Castle, as the Prince of Wales by promising them that their new Lord would be born in Wales, with an unblemished character and unable to speak a word of English.

CHIRK CASTLE

Chirk, Wrexham LL14 5AF Tel: 01691 777701 Fax: 01691 774706

Open: 1 April to 30 Sept: daily except Mon & Tues but open BH Mon; 3 Oct to 1 Nov: Sat & Sun only. Castle: 12–5. Garden: 11–6. Last admission 4.30. Events: please contact Property Manager for details of programme, which includes open-air plays, family fun days and snowdrop walks. **Admission:** £4.60, children £2.30; family ticket (max. 2 adults & 2 children) £11.50. Pre-booked parties of 15 or more £3.70 per person. Garden only, adults £2.40, children £1.20. NT members free. Parking 200m

COLBY WOODLAND GARDEN

Amroth, Narberth SA67 8PP Tel: 01834 811885

Open: 1 April to 31 Oct: daily 10–5. Walled garden: 1 April to 30 Oct: 11–5. Events: Guided walks with Gardener-in-charge held regularly throughout the season; Celtic Music evening; Shakespeare in the Meadow; Family Fun Days. **Admission:** £2.80, children £1.40; family ticket £7. Group: adult £2.30, child £1.15. Coaches welcome (narrow approaches). Open evenings by arrangement

DINEFWR PARK

Llandeilo SA19 6RT Tel: 01558 823902 Fax: 01558 822036

Open: House, garden, deer park, parkland & boardwalk: 2 April to 1 Nov: daily except Tues & Wed 11–5. Last admission 4.30. The library and old drawing room are available for conferences on Tues & Wed. Parkland also open during winter in daylight hours. Events: for details of programme please send s.a.e. marked 'Events' to Property Manager. **Admission:** £2.80, children £1.40; family ticket (max. 2 adults & 2 children) £7; 1 child (16 and under) free per paying adult from 23 July to 30 Aug. Parties £2.60, children/school groups £1.30. Coaches by prior appointment only due to narrow access. WCs in car park

ERDDIG

nr Wrexham LL13 0YT Tel: 01978 355314 Fax/Infoline: 01978 313333

Open: 21 March to 1 Nov: daily, except Thur & Fri (open Good Fri); House: 12–5; Garden: 11–6 (July & Aug: 10–6); from 3 Oct house &

garden close 1hr earlier. Last admission to house 1hr before closing. Events: 19–21 June, Craft Show in gardens (charge, incl. NT members). Also outdoor opera, jazz and Last Night of the Proms. Please send s.a.e. to Property Manager for full events programme.

PENRHYN CASTLE

Bangor LL57 4HN Tel: 01248 353084 Infoline: 01248 371337

Open: 25 March to 1 Nov: daily except Tues. Castle: 12–5 (July & Aug 11–5). Grounds and stable block exhibitions: 11–5.30 (July & Aug 10–5.30). Last admission 30min before closing (last audio tour 4). Events: a programme including open-air plays, concerts and family fun days runs throughout the season; send s.a.e. for details. Events information line (tel. 01248 371337).

PLAS NEWYDD

Llanfairpwll, Anglesey LL61 6DQ Tel: 01248 714795

Open: House: 1 April to 1 Nov: daily except Fri & Sat 12–5. Garden: same days as house 11–5.30. Last admission 30min before closing. Events: extensive programme of tours, plays, music and family events (incl. 18 July, open-air concert; 22 Aug, open-air jazz concert); please send s.a.e for full events list

PLAS YN RHIW

Rhiw, Pwllheli LL53 8AB Tel/fax: 01758 780219

Open: 1 April to 18 May: daily (except Tues & Wed) 12–5. 20 May to 30 Sept: daily (except Tues) 12–5. Last admission 4.30. Timed tickets may be in operation on BHols and during July & Aug. Events: open-air play; tel. for details

POWIS CASTLE & GARDEN

Welshpool SY21 8RF Tel: 01938 554338 Fax/Infoline: 01938 554336

Open: Castle & museum: 1 April to 28 June & 2 Sept to 1 Nov: daily except Mon & Tues 1–5; July & Aug: daily except Mon 1–5 (open BH Mon during season). Garden: same days as castle & museum, 11–6. Last admission to the garden, castle and museum each 30min before closing. Events: programme of concerts, plays, walks, talks and demonstrations throughout the year: for details tel. 01938 554338

Scotland

Southeast of the Highland boundary fault line lies a part of Scotland very different in character from its northern neighbour. If the Highlands embody the romance of Scotland, the Lowlands are the powerhouse. Lowlanders have always prospered in agriculture and more recently, in industry and commerce.

The Lowlands are traditionally all the land south of the fault line stretching north-east from Loch Lomond to Stonehaven. Confusingly, they include plenty

Above: River Tweed. Below: Forth Bridge. Bottom: Isle of Skye

of wild upland country. The region illustrates best the diversity of Scotland's magnificent scenery. The wooded valleys and winding rivers of the border give way to the stern moorland hills of the Cheviots and Lammermuirs. Lively little fishing villages cling to the rocky east coast, while the Clyde coast and its islands are dotted with cheerful holiday towns. Inland lie the Trossachs: these romantic mountains surrounding Loch Lomond are a magnet for walkers and well within reach of Glasgow.

ABBOTSFORD HOUSE

Melrose, Borders, Scotland, TD6 9BQ.
Tel: 01896 752 043 Fax: 01896 752 916
(Mrs Patricia Maxwell-Scott)

The house of Sir Walter Scott, containing many historical relics collected by him. **Location:** 3 miles W of Melrose; S of A72; 5 miles E of Selkirk. **Station(s):** No railway. **Open:** Third Monday in March–31 Oct: Mon–Sat, 10–5pm. Jun–Sept: Sun, 10–5pm. Mar–May & Oct: Sun, 2–5pm. **Admission:** Adults £3.50, children £1.80. Coach Party: Adults £2.50, children £1.30. **Refreshments:** Teashop. Gift shop. Cars with wheelchairs or disabled enter by private entrance.

AMISFIELD MAINS

Nr. Haddington, East Lothian, Scotland
Tel: 01875 870 201 Fax: 01875 870 620
(The Wemyss & March Estates Management Co. Ltd)

Georgian farmhouse with 'gothick' barn and cottage. **Location:** Between Haddington and East Linton on A1 Edinburgh-Dunbar Road. **Open:** Exteriors only. By appointment, Wemyss & March Estates, Estate Office, Longniddry, EH32 0PY, East Lothian, Scotland.

map 13
H5

ARTHUR LODGE

60 Dalkeith Road, Edinburgh, Scotland EH16 5AD
Tel: 0131 667 5163 (S. Roland Friden)

A Neo Grecian dream of a country gentleman's residence in town (Thomas Hamilton 1827). Set in a beautiful garden and imaginatively restored and decorated, an exquisite and surprising private residence. **Open:** Jun–Jul, Wed & Sat. Aug–Sept, Wed only. Tours by appointment, at 12noon, 1pm & 2pm **Admission:** £3. Concessions £2

 map 13
G5

AYTON CASTLE

Eyemouth, Berwickshire, Scotland, , TD14 5RD.
Tel: 018907 81212 Fax: 018907 81550
(Ayton Castle Maintenance Fund)

A Victorian castle built in red sandstone in 1846, which has been fully restored and is now lived in by the family owners. **Open:** 10 May – 13 Sept: Sun, 2–5pm. At other times by appointment. **Admission:** £2, Children (under 15) free. **Events/Exhibitions:** Occasionally.

 map 13
J6

BEANSTON

Nr. Haddington, East Lothian, Scotland
Tel: 01875 870 201 Fax: 01875 870 620
(The Wemyss & March Estates Management Co. Ltd)

Georgian farmhouse with Georgian orangery. **Location:** Between Haddington and East Linton on A1 Edinburgh-Dunbar Road. **Open:** Exteriors only. By appointment, Wemyss & March Estates, Estate Office, Longniddry, EH32 0PY, East Lothian, Scotland.

map 13
H5

BLAIRQUHAN CASTLE & GARDENS

Straiton, Maybole, KA19 7LZ, Ayrshire, Scotland
Tel: 016557 70239 Fax: 016557 70278 (James Hunter Blair)

Magnificent Regency Castellated mansion approached by a 3 mile long private drive beside the River Girvan. Walled gardens and pinetum. Picture gallery. **Location:** 14 miles S of Ayr, off A77. Entrance Lodge is on B7045, 1/2 mile S of Kirkmichael. **Open:** 18 July–16 Aug, daily except Mons. **Admission:** Adults £3.50, children £2, OAPs £2.50. Parties by arrangement any time of the year. **Refreshments:** Tearoom. Car parking. Wheelchair access – around gardens and principal floor of the Castle.

 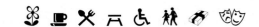 map 10
B2

BOWHILL

Selkirk, Borders TD7 5ET
Tel: 01750 22204 Fax: 01750 22204 (Buccleuch Heritage Trust)

Border home of the Scotts of Buccleuch. Paintings by Guardi, Canaletto, Claude, Gainsborough, Reynolds and Raeburn. Superb furniture, porcelain. Monmouth, Sir Walter Scott, Queen Victoria relics. Victorian kitchen. Audio visual. Theatre. Adventure Woodland. Nature trails. **Location:** 3 miles west of Selkirk, on A708. Edinburgh, Carlisle and Newcastle approx 1.5 hours by road. **Open:** House: 1–31 Jul, daily 1–4.30pm. Open by appointment at additional times for educational groups. Country park: 25 Apr–31 Aug daily except Fri, 12 noon–5pm. Open on Fridays in July with House. Last entry 45 mins before closing. **Admission:** House & Park: Adults £4, children £1, OAP and groups £3.50. Wheelchair users and children under 5 free. Park £1. **Refreshments:** Gift shop, tearoom.

map 13 H6

DALMENY HOUSE

South Queensferry, Edinburgh, Scotland, EH30 9TQ.
Tel: 0131 331 1888 Fax: 0131 331 1788 (Earl of Rosebery)

Home of the Earls of Rosebery, set in beautiful parkland on the Firth of Forth. Scotland's first gothic revival house. Rothschild Collection of 18th century French furniture and decorative art. Portraits by Reynolds, Gainsborough, Raeburn and Lawrence. Goya tapestries. Napoleonic Collection. **Location:** 7 miles N of Edinburgh, signposted off A90. **Buses:** St. Andrew Square Bus Station to Chapel Gate (1 mile from house). **Open to public:** July & August, Sun 1–5.30pm. Mon & Tue, 12–5.30pm. Special parties at other times by arrangement. **Admission:** Adults £3.60, children (10–16) £2, children under 10–free, OAPs £3.20, students £ 2.80, groups (min. 20) £3. Corporate events welcome throughout the year. **Internet:** www.edinburgh.org

map 13 G5

DRUMLANRIG CASTLE

Nr Thornhill, Dumfries & Galloway, DG3 4AQ
Tel: 01848 330248 (His Grace The Duke of Buccleuch & Queensberry K.T.)

Exquisite pink sandstone castle 1679–91. Renowned works by Holbein, Leonardo & Rembrandt, Versailles furniture, Bonnie Prince Charlie's relics, Douglas family historical exhibition, extensive gardens and woodlands superbly landscaped. **Open:** Castle: daily 2 May–23 Aug. Guided tours 12–4pm (limited tours 10–12 Jul), 11–12pm available for pre-booked groups–school groups by appointment from 9.30am. 24–31 Aug. Open by appointment only. Country Park, Gardens and Adventure Woodland 2 May–31 Aug. Daily 11–5pm. **Admission:** Adult Castle & Country Park £6, County Park £3. Child Castle & Country Park £2, Senior Citizens Castle & Country Park £4. Family (2 adults, 4 children) £14. Pre-booked groups special time 11–12pm £8, normal time 12–4pm £6. Wheelchairs free.

map 13 J6

FLOORS CASTLE

Kelso, TD5 7SF, Scotland
Tel: 01573 223 333 Fax: 01573 226 056 (Duke of Roxburghe)

Scotland's largest inhabited castle, built in 1721 by William Adam and remodelled by Playfair. Outstanding collection of French furniture, stunning tapestries and works of art. Beautiful Chinese and European porcelain and a unique Victorian collection of birds. **Location:** N of Kelso. **Station(s):** Berwick-upon-Tweed. **Open:** 5 April–25 October daily. 10am–4.30pm. **Admission:** Please contact for admission prices. Party rates on request. **Refreshments:** Restaurant and coffee shop. **Events/Exhibitions:** Pipe bands and Highland dancers throughout the year. **Accommodation:** At nearby Sunlaws House Hotel. **Conferences:** Facilities available including dinners, receptions, product launches and outdoor events. Free parking, walled garden, woodland & river walks and garden centre.

map 13 J6

GOSFORD HOUSE

Longniddry, EH32 OPY, East Lothian, Scotland Tel: 01875 870 201
Fax: 01875 870 620 (The Wemyss & March Estates Management Co. Ltd)

Robert Adam designed the Central block and Wings, which were later demolished. Two Wings rebuilt in 1890 by William Young. The 1800 roof was part burnt (military occupation) in 1940, but was restored in 1987. North Wing now roofless. South Wing is family home and contains famous Marble Hall (Staffordshire Alabaster). Parts of South Wing are open. Fine collection of paintings and works of art. Surrounding gardens redeveloping. Extensive policies, artificial ponds; geese and other wildfowl breeding. **Location:** On A198 between Aberlady and Longniddry. NW of Haddington. **Station(s):** Longniddry (2.5 miles). **Open:** June-July, Wed, Sat–Sun, 2–5pm. **Admission:** Adults £2.50, children 75p. **Refreshments:** Hotels in Aberlady.

HARELAW FARMHOUSE

Nr. Longniddry, East Lothian, Scotland
Tel: 01875 870 201 Fax: 01875 870 620
(The Wemyss & March Estates Management Co. Ltd)

Early 19th century 2-storey farmhouse built as an integral part of the steading. Dovecote over entrance arch. **Location:** Between Longniddry and Drem on B1377. **Open:** Exteriors only. By appointment, Wemyss & March Estates, Estate Office, Longniddry, EH32 0PY, East Lothian, Scotland.

map 13
H5

KELBURN CASTLE & COUNTRY CENTRE

Fairlie, KA29 0BE, Ayrshire, Scotland
Tel: 01475 568 685 Fax: 01475 568 121 (Earl of Glasgow)

Historic home of the Earls of Glasgow, Kelburn has been owned by the Boyle family for over 800 years and is famous for its spectacular scenery and beautiful Glen with walks, waterfalls and gorges. Discover Kelburn's colourful history in the Kelburn Story Exhibition, Museum and New Zealand Exhibition. There are lovely gardens, a riding centre, a nature centre and the Secret Forest – a natural wood filled with unusual follies and sculptures. Birds of Prey displays (May-Sept). **Location:** 2 miles S of Largs, North Ayrshire, On the A78. **Station(s):** Largs. **Open:** Easter-end Oct, daily, 10–6pm. **Admission:** Adults £4, Children/OAPs £2.50. Castle open for guided tours July-Aug, £1.50. Winter opening: 11–5pm. Grounds only. Riding centre open all year. **Refreshments:** Licensed cafe and tea room.

HOPETOUN HOUSE

South Queensferry, West Lothian, Scotland, EH30, 9SL
Tel: 0131 331 2451 Fax: 0131 319 1885 (Hopetoun House Preservation Trust)

Hopetoun House is a unique gem of Europe's architectural heritage and undoubtedly 'Scotland's Finest Stately Home'. Situated on the shores of the Firth of Forth, it is one of the most splendid examples of the work of Scottish architects Sir William Bruce and William Adam. The Bruce House has fine carving, wainscoting and ceiling painting, while in contrast the Adam interior, with opulent gilding and classical motifs reflect the aristocratic grandeur of the early 18th century. The House is set in 100 acres of rolling parkland including woodland walks, the Red Deer Park, The Spring Garden with a profusion of wild flowers, and numerous picturesque picnic spots. Panoramic views can be seen from the rooftop platform. **Location:** 2 miles from Forth Road Bridge. 10 miles from Edinburgh. **Open:** 10 Apr–27 Sept, daily, 10–5.30pm. Last admission 4.30pm. **Admission:** Adults £4.70, children £2.60, OAPs/students/groups £4.20, family £14.50. **Refreshments:** Delicious meals and snacks served in the recently converted Stables Restaurant.

map 13
G5

LAURISTON CASTLE
Edinburgh, Lothian, Scotland

A 1590s Scottish tower house with substantial additions from 1824 by the architect William Burn, the castle stands in 30 acres of parkland and tranquil gardens which enjoy a spectacular view across the Firth of Forth. The remarkably complete Edwardian interior was designed by the castle's last owner, William Robert Reid, who was the proprietor of the important Edinburgh cabinet making business, Morison & Company. Reid was both a connoisseur and a collector. Between 1903, when he purchased Lauriston and his death in 1919, he filled the castle with superb collections of eighteenth century Italian furniture (principally from Naples and Sicily), Derbyshire Blue John, Sheffield Plate, Caucasion carpets and rugs, clocks, porcelain, Mezzotint prints, tapestries, textiles and items of decorative art. There are also many

items of fine furniture made by Morison & Co during the 1890s. The Castle is preserved exactly as left in 1926 at the death of Reid's widow, Margaret Johnston Reid, who gave it in Trust to the Nation. To enter Lauriston is to step across a threshold in time into the home of a wealthy and cultured family in the years before the Great War. **Located:** Cramond Road South, Davidson's Mains some three miles from the centre of Edinburgh. **Open:** April–October daily, except Friday, 11–1pm, 2–5pm, November–March, Saturday and Sunday only 2–4pm. Visit is by guided tour only. Tours take about 50 minutes. Last admission 40 minutes before each closing time. **Cost:** Admission charge (concessions available). Tel: 0131 336 2060. Free admission to grounds and car parking.

map 13
G5

LENNOXLOVE HOUSE
Haddington, East Lothian, Scotland, EH41 4NZ
Tel: 01620 823 720 Fax: 01620 825 112 (Duke of Hamilton)

Lennoxlove House, home of the Duke of Hamilton, dates from the 14th century and is set in 600 acres of woodland about 20 minutes drive from Edinburgh. The original Tower with its splendid Great Hall was known as Lethington Tower, but later renamed Lennoxlove after Frances Stewart, Duchess of Lennox, a favourite of Charles II. The house is home to the Hamilton Palace collection of furniture, paintings and porcelain as well as historic mementoes of Mary, Queen of Scots, including her silver casket, sapphire ring and a death mask. **Open: House & Grounds:** Easter Weekend-end Oct. Guided tours – Wed, Sat, Sun, 2–4.30pm. Private groups by arrangement. **Refreshments:** Tearoom serves morning coffee, light lunches and afternoon tea.

map 13
H5

MANDERSTON
Duns, TD11 3PP, Berwickshire, Scotland.
Tel: 01361 883 450 Fax: 01361 882 010 (Lord & Lady Palmer)

Manderston, the home of Lord and Lady Palmer is an Edwardian mansion set in 56 acres of formal gardens (Scottish Borders). The only silver staircase in the world, insights into life at the turn of the century both 'upstairs' and 'downstairs'. Formal and woodland gardens, stables, Racing Room, Biscuit Tin Museum, Marble Dairy, lakeside walks. Tearoom serving cream teas on open days and gift shop all combine to make this a memorable day out. **Location:** 12 miles W of Berwick-upon-Tweed. **Open:** 14 May–27 Sept: Thurs & Sun, 2–5.30pm. Also Mons 25 May & 31 Aug. Group visits any time of year by appointment. **Admission:** Please phone 01361 883450 for details. **Refreshments:** Tearoom serving cream teas on open days. **Conferences:** Available as a corporate and location venue.

map 13
J5/6

PALACE OF HOLYROODHOUSE

Edinburgh EH8 8DX, Scotland
Tel: 0131 556 7371 (Her Majesty The Queen)

Buckingham Palace, Windsor Castle and the Palace of Holyroodhouse are the Official Residences of the Sovereign and are used by the Queen as both home and office. The Queen's personal standard flies when Her Majesty is in residence. Furnished with works of art from the Royal Collection, these buildings are used extensively by The Queen for State ceremonies, audiences and official entertaining and are opened to the public as much as these commitments allow. At the end of Edinburgh's Royal Mile, one of the most famous and historic streets in the world, stands the Palace of Holyroodhouse, The Queen's official residence in Scotland. Set against the spectacular backdrop of Arthur's Seat, Holyrood evolved from a medieval fortress into a baroque palace and has always been a favoured royal residence. The Royal Apartments, an extensive suite of rooms which epitomise the elegance and grandeur of this ancient and noble house, contrast with the historic tower apartments of Mary, Queen of Scots' which are steeped in intrigue and sorrow. These personal, intimate rooms, where she lived following her return from France in 1561, witnessed the murder of David Rizzio, her favourite secretary, by her jealous husband, Lord Darnley and his accomplices. **Open:** Every day (except 10 Apr, 12–23 May, 25, 26 Dec and for 10 days in Jun/Jul), 1 Nov–31 Mar: 9.30–3.45pm (last admission); 1 Apr–31 Oct: 9.30–5.15pm (last admission). Garden Open: Apr–Oct. Guided tours/exhibition: Nov–Mar. **Admission:** Adults £5.30, children (under 17) £2.60, OAPs (over 60) £3.70.

map 13
G5

MAYBOLE CASTLE

High Street, Maybole, Ayrshire KA19 7BX
Tel: 01655 883765 (The Trustees of The Seventh Marquess of Ailsa)

Historic 16th century Town house of the Kennedy family. **Location:** High Street, Maybole on A77. Open: May–Sept. Sun, 3–4pm. At other times by appointment. **Admission:** Adult £2, concs. £1.

map 10
B2

SORN CASTLE

Sorn, Mauchline, Ayrshire.
Tel: Cluttons 01505 612 124 (R. G. McIntyre's Trust)

Dating from 14th century, the Castle stands on a cliff on the River Ayr. The 18th and 19th century additions are of the same pink sandstone quarried from the river banks. The woodlands and grounds were laid out in the 18th century with fine hardwood trees, rhododendrons and azaleas. The Castle is essentially a family home with fine examples of Scottish paintings and artefacts. **Location:** 4 miles E of Mauchline, on B743. **Open:** Castle: 18 July–15 Aug, 2–5pm or by appointment. Grounds: 1 Apr–30 Oct. **Admission:** Adults £3.50.

map 12
E6

MELLERSTAIN HOUSE

Gordon, Berwickshire, Borders, Scotland, TD3 6LG
Tel: 01573 410 225 Fax: 01573 410636 (The Mellerstain Trust)

Scotland's famous Adam mansion. Beautifully decorated and furnished interiors. Terraced gardens and lake. Gift shop. **Location:** 9 miles NE of Melrose. 7 miles NW of Kelso. 37 miles SE of Edinburgh. **Open:** Easter (4 days), then May–Sept, daily except Sats. 12.30–5pm. (Last admission 4.30pm). Groups at other times by appointment. **Admission:** Adults £4.50, seniors £3.50, child £2.00. Groups (20+) £3.50 prior booking required. Apply Administrator. Free parking. **Refreshments:** Tearooms. **Events/Exhibitions:** 7 June: Vintage Car Rally. 10–12 July: Craft Festival. Permanent exhibition of Antique Dolls and Toys. Wheelchair access to principal rooms **E-Mail:** a.ashby@virgin.net **Internet:** www.calligrafix.co.uk/mellerstain

map 13
J6

POLLOK HOUSE

Pollok Country Park, Glasgow G43 1AT
Tel: 0141 6331 1854 Fax: 0141 332 9957 (Glasgow Museums)

Built in 1747–52, additions by Sir Rowland Anderson 1890–1908. Set in well-tended gardens amidst 361 acres of park and woodland. Contains Stirling Maxwell collection of Spanish and other European paintings, one of the finest in Britain; displays of furniture, ceramics, glass and silver. Nearby in Pollok Park is the world-famous Burrell Collection. **Location:** 2.5 miles south of city centre. Station: Pollokshaws West 0.5 mile. **Open:** early May–late October every year. Mon, Wed–Sat 10–5pm. Sun 11–5pm. Closed Tues. **Admission:** Free. Refreshments: Restaurant 632 0274.

map 12
E5

STEVENSON HOUSE

Haddington, East Lothian, Scotland, EH41 4PU. Tel: 0162 082 3217
(A. C. H. Dunlop, Brown Dunlop Country Houses Trust)

A family home for four centuries of charm and interest, dating from the 13th century when it belonged to the Cistercian Nunnery at Haddington, but partially destroyed on several occasions and finally made uninhabitable in 1544. Restored about 1560, the present house dates mainly from this period, with later additions in the 18th century. Fine furniture, pictures, etc. **Location:** 20 miles from Edinburgh, 1.5 miles from A1, 2 miles from Haddington. (See Historic House direction signs on A1 and in Haddington). **Open:** 4 Jul–2 Aug daily except Fri. Guided tour (1 hour) at 3pm. Admission: £2. Other times by arrangement only. Gardens open daily Apr–Oct. **Refreshments:** Appointment parties coffees and teas by arrangement at Stevenson. Nearest hotels and restaurants in Haddington (2 miles from Stevenson). Car parking. Suitable for wheelchairs in garden only.

map 13
H5

ROYAL BOTANIC GARDEN

20a Inverleith Row, Edinburgh EH3 5LR
Tel: 0131 552 7171 Fax: 0131 552 0382

Scotland's premier garden. Discover the wonders of the plant kingdom in over 70 acres of beautifully landscaped grounds including the world famous Rock Garden, the Pringle Chinese Collection and the amazing Glasshouse Experience featuring Britain's tallest palmhouse. **Location:** Off A902, 1 mile north of the city centre. **Open:** Daily. **Admission:** Free, donations welcome.

THIRLESTANE CASTLE

Lauder, Berwickshire, Scottish Borders TD2 6RU
Tel: 01578 722 430 Fax: 01578 722 761(Thirlestane Castle Trust)

One of the oldest and finest castles in Scotland, Thirlestane was the seat of the Earls and Duke of Lauderdale. It has unsurpassed 17th century ceilings, a restored picture collection, Maitland family treasures, historic toys and a country life exhibition. Woodland picnic tables, tearoom and gift shop. **Open:** 10–17 Apr and Sun, Mon, Wed & Thurs in May, June & Sept. 2–4.30pm last admission. July & Aug, Sun–Fri 12–4.30pm last admission. Adults £4.00. Family (parents and own school age children) £10. Party discounts available, also booked tours at other times by arrangement. Free parking.

map 13
H6

TRAQUAIR HOUSE

Innerleithen, Peeblesshire, Scotland EH44 6PW
Tel: 01896 830 323 Fax: 01896 830 639 (Mrs F. Maxwell Stuart)

Traquair is Scotland's oldest inhabited and most romantic house, spanning over 1000 years of Scottish history. Once a pleasure ground for Scottish kings in times of peace, then a refuge of Catholic priests in times of terror, the Stuarts of Traquair supported Mary, Queen of Scots and the Jacobite cause without counting the cost. In one of the 'modern' wings (completed in 1680) visitors can also see an 18th century working brewery, which was resurrected by the 20th Laird and now produces the world renowned Traquair House Ale. In the grounds there is also a maze, craft workshops, 1745 Cottage Restaurant and extensive woodland walks. **Open:** 11 Apr–30 Sept, daily. Oct, Fri–Sun only. 12.30–5.30pm. Jun–Aug, 10.30–5.30pm. **e-mail:** traquair.house @scotborders.co.uk

map 13
H6

WHITHORN PRIORY

Whithorn
Tel:01988 500508 (Historic Scotland)

Part of the 'Whithorn Cradle of Christianity' attraction. The site of the first Christian church in Scotland. Founded as 'Canadian Casa' by Sir Ninian in the early 5th century it later became the cathedral church of Galloway. In the museum is a fine collection of early Christian stones including the Monreith Cross. Visitor Centre and archaeological dig. **Location:** At Whithorn on the A746. **Open:** Please phone for details, 01988 500700. **Admission:** Joint ticket by Whithorn Trust gives entry to the Priory, Priory museum and archaeological dig.

YESTER HOUSE

Gifford, East Lothian EH41 4JH
Tel: 01620 810241 Fax: 01620 810650 (Francis Menotti)

Splendid neo-classical House designed by James Smith, set on the edge of the Lammermuir Hills. For centuries the seat of the Marquesses of Tweedale. Fine 18th century interiors by William and Robert Adam, including the Great Saloon which is a perfect example of their style. Formal gardens were laid out in the 17th century and provide a beautiful natural setting to this day. The House has been extensively restored and sumptuously furnished by the current owner. **Open:** House and Chapel, 12, 13, and 14 Aug, 3–6pm. **Admission:** House & Garden, adults £3, children £1.50, OAPs £1. Garden only £1. Chapel only 75p.

map 13
H5

BALCARRES

Colinsburgh, Fife, Scotland
Tel: 01333 340 206 (Balcarres Trust)

16th century house with 19th century additions by Burn and Bryce. Woodland and terraced garden. **Location:** ½ mile N of Colinsburgh. **Open:** Woodlands and Lower Garden: 9–25 Feb & 30 Mar–20 June, daily except Suns. West Garden: 8–20 Jun, daily except Suns. 2–5pm. House not open except by written appointment and 20 Apr–5 May **Admission:** Gardens Only – Adults £2.50, Children £1.50. House – £4.50. Car park. Suitable for disabled persons, no wheelchairs provided.

map 13
H4

BOLFRACKS GARDEN

Aberfeldy, Perthshire PH15 2EX
Tel: 01887 820207 (M. J. D. Hutchison)

The Garden, approximately four acres, overlooks the upper Tay Valley with splendid views over the river to the hills beyond. A walled garden of an acre contains a wide variety of flowering trees, shrubs and perennials including a good collection of old fashioned rambler and shrub roses. A less formal garden with a burn and lots of peat wall arrangements contains very many ericaceous plants including rhododendrons particularly dwarf, heaths, dwarf conifers. Primulas, moeonopisis, celmisias and gentians all do well. Masses of bulbs in spring and good autumn colour. **Open:** Apr–Oct, 10–6pm. **Admission** £2.

map 13
F3

BLAIR CASTLE

Blair Atholl, Pitlochry, Perthshire PH18 5TI Scotland.
Tel: 01796 481 207 Fax: 01796 481 487

Scotland's most visited historic house is home of the Atholl Highlanders, Britain's only private army. The Castle boasts 32 fascinating rooms containing a unique collection of beautiful furniture, fine paintings, arms and armour, china, costumes, lace, masonic regalia and other treasures. Explore extensive grounds with walks, nature trails, deer park and enjoy the rare wildlife that exists in its natural habitat. 18th century walled garden restoration project. **Location:** 8 miles NW of Pitlochry, off A9. **Station:** Blair Atholl (half a mile). **Open:** Castle & Grounds: 1 Apr–30 Oct, daily 10–6pm. Last admission 5pm. **Admission:** Castle: Adults £5.50, children £4, OAP's £4.50. Grounds £2 per car. Family tickets. Reduced rates and guided tours for parties by prior arrangements.

map 13
F2

CASTLE MENZIES

Weem, Aberfeldy, PH15 2JD, Perthshire, Scotland.
Tel: 01887 820 982 (Menzies Charitable Trust)

Magnificent example of a 16th century 'Z' plan fortified house, seat of Chiefs of Clan Menzies for over 400 years and now nearing completion of its restoration from an empty ruin. It was involved in the turbulent history of the Central Highlands. 'Bonnie Prince Charlie' was given hospitality here on his way north to Culloden in 1746. Visitors can explore the whole of the 16th century building, together with part of the 19th century addition. Small clan museum and gift shop. **Location:** 1.5 miles from Aberfeldy, on B846. **Open:** 1 Apr–17 Oct 1998, Mon–Sat, 10.30–5pm. Sun, 2–5pm. Last admission 4.30pm. **Admission:** Adult £3, OAPs £2.50, children £1.50 (Reduction for groups). **Refreshments:** Tearoom.

map 13
F3

CRAIGDARROCH HOUSE

Moniaive, DG3 4JB Dumfries & Galloway, Scotland
Tel: 01848 200 202 (J. H. A Sykes)

William Adam house built for Annie Laurie. **Location:** 2 miles W of Moniaive, on B729. **Open:** All July, 2–4pm. **Admission:** £2. Please note: no public conveniences.

map 10
C3

DRUMMOND CASTLE GARDENS

Muthill Crieff, Tayside, Scotland, PH5 2AA
Tel: 01764 681 257/433 Fax: 01764 681 550

The gardens of Drummond Castle, first laid out in the early 17th century by John Drummond, 2nd Earl of Perth, are said to be among the finest formal gardens in Europe. A spectacular view can be obtained from the upper terrace, overlooking a magnificent example of an early Victorian parterre in the form of a St. Andrew's Cross. The multi-faceted sundial by John Mylne, Master Mason to Charles 1, has been the centrepiece since 1630. The gardens recently featured in United Artists 'Rob Roy'. **Location:** Entrance 2 miles S of Crieff, on A822 Muthill Road. **Open:** May–Oct & Easter Weekend, daily, 2–6pm. (Last admission 5pm). **Admission:** Adults £3, Children £1.50, OAPs £2.

map 13
F4

GLAMIS CASTLE

Glamis, Angus, Scotland, DO8 1RJ
Tel: 01307 840 393 Fax: 01307 840 733

Family home of the Earls of Strathmore and Kinghorne and a royal residence since 1372. Childhood home of H.M. Queen Elizabeth, The Queen Mother and the legendary setting of Shakespeare's play 'Macbeth'. Five-storey L-shaped tower block dating from 15th century, remodelled in 1606, containing magnificent rooms with wide range of historic pictures, furniture and porcelain, etc. **Location:** Glamis, 6 miles W of Forfar, A94. **Open:** 29 Mar–25 Oct, daily 10.30–5.30pm (Jul & Aug open from 10am). Last admission 4.45pm **Admission:** Adults £5.20, children (5–16) £2.70, OAPs £4, family £14. Grounds only: Adults £2.40, children/OAP £1.30. Party rates (min 20), adult £4.70, OAP £3.50, child £2.40. **Facilities:** Licensed self-service restaurant, seating for 96. Picnic area, four shops, magnificent grounds, garden and nature trail. Ample parking.

RAMMERSCALES

Lockerbie, Dumfriesshire, Scotland, DG11 1LD
Tel: 01387 811 988 Fax: 011387 810 940
(M. A. Bell Macdonald)

Georgian manor house dated 1760 set on high ground with fine views over Annandale. Pleasant policies and a typical walled garden of the period. There are Jacobite relics and links with Flora Macdonald retained in the family. There is also a collection of works by modern artists. **Location:** 5 miles W of Lockerbie (M6/A74). 2.5 miles S of Lochmaben on B7020. **Open:** Last week of July–first 3 weeks of August (except Sats) 2–5pm. **Admission:** Adults £5, children/OAPs £2.50.

map 10
D3

STOBHALL

Guildtown, Perthshire, Scotland, (Earl of Perth)

Gardens and policies. Chapel with 17th century painted ceiling. Location: 8 miles N of Perth on A93. **Open:** Mid May–mid June, 1–5pm. **Admission:** Adults £2, children £1.

map 13
G3

SCONE PALACE

Scone, Perth, PH2 6BD, Perthshire.
Tel: 01738 552300 (The Earl of Mansfield) Fax: 01738 552588

Situated 2 miles outside Perth, Scone was the ancient crowning place of the Kings of Scotland and the home of the Stone of Destiny. The present Palace was remodelled in the early nineteenth century, using the structure of the 1580 Palace and remains the home of the Earl and Countess of Mansfield. The staterooms contain a unique collection of ivories, paintings, clocks, furniture, porcelain and Vernis Martin. The grounds house magnificent collections of shrubs with woodland walks through the famed pinetum; many species were first introduced by David Douglas (of Douglas Fir fame). The magnificence of the palace and its contents are complemented by an attractive gift shop, restaurants and adventure playground. Scone is ideal for any family visit and can also provide a exciting venue for corporate and incentive hospitality, both in the Palace or outside in the grounds or Parklands running down to the River Tay. **Open:** 10 Apr–12 Oct, 9.30–5.15pm (last admission 4.45pm). **Admission:** Adults £5.20, children £3, OAPs £4.40, family £16. Groups: Adults £4.70, children £2.60, OAPs £4.

map 13
G3

BALLOCH CASTLE COUNTRY PARK

Balloch, Strathclyde, Scotland.
Tel: 01389 758216 (Dumbarton District Council)

Balloch Castle is a 200 acre country park situated on the bonnie banks of Loch Lomond. Folk say that it is one of the finest parks in the whole of the country and who are we to argue. Steeped in history and with breathtaking views over Loch Lomond, this ancient seat of the Lennox offers the visitor a chance to blend the wild, natural beauty of Scotland with the formal glory of ornamental gardens and the splendid trees of former estate days. The present Balloch Castle, now the Visitor Centre, was built in 1808 and is built in the 'castle-gothic' style of architecture. It was one of the first of its type built in Scotland. We look forward to seeing you. **Location:** SE shore of Loch Lomond, off A82 for Balloch or A811 for Stirling. **Admission:** Free for both Visitor Centre and Country Park. For further information, please contact the Loch Lomond Park Authority on 01389 758216. **Open:** 10–6pm Apr–Oct.

map 12 E5

THE DOUNE OF ROTHIEMURCHUS

Rothiemurchus Estate, By Aviemore, Inverness-shire PH22 1QH.
Tel: 01479 810858. Fax: 01479 811778 (J.P. Grant of Rothiemurchus)

The family home of The Grants of Rothiemurchus was nearly lost as a ruin and has been under an ambitious repair programme since 1975. This exciting project may be visited on selected Mondays throughout the year. Book with the Visitor Centre for a longer 2 hour "Highland Lady" tour which explores the haunts of Elizabeth Grant of Rothiemurchus, born 1797, author of "Memoirs of a Highland Lady" who vividly described the Doune and its surroundings from the memories of her childhood. Pheasant shoots, multi-activity days and receptions available. **e-mail:** rothie@enterprise.net **Location:** 2 m S of Aviemore on E bank of Spey river. **Open:** Grounds: May-Aug, Mon 10–12.30pm and 2–4.30pm. Also first Monday of the month in winter. Admission: Doune Grounds: £1. Guided Highland Lady Tour: £5, min. charge of £20. Booking essential.

BRAEMAR CASTLE

Braemar, Grampian, AB35 5XR, Scotland.
Tel/Fax:013397 41219 (Braemer Castle)

Built in 1628 by the Earl of Mar. Attacked and burned by the celebrated Black Colonel (John Farquharson of Inverey) in 1689. Repaired by the government and garrisoned with English troops after the rising of 1745. Later transformed by the Farquharsons of Invercauld, who had purchased it in 1732, into a fully furnished private residence of unusual charm. L-plan castle of fairy tale proportions, with round central tower and spiral staircase. Barrel-vaulted ceilings, massive iron 'Yett' and underground pit (prison). Remarkable star-shaped defensive curtain wall. Much valuable furniture, paintings and items of Scottish historical interest. **Location:** Half a mile NE of Braemar on A93 **Open:** Easter-late Oct, daily (except Fri), 10–6pm **Admission:** Adults £2.50, children £1. Groups/OAPs/students £2. Free car and bus park. **Refreshments:** In Braemar.

map 4 C5

CALLENDAR HOUSE

Callendar Park, Falkirk, Scotland, FK1 1YR
Tel: 01324 503 770 (Falkirk Council)

Imposing mansion within attractive parkland with a 900 year history. Facilities include a working kitchen of 1825 where costumed interpreters carry out daily chores, including cooking based on 1820's recipes. **Exhibition area:** 'Story of Callendar House', plus two temporary galleries, with regularly changing exhibitions. New for 1998 Permanent Exhibition 'William Forbes Falkirk' with working 1820's general store, clockmaker and printer. There is also a history research centre, gift shop and the Georgian tea shop at the Stables. **Location:** E of Falkirk town centre, on A803 Callendar Road. **Open:** Jan-Dec: Mon-Sat, 10–5pm. Apr–Sept: Sun, 2–5pm. Open all public hols. **Admission:** Adults £1.80, Children 90p, OAPs 90p. Last admission 4.15pm.

map 13 F5

CAWDOR CASTLE

Nairn, Scotland, IV12 5RD (The Dowager Countess Cawdor)
Tel: 01667 404615 Fax: 01667 404674

The most romantic castle in the Highlands. The 14th century keep, fortified in the 15th century and impressive additions, mainly 17th century, form a massive fortress. Gardens, nature trails and splendid grounds. Shakespearean memories of Macbeth. **Location:** S of Nairn, on B9090 between Inverness and Nairn. **Station(s):** Nairn (5m) and Inverness (14m). **Open:** 1 May–11 Oct, daily, 10–5.30pm. Last admission 5pm. **Admission:** Adults £5.20, children (5–15) £2.80, OAPs & disabled £4.20. Groups: Adult (20+) £4.70, children (5–15, 20+) £2.30, family (2 adults + up to 5 children) £14. Gardens, grounds and nature trails only: £2.80. **Refreshments:** Licensed restaurant, snack bar. Gift shop, bookshop and wool shop. Picnic area, 9 hole golf course and nature trails. No dogs allowed in Castle or Grounds.

map 15 F5

CRAIGSTON CASTLE

Turriff AB5 7PX, Aberdeenshire
Tel: 01888551 228 (William Pratesi Urquhart of Craigston)

Built between 1604–1607 by John Urquhart, Craigston Castle is still owned and lived in, by the Urquhart family. The Urquharts moved there following the loss of their estate on the Black Isle. Few changes have been made to the castle's exterior since its construction. The main exterior feature is the sculptured balcony on top of a central arch. This is unique in Scottish architecture and depicts a piper, two knights and David and Goliath. The interior decoration dates mainly from the 19th century. In the 1930s the beautifully and unique carved wooden panels were mounted in the drawing rooms. A number of mirrors were brought to Craigston from the palace of Versailles in the early part of the century. Craigston's woods were almost entirely destroyed during the gale of 1950. The replanting by Bruce Urquhart (died May 1995) was aimed at achieving both commercial and amenity value.

DUFF HOUSE COUNTRY HOUSE GALLERY

Banff, Aberdeenshire, Scotland, AB45 3SX.
Tel: 01261 818 181 Fax: 01261 818 900

Duff House is one of the most imposing and palatial country houses in Scotland, with a classical facade and a grand staircase leading to the main entrance. It remained in the hands of the Duffs, Dukes of Fife, until 1906 when the family presented the house and park to Banff and Macduff, consigning its contents to the saleroom. Set in acres of parkland, by the banks of River Deveron, Duff House is one of the glories of the North East. Designed by William Adam for William Duff (1st Earl Fife), it is situated between the Royal burgh of Banff and the fishing port of Macduff and is a splendid example of Scottish baroque architecture. Duff House is now the premier outstation of the National Galleries of Scotland. **Location:** Banff. 47 miles NE of Aberdeen on A947. **Open:** 1 Apr–30 Sept, daily, 11–4pm. 1 Oct–31 Mar, Thur–Sun, 11–4pm. **Admission:** Adults £3, concessions £2. Free admission to shop, tearoom, grounds and woodland walks. **Refreshments:** Tearoom.

map 15 J5

DUNROBIN CASTLE

Golspie, Sutherland KW10 6SF Scotland
Tel: 01408 633177 Fax: 01408 634081 (The Sutherland Trust)

Dunrobin Castle is the most northerly of Scotland's Great Castles and seat of the Earls of Sutherland (Earldom created c.1235). The keep dates from c.1300 and there are additions from the 17–19th centuries, the biggest being in 1845 when the castle was remodelled by Sir Charles Barry, who had just completed the Houses of Parliament. A serious fire in 1915 caused a lot of damage and gave Sir Robert Lorimer a chance to re-design and re-decorate all the major rooms. The Castle is filled with fine furniture, superb paintings, fine china and family memorabilia. The rooms and corridors are decorated with flowers from the garden which is overlooked by most of them. The Dining room contains the outstanding family silver. The whole building has a friendly, 'lived in' atmosphere. The beautiful gardens were laid out by Barry at the same time as he re-modelled the castle and are of French formal design. In recent years, they have been improved and restored and are one of the few remaining formal gardens in Scotland. The castle and gardens are set next to the sea and there are lovely walks along the beach and the surrounding woodlands. The garden contains an eccentric museum, unlike anything else in the UK. This must be seen, even by those who disapprove of the activities it displays! **Location:** OS Ref: NC850 010.50m N of Inverness on A9. 1m NE of Golspie. **Open:** 1 Apr–31 May & 1–15 Oct: Mon–Sat 10.30–4.30pm. Sun 12–4.30pm. Last entry 4pm. 1 Jun–30 Sept; Mon–Sat 10.30–5.30pm. Sun, 12–5.30pm. Last entry 5pm. **Admission:** Adult £5, child£3.50, OAP £3.50. Groups–Adult £4.50, child £3, OAP £3. Family (2 adults and 2 children) £15. Open all year round for pre-booked groups. **Refreshments:** Tearooms seating 90. **Events**: 12 Aug Highland Games, 18 Aug Vintage Car Rally. A variety of evening and lunchtime functions can be arranged on request. All functions are accompanied by good quality local music.

map 13
F3

DUNVEGAN CASTLE

Dunvegan, Isle of Skye Scotland, IV55 8WF
Tel: 01470 521206 Fax: 01470 521205

Any visit to this enchanted Isle must be deemed incomplete without savouring the wealth of history offered by Dunvegan Castle, the home of the Chiefs of Macleod for nearly 800 years. Dunvegan Castle is a Fortress stronghold in an idyllic lochside setting with dramatic scenery where seals play and eagles soar. Other attractions include gardens, craft shops, boat trips, restaurant, loch cruises and pedigree highland cattle. **Location:** Dunvegan Village (1 mile), 23 miles W of Portree on the Isle of Skye. **Open:** Mon 23 Mar–Sat 31 Oct Mon–Sun 10–5.30pm. Last admission 5pm. **Admission:** Castle & Gardens Adults £5, children £2.50, parties/OAPs/students £4.50. Gardens only Adults £3.50, children £2.

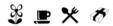

map 14
A3

FASQUE

Fettercairn, Laurencekirk, AB30 1DN, Kincardineshire,
Tel: 01561 340 202/ 340 569 Fax: 01561 340 569(Charles Gladstone)

Fasque is a spectacular example of a Victorian 'Upstairs-Downstairs' stately home. Bought by Sir John Gladstone in 1829, it was home to William Gladstone, four times Prime Minister, for much of his life. In front of the house red deer roam in the park and behind the hills dramatically towards the Highlands. Inside, very little has changed since Sir John's days. Fasque is not a museum, bur rather an unspoilt old family home. Visit the kitchen, laundry, bakery, knives hall and buttery. You'll find a wealth of domestic articles from a bygone age. Climb the famous double cantilever staircase, and wander through the magnificent drawing room, library and bedrooms. Explore a Victorian gamekeeper's hut, complete with man trap, or discover our exhibition of William Gladstone memorabilia. Groups and Coach Parties welcome.

C   map 13
J2

INVERARAY CASTLE

Cherry Park, Inveraray, Argyll, Scotland, PA32 8XE
Tel: 01499 302 203 Fax: 01499 302 421
(The Trustees of the Tenth Duke of Argyll–Home of the Duke and Duchess of Argyll)

Since the early 15th century Inveraray Castle has been the Headquarters of the Clan Campbell. The present Castle was built in the third quarter of the 18th century by Roger Morris and Robert Mylne. The Great Hall and Armoury, the Staterooms, tapestries, pictures and the 18th century furniture and Old Kitchen are shown. Those interested in Campbell Genealogy and History will find a visit to The Campbell Room especially enjoyable. **Location:** 3/4 mile NE of Inveraray by Loch Fyne. 61 miles NW of Glasgow. **Open:** 4 Apr–11 Oct. Closed Sat 18 Apr 1998.

map 12
D4

MOUNT STUART HOUSE & GARDENS

Mount Stuart, Isle of Bute, Scotland, PA20 9LR
Tel: 01700 503 877 Fax: 01700 505 313(The Mount Stuart Trust)

Spectacular High Victorian Gothic house. Ancestral home of the Marquesses of Bute. Splendid interiors, art collection and architectural detail, set in 300 acres of stunning woodlands, mature Victorian Pinetum, arboretum and exotic gardens. Tearoom, shop, scenic picnic areas and car park. Scottish Tourism Oscar winner. **Location:** 5 miles S of Rothesay Pierhead. Local bus service to house. Frequent ferry service from Wemyss Bay, Renfrewshire & Colintraive, Argyll. Only 1 hr from Glasgow Airport. **Open:** 10–13 Apr inclusive and from 1 May–18 Oct, daily except Tue & Thurs. 10–5pm (House from 11am). **Admission:** House & Gardens: Adults £6, children £2.50, family £15. Gardens: Adults £3.50, children £2, family £9. Conc. & group rates given. Pre-booked guided tours available. Guide dogs only.

map 12
D6

The National Trust for Scotland

ALLOA TOWER, Alloa, Clackmannanshire. Open: Good Fri–Easter Mon and 1 May–30 Sep, daily 1.30–5.30.

ANGUS FOLK MUSEUM, Kirkwynd, Glamis, Forfar, Angus DD8 1RT. Open: Good Fri–Easter Mon and 1 May–30 Sep, daily 11–5.

ARDUAINE GARDEN, Arduaine, By Oban, Argyll PA34 4XQ. Open: all year, daily 9.30–sunset.

BACHELORS' CLUB, Sandgate Street, Tarbolton KA5 5RB. Open: Good Fri–30 Sep, daily 11.30–5; weekends in Oct, 11.30–5

BANNOCKBURN, Glasgow Road, Stirling FK7 0LJ. Open: site, all year, daily. Heritage Centre and shop, 1–31 Mar and 1 Nov–23 Dec, daily 11–3; 1 Apr–31 Oct, daily 10–5.30.

BARRIE'S BIRTHPLACE, 9 Brechin Road, Kirriemuir, Angus DD8 4BX. Open: Good Fri–Easter Mon and 1 May–30 Sep, Mon–Sat 11–5.30 Sun 1.30–5.30.

BARRY MILL, Barry, Carnoustie, Angus DD7 7RJ. Open: Good Fri–Easter Mon and 1 May–30 Sep, daily 11–5.

BRANKLYN GARDEN, 116 Dundee Road, Perth PH2 7BB. Open: 1 Mar–31 Oct, daily 9.30–sunset.

BRODICK CASTLE AND GOATFELL, Isle of Arran, KA27 8HY. Open: castle, 1 Apr (or Good Fri if earlier)–31 Oct, daily 11.30–5.

BRODIE CASTLE, Brodie, Forres IV36 0TE. Open: castle, 1 Apr (or Good Fri if earlier)–30 Sep, Mon–Sat 11–5.30, Sun 1.30–5.30.

BROUGHTON HOUSE AND GARDEN, 12 High Street, Kirkcudbright DG6 4JX. Open: 1 Apr (or Good Fri if earlier)–31 Oct, daily 1–5.30.

CARLYLE'S BIRTHPLACE, The Arched House, Ecclefechan, Lockerbie DG11 3DG. Open: 1 May–30 Sep, Fri–Mon 1.30–5.30.

CASTLE FRASER, Sauchen, Inverurie AB51 7LD. Open: castle, Good Fri–Easter Mon, 1 May–30 Jun and 1–30 Sep, daily 1.30–5.30; 1 Jul–31 Aug, daily 11–5.30; weekends in Oct, 1.30–5.30 (last admission 4.45).

CRATHES CASTLE AND GARDEN, Banchory AB31 3QJ. Open: castle, Visitor Centre, shop and licensed restaurant, 1 Apr (or Good Fri if earlier)–31 Oct, daily 11–5.30 (last admission–castle 4.45).

CULLODEN, NTS Visitor Centre, Culloden Moor, Inverness IV1 2ED.

Open: site, all year, daily. Visitor Centre, 1 Feb–31 Mar and 1 Nov–30 Dec (except 25/26 Dec), daily 10–4; 1 Apr–31 Oct, daily 9–6.

CULROSS, Fife, off A985, 12M West of Forth Road Bridge. Open: Palace, 1 Apr (or Good Fri if earlier)–30 Sep, daily 11–5 (last admission 4). Town House and Study, same dates, 1.30–5 and weekends in Oct, 11–5.

CULZEAN CASTLE AND COUNTRY PARK, Maybole KA19 8LE. Open: castle, Visitor Centre, licensed restaurant and shops, 1 Apr (or Good Fri if earlier)–31 Oct, daily 10.30–5.30 (last admission 5)

DRUM CASTLE, Drumoak, By Banchory AB31 3EY. Open : Good Fri–Easter Mon and 1 May–30 Sep, daily 1.30–5.30; weekends in Oct, 1.30–5.30 (last admission 4.45). Garden, same dates, daily 10–6. Grounds, all year, daily 9.30–sunset.

FALKLAND PALACE, GARDEN AND TOWN HALL, Falkland, Cupar, Fife KY15 7BU. Open: palace and garden, 1 Apr (or Good Fri if earlier)–31 Oct, Mon–Sat 11–5.30, Sun 1.30–5.30 (last admission–palace 4.30,–garden 5).

FYVIE CASTLE, Fyvie, Turriff AB53 8JS. Open: castle, 1 Apr (or Good Fri if earlier)–30 Jun and 1–30 Sep, daily 1.30–5.30; 1 Jul–31 Aug daily 11–5.30; weekends in Oct, 1.30–5.30 .

THE GEORGIAN HOUSE, 7 Charlotte Square, Edinburgh EH2 4DR. Open: 1 Apr (or Good Fri if earlier)–31 Oct, Mon–Sat 10–5, Sun 2–5

GLADSTONE'S LAND, 477B Lawnmarket, Edinburgh EH1 2NT. Open: 1 Apr (or Good Fri if earlier)–31 Oct, Mon–Sat 10–5, Sun 2–5

GLENCOE, NTS Visitor Centre, Glencoe, Ballachulish PA39 4HX. Open: site, all year, daily. Visitor Centre and snack-bar, 1 Apr (or Good Fri if earlier) to 18 May and 1 Sep–31 Oct, daily 10–5; 19 May–31 Aug, daily 9.30–5.30 .

GLENFINNAN MONUMENT, NTS Information Centre, Glenfinnan PH37 4LT. Open: site, all year, daily. Visitor Centre and snack-bar, 1 Apr (or Good Fri if earlier)–18 May and 1 Sep–31 Oct, daily 10–1 and 2–5; 19 May–31 Aug, daily 9.30–6 (snack-bar 10–6).

GREENBANK GARDEN, Flenders Road, Clarkston, Glasgow G76 8RB. Open: all year, daily 9.30–sunset, except 25/26 Dec and 1/2 Jan. Shop and tearoom, 1 Apr (or Good Fri if earlier)–31 Oct, daily 11–5; 1 Nov–31 Mar, Sat/Sun 2–4. House open 1 Apr–31 Oct, Suns only 2–4 and during special events (subject–functions in progress). No dogs in garden, please.

HADDO HOUSE, Ellon, Aberdeenshire AB41 0ER. Open: house, Good Fri–Easter Mon and 1 May–30 Sep, daily 1.30–5.30; weekends in Oct, 1.30–5.30 (last admission 4.45); shop and Stables.

THE HILL HOUSE, Upper Colquhoun Street, Helensburgh G84 9AJ. Open 1 Apr (or Good Fri if earlier)–31 Oct, daily 1.30–5.30 (last admission 5); tearoom, 1.30–4.30.

HILL OF TARVIT MANSIONHOUSE, Cupar, Fife KY15 5PB. Open: house, Good Fri–Easter Mon and 1 May–30 Sep, daily 1.30–5.30; weekends in Oct, 1.30–5.30 (last admission 4.45). Garden and grounds, all year, daily 9.30–sunset.

HOUSE OF THE BINNS, Linlithgow, West Lothian EH49 7NA. Open: house, 1 May–30 Sep, daily except Fri, 1.30–5.30 (last admission 5). Parkland, 1 Apr–31 Oct, daily 9.30–7; 1 Nov–31 Mar, daily 9.30–4.

HOUSE OF DUN, Montrose, Angus DD10 9LQ. Open: house and shop, Good Fri–Easter Mon and 1 May–30 Sep, daily 1.30–5.30; weekends in Oct, 1.30–5.30 (last admission 5).

HUGH MILLER'S COTTAGE, Cromarty, IV11 8XA. Open: 1 May–30 Sep, Mon–Sat 10–1 and 2–5.30, Sun 2–5.30.

INVEREWE GARDEN, Poolewe IV22 2LQ. Open: garden, 15 March–31 Oct, daily 9.30am–9pm; 1 Nov–14 Mar, daily 9.30–5. Visitor Centre and shop, 15 Mar–31 Oct, daily 9.30–5.30. Licensed restaurant, same dates, daily 10–5. Guided garden walks, 15 Mar–30 Sep, Mon–Fri at 1.30. No dogs in garden please. No shaded car parking.

KELLIE CASTLE AND GARDEN, Pittenweem, Fife KKY10 2RF. Open castle, Good Fri–Easter Mon and 1 May–30 Sep, daily 1.30–5.30; weekends in Oct, 1.30–5.30 (last admission 4.45). Garden and grounds, all year, daily 9.30–sunset. .

KILLIECRANKIE, NTS Visitor Centre, Killiecrankie, Pitlochry PH16 5LG. Open: site, all year, daily. Visitor Centre, shop and snack-bar, 1 Apr (or Good Fri if earlier)–31 Oct, daily 10–5.30.

LEITH HALL AND GARDEN, Huntly AB54 4NQ. Open: house and tearoom, Good Fri–Easter Mon and 1 May–30 Sep, daily 1.30–5.30; weekends in Oct, 1.30–5.30 (last admission 4.45). Garden and grounds all year, daily 9.30–sunset.

PITMEDDEN GARDEN, Ellon AB41 0PD. Open: garden, Visitor Centre, museum, tearoom, grounds and other facilities, 1 May–30 Sep, daily 10–5.30 (last admission 5).

PRESTON MILL AND PHANTASSIE DOOCOT, East Linton, East Lothian, EH40 3DS. Open: Good Fri–Easter Mon, 1 May–30 Sep, Mon–Sat 11–1 and 2–5, Sun 1.30–5; weekends in Oct, 1.30–4.

PRIORWOOD GARDEN AND DRIED FLOWER SHOP, Melrose TD6 9PX. Open: 1 Apr (or Good Fri if earlier)–30 Sep, Mon–Sat 10–5.30, Sun 1.30–5.30; 1 Oct–24 Dec, Mon–Sat 10–4, Sun 1.30–4.

ROBERT SMAIL'S PRINTING WORKS, 7/9 High Street, Innerleithen EH44 6HA. Open: Good Fri–Easter Mon and 1 May–30 Sep, Mon–Sat 10–1 and 2–5, Sun 2–5; weekends in Oct, Sat 10–1 and 2–5, Sun 2–5 (last admission 45 mins before closing, morning and afternoon).

SOUTER JOHNNIE'S COTTAGE, Main Road, Kirkoswald KA19 8HY. Open: Good Fri–30 Sept, daily 11.30–5; weekends in Oct, 11.30–5 (last admission 4.30).

THE TENEMENT HOUSE, 145 Buccleuch Street, Glasgow G3 6QN. Open 1 Mar–31 Oct, daily 2–5 (last admission 4.30) Very restricted parking.

THREAVE GARDEN AND ESTATE, Castle Douglas DG7 1RX. Open: estate and garden, all year, daily 9.30–sunset. Walled garden and glasshouses, all year, daily 9.30–5.

TORRIDON, N of A896, 9M SW of Kinlochewe. Open: Countryside Centre, 1 May–30 Sep, Mon–Sat 10–5, Sun 2–5. Estate, Deer Park and Deer Museum (unstaffed), all year, daily.

WEAVER'S COTTAGE, The Cross, Kilbarchan PA10 2JG. Open: Good Fri–30 Sep, daily 1.30–5.30; weekends in Oct, 1.30–5.30

Ireland

Top: Glin Castle. Left: Mount Usher. Below: Powerscourt

Ireland is fast becoming one of most popular places to visit. For such a tiny island it has a vast history steeped in romanticisim, valour, poverty, poetry and music.

From the stark craggy cliffs on the west coast of Galway to the calm running waters of the River Liffey in Dublin, Ireland offers contrasting territory that is both breathtaking and serene. Looking out on the barren lands of Connemara is to view a land still untouched by the modern world.

Music is an integral part of Irish life and can be heard on the streets drifting from the bars – another integral part of Irish life! The joviality and talk in the pubs is mingled with the live music that is played by the locals. It would also serve music lovers who visit Ireland to attend where possible a 'Fleadh' (pronouned 'Fla') which is a festival of music offering the opportunity to find great 'craic' (fun!)

The weather can be contrary but this is a secondary concern when you discover all that Ireland has to offer.

ANTRIM CASTLE GARDENS

Randalstown Road, Antrim (Antrim Borough Council)
Tel 01849 428000   Fax: 01849 460 360

Antrim Castle Gardens boasts ownership of one of the earliest examples of an Anglo-Dutch water garden within the British Isles. It contains exceptional examples of ornamental canals, an ancient motte and a parterre garden. The parterre garden has preserved the timeless atmosphere of the 17th century formal garden. It has been planted with fine examples of 17th century plants which were originally used for culinary and medicinal purposes. The gardens can be viewed to their best advantage from the top of the motte which retains its spiral path. **Open:** Mon–Fri, 9.30–9.30pm, Sat 10–5pm. Jul–Aug, Sun 2–5pm.

map 16
D2

BENVARDEN GARDENS

Benvarden Dervock, Co Antrim, N. Ireland.
Tel: 012657 41331 Fax: 012657 41955 (H.J. Montgomery)

Benvarden House is situated on the banks of the River Bush where the river is crossed by the Coleraine-Ballycastle road (B67). The Walled Garden, about 2 acres in area, appears on a map dated 1788 and has been cultivated since then without interruption, although with alterations to the layout from time to time. The Garden is one of the finest and best maintained in the North of Ireland and ranges from beautiful rose beds to a well stocked kitchen garden. The extensive pleasure grounds stretch down to the banks of the river which is spanned by a splendid iron bridge 90 feet long, erected by Robert Montgomery in 1878. **Open:** 1 Jun–31 Aug 2–6pm. Tues–Sun. Bank Hol Mons. **Admission** £2.

map 16
D2

DUBLIN WRITERS MUSEUM

18 Parnell Square, Dublin 1, Ireland
Tel: 00 353 1 872 2077 Fax: 00 353 1 872 2231
(Dublin Tourism Enterprises)

The Dublin Writers Museum is located in a splendidly restored 18th century house. It uniquely represents that great body of Irish writers – in prose, poetry and drama – which has contributed so much to the world of literature over the years. **Location:** Dublin city centre – 5 mins. walk from O'Connell St. **Open:** All year except 24/25/26 Dec. Mon–Sat 10–5pm. Sun & Public Hols 11–5pm. Late opening Jun–Aug, Mon–Fri 10–6pm. **Admission:** Adults £2.95, children £1.30, concessions £2.50, family £8. Group rates (20+): Adults £2.50, children £1.10, concessions £2.10.

map 16
D4

FERNHILL GARDEN

Sandyford, Co. Dublin, Ireland
Tel: 00 353 12 956 000 (Mrs Sally Walker)

A garden for all seasons, 200 years old in Robinsonion style with over 4,000 species and varieties of trees, shrubs and plants. Dogs not allowed. **Location:** Sandyford, Co. Dublin. **Open:** Mar–Oct, Tue–Sat, 11am–5pm. Sun 2–6pm. **Admission:** Adults £3, Children £1, OAPs £2.

map 16
D4

BANTRY HOUSE

Bantry, Co. Cork, Ireland
Tel: 00 353 2 750 047 Fax: 00 353 2 750 795 (Egerton Shelswell-White)

Partly Georgian mansion standing at edge of Bantry Bay, with beautiful views. Seat of family of White, formerly Earls of Bantry. Unique collection of tapestries, furniture, etc. Terraces and statuary in the Italian style in the grounds. **Location:** In outskirts of Bantry (1/2 mile). 56 miles SW of Cork. **Open:** Daily, 9–6pm, Mar 17–Oct 31. **Admission: House & Grounds:** Adults £6, children (up to 14) accompanied by parents free, OAPs £4.40, students £4. **Grounds** only: £2. **Groups** (20+) House & Grounds: £4. **Grounds** only: £1.00. **Refreshments:** Tearoom, Bed & Breakfast and dinner. **Events/Exhibitions:** 1796 Bantry French Armada (permanent exhibition). West Cork Chamber Music Festival June–July. **Accommodation:** B&B and dinner. Nine rooms en suite. **Conferences:** Facilities available. Shop.

map 16
B6

GLIN CASTLE

Glin, Co Limerick Ireland
Tel: 00 353 68 34173 Fax: 00 353 68 34364 (Bob Duff)

Glin Castle, one of Ireland's most historic properties and home to the FitzGerald family, hereditary Knights of Glin. The castle, with its superb interiors, decorative plaster work and collections of Irish furniture and paintings stands on the banks of the River Shannon surrounded by formal gardens and parkland and in the middle of 500 acres of dairy farm and woodland. The beautiful walled kitchen garden supplies the castle with fresh vegetables and fruit. Castle & Gardens open to the public 1 May to 30 June 10–noon and 2–4pm daily. Castle rentals and overnight accommodation available. Glin Castle is a member of Ireland's Blue Book.

HAMWOOD

Hamwood, Dunboyne, Co Meath
Tel: (01) 8255210 (Major C.R.F. Hamilton)

Situated 3km from Dunboyne on Maynooth Road (beside Ballymacoll Stud). **Open:** House: 1 Apr–31 Aug 2–6pm. Gardens: Open 3rd Sun of each month Mar–Jul 2–6pm. Groups by arrangements. Hamwood is an 18th century house built in the Palladian style in 1779 by Charles Hamilton, wine importer and later Land Agent for the Duke of Leinster. The house was built at a cost of £2,500 with all the timber used in the construction coming from Memel in Russia and was one of the first in Ireland to be roofed with dry slating. The house contains a fine collection of 18th century furniture, mirrors and pictures of historical interest. Hamwood was also the home of Eva and Letitia Hamilton, artists of the 1920–1960 period and now the home of their nephew. The garden is one of the least known in Meath but is among the most fascinating.

THE JAMES JOYCE MUSEUM

The Joyce Tower, Sandycove, Co. Dublin, Ireland
Tel: 00 353 1 280 9265 Fax: 00 353 1 280 9265
(Dublin Tourism Enterprises)

The Joyce Tower is a Martello tower, one of 26 built around Dublin in 1804 as defence against Napoleon. The building was lived in by James Joyce in 1904 and is described in his novel 'Ulysses'. It now houses the James Joyce Museum, a modern exhibition devoted to the life and works of the famous writer. The living room upstairs, described in 'Ulysses', has recently been reconstructed. **Location:** Sandycove Point on sea front, 1 mile from Dun Laoghaire. **Station(s):** DART to Sandycove. **Buses:** 8 (to Sandycove). **Open:** Apr–Oct, Mon–Sat, 10–1pm & 2–5pm. Suns and public hols, 2–6pm. **Admission:** Adults £2.50, children £1.30, concessions £2, family £7.50. Groups prices: Adults £2, children £1, concessions £1, by prior arrangement.

JOHNSTOWN CASTLE DEMESNE

Wexford, Ireland. Tel: 00 353 53 42888 Fax: 00 353 53 42004
(Teagase Soils and Environment Centre)

Grounds and gardens only. 50 acres of well laid out grounds with artificial lakes and a fine collection of ornamental trees and shrubs. Agricultural museum. **Location:** 5 miles SW of Wexford. **Open:** All year, daily, 9am-5pm. Guidebook available at Castle. Although the grounds will continue to be open throughout the year, an admission charge will only apply from 1 May–5 Oct, 1997. **Admission:** Car (and passengers) £2.80. Large coach £20. Small coach £10. Adults (pedestrians/cyclists) £1.50, children/students 50p. Wedding parties for photography £20. Season ticket £7. **Refreshments:** Coffee shop open July–Aug at museum.

LISMORE CASTLE GARDENS

Lismore, Co. Waterford, Ireland
Tel: 00 353 58 54424 Fax: 00 353 58 54896 (Lismore Estates)

Lismore Castle has been the Irish home of the Dukes of Devonshire since 1753 and at one time belonged to Sir Walter Raleigh. The gardens are set in seven acres within the 17th century outer defensive walls and have spectacular views of the castle. There is also a fine collection of specimen magnolias, camellias, rhododendrons and a remarkable yew walk where Edmund Spenser is said to have written the "Faerie Queen". Throughout the open season there is always plenty to see in this fascinating and beautiful garden. **Location:** Lismore, 45 miles W of Waterford. 35 miles NE of Cork (1 hour). **Open:** Early Apr–end Sept. **Admission:** Adults £2.50, children (under 16) £1.50. Reduced rates for groups of 20+ – adults £2.25, children £1.30.

MALAHIDE CASTLE

Malahide, Co Dublin
Tel: 00 353 1 846 2184 Fax: 00 353 1 846 2537
(Dublin Tourism Enterprises)

Malahide Castle, set on 250 acres of parkland in the pretty seaside town of Malahide, was both a fortress and a private home for nearly 800 years and is an interesting mix of architectural styles. The Talbot family lived here from 1185 to 1973, when the last Lord Talbot died. The house is furnished with beautiful period furniture together with an extensive collection of Irish portrait paintings, mainly from the National Gallery. **Open:** Apr–Oct: Mon–Fri 10–5pm, Sat 11–6pm, Sun & Hols 11–6pm. Nov–Mar: Mon–Fri 10–5pm, Sat 2–5pm, Sun & Hols 2–5pm. Closed for tours 12.45–2pm. **Admission:** Adults £3, children (under 12) £1.65, concs (under 18) £2.50, family £8.25. Group: Adults £2.55, children £1.45, concs: £2.15.

KYLEMORE ABBEY & GARDENS

Connemara, Co Galway, Ireland
Tel: 00 353 95 41146 Fax: 00 353 95 41115

Set in the heart of the Connemara mountains is the Kylemore Abbey Estate, home of the Irish Benedictine Nuns. Visit the picturesque Abbey (reception rooms, video and exhibition) and enjoy a stroll to the beautifully restored Gothic Church; browse in the craft shop and sample our home-cooked food in the restaurant. From May 1998 you will have a unique opportunity to visit a Victorian Walled Garden under restoration. The Kylemore Abbey 6 acre Victorian Garden is the most significant walled garden in the west. Access is separate to the Abbey and is through a magnificent wilderness walk. A visit to the west of Ireland is not complete without experiencing the beauty and tranquillity that is Kylemore Abbey and Garden. **Open:** Abbey: All year. Visit Abbey reception rooms, exhibition, video, Gothic Church and lake walk. Craft shop, restaurant, pottery (Mar–Nov). Garden: (May–Nov) wilderness walk, walled garden, tea house and gift shop. **E-mail:** enquiries@kylemore abbey.ie

map 16
B4

MUCKROSS HOUSE, GARDENS & TRADITIONAL FARMS

National Park, Killarney, Kerry
Tel: 00 353 64 31440 Fax: 00 353 64 33926 (Trustees of Muckross)

Muckross House is a magnificent Victorian mansion, situated on the shores of Muckross Lake and set amidst the splendid and spectacular landscape of Killarney National Park. The exquisitely furnished rooms portray the lifestyles of the gentry, including Queen Victoria's boudoir and bedroom as it was when she visited in 1861. The basement depicts the lifestyles of the servants and today is home to Muckross Craft Workshops. The Gardens of Muckross are famed for their beauty worldwide. Muckross Traditional Farms is an exciting outdoor representation of the lifestyles and farming traditions of a rural community of the 1930s. Three separate working farms, complete with animals, poultry and traditional farm machinery will help you relive the past when all work was carried out using traditional methods. Muckross Vintage Coach, visitors to the Farms can enjoy a Free trip around the site on a beautiful Vintage Coach. Location: 3.5m from Killarney, on the Kenmare road. **Open:** Daily, all year. 9–5.30pm, 9–7pm Jul/Aug (Farms Mar–Oct) **Admission:** Adult Ir£3.80, students Ir£1.60. Group rate for 20+ Ir£2.70. Family Ir£9. Ditto for Muckross Traditional Farms. Substantial savings on joint tickets. Gardens free.

map 16
B6

221

MOUNT USHER

Ashford, Co Wicklow
Tel: 00 353 404 40205/40116 Fax: 00 353 404 4025 (Mrs Madelaine Jay)

Laid out along the banks of the river Vartry, Mount Usher represents the Robinsonian style, i.e. informality and natural design. Trees and shrubs introduced from many parts of the world are planted in harmony with woodland and shade loving plants. The river, with its weirs and waterfalls, is enchanted by attractive suspension bridges from which spectacular and romantic views may be enjoyed. The Gardens cover 20 acres and comprise of over 5000 different species of plants, most serving as host to a variety of birds and other wildlife. To the professional gardener, the lover of nature or the casual tourist, a visit to Mount Usher is sure to be a memorable one. **Location:** Ashford, 1 mile from Wicklow on Dublin-Bray Rd. **Open:** Mid Mar–end of October .

map 16 **D5**

NEWBRIDGE HOUSE

Donabate, Co. Dublin, Ireland
Tel: 00 353 1 8436534 Fax: 00 353 1 8462537(Dublin Tourism Enterprises)

This delightful 18th century mansion is set on 350 acres of parkland, 12 miles north of the city centre and boasts one of the finest Georgian interiors in Ireland. The house appears more or less as it did 150 years ago. It was built in 1737, to a design by Richard Castle, for the Archbishop of Dublin and contains elaborate stucco plasterwork by Robert West. The grounds contain a 29 acre traditional farm complete with farmyard animals, a delight to any young visitor and perfect for school tours and large groups. **Open:** Apr–Sept: Tue–Fri 10–5pm, Sat 11–6pm, Sun & Public Hols 2–5pm, closed Mons. Oct–Mar: Sat, Sun, Public Hols 2–5pm. Closed for tours daily 1–2pm. Coffee shop remains open **Admission:** Adult £2.85, children (under 12) £1.55, concs £2.50, family £7.75. Group: Adult £2.50, children £1.35, concs £2.10.

map 16 **D4**

POWERSCOURT GARDENS & WATERFALL

Enniskerry, Co. Wicklow, Ireland
Tel: 00 353 204 6000 Fax: 00 353 28 63561

Just 12 miles south of Dublin, in the foothills of the Wicklow Mountains, lies Powerscourt Estate. Its 20 hectares of gardens are famous the world over. It is a sublime blend of formal gardens, sweeping terraces, statuary and ornamental lakes, together with secret hollows, rambling walks, walled gardens and over 200 variations of trees and shrubs. The shell of the 18th century house gutted by fire in 1974 has an innovative new use: encorporating a terrace restaurant overlooking the spectacular gardens, speciality shops and an exhibition on the Estate and Gardens. Powerscourt Waterfall (5km from Gardens) is Ireland's highest.

map 16 **D4**

SEAFORDE GARDENS

Seaforde, Downpatrick, Co. Down, BT30 8PG,
Northern Ireland Tel: 01396 811 225 Fax: 01396 811 370
(Patrick Forde)

Over 600 trees and shrubs, container grown. Many camellias and rhododendrons. National collection of Eucryphius. Tropical butterfly house with hundreds of free flying butterflies. The 18th century walled gardens and pleasure grounds contain a vast collection of trees and shrubs. Many very rare. Huge rhododendrons. The Hornbeam maze is the oldest in Ireland. **Location:** On A24, Ballynahinch–Newcastle road.

map 16 **E3**

STROKESTOWN PARK HOUSE & GARDENS

Strokestown, Co Roscommon, Ireland
Tel: 00 353 78 33013 Fax: 00 353 78 33712

Strokestown Park was the family home of the Pakenham Mahon family from the 1660's up to 1979. The house retains virtually all of its original furnishings and is seen by guided tours. The Famine Museum uses original documents and letters relating to the time of the Famine on the Strokestown Park Estate to explain the history of The Great Irish Famine and to draw parallels with the occurrence of famine in the Developing World today. The 4.5 acre walled pleasure garden was opened in Aug 1997, having been faithfully restored to its original splendour. Strokestown Park is privately owned since 1979 by the Westward Group, a company based in Strokestown and its restoration is a measure of their commitment to the preservation of our heritage. Visitors can avail of this unique opportunity by visiting any or all three of these heritage attractions (discounts are available for those who visit more than one attraction).

map 16 **C4**

Bunratty Castle & Folk Park

Craggaunowen, The Living Past

SHANNON HERITAGE 'A COMMON CELTIC PAST'

Central Reservations Bunratty Castle & Folk Park, Bunratty, Co. Clare, Ireland
Tel: 00 353 61 360 788   Fax: 00 353 61 361 020

'A Common Celtic Past' is a concept which links each of the products in the Shannon Heritage portfolio together in a time line. The story which is thereby created brings the visitor into the magic and mystery of the Pre-Celtic, Celtic Viking, Norman, Anglo and native Irish societies starting 5000 years ago and continuing to the present day. **Open: Bunratty Castle & Folk Park** Open all year round, 9.30–5.30pm (Last admission 4.15pm). June–Aug; **Folk Park** open from 9.00–6.30pm (Last admission 5.30pm). Closed Good Friday, Christmas Eve, Christmas Day & St Stephens Day. **Craggaunowen, The Living Past:** Open daily from Apr–29 Oct, 10–6pm. (Last admission 5pm). Mid May–mid Aug 9–6pm. Winter season, will open on request for groups. **King John's Castle:** Open daily Apr–Oct 31st 9.30–5.30pm (Last admission 4.15pm). **Knappogue Castle:** Open daily Apr–Oct 6th 9.30–5.30pm. Will open on request for groups. **Killaloe Heritage Centre:** Open daily Apr–Sept 29th 9.30–5.30pm. **Cliffs of Moher Visitors Centre & O'Briens Tower:** O'Briens Tower Open daily Mar–Oct 29th 10–6pm. (Weather permitting). Visitor Centre open all year round from 10–6pm. **Dunguaire Castle:** Open daily May–Oct 6th 9.30–5.30pm. (Last admission 5pm). **Lough Gur:** Open daily May–Sept 29th 10–6pm.

🌸 ☕ ✕ 🎁 🎭

map 16
B5

TIMOLEAGUE CASTLE GARDENS

Timoleague, Bandon, Co Cork
Tel: 00 353 23 46116

This is a charming garden, which surrounds a 1920s house and a ruined Norman church. **Location:** 11 km south of Brandon. **Open:** June–August, Monday–Saturday, 11–5.30pm. Sunday, 2pm–5.30pm. Other times by appointment only. **Admission:** Charges apply.

TULLYNALLY CASTLE & GARDENS

Castlepollard, Co. Westmeath, Ireland.
Tel: 00 353 44 61159/61289 Fax: 00 353 44 61856
(Thomas & Valerie Palceham)

Home of the Pakenhams (later Earls of Longford) since the 17th century. The original house is now incorporated in a huge rambling neo-gothic castle. 30 acres of romantic woodland and walled gardens are also open to the public. **Location:** 1.5 miles outside Castlepollard on Granard Road. **Station(s):** Mullingar. **House open:** 15 June–30 July, 2–6pm. Pre-booked groups admitted at other times. **Gardens:** May–Sept, 2–6pm. **Admission:** House & Gardens: Adults £4, children £2, groups £3.50. Gardens only: Adults £2.50, children £1. **Refreshments:** Tearoom open May–1 Sept at weekends and Bank Hols.

🌳 🌸 ☕ 🏛 ♿ 🚶 🎭

map 16
C4

ARGORY
Moy, Dungannon BT71 6NA Tel: 01868 784753

CASTLE COOLE
Enniskillen, BT74 6JY Tel: 01365 322690 Fax: 01365 325665

CASTLE WARD
Strangford, Downpatrick, BT30 7LS Tel: 01396 881204

DOWNHILL CASTLE, MUSSENDEN TEMPLE, BISHOP'S GATE & BLACK GLEN
42 Mussenden Road, Castlerock, Coleraine BT51 4RP Tel: 01265 848728

FLORENCE COURT
Enniskillen, Co. Fermanagh BT92 1DB Tel: 01365 348249 Fax: 01365 348873

HEZLETT HOUSE
107 Sea Road, Castlerock, Co. Londonderry BT51 4TW Tel: 01265 848567

MOUNT STEWART HOUSE, GARDEN & TEMPLE OF THE WINDS
Newtownards, Co. Down BT22 2AD Tel: 012477 88387/88487

SPRINGHILL
20 Springhill Road, Moneymore, Magherafelt BT45 7NQ Tel: 01648 748210

Belgium

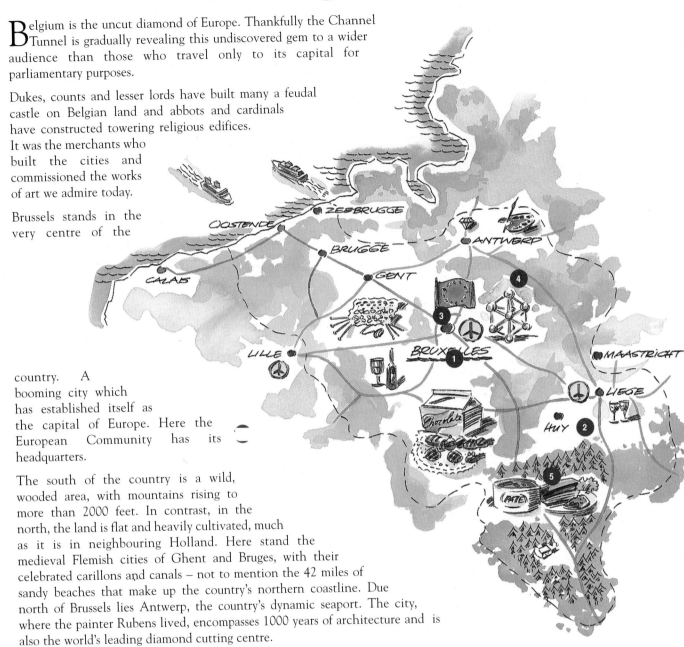

Belgium is the uncut diamond of Europe. Thankfully the Channel Tunnel is gradually revealing this undiscovered gem to a wider audience than those who travel only to its capital for parliamentary purposes.

Dukes, counts and lesser lords have built many a feudal castle on Belgian land and abbots and cardinals have constructed towering religious edifices. It was the merchants who built the cities and commissioned the works of art we admire today.

Brussels stands in the very centre of the country. A booming city which has established itself as the capital of Europe. Here the European Community has its headquarters.

The south of the country is a wild, wooded area, with mountains rising to more than 2000 feet. In contrast, in the north, the land is flat and heavily cultivated, much as it is in neighbouring Holland. Here stand the medieval Flemish cities of Ghent and Bruges, with their celebrated carillons and canals – not to mention the 42 miles of sandy beaches that make up the country's northern coastline. Due north of Brussels lies Antwerp, the country's dynamic seaport. The city, where the painter Rubens lived, encompasses 1000 years of architecture and is also the world's leading diamond cutting centre.

CHATEAU-FORT (CASTLE OF BOUILLON)

Bte Postale 13, B6830 Bouillon, Belgium
Tel: 00 32 61 466 257 Fax: 00 32 61 468 285

The most interesting feudal castle in Belgium, this fortress probably goes back to 8C, but the first records date from 988. Its existence was made immortal by heroic Godfrey of Bouillon, leader of the First Crusade in 1096 and proclaimed King of Jerusalem. The castle was militarily occupied until 1830. **Open:** Jan, weekends 10–5pm. Feb–Dec, weekdays 1–5pm, weekends 10–5pm. Mar, Oct, Nov, 10–5pm. Apr–Jun, Sep, 10–6pm. Jul, Aug, 9.30–7pm. During the Christmas hols and Spring hols, 10–5pm weather permitting. Closed 25 Dec and 1 Jan. Possibility to combine with the museums. **Admission:** Adult BEF150, child BEF80. Seniorcard BEF140 . Studentscard BEF120. Groups (20 pers.): Adult BEF130, child (6–12yrs) BEF70, student (13–18yrs) BEF100. English guide BEF30. **Events:** Night visit of the castle by torch. BEF150+BEF70 for compulsory torch.

CHÂTEAU FORT ECAUSSINNES LALAING

1, rue de Seneffe–B7191 Ecaussinnes Lalaing, Belgium
Tel/Fax: 00 32 67.44 24 90

From the 11th and 12th century, transformed into a residence in the 15th century, this castle preserves the memory of the family of the counts van der Burch, who lived there from 1624 to 1854. Furnished rooms: grand salon, bedroom, oratory. Medieval part: armoury, ancient kitchen, chapel, dungeon. Collections: portraits of the counts van der Burch; paintings, sculptures, glasses, porcelain, furniture, ancient weapons. **Location:** 7km from exit 20 on E19 (direction Ronquieres). **Open:** 10–12pm, 2–6pm. 1 Apr–2 Nov–weekends and holidays. Jul–Aug, everyday except Tues and Weds. Groups by appointment 1 Apr–2 Nov (guided tours on request).

map 224
1

CHATEAU DE MODAVE

B–4577 Modave, Belgium
Tel: 00 32 85 411 369   Fax: 00 32 85 412 676

Dating back to 13C, the castle owes its architectural appearance to the restoration by Count de Marchin from 1652–1673. Modave had many distinguished owners, before it was bought in 1941 by the 'Compagnie Intercommunale Bruxelloise des Eaux', in order to protect the impounded water. Twenty richly decorated and furnished rooms are open to the public and include remarkable ceilings, stucco works by Jean-Christian Hansche, sculptures, paintings, Brussels tapestries and 18C furniture. In 1667 Rennequin Sualem built the hydraulic wheel that was used as a pattern for the machine at Marly, bringing the water from the Seine to Versailles Palace. This technical achievement is illustrated in one of the rooms with several documents, plans and an accurate replica of the wheel, made to scale. **Open:** 1 Apr–15 Nov, 9–6pm. 16 Nov–31 Mar, by appointment.

map 224
2

NATIONAL BOTANIC GARDEN OF BELGIUM

Domein Van Bouchout–B1860 Meise, Belgium
Tel: 00 32 22 69 39 05 Fax: 00 32 2 27 015 67

At only a stones throw from Brussels, the centre of European activity, lies the National Botanic Garden of Belgium in the domain of Bouchout, Meise. The domain is closely interwoven with Belgian history. The earliest remains of the castle date back to the 12th century. In more recent times it was the refuge of the former Empress of Mexico, Charlotte, sister of King Leopold II. She died in 1927. Apart from the castle there are various smaller features. There are ice cellars, small ornamental buildings, an exquisite greenhouse by Alphonse Balat, ancient trees and wide sweeping lawns. The Botanic Garden was located to the site in 1939 and added extensive living collections. The immense Plant-Palace houses the tropical and subtropical collections and covers more than 1 hectare. The temperate collections are grouped in several locations in the park. During summer the old Orangery functions as a restaurant and the castle houses a small shop. **Open:** Easter, 30 Oct, from 1pm onwards. Closing times vary according to season and weather conditions. Call: 32 (0) 2 269 39 05 for details. **Admission:** Adult BEF200, child/student BEF100. Internet: http//www.BR.fgov.be.

map 224
3

STERCKSHOF PROVINCIAAL MUSEUM – SILVER CENTRE

Hooftvunderlei 160–B 2100 Antwerp (Deurne)
Tel: 00 32 3 360 5250   Fax: 00 32 3 360 5253

The Sterckshof Provinciaal Museum-Silver Centre is a museum in a park on the edge of the city of Antwerp. It is a journey of discovery that leads through a picturesque castle to the treasures of Belgian silver production from the 16th to the 20th centuries inclusive. At the end of the 18th century little remained of the castle built in the 16th century. On the basis of the original foundation and iconographic material, a reconstruction emerged during the thirties. The library with public reading room (Internet: www.cipal.be/digibib/home.htm), many exhibitions and the museum workshop throw further light on the art of the silversmith. The garden was relaid in 1994. The Sterckshof Museum is situated in the Provincial Domain Rivierenhof (Castle Rivierenhof, now a restaurant). **Location:** Provinciaal Domein Rivierenhof, entrance Cornelissenlaan, Antwerp (Deurne). Antwerp expressway (E 19) exit 3 and motorway Antwerp-Liège (E 313) exit 18. **Stations:** Antwerpen-Centraal and bus 18 (Collegelaan), 41 (Cogelsplein) or tram 10 (Cogelsplein), 24 (Waterbaan). Antwerpen-Berchem and bus 18 (Collegelaan). **Open:** 10–5.30pm. Closed on Mon and 25 Dec–2 Jan. **Admission:** Museum and garden free. Exhibition hall: BEF200–100. Family rate BEF300. **Events/Exhibition:** 1998 – From Belle Epoque to Art Nouveau. Belgian Silver 1868–1914, 15 Sep–13 Dec.

map 224
4

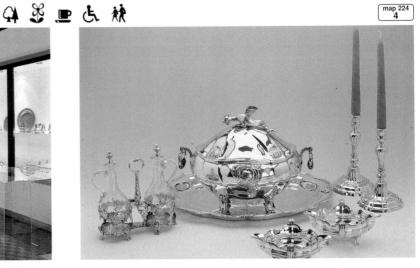

France

France is a nation of contrasting landscapes, from high mountain plateaux to lush farmland, traditional villages to chic boulevards, where heritage is set against a backdrop of ever changing vistas. This country belongs to both northern and southern Europe, encompassing Britanny with its Celtic maritime heritage, the Mediterranean sunbelt, Germanic Alsace-Lorraine and the rugged mountain resorts of the Auvergne and the Pyrénées.

Artists have always been inspired by France, especially since landscape became a legitimate subject for art in the 19th century. Art and tourism have been closely linked for over a century, when the establishment of artists' colonies in the forest of Fontainbleau, Brittany and the South of France did much to make these areas attractive to visitors. Today, one of the pleasures of touring the countryside is the recognition of landscapes made famous in paintings by artists such as Monet, Van Gogh and Cezanne.

In the North, the River Seine winds its way across the gentle landscapes of the Ile de France towards Paris – a city of stately palaces – where the tradition of the classical French garden began. Moving onwards, the rich soils of Normandy, provide a favourable climate where gardens thrive. It is here especially, that the influence of the English Garden is felt.

Nowhere in the world is a country more synonymous with wine than France. Each of the principal wine producing regions reveals its own identity, based on grape varieties, climate and local culture. The range, quality and reputation of the fine wines of Bordeaux, Dordogne, The Loire and Champagne in particular make them role models to the world, where the realm of chateaux and vineyards are inexorably linked.

An area of green valleys and majestic Chateaux, The Loire is the setting for artistic towns such as Chartres, Tours and Poitiers. Southern France, however, is steeped in an Italianate balminess where villas perch on rocky clifftops amongst beautifully tended formal gardens filled with colour.

France

LE CHÂTEAU D'ANET

28260 Anet, Ile De France, France.
Tel: 00 33 2 37 41 90 07, Fax: 00 33 2 37 41 96 45

In 1547, Diane de Poitiers, the mistress of Henry II of France, ordered the construction of The Château d' Anet. The castle is a masterpiece, a result of the work of the celebrated architect, Philbert de l'Orme and of many other artists. In the 17th century, the castle underwent numerous refurbishments including the grand staircase and the construction of the canal, built according to maps drawn up by Le Notre. The castle was considerably altered in the nineteenth century, with several generations of owners continually improving the castle, a true gem of French architecture. **Open:** 1–30 Nov and 1 Feb–31 Mar 1998, Sat and Sun, 2–5pm. 1 Apr–to 31 Oct, (every day except for Tues), 2–6.30pm. Closed in Dec and Jan. **Admission:** Adults FF36, groups (20 people or more)FF26, primary school children FF15, secondary school children Ff20.

CHÂTEAU DE BARLY

62810 Barly, France
Tel: 00 33 3 21 48 41 20

French Historians are unanimous in their view that "Barly is the most perfect example of 18th century French art in Artois". The castle features beautiful white stoned façades, fine eighteenth century panelling and a rare staircase of a particular elegance. Hour long guided tours by the owner, covering both the interiors and exteriors of the castle. English spoken. The castle has received six prizes for its restoration programme over the past quarter of a century. Received the Europa/Vestra medal in 1996. **Open:** Visits by appointment only, Apr–Oct. **Admission:** Adults FF30, children FF15, groups (min 20) FF25. Free parking adjacent to the church and castle.

map 227
2

CHÂTEAU DE BEAUMESNIL

Fondation Furstenberg-Beaumesnil, Beaumesnil, France
Tel & Fax: 00 33 2 32 444 009

Unique Louis XIII baroque style castle built 1633 to 1640. Surrounded by 80 hectares landscaped by La Quintinie, who worked with Le Nôtre at Versailles. Furnished interiors and museum of ancient bookbindings. Video on book-binding and gold decoration. **Open:** Jul, Aug, daily (except Tue), 10–12noon & 2–6pm. Apr, May, Jun, Sep, Fri–Mon, 2–6pm. **Admission:** Adults FF35, children FF15. **Location:** 15km east of Bernay.

map 227
3

CHÂTEAU DE KERLEVENAN

56370 Sarzeau, Morbihan, Brittany
Tel: 00 33 2 97 26 46 79

Kerlevenan, a magnificent château built in the style of Louis XVI, dates back to the 18th century (1780) and is set in a great park. The former stables have been transformed into living quarters for the rest of the family and the château also features a chapel and a Chinese pavilion. The white stoned building is reminiscent of the 'Petit Trianon' and the Italian palaces, with its spectacular view over the Gulf of Morbihan. **Open:** 1 Jul–30 Sept, 2–6pm, except Fris. Between Nov–Jul by prior arrangement. Please call the warden on: 0033 2 97 26 46 79. House situated at the park gates on the Route D780 just past St Colombier. **Location:** In Brittany, just off the Route 780 between Vannes and Port-Navalo, on the edge of the Gulf of Morbihan, on the Rhuys peninsula.

map 227
4

GARDENS OF NORMANDY

The 1990's have witnessed a marked revival in garden interest in France and The Seine Maritime department can claim a leading role in this movement with more than thirty gardens regularly open to the public.

Conveniently situated around Rouen, within easy driving distance from the Dieppe or Le Havre ferry terminals, here are three selected gardens designed and maintained by their owners and illustrating three contemporary horticultural talents.

Each of the gardens serves to enhance the manor house it surrounds and thereby provides an interest beyond the specialists' National Collection of Hardy Geraniums at Les Forrières du Bosc, the 2000 varieties of roses at Jardins d'Angélique or the 700 different flowers and vegetable gardens within the Château de Bosmelet walled Kitchen garden.

Visitors will enjoy discovering the typical Normandy countryside when going from one garden to the other for a pleasant one-day outing.

CHATEAU DE BOSMELET

Le Bosmelet, 76720 Auffay, France
Tel: 00 33 2 35 32 81 07 Fax: 00 33 2 35 32 84 62 (Baron de Bosmelet)

The Louis XIII Chateau is set in a classical French park designed in 1715 by Colinet to include a walled Kitchen beside the 300 year-old lime tree avenue. The present generation tackled the senescent mixed borders in 1996; then introduced the 'Rainbow Kitchen Garden' displaying vegetables and flowers in 4 colour sequences, also a Narcissus garden which becomes the Oriental Vegetable Garden, next to the 'Dahlia River' with 80+ cultivars in autumn. **Location:** Mid-way between Dieppe and Rouen leave N27 to enter Auffay. Facing the church, turn right along D96 towards Montreuil-en-Caux. **Open:** 1 May–15 Oct. Wed–Sun, 1–7pm. **Admission:** Park and garden: Adults 30FF, accompanied children under 16 free. (Guided tour of House and garden for pre-booked parties of 15 or more: FF35, grounds only: FF25).

map 229
5

FORRIERRES DU BOSC

Route De Duclair, 76150 Saint Jean Du Cardonnay, France
Tel: 00 33 2 35 33 47 06 Fax: 00 33 2 35 33 70 53 (Dr. & Mrs D. Evrard)

Only 5 minutes from the centre of Rouen you will find this enticing 5 acre garden where hardy geraniums reign supreme. Designed, planted and maintained by its owners, it extends gracefully around a 17th/19th century house whose walls are covered by numerous roses rising from amongst shrubs and flowers. The many magnificent century-old trees add to the serenity of the site and are worth a visit in themselves. The French national collection of hardy geraniums is held here and has greatly contributed to the international reputation of the garden and its owners. **Location:** From Rouen A15 towards Le Havre, 1st exit 'Maromme' straight over the roundabout, follow D43 towards Duclair. **Open:** May 15, Thurs, Sat, Sun and Bank hols, 10–6pm. Groups by arrangement. **Admission:** Adults Ff30, children under 10 free. E-mail: dr.evrard@wanadoo.fr

map 227
6

LES JARDINS D'ANGÉLIQUE

Hameau du Pigrard. 76520 Montmain
Tel: 00 33 2 35 79 08 12 (Mr & Mrs Y. LeBellegard)

Yves and Gloria LeBellegard designed this romantic garden in 1989 in memory of their deceased daughter Angélique. Playing on different shapes and colour harmonies, the lawn pathway meanders over 2 1/2 acres in front of the 17th century manor patiently restored by the owners. Best known for its remarkable collection of roses, the garden also boasts many peonies, hydrangeas and perennials. In 1996 a new garden was opened on the front side of the house with boxwood parterres and topiary yews encasing a central fountain. **Location:** Leave Rouen towards Darnetal, exit the highway towards Lyons-la-Forêt. Follow D42 until the garden on your right after Montmain. **Open:** 1 May–31 Oct, everyday except Tuesdays, 10–7pm. **Admission:** Adults Ff25, children under 12 free, guided tours for groups of minimum 15 persons. **Refreshments:** Teas.

map 227
7

France

CHÂTEAU DE LOSSE

24290 Thonac par Montignac-Lascaux, Dordogne (Périgord), France
Tel/Fax: 00 33 50 80 08 Internet: http://www.finest.tm.fr/chateau_losse

The medieval stronghold overlooks the Vézère river, it is defended by the largest gatehouse in SW France, curtain walls linked by five towers and is surrounded by deep ditches. Within the Renaissance Hall's (1576) elegant architecture lies fine decor and exceptional period furniture (16th and 17th century). These bear witness to the way of life during the reign of the last Valois and first Bourbon kings. A walk through the green bowers in the gardens, terraced above the splendid valley and on the rose lined ramparts is a delightful conclusion to an evocative tour. **Open:** Easter–30 Sept, daily & All Saints weekend. Groups by appointment at other times. **Admission:** Adult FF30, child FF15. Group rates available. **Location:** On D706, 5km from Montignac-Lascaux to Les Eyzies. Disabled access (free access to 80% of tour), guided tours in English or with English texts.

map 227
8

CHÂTEAU DU LUDE

72800 Le Lude, Sarthe, France
Tel: 00 33 243 94 60 09 Fax: 00 33 243 45 27 53

An old fortress of the Anjou dukedom dominating the Loir, transformed in the Renaissance into a country retreat by King Louis XI's chamberlain. The Château du Lude is a remarkable illustration of the way French architecture has evolved, from the Renaissance to the late 18th century. Lived in by the same family for the past 200 years, the Château contains a rich interior arrangement. Formal gardens on several terraces, kitchen garden. **Location:** 30 miles S of Le Mans and N of Tours. **Open:** 1 Apr–30 Sept (all year on request for groups). Outside 10–12am, 2–6pm. Inside guided tour 2.30–6pm. **Admission:** Ff35, reduction for children and groups. **Events:** Garden Fair, 30–31 May, 24–25 Oct. 'Cooking days' in the old kitchen and visit of the kitchen garden: 12–14 Jul, 15–16 Aug, 19–20 Sept.

map 227
9

CHATEAU DE MALLE

33210 Preignac, France
Tel: 00 33 5 56 62 36 86 Fax: 00 33 5 56 76 82 40 (Comtesse De Bournazel)

Bordeaux area. Magnificent residence surrounded by Italian style gardens, in the heart of Sauternes vineyard, 35 miles south Bordeaux, Chateau de Malle built by Jacques de Malle, direct ancestor of the Comte de Bournazel, dates from the early 17th century. The castle is tile-roofed, dominated by a Mansard one-storied slate covered central pavilion with two round towers at each end, topped with slate domes. The chapel is in one of the towers. The ceilings, furniture and paintings have remained as they were. The vineyard encompasses the region of Sauternes (Malle is a great classified vintage under the famous Imperial classification of 1855) and Graves (red and white wines).

map 227
10

CHATEAU DE MEUNG SUR LOIRE

45130 Meung Sur Loire, France
Tel: 00 33 2 38 44 36 47 Fax: 00 33 2 38 44 29 37

The oldest chateau of the Loire Valley with over 16 centuries of history. Entirely furnished–130 rooms–plus undergrounds open to the public. The only castle in the Loire Valley with an underground chapel, prisons, torture chamber and apparatus, dungeon and prison of Villon (a 15th century poet). Headquarters of the English armies during the 100 years war. Episcopal residence of the bishops of Orleans for 6 centuries, who were administrators of the crown. Centre of justice for central France. First castle of the Loire Valley south of Paris. British owned. **Open:** Jan–Mar, 10.30–12 noon & 2.30–4pm. Apr–Jun, 10–12.30pm & 2–5pm. Jul–Aug, 9–12.30pm & 1.30–6pm. Sep–Oct, 10–12noon & 2–5pm. Nov–Jan, 10.30–12noon & 2.30–4.30pm. **Location:** Situated on border of river Loire off A10 Paris to Bordeaux, outlet Meung, the medieval village immediately after Orleans.

map 227
11

CHÂTEAU ET PARC DE MARTINVAST

Domaine de Beaurepaire, 50690 Martinvast, Basse-Normandie, France
Tel: 00 33 2 33 52 02 23 Fax: 00 33 2 33 52 03 01

Listed landscaped park and neo-gothic chateau from the 11th, 16th and 19th century. At the beginning of the 19th century, Alexandre du Moncel transformed the marshes surrounding the château into an English style garden. In 1861, Baron Schickler, the new owner, created an arboretum of more than 200 species and varieties of trees, especially exotic conifers. The meadow of grass and the natural forest on the slopes were kept, as were the ponds colonised by lilies. The numerous banks of tree-like rhododendrons that grow by the conifers offer a striking perspective for all visitors. **Open:** 5 Apr–11 Nov, daily, 2–7pm. Walk at leisure with a leaflet and map. Guided tours for groups (min. 20 pers) by appointment. **Admission:** Adult FF30, teenagers FF20, child FF15. Groups FF25. Parents with children FF70. In May, add FF5 per category. **Location:** 5km from Cherbourg.

map 227
12

CHÂTEAU DE MAUPAS

Morogues 18220, France
Tel: 00 33 2 48 64 41 71 Fax: 00 33 2 48 64 19 82

The Château de Maupas was built in the 15th century by Jean Dumesnil Simon, bailiff and governor of the Berry. It was erected on the ancient site of a previous dwelling which first belonged to the Sullys (1284) then to the Mathefelons (14th century) and to the Rochechouarts. In 1682, the château became the property of Antoine Agard for the sum of 36 000F, paid in gold. Antoine Agard was ennobled by Louis XV in 1725. You may visit the different drawing rooms, a state bedroom with its games room, an old kitchen, etc... **Open:** Palm Sunday–1 Oct, daily, 2–7pm. On Sun and Bank Hols, 10–12noon. Open for groups in the morning on request. 14 Jul–1 Oct, daily, 10–12noon. 1 Oct–15 Oct, daily 2–6pm. 15 Oct–15 Nov, open Sun 2–6pm. **Location:** From Bourges the D955 (25km) then the C.D 46 or the C.D 59 (50 km).

C
map 227
13

CHÂTEAU DE CANON

14270 Mézidon-Canon, France
Tel: 00 33 2 31 20 05 07 Fax: 00 33 2 31 78 04 39

Situated between the 'Pays d'Auge' and the 'Plaine de Caen' in the heart of a country rich in Roman churches, manors and castles, Canon nestles amongst ancient trees and a cluster of bubbling springs. The château is graced with balusters, Italian statues, a Chinese kiosk, a temple and neo-classic ruins and park where the formal French garden harmonises with the more natural English garden: long sweeping avenues lead to the main courtyard. Canon still has its 'Chartreuses', an exception collection of walled herbaceous borders. Jean Baptiste Jacques Elie de Beaumont, a lawyer and treasurer of 'le comte d'Artois' (later became Charles X) designed the place and in 1775 created the famous feast of 'Bonnes Gens', a name once used by the village itself. **Open:** Easter–30 Jun, Sat, Sun and BHols, 2–6pm. 1 Jul–30 Sep, daily (except Tue), 2–7pm. Open to groups by prior arrangement.

map 227
14

CHÂTEAU DE SAGONNE

18600 Sagonne, France
Tel: 00 33 2 488 001 27 (M. Spang–Babou)

The Chateau de Sagonne stands overlooking a listed medieval village. Sagonne, with its prestigious history, occupies an area of Gallo-Roman origin. In AD832, the site was the stronghold of Agane, the daughter of Wicfred, Count of Bourges. Owned first by her descendants, the Counts of Sancerre and by the 'Amboise' family, it then belonged to: Jean Babou, General Commander of Ordnance; Charles de l'Aubespine, Saint-Simon's uncle; J.H. Mansart, architect of Versailles Palace and finally the Duchess of Mouchy, Marie Antionette's governess. The castle is still partly surrounded by defence walls and an impressive keep, adorned by a tower with a fine staircase. The castle displays medieval and 17C frescoes, tapestries, furnished rooms, weapons, portraits and historic mementoes. **Open:** 1 Jun–30 Sep, 10–12 noon & 2–6pm. **Location:** On RN76, 40km from Bourges.

map 227
15

Photograph: F. Vallon – Kipa Press

CHÂTEAU DE CHEVERNY

41700 Cheverny, France
Tel: 00 33 2 54 79 96 29 Fax: 00 33 2 54 79 25 38 (Charles Antoine de Vibraye)

Travelling along the Loire Valley is like opening a book of the history of France. The principal jewels in this rich inheritance are: Chambord, Blois, Chenonceau and Cheverny. The Chateau of Cheverny, with its immaculate façade, is noted for its architecture which is both classical and majestic. For 7 centuries the chateau has been the home of the very distinguished Hurault family, councillors to Kings Louis XII, Francois I, Henri III and Henri IV. Today their descendants still live in this great House and preside over the fortunes of the Domaine de Cheverny. The chateau has been open to visitors since 1922 and now welcomes several hundred thousand visitors per year, enchanted by the richness of its decoration and the abundance of its superb furnishings.

Cheverny is considered to be the most magnificently furnished chateau in the Loire Valley. In the park, the world's largest captive balloon lifts you to a height of 150 metres in complete silence, from the gondola, which holds up to 25 passengers, there is an unforgettable 360° view as you rise above the tops of the hundred-years old trees. The chateau slowly appears from an unusual angle, followed by the 2000 hectare forest of Cheverny. In the distance, the Loire Valley can be seen on one side and the mysterious Sologne on the other. The flights take place in complete safety. After descending from the Aero-Cheverny, you can explore the park and canal by electric car and boat, in complete silence.

map 227
16

DOMAINE DE COURSON

91680 Courson–Monteloup
Tel: 00 33 1 64 58 90 12   Fax 00 33 1 64 58 97 00

Architecture typical of the majestic country houses built in the 17th century for the wealthy officers of the Crown around Paris. Napoleonic memorabilia. Spanish, Italian and French paintings. An early 19th century beautifully landscaped park with many rare species of trees and shrubs in 80 acres of woodland. **Open:** Sun & Public Hols. Park: 1 Jan–31 Dec. Château: 15 Mar–15 Nov. **Admission:** Adult FF42, child FF29. Reduced rates for groups and grounds only. **Events/Exhibitions:** Spectacular flower shows, third weekend of May and Oct. **Location:** Near Arpajon, 20 miles SW of Paris, 4 miles from the A10 and N20. Available for exclusive corporate entertainment. Weddings, receptions and seminars in 'Les Petites Ecuries du duc de Padoue'. Dogs allowed on lead. No access for dogs during flower shows. **Email:** COURSONDOM@AOL.COM

map 227
17

CHÂTEAU DE CINQ MARS

Route de Pernay, 37130 Cinq-Mars-La-Pile, France
Tel: 00 33 2 47 96 4049 Fax: 33 2 47 96 4049

Cinq-Mars, with its towers, moat and fortification, is a classical feudal castle. Each of the two towers contains large vaulted rooms, two of which are available to rent out for receptions, lunch and special events. The owner and his children live in the last surviving wing of the 'Logis des Gardes'. The other wings were destroyed in 1840 to make way for a romantic garden. The 'Logis des Gardes' contains three bedrooms ('Chambres d'Hote'). They occupy a wonderfully peaceful location in the middle of the park and provide the perfect location for a relaxing stay. **Open:** Daily (except Tue), 9–dusk. **Admission:** FF15. Rooms FF400/440 per night. Price is for two people and includes breakfast. **Location:** Between Tours (20 mins) and Langeais.

map 227
18

LES JARDINS DU MANOIR DU PONTGIRARD

61290 Monceaux-au-Perche, France
Tel: 00 33 2 33 73 61 49

In the listed setting of the Réno-Valdieu forest overlooking the Jambée river valley. The 16th century Pontgirard manor sits amidst its terraced gardens highlighted by yew topiary. The promenade begins with the euphorbia border, continues through the pergola and up to the herb garden. The oak avenue is lined by a terraced water way. A 200 year old lime tree dominates the fountain of Plato garden which overlooks the formal walled garden and its four seasons mixed borders below. The visit ends at the recently landscaped duck pond with cascade. **Open:** 1 May–30 Oct. Sat, Sun & Bank Hols. 2.30–6.30pm. **Admission:** Adults FF20. Children (under 16 years) free. Groups FF15 (min. 10 pers.) by appointment.

map 227
19

The 'Monuments d'Exception' offer all the comfort and qualities asscociated with British properties. These monuments, famous for their history, architecture, works of art and gardens, exude a unique style and charm. A visit any of these properties is bound to be a lively and interesting one.

CHATEAU DES BAUX DE PROVENCE
13520 Les Baux de Provence
Tel: 00 33 4 90 54 55 56 Fax: 00 33 4 90 54 55 00

The Baux Château was constructed on one of the most beautiful sites in France, overlooking Provence as far as the sea. The Baux history museum retraces the turbulent history of this 1000yr old town, the imposing remains of the château and the ancient fortified town of Baux, (dungeon, fortified towers, columbarium, hospital, caves). Life-size medieval siege machines create a vivid impression of warfare in the middle ages. **Location:** 25km from Avignon, 15km from Arles, 40km from Nice. Off A7 at Avignon Sud or Salon de Provence exits. On A9 at Nimes exit, in direction of Arles. **Open:** Every day. Spring 9–7.30pm, Summer 9–8.45pm, Autumn 9–6.30pm. Winter 9–5pm.

map 227
20

MUSEE JACQUEMART-ANDRE
158 bd Haussmann, 75008 Paris
Tel: 00 33 01 42 89 04 91 Fax: 00 33 01 42 25 09 23

The Jacquemart-Andre Museum presents collections worthy of the greatest museums in a magnificent private mansion dating from the end of the 19th century, with all the atmosphere of a great residence. This sumptuous palace, property of Institut de France, allows the visitor to discover magnificent, intimate areas which are characteristic of Edouard André and his wife, Nélie Jacquemart: large function rooms, monumental staircase, winter garden, 'Italian Museum', private apartments. United by their passion for art, they created together one of the most beautiful collections in France, particularly for the Italian Renaissance, the Great Flemish Masters and the 18th century French School. **Location:** In the heart of Paris, 5 minutes from the Champs Elysées. **Open:** Every day, throughout the year, 10–6pm.

map 227
21

CHÂTEAU DE VALENCAY
36600 Valencay
Tel: 00 33 2 54 00 15 69   Fax: 00 33 2 54 00 02 37

The Valencay Chateau, one of the most beautiful French Renaissance monuments, was the residence of the Prince of Talleyrand, one of Napoleon Bonaparte's ministers. The castle guarantees a fascinating visit for all the family. The most remarkable architectural feature is undoubtedly the imposing Keep. The Great Function Rooms and furnished private suites retain the memories of Talleyrand and his illustrious guests. The castle is surrounded by magnificent gardens and a park featuring wild animals. Special events. **Location:** 220km from Paris, 50km from Blois, 70km from Tours on the D956 and the D960. **Open:** Every day, throughout the year: 1–31 Mar, 9.30–noon & 2–5pm. 1 Apr–30 Jun, 9.30–6pm. 1 Jul–31 Aug 9.30–7.30pm. 1 Sept–15 Nov, 9.30–6pm. 16 Nov–28 Feb, 2–5pm.

map 227
22

VILLA EPRUSSI DE ROTHSCHILD
06230 Saint Jean Cap Ferrat
Tel: 00 33 4 93 01 33 09 Fax: 00 33 4 93 01 31 10

Built by Baroness Ephrussi de Rothschild during the Belle Epoque, the villa is surrounded by seven glorios gardens, decorated with ornamental lakes, waterfalls, patios, flower beds, shady paths and rare types of trees. Overlooking the sea and offering a unique view over the French Riveria, this palace has retained all the atmosphere of an inhabited residence. The Villa, inspired by the great residences of the Italian Renaissance, houses private function rooms and apartments with high quality works of art, collected by Beatrice Ephrussi throughout her life. A free English guide book is given to each visitor. In the summer, a series of concerts enlivens the gardens. **Location:** Between Nice and Monaco, on the coast road (N 98). **Open:** Everyday throughout the year, 15 Feb–1 Nov, 10–6pm and 2 Nov–14 Feb 1998. Weekends and school hols 10–6pm. Weekdays 2–6pm.

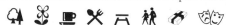

map 227
23

CLAUDE MONET FOUNDATION

27620, Giverny, France
Tel: 00 33 2 32 51 28 21 Fax: 00 33 2 32 51 54 18

Claude Monet's property opened to the public in 1980 after completion of large-scale restoration work. Claude Monet's collection of Japanese wood prints is displayed in several rooms of the House. The water lily studio opened to visitors and Monet's flowers and water-garden are as they were in his time. **Open:** 1 Apr–Nov 1, 10–6pm. Closed on Mondays except Easter and Whitweekend. **Admission:** 35 FF per person. Groups by reservation only (minimum 20 Persons) 25 FF Per person.

JARDINS DU CHÂTEAU DE VILLIERS

18800 Chassy, France
Tel: 00 33 2 48 80 21 42   Fax: 00 33 2 48 80 22 04

A Berry manor house dating back to 15 C, the Château de Villiers has been a family home for 350 years. Although the house itself is closed, the gardens are open to the public. After passing the dovecote upon entering and crossing a series of courtyards, your journey takes you to the beautiful secret garden, with its flowering shrubs, clematis and hardy perennials. The large lake awaits you, dominated by an old, recently restored, windmill. In springtime, enjoy the lilacs growing in the orchard, the rose-filled clearing and rows of Medlar trees. **Location:** 38km E of Bourges by D976 to Nérondes. Then 5km N by D6. **Station:** Nérondes. **Open:** 12 Apr–1 Nov, 10–7pm. **Admission:** Ff35, child under 7 free, half price for under 18s. Ff45 for groups by written arrangement, guided visit by owner. **Refreshments:** Tea and drinks. Home-made cakes are available in the afternoon.

NACQUEVILLE CHÂTEAU & GARDENS

50460 Urville-Nacqueville, France
Tel: 00 33 2 33 03 56 03 (Mr & Mrs F Azan)

Construction of the château began in 1510 as a fortified manor. Partly modified during the 18th and 19th centuries, it displays granite walls and stone roofs and is, therefore, characteristic of the finest Cotentin manors. The park, created in the 1830s by an English landscape gardener, is romantic and most delightful. A stream runs down to an enchanting lake in which the château is reflected. Many varieties of rhododendrons, azaleas, hydrangeas and ornamental trees are spread over the large lawns. **Open:** Easter–30 Sept, every day except Tuesday & Friday. Guided visits at 2, 3, 4 & 5pm only. **Admission:** Adults FF30, children FF10. **Location:** On North Cotentin coastal road, 5km West of Cherbourg.

CHÂTEAU DE THOIRY

78770, Thoiry, France
Tel: 00 33 1 3487 5225 Fax: 00 33 1 3487 5412

Thoiry, a listed Renaissance monument, was built in 1559 by Philibert de l'Orme. Home of the Counts of La Panouse for 440 yrs, Thoiry has fine furniture, tapestries, portraits and 950 years of archives. 300 acres of parterres by Le Nôtre and Desgot, Autumn Garden, roses, a bluebell wood with huge rhododendrons by Varé, magnolias, prunus, peony border, labyrinth, hortensias and many new creations each year. 'The Talking Trees' audio guide, train tours in the botanical and zoological gardens, new European River Otter biotope and 1000 free-roaming animals with English taped guide of the Wildlife Park. **Open:** Animal reserve and gardens open every day of the year. **Admission:** Castle: Adult FF38, child FF30. Reserve and gardens: Adult FF100, child (3–12 yr) FF79. **Location:** 25m W of Paris by A13, A12, N12, D11. 30mins from Versailles or Giverny. **Website:** www.thoiry.tm.fr

Germany

Time stands still in much of Germany. You notice this in much of the architecture seen throughout this enchanting land and in the variety of castles which beautify its rural landscape.

The huge number of castles in Germany are legacies of the old German Empire, which comprised of over 300 individual states. Perhaps no other country in Western Europe has such a complex past and modern history. Much of this history can be viewed by visitors today, in a country of sheer beauty where outdoor activity is a way of life and there is a wealth of places to visit.

The heyday of castle construction came in the Middle Ages – the days of Chivalry. The thousands of castles that were built at this time all share the same defensive style of architecture, with their distinctive romantic walls and towers. In mountainous regions of Germany, castles cling to hill tops dominating the countryside below, whereas in the plains, moated castles are reflected in lakes and rivers.

As in most countries in Europe, the best way to discover the places and the people is on foot. Walking trails criss-cross the German landscape with more than 80,000 miles of marked paths. Popular areas for hiking include the wonderful Black Forest, Hartz Mountains, the Bavarian Forest, the so-called Saxon Switzerland area and the Thuringen Forest. The Bavarian Alps offer the most inspiring scenery and are the centre of mountaineering in Germany, if you are admirably energetic. A picturesque river voyage on the Rhine accompanied by the local wines may be more suitable for the rest of us.

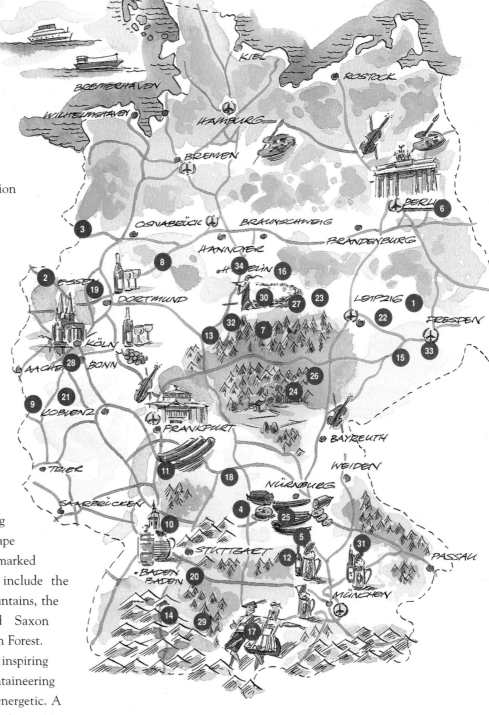

ALBRECHTSBURG MEISSEN

Domplatz 1, 01662 Meissen, Germany
Tel: 00 49 35 21 4 70 70   Fax: 00 49 35 21 4 70 11

Situated on the left of the river Elbe, the Albrechtsburg rises high above the city of Meissen. This imposing structure was commissioned by the brothers Ernst and Albrecht von Wettin, who ruled together over Saxony and Thuringia. The construction of the new residence began in 1471 under the leadership of the masterbuilder Arnold von Westfalen. The fortress, one of his architectural masterpieces, is classified as the first German castle. It is built in late Gothic style with some Renaissance elements also being apparent. <u>Open:</u> Daily 10–6pm. Dec–Feb 10–5pm (1–19 Jan closed). <u>Admission:</u> Adults DM6, reduced DM3, guided tour DM2 in addition to entry fee (tour groups only with reservation).

ANHOLT CASTLE

Wasserburg Anholt, Postfach 2226, D–46417 Isselburg
Tel: 00 49 2874 45353 4 Fax: 00 49 2874 45356

Moated Anholt Castle, set in the Rhine downstream landscape. Residence of the Princes of Salm-Salm. Unique setting with museum, park (35 acres), hotel-restaurant, golf course (18 holes) and rock-garden of 1894 (60 acres). Main castle with 'Broad Tower' from the 12th century. Enlarged into a barrack house in 1700. Since 1966, museum with historic furniture and the Princes' art gallery (700 works of art): Rembrandt, Van Goyen, Murillo, Breughel, Teniers, Terborch. Tapestries, porcelain collection, library, dining rooms, medieval kitchen, coinage, armour and weapons, rooms with fine plasterwork. French gardens with baroque ornaments, maze, tea house, arboretum and rose garden. English landscape gardens by Weyhe (1835) and Edward Milner (1858). The economic building, built in 1700, has been used as a hotel restaurant since 1968.

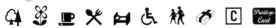

BENTHEIM CASTLE

Burg Bentheim, D-48455 Bad Bentheim, Niedersachsen, District Osnabruck Germany
Tel/Fax: 00 49 5922-5011 (Furst zu Bentheim und Steinfurt)

Situated on a rocky hill, the castle has overlooked the picturesque town and an immense area of 40 miles in each direction for almost 1000 years. Bentheim Castle dates back to the times of the Saxon dukes in the 10th and 11th centuries. At the beginning of the 12th century, the castle became the residence of the counts of Holland. Bentheim Castle offers a medieval keep, the impressive sculpture of the "good lord of Bentheim", one of the most ancient documents of Christian life in northern Germany, the round tower with its dungeons and prisons as well as the tudor style re-erected palace with its magnificent grand staircase and staterooms built for the late Queen Emma of the Netherlands. The little museum displays unique documents of family history. <u>Location:</u> Amsterdam-Osnabruck A30 8km ahead of the Dutch border, exit Bad Bentheim and the motorway Oberhausen-Emden A31 exit Ochtrup 5km. <u>Open:</u> 1 Mar–1 Nov. Daily 10–6pm last admission 5.15pm. In Nov, Jan and February. On weekends from 10–sunset. Closed in Dec. <u>Admission:</u> Adults DM4, children and groups DM3.

BALDERN CASTLE

D–73441 Bopfingen, Germany
Tel 00 49 7362 9688 0 (Prince zu Oettingen-Wallerstein)

Baldern Castle, rebuilt in the early 18th century on the ground plans of the original fortress, houses one of the most extensive private collections of Arms and Armour in Germany from the 16th to 18th century, all still in good working order. Further highlights of the tour are the precious drawing rooms, a dining room and particularly the Ballroom with exceptional stucco decoration. Baldern offers a spectacular view over the surrounding countryside. **Location:** Just off the Romantic Road (leave B25 in Wallerstein) close to A7 Exit Ellwangen or Nordlingen. **Open:** Mid Mar–Oct 9–5pm (closed Mons) **Admission:** Adult Dm6, child Dm3, group Dm5. **Refreshments:** Schloss-Schenke zum Marstall in the baroque stables. **Weddings:** Chapel can be hired for weddings (100 persons).

map 235
4

LEITHEIM PALACE

Jutta v. Tucher, 86687 Kaisheim-leitheim
Tel: 00 49 9097/1016 Fax: 00 49 9097/1019

The Cistercian Monks of Kaisheim under Abbot Elias Götz built Schloss Leitheim between 1681 and 1696. Abbot Cölestin Meermoos added a third floor to the castle in 1751 and commissioned the artist Godefried Berhard Göz to decorated the rooms and festive halls with frescos. Along with classic stucco pieces of Anton Landes of Wessobrunn, they form the most meaningful development of south German Rococo art. **Location:** 10km east of Donauwörth. Jun–Sept the Leitheim Palace concerts take place in the Rococo festival hall. The palace is available for tours, weddings and festivals.

map 235
5

BRANITZ CASTLE

Kastanienallee 11, 03042 Cottbus
Tel: 00 49 355 751 521 Fax: 00 49 355 713 179

Branitz Castle stands in a historic English garden. The park (approx. 100 hectares) was laid by Herman Furst of Puckler–Muskau (1785–1871) a landscape gardener of the European circle. With its ponds, small water ways, hills, ornamental trees and bushes, the gardens have a very distinctive character. Rather unique pyramids lie deep within the garden. Inside the late Baroque style castle and stable are the historically furnished rooms (from 19th century) which contain different exhibitions depicting the life and work of the Princes of Puckler. From June 1998 the Cottbus collection of the romantic painter Carl Blechen will be exhibited in the restored castle rooms. **Locations:** Cottbus, around 100km S of Berlin on A15. **Open:** Summer, daily 10–6pm. Winter, daily except for Mons, 10–5pm. Special events include theatre, concerts and readings.

map 235
6

CREUZBURG CASTLE

Fremdenverkehrsbuero Creuzburg, Markt 4, D–99831 Creuzburg
Tel: 00 49 36926 98047   Fax: 00 49 36926 82380

Our Castle is situated only 12km away from the well-known Wartburgstadt Eisenach, on the road B7. Creuzburg is one of the oldest towns in Thuringia. It was founded by landgrave Hermann I in 1213. The Creuzburg Castle was one of the main residences of the Thuringian landgraves and gave the town its name. The famous 'Holy Elizabeth' stayed within the castle's walls on several occasions. In 1571 the musician and composer Michael Praetorius was born in Creuzburg. For more detailed information please contact the above.

map 235
7

DETMOLD CASTLE

D–32156 Detmold, Germany
Tel: 00 49 5231 70020 Fax: 00 49 5231 700249 (The Prince of Lippe)

The Castle in the centre of the town of Detmold has been used as the governing offices of the ruling Nobles and Princes of Lippe for hundreds of years. Indeed, it is still the home of the Noble Family. The state of Lippe was one of the small German Monarchy states up until 1918. The façade that encloses a rectangular courtyard is built in the 'Weser Renaissance' style. The old fortifications are still partly intact. The most noteworthy part of the historic furnishings are the tapestries dating from 1675, depicting in glowing colours, the military campaigns of Alexander the Great. **Admission:** Adults DM6, children DM3 and group DM4.50 per person. **Events:** Tours of the castle are between 10–12am, 2–5pm daily.

map 235
8

EHRENBURG

56332 Brodenbach/Mosel
Tel: 00 49 2605 2432 (Thomas Schulz-Anschütz)

Ehrenburg Castle was built in the early 12th century by the Archbishops of Trier. Strongest castle of the Mosel River. Huge circular Renaissance bastion. Attacked and burnt by the soldiers of Louis XIV in 1689. The magic medieval castle is hidden in a secret wooded valley near Koblenz. **Open:** Apr–Oct, daily except Tue, 10–4pm. **Admission:** Adults DM7, children DM5. **Refreshments:** Refreshments served by Ehrenburg staff in medieval costumes, home-made hot and cold dishes. Catering for weddings and groups, medieval banquets in the original Knights Hall. Five romantic hotel rooms inside the castle, special medieval candle-light dinners for hotel guests can be arranged. **Events/Exhibitions:** Special events and medieval castle-fair Apr–Oct, every Sun.

CASTLES OF THE PRINCE OF HOHENLOHE – OEHRINGEN

Wald & Schlosshotel – D–74639 Friedrichsruhe / Zweiflingen, Germany Tel: 00 49 7941 60870 Fax: 00 49 7941 61468
Schloss Neuenstein – D–74632 Neuenstein, Germany Tel: 00 49 7942–2209/49 7941–60990 Fax: 00 49 7941–609920

Wald & Schlosshotel: This graceful hunting castle, once the summer residence of Prince Johann-Friedrich of Hohenlohe-Oehringen, is now part of an elegant hotel in a magnificent park. Visitors will appreciate the handsome reception rooms, with their splendid family portraits and gilt mirrors. The guest rooms are decorated in harmonious colours and extremely comfortable. The Michelin star restaurant, decorated with candles and chandeliers providing attractive lighting, offers a sensational international menu and first-class wines. Leisure facilities include indoor and outdoor pools, tennis, fishing, riding and an 18-hole golf course. Directions: BAB 6, Exit Öhringen, follow signs towards Zweiflingen; find signs to the Wald & Schlosshotel at Friedrichsruhe.

Schloss Neuenstein: Schloss Neuenstein, a water castle from the 11th century, was developed 500 years later into a noble residence in the Renaissance style. The castle houses the Hohenlohe Museum which has an extensive historic collection which reflects the art and culture of the Hohenlohe region. One can, amongst other things, visit the splendid Knights Hall, the Kaiser Hall with its rich collection of weapons and the art and rarity cabinet containing finely crafted goldsmiths work and ivory carvings. A special attraction is the fully functioning castle kitchen from 1485, which remains in its original condition. **Location:** BAB 6, exit Neuenstien, B19 Burgenstrasse. **Open:** 16 Mar–15 Nov, daily except Monday (when it is not a Bank Holiday), 9–12am and 1–6pm.

GUTTENBERG CASTLE

D–74855 Hassmersheim–Neckarmühlbach
Tel: 00 49 6266 228 Fax: 00 49 6266 1697

The 12th century castle is a great example of medieval castle architecture in the South of Germany. Built by the Staufen Emperors, it has never been destroyed and is still inhabited. It contains an attractive castle museum and a spectacular bird show. The view over the Neckarvalley from the high tower and the restaurants is very popular. **Location:** Between Heidelberg and Stuttgart on the Neckar river. A6 exit Bad Rappenau. **Open:** Mar–Nov, 10–5pm. The restaurant opens until 10pm. **Admission:** Adults Dm15, children Dm10. **Refreshments:** The kitchen specialises in venison, vegetables, fruit and herbs from the regional gardens to complement the famous local wines. **Internet:** http//burg-guttenberg.neckar.com

HARBURG CASTLE

D–86655 Harburg, Germany
Tel: 00 49 9080 9686 0 (Prince zu Oettingen-Wallerstein)

At Harburg visitors enter one of the earliest and best-preserved fortresses in southern Germany, built before 1100 and owned by the Counts and then the Princes of Oettingen since 1299. From the height of an imposing rock, it defends the entrance to the most researched meteor crater in the world, the 'Ries'. A tour around the fine Inner Court is a rendezvous with history. Along the wall walk visitors pass through a medieval world of prison cells, courtroom, keeps and towers. The highlight of every tour is the Great Ballroom and the Fortress Church. **Location:** On Romantic Road (B25) between Nördlingen and Donauwörth. **Open:** Mid Mar–Oct, 9–5pm (closed Mon). **Admission:** Adult DM6, child DM3, group DM5. **Refreshments:** Burgschenke in historic ambience. Accommodation: Hotel in the castle. Church can be hired for weddings (150 people).

map 235
12

HERZBERG CASTLE

bei Breitenbach/Herzberg, Verwaltung 36280 Oberaula
Tel: 00 49 6628 236 Fax: 00 49 6628 8601

The castle once served as protector for the old Handels and Heer roads between Frankfurt and Leipzig. It is the largest 'high' castle in Hessen. The oldest part dates from the 13th century with further developments made in the 15th century. Today it is partly ruined with other parts still in good order. The castle was also used to protect the 'ordinary' people during conflicts. In the 18th and 19th centuries the castle fell into dilapidation, but is currently under continuous renovation. **Location:** Off the Autobahn Kassel-Würzburg, (Niederaula exit, 8km west). Parking available at the castle. **Open:** For tours between 10.30–7pm. Open all year with the exception of Nov and Weds. **Admission:** DM3 with discounts for children and groups. **Events/Exhibitions:** Summer concerts, Castle market and Knight's games in June, Hippy Open Air Festival in July.

map 235
13

HOHENZOLLERN CASTLE

Burg Hohenzollern–Verwaltung, 72379 Hechingen, Germany
Tel: 00 49 7471 2428 Fax: 00 49 7471 6812

The majestic castle with its fantastic view is the ancestral seat of the Hohenzollern Dynasty, the Prussian Royal Family (Frederick the Great) and the German Emperors. Guided tours, showing a valuable collection of artwork and treasures, including the Prussian King's Crown, offer an insight into 19th century architecture and into Prussian and German history. **Location:** 5km from Hechingen town centre. **Open:** Daily all year except 24 Dec, 16 Mar–15 Oct. 9–5.30pm. 16 Oct–15 Mar, 9–4.30pm. Guided tours every 15 to 30 minutes, English tours on prior arrangement. **Admission:** Castle grounds and house: Adults DM9, groups DM6, children DM3. Castle grounds DM4. **Refreshments:** Snack bar, and restaurant open daily in summertime.

map 14
14

KRIEBSTEIN CASTLE

09648 Kriebstein, Saxony
Tel: 00 49 34327 952 0 Fax: 00 49 34327 952 22

Rising high over the Zschopau river Kriebstein Castle is situated on a steep rock, 3km S of Waldheim. The castle dates back to 1384, when Knight Dietrich of Beerwalde gained the rights from the Margrave Wilhelm I of Meissen. The main part of the castle stems from the 14C. By the end of the 15C the castle had most of its sides that are visible today. The residential tower is unique as its furniture and paintings are an example of the style of living in the late middle ages. **Location:** From S over BAB4 Mittweida–Talsperre Kriebstein from N over BAB14 Döllen/Nord–Dobeln–Waldheim. **Open:** Daily except Mon. Mar–Apr, Oct–Nov, 10–4pm. May–Sept,weekdays 9–5pm, weekends 10–6pm and public hols. **Admission:** Adult Dm5, child Dm2.50 Guided tour by arrangement for 10–40 people. **Refreshments:** Tearoom, meals, picnic area. Hall renting.

map 235
15

KONRADSBURG

Förderkreis Konradsburg, e. V 06463 Ermsleben
Tel: 00 49 3 47 43 92 565

Castle complex with a varied history in the heart of Germany. Possibly founded by Heinrich I it is situated on the place of a prehistoric settlement from the Bronze Age. First built to defend against Hungarian attacks it later served to protect the King's estate Harz Mountains and Quedlinburg, the main seat of the first German king. In 1125 it became a Benedictines' monastery (later Carthusian) after the lord changed residence. Destroyed during the Peasant Wars in 1525 it had been used for agricultural purposes up until the last decades of this century. The complex is being specifically restored to fight the dilapidation since 1982. The registered society 'Förderkreis Konradburg' has been the curator since 1990. Nowadays one can visit a late romanesque church with crypt, remains of the monastery, the 'Black kitchen", a herb garden and a house containing the well with a treadmill formerly driven by a donkey. There is a gallery with a stylish café and many various cultural highlights throughout the year. A windmill and an old brickworks also reconstructed by the society are nearby. The former forest warden's, a place for accommodation, offers ecologically interested visitors the demonstration of traditional agricultural techniques. The natural beauty of the north-eastern Harz Mountains stimulates to go for a walk or to cycle into the romantic valleys. In this area one can find numerous samples of a long cultural history, e.g. well-maintained medieval castles, churches and wide parks – a delight for art lovers. The hotels, often situated in historical palaces, are of a good or even excellent standard. Leisure activities include riding, tennis and golf. <u>Open:</u> Apr–Oct, 10–5pm. Nov–Mar 10–4pm. <u>Admission:</u> By donation.

map 235
16

KRONBURG CASTLE

Burgstrasse 1, 87758 Kronburg, Bavaria
Tel: 00 49 8394/271 Fax: 00 49 8394/1671

Built on a picturesque hill in the Allgäu, Kronburg Castle has been the property of Baron of Vequel-Westernach for 375 years. This fine four-winged Renaissance style castle is mentioned first in documents from 1227. Part of the building is open to visitors from May–Oct (if booked in advance). The Baron and Baroness guide you personally through some superb rooms. (The German Master Hall, with rich stucco work, the Red drawing room with its original Renaissance ceiling, the Hunting room, Visionary gallery, many rooms with 300 yr old linen wallpaper and the Rococo style chapel).There are chamber and castle-yard concerts during the summer. A newly built guesthouse houses exclusive holiday apartments. **Location:** Nr Memmingen, 5km W on A7 (direction of Konigsschlossern), taking the exit Woringen. **Admission:** Adult DM7, child DM3.50.

map 235
17

LANGENBURG CASTLE

Fürstliche Verwaltung, Schloss Langenburg, 74595 Langenburg
Tel: 00 49 7905 1041 Fax: 49 07905 1040

With parts of the castle dating back to the 12C it is remarkable that this castle is still home to the noble family Hohenlohe-Langenburg. Offering one of the nicest Renaissance courtyards in Germany, a chapel and a Baroque garden, the former stables also house a classic car museum. In an area almost 2,000m^2, there are approx. 80 legendary cars from 1899 up to the modern Formula 1 racing car. The castle tour displays the superb Baroque hall, different museum rooms with fine stucco ceilings and the equally splendid furnishings of the Langenburg family. **Castle Tours:** Good Fri–1 Nov, daily, 10–5pm. Tours every hour on the hour. Groups should contact the castle for advance bookings. Groups can also visit at times outside the hours above and tours can also be in English. Castle concerts, stately rooms for weddings and events. Attractive walk, museum shop and cafe situated in rose garden.

map 235
18

LEMBECK CASTLE

46286 Dorsten-Lembeck, Nordrhein–Westfalen, Germany
Tel: 00 49 23697167 Fax: 00 49 236977391 (Ferdinand Graf von Merveldt)

A fine example of an early Baroque Westphalian moated castle built in 1692 on the foundations of a medieval fortress. The northwest wing was re-modelled in 1730 by the eminent architect Johann-Conrad Schlaun who worked extensively on other important houses in the region. The home of Graf Merveldt, whose family and ancestors have owned Lembeck since the Middle Ages, the castle is now a museum and hotel. It contains a substantial collection of Chinese porcelain, Flemish Tapestries, Dutch furniture and items of local cultural and historic interest and stands in extensive grounds which include a fine rhododendron park. **Location:** From Autobahn 43 Haltern exit or Autobahn 31 Lembeck exit. Station: Lembeck, **Open:** Daily Mar–Nov from 10–6pm. **Admission:** Adult DM7, child DM4.50.

map 235
19

LICHTENSTEIN PALACE

D–7414 Lichtenstein
Tel: 00 49 7129 4102

Lichtenstein Palace, built on the 817m steep rock face, provides visitors with a wonderful view of the Echaz valley and its surroundings. Inspired by the novel 'Lichtenstein' by Wilhelm Hauff, the palace was built in around 1840/42 following plans which were drawn up by the architect Heideloff. The plans were based on an idea of Count Wilhelm Von Wuttemberg who wished to build a medieval style German Knights Stronghold. Rooms on display for visitors include: The Weapons Hall, the Drinks Room, the Castle Chapel. The Kings Room and the Knights Hall with its valuable glass paintings and pictures dating from the 14th and 15th centuries. **Open:** Daily, Apr–Oct, 9–12pm, 1–5.30pm. Sun & Hols open throughout the year. Nov, February, Mar, open Sat & Sun only. 9–12, 1–5pm. Closed in Dec & Jan.

map 235
20

MARKSBURG CASTLE

D–56338 Braubach, Germany
Tel: 00 49 26 27 206 Fax: 00 49 26 27 88 66 E-mail: DBV.Marksburg@t-online.de

The imposing Marksburg, known as the jewel of the Rhine Valley, is the only castle on the cliffs of the Rhine that has never been destroyed. Dating back to the 12th century, the castle has maintained its medieval character. The high Keep is surrounded by the Romanesque Palace and the Gothic Hall with the Chapel Tower. Of special interest are the horse steps carved out of the rock, the Great Battery and the medieval Herb Garden with its spectacular view, the Gothic Kitchen, Knights' Hall, Armoury and Torture Chamber. The Marksburg is the seat of the German Castles Association. **Location:** Braubach, 12 km south of Koblenz on B42. **Open:** Daily from 10–5pm, Nov–Easter 11–4pm. **Admission:** Adult DM7, child DM4 (guided tours also in English).

map 235
21

MILDENSTEIN CASTLE

Burglehn 6, D 04703 Leisnig
Tel: 00 49 34321 / 12652

A Medieval castle in the heart of Sachsen. The Romanesque chapel with its late Gothic sculptures and the powerful central keep which provides a wonderful view of the surrounding countryside are worth seeing. Possibly the nicest room is the Knight's Hall which houses a collection from the castle museum. **Open:** Apr–Oct, Tue–Sun 9–5pm. Nov–Mar, Tue–Fri 9–4pm, Sat–Sun 9–5pm. **Admission:** Adults DM4, concs DM2.

map 235
22

MORITZBURG HALLE

Friedemann-Bach-Platz 5, 06108 Halle (Saale)
Tel: 00 49 345 281 20 10 Fax: 00 49 345 202 99 90

The late medieval Moritzburg was built between 1484 and 1513 as a residence for the Archbishop of Magdeburg. The Cardinal Albredit, Elector of Brandenburg and Archbishop of Hagdeburg and Mainz lived here and in the neighbouring new residence for three decades (1514–1541). During his administration he developed the city of Halle with the Moritzburg (as it was the preferred residence) into a significant centre piece for early renaissance architecture in Germany. One finds the Moritzburg in the city centre of Halle which today houses the State Art Museum of Saxony-Anholt. The valuable collection stems from medieval times right up to the present day. The collection includes paintings, sculptures, handcrafts, photographs, coins and medals. Beside the exquisite historic collection, principally the handcrafts, the castle has an impressive stock of classic modern works and their forerunners from the 19th century. A selection of this stock is on constant display, during the continuously changing special exhibitions of German and international art. **Open:** Tue 11–8.30pm (free), Wed–Sun & Bank Hols 10–6pm (DM5, reduced to DM3). Tours: Following prior bookings: Tue, DM30. Wed–Fri, DM30 plus DM3 per person. Sat, Sun & Bank Hols, DM45 plus DM3 per person. **Events/Exhibitions:** Festivals or events in a historic atmosphere by arrangement. Facilities: The Museum Café is situated in two splendid rooms which date from the 16th century with rich wall and ceiling decorations of wood carvings. Opening times are the same as the museum. There is a public car park directly in front of the Moritzburg.

map 235
23

OSTERBURG

Schlosberg 14, 07570 Weida
Tel: 00 49 1409 36603 62775

The old town Weida, 'Cradle of the Vogtland', houses the fortress Osterburg with its superb 54metre terraced keep. Until the late Middle Ages Osterburg was the ancestral seat of the landvogts. Every last weekend in June, the citizens of Weida celebrate the festival of the Osterburg and the region in the fortress. Visit Weida, the museum of the fortress and the art galleries all year round. Built from 1163–1193, the fortress was the ancestral seat of the feudal lords and governors of Weida until early 15C. The castle incorporates the standard type of a German feudal castle. Its importance, development and origin reflects a multitude of tendencies of social development and is now a meeting place of art and culture. **Open:** Tue–Sun throughout the year (closed Mon), 10–5pm. **Admission:** Adult DM4, child DM1. **Location:** Centre of East Thuringia, 6m from Gera (A9, A4).

map 235
24

PAPPENHEIM CASTLE

Neues Schloß, 91788 Pappenheim, Germany
Tel: 00 49 9143 83 890   Fax: 00 49 9143 6445 (Gräfliche Verwaltung)

An imposing 12th century castle, extension 300m long, overlooking the picturesque former residence city of the Hereditary Marshals of the Holy Roman Empire, the Marchesses Pappenheim, with important historic buildings, enlarged during the following centuries; partly destroyed since the 30-years-war, an economical building and the arsenal of the 15th century contain a small museum, keep, long fortification walls, falconry, twice a day demonstrations and a zoo with eagles, hawks, falcons and owls, herb garden, aboretum with collection of trees, shrubs and plants of the area, medieval tournament last weekend in June. **Location:** 35 miles W of Eichstaett. **Open:** Easter–5 Nov, Tue–Sun, 10–5pm. **Admission:** Adults DM9, children DM7.

map 235
25

POSTERSTEIN CASTLE

D–0426 Posterstein/Thuringia Germany
Tel/Fax: 00 49 34496 22595

Going to Saxony's capital Dresden on the busy motorway A4 you will pass Burg Posterstein which is situated halfway between Thuringia's capital Erfurt and Dresden. Burg Posterstein is located in Eastern Thuringia, bordering on the classical Thuringia, marked by Goethe. The first information about the castle dates from 1191. The first owner Knight Stein, got his landed property from King Friedrich I; Barbarossa. In the 16th and 17th century the old castle was rebuilt and became a little palace. The last restoration work took place from 1984 to 1991. Since 1953 there has been a museum. **Open:** Tues–Sat, 10–5pm, Sun 10–6pm. Nov–Feb: Tues–Fri 10–4pm. Sat–Sun 10–5pm. **Admission:** Adults DM5, students DM2, children under 14, free. Exhibitions: History of the region; gallery of art. Nearby the castle you can visit the church of the castle with a very famous wood carving from 1689. Services: Hotel, gastronomy, garden, special events, parking.

map 235
26

Germany

QUERFURT CASTLE

06268 Querfurt, Germany
Tel: 00 49 34 771/22064

Gracing the southern slope of the Quernebach Valley, the castle is one of the oldest in Germany. Its first documented mention occurred in the Hersfeld tithe register (866–899). In fact, this is also one of the largest castle compounds in the land, with an area almost seven times as large as that of the Wartburg. Presumably, Querfurt Castle served as a haven for refugees in Carolingian times. Evidence of stone buildings exists from the late 10th century onwards. The most conspicuous features of the castle are its three towers: 'Dicker Heinrich', 'Marterturm' and 'Pariser Turm'. At the centre is the Romanesque church built in the latter half of the 12th century, a crosshoped edifice with three semicircular apses and an octagonal crossing tower. **Open:** Tue–Sun, 9–5pm. Closed Mon. Admission: DM5, reduced to DM3.

map 235 **27**

SAYN CASTLE & BUTTERFLY GARDEN

D–56170 Bendorf-Sayn Germany
Tel: 00 49 2622 15478 (The Prince & The Princess zu Sayn-Wittgenstein-Sayn)

Burg Sayn, built before 1200 by the sovereign Counts of Sayn, was destroyed in 1633 and recently restored. Spectacular view on romanesque Sayn abbey, Rhine Valley and volcanic Eifel mountains. A Turmuhrenmuseum contains fine collection of tower clocks. Castellated terraces descend to Schloss Sayn, a palace severely damaged during WWII. Landscaped park with rare trees, ponds, playgrounds and Garten der Schmetterlinge, an exotic dreamland with hundreds of live tropical butterflies. **Location:** Bendorf-Sayn, 10km NE of Koblenz on A48 and B42. **Open:** Mid Mar–Oct. Butterfly garden daily from 9–6pm. **Admission:** Butterfly garden: Adult DM8, Child DM5. **Refreshments:** Burgschanke open 11–6pm (closed Mons). Cafeteria at butterfly garden.

map 235 **28**

SIGMARINGEN CASTLE

F.H Sclossverwaltung, 72488 Sigmaringen
Tel: 00 49 7571 729 230   Fax: 07571 729 105

Sigmaringen Castle is, to this day, the home of the descendants of the Earls of Hohenzollern. The castle majestically overlooks the town of Sigmaringen and its surrounding countryside. There are many fascinating things to see in the castle; the Hubertus hall houses a large collection of hunting trophies and over 3,000 historic weapons of all types (one of the largest private collections of its kind in Europe). Art is indestructible, but it has found a safe hiding place here in Hohenzollern's castle; valuable tapestries and paintings, priceless porcelain pieces, elegant and tasteful furniture, which capture a calm and still ambience, can be found here. **Open:** For guided tours: Nov, Feb–Apr, daily, 9.30–4.30pm; May–Oct, daily, 9–4.45pm; Dec–Jan, only organised tours with prior bookings, until 4pm.

map 235 **29**

SONDERHAUSEN CASTLE

Box 83 99702 Sonderhausen (Siftung Thüringer Schlösser und Gärten)
Tel: 00 49 36 32 6630

The former residence of the Counts (since 1697 Princes) of Schwarzburg-Sonderhausen is the many-sided and in historical and artistical terms, the most interesting building in the north of Thuringia to experience about 600 years of architecture. The castle is situated on a rise above the town, surrounded by a 19C park covering 30 hectares. **Location:** 60km N of Erfurt on B4, parking near castle; railway-line: Intercity to Erfurt, regional-line to Sondershausen. **Open:** Residence-museum Tues–Sun 10–4pm, closed Mon; guided tours 10am & 2pm and by arrangements; special tours by arrangement (contact museum Tel: +49 3632 663 120). **Admission:** Adult DM6, seniors/student DM4, child (under 6) free, groups (min 15 pers.) DM3. Restaurants in historical rooms daily 11–12pm. Concerts in historic rooms (symphonic and chamber music, organ recitals) and exhibitions.

map 235 **30**

THE PRINCELY CASTLE OF THURN UND TAXIS

Emmeramsplatz 5, D-93047 Regensburg, Bavaria
Tel: 49 0941 5048133 Fax: 49 0941 5048256

Since 1812, this has been the home of the Princes of Thurn und Taxis, who reconstructed parts of the former Benedictine monastery of St. Emmeram as their residence. Besides the palace staterooms, furnished in different styles (rococo, neo-rococo, classic, historic), you can visit the medieval cloister (11–14th centuries) with the mortuary chapel (19th century) and the carriage museum (carriages, sleighs, sedan chairs, harnesses) in the former princely stables and riding hall. <u>Location:</u> A93, Exit Regensburg-Konigswiesen, then direction "Regensburg centre" <u>Open:</u> Apr–Oct daily 11am, 2, 3, 4pm, on Sats and Suns also 10am, Nov–Mar, Sats, Suns, Bank Hols 10, 11, 2, 3pm (guided tours only), tours for groups by appointment. <u>Admission:</u> Adults DM12, reduced fee DM10.

map 235
31

WALDECK CASTLE

34513 Waldeck Am Ederseek, Germany
Tel: 00 49 5623 589 0 Fax: 00 49 5623 589 289 (European Castle Hotels & Restaurants Group)

Waldeck Castle was the main castle of the Princes of Waldeck and Pyrmont. The early medieval castle complex was built on a rounded stone hilltop overlooking the 27km long Eder lake in the centre of Germany. One can visit the castle dungeons, the kitchen, the court hall from the 13th century, the examples of witchcraft, the prison, the 120m deep castle well and the castle centre courtyard with a view of the Eder Lake (one of the largest reservoirs in Europe). Throughout the summer months there are special events held at the castle. In the castle itself there is a hotel with 41 comfortable rooms, 2 restaurants, a drawing room and banquet and conference rooms. Weddings and receptions can be booked directly in the castle.

map 235
32

WALLERSTEIN CASTLE AND RIDING SCHOOL

D–86757 Wallerstein, Germany
Tel: 00 49 9080 9686 0 (Prince zu Oettingen–Wallerstein)

The 'New Castle' in Wallerstein arose after the thirty year war when the fortress on the Wallerstein Cliffs was destroyed by Swedish troops. In its empire staterooms the fine porcelain and glass collection of the Princes of Oettingen is exhibited. A walk in the park will bring the visitor to the most impressive building, the Riding School which houses the stable – carriage – and tack museum as well as items of the original fire department. <u>Location:</u> On the Romantic Road (B25) between Dinkelsbuhl and Nordlingen. Open: Mid Mar–Oct, 9–5pm (closed Mons). <u>Admission:</u> Adult DM6, child DM3, group DM5. <u>Refreshments:</u> Restaurant of Prince Oettingen–Wallersteins brewery at the Wallerstein Cliff.

map 235
4

WEESENSTEIN CASTLE

Am Schlossberg 1, 1809 Müglitztal, Sachsen
Tel: 0049 3 50 275436

Weesenstein Castle is an architectural curiosity, situated in the picturesque Müglitz Valley. The castle was transformed in the nineteenth century from the private residence of King Johanns of Saxony to the famous stone building of today. The visitor will experience a fascinating stroll through 700 years of history, from early stronghold to romantic royal castle. Events include, concerts, theatre and a medieval feast at Whitsun. Open: Throughout the year. November to Easter, 9-5pm. Easter to October, 9-6pm, closed 24th December. Guided tours available.

map 235
33

WERNIGERODE CASTLE

Schloss Wernigerode GmbH, Am Schloss 1, 38855 Wernigerode
Tel: 00 49 39 43 50 03 96   Fax: 00 49 39 43 50 03 99

The original Romanesque castle dating from the 12th century, extensively altered over the years, was up to 1945 the residential palace of the Earls of Stolberg, who took the name 'von Stolberg-Wernigerode' from their principality, the earldom of Wernigerode. The grand turreted stone and half-timber castle with magnificent views over the medieval town of Wernigerode today ranks as a major example of the North German "Historismus" building style. The remarkable rise to political power of Earl. Otto, who became Vice Chancellor of Germany under Bismarck, gave impetus to the sumptuous late 19th century remodelling seen today, including the original staterooms of Europe's highest ranking nobility of that day. Changing exhibits, a variety of events and scientific symposiums fulfil the Scholssmuseum's aim to become a centre of artistic and cultural history of the 19th century. Weddings: in the Chapel, banquets in the Dining Hall, receptions, conferences and parties in the grandly appointed staterooms by arrangement. **Location:** Above Wernigerode, 70km south of Brunswick. Transfer service every 20 minutes from the Town Centre. **Open:** May–Oct daily 10–6pm, last admission 5.30pm, Nov–Apr closed Mon. **Admission:** Adults DM8, children DM4. Gardens and panorama terrace free. **Refreshments:** Restaurant and tearoom open daily except Mondays. **Exhibitions/Events:** Open air opera, theatre, concerts and ballet on the central terrace, shop.

map 235
34

'THE VALUE OF
LIFE CAN
BE MEASURED BY
HOW MANY
TIMES YOUR SOUL
HAS BEEN
DEEPLY STIRRED.'

Soichiro Honda

Soichiro Honda was the inspiration behind what is now the world's largest engine manufacturer. His concern for man and the environment led us to build not only the world's most fuel-efficient car (9426 mpg) but also the winner of the Darwin to Adelaide race for solar-powered vehicles. His search for excellence gave rise to us winning 6 consecutive Formula 1 constructor's championships. It also led to the all-aluminium NSX, a car capable of 168mph and in which, at 70mph with the roof off, you don't need to raise your voice. Soichiro Honda, a softly spoken man, would have approved. For more information on our current range of cars, call **0345 159 159.**

HONDA

First man, then machine.

HILDON LTD.
Hildon House, Broughton, Hampshire SO20 8DG
☎ 01794-301 747, Fax 01794-301 718

Heritage Education Trust

Sandford Award Holders

The following properties received Sandford Awards in the years in brackets after their names in recognition of the excellence of their educational services and facilities and their outstanding contribution to Heritage Education. Two or more dates indicate that the property has been reviewed and received further recognition under the system of quinquennial review introduced by the Heritage Education Trust in 1986.

The Argory, Co. Tyrone, Northern Ireland (1995)

Aston Hall, Birmingham (1993)

Avoncroft Museum of Buildings, Bromsgrove, Worcs. (1988, 1993)

Bass Museum Visitor Centre and Shire Horse Stables, Burton upon Trent, Staffs. (1990)

Beaulieu Abbey, Nr Lyndhurst, Hants. (1978, 1986, 1991)

Bewdley Museum, Worcs (1992)

Bickleigh Castle, Nr Tiverton, Devon (1983, 1988)

Blakesley Hall Museum, Birmingham (1993)

Blenheim Palace, Woodstock, Oxon (1982, 1987, 1992)

Bodiam Castle, East Sussex (1995)

Boughton House, Kettering, Northants (1988,1993)

Bowhill House & Country Park, Bowhill, Nr Selkirk, Borders, Scotland (1993)

Bronte Parsonage Museum, Haworth, Nr Keighley, West Yorks (1993)

Buckfast Abbey, Buckfastleigh, Devon (1985, 1990,1995)

Buckland Abbey, Yelverton, Devon (1995, 1996)

Cannock Hall, Barnsley (1997)

Canterbury Cathedral, Canterbury, Kent (1988, 1993)

Castle Museum, York, North Yorks (1987, 1993)

Castle Ward, County Down, Northern Ireland (1980, 1987, 1994)

Cathedral & Abbey Church of St. Alban, St Albans, Herts (1986, 1991, 1996)

Chiltern Open Air Museum, Chalfont St Giles, Bucks (1994)

Chirk Castle, Chirk, Clwyd, Wales (1994)

Clive House Museum, Shrewsbury, Salop (1992)

Coldharbour Mill, Working Wood Museum, Cullompton, Devon (1989,1994)

Combe Sydenham, Nr Taunton, Somerset (1984, 1989, 1994)

Crathes Castle and Gardens, Kincardineshire, Scotland (1992)

Croxteth Hall and Country Park, Liverpool, Merseyside (1980, 1989, 1994)

Culzean Castle and Country Park, Ayrshire, Scotland (1984, 1989, 1994)

Dove Cottage and the Wordsworth Museum, Grasmere, Cumbria (1990)

Drumlanrig Castle and Country Park, Dumfriesshire, Scotland (1989)

Dulwich Picture Gallery, London (1990)

Dunham Massey, Altrincham, Cheshire (1994)

Erddig Hall, Nr Wrexham, Clwyd, Wales (1991, 1996)

Exeter Cathedral, Devon (1995)

Flagship Portsmouth, Portsmouth (1996)

Ford Green Hall, Stoke-on-Trent (1996)

Florence Courthouse, Co Fernanagh, Northern Ireland (1995)

Gainsborough Old Hall, Gainsborough, Lincs (1988, 1993)

Georgian House, Edinburgh, Lothian, Scotland (1978)

Gladstone's Land, Edinburgh, Scotland (1995)

Godolphin, Helston, Cornwall (1993)

Glamis Castle, Angus, Scotland (1997)

Harewood House, Leeds, West Yorks (1979, 1989, 1994)

Sir Harold Hillier Gardens and Arboretum, Ampfield, Nr Romsey, Hants (1993)

Holdenby House, Northampton, Northants (1985, 1990, 1995)

Hopetoun House, South Queensferry, Lothian, Scotland (1983, 1991)

Jewellery Quarter Discovery Centre, Birmingham (1996)

Museum of Kent Life, Cobtree, Kent (1995)

Kingston Lacy House, Wimborne, Dorset (1990)

Laundry Cottage, Normandby Hall Country Park, South Humberside (1994)

Lichfield Cathedral and Visitors' Study Centre, Lichfield, Staffs (1991, 1996)

Blenheim Palace, Oxfordshire

Llancaiach Fawr Manor, Nelson, Mid Glamorgan (1994)

Macclesfield Museums, Macclesfield, Cheshire (1988, 1993)

Moseley Old Hall, Wolverhampton, West Midlands (1984, 1989, 1994)

Norton Priory, Cheshire (1992)

Oakwell Hall Country Park, Birstall, West Yorks. (1988, 1993)

Penhow Castle, Nr Newport, Gwent, Wales (1980, 1986, 1991)

The Priest's House Museum, Wimborne Minster, Dorset (1993)

Quarry Bank Mill, Styal, Cheshire (1987, 1992)

The Queen's House, Greenwich (1995)

Rockingham Castle, Nr Corby, Northants (1980, 1987, 1992)

Rowley's House Museum, Shrewsbury, Salop (1993)

The Shugborough Estate, Stafford, Staffs (1987, 1992)

South Shields Museum and Art Gallery, (Arbeia Roman Fort), Arbeia (1996)

Sutton House, Hackney (1996)

Tatton Park, Knutsford, Cheshire (1979, 1986, 1991, 1996)

Tenement House, Glasgow(1996)

Tower of London, Tower Bridge, London (1978, 1986, 1991, 1996)

Weald and Downland Open Air Museum, Chichester (1996)

Wightwick Manor, Wolverhampton, West Midlands (1986, 1991, 1996)

Wilberforce House and Georgian Houses, Hull, Humberside (1990)

Wimpole Hall, Near Cambridge, Cambs (1988, 1993)

Supplementary List of Properties

The list of houses in England, Scotland and Wales printed here are those which are usually open 'by appointment only' with the owner, or open infrequently during the summer months. These are in addition to the Houses and Gardens which are open regularly and are fully classified. Where it is necessary to write for an appointment to view, see code (WA). * denotes owner/address if this is different from the property address. The majority of these properties have received a grant for conservation from the Government given on the advice of the Historic Buildings Councils. Public buildings, almshouses, tithe barn, business premises in receipt of grants are not usually included, neither are properties where the architectural features can be viewed from the street.

ENGLAND

AVON

Birdcombe Court, (Mr & Mrs P. C. Sapsed.) (WA), Wraxall, Bristol

Eastwood Manor Farm, (A. J. Gay), East Harptree

Partis College, (The Bursar.) (WA), Newbridge Hill, Bath, BA1 3QD Tel: 01225 421 532

The Refectory, (Rev. R. Salmon), The Vicarage Tel: 01934 833 126

Woodspring Priory, (WA), Kewstoke, Weston-Super-Mare.*The Landmark Trust.

BEDFORDSHIRE

The Temple, (The Estate Office) (WA), Biggleswade

Warden Abbey, (WA), Nr. Biggleswade
* The Landmark Trust.

BERKSHIRE

High Chimneys, (Mr & Mrs S. Cheetham) (WA), Hurst, Reading Tel: 01734 34517

St. Gabriel's School, (The Headmaster), Sandleford Priory, Newbury Tel: 01635 40663

BUCKINGHAMSHIRE

Bisham Abbey, (The Director), Marlow Tel: 01628 476 911

Brudenell House, (Dr H. Beric Wright) (WA), Quainton, Aylesbury, HP22 4AW

Church of the Assumption, (Friends of Friendless Churches), Harmead, Newport Pagnell Tel: 01234 39257 * For Key: Apply to H. Tranter, Manor Cottage, Hardmead, by letter or phone on 01234 39257.

Iver Grove, (Mr & Mrs T. Stoppard) (WA), Shreding Green, Iver

Repton's Subway Facade, (WA), Digby's Walk, Gayhurst Tel: 01908 551 564* JH Beverly, The Bath House, Gayhurst.

CAMBRIDGESHIRE

The Chantry, (Mrs T. A. N. Bristol) (WA), Ely, Cambridge

The Church of St. John the Baptist, (Friends of Friendless Churches), Papworth St. Agnes * For Key: Apply to Mrs P. Honeybane, Passhouse Cottage, Papworth St. Agnes, by letter or phone on 01480 830 631.

The King's School, Ely, (WA) Bursars Office, The King's School, Ely, CB7 4DB Tel: 01353 662 837, Fax: 01353 662 187

Leverington Hall, (Professor A. Barton) (WA), Wisbech, PE13 5DE

The Lynch Lodge, (WA), Alwalton, Peterborough
* The Landmark Trust

CHESHIRE

Bewsey Old Hall, (The Administrator) (WA), Warrington

Crown Hotel, (Proprietor: P. J. Martin), High Street, Nantwich, CW5 5AS Tel: 01270 625 283, Fax: 01270 628 047

Charles Roe House, (McMillan Group Plc) (WA), Chestergate, Macclesfield, SK11 6DZ

Shotwick Hall, (Tenants: Mr & Mrs G. A. T. Holland), Shotwick Tel: 01244 881 717
* R. B. Gardner, Wychen, 17 St. Mary's Road, Leatherhead, Surrey. By appointment only with the tenants, Mr & Mrs G. A. T. Holland.

Tudor House, Lower Bridge Street, Chester Tel: 01244 20095

Watergate House, (WA), Chester Tel: 01352 713353 * Ferry Homes Ltd, 49 High Street, Holywell, Clywd, Wales, CH8 9TF.

CLEVELAND

St. Cuthbert's Church & Turner Mausoleum, (Kirkleatham Parochial Church Council), Kirkleatham Tel: Contact Mrs R. S. Ramsdale on 01642 475 198 or Mrs D. Cook, Church Warden on 01642 485 395

CORNWALL

The College, (WA), Week St. Mary
* The Landmark Trust.

Town Hall, (Camelford Town Trust), Camelford

Trecarrel Manor, (N. H. Burden), Trebullett, Launceston Tel: 01566 82286

CUMBRIA

Coop House, (WA), Netherby
* The Landmark Trust.

Preston Patrick Hall, (Mrs J. D. Armitage) (WA), Milnthorpe, LA7 7NY Tel: 01539 567 200, Fax: 01539 567 200

Whitehall, (WA), Mealsgate, Carlisle, CA5 1JS
* Mrs S. Parkin-Moore, 40 Woodsome Road, London, NW5 1RZ.

DERBYSHIRE

Elvaston Castle, (Derbyshire County Council), Nr. Derby, DE72 3EP Tel: 01332 571 342

10 North Street, (WA), Cromford
* The Landmark Trust.

Swarkestone Pavilion, (WA), Ticknall
* The Landmark Trust.

DEVON

Bindon Manor, (Sir John & Lady Loveridge) (WA), Axmouth

Bowringsleigh, (Mr & Mrs M. C. Manisty) (WA), Kingbridge

Endsleigh House, (Endsleigh Fishing Club Ltd), Milton Abbot, Nr. Tavistock Tel: 01822 870 248, Fax: 01822 870 502

Hareston House, (Mrs K. M. Basset), Brixton, PL8 2DL Tel: 01752 880 426

The Library, (WA), Stevenstone, Torrington
* The Landmark Trust.

Sanders, (WA), Lettaford, North Bovey
* The Landmark Trust.

The Shell House, (Endsleigh Fishing Club Ltd), Milton Abbot, Nr. Tavistock Tel: 01822 870 248, Fax: 01822 870 502

Shute Gatehouse, (WA), Shute Barton, Nr. Axminster
* The Landmark Trust.

Town House, (Tenant: Mr & Mrs R. A. L. Hill), Gittisham, Honiton Tel: 01404 851 041
* Mr & Mrs R. J. T. Marker

Wortham Manor, (WA), Lifton
* The Landmark Trust.

DORSET

Bloxworth House, (Mr T. A. Dulake) (WA), Bloxworth

Clenston Manor, Winterborne, Clenston, Blandford Forum

Higher Melcombe, (M. C. Woodhouse) (WA), Dorchester, DT2 7PB

Moignes Court, (A. M. Cree) (WA), Owermoigne

Smedmore House, Kimmeridge, BH20 5PG

Stafford House, (Mr & Mrs Richard Pavitt), West Stafford, Dorchester Tel: 01305 263 668

Woodsford Castle, (WA), Woodsford, Nr. Dorchester
* The Landmark Trust.

COUNTY DURHAM

The Buildings in the Square, (Lady Gilbertson) (WA), 1 The Square, Greta Bridge, DL12 9SD Tel: 01833 27276

ESSEX

Blake Hall, Battle of Britain Museum & Gardens, (Owner: R. Capel Cure), Chipping Ongar, CM5 0DG Tel: 01277 362 502

Church of St. Andrews and Monks Tithe Barn, (Harlow District Council), Harlow Study & Visitors Centre, Netteswellbury Farm, Harlow, CM18 6BW Tel: 01279 446 745, Fax: 01279 421 945

Grange Farm, (J. Kirby), Little Dunmow, CM6 3HY Tel: 01371 820 205

Great Priory Farm, (Miss L. Tabor), Panfield, Braintree, CM7 5BQ Tel: 01376 550 944

The Guildhall, (Dr & Mrs Paul Sauven), Great Waltham Tel: 01245 360 527

Old All Saints, (R. Mill), Old Church Hill, Langdon Hills, SS16 6HZ Tel: 01268 414 146

Rainham Hall, (The National Trust. Tenant: D. Atack), Rainham

Rayne Hall, (Mr & Mrs R. J. Pertwee) (WA), Rayne, Braintree

The Round House, (M. E. W. Heap), Havering-atte-Bower, Romford, RM4 1QH Tel: 01708 728 136

GLOUCESTERSHIRE

Abbey Gatehouse, (WA), Tewksbury
* The Landmark Trust.

Ashleworth Court, (H. J. Chamberlayne), Gloucester Tel: 01452 700 241

Ashleworth Manor, (Dr & Mrs Jeremy Barnes) (WA), Ashleworth, Gloucester, GL19 4LA Tel: 01452 700 350

Bearland House, (The Administrator) (WA), Longsmith Street, Gloucester, GL1 2HL, Fax: 01452 419 312

Castle Godwyn, (Mr & Mrs J. Milne) (WA), Painswick

Chaceley Hall, (W. H. Lane), Tewkesbury Tel: 01452 28205

Cheltenham College, (The Bursar), The College, Bath Road, Cheltenham, GL53 7LD Tel: 01242 513 540

The Cottage, (Mrs S. M. Rolt) (WA), Stanley Pontlarge, Winchcombe, GL54 5HD

East Banqueting House, (WA), Chipping Camden
* The Landmark Trust.

Minchinhampton Market House, (B. E. Lucas), Stroud Tel: 01453 883 241

The Old Vicarage, ('Lord Weymyss' Trust), The Church, Stanway Tel: 01386 584 469
* Apply to Stanway House, Stanway, Cheltenham:

St. Margaret's Church, (The Gloucester Charities Trust), London Road, Gloucester Tel: 01452 23316
By appointment with the Warden on 01831 470 335.

Tyndale Monument, (Tyndale Monument Charity), North Nibley, GL11 4JA Tel: 01453 543 691
For Key: See notice at foot of Wood Lane.

GREATER MANCHESTER

Chetham's Hospital & Library, (The Feoffees of Chetham's Hospital & Library), Manchester, M5 1SB Tel 0161 834 9644, Fax: 0161 839 5797

Slade Hall, (Manchester & District Housing Assn.) (WA), Slade Lane, Manchester, M13 0QP

HAMPSHIRE

Chesil Theatre (formerly 12th century Church of St. Peter Chesil), (Winchester Dramatic Society), Chesil Street, Winchester, SO23 0HU Tel: 01962 867 086

The Deanery, (The Dean & Chapter), The Close, Winchester, SO23 9LS Tel: 01962 853 137, Fax: 01962 841 519

Greywell Hill, near Hook (PR FitzGerald, Wilsons)(WA) Steynings House, Fisherton Street, Salisbury SP2 7RJ

Manor House Farm, (S. B. Mason), Hambledon Tel: 01705 632 433

Moyles Court, (Headmaster, Moyles Court School) (WA), Moyles Court, Ringwood, BH24 3NF Tel: 01425 472 856

HEREFORD & WORCESTER

Britannia House, (The Alice Ottley School), The Tything, Worcester. Apply to the Headmistress.

Church House, (The Trustees), Market Square, Evesham

Grafton Manor, (J. W. Morris, Lord of Grafton), Bromsgrove Tel: 01527 31525

Newhouse Farm, (The Administrator) (WA), Goodrich, Ross-on-Wye

The Old Palace, (The Dean & Chapter of Worcester) (WA), Worcester.

Shelwick Court, (WA), Hereford * The Landmark Trust.

HERTFORDSHIRE

Heath Mount School, (The Abel Smith Trustees), Woodhall Park, Watton-at-Stone, Hertford, SG14 3NG Tel: 01920 830 286, Fax: 01920 830 357

Northaw Place, (The Administrator), Northaw Tel: 01707 44059

KENT

Barming Place, (Mr J. Peter & Dr Rosalind Bearcroft), Maidstone Tel: 01622 727 844

Bedgebury National Pinetum, (Forestry Enterprise), Nr. Goudhurst Tel: 01580 211 044, Fax: 01580 212 523

Foord Almshouses, (The Clerk to the Trustees) (WA), Rochester

Mersham-le-Hatch, (The Hon. M. J. Knatchbull), Nr. Ashford, TN25 5NH Tel: 01233 503 954, Fax: 01233 611 650. Apply to the tenant: The Directors, Caldecott Community.

Nurstead Court, (Mrs S. M. H. Edmeades-Stearns), Meopham Tel: 01474 812 121

Old College of All Saints, Kent Music Centre, Maidstone Tel: 01622 690 404
Apply to the Regional Director.

The Old Pharmacy, (Mrs Peggy Noreen Kerr), 6 Market Place, Faversham, ME13 7EH

Prospect Tower, (WA), Belmont Park, Faversham
* The Landmark Trust.

Yaldham Manor, (Mr & Mrs J. Mourier Lade) (WA), Kemsing, Sevenoaks, TN15 6NN Tel: 01732 761 029

LANCASHIRE

Properties by Appointment

The Music Room, (WA), Lancaster
* The Landmark Trust.

Parrox Hall, (Mr & Mrs H. D. H. Elleston) (WA), Preesall, Nr. Poulton-le-Fylde, FY6 0NW Tel: 01253 810 245, Fax: 01253 811 223

LEICESTERSHIRE

Launde Abbey, (Rev. Graham Johnson), East Norton

The Moat House, (Mrs H. S. Hall), Appleby Magna Tel: 01530 270 301

Old Grammar School, Market Harborough Tel: 01858 462 202

Staunton Harold Hall, (Ryder-Cheshire Foundation), Ashby-de-la-Zouch Tel: 01332 862 798

LINCOLNSHIRE

Bede House, Tattershall

The Chateau, (WA), Gate Burton, Gainsborough
* The Landmark Trust.

East Lighthouse, (Cdr. M. D. Joel R.N.) (WA), Sutton Bridge, Spalding, PE12 9YT

Fulbeck Manor, (J. F. Fane) (WA), Grantham, NG32 3JN Tel: 01400 272 231

Harlaxton Manor, (University of Evansville) (WA), Grantham

House of Correction, (WA), Folkingham
* The Landmark Trust.

The Norman Manor House, (Lady Netherthorpe) (WA), Boothby Pagnell

Pelham Mausoleum, (The Earl of Yarborough), Limber, Grimsby

Scrivelsby Court, (Lt. Col. J. L. M. Dymoke M.B.E. DL.) (WA), Nr. Horncastle, LN9 6JA Tel: 01507 523 325

LONDON

All Hallows Vicarage, (Rev. R. Pearson), Tottenham, London, N17

69 Brick Lane, (The Administrator) (WA), London, E1

24 The Butts, 192, 194, 196, 198, 202, 204-224 Cable Street, (Mrs Sally Mills) (WA), London

11-13 Cavendish Street, (Heythrop College) (WA), London

Celia & Phillip Blairman Houses, (The Administrator) (WA), Elder Street, London, E1

Charlton House, (London Borough of Greenwich) (WA), Charlton Road, Charlton, London, SE7 8RE Tel: 0181 856 3951

Charterhouse, (The Governors of Sutton Hospital), Charterhouse Square, London, EC1

17-27 Folgate Street, (WA), London, E1

36 Hanbury Street, (WA), London, E1

Heathgate House, (Rev. Mother Prioress, Ursuline Convent), 66 Crooms Hill, Greenwich, London, SE10 8HG Tel: 0181 858 0779

140, 142, 166 168 Homerton High Street, (WA), London, E5

Properties by Appointment Only

House of St. Barnabas-in-Soho, (The Warden of the House) (WA), 1 Greek Street, Soho, London, W1V 6NQ Tel: 0171 437 1894

Kensal Green Cemetery, (General Cemetery Company), Harrow Road, London, W10 4RA Tel: 0181 969 0152, Fax: 0181 960 9744

69-83 Paragon Road, (WA), London, E5

Red House, (Mr & Mrs Hollamby) (WA), Red House Lane, Bexleyheath

Sunbury Court, (The Salvation Army), Sudbury-on-Thames Tel: 01932 782 196

Vale Mascal Bath House, (Mrs F. Chu), 112 North Cray Road, Bexley, DA5 3NA Tel: 01322 554 894

Wesley's House, (The Trustees of the Methodist Church), 47 City Road, London, EC1Y 1AU Tel: 0171 253 2262, Fax: 0171 608 3825

MERSEYSIDE

The Turner Home, (R. A. Waring RGN., CGN), Dingle Head, Liverpool Tel: 0151 727 4177

NORFOLK

All Saints' Church, (Norfolk Churches Trust) , Barmer Keyholder – No 5, The Cottages.

All Saints' Church, (Norfolk Churches Trust) , Cockthorpe. Keyholder - Mrs Case at farmhouse.

All Saints' Church, (Norfolk Churches Trust) , Dunton Key of Tower at Hall Farm.

All Saints' Church, (Norfolk Churches Trust) , Frenze Keyholder - Mrs Alston at farmhouse.

All Saints' Church, (Norfolk Churches Trust) , Hargham Keyholder – Mrs Clifford, Amost, Station Road, Attleborough.

All Saints' Church, (Rector, Churchwardens and PCC) , Weston Longville, NR9 5JU Keyholder - Rev. J. P. P. Illingworth.

All Saints' Church, (Norfolk Churches Trust) , Snetterton Keyholder - at Hall Farm.

Billingford Mill, (Norfolk County Council), Scole

6 The Close, (The Dean & Chapter of Norwich Cathedral) (WA), Norwich

Fishermen's Hospital, (J. E. C. Lamb F.I.H., Clerk to the Trustees), Great Yarmouth Tel: 01493 856 609

Gowthorpe Manor, (Mrs Watkinson) (WA), Swardeston, NR14 8DS Tel: 01508 570 216

Hales Hall, (Mr & Mrs T. Read) (WA), London, NR14 6QW Tel: 0150 846 395

Hoveton House, (Sir John Blofeld), Wroxham, Norwich, NR12 8JE

Lattice House, (Mr & Mrs T. Duckett) (WA), King's Lynn Tel: 01553 777 292

Little Cressingham Mill, (Norfolk Mills & Pumps Trust), Little Cressingham, Thetford Tel: 01953 850 567

Little Hautbois Hall, (Mrs Duffield) (WA), Nr. Norwich, NR12 7JR Tel: 01603 279 333, Fax: 01603 279 615

The Music House, (The Warden), Wensum Lodge, King Street, Norwich Tel: 01603 666 021/666022, Fax: 01603 765 633

Norwich Cathedral Close, (WA), The Close, Norwich Apply to the Cathedral Steward's Office, Messrs. Percy Howes & Co, 3 The Close, Norwich.

The Old Princes Inn Restaurant, 20 Prince Street, Norwich Tel: 01603 621 043

The Old Vicarage, (Mr & Mrs H. C. Dance), Crown St. Methwold, Thetford, IP25 ANR

St. Andrew's Church, (Norfolk Churches Trust), Frenze Keyholder - Mrs Altston at farmhouse opposite.

St. Celia's Church, West Bilney Keyholder - Mr Curl, Tanglewood, Main Road, West Bilney.

St. Margaret's Church, (Norfolk Churches Trust), Morton-on-the-Hill, NR9 5JS Keyholder - Lady Prince-Smith at the Hall.

St. Mary's Church, (Norfolk Churches Trust), Dunton

St. Peter's Church, (Norfolk Churches Trust), The Lodge, Millgate, Aylsham, NR11 6HX Keyholder - Lord & Lady Romney at Wesnum Farm or Mrs Walker at Pocklethorpe Cottages.

Stracey Arms Mill, (Norfolk County Council), Nr. Acle Tel: 01603 611122 Ext 5224

The Strangers' Club, 22, 24 Elm Hill, Norwich Tel: 01603 623 813

Thoresby College, (King's Lynn Preservation Trust) (WA), Queen Street, King's Lynn, PE30 1HX

Wiveton Hall, (D. MacCarthy) (WA), Holt

NORTHAMPTONSHIRE

Courteenhall, (Sir Hereward Wake Bt. MC) (WA), Northampton

Drayton House, (L. G. Stopford Sackville) (WA), Lowick, Kettering, NN14 3BG Tel: 01832 732 405

The Monastery, (Mr & Mrs R. G. Wigley) (WA), Shutlanger, NN12 7RU Tel: 01604 862 529

Paine's Cottage, (R. O. Barber) (WA), Oundle

Weston Hall, (Mr & Mrs Francis Sitwell) (WA), Towcester

NORTHUMBERLAND

Brinkburn Mill, (WA), Rothbury * The Landmark Trust.

Capheaton Hall, (J. Browne-Swinburne) (WA), Newcastle-upon-Tyne, NE19 2AB

Causeway House, (WA), Bardon Mill

Craster Tower, (Col. J. M. Craster, Miss M. D. Craster & F. Sharratt) (WA), Alnwick

Netherwitton Hall, (J. C. R. Trevelyon) (WA), Morpeth, NE61 4NW Tel: 01670 772 219 Fax: 01670 772 332

NOTTINGHAMSHIRE

Winkburn Hall, (R. Craven-Smith-Milnes), Newark, NG22 8PQ Tel: 01636 636 465, Fax: 01636 636 717

Worksop Priory Church & Gatehouse, The Vicarage, Cheapside Tel: 01909 472 180

OXFORDSHIRE

26-27 Cornmarket Street & 26 Ship Street, (Home Bursar), Jesus College, Oxford Shop basement by written appointment to: Laura Ashley Ltd, 150 Bath Road, Maidenhead, Berks, SL6 4YS.

Hope House, (Mrs J. Hageman), Woodstock

The Manor, (Mr & Mrs Paul L. Jacques) (WA), Chalgrove, OX44 7SL Tel: 01865 890 836, Fax: 01865 891 810

Monarch's Court House, (R. S. Hine) (WA) Benson

Ripon College, (The Principal) (WA), Cuddesdon

30-43 The Causeway, (Mr & Mrs R. Hornsby), 39-43 The Causeway, Steventon

SHROPSHIRE

Bromfield Priory Gatehouse, (WA), Ludlow Tel: 01628 825 925* The Landmark Trust.

Halston, (Mrs J. L. Harvey) (WA), Oswestry

Hatton Grange, (Mrs P. Afia) (WA), Shifnal

Langley Gatehouse, (WA), Acton Burnell Tel: 01628 825 925 * The Landmark Trust, Shottesbrooke, nr. Maidenhead, Berks, SL6 3SW.

Oakley Manor, (Shrewsbury & Atcham Borough Council), Belle Vue Road, Shrewsbury, SY3 7NW Tel: 01243 231 456, Fax: 01243 271 598

St. Winifred's Well, (WA), Woolston, Oswestry * The Landmark Trust, Shottesbrooke, nr. Maidenhead, Berks, SL6 3SW.

Stanwardine Hall, (P. J. Bridge), Cockshutt, Ellesmere Tel: 01939 270 212

SOMERSET

Cothelstone Manor & Gatehouse, (Mrs J. E. B. Warmington) (WA), Cothelstone, Nr. Taunton, TA4 3DS Tel: 01823 432 200

Fairfield, (Lady Gass), Stogursey, Bridgwater, TA5 1PU Tel: 01278 732 251 Fax: 01278 732277

Gurney Manor, (WA), Cannington Tel: 01628 825 925 * The Landmark Trust, Shottesbrooke, nr. Maidenhead, Berks, SL6 3SW.

The Old Drug Store, (Mr & Mrs E. D. J. Schofield) (WA), Axbridge

The Old Hall, (WA), Croscombe * The Landmark Trust, Shottesbrooke, nr. Maidenhead, Berks, SL6 3SW.

The Priest's Hole, (WA), Holcombe Rogus, Nr. Wellington * The Landmark Trust, Shottesbrooke, nr. Maidenhead, Berks, SL6 3SW.

Stogursey Castle, (WA), Nr. Bridgwater * The Landmark Trust, Shottesbrooke, nr. Maidenhead, Berks, SL6 3SW.

West Coker Manor, (Mr & Mrs Derek Maclaren), West Coker, BA22 9BJ Tel: 01935 862 646

Whitelackington Manor, (E. J. H. Cameron), Dillington Estate Office, Illminster, TA19 9EQ Tel: 01460 54614

Properties by Appointment

STAFFORDSHIRE

Broughton Hall, (The Administrator) (WA), Eccleshall

Dunwood Hall, (Dr R. Vincent-Kemp FRSA), Longsdon, Nr. Leek, ST9 9AR Tel: 01538 385 071

The Great Hall in Keele Hall, (The Registrar, University of Keele) (WA), Keele

Ingestre Pavilion, (WA), Nr. Stafford
* The Landmark Trust, Shottesbrooke, nr. Maidenhead, Berks, SL6 3SW.

Old Hall Gatehouse, (R. M. Eades), Mavesyn Ridware Tel: 01543 490 312

The Orangery, (Mrs M Philips), Heath House, Tean, Stoke-on-Trent, ST10 4HA Tel: 01538 722 212

Park Hall, (E. J. Knobbs) (WA), Leigh

Tixall Gatehouse, (WA), Tixall, Nr. Stafford
* The Landmark Trust, Shottesbrooke, Nr. Maidenhead, Berks, SL6 3SW.

SUFFOLK

The Deanery, (The Dean of Bocking), Hadleigh, IP7 5DT Tel: 01473 822 218

Ditchingham Hall, (The Rt. Hon. Earl Ferrers), Ditchingam, Bungay

The Hall, (Mr & Mrs R. B. Cooper) (WA), Great Bricett, Ipswich

Hengrave Hall Centre, (The Warden), Bury St. Edmunds, IP28 6LZ Tel: 01284 701 561

Martello Tower, (WA), Aldeburgh
* The Landmark Trust.

Moat Hall, (J. W. Gray), Woodbridge, IP13 9AE Tel: 01728 746 317

The New Inn, (WA), Peasenhall
* The Landmark Trust.

Newbourne Hall, (John Somerville) (WA), Woodbridge

Worlingham Hall, (Viscount Colville of Culross) (WA), Beccles

SURREY

Crossways Farm, (Tenant: C. T. Hughes) (WA), Abinger Hammer

Great Fosters Hotel, (Manager: J. E. Baumann), Egham, TW20 9UR Tel: 01784 433 822

St. Mary's Home Chapel, Church Lane, Godstone Tel: 01883 742 385

SUSSEX

Ashdown House, (The Headmaster), Ashdown House School, Forest Row, RH18 5JY Tel: 01342 822 574, Fax: 01342 824 380

Chantry Green House, (Mr & Mrs G. H. Recknell), Steyning Tel: 01903 812 239

The Chapel, Bishop's Palace, (Church Commissioners), The Palace, Chichester

Christ's Hospital, (WA), Horsham Tel: 01403 211 293

Laughton Tower, (WA), Lewes * The Landmark Trust.

WARWICKSHIRE

Bath House, (WA), Walton, Stratford-upon-Avon
* The Landmark Trust, Shottesbrooke, nr. Maidenhead, Berks, SL6 3SW.

Binswood Hall, (North Leamington School) (WA), Binswood Avenue, Leamington Spa, CV32 5SF Tel: 01926 423 686

Foxcote, (C. B. Holman) (WA), Shipton-on-Stour

Nicholas Chamberlain's Almshouses, (The Warden), Bedworth Tel: 01203 312 225

Northgate, (R. E. Phllips) (WA), Warwick, CV34 4JL

St. Leonard's Church, (WA), Wroxall
Apply to Mrs J. M. Gowen, Headmistress, Wroxall Abbey School, Warwick, CV35 7NB.

War Memorial Town Hall, (The Secretary, D. R. Young), 27 Henley Street, Alcester, B49 5QX Tel: 01789 765 198

WILTSHIRE

Bradley House, Maiden Bradley, Warminster Tel: 01803 866633 (The Estate Office)

Chinese Summerhouse, Amesbury Abbey, Amesbury Tel: 01980 622 957

Farley Hospital, (The Warden), Church Road, Farley, SP5 1AH Tel: 01722 712 231

Milton Manor, (Mrs Rupert Gentle), The Manor House, Milton Lilbourne, Pewsey, SN9 5LQ Tel: 01672 563 344, Fax: 01672 564 136

Old Bishop's Palace, (The Bursar, Salisbury Cathedral School), 1 The Close, Salisbury Tel: 01722 322 652

The Old Manor House, (J. Teed) (WA), 2 Whitehead Lane, Bradford-upon-Avon

Orpins House, (J. Vernon Burchell) (WA), Church Street, Bradford-upon-Avon

The Porch House, (Tim Vidal-Hall) (WA), 6 High Street, Potterne, Devizes, SN10 5NA

YORKSHIRE

Beamsley Hospital, (WA), Skipton
* The Landmark Trust.

Busby Hall, (G. A. Marwood) (WA), Carlton-in-Cleveland

Calverley Old Hall, (WA), Nr. Leeds
* The Landmark Trust.

Cawood Castle, (WA), Nr. Selby
* The Landmark Trust.

Chapel & Coach House, Aske, Richmond

The Church of Our Lady & St. Everilda, (WA), Everingham Tel: 01430 860 531

The Culloden Tower, (WA), Richmond
* The Landmark Trust.

The Dovecote, (Mrs P. E. Heathcote), Forcett Hall, Forcett, Richmond Tel: 01325 718 226

Home Farm House, (G. T. Reece) (WA), Old Scriven, Knaresborough

Moulton Hall, (The National Trust. Tenant: The Hon. J. D. Eccles) (WA), Richmond

The Old Rectory, (Mrs R. F. Wormald) (WA), Foston, York

The Pigsty, (WA), Robin Hood's Bay
* The Landmark Trust.

Fulneck Boys' School, (I. D. Cleland, BA, M. Phil, Headmaster) (WA), Pudsey

Grand Theatre & Opera House, (General Manager: Warren Smith), 46 New Briggate, Leeds, LS1 6NZ Tel: 0113 245 6014, Fax: 0113 246 5906

Horbury Hall, (D. J. H. Michelmore), Horbury, Wakefield Tel: 01924 277 552

Town Hall, (Leeds City Council), Leeds Tel: 0113 247 7989

Weston Hall, (Lt. Col. H. V. Dawson) (WA), Nr. Otley, LS21 2HP

WALES

CLYWYD

Fferm, (Dr M. C. Jones-Mortimer), Pontblyddyn, Mold, CH7 4HN Tel: 01352 770 876

Golden Grove, (N. R. & M. M. J. Steele-Mortimer) (WA), Llanasa, Nr. Holywell, CH8 9NE Tel: 01745 854 452, Fax: 01745 854 547

Halghton Hall, (J. D. Lewis) (WA), Bangor-on-Dee, Wrexham

Lindisfarne College, (The Headmaster) (WA), Wynnstay Hall, Ruabon Tel: 01978 810 407

Pen Isa'r Glascoed, (M. E. Harrop), Bodelwyddan, LL22 9D745 583 501D Tel: 01 45 583501

DYFED

Monkton Old Hall, (WA), Pembroke
* The Landmark Trust.

Taliaris Park, (J. H. Spencer-Williams) (WA), Llandeilo

University of Wales Lampeter, (Prof. Keith Robbins), Lampeter, SA48 7ED Tel: 01570 422 351, Fax: 01570 423 423

West Blockhouse, (WA), Haverfordwest, Dale
* The Landmark Trust.

SOUTH GLAMORGAN

Fonmon Castle, (Sir Brooke Boothby, Bt.), Barry, CF6 9ZN Tel: 01446 710 206, Fax: 01446 711 687

GWENT

Blackbrook Manor, (Mr & Mrs A. C. de Morgan), Skenfrith, Nr. Abergavenny, NP7 8UB Tel: 01600 84453, Fax: 01600 84453

Castle Hill House, (T. Baxter-Wright) (WA), Monmouth

Clytha Castle, (WA), Abergavenny
* The Landmark Trust.

Great Cil-Lwch, (J. F. Ingledew) (WA), Llantilio Crossenny, Abergavenny, NP7 8SR Tel: 01600 780 206

Kemys House, (I. S. Burge) (WA), Keyms Inferior, Caerleon

Llanvihangel Court, (Mrs D. Johnson) (WA), Abergavenny, NP7 8DH

Overmonnow House, (J. R. Pangbourne) (WA), Monmouth

Properties by Appointment Only

3-4 Priory Street, (H. R. Ludwig), Monmouth

Treowen, (John Wheelock), Wonastow, Monmouth, NP5 4DL Tel: 01600 712 031

GWYNEDD

Cymryd, (Miss D. E. Glynne) (WA), Cymryd, Conwy, LL32 8UA

Dolaugwyn, (Mrs S. Tudor) (WA), Towyn

Nannau, (P. Vernon) (WA), Dolgellau

Penmynydd, (The Rector of Llanfairpwll) (WA), Alms House, Llnafairpwll

Plas Coch, (Mrs N. Donald), Llanedwen, Llanfairpwll Tel: 01248 714272

POWYS

Abercamlais, (Mrs J. C. R. Ballance) (WA), Brecon

Abercynrig, (Mrs W. R. Lloyd) (WA), Brecon

1 Buckingham Place, (Mrs Meeres) (WA), 1 Buckingham Place, Brecon, LD3 7DL Tel: 01874 623 612

3 Buckingham Place, (Mr & Mrs A. Whiley) (WA), 3 Buckingham Place, Brecon, LD3 7DL

Maesmawr Hall Hotel, (Mrs M. Pemberton & Mrs I. Hunt), Caersws Tel: 01686 688 255

Newton Farm, (Mrs Ballance. Tenant: D. L. Evans), Brecon

Pen Y Lan, (J. G. Meade), Meifod, Powys, SY22 6DA Tel: 01938 500 202

Plasdau Duon, (E. S. Breese), Clatter

Poultry House, (WA), Leighton, Welshpool
* The Landmark Trust..

Rhydycarw, (M. Breese-Davies), Trefeglwys, Newton, SY17 5PU Tel: 01686 430 411, Fax: 01686 430 331

Ydderw, (D. P. Eckley) (WA), Llyswen

SCOTLAND

BORDERS

Old Gala House, (Ettrick & Lauderdale District Council), Galashiels Tel: 01750 20096

Sir Walter Scott's Courtroom, (Ettrick & Lauderdale District Council)), Selkirk Tel: 01750 20096

Wedderlie House, (Mrs J. R. L. Campbell) (WA), Gordon, TD3 6NW Tel: 0157 874 0223

DUMFRIES & GALLOWAY

Bonshaw Tower, (Dr J. B. Irving) (WA), Kirtlebridge, Lockerbie, DG11 3LY Tel: 01461 500 256

Carnsalloch House, (The Leonard Cheshire Foundation), Carnsalloch, Kirkton, DG1 1SN Tel: 01387 254 924, Fax: 01387 257 971

Kirkconnell House, (F. Maxwell Witham), New Abbey, Dumfries Tel: 0138 785 276

FIFE

Bath Castle, (Angus Mitchell), Bogside, Oakley, FK10 3RD Tel: 0131 556 7671

The Castle, (J. Bevan) (WA), Elie

Castle of Park, (WA), Glenluce, Galloway
* The Landmark Trust.

Charleton House, (Baron St. Clair Bonde), Colinsburgh Tel: 0133 334

GRAMPIAN

Balbithan House, (J. McMurtie), Kintore Tel: 01467 32282

Balfluig Castle, (Mark Tennant) (WA), Grampian Apply to 30 Abbey Gardens, London, NW8 9AT

Barra Castle, (Dr & Mrs Andrew Bogdan) (WA), Old Meldrum

Castle of Fiddes, (Dr M. Weir), Stonehaven Tel: 01569 740 213

Church of the Holy Rude, St. John Street, Stirling

Corsindae House, (R. Fyffe) (WA), Sauchen by Inverurie, Inverurie, AB51 7PP Tel: 01330 833 295, Fax: 01330 833 629

Drumminor Castle, (A. D. Forbes) (WA), Rhynie

Erskine Marykirk - Stirling Youth Hostel, St. John Street, Stirling

Gargunnock House, (Gargunnock Estate Trust) (WA), Stirling

Gordonstoun School, (The Headmaster) (WA), Elgin Moray

Grandhome House, (D. R. Patton), Aberdeen Tel: 01224 722 202

Guildhall, (Stirling District Council), Municipal Buildings, Stirling Tel: 01786 79000

Old Tolbooth Building, (Stirling District Council), Municipal Buildings, Stirling Tel: 01786 79000

Phesdo House, (J. M. Thomson) (WA), Laurencekirk

The Pineapple, (WA), Dunmore, Airth, Stirling
* The Landmark Trust.

Tolbooth, (Stirling District Council), Broad Street, Stirling Tel: 01786 79400

Touch House, (P. B. Buchanan) (WA), Stirling, FK8 3AQ Tel: 01786 464 278

HIGHLANDS

Embo House, (John G. Mackintosh), Dornoch Tel: Dornoch 810 260

LOTHIAN

Cakemuir, (M. M. Scott) (WA), Parthhead, Tynehead, EH3 5XR

Castle Gogar, (Lady Steel-Maitland), Edinburgh Tel: 0131 339 1234

Ford House, (F. P. Tindall ,OBE) (WA), Ford

Forth Road Bridge, (The Bridgemaster), South Queensferry Tel: 0131 319 1699

Linnhouse, (H. J. Spur(wa)y) (WA), Linnhouse, Livingstone, EH54 9AN Tel: 01506 410 742, Fax: 01506 416 591

Newbattle Abbey College, (The Principal), Dalkeith, EH22 3LL Tel: 0131 663 1921, Fax: 0131 654 0598

Penicuik House, (Sir John Clerk, Bt.), Penicuik

Roseburn House, (M. E. Sturgeon) (WA), Murrayfield

Townhouse, (East Lothian District Council), Haddington Tel: Haddington 4161

SHETLAND ISLES

The Lodberrie, (Thomas Moncrieff), Lerwick

STRATHCLYDE

Ascog House, (WA), Rothsa* The Landmark Trust.

Barcaldine Castle, (Roderick Campbell) (WA), Benderloch

Craufurdland Castle, (J. P. Houison Craufurdland), Kilmarnock, KA3 6BS Tel: 01560 600 402

Dunstrune Castle, (Robin Malcolm of Poltallock) (WA), Lochgilphead

Kelburn Castle, (The Earl of Glasgow) (WA), Fairlie, Ayrshire, KA29 0BE Tel: Country Centre: 01475 568 685 Kelburn Castle: 01475 568 204, Fax: Country Centre: 01475 568 121 Kelburn Castle: 01475 568 328

New Lanark, (New Lanark Conservation Trust), New Lanark Mills, Lanark, ML11 9DB Tel: 01555 661 345, Fax: 01555 665 738

The Place of Paisley, (Paisley Abbey Kirk Session), Paisley Abbey, Abbey Close, Paisley, PA1 1JG Tel: 0141 889 7654

Saddell Castle, (WA), Campbeltown, Argyll
* The Landmark Trust.

Tangy Mill, (WA), Campbeltown, Kintyre, Argyll
* The Landmark Trust.

Tannahill Cottage, (Secretary, Paisley Burns Club), Queen Street, Paisley Tel: 0141 887 7500

TAYSIDE

Ardblair Castle, (Laurence P. K. Blair Oliphant), Blairgowrie, PH10 6SA Tel: 01250 873 155

Craig House, (Charles F. R. Hoste), Montrose Tel: 01674 722 239

Kinross House, (Sir David Montgomery, Bt.) (WA), Kinross

Michael Bruce Cottage, (Michael Bruce Trust), Kinnesswood

The Pavilion, Gleneagles, (J. Martin Haldane of Gleneagles) (WA), Gleneagles, Auchterarder, PH3 1PJ

Tulliebole Castle, (The Lord Moncrieff), Crook of Devon

Halliday Meecham

ARCHITECTS • INTERIOR DESIGNERS

JOHANSENS PREFERRED ARCHITECTURAL ADVISOR PARTNER

A complete architectural and interior design service for hoteliers and restauranteurs supported by a truly personal and professional practice founded in 1908.

We take great care in the design and management of contracts for the repair, refurbishment, extension and interior design of contemporary, period and listed buildings, and in the design of new uses for old buildings.

Our experience extends to hotels, restaurants and bars, swimming and leisure facilities, conference and seminar venues.

We work nationally and are interested in projects of all sizes. The hallmark of our work is an attractive project finished on time, within cost and without disruption.

Why not have an exploratory discussion to see how we can help you achieve your objectives?

RECIPIENTS OF OVER TWENTY AWARDS IN THE LAST TEN YEARS

0161 661 5566

Peter House, St. Peter's Square

Oxford Street

Manchester M1 5AN

Universities

CAMBRIDGE

Note: Admission to the Colleges means to the Courts, not to the staircases and students' rooms. All opening times are subject to closing for College functions etc. on occasional days. Halls normally close for lunch (12–2pm) and many are not open during the afternoon. Chapels are closed during services. Libraries are not usually open, special arrangements are noted. Gardens do not usually include the Fellows' garden. Figures denote the date of foundation and existing buildings are often of later date. Daylight hours – some colleges may not open until 9.30am or later and usually close before 6pm – many as early as 4.30pm. All parties exceeding 10 persons wishing to tour the college between Easter and October are required to be escorted by a Cambridge registered Guide. All enquires should be made to the Tourist Information Centre, Wheeler Street, Cambridge CB2 3QB. Terms: Lent: Mid-January to Mid-March. Easter: April to June. Michaelmas: 2nd week October to 1st week December. Examination Period closures which differ from one college to another now begin in early April and extend to late June. Notices are usually displayed. Admission charges vary from college to college. **Visitors and especially guided parties should always call at the Porters' Lodge before entering the College.**

CHRIST'S COLLEGE (1505)
Porter's Lodge, St.Andrew's Street CB2 3BU
Tel:(01223) 334900 Fax: (01223) 334967

CLARE COLLEGE (1326)
Trinity Lane

CORPUS CHRISTI COLLEGE (1352)
Porter's Lodge, Trumpington Street CB2 1RH
Tel: (01223) 338000 Fax: (01223) 338061

DOWNING COLLEGE (1800)
Downing College, Regent Street CB2 1DQ
Tel: (01223) 334800 Fax: (01223) 467934

EMMANUEL COLLEGE (1584)
Porter's Lodge, St. Andrew's Street CB2 3AP
Tel: (01223) 334200 Fax: (01223) 334426

GONVILLE & CAIUS COLLEGE (1348)
Porter's Lodge, Trinity Street CB2 1TA
Tel: (01223) 332400

JESUS COLLEGE (1496)
Porter's Lodge, Jesus Lane CB5 8BL
Tel: (01223) 339339

KING'S COLLEGE (1441)
Porter's Lodge, King's Parade CB2 1ST
Tel: (01223) 331212 Fx:(01223) 331315

MAGDALENE COLLEGE (1542)
Porter's Lodge, Magdalene Street

NEWNHAM COLLEGE (1871)
Sidgewick Avenue

PEMBROKE COLLEGE(1347)
Trumpington Street

PETERHOUSE (1284)
Porter's Lodge, Trumpington Street CB2 1RD
Tel: (01223) 338200 Fax: (01223) 337578

QUEENS' COLLEGE (1448)
Porter's Lodge, Silver Street CB3 9ET
Tel: (01223) 335511 Fax:(01223) 335566

SIDNEY SUSSEX COLLEGE (1596)
Porter's Lodge, Sidney Street CB2 3HU
Tel: (01223) 338800 Fax: (01223) 338884

ST. CATHARINE'S COLLEGE (1473)
Porter's Lodge, Trumpington Street

ST. JOHN'S COLLEGE (1511)
Tourist Liaison Office, St. John Street CB2 1TP

TRINITY COLLEGE (1546)
Porter's Lodge, Trinity Street

Conducted Tours in Cambridge: Qualified badged, local guides may be obtained from: Tourist Information Centre, Wheeler Street, Cambridge CB2 3QB. Tel: (01223) 322640 or Cambridge Guide Service, 2 Montague Road, Cambridge CB4 1BX. We normally obtain the Passes and make all negotiations regarding these with the Tourist Office, so separate application is not needed. We have been providing guides for English, Foreign language and special interest groups since 1950. We supply couriers for coach tours of East Anglia, visiting stately homes etc. As an alternative to the 2 hour walking tour we can now offer half hour panoramic in clients' coach (providing there is an effective public address system) followed by a 1.5 hour tour on foot, or 1 hour panoramic only, special flat rate for up to 55 people.

OXFORD

NOTE: Admission to Colleges means to the Quadrangles, not to the staircases and students' rooms. All opening times are subject to closing for college functions etc., on occasional days. Halls normally close for lunch (12–2pm). Chapel usually closed during services. Libraries are not usually open, special arrangements are noted. Gardens do not usually include the Fellows' garden. Figures denote the date of foundation and existing buildings are often of later date. Terms: Hilary: Mid-January to Mid-March. Trinity: 3rd week April to late June. Michaelmas: Mid October to 1st week December. **Visitors and especially guided parties should always call at the Porter's Lodge before entering the College.**

ALL SOULS COLLEGE (1438)
Porter's Lodge, High Street OX1 4AL
Open: College Weekdays: 2-4.30. (2-4pm Oct-Mar).

BALLIOL COLLEGE (1263)
Porter's Lodge, Broad Street
Open: Hall Chapel & Gardens Daily 2-5. Parties limited to 25.

BRASENOSE COLLEGE (1509)
Radcliffe Square
Open: Hall Chapel & Gardens Tour parties: Daily 10-11.30 2-5 (summer) 10-dusk (winter). Individuals 2-5. College closed 11.30-2.

CHRIST CHURCH (1546)
St. Aldate's , Enter via Meadow Gate OX1 1DP
Tel: (01865) 276499
Open: Cathedral daily 9-4.30 (winter) 9-5.30 (summer). Hall daily 9.30-12,2-5.30. Picture Gallery weekdays 10.30-1, 2-4.30. Meadows daily 7-dusk. Tourist Information-(01865) 276499.

CORPUS CHRISTI COLLEGE (1517)
Porter's Lodge, Merton Street
Open: College, Chapel & Gardens Term and vacations - daily.

EXETER COLLEGE (1314)
Porter's Lodge, Turl Street OX1 3DP
Tel: (01865) 279600 Fax:(01865) 279630
Open: College & Chapel, Fellows' Garden term and vacations daily 2-5. (Except Christmas and Easter).

HERTFORD COLLEGE (1284, 1740 & 1874)
Porter's Lodge, Catte Street OX1 3BW
Tel: (01865) 279400 Fax: (01865) 279437
Open: Quadrangle & Chapel Daily 10-6

JESUS COLLEGE (1571)
Turl Street
Open: College, Hall & Chapel Daily 2.30-4.30.

KEBLE COLLEGE (1868)
Porter's Lodge, Parks Road
Open: College & Chapel Daily 10-7 (or dusk if earlier)

LADY MARGARET HALL (1878)
Porter's Lodge, Norham Gardens
Open: College & Gardens Daily 2-6 (or dusk if earlier). The chapel is also open to the public.

LINCOLN COLLEGE (1427)
Porter's Lodge, Turl Street
Open: College & Hall weekdays 2-5. Suns 11-5. Wesley Room All Saints Library Tues & Thurs 2-4.

MAGDALEN COLLEGE (1458)
High Street OX1 4AU
Tel: (01865) 276000 Fax:(01865) 276103
Open: College Chapel Deer Park & Water Walks daily 2-6 June-Sept 11-6.

MANSFIELD COLLEGE (1886)
Porter's Lodge, Mansfield Road
Open: College, May-July, Mon-Sat, 9-5.

MERTON (1264)
Merton Street OX1 4JD
Tel: (01865) 276310 Fax:(01865) 276361
Open: Chapel & Quadrangle Mon-Fri 2-4 Oct-June: Sat & Sun 10-4. Mon-Fri 2-5. Jul-Sept: Sat & Sun 10-5. Library not open on Sat Nov-Mar.

NEW COLLEGE (1379)
New College Lane
Open: Hall, Chapel, Cloister, Gardens daily. Oct-Easter in Holywell Street Gate 2-4. Easter - Early Oct, in New College Lane Gate (11-5)

NUFFIELD COLLEGE (1937)
Porter's Lodge, New Road
Open: College only, daily 9-5

ORIEL COLLEGE (1326)
Oriel Square OX1 4EW
Tel: (01865) 276555 Fax:(01865) 276532
Open: College daily 2-5.

PEMBROKE COLLEGE (1624)
Porter's Lodge, St.Aldate's
Open: College, Hall & Chapel & Gardens Term - daily on application at the Porter's Lodge.

THE QUEEN'S COLLEGE (1340)
High Street OX1 4AW
Tel: (01865) 279120 Fax:(01865) 790819
Open: Hall Chapel Quadrangles & Garden Open to public by apt.

ST. EDMUNDS HALL (1270)
Queen's Lane OX1 4AR
Tel: (01865) 279000
Open: On application to Porter

ST. JOHN'S COLLEGE (1555)
St. Giles' OX1 3JP
Tel: (01865) 277300 Fax:(01865) 277435
Open: College & Garden, Term & Vacation, daily 1-5. Hall & Chapel summer 2.30-4.30.

TRINITY COLLEGE (1554)
Main Gate, Broad Street OX1 3BH
Tel: (01865) 277300 Fax: (01865) 279898
Open: Hall, Chapel & Gardens daily during daylight hours.

UNIVERSITY COLLEGE (1249)
Porter's Lodge, High Street OX1 4BH
Open: College, Hall & Chapel Term 2-4.

WADHAM COLLEGE (1610)
Parks Road, Oxford

WORCESTER COLLEGE (1714)
Porter's Lodge, Worcester Street OX1 2HB
Tel: (01865) 278300 Fax:(01865) 278387
Open: College & Gardens Term daily, 2-6. Vacation daily 9-12 &2-6. Hall & Chapel Apply Lodge.

GUIDED WALKING TOURS OF THE COLLEGES & CITY OF OXFORD. Tours conducted by the Oxford Guild of Guides. Lectures are offered by The Oxford Information Centre, mornings for much of the year, afternoons, tours daily. For tour times please ring (01865) 726871. Tours are offered for groups in English, French, German, Spanish, Russian, Japanese, Polish and Serbo-Croat. Chinese by appointment. The most popular tour for groups, Oxford Past and Present, can be arranged at any time. The following special interest tours are available in the afternoon only: Alice in Oxford; Literary Figures in Oxford; American Roots in Oxford; Oxford Gardens; Modern Architecture in Oxford; Architecture in Oxford (Medieval, 17th century and Modern); Oxford in the Civil War and 17th century. Further details are available from the Deputy Information Officer.

Garden Specialists

If you have been inspired by some of the wonderful gardens contained in this guide, why not recreate some of their beauty in your own garden? Whether you seek to create the traditional elegance of the English Rose Garden, the mass of glorious colour associated with Herbaceous Borders or perhaps are looking for particular varieties, the following specialists offer a range of plants to suit gardeners everywhere.

Right: Waterperry Gardens, Oxfordshire

APULDRAM ROSES

Apuldram Lane, Dell Quay, Chichester, West Sussex
Tel: 01243 785 769 Fax: 01243 536 973 (Mrs D. R. Sawday)

Specialist Rose Nursery growing over 300 varieties of Hybrid Teas, Floribundas, Climbers, Ramblers, Ground Cover, Miniature and Patio Roses. Also a large selection of shrub roses, both old and new. Mature Rose Garden to view. Field open during summer months. Suitable for disabled, but no special toilet. **Location:** 1 mile SW of Chichester. A286 Birdham–Wittering Road from Chichester. Turn right into Dell Quay Road and then right again into Apuldram Lane. **Open:** 8 Jan–22 Dec, daily. Mon–Sat, 9am–5pm. Sun & Bank Hols, 10.30am–4.30pm. Parties can be taken around by prior arrangement with guided tour of roses, June–Sept. **Refreshments:** Ice creams. **Events/Exhibitions:** Open evenings, 25 June & 1 July. Ample car parking.

map 4
D6

AYLETT NURSERIES LTD

North Orbital Road, St. Albans, Herts
Tel: 01727 822255. Fax: 01727 823024 (Mr and Mrs R S Aylett)

Aylett Nurseries of St Albans is a well-known family business with a reputation of high quality plants and service. Famous for dahlias– having been awarded a Gold Medal by the Royal Horticultural Society every year since 1961. In the spring our greenhouses are full of all popular bedding plants. Facilities also include spacious planteria, garden shop, coffee and gift shop, houseplants, florist, garden furniture. From the middle of October do not miss our Christmas Wonderland. **Location:** 2 miles out of St Albans, 1 mile from M10, M1, M25 & A1. **Open:** Daily (excl. Christmas). Mon–Sat 8.30–5 Sun 10–4. **Admission:** Free. Events: Dahlia Festival–end Sept.

map 4
E3

By Appointment to
Her Majesty Queen Elizabeth
The Queen Mother

J. W. BOYCE

Bush Pasture, Carter Street, Fordham, Ely,
Cambridgeshire, CB7 5JU.
Tel: 01638 721 158 (Roger Morley)

Specialists in garden seeds for over 80 years. Specialising in the production of pansy seed and plants. Also over 1,000 items of seed which includes a wide range of separate colours for cut flowers, bedding and drying. Also old and unusual vegetables. Seed list free on request. (Write or telephone as above).

map 5
G1

BURNCOOSE NURSERIES & GARDEN

Gwennap, Redruth TR16 6BJ
Tel: 01209 861112 Fax: 01209 860011 (C H Williams)

The Nurseries are set in the 30 acre woodland gardens of Burncoose. Some 12 acres are laid out for nursery stock production of over 3000 varieties of ornamental trees, shrubs and herbaceous plants. Specialities include camellias, azaleas, magnolias, rhododendrons and conservatory plants. The Nurseries are widely known for rarities and for unusual plants. Full mail order catalogue £1 (posted). **Location:** 2 miles southwest of Redruth on the main A393 Redruth to Falmouth road between the villages of Lanner and Ponsanooth. **Open:** Mon–Sat 9–5pm, Sun 11–5pm. Gardens and tearooms open all year (except Christmas Day). **Admission:** Nurseries free, Gardens £2.00.

map 2
C6

DEACONS NURSERY (H.H)

Moor View, Godshill, PO38 3HW, Isle of Wight
Tel: 01983 840 750 Fax: 01983 523 575 (G. D. Deacon & B. H. Deacon)

Specialist national fruit tree growers. Trees and bushes sent anywhere so send NOW for a FREE catalogue. Over 250 varieties of apples on various types of root stocks from M27 (4ft), M26 (8ft) to M25 (18ft). Plus pears, peaches, nectarines, plums, gages, cherries, soft fruits and an unusual selection of family trees. Many special offers. Catalogue always available (stamp appreciated). Many varieties of grapes; dessert and wine, plus hybrid hops and nuts of all types. **Location:** The picturesque village of Godshill. Deacons Nursery is in Moor View off School Crescent (behind the only school). **Open:** Winter – Mon–Fri, 8–4pm. Summer – Mon–Fri, 8–5pm. Sat, 8–1pm.

map 4
C7

FAMILY TREES

Sandy Lane, Shedfield, Hampshire, SO32 2HQ
Tel: 01329 834 812
(Philip House)

Wide variety of fruit for the connoisseur. Trained tree specialists; standards, espaliers, cordons etc. Other trees and old roses. Free catalogue of mail order trees of good size from Family Trees (as above). **Location:** See map in free catalogue. **Station(s):** Botley (2.5 miles). **Open:** Mid Oct–end Apr, Wed & Sat, 9.30am–12.30. **Admission:** No charge. No minimum order. Courier dispatch for next day delivery – UK and Europe.

map 5
V20

HADDONSTONE SHOW GARDEN

The Forge House, Church Lane, East Haddon, Northampton, NN6 8DB
Tel: 01604 770711 Fax: 01604 770027 (Haddonstone Limited)

See Haddonstone's classic garden ornaments in the beautiful setting of the walled manor gardens – including urns, troughs, fountains, statuary, bird baths, sundials and balustrading. Featured on BBC Gardeners' World, the garden is on different levels with shrub roses, ground cover plants, conifers, clematis and climbers. As part of Haddonstone's Silver Jubilee Celebrations, the garden was substantially expanded to allow a temple and pavilion to be displayed. **Location:** 7 miles NW of Northampton off A428. **Open:** Mon–Fri 9–5.30pm closed weekends, Bank Hols and Christmas period. **Admission:** Free. Groups must apply in writing for permission to visit.

map 4
D1

KAYES GARDEN NURSERY

1700 Melton Road, Rearsby, Leicester, Leicestershire LE7 4YR
Tel: 01664 424578 (Mrs Hazel Kaye)

Hardy herbaceous perennials and good selection of climbers and shrubs. The garden and nursery are in Rearsby, in the lovely Wreake valley. Once an orchard, the one acre garden houses an extensive selection of hardy herbaceous plants. Mixed borders and fine pergola, informal herb garden and a new water garden provide year-round interest, while the nursery offers an excellent range of interesting plants. Location: Just inside Rearsby village, N of Leicester on A607, on L.H. side approaching from Leicester. **Open:** Mar–Oct inclusive Tues–Sat 10–5pm Sun 10am–Noon. Nov–Feb inclusive Fri and Sat 10–4.30. Closed Dec 25–Jan 31 inclusive.

map 8
D6

A BRONZE ARMILLARY SPHERE OF DISTINCTION

by Sally Hersh, Sculptor & Tony Brooks, Dialist
Offered in a Limited Edition of 9. Diameter 27"
Mounted on a Bronze Turtle: the Symbol of Eternity, and Showing
The Calendar, Equation of Time, The Zodiac and Solar Time on the Sundial

Armillaries, Individually Designed Sundials and Sculpture in Stone & Bronze
Sycamores Studio, School Lane, Lodsworth, Petworth, West Sussex GU28 9DH
Telephone: 01798 861 248   Fax: 01798 861 355

LANGLEY BOXWOOD NURSERY

Rake, Nr Liss, Hampshire GU33 7JL
Tel: 01730 894467 Fax: 01730 894703 (Elizabeth Braimbridge)

This small nursery, in a beautiful setting, specialises in box-growing, offering a chance to see together a unique range of old and new varieties, hedging, topiary, specimens and rarities. Some taxus also. Descriptive list available (4 x 1st class stamps). **Location:** On B2070 (old A3) 3 miles S of Liphook. **Open:** Mon–Fri 9–4.30pm, Sat – enquire by telephone first. National Collection – Buxus.

map 4
D6

MILLAIS RHODODENDRONS

Crosswater Farm, Crosswater Lane, Churt, Farnham, GU10 2JN
Tel: 01252 792698, Fax: 01252 792526 (The Millais Family)

Six acre woodland garden and specialist nursery growing over 650 varieties of rhododendrons and azaleas. The nursery grows a selection of the best hybrids from around the world and also rare species collected in the Himalayas and available for the first time. Mail order catalogue 5 x 2nd class stamps. The gardens feature a plantsman's collection of rhododendrons and azaleas, with ponds, a stream and companion plantings. Trial garden displays hundreds of new varieties. **Location:** From Churt, take A287 1/2 mile towards Farnham. Turn right into Jumps Road and after 1/2 mile left into Crosswater Lane. **Open:** Nursery: Mon–Fri 10–1, 2–5pm. Plus Saturdays in Spring and Autumn. Garden and nursery open daily in May. Teas available on National Gardens Scheme Charity Days 4 & 25 May '98.

PERHILL PLANTS

Perhill Nurseries, Worcester Road, Great Witley, Worcestershire
Tel: 01299 896 329 Fax: 01299 896 990 (Perhill Plants)

Specialist growers of 2,500 varieties of alpines, herbs and border perennials. Many rare and unusual. Specialties include penstemons, salvias, osteospermums, dianthus, alpine, phlox, alliums, campanulas, thymes, helianthemums, diascias, lavenders, artemesias, digitals and scented geraniums. **Location:** 10 miles NW of Worcester, on main Tenbury Wells Road (A443). **Open:** 1 Feb–15 Oct, daily, 9–5pm. Sun 10.30–4.30pm. Closed 16 Oct–31 Jan except by appointment.

map 4
A1

PERRYHILL NURSERIES

Hartfield, East Sussex, TN7 4JP
Tel: 01892 770 377 Fax: 01892 770 929 (Mrs S. M. Gemmell)

The Plant Centre for the discerning gardener, with the widest range of plants in the south east of England. Old-fashioned and shrub roses a speciality, also herbaceous plants. Trees, shrubs, alpines, fruit trees and bushes, bedding plants in season. No mail order. Catalogues £1.65 incl. postage. **Location:** 1 mile N of Hartfield on B2026. **Open:** Mar–Oct, 9–5pm. Nov–Feb, 9–4.30pm. Seven days a week.

map 5
F5

Plants for Sale

ENGLAND

BEDFORDSHIRE

Woburn Abbey, Woburn MK43 07P Tel: 01525 290666

BERKSHIRE

The Savill Garden, Windsor Great Park, Berkshire.
Tel: 01753 860222

Dorney Court, Dorney, Nr Windsor SL4 6QP.
Tel: 01628 604638, Fax: 01628 665772

BUCKINGHAMSHIRE

Waddesdon Manor, Nr. Aylesbury HP18 OJW.
Tel: 01296 651236

CAMBRIDGESHIRE

The Manor, Hemingford Grey, Huntingdon PE18 9BN.
Tel: 01480 463134, Fax: 01480 465026

CHESHIRE

Arley Hall & Gardens, Arley, Northwich CW9 6NA.
Tel: 01565 777353, Fax: 01565 777465

Dunham Massey Hall, Altrincham.
Tel: 0161 941 1025, Fax: 0161 029 7508

Little Moreton Hall, Congleton. Tel: 01260 272018

Norton Priory Museum & Gardens, Tudor Road, Manor
Park, Runcorn WA7 1SX. Tel: 01928 569895

Rode Hall, Church Lane, Scholar Green ST7 3QP.
Tel: 01270 873237, Fax: 01270 882962

Tatton Park, Knutsford WA16 6QN. Tel: 01565 750250,

CORNWALL

Bosvigo Plants, Bosvigo Lane, Truro TR1 3NH
Tel: 01872 275774

Burncoose Nurseries & Garden, Gwennap, Redruth
TR16 6BJ Tel: 01209 861112, Fax: 01209 860011

Caerhays Castle & Gardens, Gorran, St Austell PL26
6LY Tel: 01872 501310, Fax: 01872 501870

Godolphin House, Godolphin Cross, Helston TR13 9RE
Tel: 01730 762409

Lanhydrock House, Bodmin. Tel: 01208 73320

Mount Edgcumbe House & Country Park, Cremyll,
Torpoint PL10 1HZ Tel: 01752 822236

Pencarrow, Washaway, Bodmin PL30 3AG.
Tel: 01208 841369

Trebah Garden Trust, Mawnon Smith, Nr. Falmouth.
Tel: 01326 250448

Trelowarren House & Chapel, Mawgan-in-Maneage,
Helston TR12 6AD Tel: 01326 221 366

CUMBRIA

Acorn Bank Garden & Waterfall, Temple Sowerby,
Penrith, CA10 1SP Tel: 017683 61893

Appleby Castle, Appleby-in-Westmorland, CA16 6XH.
Tel: 01768 351082

Dalemain, Penrith, CA11 OHB Tel: 01768 486450

Levens Hall, Kendal LA8 OPD Tel: 015395 60321

Muncaster Castle, Ravenglass CA18 1RQ.
Tel: 01229 717614, Fax: 01229 717010

Sizergh Castle, Nr. Kendal LA8 8AE Tel: 01539 560070

DERBYSHIRE

Carnfield Hall, South Normanten, Nr. Alfreton DE55
2BE. Tel: 01773 520084

Lea Gardens, Lea, Matlock DE4 5GH Tel: 01629 534380

Renishaw Hall, Sheffield S31 9WS Tel: 01246 432310

DEVON

Bickleigh Castle, Bickleigh, Nr. Tiverton EX16 8RP.
Tel: 01884 855363

Cadhay, Ottery St. Mary, EX11 1QT. Tel: 01404 812432

Castle Drogo, Drewsteignton, Exeter EX6 6PB.
Tel: 01647 433306, Fax: 01647 433186

Torre Abbey, The Kings Drive, Torquay TQ2 5JX.
Tel: 01803 293593, Fax: 01803 201154

DORSET

Athelhampton House & Gardens, Athelhampton,
Dorchester. Tel: 01305 848363, Fax: 01305 848135

Chiffchaffs, Chaffeymoor, Bourton, Gillingham SP8 5BY
Tel: 01747 840841

Compton Acres Gardens, Canford Cliffs Road, Poole.
Tel: 01202 700778, Fax: 01202 707537

Cranborne Manor Garden, Cranborne, BH21 5PP.
Tel: 01725 517248, Fax: 01725 517862

Forde Abbey & Gardens, Chard TA20 4LU
Tel: 01460 221290, Fax: 01460 220296

Horn Park Gardens, Horn Park, Beaminster, Dorset.
Tel: 01308 862212

Knoll Gardens & Nursery, Stapehill Road, Hampreston,
Wimborne BH21 7ND Tel: 01202 873931

Mapperton, Mapperton, Beaminster DT8 3NR.
Tel: 01308 862645, Fax: 01308 863348

Deans Court, Wimborne, BH21 1EE. Tel: 01202 886116

CO DURHAM

Raby Castle, Staindrop, Darlington, DL2 3AY
Tel: 01833 660202

GLOUCESTERSHIRE

Barnsley House Garden, The Close, Barnsley, Nr.
Cirencester GL7 5EE. Tel/Fax: 01285 740281

Berkeley Castle, Gloucestershire GL13 9BQ
Tel: 01453 810332

Frampton Court, Frampton-on-Severn GL2 7EU.
Tel: 01452 740267

Kiftsgate Court Gardens, Chipping Campden GL55
6LW. Tel: 01386 438777

Painswick Rococo Gardens, The Stables, Painswick GL6
6TH. Tel/Fax: 01452 813204

Sudeley Castle, Winchcombe GL54 5JD
Tel: 01242 602308

HAMPSHIRE

Gilbert White's House & Garden & The Oates
Museum, 'The Wakes', Selborne, Nr. Alton GU34 3JH
Tel: 01420 511275

Houghton Lodge Gardens, Stockbridge SO20 6LQ
Tel: 01264 810177, Fax: 01794 388072

Langley Boxwood Nursery, Rake, Nr. Liss GU33 7JL
Tel: 01730 894467. Fax: 01730 894703

Mottisfont Abbey, Nr. Romsey SO51 OLP
Tel: 01794 340757, Fax: 01794 341492

Spinners Garden, Boldre, Lymington. Tel: 01590 673347

Stratfield Saye House, Stratfield Saye, Reading RE7 2BT
Tel: 01256 882882

HEREFORD & WORCESTER

Eastnor Castle, Eastnor, Nr. Ledbury, HR8 1RL
Tel: 01531 633160 , Fax: 01531 631776

Dinmore Manor & Gardens, Nr Hereford HR4 8EE
Tel: 01432 830322

Hergest Croft Gardens, Kington.
Tel: 01544 230160, Fax: 01544 230160

How Caple Court Garden, How Caple HR1 4SX.
Tel: 01989 740 612, Fax: 01989 740 611

Kinnersley Castle, Kinnersley HR3 6QF.
Tel: 01544 327407, Fax: 01544 327663

Perhill Plants, Penhill Nurseries, Worcester Road, Great
Witley. Tel: 01299 896329, Fax: 01299 896990

HERTFORDSHIRE

Aylett Nurseries, North Orbital Road, St. Albans.
Tel: 01727 822255

The Gardens Of The Rose, Chiswell Green, St. Albans
AL2 3NR. Tel: 01727 850461, Fax: 01727 850360

Hatfield House, Hatfield AL9 5NQ.
Tel: 01707 262823, Fax: 01707 275719

ISLE OF WIGHT

Deacons Nursery (H.H.), Moor View, Godshill, PO38
3HW.

KENT

Belmont, Belmont Park, Throwley, Faversham ME13
OHH. Tel: 01795 890202.

Cobham Hall, Cobham, Nr Gravesend DA12 3BL
Tel: 01474 824319, Fax: 01474 82299

Finchcocks, Goudhurst TN17 1HH
Tel: 01580 211702, Fax: 01580 211007

Great Comp Garden, Comp Lane, St. Mary's
Platt,Borough Green, Sevenoaks, TN15 9QS.
Tel: 01732 886 154/882

Groombridge Place Gardens, Groombrdige Place,
Groombridge, Nr Royal Tunbridge Wells
Tel: 01892 863999

Ladham House, Goudhurst. Tel: 01580 212674

Lullingstone Castle, Eynsford DA14 OJA
Tel: 01322 862114

LANCASHIRE

Towneley Hall Art Gallery & Museums, Burnley BB11
3RQ. Tel: 01282 42413, Fax: 01282 436138

LEICESTERSHIRE

Kayes Garden Nursery, 1700 Melton Road, Rearsby,
Leicester LE7 4YR. Tel: 01664 424578

LINCOLNSHIRE

Elsham Hall Country & Wildlife Park & Elsham Hall
Barn Theatre, Brigg, Humberside DN20 0QZ
Tel: 01652 688698

LONDON

Chelsea Physic Garden, 66 Royal Hospital Road, London
SW3 4HS Tel: 0171 352 5646

Syon Park, Brentford, Middlesex TW8 8JF
Tel: 0181 560 0881

NORFOLK

The Fairhaven Garden Trust, South Walsham, Nr Norwich NR13 6EA Tel/Fax: 01603 270449

Holkham Hall, Well-next-the-Sea, Norfolk NR23 1AB. Tel: 01328 710227.

Hoveton Hall Gardens, Wroxham, Norwich NR12 8RJ. Tel: 01603 782798, Fax 01603 784584.

Mannington Hall, Saxthorpe. Tel: 01263 584175

NORTHAMPTONSHIRE

Coton Manor Garden, Nr Guilsborough, Northampton, NN6 8RQ. Tel: 01604 740219, Fax: 01604 740838

Cottesbrooke Hall & Gardens, Nr Northampton NN6 8PF Tel: 01604 505808, Fax: 01604 505619

The Menagerie, Horton, Horton, Northampton. NN7 2BX Tel: 01604 870957

The Prebendal Manor House, Nassington, Nr Peterborough PE8 1QG. Tel: 01780 782575

NORTHUMBERLAND

Chipchase Castle & Gardens, Wark on Tyne, Hexham Tel: 01434 230203, Fax: 01434 230740

OXFORDSHIRE

Broughton Castle, Banbury, Oxfordshire OX15 5EB Tel: 01295 262624

Waterperry Gardens, Nr Wheatley, Oxfordshire Tel: 01844 339226/254

SHROPSHIRE

Burford House Gardens, Tenbury Well WR15, 8HQ. Tel: 01584 810777, Fax: 01584 810673

SOMERSET

Gaulden Manor, Tolland, Lydeard St Lawrence, Nr Taunton TA4 3PN. Tel: 01984 667213

Hatch Court, Hatch Beauchamp, Taunton TA3 6AA. Tel: 01823 480120, Fax: 01823 480058

Hestercombe Gardens, Cheddon Fitzpaine, Taunton TA2 8LG. Tel: 01823 423923

Milton Lodge Gardens, Old Bristol Road, Wells. Tel: 01749 672168.

Sherborne Garden (Pear Tree House), Litton BA3 4PP Tel: 01761 241220

STAFFORDSHIRE

The Shugborough Estate, Milford, Nr Stafford ST17 OXB. Tel: 01889 881388

SUFFOLK

Somerleyton Hall & Gardens, Somerleyton, Lowestoft NR32 5QQ. Tel: 01502 730224, Fax: 01502 732143

SURREY

Millais Rhododendrons, Crosswater Farm, Crosswater Lane, Churt, Farnham GU10 2JN. Tel: 01252 792698

SUSSEX

Bentley House & Gardens, Halland, Nr Lewes BN8 5AF Tel: 01825 840573

Borde Hill, Balcombe Road, Haywards Heath S16 1XP. Tel: 01444 450326.

Denmans Garden, Denmans Lane, Fontwell, Nr Arundel BN18 OSU Tel: 01243 542808, Fax: 01243 544064

Fishbourne Roman Palace, Salthill Road, Fishbourne, Chichester PO19 3QR. Tel: 01243 785859

Bosvigo, Cornwall

Glynde Place, Glynde, Lewes BN8 6SX. Tel: 01273 858224, Fax: 01273 858224.

Great Dixter House & Gardens, Northam, Nr Rye TN31 6PH. Tel: 01797 252878, Fax: 01797 252879

Leonardslee Gardens, Lower Beeding, Nr Horsham RH13 6PP Tel: 01403 891212, Fax: 01403 891305

Michelham Priory, Upper Dicker, Hailsham BN27 3QS. Tel: 01323 844224, Fax: 01323 844030

Parnham House, Pulborough RH20 4HS Tel: 01903 744888, Fax: 01903 746557

Pashley Manor Gardens, Pashley Manor, Ticehurst. Tel: 01580 200692, Fax: 01580 200102

Perryhill Nurseries, Hatfield, East Sussex TN7 4JP Tel: 01892 770377, Fax: 01892 770929

West Dean Gardens, The Edward James Foundation, Estate Office, West Dean, Chichester PO18 0QZ. Tel: 01243 818210, Fax: 01243 811342

WARWICKSHIRE

Coughton Court, Alcester, B49 5JA Tel: 01789 400777

Lord Leycester Hospital, High Street, Warwick CV34 4BH. Tel/Fax: 01926 491422

WEST MIDLANDS

Birmingham Botanical Gardens & Glasshouse, Westbourne Road, Edgbaston, Birmingham B15 3TR. Tel: 0121 454 1860, Fax: 0121 454 7835

YORKSHIRE

Burton Agnes Hall, Burton Agnes, Duffield YO25 OND Tel: 01262 490 324, Fax: 01262 490513

Duncombe Park, Helmsley, Ryedale, York, YO6 5EB. Tel: 01439 770213, Fax: 01439 771114

Harewood House, The Harewood Estate, Leeds LS17 9LQ Tel: 0113 288 6331, Fax: 0113 288 6467

Helmsley Walled Garden Restoration Project, Cleveland Park, Helmsley, York YO6 5AH Tel: 01439 771427, Fax: 01439 771427

Newby Hall & Gardens, Ripon HG4 5AE. Tel: 01423 322583, Fax: 01423 324452

Norton Conyers, Ripon HG4 5EQ Tel: 01765 640333

Sewerby Hall & Gardens, Church Lane, Sewerby, Bridlington YOQT 1EA. Tel: Estate Office: 01262 673769, Hall: 01262 673769

Shandy Hall, Coxwold, York YO6 4AD Tel: 01347 868465

Sion Hill Hall, Kirby Wiske, Nr Thirsk YO7 4EU. Tel: 01845 587206, Fax: 01845 587486

Skipton Castle, Skipton BD23 1AQ. Tel: 01756 792442, Fax: 01756 796100

WALES

Colby Woodland Gardens, Stepaside, Narberth. Tel: 01834 811885

Dyffryn Gardens, St Nicholas, Cardiff SF5 6SU Tel: 01222 593 328, Fax: 01222 591 966

Picton Castle & Woodland Gardens, Haverfordwest SA62 4AS. Tel: 01437 751326, Fax: 01437 751326

Tredegar House & Park, Newport NP1 9YW Tel: 01633 815880, Fax: 01633 815895

SCOTLAND

Floors Castle, Kelso TD5 7SF. Tel: 01573 223333

Bolfracks Garden, Aberfeldy, Perthshire, PH15 2EX.

Bowhill House & Country Park, Bowhill, Nr Selkirtk TD7 5ET Tel: 01750 22204, Fax: 01750 22204

Glamis Castle, Glamis, Angus DO8 1RJ. Tel: 01307 840393, Fax: 01307 840733

Mount Stuart House & Gardens, Mount Stuart, Isle of Bute PA20 9LR Tel: 01700 503877, Fax: 01700 505313

IRELAND

Bantry House, Bantry, Co. Cork Tel: 00 353 2 750 047, Fax: 00 353 2 750 795

Benvarden Garden, Dervock, Ballymoney, Co. Antrum Tel: 01265 41331

Mount Usher, Ashford, Co. Wicklow Tel: 0404 40205/40116, Fax: 0404 40205

Powerscourt Gardens & Waterfall, Enniskeryy, Co. Wicklow. Tel: 00 353 204 6000, Fax: 00 353 28 63561

Strokestown Park House, Strokestown, Co. Roscommon Tel: 00353 78 33013, Fax: 00353 78 33712

Tullynaly Castle & Gardens, Castlepollan, Co Westmeath. Tel: 00 353 44 61, Fax: 00 153 44 61850

PARTNERS IN INSURANCE

Lakesure is the Exclusive Partner to
Historic Houses, Castles & Gardens and offers
SAVINGS ON YOUR PREMIUMS

We understand the market and have developed a
number of schemes giving extremely wide cover at a
competitive price and with first class security.

We also offer a special basis of quoting each risk using
'OUR UNIQUE NO CLAIMS
BONUS AT INCEPTION'.

Call 01702 471135 or 471185 (Phone and fax)
Talk to Bruce Thompson for further details

WE KNOW OUR BUSINESS

Properties Licensed for Civil Marriages

Bentley House, Sussex

ENGLAND

BEDFORDSHIRE

Woburn Abbey Woburn MK43 OTP. Tel: 01525 290666; Catering 01525 290662; Antiques Centre 01525 290350

BERKSHIRE

Swallowfield Park Swallowfield KG7 1TG. Tel: 01734 883815

BUCKINGHAMSHIRE

Stowe Landscape Gardens Nr Buckingham MK18 SEH. Tel: 01280 822850

Stowe School Buckingham MK18 5EH. Tel: 01280 813650 House

Waddesdon Manor The Dairy, Nr Aylesbury HP18 OJW. Tel: 01296 651236 Fax: 651142

CHESHIRE

Arley Hall and Gardens nr Great Budworth, Northwich CW9 6NA. Tel: 01565 777353

Bramall Hall Bramall Park, Stockport SK7 3NX. Tel: 0161 485 3708

Tabley House Collection Tabley House, Knutsford WA16 OHB. Tel: 01565 750151

Tatton Park Knutsford WA16 6QN. Tel: 01565 654822

CUMBRIA

Appleby Castle Appleby-in-Westmorland, CA16 6XH. Tel: 017683 51402

Muncaster Castle Ravenglass CA18 1RQ. Tel: 01229 717614

Naworth Castle The Gatehouse, Naworth, Brampton CA8 2HE. Tel: 016977 3229 /2761

DERBYSHIRE

Elvaston Castle Derby DE72 3EP. Tel: 01332 571342

Kedleston Hall Quarndon, Derby DE22 5JH. Tel: 01332 842191

DEVON

Bickleigh Castle Bickleigh, Tiverton EX16 8RP. Tel: 01884 855363

Buckfast Abbey Buckfastleigh TQ11 OEE. Tel: 01364 643891

Powderham Castle Kenton, Exeter EX6 8JQ. Tel: 01626 890243

Tiverton Castle Tiverton EX16 6RP. Tel: 01884 253200

ESSEX

Layer Marney Tower Colchester CO5 9US. Tel: 01206 330784

GREATER MANCHESTER

Heaton Hall Heaton Park, Prestwick, Manchester, Manchester M25 5SW. Tel: 0161 773 1231

HAMPSHIRE

Beaulieu Montagu Ventures Ltd, Beaulieu, Brockenhurst SO42 7ZN. Tel: 01590 612345 Fax: 612624

Highclere Castle Newbury RG15 9RN. Tel: 01635 253210

Mottisfont Abbey Garden Mottisfont, SO51 0LP. Tel: 01794 341220

HEREFORD & WORCESTER

Avoncroft Museum of Buildings Stoke Heath, Bromsgrove B60 4JR. Tel: 01527 831886 or 831363

Eastnor Castle Nr Ledbury, Hereford HR8 1RD. Tel: 01531 633160/632302

Worcester Cathedral 10A College Green, Worcester WR1 2LH. Tel: 01905 28854

HERTFORDSHIRE

Hatfield House Hatfield AL9 5NQ. Tel: 01707 262823 Fax: 275719

Knebworth House, Knebworth. Tel: 01438 812661

KENT

Cobham Hall Cobham, Nr. Gravesend DA12 3BL. Tel: 01474 824319/823371

Finchcocks Goudhurst TN7 1HH. Tel: 01580 211702

Gad's Hill Place Gads Hill School, Rochester ME3 7AA. Tel: 01474 822366

Groombridge Place Gardens Groombridge TN3 9QG. Tel: 01892 863999

Lympne Castle Nr Hythe CT21 4LQ. Tel: 01303 267571

Penshurst Place Penshurst, Tunbridge Wells TN11 8DG. Tel: 01892 870307

Tonbridge Castle Tonbridge TN9 1BG Tel: 01732 770929

LONDON

Burgh House New End Square, Hampstead NW3 1LT. Tel: 0171 431 0144

Greenwich Observatory Queens House, National Maritime Museum, Romney Road, Greenwich SE10 9NF. Tel: 0181 858 4422

Royal Botanic Gardens at Kew Gardens Kew, Richmond, London TW9 3AB. Tel: 0181 940 1171 recorded message

NORTHAMPTONSHIRE

Castle Ashby House Castle Ashby, Northampton NN7 1LQ. Tel: 01604 696696

Lamport Hall and Gardens Northampton NN6 9HD. Tel: 01604 686272

The Prebendal Manor House Nassington. Tel: 01780 782575

SHROPSHIRE

Adcote Little Ness, Nr Shrewsbury SY4 2JY. Tel: 01939 260202

Burford House Gardens Tenbury Wells WR15 8HQ. Tel: 01584 810777

Shrewsbury Castle & Shropshire Regimental Museum Castle Street, Shrewsbury SY1 2AT.

Walcot Hall Nr Bishops Castle, Lydbury North SY7 8AZ. Tel: 0171 581 2782

Weston Park Weston under Lizard, nr Shifnal TF11 8LE. Tel: 01952 850207

STAFFORDSHIRE

Ford Green Hall Ford Green Road, Smallthorne, Stoke-on-Trent ST6 1NG. Tel: 01782 233195

Shugborough Estate Milford, Stafford ST17 0XB. Tel: 01889 881388

SUFFOLK

Somerleyton Hall nr Lowestoft. Tel: 01502 730224

SURREY

Clandon Park West Clandon, Guildford GU4 7RQ. Tel: 01483 222482

SUSSEX

Anne of Cleves House 52 Southover High Street, Lewes BN7 1JA. Tel: 01273 474610 Fax: 01273 486990

Bentley House & Gardens Halland, Nr Lewes BN8 5AF. Tel: 01825 840573

Glynde Place Nr Lewes BN8 6SX. Tel: 01273 858224

Goodwood House Goodwood, Chichester PO18 0PX. Tel: 01243 774107

Royal Pavilion Brighton BN1 1EE. Tel: 01273 290900

WARWICKSHIRE

Coughton Court Alcester B49 5JA. Tel: 01789 400777 01789 762435 visitor information

WEST MIDLANDS

Birmingham Botanical Gardens and Glasshouses Westbourne Road, Edgbaston, Birmingham B15 3TR. Tel: 0121 454 1860

WILTSHIRE

Longleat House The Estate Office, Warminster BA12 7NN. Tel: 01985 844400

YORKSHIRE

The Bar Convent 17 Blossom Street, York Y02 2AH. Tel: 01904 643238

Bolton Abbey Estate Skipton BD23 6EX. Tel: 01756 710533

Bolton Castle Leyburn DL8 4ET. Tel: 01969 623981 Fax: 623332

Duncombe Park Helmsley, York, YO6 5EB. Tel: 01439 770213

Elsham Hall Country and Wildlife Park The Estate Office, Brigg DN20 0QZ. Tel: 01652 688698

Newburgh Priory Coxwold YO6 4AS. Tel: 01347 868435

Oakwell Hall Birstall WF19 9LG. Tel: 01924 474926

Ripley Castle Ripley HG3 3AY. Tel: 01423 770152

Sewerby Hall and Gardens Church Lane, Sewerby, Bridlington YO15 1EA. Tel: 01262 677974

WALES

Cardiff Castle Mrs Sally Hart, Leisure Services Department, Cardiff. Tel: 01222 878100 Fax: 01222 231 417

Gwydir Castle Llanrwst. Tel: 01492 641 687

Tredegar House Newport, Newport NP1 9YW. Tel: 01633 815880

SCOTLAND

Braemar Castle Braemar AB35 5XR. Tel: 013397 41219

Dalmeny House Charisma, South Queensferry EH30 9TQ. Tel: 0131 331 1888

Fasque Fettercairn, Laurencekirk AB30 1DN. Tel: 01561 340202 or 01561 340569

Floors Castle Kelso TD5 7SF. Tel: 01573 223333

Traquair Innerleithen EH44 6PW. Tel: 01896 830323

Scone Palace Perth PH2 6BD. Tel: 01738 552300

IRELAND

Strokestown Park House Strokestown, Co. Roscommon. Tel: 00 353 78 33013

HIGHLAND.
An almost feminine charm and character all of its own. Light and aromatic, the Gentle Spirit is rich in body with a soft heather honey finish.

ISLE OF SKYE.
Assertive but not heavy. Fully flavoured with a pungent, peaty ruggedness. It explodes on the palate and lingers on. Well balanced. A sweetish seaweedy aroma.

SPEYSIDE.
Finely balanced with a dry, rather delicate aroma, good firm body and a smoky finish. A pleasantly austere malt of great distinction with a character all its own.

WEST HIGHLAND.
Oban is the West Highland malt. A singular, rich and complex malt with the merest suggestion of peat in the aroma, slightly smoky with a long smooth finish.

ISLE OF ISLAY.
Seaweed, peat, smoke and earth are all elements of the assertive Islay character. Pungent, an intensely dry 16 year old malt with a firm robust body and powerful aroma.

LOWLAND.
Typically soft, restrained and with a touch of sweetness. An exceptionally pale smooth malt which, experts agree, reaches perfection at 10 years maturity.

DALWHINNIE	TALISKER	CRAGGANMORE	OBAN	LAGAVULIN	GLENKINCHIE
15 YEARS OLD	10 YEARS OLD	12 YEARS OLD	14 YEARS OLD	16 YEARS OLD	10 YEARS OLD
HIGHLAND	SKYE	SPEYSIDE	WEST HIGHLAND	ISLAY	LOWLAND

Les grands crus de Scotland.

In the great wine-growing regions, there are certain growths from a single estate that are inevitably superior.

For the Scots, there are the single malts. Subtle variations in water, weather, peat and the distilling process itself lend each single malt its singular character.

Each Malt is an authentic, traditional malt with its own identity, inherent in both taste and aroma.

The Classic Malts are the finest examples of the main malt producing regions. To savour them, one by one, is a rare journey of discovery.

SIX OF SCOTLAND'S FINEST MALT WHISKIES

Art Collections

Many properties throughout the guide contain notable works of art. The properties listed here have special collections.

ENGLAND

BEDFORDSHIRE

Woburn Abbey, Woburn, Beds. MK43 0TP
Tel: 01525 290666. Canaletto, Van Dyck, Reynolds

BERKSHIRE

Dorney Court, Dorney, Nr Windsor, Berkshire SL4 6QP
Tel: 01628 604638, Fax: 01628 665772
Eton College, Windsor, Berkshire SL4 6DW
Tel: 01763 671177, Fax: 01753 671 265
Brew House Gallery, Exhibitions change
Highclere Castle, Nr Newbury, Berks. RG20 9RN
Tel: 01635 253210. Old masters including Van Dyck

BUCKINGHAMSHIRE

Windsor Castle, Windsor, Berkshire SL4 1NJ
Tel: 01753 568286

CHESHIRE

Capesthorne Hall, Capesthorne, Siddington,
Nr. Macclesfield, Cheshire SK11 9JY. Tel: 01625 861221. Caravan
Park – 01625 861779, Fax: 01625 861619
Norton Priory Museum & Gardens, Tudor Road, Manor Park,
Runcorn, Cheshire WA7 1SX. Tel: 01928 569895
Contemporary sculpture
Tabley House, Knutsford, Cheshire WA16 OHB
Tel: 01565 750151, Fax: 01565 653230
Lely, Lawrence, Opie, Ward, Owen, Devis, Turner
Tatton Park, Knutsford, Cheshire WA16 6QN
Tel: 01565 750 250, Fax: 01565 654 822

CORNWALL

Mount Edgcumbe House & Country Park, Cremyll, Torpoint
PL10 1HZ Tel: 01752 822236
Pencarrow, Washaway, Bodmin PL30 3AG
Tel: 01208 841369. 18th century paintings

CUMBRIA

Appleby Castle, Boroughgate, Appleby-In-Westmorland CA16
6XH. Tel: 017683 51402, Fax: 017683 51082
Clifford Family Portraits
Hutton-In-The-Forest, Penrith. Tel: 01768 484449

DERBYSHIRE

Calke Abbey, Ticknall, Derby DE73 1LE
Tel: 01332 863822, Fax: 01332 865272
Kedleston Hall, Derby, DE22 5JH
Tel:: 01332 842191, Fax: 01332 841972
17th & 18th century Italian / Dutch collection

DEVON

Powderham Castle, Kenton, Exeter EX6 8JQ
Tel: 01626 890 243, Fax: 01626 890729
Cosway, Hudson, Reynolds
Torre Abbey, The Kings Drive, Torquay TQ2 5JX
Tel: 01803 293593, Fax: 01803 201154
Pre-Raphaelites ; 19th century

DORSET

Athelhampton House & Gardens, Athelhampton, Dorchester.
Tel: 01305 848363, Fax: 01305 848135
A.W.Pugin
Wolfeton House, Dorchester DT2 9QN
Tel: 01305 263500

CO DURHAM

Raby Castle, Staindrop, Darlington, Co Durham DL2 3AY Tel:
01833 660 202

ESSEX

The Sir Alfred Munnings Art Museum, Castle House, Dedham
CO7 6AZ Tel: 01206 322127

GLOUCESTERSHIRE

Berkeley Castle, Gloucestershire GL13 9BQ
Tel: 01453 810332
Frampton Court, Frampton-on-Severn, Gloucestershire GL2 7EU.
Tel: 01452 740267
Sudeley Castle, Winchcombe, Gloucs. GL54 5JD
Tel: 01242 602308. Van Dyck, Ruben

HAMPSHIRE

Mottisfont Abbey, Nr. Romsey, Hampshire SO51 OLP
Tel: 01794 340757, Fax: 01794 341492
Dereck Hill collection
Stratfield Saye House, Stratfield Saye, Reading, Hampshire RE7
2BT. Tel: 01256 882882

HEREFORD & WORCESTER

Eastnor Castle, Eastnor, Nr Ledbury, HR8 1RL
Tel: 01531 633160, Fax 01531 631776

HERTFORDSHIRE

Hatfield House, Hatfield, Hertfordshire AL9 5NQ.
Tel: 01707 262823, Fax: 01707 275719

KENT

Cobham Hall, Cobham, Nr Gravesend, Kent DA12 3BL.
Tel: 01474 824319, Fax: 01474 822995
Finchcocks, Goudhurst, Kent TN17 1HH
Tel: 01580 211702, Fax: 01580 211007
18th century, musical theme
Squerryes Court, Westerham, Kent TN16 ISJ
Tel: 01959 562345, Fax: 01959 565949
Old masters from Italian schools, 17th century Dutch.

LANCASHIRE

Towneley Hall Art Gallery & Museums, Burnley, Lancs BB11
3RQ. Tel: 01282 42413, Fax: 01282 436138

LEICESTERSHIRE

Belvoir Castle, Nr Grantham, Lincolnshire. NG32 1PD
Tel: 01476 870262

LINCOLNSHIRE

Grimsthorpe Castle, Grimsthorpe, Bourne
Family portraits

LONDON

Apsley House, The Wellington Museum, 149 Piccadilly, Hyde
Park Corner, London SW1.
Tel: 0171 499 5676, Fax: 0171 493 6576
Buckingham Palace, London SW1A 1AA
Tel: 0171 839 1377
Greenwich – Observatory, National Maritime Museum, Romney
Road, Greenwich SE10 9NF.
Tel: 0181 858 4422, Fax: 0181 312 6632
Maritime & Marine oil paintings
Leighton House Museum & Art Gallery, 12 Holland Park Road,
London W14 8LZ
Tel: 0171 602 3316, Fax: 0171 371 2467. Pre-Raphaelite
Syon Park, Brentford, Middlesex TW8 8JF
Tel: 0181 560 0881
The Wallace Collection, Hertford House, Manchester Square. Tel:
0171 935 0687, Fax: 0171 224 2155

MANCHESTER

Heaton Hall, Heaton Park, Prestwich, Manchester, Lancashire M25
5SW. Tel: 0161 773 1231 / 236 5744, Fax: 0161 236 7369
Part of Manchester City Art Galleries. 18th century art.

NORFOLK

Holkham Hall, Wells-next-the-Sea, Norfolk NR23 1AB
Tel: 01328 710227, Fax: 01328 711707
Rubens, Van Dyck, Claude, Poussin and Gainsborough
Norwich Castle Museum, Norwich NR1 3JU
Tel: 01603 223674
Wolterton Park, Erpingham, Norfol
Tel: 01263 584175, Fax: 01263 761214

NORTHAMPTONSHIRE

Castle Ashby House, Castle Ashby, Northampton NN7 1LQ Tel:
01604 696696, Fax: 01604 696516
Reynolds, Van Dyck
Cottesbrooke Hall & Gardens, Nr Northampton, NN6 8PF. Tel:
01604 505808, Fax: 01604 505619
Munnings, Gainsborough, Lionel Edwards
Lamport Hall & Gardens, Northampton, NN6 9HD
Tel: 01604 686272, Fax: 01604 686224

NORTHUMBERLAND

Alnwick Castle, Alnwick, Northmberland NE66 1NQ
Tel: 01665 510777, Fax: 01665 510876
Titian, Van Dyck, Canelleto

OXFORDSHIRE

Blenheim Palace, Woodstock, Oxon OX20 1PX
Tel: 01993 811325, Fax: 01993 813527
Waterperry Gardens, Nr. Wheatley, Oxon.
Tel: 01844 339226/254. Art Gallery

SHROPSHIRE

Burford House Gardens, Tenbury Well, Worcestershire, WR15,
8HQ. Tel: 01584 810777, Fax: 01584 810673
Botanical, contemporary

STAFFORDSHIRE

Sandon Hall, Sandon, Stafford , Staffordshire
Tel: 01889 508004, Fax: 01889 508586

The Shugborough Estate, Milford, Nr. Stafford ST17 Tel: 01889
881388

SUFFOLK

Christchurch Mansion, Christchurch Park, Ipswich
Tel: 01473 253246, Fax: 01473 281274
Gainsborough's House, 46 Gainsborough Street, Sudbury, Suffolk
CO10 6EU Tel: 01787 372958
Somerleyton Hall & Gardens, Somerleyton, Lowestoft, Suffolk
NR32 5QQ. Tel: 01502 730224
Wingfield Old College, Wingfield, Nr Eye, Suffolk
IP21 5RA Tel: 01379 384888, Fax: 01379 384034

SURREY

Clandon Park, West Clandon, Guildford GU4 7RQ
Tel: 01483 222 482
Gubbay Collection, Porcelain, Needlework & Furniture
Guildford House Gallery, 155 High Street, Guildford Tel: 01483
444740, Fax: 01483 444742

SUSSEX

Arundel Castle, Arundel. West Sussex.
Tel: 01903 883136
Charleston Farmhouse, Firle, nr Lewes
Tel: 01323 811265, Fax: 01323 811628
Firle Place, Nr Lewes, East Sussex, BN8 6LP
Tel/Fax: 01273 858188. Van Dyck, Reynolds, Rubens,
Gainsborough, Guardi, Seargeant, Tenniers, Puligo, Larkin plus
many others
Pallant House, 9 North Pallant, Chichester PO19 1TJ
Tel: 01243 774557 Modern British
Parnham House, Pulborough, West Sussex RH20 4HS
Tel: 01903 744888, Fax: 01903 746557
The Royal Pavilion, Brighton, East Sussex BN1 1EE
Tel: 01273 290900, Fax: 01273 292871. The largest collection of
Regency silver gilt on public display

WARWICKSHIRE

Coughton Court, Alcester, B49 5JA
Tel: 01789 400777, Fax: 01789 765544

WEST MIDLANDS

Birmingham Botanical Gardens & Glasshouse, Westbourne Road,
Edgbaston, Birmingham B15 3TR.
Tel: 0121 454 1860, Fax: 0121 454 7835

WILTSHIRE

Corsham Court, Corsham, Wilts SN13 OBZ
Tel: 01249 701610/701611. Van Dyck, Carlo Dolei
Malmesbury House, The Close, Salisbury SP1 2EB
Tel: 01722 327027, Fax: 01722 334414
Wilton House, Wilton, Salisbury, SP2 OBJ.
Tel: 01722 746720, Fax: 01722 744447

YORKSHIRE

Aske Hall, Aske, Richmond, North Yorkshire DL10 5HJ
Tel: 01748 850391 , Fax: 01748 823252
Burton Agnes Hall, Burton Agnes, Duffield, East Yorks
Tel: 01262 490 324, Fax: 01262 490513
Modern & Impressionist
Cannon Hall, Cawthorne, Barnsley S75 4AT
Tel: 01226 790 270
Harewood House, The Harewood Estate, Leeds LS17 9LQ Tel:
0113 286 6331, Fax: 0113 288 6467
Lotherton Hall, Aberford, Yorkshire L25 3EB
Tel: 0113 281 3259, Fax: 0113 281 2100
Norton Conyers, Ripon HG4 5EQ. Tel: 01765 640333
18th century portraits, 19th century hunting pictures
Sewerby Hall & Gardens, Church Lane, Sewerby, Bridlington,
East Yorks YOQT 1EA.
Tel: Estate Office: 01262 673769
Temple Newsam House, Leeds LS15 OAE
Tel: 0113 264 7321, Fax: 0113 260 2285

SCOTLAND

Bowhill House & Country Park, Bowhill, Nr. Selkirk, TD7 5ET
Scottish Borders. Tel/Fax: 01750 22204
Gainsborough, Canaletto
Dalmeny House, South Queensferry, Edinburgh, EH30 9TQ. Tel:
0131 331 1888, Fax: 0131 331 1788
Floors Castle, Kelso TD5 7SF Scottish Borders
Tel: 01573 223333, Fax: 01573 226056
Mount Stuart House & Gardens, Mount Stuart, Isle of Bute, PA20
9LR. Tel: 01700 503877, Fax: 01700 505 313

WALES

Dinefwr Park, Llandeilo, Carmarthenshire
Tel: 01558 823902

Properties offering Top Teas!

ENGLAND

BEDFORDSHIRE
Woburn Abbey Woburn MK43 OTP. Tel: 01525 290666

BERKSHIRE
Dorney Court Windsor SL4 6QP. Tel: 01628 604638
Savill Garden Crown Estate Office, Windsor Great Park, Windsor SL7 2HT. Tel: 01753 860222

CHESHIRE
Arley Hall and Gardens Nr Great Budworth, Northwich CW9 6NA. Tel: 01565 777353
Dunham Massey Altrincham WA14 4SJ. Tel: 0161 9411025
Little Moreton Hall Congleton CW12 4SD. Tel: 01260 272018
Tabley House Collection Tabley House, Knutsford WA16 OHB. Tel: 01565 750151
Tatton Park Knutsford WA16 6QN. Tel: 01565 654822

CORNWALL
Mount Edgcumbe House & Park Cremyll, Nr. Plymouth PL10 1HZ. Tel: 01752 822236
Pencarrow Washway, Bodmin PL30 5AG. Tel: 01208 841449
Trebah Garden Trust Mawnan Smith TR11 5JZ. Tel: 01326 250448
Lanhydrock Bodmin PL30 5AD. Tel: 01208 73320 Restaurant 01208 74331
Trelissick Garden Feock, Nr Truro TR3 6QL. Tel: 01872 862090; Restaurant 01872 863486

CUMBRIA
Appleby Castle Appleby-in-Westmorland, CA16 6XH. Tel: 017683 51402
Hutton-in-the-Forest Skelton, Penrith CA1 9TH. Tel: 017684 84449

DERBYSHIRE
Haddon Hall Estate Office, Bakewell DE45 1LA. Tel: 01629 812855

DEVON
Bickleigh Castle Bickleigh, Tiverton EX16 8RP. Tel: 01884 855363
Buckfast Abbey Buckfastleigh TQ11 OEE. Tel: 01364 643891
Castle Drogo Drewsteignton, Exeter EX6 6PB. Tel: 0164 743 3306
Endsleigh House The Endsleigh Charitable Trust, Milton Abbot, nr. Tavistock PL19 0PQ. Tel: 01822 870248
Powderham Castle Kenton, Exeter EX6 8JQ. Tel: 01626 890243
Torre Abbey The Kings Drive, Torquay TQ2 5JX. Tel: 01803 293593

DORSET
Athelhampton House & Gardens Athelhampton, Dorchester DT2 7LG. Tel: 01305 848363
Horn Park Beaminster DT8 3HB. Tel: 01308 862212
Knoll Gardens & Nursery Hampreston, Nr Wimborne BH21 7ND. Tel: 011202 873931
Wolfeton House Dorchester. Tel: 01305 263500

ESSEX
Hedingham Castle Castle Hedingham, nr Halstead CO9 3DJ. Tel: 01787 460261 fx 01787 461473
Layer Marney Tower Colchester CO5 9US. Tel: 011206 330784

GLOUCESTERSHIRE
Berkeley Castle Berkeley GL13 9BQ. Tel: 01453 810332
Chavenage Tetbury GL8 8XP. Tel: 01666 502329
Owlpen Manor Uley, nr Dursley GL11 5BZ. Tel: 01453 860261
Painswick Rococo Garden The Stables, Painswick House, Painswick GL6 6TH. Tel: 01452 813204 Fax: 813204
Sudeley Castle Winchcombe GL54 5JD. Tel: 01242 602308

HAMPSHIRE
Avington Park Winchester SO21 1DD. Tel: 01962 779260

Gilbert White's House & Garden and the Oates Museum The Wakes, Selborne GU34 3JH. Tel: 01420 511275
Mottisfont Abbey Garden Mottisfont, SO51 0LP. Tel: 011794 341220

HEREFORD & WORCESTER
Burton Court Eardisland, Leominster HR6 9DN. Tel: 01544 388231
Eastnor Castle Nr Ledbury, Hereford HR8 1RD. Tel: 01531 633160/632302
Hergest Croft Gardens Kington. Tel: 01544 230160
Kentchurch Court Nr Pontrilas, Hereford. Tel: 01981 240228
Kinnersley Castle Kinnersley HR3 6QF. Tel: 011544 327407

HERTFORDSHIRE
Gardens of the Rose Chiswell Green, St. Albans AL2 3NR. Tel: 01727 850461
Hatfield House Hatfield AL9 5NQ. Tel: 01707 262823 Fax: 275719

KENT
Belmont Throwley, Nr Faversham ME13 0HH. Tel: 01795 890202
Cobham Hall Cobham, Nr Gravesend DA12 3BL. Tel: 01474 824319/823371
Doddington Place Gardens Doddington, Sittingbourne ME9 0BB. Tel: 01795 886101
Gad's Hill Place Gad's Hill School, Rochester ME3 7AA. Tel: 01474 822366
Groombridge Place Gardens Groombridge TN3 9QG. Tel: 01892 863999
Ladham House, Goudhurst. Tel: 01580 211203
Lullingstone Castle Eynsford DA14 0JA. Tel: 01322 862114
Penshurst Place Penshurst, Tunbridge Wells TN11 8DG. Tel: 01892 870307
Squerryes Court Westerham TN16 1SJ. Tel: 01959 562345 or 563118

LANCASHIRE
Gawthorpe Hall Padiham, Nr Burnley BB12 8UA. Tel: 011282 770353
Towneley Hall Art Gallery Burnley BD11 3RQ. Tel: 01282 424213

LEICESTERSHIRE
Kayes Garden Nursery 1700 Melton Rd, Rearsby, Leicester LE7 4YR. Tel: 01664 424578
The Manor House Donington-le-Heath.
Stanford Hall Stanford Park, Lutterworth LE17 6DH. Tel: 01788 860250

NORFOLK
Hoveton Hall Gardens Wroxham NR11 7BB.

NORTHAMPTONSHIRE
Lamport Hall and Gardens Northampton NN6 9HD. Tel: 01604 686272

NOTTINGHAMSHIRE
Norwood Park Holme Pierrepont, Nr Southwell NG12 2LD.

OXFORDSHIRE
Waterperry Gardens Waterperry Horticultural Centre, Nr Wheatley OX9 1SZ. Tel: 01844 339226/339254

SHROPSHIRE
Burford House Gardens Tenbury Wells WR15 8HQ. Tel: 01584 810777
Hodnet Hall Gardens Nr Market Drayton TF9 3NN. Tel: 01630 685202

SOMERSET
Gaulden Manor Tolland, Nr Taunton TA4 3PN. Tel: 019847 213
Hestercombe House Gardens Cheddon Fitzpaine, Taunton TA2 8LQ. Tel: 01823 413923

STAFFORDSHIRE
Dunwood Hall Longsdon, Nr. Leek ST9 9AR. Tel: 01538 385071
Sandon Hall Sandon ST18 0BZ. Tel: 01889 508004

SUFFOLK
Kentwell Hall Long Melford, Nr. Sudbury CO10 9BA. Tel: 01787 310207
Somerleyton Hall nr Lowestoft. Tel: 011502 730224
Wingfield Old College Wingfield, Eye IP21 5RA. Tel: 011379 384888

SURREY
Clandon Park West Clandon, Guildford GU4 7RQ. Tel: 01483 222482
Loseley House Estate Office, Guildford GU3 1HS. Tel: 01483 304440

SUSSEX
Bentley House & Gardens Halland, Nr Lewes BN8 5AF. Tel: 01825 840573
Borde Hill Garden Haywards Heath RH16 1XP. Tel: 01444 450326
Denmans Garden Clock House, Denmans, Fontwell BN18 0SU. Tel: 01243 542808
Firle Place Nr Lewes BN8 6LP. Tel: 01273 858188
Fishbourne Roman Palace Salthill Road, Fishbourne, Chichester PO19 3QR. Tel: 01243 785859
Glynde Place Nr Lewes BN8 6SX. Tel: 01273 858224
Hammerwood Park East Grinstead RH19 3QE. Tel: 01342 850594
Leonardslee Gardens Lower Beeding, Horsham RH13 6PP. Tel: 01403 891212
Michelham Priory Upper Dicker, Hailsham BN27 3QS. Tel: 01323 844224 FX- 844030
Pashley Manor Gardens Ticehurst, Wadhurst TN5 7HE. Tel: 01580 200692
Royal Pavilion Brighton BN1 1EE. Tel: 01273 290900
Sewerby Hall and Gardens Church Lane, Sewerby, Bridlington YO15 1EA. Tel: 01262 677974
West Dean Gardens West Dean Estate, Nr Chichester PO18 0QZ. Tel: 01243 818210

WARWICKSHIRE
Coughton Court Alcester B49 5JA. Tel: 01789 400777 01789 762435 (visitor information)
Lord Leycester Hospital High Street, Warwick CV34 4BH. Tel: 011926 492797

YORKSHIRE
Aske Hall Aske, Rickmond DL10 5HJ. Tel: 01748 823222 Fax: 01748 823252
Bolton Castle Leyburn DL8 4ET. Tel: 01969 623981
Brodsworth Hall Brodsworth. Tel: 01302 722598
Elsham Hall Country and Wildlife Park The Estate Office, Brigg DN20 0QZ. Tel: 01652 688698
Helmsley Walled Garden Cleveland Way, Helmsley, York YO6 5AH. Tel: 01439 771427
Oakwell Hall Birstall WF19 9LG. Tel: 01924 474926

WALES
Colby Woodland Garden Amroth, Narbeth SA67 8PP. Tel: 01558 822800/01834 811885
Dinefwr Park Llandeilo SA19 6RT. Tel: 011558 823902
Picton Castle Picton Castle Trust, Haverfordwest SA62 4AS. Tel: 01437 751326
Tredegar House Newport, Newport NP1 9YW. Tel: 01633 815880

SCOTLAND
Cawdor Castle Nairn, Inverness IV12 5RD. Tel: 01667 404615
Dalmeny House Charisma, South Queensferry EH30 9TQ. Tel: 031-331 1888
Manderston Duns, Berwickshire TD11 3PP. Tel: 011361 882636

IRELAND
Bantry House Bantry, Co. Cork. Tel: 00353 2750047 fx 2750795
Benvarden Garden Dervock, Ballymoney, CO. Antrim. Tel: 012657 41331
Kylemore Abbey Kylemore, Connemara. Tel: 0195 41146, or shops 0195 41113
Mount Usher Gardens Ashford. Tel: 00353 404 40205 /40116
Powerscourt Gardens & Waterfall Enniskerry, Co. Wicklow. Tel: 00353 1 204 6000

Properties Open All Year

ENGLAND

BERKSHIRE

The Savill Garden, Windsor Great Park,
Tel: 01753 860222 (Crown Property).
Windsor Castle, Windsor, SL4 INJ Tel: 01753 868286

BUCKINGHAMSHIRE

Stowe Landscape Garden, Buckingham, Buckinghamshire
MK18 5EH Tel: 01280 822850

CAMBRIDGESHIRE

Oliver Cromwell's House, 29 Mary Street, Ely CB7 4DF
Tel: 01353 665555 ext.294, Fax: 01353 668518

CORNWALL

Burncoose Nurseries & Garden, Gwennap, Redruth
TR16 6BJ Tel: 01209 861112
Mount Edgcumbe House & Country Park, Cremyll,
Torpoint PL10 1HZ Tel: 01752 822236

CUMBRIA

Hutton-In-The-Forest, Penrith Tel: 017684 84449
Naworth Castle, Brampton CA8 2HF Tel: 0169 773229

DERBYSHIRE

Carnfield Hall, S. Normanton, Nr Alfreton, Derbeyshire
Tel: 01773 520084
Elvaston Castle, Burrowash Road, Elvaston, DE72 3EP

DEVON

Buckfastleigh Abbey, Totnes, Devon.

DORSET

Athelhampton House & Gardens, Athelhampton,
Dorchester Tel: 01305 848363, Fax: 01305 848135
Christchurch Priory, Quay Road, Christchurch, BH23 1BU.
Tel: 01202 485804, Fax: 01202 488645
Forde Abbey, Chard Tel: 01460 220231

GLOUCESTERSHIRE

Barnsley House Garden, The Close, Barnsley,
Nr Cirencester GL7 5EE.
Frampton Court, Frampton-on-Severn
Gloucester GL2 7EU Tel: 01452 740267

HAMPSHIRE

Beaulieu, Brockenhurst, SO42 7ZN Tel: 01590 612345
Langley Boxwood Nursery, Rake, Nr. Liss, GU33 7JL
Tel: 01730 894467, Fax: 01730 894703
Spinners Garden, Boldre, Lymington, SO41 5QE.
Tel: 01590 673347
Gilbert White's House & Garden & The Oates Museum,
'The Wakes' Selborne, Nr Alton, GU34 3JH

HERTFORDSHIRE

Cathedral & Abbey Church Of St. Alban, St. Albans,
Hertfordshire AL1 1BY.

HEREFORD & WORCESTER

Dinmore Manor & Gardens, Nr Hereford HR4 8EE
Tel: 01432 830322

KENT

Hall Place, Bourne Road, Bexley, DA5 1PQ.
Tel: 01322 526574, Fax: 10322 522921
Ladham House, Gouldhurst, Tel: 01580 212674
Leeds Castle, Maidenhead.
Lullingstone Castle, Eynsford, Kent DA14 OJA.
Tel: 01322 862114
The New College Of Cobham, Cobham, Nr Gravesend,
DA12 3BX Tel: 01474 812503
Owl House Gardens, Lamberhurst, Tel: 01892 890962
The Theatre Royal, 102 High Street, Chatham, ME4 4BY
Tel: 01634 831028

LANCASHIRE

Towneley Hall Art Gallery & Museums, Burnely, BB11
3RQ Tel: 01282 424213

LONDON

Buckingham Palace, The Queens Gallery, SW1A 1AA
Tel: 0171 839 1377
Burgh House, New End Square, Hampstead,
Tel: 0171 431 0144
College Of Arms, Queen Victoria Stret Tel: 0171 248 2762
Greenwich – Observatory, National Marime Museum,
Romney Road, Greenwich SE10 9NF. Tel: 0181 858 4422
Kew Gardens, Royal Botanic Gardens, Kew, Richmond
Tel: 0181 940 1171
Syon Park, Brentford TW8 8JF. Tel: 0181 560 0881
Tower of London, Tower Hill Tel: 0171 709 0765
Wallace Collection, Hertford House, Manchester Square
Tel: 0171 935 0687, Fax: 0171 224 2155

NORFOLK

Norwich Castle Museum, Norwich NR1 3JU
Tel: 01603 223624
Walsingham Abbey Grounds, Walsingham, NR22 6BP.
Tel: 01328 820 259
Wolterton Park, Erpingham Tel: 01263 584175

NORTHAMPTONSHIRE

Castle Ashby House, Castle Ashby, Northampton NN7
1LQ. Tel: 01604 696696, Fax: 01604 696516

NOTTINGHAMSHIRE

Norwood Park, Southwell, Nottingham NG25 OP
Tel: 01636 815649, Fax: 01636 815649

OXFORDSHIRE

Broughton Castle, Banbury, OX15 5EB Tel: 01295 262624
Rousham House, Rousham, Steeple Aston, OX6 3QX.
Tel: 01869 347110
University Of Oxford Botanic Gardens, Rose Lane, Oxford
OX1 4AX.
Wallingford Castle Gardens, Castle Street, Wallingford
Tel: 01491 835373
Waterperry Gardens Ltd, Nr Wheatley, Oxfordshire
Tel: 01844 339226/254

SHROPSHIRE

Ludlow Castle, Castle Square, Ludlow
Tel – Custodian: 01584 873947.
Shipton Hall, Much Wenlock TE13 6JZ. Tel: 01746 785 225
Walcot Hall, Lydbury North, Nr. Bishops Castle, SY7 8AZ
Tel: 0171 581 2782

SOMERSET

Hestercombe Gardens, Cheddon Fitzpain, Taunton,
TA2 8LG Tel: 01823 423923

STAFFORDSHIRE

Dunwood Hall, Longsdon, Nr. Leek ST9 9AR
Tel: 01538 385071
Ford Green Hall, Ford Green Road Smallthorne,
Stoke-on-Trent. Tel: 01782 233195
Sandon Hall, Sandon, Stafford Tel: 01889 508004

SUFFOLK

Christchurch Mansion, Christchurch Park, Ipswich
Tel: 01473 253246, Fax: 01473 281274
Gainsborough's House, 46 Gainsborough Street, Sudbury
CO10 6EU Tel: 01787 372958, Fax: 01787 376991
Ipswich Museum, Ipswich IP1 3QH Tel: 01473 213761

SURREY

Claremont Landscape Garden, Portsmouth Road, Esher
Tel: 01372 467842
Painshill Landscape Gardens, Portsmouth Road, Cobham
KT11 1JE. Tel: 01932 868113, Fax: 01932 868001

SUSSEX

Anne Of Cleves House, 52 Southover High Street, Lewes
BN7 1JA. Tel: 01273 474610, Fax: 01273 486990
Borde Hill, Balcombe Road, Haywards Heath S16 1XP.
Tel: 01444 450326
Chichester Cathedral, West Street, Chichester PO19 1PX.
Tel: 01243 782595, Fax: 01243 536190

Lewes Castle, Barbican House, 169 High Street, Lewes
BN7 1YE. Tel: 01273 486290, Fax: 01273 486990
Pallant House,, 9 North Pallant, Chichester PO19 1TJ
Tel: 01243 774557
Preston Manor, Preston Drove, Brighton BN1 6SD
Tel: 01273 290900, Fax: 01273 292871
Royal Botanic Gardens, Kew At Wakehurst Place, Ardingly,
Nr Haywards Heath RH17 6TN Tel: 01444 894066
The Royal Pavilion, Brighton, East Sussex BN1 1EE
Tel: 01273 290900, Fax: 01273 292871
Saint Hill Manor, Sant Hill Road, East Grinstead
RH19 4JY Tel: 01342 326711

WARWICKSHIRE

Lord Leycester Hospital, High Street, Warwick, CV34 4BH.
Shakespeare Birthplace Trust, 38/39 Henley Street, Stratford
upon Avon. Tel: 01789 204016
Warwick Castle, Warwick, CV34 4QU. Tel: 01976 406600

WEST MIDLANDS

Birmingham Botanical Gardens & Glasshouses, Westbourne
Road, Edgbaston, Birmingham, B15 3TR.
Tel: 0121 454 1860, Fax: 0121 454 7835
Soho House, Soho Avenue, Handsworth, Birmingham
B18 5LB Tel: 0121 554 9122

WILTSHIRE

Stourhead, Stourton, Mere BA12 6QH Tel: 01747 841152

YORKSHIRE

Aske Hall, Aske, Richmond DL10 5HJ. Tel: 01748 850391
Bolton Abbey, Skipton, North Yorkshire BD23 6EX.
Tel: 01756 710227, Fax: 01756 710535
Oakwell Hall, Nutter Lane, Birstall, Batley
Tel: 01924 326240
Red House, Oxford Road, Gomersal, Cleckheaton
Tel: 01274 335100
Sewerby Hall & Gardens, Church Lane, Sewerby,
Bridlington, YO15 1EA. Tel: 01262 673769
Skipton Castle, Skipton, North Yorkshire BD23 1AQ.
Tel: 01756 792442, Fax: 01756 796100
Wilberforce House, 25 High Street, Kingston-upon-Hull,
HU1 1EP. Tel: 01482 613902

WALES

St. Davids Cathedral, The Deanery, The Close, St. Davids,
Pembrokeshire. Tel: 01437 720202, Fax: 01437 721 885

IRELAND

Antrim Castle Gardens, Antrim Tel: 01849 428000
Dublin Writers Museum, 18 Parnell Square, Dublin 1.
Tel: 00 353 1 872 2077, Fax: 00 353 1 872 2231
Kylemore Abbey, Conemara, Co. Galway.
Tel: 00 353 95 41146, Fax: 00 353 95 41123
Malahide Castle, Malahide, Co. Dublin.
Tel: 00 353 1 846 2184, Fax: 00 353 1 846 2537
Powerscourt Gardens & Waterfall, Enniskerry, Co. Wicklow.
Tel: 00 353 204 6000, Fax: 00 353 28 63561
Newbridge House, Donabate, Co Dublin.
Tel: 00 353 1 8436534, Fax: 00 353 1 8462537
Johnstown Castle Demesne, Wexford.
Tel: 00 353 53 42888, Fax: 00 353 53 42004

SCOTLAND

Ayton Castle, Eyemouth, Berwickshire TD14 5RD.
Tel: 018907 81212, Fax: 018907 81550
Dalmeny House, South Queensferry, Edinburgh EH30 9TQ
Tel: 0131 331 1888, Fax: 0131 331 1788
Palace Of Holyroodhouse, Edinburgh, EH8 8DY
Tel: 0131 556 7371.

FRANCE

Chateau Des Baux, 13520 Les Baux de Provence, Provence
Chateau De Martinvast, 50690 Martinvast, Normandy
Chateau De Thoiry, 78770 Thoiry
Chateau De Valencay, 36600 Valencay
Eprussi de Rothschild Villa, 06230 St Jean Cap Ferrat
Musée Jacquemart–André, 158, bd Haussmann, 75008 Paris

Properties with Conference Facilties

ENGLAND

BEDFORDSHIRE

Woburn Abbey Woburn MK43 OTP. Tel: 01525 290666; Catering 01525 290662; Antiques Centre 01525 290350

BERKSHIRE

Eton College The Visits Office, Windsor . Tel: 01753 671177

Highclere Castle Newbury RG15 9RN Tel: 01635 253210

BUCKINGHAMSHIRE

Stowe School Buckingham MK18 5EH. Tel: 01280 813650 house 822850 gardens

Waddesdon Manor The Dairy, Nr Aylesbury HP18 OJW. Tel: 01296 651236 Fax: 651142

CAMBRIDGESHIRE

Kimbolton Castle Kimbolton School, Kimbolton PE18 OAE. Tel: 01480 860505

CHESHIRE

Adlington Hall Macclesfield SK10 4LF. Tel: 01625 829206

Arley Hall and Gardens Nr Great Budworth, Northwich CW9 6NA. Tel: 01565 777353

Capesthorne Hall Siddington, Macclesfield SK11 9JY. Tel: 01625 861221 Fax: 01625 861619

Tabley House Knutsford WA16 OHB. Tel: 01565 750151

Tatton Park Knutsford WA16 6QN. Tel: 01565 654822

CORNWALL

Trelissick Garden Feock, Nr Truro TR3 6QL. Tel: 01872 862090; Restaurant 01872 863486

COUNTY DURHAM

Auckland Castle Bishop Auckland DL14 7NR. Tel: 01388 601627

Durham Castle University of Durham, Durham DH1 3RW. Tel: 0191 374 3864

CUMBRIA

Appleby Castle Appleby-in-Westmorland, CA16 6XH. Tel: 017683 51402

Dalemain Nr Penrith CA11 0HB. Tel: 017684 86450

Muncaster Castle Ravenglass CA18 1RQ. Tel: 01229 717614

Naworth Castle The Gatehouse, Naworth, Brampton CA8 2HE. Tel: 016977 3229 /2761

DERBYSHIRE

Elvaston Castle Derby DE72 3EP. Tel: 01332 571342

DEVON

Bickleigh Castle Bickleigh, Tiverton EX16 8RP. Tel: 01884 855363

Buckfast Abbey Buckfastleigh TQ11 OEE. Tel: 01364 643891

Naworth Castle, Cumbria

Endsleigh House The Endsleigh Charitable Trust, Milton Abbot, Nr. Tavistock PL19 0PQ. Tel: 01822 870248

Powderham Castle Kenton, Exeter EX6 8JQ. Tel: 01626 890243

Tiverton Castle Tiverton EX16 6RP. Tel: 01884 253200

Torre Abbey The Kings Drive, Torquay TQ2 5JX. Tel: 01803 293593

Ugbrooke House Chudleigh TQ13 OAD. Tel: 01626 852179

DORSET

Athelhampton House & Gardens Athelhampton, Dorchester DT2 7LG. Tel: 01305 848363

Knoll Gardens & Nursery Hampreston, Nr Wimbourne BH21 7ND. Tel: 011202 873931

ESSEX

Gosfield Hall Halstead, CO9 1SF (Limited facilities). Tel 01787 472914

Layer Marney Tower Colchester CO5 9US. Tel: 01206 330784

GLOUCESTERSHIRE

Chavenage Tetbury GL8 8XP. Tel: 01666 502329

Owlpen Manor Uley, Nr Dursley GL11 5BZ. Tel: 01453 860261

Sudeley Castle Winchcombe GL54 5JD. Tel: 01242 602308

HAMPSHIRE

Avington Park Winchester SO21 1DD. Tel: 01962 779260

Beaulieu Montagu Ventures Ltd, Beaulieu, Brockenhurst SO42 7ZN. Tel: 01590 612345 Fax: 612624

Mottisfont Abbey Garden Mottisfont, SO51 0LP. Tel: 01794 341220

Stratfield Saye House Reading RG7 2BT. Tel: 01256 882882

HEREFORD & WORCESTER

Avoncroft Museum of Buildings Stoke Heath, Bromsgrove B60 4JR. Tel: 01527 831886 or 831363

Dinmore Manor Nr Hereford HR4 8EE. Tel: 01432 830503

Eastnor Castle Nr Ledbury, Hereford HR8 1RD. Tel: 01531 633160/632302

HERTFORDSHIRE

Gardens of the Rose Chiswell Green, St. Albans AL2 3NR. Tel: 01727 850461

Hatfield House Hatfield AL9 5NQ. Tel: 01707 262823 Fax: 275719

KENT

Cobham Hall Cobham, Nr. Gravesend DA12 3BL. Tel: 01474 824319/823371

Finchcocks Goudhurst TN7 1HH. Tel: 01580 211702

Gad's Hill Place Gad's Hill School, Rochester ME3 7AA. Tel: 014748 22366

Hever Castle & Gardens Hever, Nr Edenbridge TN8 7NG. Tel: 01732 865224 DIRECT 861709

Leeds Castle Maidstone ME17 1PL. Tel: 01622 765400 Fax: 735616

Penshurst Place Penshurst, Tunbridge Wells TN11 8DG. Tel: 01892 870307

Squerryes Court Westerham TN16 1SJ. Tel: 01959 562345 or 563118

LANCASHIRE

Towneley Hall Art Gallery & Museum and Museum of Local Crafts & Industries Burnley BD11 3RQ. Tel: 01282 424213

LEICESTERSHIRE

Belvoir Castle The Estate Office, Grantham NG32 1PD.

Stanford Hall Stanford Park, Lutterworth LE17 6DH. Tel: 01788 860250

LINCOLNSHIRE

Grimsthorpe Castle and Gardens Grimsthorpe, Bourne PE10 ONB. Tel: 01778 591205

LONDON

Banqueting Hall Whitehall Palace. Tel: 0171 839 8919

Boston Manor Brentford. Tel: 0181 570 0622

Chelsea Physic Garden 66 Royal Hospital Road, Chelsea SW3 4HS. Tel: 0171 352 5646

Greenwich Observatory Queens House, National Maritime Museum, Romney Road, Greenwich SE10 9NF. Tel: 0181 858 4422

Museum of Fulham Palace Bishops Avenue, Fulham SW6 6EA. Tel: 0171 736 3233 General enquiries: 0171 736 3233 Museum & tours

Strawberry Hill House St. Mary's College, Waldegrave Road, Twickenham TW1 4SX. Tel: 0181 240 4000

Syon Park Brentford TW8 8JF. Tel: 0181 560 0881

MERSEYSIDE

Meols Hall Churchtown, Southport PR9 7LZ. Tel: 01704 28326

NORFOLK

Mannington Hall Saxthorpe, Norwich NR11 7BB. Tel: 01263 584175

Wolterton Park Erpingham NR11 7BB. Tel: 01263 584175

NORTHAMPTONSHIRE

Castle Ashby House Castle Ashby, Northampton NN7 1LQ. Tel: 01604 696696

Deene Park Corby NN17 3EW. Tel: 01780 450361 /450278 Fax: 450282

Holdenby House Gardens Holdenby, Northampton NN6 8DJ. Tel: 01604 770074

Lamport Hall and Gardens Northampton NN6 9HD. Tel: 01604 686272

NORTHUMBERLAND

Alnwick Castle Estate Office, Alnwick NE66 1NQ. Tel: 01665 510777

Chillingham Castle & Gardens Chillingham, Alnwick NE66 5NJ. Tel: 01668 215359

NOTTINGHAMSHIRE

Norwood Park Holme Pierrepont, Nr Southwell NG12 2LD.

OXFORDSHIRE

Blenheim Palace Woodstock OX20 1PX. Tel: 01993 811091 Fax: 813527

SHROPSHIRE

Burford House Gardens Tenbury Wells WR15 8HQ. Tel: 01584 810777

Hawkstone Hall and Gardens Weston-U-Redcastle, Shrewsbury SY4 5LG. Tel: 01630 685242

Hawkstone Park Weston-under-Redcastle SY4 5UY. Tel: 01939 200300/200611

Weston Park Weston under Lizard, Nr Shifnal TF11 8LE. Tel: 01952 850207

SOMERSET

Bishop's Palace Wells BA5 2PD. Tel: 01749 678691 The Manager; The Henderson Rooms

Hatch Court Hatch Beauchamp, Taunton TA3 6AA. Tel: 01823 480120

STAFFORDSHIRE

Sandon Hall Sandon ST18 0BZ. Tel: 01889 508004

Shugborough Estate Milford, Stafford ST17 0XB. Tel: 01889 881388

Whitmore Hall Hillside Farm, Whitmore, Newcastle-under-Lyme . Tel: 01782 680478

SUFFOLK

Hengrave Hall Centre Bury St Edmunds IP28 6LZ. Tel: 01284 701561

Kentwell Hall Long Melford, Nr. Sudbury CO10 9BA. Tel: 01787 310207

Somerleyton Hall Nr Lowestoft . Tel: 01502 730224

Wingfield Old College Wingfield, Eye IP21 5RA. Tel: 01379 384888

SURREY

Clandon Park West Clandon, Guildford GU4 7RQ. Tel: 01483 222482

Farnham Castle Farnham GU7 0AG. Tel: 01252 721194

Loseley House Estate Office, Guildford GU3 1HS. Tel: 01483 304440

SUSSEX

Arundel Castle Arundel, Arundel . Tel: 01903 883136

Bentley House & Gardens Halland, Nr Lewes BN8 5AF. Tel: 01825 840573

Borde Hill Garden Haywards Heath RH16 1XP. Tel: 01444 450326

Firle Place Nr Lewes BN8 6LP. Tel: 01273 858188

Goodwood House Goodwood, Chichester PO18 OPX. Tel: 01243 774107

Leonardslee Lower Beeding, Horsham RH13 6PP. Tel: 01403 891212

Preston Manor Preston Drove, Brighton BN1 6SD. Tel: 01273 603005 Fax: 779108

Royal Pavilion Brighton BN1 1EE. Tel: 01273 290900

Saint Hill Manor Saint Hill Road, East Grinstead RH19 4JY. Tel: 01342 326711

West Dean Gardens West Dean Estate, Nr Chichester PO18 0QZ. Tel: 01243 818210

WARWICKSHIRE

Coughton Court Alcester B49 5JA. Tel: 01789 400777 01789 762435 visitor information

Lord Leycester Hospital High Street, Warwick CV34 4BH. Tel: 01926 492797

Warwick Castle Warwick CV34 4QV. Tel: 01926 495421

WEST MIDLANDS

Birmingham Botanical Gardens and Glasshouses Westbourne Road, Edgbaston, Birmingham B15 3TR. Tel: 0121 454 1860

WILTSHIRE

Longleat House The Estate Office, Warminster BA12 7NN. Tel: 01985 844400

Wilton House Wilton, Salisbury . Tel: 01722 743115

YORKSHIRE

Aske Hall Aske, Rickmond DL10 5HJ. Tel: 01748 823222 Fax 01748 823252

The Bar Convent 17 Blossom Street, York Y02 2AH. Tel: 01904 643238

Bolton Abbey Estate Bolton Abbey, Skipton BD23 6EX. Tel: 01756 710533

Bolton Castle Leyburn DL8 4ET. Tel: 01969 623981 Fax: 623332

Cannon Hall Museum Cawthorne S75 4AT. Tel: 01226 790270

Duncombe Park Helmsley, York, Helmsley YO6 5EB. Tel: 01439 770213

Elsham Hall Country and Wildlife Park The Estate Office, Brigg DN20 0QZ. Tel: 01652 688698

Fairfax House Castlegate, York YO1 1RN. Tel: 01904 655543

Harewood House and Bird Garden The Estate Office, Harewood, Leeds LS17 9LQ. Tel: 0113 288 6331

Hovingham Hall Hovingham, York YO6 4LU. Tel: 01653 628206

Newby Hall & Gardens Ripon HG4 5AE. Tel: 01423 322583

Ripley Castle Ripley, Harrogate HG3 3AY. Tel: 01423 770152

Sewerby Hall and Gardens Church Lane, Sewerby, Bridlington YO15 1EA. Tel: 01262 677974

WALES

Cardiff Castle Mrs Sally Hart, Leisure Services Department, Cardiff . Tel: 01222 878100 Fax: 01222 231417

Dinefwr Park Llandeilo SA19 6RT. Tel: 01558 823902

Tredegar House Newport, Newport NP1 9YW. Tel: 01633 815880

SCOTLAND

Ayton Castle Estate Office, Eyemouth TD14 5RD. Tel: 018907 81212

Bowhill Nr Selkirk TD7 5ET. Tel: 01750 22204

Callendar House Falkirk FK1 1YR. Tel: 01324 612134

Dalmeny House Charisma, South Queensferry EH30 9TQ. Tel: 0131 331 1888

Dunrobin Castle Golspie, Sutherland KW10 6SF. Tel: 01408 633177/633268

Fasque Fettercairn, Laurencekirk AB30 1DN. Tel: 01561 340202 or 01561 340569

Floors Castle Roxburghe Estates Office, Kelso TD5 7SF. Tel: 01573 223333

Glamis Castle Estate Office, Glamis DD8 1RT. Tel: 01307 840393/242

Manderston Duns, Berwickshire TD11 3PP. Tel: 01361 882636

Traquair Innerleithen EH44 6PW. Tel: 01896 830323

IRELAND

Antrim Castle Gardens Antrim . Tel: 01849 428000

Bantry House Bantry, Co. Cork . Tel: 00353 2750047 Fax 2750795

Dublin Writer's Museum 18 Parnell Square, Dublin 1 . Tel: 00353 1 872077

SMOKING DAMAGES THE HEALTH
OF THOSE AROUND YOU

Chief Medical Officers' Warning

Properties Offering Accommodation

ENGLAND

BERKSHIRE

Swallowfield Park, Swallowfield, RG7 1TG
Tel: 01734 883815

BUCKINGHAMSHIE

Waddesdon Manor, Nr. Aylesbury, HP18 OJW
Tel: 01296 651236, Fax: 01296 651 142

CORNWALL

Tregrehan, Par, PL24 25J Tel: 01726 814 389/812 438
Accommodation: Self-catering cottages available

CUMBRIA

Appleby Castle, Boroughgate, Appleby-in-Westmorland,
CA16 6XH Tel: 01763 51402

Dalemain, Nr. Penrith, CA11 0HB Tel: 017684 86450
Accommodation: B&B, Parkhouse Farm, Dalemain
Tel: 017684 86212

Naworth Castle, Brampton Castle, Brampton CA8 2HE
Tel: (016977) 3229 Accommodation: There are 10
bedrooms available for overnight parties.

DEVON

Buckfast Abbey, Buckfastleigh TQ11 OEE
Tel: 01364 642519, Fax: 01364 643891

Endsleigh House, Milton Abbot, Tavistock PL19 OPQ
Tel: 01822 870248, Fax: 01822 870502

Flete, Ermington, Ivybridge, Plymouth, PL21 9NZ
Tel: 01752 830 308, Fax: 01752 830 309

Fursdon, Cadbury, Thorverton, Exeter EX5 JS
Tel: 01392 860860

Kingston House, Staverton, Totnes,TQ9 6AR
Tel: 01803 762235 Luxury accommodation in house and
self-contained cottages.

Tiverton Castle, Tiverton EX16 6RP Tel: 01884 253200
Accommodation: 3 superb self-catering holiday
apartments inside Castle available weekly, short breaks,
or winter lettings. Graded 4 Keys Highly Commended.

Yarde, Marlborough, Nr Salcombe TQ7 3BY
Tel: 01548 842367

DORSET

Smedmore House, Kimmeridge BH20 5PG
Tel: 01929 480719

COUNTY DURHAM

Durham Castle, Durham Tel: 0191 374 3863
Accommodation: Contact 0191-374 3863

ESSEX

Gosfield Hall, Halstead, CO9 1SF Tel: 01787 472 914

GLOUCESTERSHIRE

Owlpen Manor, Uley, nr Dursley GL11 5BZ
Tel: 01453 860261 Accommodation: Nine period
cottages available, including listed buildings.

Sudeley Castle and Gardens, Winchcombe, GL54 5JD
Tel: 01242 603197/602308 Accommodation: 14 romantic
Cotswold Cottages on Castle Estate. Private guided tours
of Castle Apartments and Gardens by prior arrangement.
Schools educational pack available.

HEREFORD & WORCESTER

Bernithan Court, Llangarron
Accommodation: On application.

Brobury House & Garden, Borbury, Nr Hereford, HR3
6BS Tel: 01981 500 229

Burton Court, Eardisland HR6 9DN Tel: 01544 388231
Accommodation: Holiday flat, self contained – sleeps 7.

Eastnor Castle, Nr Ledbury, HR8 1RD
Tel: 01531 633160/632302, Fax: 01531 631766
Luxury accommodation for select groups.

Hergest Croft Gardens, Kington Tel: 01544 230160
Accommodation: Self-catering house – nursery sleeps 7.

Kentchurch Court, Hereford Tel: 01981 240228
Accommodation by appointment.

Kinnersley Castle, Kinnersley Tel: 01544 327407
Accommodation for residential groups by arrangement,
retreats etc.

Moccas Court, Moccas HR2 9LH Tel: 01981 500381
Accommodation: Available at The Red Lion Hotel,
Bredwardine.

KENT

Cobham Hall, Cobham, nr. Gravesend, DA12 3BL
Tel: 01474 824319/823371 Accommodation: The house,
grounds, accommodation (250 beds) and sports facilities
are available for private hire, wedding receptions, business
conferences, residential and non-residential courses and
film and photographic location.

Great Maytham Hall, Rolvenden, Cranbrook, TN17 4NE
Tel: 01580 241 346, Fax: 01580 241 038

NORFOLK

Walsingham Abbey, Estate Office, Walsingham, NR22
6BP Tel: 01328 820259 Accommodation: Also available
in the village (Hotel, B&B etc.).

NORTHAMPTONSHIRE

Castle Ashby House, Castle Ashby, Northampton NN7
1LQ Tel: 01604 696696
Accommodation: Holiday cottages.

Deene Park, Corby, Northants Tel: 01780 450278

The Prebendal Manor House, Nassington
Tel: 01780 782575 Accommodation: Bed & Breakfast in
the 15th C Lodgings building.

NORTHUMBERLAND

Alnwick Castle, Alnwick, Northumberland NE66 1NQ
Tel: 01665 510777 Accommodation: Holiday cottages.

Chillingham Castle and Gardens, Alnwick
Tel: 01668 215359 Accommodation: Private family suites
of rooms available.

NOTTINGHAMSHIRE

Carlton Hall, Carlton-On-Trent, Newark NG23 6NW
Tel: 01636 821421 Accommodation: Self-catering by
appointment.

Norwood Park, Southwell, Nottingham NG25 OPF
Tel: 01636 815649

Papplewick Hall, Near Nottingham NG15 8FE
Tel: 0115 9633491 Accommodation: Country House
hospitality, full breakfast and dinner, prices on request.

OXFORDSHIRE

Aynhoe Park, Suite 10, Aynho, Banbury, Oxfordshire,
OX17 3BQ Tel: 01869 810 636

Mapledurham House and Watermill, Mapledurham RG4
7TR Tel: (01734) 723350 Accommodation: Eleven self
catering holiday cottages.

SHROPSHIRE

Upton Cressett Hall, Bridgnorth Tel: 01746 714307,
Accommodation: Self catering accommodation available
in Gatehouse.

Walcot Hall, Lydbury North, Nr Bishops Castle SY7 8AZ
Tel: 0171 581 2782 Accommodation: 3 flats and Ground
Floor wing available all year.

Weston Park, Nr Shifnal TF11 8LE Tel: 01952 850207
Accommodation: Luxury rooms in the house.

STAFFORDSHIRE

Dunwood Hall, Longsdon, Nr Leek, Staffordshire, ST9
9AR Tel: 01538 385071

Shugborough, Stafford ST17 OXB Tel: (01889) 881388
Accommodation: Details of group accommodation can be
obtained from the booking office

SURREY

Albury Park, Albury, Guildford GU5 9BB
Tel: 01483 202 964, Fax: 01483 205 013

Greathed Manor, Dormansland, Lingfield, RH7 6PA
Tel: 01342 832 577, Fax: 01342 836 207

SUSSEX

Danny, Hurstpierpoint, Hassocks BN6 9BB
Tel: 01273 833 000, Fax: 01273 832 436

Goodwood House, Chichester PO18 OPX
Tel: (01243) 774107 Accommodation: Goodwood Park
Hotel, Golf and Country Club- reservations (01345)
123333/(01243) 775537

Hammerwood Park, nr East Grinstead RH19 3QE
Tel: 01342 850594, Fax: 01342 850864
Accommodation: B&B with a difference in an idyllically
peaceful location only 20 minutes from Gatwick.

WARWICKSHIRE

Coughton Court, Alcester B49 5JA Tel: 01789 400777
(01789) 762435 (Visitor information) Accommodation:
Luxury accommodation available for select groups.

WILTSHIRE

Pythouse, Tisbury, Salisbury SP3 6PB
Tel: 01747 870 210, Fax: 01747 871 786

YORKSHIRE

The Bar Convent, 17 Blossom Street, York YO2 2AH
Tel: 01904 643238

Bolton Abbey, Skipton, North Yorkshire, BD23 6EX
Tel: 01756 710 535

Ripley Castle, Ripley HG3 3AY Tel: 01423 770152
Accommodation: 25 deluxe bedrooms at the Estate owned
Boar's Head Hotel, 100 yards from the Castle in Ripley
village. The hotel is rated RAC****.

IRELAND

Bantry House, Bantry, Co. Cork. Tel: (027) 50047
Accommodation: Bed & Breakfast and dinner. Nine
rooms en suite.

Glin Castle, Glin Tel: (068) 34173/34112
Accommodation: Overnight stays arranged. Castle can be
rented.

Powerscourt Gardens & Waterfall, Enniskerry, Co.
Wicklow, Ireland Tel: 00353 204 6000

SCOTLAND

Ayton Castle, Eyemouth, Berwickshire TD14 5RD
Tel: 018907 812812

Dunvegan Castle, Isle Of Skye Tel: (01470) 521206
Accommodation: Self catering cottages within grounds.

Manderston, Duns, Berwickshire TD11 3PP
Tel: (01361) 883450 Accommodation: By arrangement.

Sorn Castle, Sorn, Mauchline Tel: (01505) 612124
Accommodation: Available - contact Cluttons.

Traquair, Innerleithen EH44 6PW Tel: (01896) 830323,
Accommodation: 2 rooms B&B and Holiday flat to rent.

WALES

Gwydir Castle, Llanrwst, Gwynedd Tel: 01492 641 687

271

Johansens Recommendations

Alphabetical list of Johansens Recommendations in Great Britain & Ireland

HOTELS

ENGLAND

AVON/BATH – Please refer to Somerset Listing

BEDFORDSHIRE

Flitwick Manor	Flitwick	01525 712242
Moore Place Hotel	Milton Keynes	01908 282000
Woodlands Manor	Bedford	01234 363281

BERKSHIRE

Chauntry House Hotel & Restaurant	Bray-on-Thames	01628 73991
Cliveden	Maidenhead	01628 668561
Donnington Valley Hotel & Golf Course	Newbury	01635 551199
Elcot Park Hotel & Country Club	Newbury	01488 658100
Fredrick's Hotel & Restaurant	Maidenhead	01628 635934
The French Horn	Sonning-On-Thames	01734 692204
Hollington House Hotel	Newbury	01635 255100
Monkey Island Hotel	Bray-on-Thames	01628 23400
Oakley Court	Windsor	01753 609988
Royal Berkshire	Ascot	01344 23322
Swan Diplomat	Streatley-On-Thames	01491 873737

BRISTOL

Swallow Royal Hotel	Bristol	0117 9255200

BUCKINGHAMSHIRE

Danesfield House	Marlow-On-Thames	01628 891010
Hartwell House	Aylesbury	01296 747444
The Priory Hotel	Aylesbury	01296 641239
Stoke Park	Slough	01753 717171

CAMBRIDGESHIRE

The Haycock	Peterborough	01780 782223
The Old Bridge Hotel	Huntingdon	01480 452681

CHESHIRE

The Alderley Edge Hotel	Alderley Edge	01625 583033
The Bridge Hotel	Prestbury	01625 829326
Broxton Hall Country House Hotel	Chester	01829 782321
The Chester Grosvenor	Chester	01244 324024
Crabwall Manor	Chester	01244 851666
Nunsmere Hall	Chester	01606 889100
Rookery Hall	Nantwich	01270 610016
Rowton Hall Hotel	Chester	01244 335262
The Stanneylands Hotel	Manchester	01625 525225
Willington Hall Hotel	Willington	01829 752321
Woodland Park Hotel	Altrincham	0161 928 8631

CORNWALL

Alverton Manor	Truro	01872 276633
Budock Vean Golf & Country Club	Falmouth	01326 250288
The Garrack Hotel	St Ives	01736 796199
The Lugger Hotel	Portloe	01872 501322
Meudon Hotel	Falmouth	01326 250541
Nansidwell Country House	Falmouth	01326 250340
The Nare Hotel	Veryan	01872 501279
Penmere Manor	Falmouth	01326 211411
Rose-in-Vale Country House Hotel	St Agnes	01872 552202
Talland Bay Hotel	Talland-By-Looe	01503 272667
The Well House	St Keyne	01579 342001

CO DURHAM

Headlam Hall	Darlington	01325 730238
Lumley Castle Hotel	Durham	0191 389 1111
Redworth Hall Hotel & Country Club	Newton Aycliffe	01388 772442

CUMBRIA

Appleby Manor Country House Hotel	Appleby-in-Westmorland	017683 51571
The Borrowdale Gates Hotel	Keswick	017687 77204
Farlam Hall Hotel	Brampton	016977 46234
Gilpin Lodge	Windermere	015394 88818
Graythwaite Manor	Grange-Over-Sands	015395 32001
Holbeck Ghyll Country House Hotel	Ambleside	015394 32375
Lakeside Hotel On Lake Windermere	Windermere	015395 31207
Langdale Chase	Windermere	015394 32201
Langdale Hotel & Country Club	Ambleside	015394 37302
Linthwaite House Hotel	Windermere	015394 88600
Michaels Nook	Grasmere	015394 35496
Nanny Brow Country House Hotel	Ambleside	015394 32036
The Old Vicarage Country House Hotel	Witherslack	015395 52381
Rampsbeck Country House Hotel	Lake Ullswater	017684 86442
Rothay Manor	Ambleside	015394 33605
Sharrow Bay Country House Hotel	Lake Ullswater	017684 86301
Temple Sowerby House Hotel	Penrith	017683 61578
Tufton Arms Hotel	Appleby-In-Westmorland	017683 51593
The Wordsworth Hotel	Grasmere	015394 35592

DERBYSHIRE

Callow Hall	Ashbourne	01335 343403
The Cavendish Hotel	Baslow	01246 582311
Fischer's	Baslow	01246 583259
George Hotel	Hathersage	01433 650436
Hassop Hall	Bakewell	01629 640488
Makeney Hall Country House Hotel	Derby	01332 842999
Mickleover Court	Derby	01332 521234
Riber Hall	Matlock	01629 582795
Riverside Country House Hotel	Ashford-In-The-Water	01629 814275
The Wind In The Willows	Glossop	01457 868001

DEVON

The Arundell Arms	Lifton	01566 784666
Bolt Head Hotel	Salcombe	01548 843751
Brookdale House Restaurant & Hotel	North Huish	01548 821661
Combe House Hotel	Gittisham	01404 42756
Gidleigh Park	Chagford	01647 432367
Holne Chase Hotel	Ashburton	01364 631471
The Horn Of Plenty	Tavistock	01822 832528
Hotel Riviera	Sidmouth	01395 515201
Ilsington Country Hotel	Ilsington	01364 661452
Kitley	Plymouth	01752 881555
Lewtrenchard Manor	Lewdown	01566 783 256
Northcote Manor	South Molton	01769 560501
Orestone Manor Hotel & Restaurant	Torquay	01803 328098
The Osborne Hotel	Torquay	01803 213311
The Palace Hotel	Torquay	01803 200200
Passage House Hotel	Newton Abbot	01626 55515
Percy's at Coombeshead	Launceston	01409 211236
Tytherleigh Cot Hotel	Axminster	01460 221170
Watersmeet Hotel	Woolacombe	01271 870333
Woolacombe Bay Hotel	Woolacombe	01271 870388
Whitechapel Manor	South Molton	01769 573377
Bel Alp House	Haytor	01364 661217
The Edgemoor	Bovey Tracey	01626 832466
Soar Mill Cove Hotel	Salcombe	01548 561566

DORSET

Bridge House Hotel	Beaminster	01308 862200
The Haven Hotel	Poole	01202 707333
The Mansion House Hotel	Poole	01202 685666
Moonfleet Manor	Weymouth	01305 786948
The Norfolk Royale Hotel	Bournemouth	01202 551521
Plumber Manor	Sturminster Newton	01258 472507
The Priory	Wareham	01929 551666
Summer Lodge	Evershot	01935 83424

EAST SUSSEX

Ashdown Park Hotel	Forest Row	01342 824988
Broomhill Lodge	Rye	01797 280421
Buxted Park Country House Hotel	Buxted,Near Uckfield	01825 732711
Dale Hill Hotel And Golf Club	Ticehurst	01580 200112
Horsted Place Sporting Estate And Hotel	Uckfield	01825 750581
Netherfield Place	Battle	01424 774455
Powdermills Hotel	Battle	01424 775511
Topps Hotel	Brighton	01273 729334
White Lodge Country House Hotel	Alfriston	01323 870265

ESSEX

Five Lakes Hotel Golf & Country Club	Colchester	01621 868888
Maison Talbooth	Dedham	01206 322367
Pontlands Park Country Hotel	Chelmsford	01245 476444
The White Hart Hotel & Restaurant	Colchester	01376 561654
Whitehall	Stansted	01279 850603

GLOUCESTERSHIRE

Calcot Manor	Tetbury	01666 890391
Charingworth Manor	Chipping Campden	01386 593555
The Cheltenham Park Hotel	Cheltenham	01242 222021
The Close Hotel	Tetbury	01666 502272
Corse Lawn House Hotel	Tewkesbury	01452 780479
The Cotswold House	Chipping Campden	01386 840330
The Grapevine Hotel	Stow-On-The-Wold	01451 830344
The Greenway	Cheltenham	01242 862352
Hatton Court Hotel	Gloucester	01452 617412
Hotel On The Park	Cheltenham	01242 518898
Lords Of The Manor Hotel	Upper Slaughter	01451 820243
Lower Slaughter Manor	Lower Slaughter	01451 820456
The Manor House Hotel	Moreton-In-Marsh	01608 650501
The Painswick Hotel	Painswick	01452 812160
The Snooty Fox	Tetbury	01666 502436
Stonehouse Court	Stonehouse	01453 825155
The Swan Hotel At Bibury	Bibury	01285 740695
Washbourne Court Hotel	Lower Slaughter	01451 822143
Wyck Hill House	Stow-On-The-Wold	01451 831936

GREATER MANCHESTER

Etrop Grange	Manchester Airport	0161 499 0500

HAMPSHIRE

Careys Manor Hotel	Brockenhurst	01590 623551
Chewton Glen	New Milton	01425 275341
Esseborne Manor	Andover	01264 736444
Fifehead Manor	Middle Wallop	01264 781565
Hotel Du Vin & Bistro	Winchester	01962 841414
Lainston House Hotel	Winchester	01962 863588
The Montagu Arms Hotel	Beaulieu	01590 612324
New Park Manor	Brockenhurst	01590 623467
Parkhill Hotel	Lyndhurst	01703 282944
Passford House Hotel	Lymington	01590 682398
Rhinefield House Hotel	Brockenhurst	01590 622922
Stanwell House	Lymington	01590 677123
Tylney Hall	Basingstoke	01256 764881

HEREFORDSHIRE

The Chase Hotel	Ross-On-Wye	01989 763161
Hope End Hotel	Ledbury	01531 633613
Pengethley Manor	Ross-On-Wye	01989 730211
Penrhos Court	Kington	01544 230720

HERTFORDSHIRE

Down Hall Country House Hotel	Bishop's Stortford	01279 731441
Hanbury Manor	Ware	01920 487722
The Manor of Groves Hotel	Harlow	01279 600777
Pendley Manor Hotel	Tring	01442 891891
Sopwell House Hotel & Country Club	St Albans	01727 864477
Stocks Hotel Golf & Country Club	Hemel Hempstead	01442 851341
West Lodge Park	Hadley Wood	0181 440 8311

ISLE OF WIGHT

The George Hotel	Yarmouth	01983 760331

KENT

Brandshatch Place Hotel	Fawkham	01474 872239
Bridgewood Manor Hotel	Rochester	01634 201333
Chilston Park	Maidstone	01622 859803
Eastwell Manor	Ashford	01233 219955
Hotel Du Vin & Bistro	Tunbridge Wells	01892 526455
Howfield Manor	Canterbury	01227 738294
Hythe Imperial Hotel	Hythe	01303 267441
Rowhill Grange	Dartford	01322 615136
The Spa Hotel	Tunbridge Wells	01892 520331

LANCASHIRE

The Gibbon Bridge Hotel	Preston	01995 61456

LONDON

The Ascott Mayfair	Mayfair	0171 499 6868
Basil Street Hotel	Knightsbridge	0171 581 3311
The Beaufort	Knightsbridge	0171 584 5252
Beaufort House Apartments	Knightsbridge	0171 584 2600
Blakes Hotel	South Kensington	0171 370 6701
The Cadogan	Knightsbridge	0171 235 7141
Cannizaro House	Wimbledon Common	0181 879 1464
The Cliveden Town House	Knightsbridge	0171 730 6466
The Dorchester	Mayfair	0171 629 8888
Draycott House Apartments	Chelsea	0171 584 4659
The Halcyon	Holland Park	0171 727 7288
Harrington Hall	Kensington	0171 396 9696
The Hempel	Lancaster Gate	0171 298 9000
The Leonard	Portman Square	0171 935 2010
The London Outpost of the Carnegie Club	Knightsbridge	0171 589 7333
The Milestone	Kensington	0171 917 1000
Number Eleven Cadogan Gardens	Knightsbridge	0171 730 7000
Number Sixteen	South Kensington	0171 589 5232
Park Consul Hotel	Chelsea	0171 225 7500
Pembridge Court Hotel	Kensington	0171 229 9977
The Ritz	St James	0171 493 8181

LEICESTERSHIRE

Barnsdale Lodge	Rutland Water	01572 724678
The Lake Isle	Uppingham	01572 822951
Normanton Park Hotel	Rutland Water	01780 720315
The Priest House On the River	Castle Donington	01332 810649
Quorn Country Hotel	Leicester	01509 415050
Stapleford Park, An Outpost of The Carnegie Club	Stapleford	01572 787522

LINCOLNSHIRE

Belton Woods	Grantham	01476 593200
The George Of Stamford	Stamford	01780 755171

MERSEYSIDE

The Woolton Redbourne Hotel	Liverpool	0151 421 1500/428 2152

NORFOLK

Congham Hall	King's Lynn	01485 600250
Park Farm Hotel & Leisure	Norwich	01603 810264
Petersfield House Hotel	Norwich	01692 630741
Sprowston Manor Hotel	Norwich	01603 410871

NORTH YORKSHIRE

The Balmoral Hotel	Harrogate	01423 508208
The Boar's Head Hotel	Harrogate	01423 771888
Crathorne Hall Hotel	Crathorne	01642 700398
The Devonshire Arms Hotel	Bolton Abbey	01756 710441
The Grange Hotel	York	01904 644744
Grants Hotel	Harrogate	01423 560666
Hackness Grange	Scarborough	01723 882345
Hazlewood Castle	Hazlewood	01937 530530
Hob Green Hotel & Restaurant	Harrogate	01423 770031
Middlethorpe Hall	York	01904 641241
Monk Fryston Hall	Leeds	01977 682369
Mount Royale Hotel	York	01904 628856
The Pheasant	Helmsley	01439 771241 /770416
Rudding Park House & Hotel	Harrogate	01423 871350
The Worsley Arms Hotel	Hovingham	01653 628234
Wrea Head Country Hotel	Scarborough	01723 378211
York Pavilion Hotel	York	01904 622099

NORTHAMPTONSHIRE

Hellidon Lakes Hotel & Country Club	Banbury	01327 262550

NORTHUMBERLAND

Linden Hall Hotel	Newcastle-Upon-Tyne	01670 516611
Marshall Meadow Country House Hotel	Berwick-Upon-Tweed	01289 331133
Slaley Hall Hotel Golf Resort & Spa	Newcastle-Upon-Tyne	01434 673350
Tillmouth Park	Berwick-Upon-Tweed	01890 882255

NOTTINGHAMSHIRE

Langar Hall	Nottingham	01949 860559

OXFORDSHIRE

The Bay Tree Hotel & Restaurant	Burford	01993 822791
The Feathers Hotel	Woodstock	01993 812291

- Le Manoir Aux Quat' Saisons ... Oxford ... 01844 278881
- Mill House Hotel ... Kingham ... 01608 658188
- Phyllis Court Club ... Henley-On-Thames ... 01491 574366
- The Plough at Clanfield ... Clanfield ... 01367 810222
- The Springs Hotel ... Wallingford ... 01491 836687
- Studley Priory ... Oxford ... 01865 351203
- Weston Manor ... Oxford ... 01869 350621
- Wroxton House Hotel ... Banbury ... 01295 730777

RUTLAND
- Hambleton Hall ... Oakham ... 01572 756991

SHROPSHIRE
- Albrighton Hall Hotel & Restaurant ... Shrewsbury ... 01939 291000
- Dinham Hall ... Ludlow ... 01584 876464
- Hawkstone Park Hotel ... Shrewsbury ... 01939 200611
- Madeley Court ... Telford ... 01952 680068
- The Old Vicarage Hotel ... Wolverhampton ... 01746 716497
- Rowton Castle Hotel & Restaurant ... Shrewsbury ... 01743 884044

SOMERSET
- The Bath Spa ... Bath ... 01225 444424
- Bindon Country House Hotel ... Taunton ... 01823 400070
- The Castle At Taunton ... Taunton ... 01823 272671
- Charlton House ... Shepton Mallet ... 01749 342008
- Combe Grove Manor & Country Club ... Bath ... 01225 834644
- Daneswood House Hotel ... Bristol South ... 01934 843145
- Homewood Park ... Bath ... 01225 723731
- Hunstrete House ... Bath ... 01761 490490
- Langley House Hotel ... Wiveliscombe ... 01984 623318
- The Mount Somerset Hotel ... Taunton ... 01823 442500
- Periton Park Hotel ... Middlecombe ... 01643 706885
- The Priory ... Bath ... 01225 331922
- The Queensberry ... Bath ... 01225 447928
- The Royal Crescent ... Bath ... 01225 823333
- Rumwell Manor Hotel ... Taunton ... 01823 461902
- Ston Easton Park ... Bath ... 01761 241631

SOUTH YORKSHIRE
- Charnwood Hotel ... Sheffield ... 0114 258 9411
- Whitley Hall Hotel ... Sheffield ... 0114 245 4444

STAFFORDSHIRE
- The Brookhouse ... Burton upon Trent ... 01283 814188
- Hoar Cross Hall Health Spa Resort ... Lichfield ... 01283 575671
- Swinfen Hall ... Lichfield ... 01543 481494

SUFFOLK
- The Angel Hotel ... Bury St Edmunds ... 01284 753926
- Belstead Brook Manor Hotel ... Ipswich ... 01473 684241
- Cornwallis Arms ... Diss ... 01379 870326
- Hintlesham Hall ... Ipswich ... 01473 652268
- Ravenwood Hall ... Bury St Edmunds ... 01359 270345
- Seckford Hall ... Woodbridge ... 01394 385678
- The Swan Hotel ... Southwold ... 01502 722186
- Swynford Paddocks Hotel & Restaurant ... Newmarket ... 01638 570234
- Wentworth Hotel ... Aldeburgh ... 01728 452312

SURREY
- The Angel Posting House And Livery ... Guildford ... 01483 564555
- Coulsdon Manor Hotel ... Croydon ... 0181 668 0414
- Grayshott Hall Health Fitness Retreat ... Grayshott ... 01428 604331
- Great Fosters ... Egham ... 01784 433822
- Langshott Manor ... Gatwick ... 01293 786680
- Lythe Hill Hotel ... Haslemere ... 01428 651251
- Nutfield Priory ... Redhill ... 01737 822066
- Oatlands Park Hotel ... Weybridge ... 01932 847242
- Pennyhill Park Hotel ... Bagshot ... 01276 471774
- The Richmond Gate Hotel ... Richmond-Upon-Thames ... 0181 940 0061
- Woodlands Park Hotel ... Cobham ... 01372 843933

WARWICKSHIRE
- Billesley Manor ... Stratford-Upon-Avon ... 01789 279955
- Coombe Abbey ... Coventry ... 01203 450450
- Ettington Park Hotel ... Stratford-Upon-Avon ... 01789 450123
- The Glebe At Barford ... Warwick ... 01926 624218
- Mallory Court ... Leamington Spa ... 01926 330214
- Nailcote Hall ... Coventry ... 01203 466174
- Nuthurst Grange ... Hockley Heath ... 01564 783972

WEST MIDLANDS
- The Burlington Hotel ... Birmingham ... 0121 643 9191
- The Mill House Hotel ... Birmingham ... 0121 459 5800
- New Hall ... Birmingham ... 0121 378 2442
- The Swallow Hotel ... Birmingham ... 0121 452 1144

WEST SUSSEX
- Alexander House ... Gatwick ... 01342 714914
- Amberley Castle ... Amberley ... 01798 831992
- The Angel Hotel ... Midhurst ... 01730 812421
- Bailiffscourt ... Arundel ... 01903 723511
- Little Thakeham ... Storrington ... 01903 744416
- The Millstream Hotel ... Chichester ... 01243 573234
- Ockenden Manor ... Cuckfield ... 01444 416111
- South Lodge Hotel ... Horsham ... 01403 891711
- The Spread Eagle Hotel ... Midhurst ... 01730 816911

WEST YORKSHIRE
- 42 The Calls ... Leeds ... 0113 244 0099
- Bagden Hall Hotel & Golf Course ... Huddersfield ... 01484 865330
- The Carlton Hotel ... Hebden Bridge ... 01422 844400
- Chevin Lodge Country Park Hotel ... Otley ... 01943 467818
- Haley's Hotel and Restaurant ... Leeds ... 0113 278 4446
- Holdsworth House ... Halifax ... 01422 240024
- Linton Springs ... Wetherby ... 01937 585353
- Oulton Hall ... Leeds ... 0113 282 1000
- Rombalds Hotel ... Ilkley ... 01943 603201
- The Victoria Hotel ... Bradford ... 01274 728706
- Wood Hall ... Wetherby ... 01937 587271

WILTSHIRE
- Beechfield House ... Lacock ... 01225 703700
- Bishopstrow House ... Warminster ... 01985 212312
- Crudwell Court Hotel ... Malmesbury ... 01666 577194
- Ivy House Hotel ... Marlborough ... 01672 515333
- Lucknam Park ... Bath ... 01225 742777
- The Manor House ... Castle Combe ... 01249 782206
- The Old Bell ... Malmesbury ... 01666 822344
- The Pear Tree at Purton ... Swindon ... 01793 772100
- Whatley Manor ... Malmesbury ... 01666 822888
- Woolley Grange ... Bradford-On-Avon ... 01225 864705

WORCESTERSHIRE
- Brockencote Hall ... Chaddesley Corbett ... 01562 777876
- The Colwall Park Hotel ... Malvern ... 01684 540206
- The Cottage In The Wood ... Malvern Wells ... 01684 575859
- Dormy House ... Broadway ... 01386 852711
- The Elms ... Abberley ... 01299 896666
- The Evesham Hotel ... Evesham ... 01386 765566
- Grafton Manor Country House Hotel ... Bromsgrove ... 01527 579007
- The Lygon Arms ... Broadway ... 01386 852255
- Salford Hall Hotel ... Stratford-Upon-Avon ... 01386 871300
- Wood Norton Hall ... Evesham ... 01386 420007

WALES

CEREDIGION
- Bodysgallen Hall ... Llandudno ... 01492 584466
- Conrah Country House Hotel ... Aberystwyth ... 01970 617941

DENBIGHSHIRE
- Bodidris Hall ... Llandegla ... 01978 790434
- Bryn Howel Hotel & Restaurant ... Llangollen ... 01978 860331
- Tyddyn Llan Country House Hotel ... Corwen ... 01490 440264

FLINTSHIRE
- Soughton Hall Country House Hotel ... Chester ... 01352 840811

GWENT
- The Celtic Manor Hotel & Golf Club ... Newport ... 01633 413000
- The Crown At Whitebrook ... Monmouth ... 01600 860254
- The Cwrt Bleddyn Hotel ... Usk ... 01633 450521
- Llansantffraed Court Hotel ... Abergavenny ... 01873 840678

GWYNEDD
- Bontddu Hall ... Barmouth ... 01341 430661
- Bron Eifion Country House Hotel ... Criccieth ... 01766 522385
- Gwesty Seiont Manor Hotel ... Caernarfon ... 01286 673366
- Hotel Maes-Y-Neuadd ... Harlech ... 01766 780200
- The Hotel Portmeirion ... Portmeirion Village ... 01766 770228
- Palé Hall ... Bala ... 01678 530285
- Penmaenuchaf Hall ... Dolgellau ... 01341 422129
- Porth Tocyn Country House Hotel ... Abersoch ... 01758 713303
- St Tudno Hotel ... Llandudno ... 01492 874411
- Trearddur Bay Hotel ... Anglesey ... 01407 860301
- Tynycornel Hotel ... Tywyn ... 01654 782282

HEREFORDSHIRE
- Allt-Yr-Ynys Hotel ... Abergavenny ... 01873 890307

MID GLAMORGAN
- Coed-Y-Mwstwr Hotel ... Bridgend ... 01656 860621
- Miskin Manor ... Cardiff ... 01443 224204

MONTGOMERYSHIRE
- Lake Vyrnwy Hotel ... Lake Vyrnwy ... 01691 870 692

PEMBROKESHIRE
- The Court Hotel & Restaurant ... Pembroke ... 01646 672273
- Penally Abbey ... Tenby ... 01834 843033
- Warpool Court Hotel ... St David's ... 01437 720300

POWYS
- Gliffaes Country House Hotel ... Crickhowell ... 01874 730371
- The Lake Country House ... Llangammarch Wells ... 01591 620202
- Llangoed Hall ... Brecon ... 01874 754525
- Peterstone Court ... Brecon ... 01874 665387
- Ynyshir Hall ... Machynlleth ... 01654 781209

VALE OF GLAMORGAN
- Egerton Grey Country House Hotel ... Cardiff ... 01446 711666

WEST GLAMORGAN
- Norton House Hotel & Restaurant ... Swansea ... 01792 404891

SCOTLAND

ABERDEENSHIRE
- Ardoe House Hotel & Restaurant ... Aberdeen ... 01224 867355
- Darroch Learg Hotel ... Ballater ... 013397 55443
- Kildrummy Castle Hotel ... Kildrummy ... 019755 71288
- Thainstone House Hotel ... Aberdeen ... 01467 621643

ARGYLL
- Ardanaiseig ... Kilchrenan by Taynuilt ... 01866 833333
- Enmore Hotel ... Dunoon ... 01369 702230
- Invercreran Country House Hotel ... Appin ... 01631 730 414
- Isle Of Eriska ... Isle Of Eriska, by Oban ... 01631 720371
- Knipoch Hotel ... Oban ... 01852 316251
- Western Isles Hotel ... Isle Of Mull ... 01688 302012

AYRSHIRE
- Montgreenan Mansion House Hotel ... Irvine ... 01294 557733
- Piersland House Hotel ... Troon ... 01292 314747

BANFFSHIRE
- Craigellachie Hotel ... Craigellachie ... 01340 881204

DUMFRIES & GALLOWAY
- Balcary Bay Hotel ... Auchencairn ... 01556 640217
- Cally Palace Hotel ... Gatehouse Of Fleet ... 01557 814341
- Corsewall Lighthouse Hotel ... Stranraer ... 01776 853220

DUNBARTONSHIRE
- Cameron House ... Loch Lomond ... 01389 755565

EAST LOTHIAN
- Greywalls ... Gullane ... 01620 842144

EDINBURGH
- Borthwick Castle ... Edinburgh ... 01875 820514
- Channings ... Edinburgh ... 0131 315 2226
- The Norton House Hotel ... Edinburgh ... 0131 333 1275
- The Albany Townhouse Hotel ... Edinburgh ... 0131 556 0397
- Dalhousie Castle Hotel & Restaurant ... Edinburgh ... 01875 820153
- The Howard ... Edinburgh ... 0131 557 3500
- Johnstounburn House ... Edinburgh ... 01875 833696

FIFE
- Rufflets Country House ... St Andrews ... 01334 472594
- St. Andrews Golf Hotel ... St. Andrews ... 01334 472611

GLASGOW
- The Beardmore Hotel ... Glasgow ... 0141 951 6000
- Gleddoch House ... Glasgow ... 01475 540711

INVERNESS-SHIRE
- Allt-nan-Ros Hotel ... Fort William ... 01855 821210
- Arisaig House ... Beasdale By Arisaig ... 01687 450622
- Bunchrew House Hotel ... Inverness ... 01463 234917
- Craigdarroch House Hotel ... Loch Ness ... 01456 486 400
- Culloden House Hotel ... Inverness ... 01463 790461
- Kingsmills Hotel ... Inverness ... 01463 237166
- Knockie Lodge Hotel ... Fort Augustus ... 01456 486276
- Loch Torridon Hotel ... Torridon ... 01445 791242
- Mansion House Hotel & Country Club ... Elgin ... 01343 548811

KIRKCUDBRIGHTSHIRE
- Baron's Craig Hotel ... Dalbeattie (Rockcliffe) ... 01556 630 225

LANARKSHIRE
- Shieldhill ... Biggar ... 01899 220035

MORAYSHIRE
- Rothes Glen ... Elgin ... 01340 831254

PEEBLESHIRE
- Cringletie House Hotel ... Peebles ... 01721 730233

PERTHSHIRE
- Ballathie House Hotel ... Perth ... 01250 883268
- Cromlix House ... Kinbuck Nr Stirling ... 01786 822125
- Dalmunzie House ... Glenshee ... 01250 885224
- Farleyer House Hotel ... Aberfeldy ... 01887 820332
- Huntingtower Hotel ... Perth ... 01738 583771
- Kinfauns Castle ... Perth ... 01738 620777
- Kinloch House Hotel ... Blairgowrie ... 01250 884237
- Murrayshall House Hotel & Golf Course ... Scone ... 01738 551171
- Parklands Hotel & Restaurant ... Perth ... 01738 622451
- Roman Camp Hotel ... Callander ... 01877 330003

ROSS-SHIRE
- Coul House Hotel ... Strathpeffer ... 01997 421487

ROXBURGHSHIRE
- Ednam House Hotel ... Kelso ... 01573 224168
- Sunlaws House Hotel and Golf Course ... Kelso ... 01573 450331

STERLINGSHIRE
- The Gean House ... Alloa ... 01259 219275

SUTHERLAND
- Inver Lodge Hotel ... Lochinver ... 01571 844496

WEST LOTHIAN
- Houstoun House ... Uphall ... 01506 853831

WIGTOWNSHIRE
- Kirroughtree House ... Newton Stewart ... 01671 402141
- Knockinaam Lodge ... Portpatrick ... 01776 810471

IRELAND

CO. ANTRIM
- Galgorm Manor ... Ballymena ... 01266 881001

CO. CLARE
- Dromoland Castle ... Newmarket-On-Fergus ... 00 353 61 368144

CO. DOWN
- Culloden Hotel ... Belfast ... 01232 425223

CO. DUBLIN
- The Hibernian ... Dublin ... 00 353 1 668 7666
- The Merrion Hotel ... Dublin ... 00 353 1 603 0600
- Portmarnock Hotel & Golf Links ... Dublin ... 00 353 1 846 0611

CO. GALWAY
- Renvyle House Hotel ... Connemara ... 00 353 95 43511

CO. KERRY
- Aghadoe Heights Hotel ... Killarney ... 00 353 64 31766
- Dunloe Castle ... Killarney ... 00 353 64 44111
- Muckross Park Hotel ... Killarney ... 00 353 64 31938
- Parknasilla Hotel ... Parknasilla ... 00 353 64 45122
- Sheen Falls Lodge ... Kenmare ... 00 353 64 41600

CO. KILDARE
- Barberstown Castle ... Dublin ... 00 353 1 6288157
- Kildare Hotel & Country Club ... Dublin ... 00 353 1 601 7200

CO. LONDONDERRY
- Radisson Roe Park Hotel & Golf Resort ... Limavady ... 015047 22222

CO. MAYO
- Ashford Castle ... Cong ... 00353 92 46003

CO. MONAGHAN
- Nuremore Hotel & Country Club ... Carrickmacross ... 00 353 42 61438

Johansens Recommendations

CO. WEXFORD

Kelly's Resort Hotel	Rosslare	00 353 53 32114
Marlfield House	Gorey	00 353 55 21124

CO. WICKLOW

Hunter's Hotel	Rathnew	00 353 404 40106
Tinakilly Country House Hotel	Wicklow	00 353 40469274

JERSEY

The Atlantic Hotel	St Brelade	01534 44101
Château La Chaire	Rozel	01534 863354
Hotel L'Horizon	St Brelade	01534 43101
Longueville Manor	Jersey (St Saviour)	01534 25501

COUNTRY HOUSES

ENGLAND

B & NE SOMERSET

Apsley House	Bath	01225 336966
Bath Lodge Hotel	Bath	01225 723040

BRISTOL

Chelwood House	Bristol	01761 490730

CAMBRIDGESHIRE

Melbourn Bury	Cambridge	01763 261151
Olivers Lodge Hotel & Restaurant	St. Ives	01480 463252

CO. DURHAM

Grove House	Hamsterley Forest	01388 488203

CORNWALL

Allhays Country House	Looe	01503 272434
Coombe Farm	Looe	01503 240223
The Cormorant Hotel	Golant by Fowey	01726 833426
The Countryman At Trink Hotel	St Ives	01736 797571
The Hundred House Hotel	St Mawes	01872 501336
Nansloe Manor	Helston	01326 574691
The Royal Hotel	Truro	01872 270345
Trebrea Lodge	Tintagel	01840 770410
Tregildry Hotel	Helford River	01326 231378
Trelawne Hotel-The Hutches	Falmouth	01326 250226
Tye Rock Hotel	Porthleven	01326 572695

CUMBRIA

Aynsome Manor Hotel	Cartmel	015395 36653
Braemount House Hotel	Windermere	015394 45967
Crosby Lodge Country House Hotel	Carlisle	01228 573618
Dale Head Hall Lakeside Hotel	Keswick	017687 72478
Fayrer Garden House Hotel	Windermere	015394 88195
Grange Country House Hotel	Keswick-On-Derwentwater	017687 72500
Hipping Hall	Kirkby Lonsdale	015242 71187
Lovelady Shield Country House Hotel	Alston	01434 381203
Number Thirty One	Carlisle	01228 597080
Quarry Garth Country House Hotel	Windermere	015394 88282
Swinside Lodge Hotel	Keswick	017687 72948
White Moss House	Grasmere	015394 35295

DERBYSHIRE

The Beeches Farmhouse	Ashbourne	01889 590288
Biggin Hall	Biggin-By-Hartington	01298 84451
Dannah Farm Country Guest House	Belper	01773 550273 / 630
East Lodge Country House Hotel	Bakewell	01629 734474
The Manor Farmhouse	Matlock	01609 534246
Manor House Hotel & Restaurant	Dronfield	01246 413971
The Peacock Hotel at Rowsley	Bakewell	01629 733518
Underleigh House	Hope	01433 621372
The Wind In The Willows	Glossop	01457 868001

DEVON

Ashelford	Combe Martin	01271 850469
Bel Alp House	Haytor	01364 661217
The Belfry Country Hotel	Honiton	01404 861234
Blagdon Manor Country Hotel	Ashwater	01409 211224
Coombe House Country Hotel	Crediton	01363 84487
Easton Court Hotel	Chagford	01647 433469
Hewitt's Hotel	Lynton	01598 752293
Kingston House	Staverton	01803 762 235
The Lord Haldon Hotel	Exeter	01392 832483
Marsh Hall Country House Hotel	South Molton	01769 572666
Moor View House	Lydford	01822 820220
Preston House Hotel	Saunton	01271 890472
Prince Hall Hotel	Dartmoor	01822 890403
The Thatched Cottage Country Hotel	Lifton	01566 784224
Venn Ottery Barton	Venn Ottery	01404 812733
The White House	Kingsbridge	01548 580580
Wigham	Morchard Bishop	01363 877350
Yeoldon House Hotel	Bideford	01237 474400

DORSET

Beechleas	Wimborne Minster	01202 841684
The Eastbury Hotel	Sherborne	01935 813131
Kemps Country House Hotel	Wareham	01929 462563
Langtry Manor	Bournemouth	01202 553887
Thatch Lodge Hotel	Lyme Regis	01297 560407
Yalbury Cottage Hotel	Dorchester	01305 262382

EAST SUSSEX

The Country House At Winchelsea	Winchelsea	01797 226669
Hooke Hall	Uckfield	01825 761578
White Vine House	Rye	01797 224748

ESSEX

Hockley Place	Colchester	01206 251703

GLOUCESTERSHIRE

Bibury Court	Bibury	01285 740337
Burleigh Court	Minchinhampton	01453 883804
Charlton Kings Hotel	Cheltenham	01242 231061
Dial House Hotel	Bourton-On-The-Water	01451 822244
Halewell	Cheltenham	01242 890238
Lower Brook House	Blockley	01386 700286
The Malt House	Chipping Campden	01386 840295
The Old Rectory	Broadway	01386 853729
Owlpen Manor	Owlpen	01453 860261
Tudor Farmhouse Hotel & Restaurant	Clearwell	01594 833046
Upper Court	Tewkesbury	01386 725351

HAMPSHIRE

The Beaufort Hotel	Portsmouth	01705 823707
The Gordleton Mill Hotel	Lymington	01590 682219
Thatched Cottage Hotel & Restaurant	Brockenhurst	01590 623090
Whitley Ridge & Country House Hotel	Brockenhurst	01590 622354

HEREFORDSHIRE

The Bowens Country House	Hereford	01432 860430
Glewstone Court	Ross-On-Wye	01989 770367
Lower Bache	Leominster	01568 750304
The Steppes	Hereford	01432 820424

HERTFORDSHIRE

Little Offley	Luton	01462 768243
Redcoats Farmhouse Hotel	Stevenage	01438 729500

ISLE OF WIGHT

Peacock Vane Hotel	Bonchurch	01983 852019

KENT

The Garden Hotel	Canterbury	01227 751411
Romney Bay House	New Romney	01797 364747
Tanyard	Maidstone	01622 744705
Wallett's Court	Dover	01304 852424
The Woodville Hall	Dover	01304 825256

LANCASHIRE

Mains Hall Hotel & Brasserie	Blackpool	01253 885130
Quarlton Manor Farm	Bolton	01204 852277

LEICESTERSHIRE

Abbots Oak	Coalville	01530 832 328
White Wings	Fenny Drayton	01827 716100

LINCOLNSHIRE

D'Isney Place Hotel	Lincoln	01522 538881
Midstone House	Peterborough	01780 740136
The Old Mill	Stamford	01780 740815
The Priory	Stamford	01780 720215
Washingborough Hall	Lincoln	01522 790340

MIDDLESEX

Oak Lodge Hotel	Enfield	0181 360 7082

NORFOLK

The Beeches Hotel	Norwich	01603 621167
Beechwood Hotel	North Walsham	01692 403231
Broom Hall	Saham Toney	01953 882125
Catton Old Hall	Norwich	01603 419379
Elderton Lodge Hotel & Restaurant	North Walsham	01263 833547
The Moat House	Norwich	01508 570149
Norfolk Mead Hotel	Norwich	01603 737531
The Old Rectory	Great Snoring	01328 820597
The Old Rectory	Norwich	01603 700772
Salisbury House	Diss	01379 644738
The Sedgeford Estate	Sedgeford	01485 572855
The Stower Grange	Norwich	01603 860210
Titchwell Manor Hotel	Titchwell	01485 210221
Vere Lodge	Fakenham	01328 838261

NORTH YORKSHIRE

Appleton Hall	Appleton-Le-Moors	01751 417227
Dunsley Hall	Whitby	01947 893437
Millers House Hotel	Middleham	01969 622630
Newstead Grange	Malton	01653 692502
The Parsonage Country House Hotel	York	01904 728111
Rookhurst Georgian Country House	Hawes	01969 667454
The White House	Harrogate	01423 501388
Simonstone Hall	Hawes	01969 667255

NORTHUMBERLAND

Waren House Hotel	Bamburgh	01668 214581

NOTTINGHAMSHIRE

The Cottage Country House Hotel	Nottingham	01159 846882

OXFORDSHIRE

Conygree Gate Hotel	Stow-On-The-Wold	01608 658389
Fallowfields	Oxford	01865 820416
The Shaven Crown Hotel	Shipton-Under-Wychwood	01993 830330
The Stonor Arms	Stonor	01491 638866

SHROPSHIRE

Cross Lane House Hotel	Bridgnorth	01746 764887
Delbury Hall	Ludlow	01584 841267
Overton Grange Hotel	Ludlow	01584 873500
Pen-y-Dyffryn Country Hotel	Oswestry	01691 653700

SOMERSET

Ashwick Country House Hotel	Dulverton	01398 323868
The Beacon Country House Hotel	Minehead	01643 703476
Beryl	Wells	01749 678738
Bloomfield House	Bath	01225 420105
Channel House Hotel	Minehead	01643 703229
The Cottage Hotel	Porlock Weir	01643 863300
The Crown Hotel	Exford	01643 831554/5
Eagle House	Bath	01225 859946
The Exmoor House Hotel	Dunster	01643 821268
Glencot House	Wells	01749 677160
Higher Vexford House	Taunton	01984 656267
Holbrook House Hotel	Wincanton	01963 32377
Langford Manor	Taunton	01460 281674
Little Barwick House	Barwick Village	01935 423902
The Oak House Hotel	Cheddar	01934 732444
The Old Priory	Midsomer Norton	01761 416784
Oldfields	Bath	01225 317984
Paradise House	Bath	01225 317723
Periton Park Hotel	Middlecombe	01643 706885
The Pheasant Hotel	Seavington St Mary	01460 240502
Simonsbath House Hotel	Simonsbath	01643 831259
Woolverton House	Bath (Woolverton)	01373 830415

SOUTH YORKSHIRE

Staindrop Lodge	Sheffield	0114 284 6727

STAFFORDSHIRE

Porch Farmhouse	Ashbourne	01538 304545

SUFFOLK

Chippenhall Hall	Fressingfield	01379 588180 / 586733
Gladwins Farm	Dedham Vale	01206 262261
Hope House	Yoxford	01728 668281
Ivy House Farm	Oulton Broad	01502 501353
Lavenham Priory	Lavenham	01787 247404
The Old Rectory	Hadleigh	01449 740745
Tarantella Hotel & Restaurant	Sudbury	01787 378879
Wood Hall Hotel & Country Club	Woodbridge	01394 411283

SURREY

Chase Lodge	Hampton Court	0181 943 1862
Stanhill Court Hotel	Gatwick	01293 862166

WARWICKSHIRE

The Ardencote Manor Hotel	Warwick	01926 843111
Arrow Mill Hotel And Restaurant	Alcester	01789 762419
Chapel House	Atherstone	01827 718949
Glebe Farm House	Stratford-upon-Avon	01789 842501
Marston Farm Country Hotel	Sutton Coldfield	01827 872133

WEST SUSSEX

Burpham Country House Hotel	Arundel	01903 882160
Chequers Hotel	Pulborough	01798 872486
Crouchers Bottom	Chichester	01243 784995
Woodstock House Hotel	Chichester	01243 811666

WILTSHIRE

Stanton Manor	Chippenham	01666 837552
Widbrook Grange	Bath	01225 864750 / 863173

WORCESTERSHIRE

The Mill At Harvington	Evesham (Harvington)	01386 870688
The Old Rectory	Redditch (Ipsley)	01527 523000

WALES

ABERCONWY

Tan-y-Foel	Betws-y-Coed	01690 710507

CONWY

The Old Rectory	Conwy	01492 580611

DYFED

The Pembrokeshire Retreat	Cardigan	01239 841387

GWENT

Llanwenarth House	Abergavenny	01873 830289
Parva Farmhouse and Restaurant	Tintern	01291 689411
Penyclawdd Court	Abergavenny	01873 890719

GWYNEDD

Aber Artro Hall	Harlech	01341 241374
Berthlwyd Hall Hotel	Conwy	01492 592409
Dolmelynllyn Hall	Dolgellau	01341 440273
Plas Penhelig Country House Hotel	Aberdovey	01654 767676
Ty'n Rhos Country House	Caernarfon	01248 670489

PEMBROKESHIRE

Waterwynch House Hotel	Tenby	01834 842464

POWYS

Glangrwyney Court	Abergavenny	01873 811288
Old Gwernyfed Country Manor	Brecon	01497 847376

SCOTLAND

ABERDEENSHIRE

Meldrum House	Old Meldrum	01651 872294
Balgonie Country House	Ballater	013397 55482
The Old Manse of Marnoch	Huntly	01466 780873

ARGYLLSHIRE

Ardsheal House	Kentallen Of Appin	01631 740227
Druimneil	Port Appin	01631 730228
Dungallen House Hotel	Oban	01631 563799
Killiechronan	Isle Of Mull	01680 300403
The Manor House Hotel	Oban	01631 562087

AYRSHIRE

Chapeltoun House	Glasgow	015604 82696

DUMFRIES & GALLOWAY

Broomlands House	Dalbeattie	01556 611463
Well View Hotel	Moffat	01683 220184

FIFE

Chapel House	Fife	01337 831790

INVERNESS-SHIRE

Boath House	Nairn	01667 454896
Ashburn House	Fort William	01397 706000
Culduthel Lodge	Inverness	01463 240089
Polmaily House Hotel	Drumnadrochit	01456 450343

KINROSS-SHIRE

Nivingston Country House	Kinross	01577 850216

KIRKCUDBRIGHTSHIRE

Auchenskeoch Lodge	Dalbeattie	01387 780277

LOTHIAN

No 22 Murrayfield Gardens	Edinburgh	0131 337 3569

MORAYSHIRE

Ardconnel House	Grantown-on-Spey	01479 872104

PERTHSHIRE

Dunfallandy House	Pitlochry	01796 472648
Dupplin Castle	Perth	01738 623224
The Killiecrankie Hotel	Killiecrankie,By Pitlochry	01796 473220
The Lake Hotel	Port Of Menteith	01877 385258
Newmiln Country House	Perth	01738 552364
Queen's View Hotel	Strathtummel	01796 473291

ROSS-SHIRE

Kinkell House	Dingwall	01349 861270

STIRLINGSHIRE

Blairlogie House	Blairlogie	01259 761441
Culcreuch Castle Hotel	Fintry	01360 860555

SUTHERLAND

The Kinlochbervie Hotel	Kinlochbervie	01971 521275
Borgie Lodge Hotel	Tongue	01641 521332

WESTERN ISLES

Ardvourlie Castle	Isle Of Harris	01859 502307

IRELAND

CO. CLARE

Halpins Hotel & Vittles Restaurantx	Kilkee	00 353 65 56032

CO. CORK

Liss Ard Lake Lodge	Skibbereen	00 353 28 22365

CO. DONEGAL

Castle Grove Country House	Letterkenny	00 353 745 1118

CO. DOWN

Glassdrummand Lodge Country House	Annalong	013967 68451
Portaferry Hotel	Portaferry	012477 28231

CO. KERRY

Ard na Sidhe	Caragh Lake	00 353 66 69105
Caragh Lodge	Caragh Lake	00 353 66 69115
Earls Court House	Killarney	00 353 64 34009

CO. SILGO

Coopershill House	Riverstown	00 353 71 65108
Markree Castle	Sligo	00 353 71 67800

CO. TIPPERARY

Cashel Palace Hotel	Cashel	00 353 62 62707

CO. WICKLOW

The Old Rectory	Wicklow	00 353 404 67048

CO. DUBLIN

Aberdeen Lodge	Dublin	00 353 1 2838155

CHANNEL ISLANDS

JERSEY

Hotel La Tour	St Aubin	01534 43770

GUERNSEY

Bella Luce Hotel & Restaurant	St Martin	01481 38764
Hotel Hougue Du Pommier	Castel	01481 56531
La Favorita Hotel	Fermain Bay	01481 35666

INNS WITH RESTAURANTS

ENGLAND

BERKSHIRE

Boulters Lock Hotel	Maidenhead	01628 21291
The Christopher Hotel	Eton/Windsor	01753 811677 / 852359
The Leatherne Bottel Riverside Inn	Goring-On-Thames	01491 872667
The Royal Oak Hotel	Yattendon	01635 201325
The Swan Hotel	Newbury	01635 298314

BUCKINGHAMSHIRE

The Different Drummer	Milton Keynes	01908 564733
The Fox Country Hotel	Henley	01491 638289

CAMBRIDGESHIRE

Panos Hotel & Restaurant	Cambridge	01223 212958

CHESHIRE

Longview Hotel And Restaurant	Knutsford	01565 632119
The Swan Hotel	Chester	01829 733838
Wild Boar Hotel & Restaurant	Chester	01829 260309

CORNWALL

The Harbour Inn	Porthleven	01326 573876
Jubilee Inn	Pelynt	01503 220312
The Old Custom House Hotel	Padstow	01841 532359
The Port William	Tintagel	01840 770230
The Rising Sun	St Mawes	01326 270233
Trengilly Wartha Country Inn	Falmouth	01326 340332
Tyacks Hotel	Camborne	01209 612424

CUMBRIA

The Mortal Man Hotel	Troutbeck	015394 33193
The New Dungeon Ghyll Hotel	Ambleside	015394 37213
The Pheasant Inn	Bassenthwaite Lake	017687 76234
The Royal Oak Inn	Appleby-In-Westmorland	017683 51463
The Swan Hotel	Newby Bridge	015395 31681
The Tarn End House Hotel	Carlisle	016977 2340
Whoop Hall Inn	Kirkby Lonsdale	015242 71284

DERBYSHIRE

Boar's Head Hotel	Burton Upon Trent	01283 820344
The Bulls Head Inn	Eyam	01433 630873
The Chequers Inn	Calver,Nr Bakewell	01433 630231
Donington Manor Hotel	Castle Donington	01332 810253
The Maynard Arms	Grindleford	01433 630321
The Plough Inn	Hathersage	01433 650319
Red Lion Inn	Ashbourne	01335 370396
The Waltzing Weasel	Hayfield	01663 743402

DEVON

The Barn Owl Inn	Torquay	01803 872130
The George Hotel	Hatherleigh	01837 810454
Home Farm Hotel	Honiton	01404 831278
New Inn Hotel	Clovelly	01237 431303
The Old Church House Inn	Torbryan Nr Totnes	01803 812372
The Rising Sun	Lynmouth	01598 753223
The Sea Trout Inn	Totnes	01803 762274
Thelbridge Cross Inn	Thelbridge	01884 860316
The Victoria Hotel	Dartmouth	01803 832572
The White Hart Hotel	Moretonhampstead	01647 440406
Ye Olde Churston Court Inn	Brixham	01803 842186

DORSET

The Coppleridge Inn	Shaftesbury	01747 851980
The Manor Hotel	Bridport	01308 897616

EAST SUSSEX

Winston Manor	Crowborough	01892 652772

ESSEX

The Cricketers	Clavering	01799 550442
The Red Lion Hotel	Colchester	01206 577986

GLOUCESTERSHIRE

The Horse and Groom Inn	Stow-on-the-Wold	01451 830584
Kingshead House Restaurant	Cheltenham	01452 862299
The Masons Arms	Cirencester	01285 850164
The New Inn at Coln	Cirencester	01285 750651
The Noel Arms	Chipping Campden	01386 840317
The Old Manse	Bourton-On-The-Water	01451 820082
The Ragged Cot	Minchinhampton	01453 884643/731333
The Royalist Hotel	Stow-On-The-Wold	01451 830670

HAMPSHIRE

The Woodfalls Inn	Fordingbridge	01725 513222

HEREFORDSHIRE

Feathers Hotel	Ledbury	01531 635266
Rhydspence Inn	Hay-On-Wye	01497 831262
Wheelbarrow Castle	Leominster	01568 612219
Ye Olde Salutation Inn	Weobley	01544 318443

KENT

The Harrow At Warren Street	Maidstone	01622 858727
Ringlestone Inn	Maidstone	01622 859900
The Royal Oak	Sevenoaks	01732 451109
The Royal Wells Inn	Tunbridge Wells	01892 511188

LANCASHIRE

Fence Gate Inn	Burnley	01282 618101
The Inn At Whitewell	Whitewell	01200 448222
The Old Bell Inn Hotel	Saddleworth	01457 870130
Tree Tops Country House Hotel	Southport	01704 879651
Ye Horn's Inn	Preston	01772 865230

LEICESTERSHIRE

Barnacles Restaurant	Hinkley	01455 633220

LINCOLNSHIRE

The Black Horse Inn	Grimsthorpe	01778 591247
Hare & Hounds	Fulbeck	01400 272090

NORFOLK

The Barton Angler Country Inn	Wroxham	01692 630740
The Garden House Hotel	Norwich	01603 720007
Green Farm Restaurant And Hotel	Thorpe Market	01263 833602
The Hoste Arms Hotel	Burnham Market	01328 738777
The Lifeboat Inn	Thornham	01485 512236
The Old Brewery House Hotel	Reepham	01603 870881
White Horse Hotel	Blakeney	01263 740574

NORTH CORNWALL

The Port Gaverne Hotel	Port Gaverne	01208 880244

NORTH YORKSHIRE

The Blue Lion	East Witton	01969 624273
The Boar's Head Hotel	Harrogate	01423 771888
The Crown Hotel	Boroughbridge	01423 322328
The Feathers Hotel	Helmsley	01439 770275
The Feversham Arms Hotel	Helmsley	01439 770766
The George at Easingwold	York	01347 821698
The Jefferson Arms	York	01904 448316
The Kings Arms Hotel And Restaurant	Askrigg	01969 650258
The Low Hall Hotel	Harrogate	01423 508598
Mallyan Spout Hotel	Goathland	01947 896486
The New Inn Hotel	Settle	015242 51203
The Red Lion	Burnsall	01756 720204
The Wensleydale Heifer Inn	West Witton	01969 622322
The Wheatsheaf Inn	Egton	01947 895271
The White Swan	Pickering	01751 472288

NORTHAMPTONSHIRE

The Falcon Hotel	Castle Ashby	01604 696200
The Windmill At Badby	Badby Nr Daventry	01327 702363

NORTHUMBERLAND

The Blue Bell Hotel	Belford	01668 213543

NOTTINGHAMSHIRE

Hotel Des Clos	Nottingham	01159 866566
The Willow Tree	Newark	01636 626613

OXFORDSHIRE

The George Hotel	Dorchester-On-Thames	01865 340404
Cotswold Gateway Hotel	Burford	01993 822695
Holcombe Hotel	Oxford	01869 338274
The Jersey Arms	Oxford	01869 343234
The Kings Head Inn & Restaurant	Stow-On-The-Wold	01608 658365
The Lamb Inn	Burford	01993 823155
The Lamb Inn	Shipton-Under-Wychwood	01993 830465
The Mill & Old Swan	Oxford	01993 774441
The Shaven Crown Hotel	Shipton Under Wychwood	01993 830330
The Talkhouse	Oxford	01865 351648

RUTLAND

The Whipper-In Hotel	Oakham	01572 756971

SHROPSHIRE

The Hundred House Hotel	Telford	01952 730353
The Nesscliffe	Shrewsbury	01743 741430
The Redfern Hotel	Cleobury Mortimer	01299 270 395
The Roebuck Inn	Ludlow	01584 711230

SOMERSET

The Anchor Country Inn & Hotel	Dulverton	01398 323433
The King's Arms Inn & Restaurant	Montacute	01935 822513
The Royal Oak Inn	Exmoor	01643 831506/7
The Talbot Inn at Mells	Mells Nr Bath	01373 812254
Walnut Tree	Sherborne	01935 851292
The Woolpack Inn	Beckington Nr Bath	01373 831244

STAFFORDSHIRE

The Dower House	Stafford	01889 270707
The George Hotel	Eccleshall	01785 850300
The Old Vicarage Restaurant	Burton Upon Trent	01283 533222
The Three Horseshoes Inn	Leek	01538 300296
The Wheatsheaf Inn At Onneley	Onneley	01782 751581

SUFFOLK

The Countrymen	Long Melford	01787 312356

SURREY

Inn On The Lake	Godalming	01483 415575

WARWICKSHIRE

The Coach House Hotel	Stratford-upon-Avon	01789 204109 / 299468
The Golden Lion Inn of Easenhall	Rugby	01788 832265

WEST SUSSEX

Badgers	Petworth	01798 342651
The Boathouse Brasserie	Amberley,Near Arundel	01798 831059
The Chequers At Slaugham	Handcross	01444 400239
The Old TollgateHotel	Worthing	01903 879494
White Horse Inn	Petworth	01798 869 221
The Woodcock Inn & Restaurant	East Grinstead	01342 325859

WEST YORKSHIRE

Old White Lion Hotel	Haworth	01535 642313
The Rock Inn Hotel	Halifax/Huddersfield	01422 379721

WILTSHIRE

The Castle Inn	Castle Combe	01249 783030
The Horse And Groom Inn	Malmesbury	01666 823904

WORCESTERSHIRE

The Broadway Hotel	Broadway	01386 852401
Crown At Hopton	Cleobury Mortimer	01299 270372
The Old Schoolhouse	Worcester	01905 371368
Riverside Restaurant And Hotel	Evesham	01386 446200
The Talbot	Worcester	01886 821235
The White Lion Hotel	Upton-Upon-Severn	01684 592551

WALES

CARMARTHENSHIRE

The Plough Inn	Llandeilo	01558 823431

DENBIGHSHIRE

The West Arms Hotel	Llanarmon Dyffryn Ceiriog	01691 600665
Ye Olde Anchor Inn	Ruthin	01824 702813

GWENT

The Castle View Hotel	Chepstow	01291 620349

MONTGOMERYSHIRE

The Lion Hotel And Restaurant	Welshpool	01686 640452
The Royal Oak Hotel & Restaurant	Welshpool	01938 552217

SCOTLAND

CLACKMANNANSHIRE

Whinsmuir Country Inn	Powmill (Nr Kinross)	01577 840595

DUMFRIESSHIRE

Annandale Arms Hotel	Moffatt	01683 220013

ISLE OF SKYE

Hotel Eilean Iarmain	Isle Of Skye	01471 833332
Uig Hotel	Isle Of Skye	01470 542205

KINCARDINESHIRE

Potarch Hotel	Banchory	013398 84339

PERTHSHIRE

The Glenisla Hotel	Blairgowrie	01575 582223
The Loft Restaurant	Blair Atholl	01796 481377
The Moulin Hotel	Pitlochry	01796 472196

IRELAND

CO. DOWN

The Old Inn, Crawfordsburn	Crawfordsburn	01247 853255

CHANNEL ISLANDS

The Moorings Hotel	Jersey	01534 853633
Sea Crest Hotel And Restaurant	Jersey (St Brelade)	01534 46353

Calendar of Events

Wilton House, Wiltshire

Kentwell Hall, Suffolk

Hawkstone Historic Park, Shropshire

MARCH

28 Feb–1	Siberian Husky Rally	Grimsthorpe Castle, Lincolnshire (01778 591205)
–20 March	An Exhibition about the year the American Civil War came to Hampstead	Burgh House, Hampstead, London
1	Daffy Down Dilly Day – FREE ENTRY	Trebah Garden, Cornwall
6–8	21st Annual Antiques Fair	Wilton House, Wiltshire (01722 746720)
12–15	Twilight Tours – Enjoy the lights & views of London at Sunset	Tower Bridge Experience, London (0171 403 3761)
18	Garden Special – A Spring Workshop with Beth Rothschild	Waddesdon Manor, Buckinghamshire (01296 651226)
19–21	Engineers Evening Tours–Behind the scenes	Tower Bridge Experience, London (0171 403 3761)
21–22	Countrywide Fair – Fashion & Crafts	Tatton Park, Cheshire (01565 654822)
27–29	Galloway Antiques Fair	Naworth Castle, Cumbria (016977 3229)
28–29	Armada! 1588 as Penshurst Place prepares for Spanish Invasion	Penshurst Place, Kent
28–29	Mountain Bike Race	Hawkstone Historic Park, Shropshire (01939 200611)
30	Clandon Park Designer Clothes Sale	Clandon Park, Surrey (Enq 01483 222482)

APRIL

April	'Singing the Blues' – exhibition of ceramics, textiles, jewellery and glass	Waterperry Gardens, Oxfordshire (01844 339226)
1–5	Spring Plant Sale	Coton Manor Garden, Northamptonshire
2–30	Special Exhibition, Gillian Clarke	Museum of Garden History, London
4–26	Young Adventurers, exciting tour for children	Penhow Castle, Gwent
9–26	Easter Egg Hunt	Trebah Garden, Cornwall
10–13	Easter Craft Festival	Duncombe Park, Yorkshire
10–13	Easter Egg Hunt	Hawkstone Historic Park, Shropshire (01939 200611)
10–13	Great Easter Egg Quiz & Tudor Re-Creation	Kentwell Hall, Suffolk
10–14	The Kings Progress	Warwick Castle, Warwickshire
11–12	Easter Steam Rally with Medieval Crafts Fair	Avoncroft Museum, Hereford & Worcester
11–13	Craft Fayre	Dyffryn Gardens, Wales
11–13	Easter Festival	Tatton Park, Cheshire (01565 654822)
11–13	A Celebration of Easter	Leeds Castle, Kent
12	Easter Egg Extravaganza	Traquair House, Peeblesshire, Scotland
12	Easter Egg Hunt	The Vyne, Hampshire (01256 881337)
12–13	A Victorian Easter – the house is open on the Monday 11am-6pm	Holdenby House, Northants
12–13	Antique Fair	Lamport Hall, Northamptonshire
12–13	Easter at Penshurst inc. Free Easter Eggs for Children	Penshurst Place, Kent
12–13	Traditional Food Fair	Weald & Downland Open Museum, Sussex
13	Daffodil Time	High Beeches, W Sussex
13	Easter Egg Hunt	Ludlow Castle, Shropshire
16	Family Fun Day	Colby Woodland Gardens, Pembrokeshire
16–18	Homes and Gardens Spring Grand Sale	Sudeley Castle, Gloucestershire
17–19	Country Lifestyle Fair	Highclere Castle, Berkshire (01635 253210)
18–19	Craft Fair	Elton Hall, Cambs
18–19	Garden Festival	Borde Hill, Sussex
18–19	Pembrokeshire Horticultural Society Spring Show	Picton Castle, Wales
18–19	Celebration of Shakespeare	Wilton House, Wiltshire (01722 746720)
19	Open Day organised by the Rotary	Naworth Castle, Cumbria (016977 3229)
19	Daffodil Sunday, tours every hour 12–4pm	Thorp Perrow Arboretum, North Yorkshire
20	Private Garden open (NGS)	Woburn Abbey, Bedfordshire
22	Garden Special – Planting in Pots with Sue Dickinson	Waddesdon Manor, Buckinghamshire (01296 651226)
25	Spring Plant Fair	Pashley Manor Gardens, E Sussex
26	Special Plants Fair	Spetchley Park, Worcester
26	Children's Animal Fair	Borde Hill, Sussex
26	Spring Fair	Museum of Garden History, London
30–4 May	Tulip Festival	Pashley Manor Gardens, E Sussex

MAY

May	'Spring Fever' – exhibition of glass, ceramics and etchings	Waterperry Gardens, Oxfordshire (01844 339226)
2–4	Craft Fair	Blenheim Palace, Oxfordshire
2–4	Weald of Kent Craft Show	Penshurst Place, Kent
2–4	Bonsai Weekend, Demonstrations and advice	Leonardslee Gardens, W Sussex
2–4	Tonbridge Gardening Show	Tonbridge Castle Lawn, Kent (01732 357872)
2–4	Home & Garden Exhibition	Dyffryn Gardens, Wales
2–4	'Dining in Style' Victorian banqueting display in Syon House	Syon Park, London (0181 560 0881)
3	Rare Plant Fair	Castle Bromwich, W Midlands
3	Volkswagen Owners Club Rally	Stanford Hall, Leics (01788 860250)
3–4	Jousting Tournament 'The Knights of Royal England'	Hedingham Castle, Essex (01787 460261)
3–4	Historical Re-enactment by The Red Wyvern Society	Appleby Castle, Cumbria (Enq 017683 51402)
3–4	Spring Country Craft Fair	Eastnor Castle, Hereford & Worcester
3–4	Garden Festival for Charity	Haddonstone Show Garden, Northamptonshire
3–4 Oct	Exhibition – Military Munnings 1917–1918	The Sir Alfred Munnings Art Museum, Essex
4	Bluebell Time	High Beeches, W Sussex
4	Circus Workshop	Hawkstone Historic Park, Shropshire (01939 200611)
4	Flower Fair, Trade Stands, Crafts, Talks & Walks	Hergest Estate, Hereford & Worcester
7–10	Living Crafts, Europe's Largest & Most Prestigious Crafts Event	Hatfield House, Hertfordshire (01705 426523)
8	Opera Through the Looking Glass	Clandon Park, Surrey (Enq 01372 451596
8–10	Home Design and Interiors Exhibition	Elton Hall, Cambridgeshire
9–10	Spring Autojumble	Beaulieu, Hampshire (01590 612624)
9–10	Museum Working Weekend	Breamore House, Hampshire
9–10	Country Garden Festival	Lulworth Castle, Dorset
10	Spring Plant Fair	Newby Hall, N Yorkshire
10	New Homes Exhibition	Ingatestone Hall, Essex (01277 353010)
12	Guided Evening Tour and Wine Reception	Mount Usher Gardens, Ireland
16–17	Festival of English Food & Wine	Leeds Castle, Kent
17	Spring Plant Fair	Colby Woodland Gardens, Pembrokeshire
17	Gardens open under the National Gardens Scheme	Deene Park, Northamptonshire

Warwick Castle, Warwickshire

17	Model Soldiers Day 25th Anniversary–display of 8000–to include valuations	Hatfield House, Hertfordshire (0181 979 7137)
17	An Afternoon's Adventure with Alice. Audience participation.	Penshurst Place, Kent (01892 870307)
17	Spring Tour, 2pm	Thorp Perrow Arboretum, N Yorkshire
18–22	Chelsea Flower Show	Special Opening at the Chelsea Physic Garden
21–25	Charleston Festival – Writers/artists-work today & the heritage of Bloomsbury	Charleston Farmhouse, Sussex
23	Atholl Highland Games	Blair Castle, Scotland (01796 481207)
23	London Opera Players 'Ring Up the Curtain'	Doddington Hall, Lincs (B/0 01522 694308)
23–25	'History Mystery' as part of Museum week	Avoncroft Museum of Historic Buildings, Hereford & Worcester
23–25	Craft Fair	Ludlow Castle, Shropshire
23–25	Fireservice Preservation Group 30th Anniversary	Blenheim Palace, Oxfordshire
23–25	Craft Show	Breamore House, Hampshire
23–25	Merrie England Weekend, including medieval stalls & archery	Hever Castle, Kent
23–25	Jousting Weekend	Warwick Castle, Warwickshire
23–25	Scottish Beer Festival	Traquair House, Peeblesshire, Scotland
24	Blair Castle Highland Games	Blair Castle, Scotland (01796 481207)
24	Teeside Yesteryear Car Club Rally and display	Appleby Castle, Cumbria (Enq 017683 51402)
24	TV/Film Memorabilia Fair	Castle Bromwich, W Midlands
24	Countryside Day	Mannington Hall, Norfolk
24	Country Fair	Duncombe Park, Yorkshire
24–25	Country Fair	Broadlands, Hampshire (01794 517888)
24–25	Live Re-Enactment of Battle with King Arthur	Hawkstone Historic Park, Shropshire (01939 200611)
24–25	Medieval Entertainment, dancing, games, archery, Knights in combat	Hedingham Castle, Essex (01787 460261)
24–28	Flower Festival, 10–5.30pm	Athelhampton House & Gardens, Dorset
24–25	Southern Counties Country Show	Highclere Castle, Berkshire (01635 253210)
24–25	Lamport Country Festival	Lamport Hall, Northamptonshire (01604 686272)
24–25	Penshurst Place Classic Motor Show	Penshurst Place, Kent (01892 870307)
29–31	The Fabulous Holker Garden Festival	Holker Hall, Cumbria (015395 58838)
29–31	Live Crafts	Loseley Park, Surrey
29–31	The Longleat Horse Trials	Longleat, Wiltshire
30–31	Flower and Garden Show	Eastnor Castle, Hereford & Worcester
30–31	National Pet Event	Highclere Castle, Berkshire (01635 253210)
30–31	Quality Craft Fair	Tatton Park, Cheshire (01565 654822)

JUNE

Holker Hall, Cumbria

1–5	Special Chelsea Festival Openings, 12–5pm	Chelsea Physic Garden, London
5	Hamlet	Ludlow Castle, Shropshire (B/O 01584 872150)
5–7	Homes Design Exhibition	Ingatestone Hall, Essex (01277 353010)
5–7	Wessex Craft & Flower Fayre	Wilton House, Wiltshire (01722 746720)
6	Shirley Bassey Concert	Highclere Castle, Berkshire (01635 253210)
6	Jazz at the Vyne	The Vyne, Hampshire (01256 881337)
6	The Taming of the Shrew, 8pm by Illyria	Uppark, Hampshire (B/O 01730 825415)
6–7	Balloon & Vintage Car Fiesta	Leeds Castle, Kent
6–7	Gardeners' Fair	Burton Agnes Hall, E Yorkshire
6–7	Rainbow Craft Fair	Newby Hall, N Yorkshire
6–7	Special Garden Weekend with the Head Gardener	Cawdor Castle, Nairn, Scotland
7	Arbury Motor Transport Spectacular	Arbury Hall, Warwickshire
7	Classic Car Rally	Ripley Castle, N Yorkshire (01423 770152)
7	Heavy Horse Spectacular	Weald & Downland Open Museum, Sussex
7	D-Day Commemoration	Trebah Garden, Cornwall
7	Syon Family Day 'Music, Madness & Mayhem'	Syon Park, London (0181 560 0881)
10	'A Midsummer's Night Dream'	Painswick Rococo Garden, Glos
11–14	Art of Living–Decorative Arts Fair	Eastnor Castle, Hereford & Worcester
11–14	Homes & Garden Grand Summer Sale	Ripley Castle, N Yorkshire (01423 770152)
12–14	Goodwood Festival of Speed	Goodwood, West Sussex
12–14	Needlecraft and Beading Exhibition in Longleat House	Longleat, Wiltshire
13–14	Beaulieu Classic Boat Festival (at Buckler's Hard)	Beaulieu, Hampshire (01590 612624)
13–14	Rainbow Craft Fair	Arbury Hall, Warwickshire
13–14	Knights in Combat	Warwick Castle, Warwickshire
13–14	Carriage Driving Event	Tatton Park, Cheshire (01565 654822)
13	Last Night at the Proms with Fireworks Finale	Blenheim Palace, Oxfordshire (B/O 01625 560000)
13	Bournemouth Sinfonietta Open Air Concert	Lulworth Castle (B/O 01929 400352)
14	Father's Day Treasure Trail	Hawkstone Historic Park, Shropshire (01939 200611)
14	Rare Plant Fair	Colby Woodland Gardens, Pembrokeshire
14	Tudor Dancing on the South Lawn	Penshurst Place, Kent (01892 870307)
14	Horse & Carriage Driving	Syon Park, London (0181 560 0881)
14–5 July	Great Annual Re-Creation of Tudor Life	Kentwell Hall, Suffolk
15–24	Flower Festival	Haddon Hall, Derbyshire
18–21	Rose & Summer Flower Festival	Pashley Manor Gardens, E Sussex
19	SSAFA Band Concert & Beating Retreat	Blenheim Palace, Oxfordshire
20	Midsummer Music on the Lawns of Stourhead	Stourhead, Wilts (01747 841152)
20	Performing Arts Open Air Concert	Grimsthorpe Castle, Lincolnshire (01778 591205)
20	Concert with Ashley Wass	Doddington Hall, Lincs (B/0 01522 694308)
20	Woodstock Carnival	Woodstock, Oxfordshire
20–21	Festival of Gardening	Hatfield House, Hertfordshire (01707 262823)
21	Gardens open for the National Garden Scheme	Cottesbrooke Hall, Northamptonshire
25	Thomson Roddick & Laurie Fine Art & Furniture Auction	Naworth Castle, Cumbria (016977 3229)
25–28	Marie Curie Cancer Care Flower Exhibition	Avington Park, Hampshire
26–28	Gardeners' Weekend	Hever Castle, Kent
26–28	Home Design & Interiors Exhibition	Penshurst Place, Kent (01892 870307)
27	Sudeley Rose Festival	Sudeley Castle, Gloucestershire
27–28	Historical Re-enactment by The Red Wyvern Society	Appleby Castle, Cumbria (Enq 017683 51402)
27–28	'Animals Everywhere!'	Avoncroft Museum , Hereford & Worcester
27–28	The Arley Garden Festival	Arley Hall, Cheshire (01565 777284)
27–28	Usk Town Gardens Open, NGS 10am-6pm	The Castle House, Gwent, Wales
27–28	West Sussex Country Craft Fair	Leonardslee Gardens, W Sussex
27–28	The National Southern Rose Show	Shepperton (Enq. 01727 850461)
27–28	The Garden Event	West Dean Gardens, W Sussex
27–28	Wilton Horse Trials	Wilton House, Wiltshire (01722 746720)
28	Charity Opening for St John's Ambulance 2–5pm	Norton Conyers, N Yorkshire
28	The Radio Rally	Longleat, Wiltshire
28	The Game Show	Broughton Hall, N Yorkshire

Eastnor Castle, Hereford & Worcester

Calendar of Events

Borde Hill, Sussex

Traquair House, Scotland

Stourhead, Wiltshire

JULY

3–5	Open Air Picnic Concerts on the lawns	Hatchlands, Surrey
4	The Proms Concert	Longleat, Wiltshire
4	The Orchestral and Fireworks Concert	Arley Hall, Cheshire (B/O 01625 583453)
4	Tower Bridge's 104th Birthday Party	Tower Bridge Experience, London (0171 403 3761)
4–5	Grand Fireworks Concert	Warwick Castle, Warwickshire
4–5	BHTA Borde Hill Horse Trials	Borde Hill, Sussex
5	Grimsthorpe Summer Fayre	Grimsthorpe Castle, Lincolnshire (01778 591205)
5	Performing Arts Viennese Concert	Ripley Castle, N Yorkshire (01423 770152)
5–18	The Pergola Open Air Theatre	West Dean Gardens, W Sussex
7–12	The Hampton Court Palace Flower Show	Hampton Court, London
11	Palace House Proms	Beaulieu, Hampshire (01590 612624)
11	BBC Big Band Concert	Broadlands, Hampshire (01794 517888)
11	Play performed in the Gardens	Lamport Hall, Northamptonshire (01604 686272)
11	Garden Party at Deans Court including stands	Deans Court, Dorset
11	Orchestral Concert and Fireworks	Sudeley Castle, Gloucestershire (B/O 01242 602308)
11	Alice in Wonderland, 7pm by Illyria	Uppark, Hampshire (B/O 01730 825415)
11	The Baron's Treat-Music & Family fun with Victorian Games	Waddesdon Manor, Buckinghamshire
11–12	Gardeners Weekend	Castle Bromwich, W Midlands
11–12	Grimsthorpe Antiques Festival and Fair	Grimsthorpe Castle, Lincolnshire (01778 591205)
11–12	Large Birds of Prey	Warwick Castle, Warwickshire
11–12	Torbay Flower Club	Torre Abbey, Devon
11–12	Balloon Fiesta	Penshurst Place, Kent (01892 870307)
11–12	Historic Vehicle Gathering	Powderham Castle, Devon
11–12	Fuchsia Fanfare '98 10–5pm	Borde Hill, Sussex
12	Family Fun Day Out	Dyffryn Gardens, Wales
12– 6 Sept	Summer Exhibition 'Art and Healing in Ghana'	Chelsea Physic Garden, London
16–19	Galloway Antiques Fair	Ripley Castle, N Yorkshire (01423 770152)
17	Maze Open	Woburn Abbey, Bedfordshire
17–18	Classical Music with Fireworks	The Vyne, Hampshire (01256 881337)
18	Classic Pops with Fireworks	Lulworth Castle (B/O 01929 400352)
18	Open Air Extravaganza with Fireworks	Wilton House, Wiltshire (01722 746720)
18–19	Rainbow Craft Fair	Dalemain, Cumbria
18–19	A Tudor Revel- Jousting, Archery, Falconry, Jesters, Clowns	Hatfield House, Hertfordshire (01707 262055)
19	Vintage Car Rally	Doddington Place, Kent
19	Historic Vehicle Rally	Newby Hall, N Yorkshire
19	Charity Opening for Guide Dogs for the Blind, 2–5pm	Norton Conyers, N Yorkshire
19	Show for Rare & Traditional Breeds	Weald & Downland Open Museum, Sussex
21	Last Night of the Proms Concert	Woburn Abbey, Bedfordshire
21–25	Shakespearean Production by Gloucestershire Drama Assoc.	Painswick Rococo Garden, Gloucestershire
22	Evening Gardens Tour	Tatton Park, Cheshire (01565 654822)
24	Stowe Annual Summer Ball	Stowe Schools, Buckinghamshire (01280 813650)
24–25	Open Air Shakespeare 'Antony & Cleopatra'	Kentwell Hall, Suffolk (B/O 01787 310207)
24–25	Longleat Balloon Festival	Longleat, Wiltshire
24–26	Loseley Garden Festival	Loseley Park, Surrey
25	Fireworks Concert, 8pm	Coughton Court, Warwickshire (B/O 0500 661812)
25	Madam Butterfly performed by Opera Box	Dyffryn Gardens, Wales (01446 709528)
25–26	English Playtour Theatre-Jabberwocky with Alice Through the Looking Glass	Duncombe Park, Yorkshire (B/O 01439 770213)
25–26	Re-creation of the Visit of King Henry VII to Hedingham Castle	Hedingham Castle, Essex (01787 460261)
25–26	The National Northern Show, Gateshead	The Royal National Rose Society (Enq. 01727 850461)
25–26	Fuchsia & Pelargonium Show	Torre Abbey, Devon
25–13 Sept	Home of Football	Callendar House Large Gallery, Falkirk, Scotland
26	Buckler's Hard Village Festival	Beaulieu, Hampshire (01590 612624)
26	Rothiemurchus Highland Games	Rothiemurchus, Aviemore, Scotland (01479 810858)
26	Sheringham Little Theatre Day	Mannington Hall, Norfolk
26	Seafarers Day	Sewerby Hall, Yorkshire
28–1	Festival Meeting, Goodwood racecourse	Goodwood, West Sussex
31 & 1 Aug	2 Classical Spectacular Concerts	Avington Park, Hampshire (B/O 01962 779260)
31–2 Aug	Summer Craft Show	Broadlands, Hampshire (01794 517888)

AUGUST

Every Saturday	Knights of the Royal England Jousting	Hever Castle, Kent
Every Sunday	Longbow Archery	Hever Castle, Kent
1	Open Air Concert with Fireworks	Powderham Castle, Devon
1	The Hatfield Park Prom	Hatfield House, Hertfordshire (01952 810428)
1	BBC Big Band Concert	Ripley Castle, N Yorkshire (01423 770152)
1–2	Traquair Fair	Traquair House, Peeblesshire, Scotland
1–2	QEF Classic Car Show	Loseley Park, Surrey
1–2	Live Steam Model Show	Breamore House, Hampshire
1–2	Have a go at Archery	Wilton House, Wiltshire (01722 746720)
1–31	Young Adventurers, exciting tour for children	Penhow Castle, Gwent, Wales
2	Festival of Transport	Highclere Castle, Berkshire (01635 253210)
7–9	Art in Clay	Hatfield House, Hertfordshire
7–9	Pembrokeshire Horticultural Society Summer Show	Picton Castle, Wales
8	Shakespeare play on the Lawns – 'Antony and Cleopatra'	Stourhead, Wiltshire
8	The 1998 Music and Fireworks Spectacular	Stanford Hall, Leics (01788 860250)
8–9	Rainbow Craft Fair	Grimsthorpe Castle, Lincolnshire
8–9	The National Show for Miniature Roses	The Gardens of the Rose, Hertfordshire
9	Gardens open for the National Garden Scheme	Cottesbrooke Hall, Northamptonshire (01604 505808)
9	Annual Dog Show	Tatton Park, Cheshire
10–30 Sept.	Annual Summer Opening of the State Rooms	Buckingham Palace, London
12	A Traditional style Highland Games	Dunrobin Castle, Sutherland, Scotland
14–15	Illyria- Open Air Shakespeare-Taming of the Shrew	The Vyne, Hampshire (01256 881337)
15	'Last Night at the Proms' Concert	Broadlands, Hampshire (01794 517888)
15	Concert in Stourhead Park	Stourhead, Wiltshire
15–16	Hampshire Flower Show	Broadlands, Hampshire (01794 517888)
15–16	MG Rally	Ripley Castle, N Yorkshire (01423 770152)
15–16	Chilli Fiesta	West Dean Gardens, W Sussex
15–16	Children's Activity Weekend	Weald & Downland Open Museum, Sussex
16	Summer Plant Fair	Pashley Manor Gardens, E Sussex
16	Vintage Car Rally	Dunrobin Castle, Sutherland, Scotland

17–21	Children's Fun Week	Eastnor Castle, Hereford & Worcester
18	Evening tour by the Head Gardener in the "Eucryphia Season"	Mount Usher Gardens, Ireland
21–24	Bowmore Blair Castle Horse Trials, International 3 Day Event	Blair Castle, Scotland (01796 481207)
22	Lesley Garrett in the Park & Fireworks	Hatfield House, Hertfordshire (0171 957 4041)
22	Courtyard Fair	Mapperton Gardens, Dorset
22–23	Rainbow Craft Fair	Arbury Hall, Warwickshire
22–23	Antiques Fair	Elton Hall, Cambridgeshire
22–26	Then & Now- 1958 joins 1998 for the Hall's 4 Centenary celebrations	Burton Agnes Hall, E Yorkshire
23	Jaguar Car Rally	Highclere Castle, Berkshire
23	Classic Car Event	Lulworth Castle, Dorset
24	St John Fun Day	Grimsthorpe Castle, Lincolnshire (01778 591205)
29–31	Historical Re-enactment by The Red Wyvern Society	Appleby Castle, Cumbria (Enq 017683 51402)
29–31	Craft Fair	Blenheim Palace, Oxfordshire
29–31	Craft Fair	Highclere Castle, Berkshire (01635 253210)
29–31	The Medieval Weekend	Warwick Castle, Warwickshire
30	MG Rally	Holker Hall, Cumbria (015395 58328)
30–31	Victorian Fun Day	Hawkstone Historic Park, Shropshire (01939 200611)
30–31	'Flowers at Syon' Spectacular floral displays within Syon House	Syon Park, London (0181 560 0881)
30–31	International Horse Trials	Highclere Castle, Berkshire (01635 253210)

SEPTEMBER

5–6	Autojumble & Automart	Beaulieu, Hampshire (01590 612624)
5–6	Rainbow Craft Fair	Newby Hall, N Yorkshire
5–6	Autumn Gardening Show	Tonbridge Castle Lawn, Kent (01732 357872)
6	Charities Day	Mannington Hall, Norfolk
6	Horticultural and Craft Show	Dyffryn Gardens, Wales
10–13	Blenheim International Vauxhall Horse Trials	Blenheim Palace, Oxfordshire
11–13	Country Lifestyle Fair	Hatfield House, Hertfordshire (01494 450504)
11–13	Patchwork and Quilting Exhibition	Hever Castle, Kent
11–14	Torre Abbey Flower Festival	Torre Abbey, Devon
12–13	Heritage Days	Grimsthorpe Castle, Lincolnshire (01778 591205)
12–14	Weald of Kent Craft Show	Penshurst Place, Kent (01892 870307)
18–20	The Great Autumn Rose Show	The Gardens of the Rose, Hertfordshire (Enq. 01727 850461)
19	Old Time Musical Hall Evening. Celebration of traditional Edwardian England	Clandon Park, Surrey (Enq 01372 451596
19–20	Dahlia Festival	Aylett Nurseries, Hertfordshire
19–20	Re-Opening of Goodwood Motor Circuit	Goodwood, West Sussex
19–20	Annual Plant Sale-FREE GARDEN ENTRY	Trebah Garden, Cornwall
19–20	Somerleyton Horse Trials	Somerleyton Hall, Suffolk
19–20	Wood Weekend	Tatton Park, Cheshire
24	Old Time Musical Hall Evening	Clandon Park, Surrey (Enq 01372 451596
26–27	Dahlia Festival	Aylett Nurseries, Hertfordshire

OCTOBER

October	'Ark in Action'- exhibition of animals in various media	Waterperry Gardens, Oxfordshire (01844 339226)
1–18	Special Exhibition, Linda Chiltern	Museum of Garden History, London
2–4	Special Needlework and Lace Exhibition	Blair Castle, Scotland (01796 481207)
3–4	Crafts at Stanford Hall	Stanford Hall, Leics (01788 860250)
3–4	Christmas Craft Fair	Eastnor Castle, Hereford & Worcester
4	Bridal Fair	Tatton Park, Cheshire
7	The Sincerest Form of Flattery-Burgundy vs. The New World	Clandon Park, Surrey (B/O 01483 222482)
10	Evening tour with Head Gardener & wine reception	Mount Usher Gardens, Ireland
11	Autumn Tour, 2pm	Thorp Perrow Arboretum, N Yorkshire
13–15	Robert Bailey Antiques Fair	Holker Hall, Cumbria (015395 58328)
15	Autumn Splendour & Covered Bazaar	High Beeches, W Sussex
18	Apple Day	West Dean Gardens, W Sussex
22	Thomson Roddick & Laurie Fine Art & Furniture Sale	Naworth Castle, Cumbria (016977 3229)
23–25	Antiques Fair	Deene Park, Northamptonshire
24	Decorations for Celebrations	Waddesdon Manor, Buckinghamshire (01296 651226)
24–25	Apple Day, tasting and traditional children's games	Waterperry Gardens, Oxfordshire (01844 339226)
24–25	Gifts & Crafts Fair	Lamport Hall, Northamptonshire (01604 686272)
24–1 Nov	Puritans, Daggers & Witchcraft	Warwick Castle, Warwickshire
31	Fireworks Fair	Beaulieu, Hampshire (01590 612624)
31–1 Nov	Glenfiddich World Piping Championships	Blair Castle, Scotland (01796 481207)
31–1 Nov	Stowe Christmas Craft, Gift & Food Fayre	Stowe Schools, Buckinghamshire (01280 813650)

NOVEMBER

Nov & Dec	'Fantasia'- exhibition of Russian boxes, silk textiles, porcelain and jewellery	Waterperry Gardens, Oxfordshire (01844 339226)
1	Autumn Tour,2pm	Thorp Perrow Arboretum, N Yorkshire
6	Charity Fireworks Display	Broadlands, Hampshire (01794 517888)
6–8	Christmas Food & Gift Fair	Loseley Park, Surrey
7	Grand Fireworks Spectacular	Leeds Castle, Kent
14–15	Christmas Craft Fair	Broadlands, Hampshire (01794 517888)
15–5 Jan	Christmas Tours in the evening with carols, hot pies & punch	Penhow Castle, Gwent, Wales
27–29	Live Crafts	Loseley Park, Surrey
28–29	Avoncroft Craft Show	Avoncroft Museum, Hereford & Worcester

DECEMBER

4–6	Christmas Fair	Highclere Castle, Berkshire (01635 253210)
5–6	Santa Claus Weekends	Tower Bridge Experience, London (0171 403 3761)
5–6	Christmas Craft Festival	Duncombe Park, Yorkshire
6–13	Christmas Days & Evenings at Arley	Arley Hall, Cheshire (01565 777284)
8–13	Candlelight Tours of the Mansion	Tatton Park, Cheshire
11	Christmas at Stourhead	Stourhead, Wiltshire
12–24	Christmas at the Castle	Leeds Castle, Kent
13–15	Phillips Fine Art Sale	Powderham Castle, Devon

Appleby Castle, Cumbria

Beaulieu, Hampshire

Waterperry Gardens, Oxfordshire

Claim Your Free Privilege Card

And benefit from...

- 10% Discount
- A room upgrade (when available)
- VIP Service

at selected Johansens Recommended Hotels, Country Houses and Inns, in Great Britain, Ireland and also Europe. Participating places are listed at the back of each corresponding guide.

ALSO get special deals at selected Historic Houses, Castles and Gardens establishments. Participating places feature the Symbol 🏷

Yes, I would like to receive my free Privilege Card.

Return this coupon Freepost to Johansens, FREEPOST (CB264), 43 Millharbour, London E14 9BR

Name --

Address --

Postcode --

See page 246 for more information on Johansens Guides and CD ROMS

Order Coupon

save £10

To order Johansens guides, simply indicate which publications you require by putting the quantity(ies) in the boxes provided. Choose you preferred method of payment and return this coupon (NO STAMP REQUIRED). You may also place your order using FREEPHONE 0800 269397 or by fax on 0171 251 6113.

❏ I enclose a cheque for £_____ payable to Johansens.

❏ I enclose my order on company letterheading, please invoice me. (UK companies only)

❏ Please debit my credit/charge card account (please tick)

❏ MASTERCARD ❏ VISA ❏ DINERS ❏ AMEX ❏ SWITCH

Switch Issue Number ☐

Card No ☐☐☐☐

Signature _____ Expiry Date _____

Name (Mr/Mrs/Miss) _____

Address_____

_____ Postcode _____

(We aim to despatch your order within 10 days, but please allow 28 days for delivery)

Post free to: Johansens, FREEPOST (CB264), 43Millharbour, London E14 9BR

Occasionally we may allow reputable organisations to write to you with offers which may interest you. If you prefer not to hear from them, tick this box ❏

	PRICE	QTY	TOTAL
The Collection of 4 Johansens Guides + Recommended Hotels & Inns – North America FREE £53.80	£43.80		
The Collection in a Presentation Boxed Set £58.80 + Recommended Hotels & Inns – N. America FREE	£48.80		
The 2 CD ROMS £49.90	£39.00		
Recommended Hotels – Great Britain & Ireland 1998	£18.95		
Recommended Country Houses and Small Hotels – GB & Ireland 1998	£10.95		
Recommended Inns with Restaurants – GB & Ireland 1998	£9.95		
Recommended Hotels – Europe 1998	£13.95		
Recommended Hotels – North America 1998	£9.95		
Historic Houses Castles & Gardens	£6.95		
CD ROM – Hotels, Country Houses & Inns Great Britain & Ireland 1998 with Historic Houses Castles & Gardens	£29.95		
CD ROM – Recommended Hotels & Inns N. America and Recommended Hotels Europe 1998	£19.95		
1998 Privilege Card – 10% discount, room upgrade when available. VIP Service at participating establishments	FREE		
The Independent Traveller – Johansens newsletter including many special offers	FREE		
Postage & Packing UK: £4 – or £2 for single orders and CD-Roms Outside UK: Add £5 – or £3 for single orders and CD-Roms			
	TOTAL £		

CALL THE JOHANSENS CREDIT CARD ORDER SERVICE FREE ☎ **0800 269397**

PRICES VALID UNTIL 31/12/98 2J1

Order Coupon

save £10

To order Johansens guides, simply indicate which publications you require by putting the quantity(ies) in the boxes provided. Choose you preferred method of payment and return this coupon (NO STAMP REQUIRED). You may also place your order using FREEPHONE 0800 269397 or by fax on 0171 251 6113.

❏ I enclose a cheque for £_____ payable to Johansens.

❏ I enclose my order on company letterheading, please invoice me. (UK companies only)

❏ Please debit my credit/charge card account (please tick)

❏ MASTERCARD ❏ VISA ❏ DINERS ❏ AMEX ❏ SWITCH

Switch Issue Number ☐

Card No ☐☐☐☐

Signature _____ Expiry Date _____

Name (Mr/Mrs/Miss) _____

Address_____

_____ Postcode _____

(We aim to despatch your order within 10 days, but please allow 28 days for delivery)

Post free to: Johansens, FREEPOST (CB264), 43Millharbour, London E14 9BR

Occasionally we may allow reputable organisations to write to you with offers which may interest you. If you prefer not to hear from them, tick this box ❏

	PRICE	QTY	TOTAL
The Collection of 4 Johansens Guides + Recommended Hotels & Inns – North America FREE £53.80	£43.80		
The Collection in a Presentation Boxed Set £58.80 + Recommended Hotels & Inns – N. America FREE	£48.80		
The 2 CD ROMS £49.90	£39.00		
Recommended Hotels – Great Britain & Ireland 1998	£18.95		
Recommended Country Houses and Small Hotels – GB & Ireland 1998	£10.95		
Recommended Inns with Restaurants – GB & Ireland 1998	£9.95		
Recommended Hotels – Europe 1998	£13.95		
Recommended Hotels – North America 1998	£9.95		
Historic Houses Castles & Gardens	£6.95		
CD ROM – Hotels, Country Houses & Inns Great Britain & Ireland 1998 with Historic Houses Castles & Gardens	£29.95		
CD ROM – Recommended Hotels & Inns N. America and Recommended Hotels Europe 1998	£19.95		
1998 Privilege Card – 10% discount, room upgrade when available. VIP Service at participating establishments	FREE		
The Independent Traveller – Johansens newsletter including many special offers	FREE		
Postage & Packing UK: £4 – or £2 for single orders and CD-Roms Outside UK: Add £5 – or £3 for single orders and CD-Roms			
	TOTAL £		

CALL THE JOHANSENS CREDIT CARD ORDER SERVICE FREE ☎ **0800 269397**

PRICES VALID UNTIL 31/12/98 2J1

Index to Properties

Indexes

Indexes

Indexes

Key to Map Pages

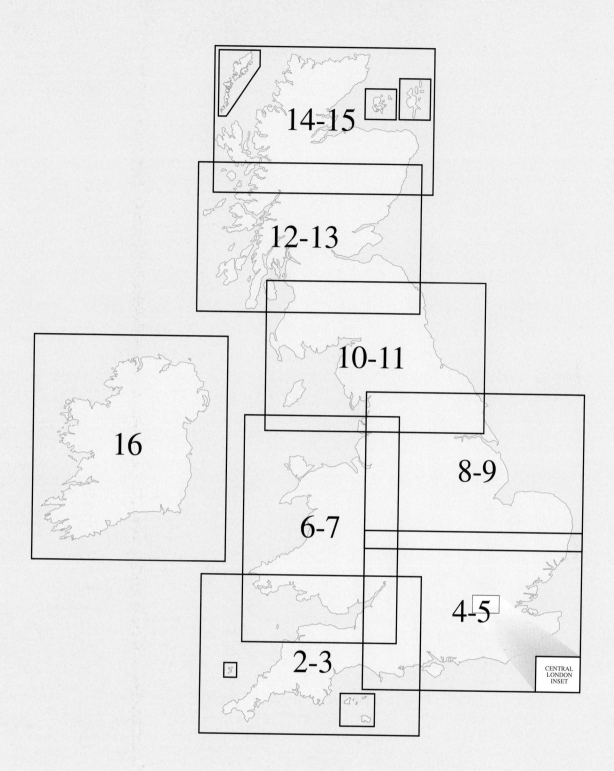

14-15

12-13

10-11

16

8-9

6-7

2-3

4-5

CENTRAL
LONDON
INSET

Key to Map Symbols

M62 12	Motorway		♯	Property in the care of English Heritage		🏠	House with or without garden
A55	Primary Route		🍀	Property in the care of The National Trust		🏰	Castle with or without garden
	A Roads						
	B Roads			Property in the care of The National Trust for Scotland		❀	Garden

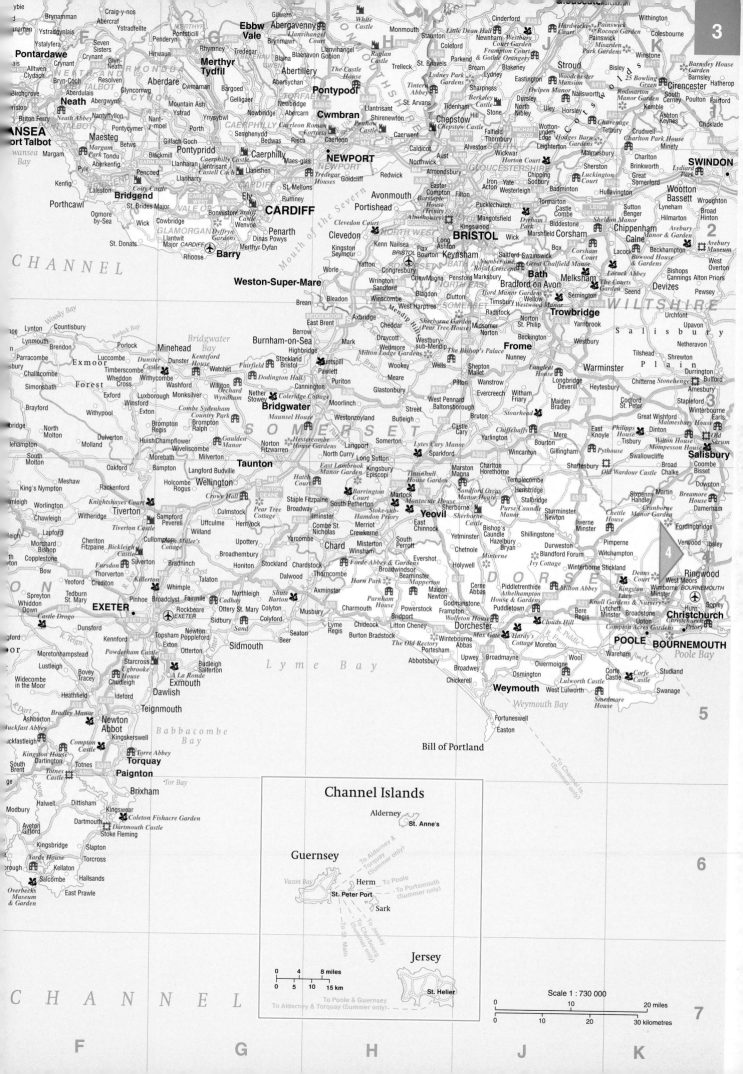

4

Amblecote
Kinver
Stourbridge
Halesowen
Kidderminster
Harrington Hall
Catshill
Kings Norton
Solihull
Knowle
Baddesley Clinton
Kenilworth Castle
BIRMINGHAM
Birmingham Botanical Gardens
Meriden
Coventry Cathedral
COVENTRY
Rugby
Fillongley
Bedworth
Wolvey
Ansty
Paulton
Brinklow
Ullesthorpe
Gilmorton
Lutterworth
Stanford Hall
Swinford
Husbands Bosworth
North Kilworth
Welford
Market Harborough
Kelmarsh Hall & Gardens
Rothwell
Lamport Hall & Gardens
Broughton
Desborough
Geddington
Kettering
Thrapston
Great Gidding
Sawtry

Bewdley
Hartlebury Castle
Chaddesley Corbett
Bromsgrove
Alvechurch
Packwood House
Kenilworth
Warwick Castle
Warwick
Dorridge
Baddesley Clinton
Coventry Airport
Dunchurch
Kilsby
Crick
Yelvertoft
Naseby
Cottesbrooke Hall & Gardens
Coton Manor Garden
Lamport
Holdenby House Gardens
Wellingborough
Rushden
Higham Ferrers
Irchester
Swineshead
Raunds
Grafham Water
Kimbolton Castle
Great Staughton
Spaldwick
Huntingdon

Clows Top
Stourport-on-Severn
Witley Court
Hanbury Hall
Stoke Prior
Redditch
Henley-in-Arden
Lord Leycester Hospital
Wootton Wawen
Claverdon
Snitterfield
Royal Leamington Spa
Southam
Daventry
Princethorpe
Long Buckby
Althorp Park
Weedon Bec
Stony Stratford
NORTHAMPTON
Castle Ashby
Bozeat
Harrold
Sharnbrook
Broadfields

Clifton upon Teme
Droitwich
Astwood Bank
Feckenham
Inkberrow
Alcester
The Shakespeare Birthplace Trust
Stratford-upon-Avon
Wellesbourne
Charlecote Park
Kineton
Farnborough Hall
Upton House
Cropredy
Canons Ashby House
Byfield
Woodford Halse
Charwelton
Blisworth
Roade
Cowper & Newton Museum
Olney
Turvey
Bedford
Cardington
Great Barford
Biggleswade

Worcester
Worcester Cathedral
Spetchley Park
Hillier Garden
Bishampton
Crowle
Powick
Pershore
Defford
Bredon
Ashton under Hill
Broadway
Snowshill Manor
Blockley
Blockley Gardens
Chipping Campden
Mickleton
Hidcote Manor Garden
Honington Hall
Middle Tysoe
Halford
Shipston on Stour
Tidmington
Long Compton
Broughton Castle
Banbury
Swalcliffe
Hook Norton
Bloxham
Deddington
Aynho
Aynhoe Park
King's Sutton
Croughton
Brackley
Beachampton
Buckingham
Stowe Landscape Gardens
Stowe (Stowe School)
Padbury
Steeple Claydon
Winslow Hall
Winslow
Great Brickhill
MILTON KEYNES
Bletchley
Woburn
Woburn Abbey
Woburn Sands
Milton Bryan
Toddington
Wrest Park House & Gardens
Flitwick
Clophill
Shillington
Ampthill
Ridgmont
Barton-le-Clay

Great Malvern
Little Malvern Court & Gardens
Malvern Link
Kempsey
Upton upon Severn
Welland
Eastnor
Staunton
Newent
Tewkesbury
Bredon
Leigh
Willersey
Sezincote
Stanway House
Snowshill Manor
Great Wolford
Great Tew
Enstone
Lower Heyford
Rousham House
Middleton Stoney
Ardley
Bicester
Stratton Audley
Marsh Gibbon
North Marston
Claydon House
Whitchurch
Wing
Linslade
Leighton Buzzard
Wingrave
Mentmore
Ivinghoe
Aston Abbotts
Aston Clinton
Dagnall
Whipsnade
Dunstable
Harpenden
Redbourn
Wheathampstead
LUTON
Knebworth
Luton Airport

Eastnor
Little Malvern
Upton upon Severn
Ashton under Hill
Bishop's Cleeve
Sudeley Castle
Guiting Power
Stow-on-the-Wold
Whittington Court
Bledington
Bourton-on-the-Water
Chipping Norton
Charlbury
Ditchley Park
Kirtlington
Charlton-on-Otmoor
Waddesdon Manor
Brill
Oakley
Long Crendon
Nether Winchendon House
Haddenham
Stone
Wendover
Ashridge
Berkhamsted
Gorhambury
St. Albans Cathedral

Gloucester
Gloucester & Cheltenham Airport
Churchdown
Cheltenham
Charlton Kings
Withington
Chedworth Roman Villa
Colesbourne
Northleach
Aldsworth
Burford
Witney
Ducklington
Eynsham
Leafield
Bladon
Blenheim Palace
Woodstock
Kidlington
Islip
Stanton St. John
Waterperry Gardens
Thame
Tetsworth
Chinnor
Stokenchurch
Princes Risborough
Hampden Manor House
Great Missenden
Chesham
Little Missenden
Chenies Manor House
The Gardens of the Rose
Amersham
Chalfont St. Giles
Chiltern Open Air Museum
Hemel Hempstead
Watford
Rickmansworth
HARROW
Uxbridge

Huntley
Hardwicke Court
Painswick Rococo Garden
Painswick
Stroud
Woodchester Mansion
Misarden Park Gardens
Bisley
Winstone
Barnsley House Garden
Barnsley
Bibury
Hatherop
Fairford
Lechlade
Kelmscott Manor
Buscot Old Parsonage
Buscot Park
Faringdon
Bampton
Stanton Harcourt
Cumnor
OXFORD
University of Oxford Botanic Garden
Wheatley
Stadhampton
Dorchester
Benson
Ewelme
Princes Risborough
West Wycombe Park (1750)
High Wycombe
Stonor Park
Beaconsfield
Marlow
Bourne End
Stoke Poges
SLOUGH
Iver
Pitshanger Manor Museum
Southall Acton

Eastington
Owlpen Manor
Uley
North Nibley
Wotton-under-Edge
Leighterton
Horsley
Nailsworth
Rodmarton Manor Garden
Woodchester Mansion
Cirencester
Poulton
South Cerney
Cricklade
Ashton Keynes
Minety
Purton
Highworth
Buckland
East Hanney
Steventon
Harwell
Didcot
Wallingford
Wallingford Castle Gardens
Cholsey
Woodcote
Goring
Nuffield Place
Greys Court
Mapledurham House & Watermill
Henley-on-Thames
Cookham
Cliveden
Wargrave
Maidenhead
Dorney Court
Eton College
Windsor
Windsor Castle
Windsor
Hounslow
Heathrow
Richmond

Yate
Chipping Sodbury
Badminton
Tormarton
Leigh Delamere
Great Somerford
Sutton Benger
Hullavington
Luckington Court
Chavenage
Tetbury
Malmesbury
Charlton Park House
Charlton
Brinkworth
Lydiard Park
SWINDON
Wanborough
Wroughton
Wootton Bassett
Broad Hinton
Lyneham
Hilmarton
Ashbury
Ashdown House
Lambourn
Baydon
Aldbourne
Ramsbury
Chaddleworth
Great Shefford
Chieveley
Yattendon
Welford Park
Pangbourne
Basildon Park
Theale
READING
Twyford
Wokingham
Bracknell
Ascot
Sunningdale
Staines
Egham
Savill Garden
Chertsey
Esher
Weybridge

Wick
Marshfield
Corsham
Dyrham Park
Castle Combe
Biddestone
Chippenham
Sheldon Manor
Avebury Manor & Garden
Avebury
Avebury Museum
Calne
Beckhampton
Bowood House & Gardens
West Overton
Marlborough
Froxfield
Great Bedwyn
Newbury
Shalbourne
Kintbury
Hungerford
Brimpton
Aldermaston
Thatcham
Burghfield
Tadley
Silchester
Swallowfield Park
Sherfield on Loddon
Stratfield Saye House
Mortimer
Crowthorne
Sandhurst
Bagshot
Camberley
Bisley
Pirbright
RHS Garden Wisley
Ripley
Windlesham
Chobham
Woking
Byfleet
Leatherhead
East Horsley

Bath
Number one, Royal Crescent
Great Chalfield Manor
Corsham Court
Box
Lacock
Lacock Abbey
Bishops Cannings
Devizes
Seend
Melksham
Bromham
The Courts Garden
Semington
Alton Priors
Pewsey
Burbage
East Grafton
Collingbourne Kingston
Ludgershall
Vernham Dean
Highclere Castle
Kingsclere
Hannington
Overton
Basing House Ruins
Basingstoke
The Vyne
Hartley Wintney
Sherfield
Hook
Odiham
Cliddesden
Crondall
Farnborough
Aldershot
Tongham
Worplesdon
Ash
Guildford
Guildford
Clandon Park
Dorking
Polesden Lacey

Trowbridge
Yarnbrook
Norton St. Philip
Westwood Manor
Iford Manor Gardens
Wellow
Westbury
Warminster
Heytesbury
Longbridge Deverill
Codford St. Peter
Upavon
Everleigh
Cholderton
Weyhill
Thruxton
Hurstbourne Tarrant
Andover
Whitchurch
Hurstbourne Priors
St Mary Bourne
Overton
Sutton Scotney
Micheldever
Preston Candover
Lasham
Alton
Bentley
Frensham
Millais Nurseries
Elstead
Farnham
Farnham Castle
Milford
Godalming
Winkworth Arboretum
Wonersh
Goddards
Cranleigh
Ewhurst
Horsham

Frome
Beckington
Nunney
Mells
Wanstrow
Longleat House
Maiden Bradley
Stourhead
Mere
Zeals
Chicklade
Tisbury
Hindon
Philipps House
Dinton
Old Sarum
Wilton House
Salisbury Plain
West Lavington
Tilshead
Shrewton
Chitterne
North Tidworth
Bulford
Amesbury
Stonehenge
Durrington
Middle Wallop
Stockbridge
King's Somborne
Houghton Lodge Gardens
Crawley
Easton
New Alresford
Bramdean House
Ropley
Chawton
Selborne
Gilbert White's House & Garden and the Oates Museum
Bordon
Liphook
Hollycombe Steam Collection
Liss
Haslemere
Northchapel

Wincanton
Gillingham
Shaftesbury
Hazelbury Bryan
Sturminster Newton
Marnhull
Iwerne Minster
Shillingstone
Pimperne
Chettle House
Cranborne Manor Garden
Verwood
Fordingbridge
Rockbourne
Breamore House & Gardens
Downton
Redlynch
West Wellow
Bramshaw
Romsey
Mottisfont Abbey Garden
Winchester
Braishfield
Twyford
Bishop's Waltham
Hinton Ampner Garden
West Meon
East Meon
Langley Boxwood Nursery
Meonstoke
Petersfield
South Harting
Cocking
Midhurst
Easebourne
Fittleworth
Pulborough
Washington

POOLE
BOURNEMOUTH
Compton Acre Gardens
Broadstone
Wimborne Minster
Kingston Lacy
Witchampton
Horton
Blandford Forum
Winterborne Stickland
Winterborne Kingston
Bere Regis
Lytchett Minster
Christchurch
Christchurch Priory
Hurn
Sopley
New Milton
Lymington
Brockenhurst
Lyndhurst
Beaulieu
Exbury Gardens
Fawley
Hythe
SOUTHAMPTON
Totton
Southampton Airport
Netley
Hamble
Botley
Wickham
Titchfield
Fareham
Porchester Castle
Gosport
PORTSMOUTH
Havant
Emsworth
Apuldram Roses
Chichester
Chichester Cathedral
Pallant House
Bosham
Goodwood
Denmans Garden
Arundel
Arundel Castle & Gardens
Littlehampton
Angmering
Bognor Regis
Worthing

Weymouth Bay
Puddletown
Hardy's Cottage
Moreton
Bovington
Wool
Wareham
Corfe Castle
Studland
Swanage
The Needles
The Needles Old Battery
Yarmouth
Freshwater
Totland
Brighstone
Brook
Shorwell
Godshill
Carisbrooke Castle
Newport
Cowes
East Cowes
Osborne House
Ryde
Seaview
St. Helens
Bembridge
Sandown
Shanklin
Ventnor
St. Catherine's Point

South Downs
West Dean Gardens
Singleton
Weald and Downland Open Air Museum
Fishbourne Roman Palace
Mid Lavant
Selsey
Selsey Bill

To St. Malo (Summer only)
To Cherbourg
To Caen, Cherbourg, Le Havre.
St. Malo & Bilbao
Santander (winter only)

Isle of Wight

5

Numbered Sites Within the M25

1. Fenton House
2. Burgh House
3. Keats House
4. Kenwood, The Iveagh Bequest
5. Capel Manor
6. Rose Cottage
7. Sutton House
8. Hall Place
9. The Old Palace
10. Southside House
11. Royal Botanic Gardens, Kew
12. Syon House
13. Syon Park Gardens
14. Strawberry Hill
15. Marble Hill House
16. Ham House
17. Hampton Court Palace
18. Osterley Park
19. Boston Manor
20. Claremont Landscape Garden
21. Claremont
22. Painshill Park
23. 2 Willow Road

Central London Inset

Scale 1 : 730 000

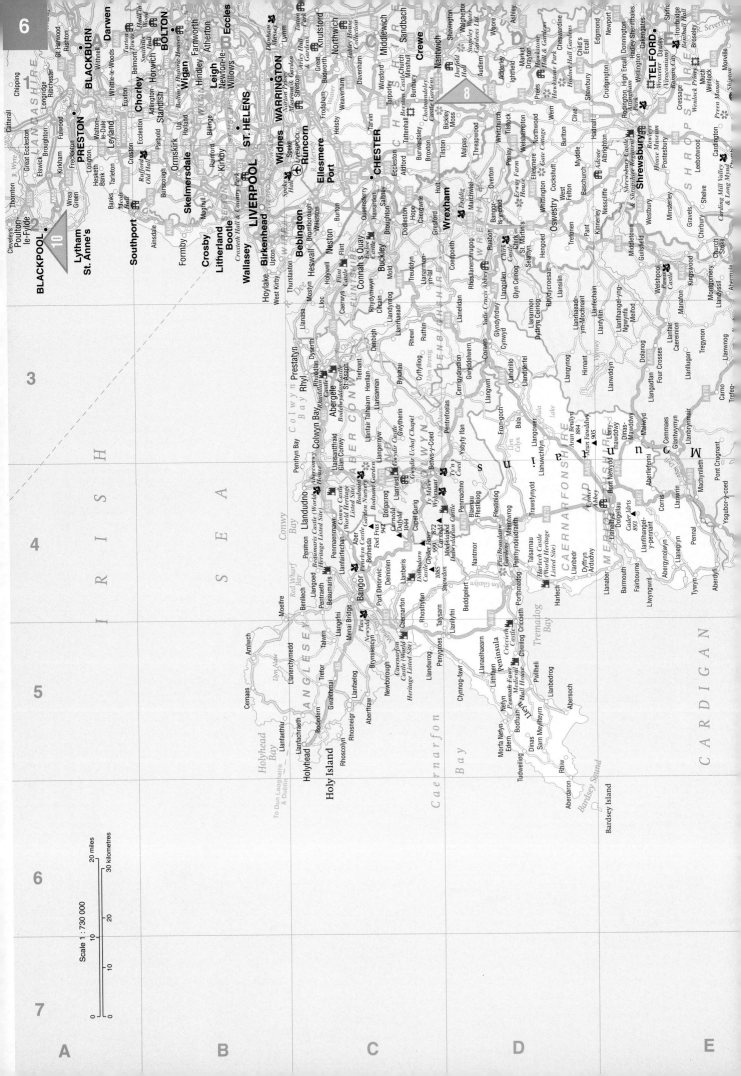

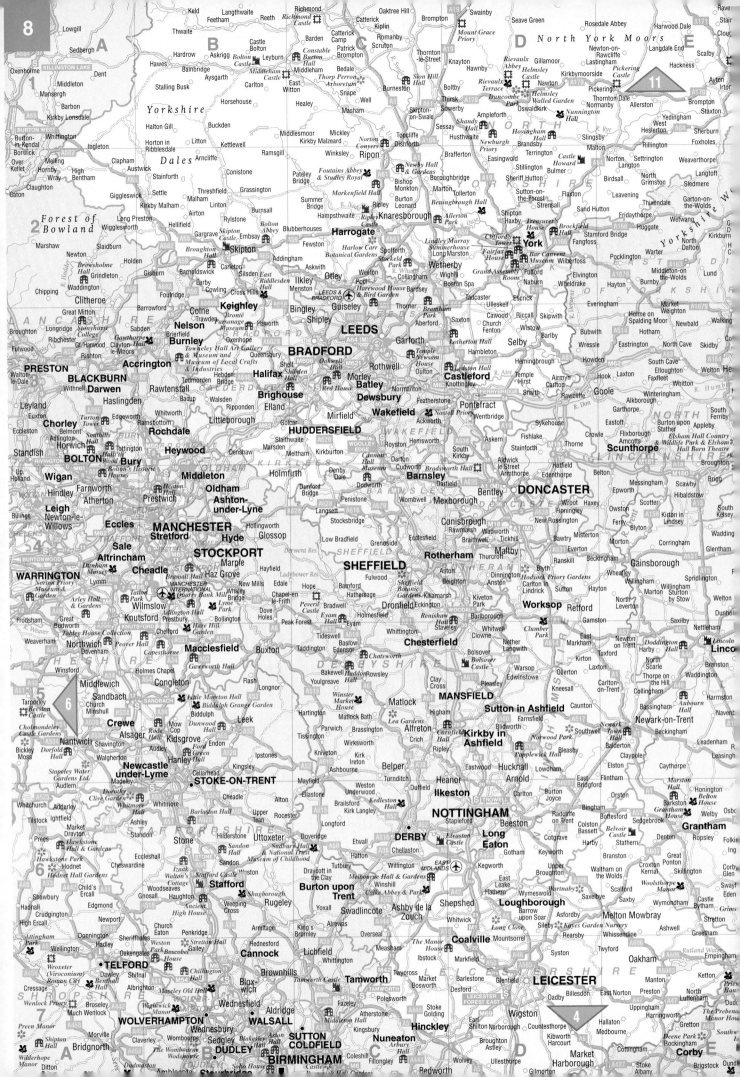

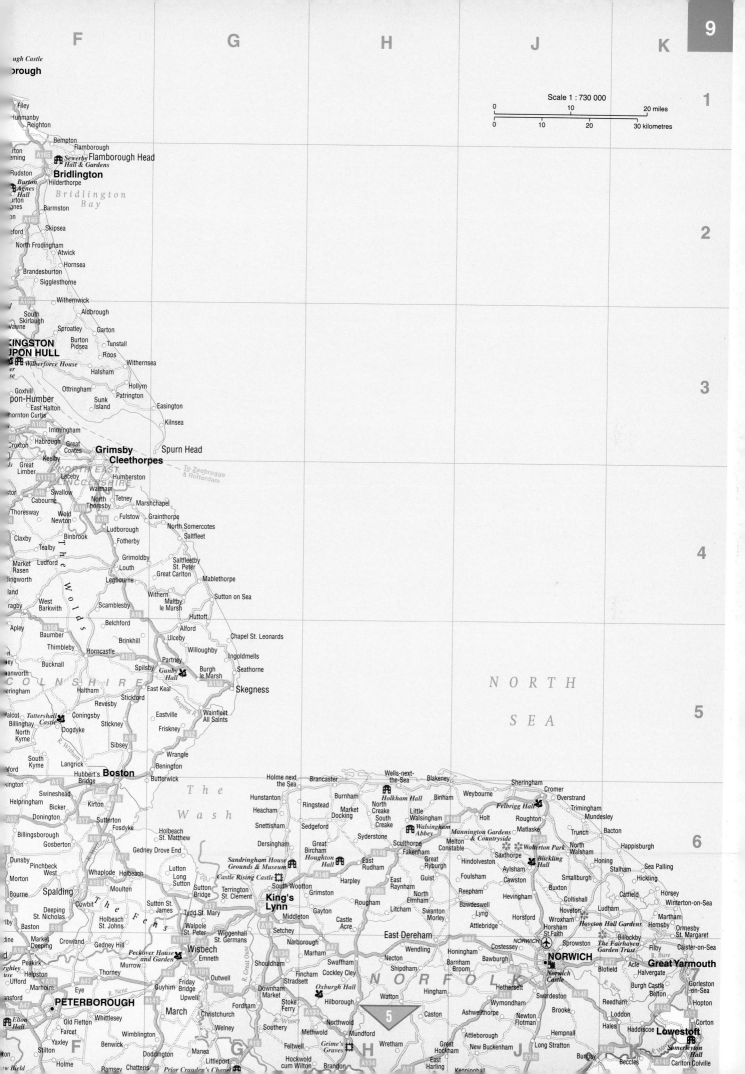

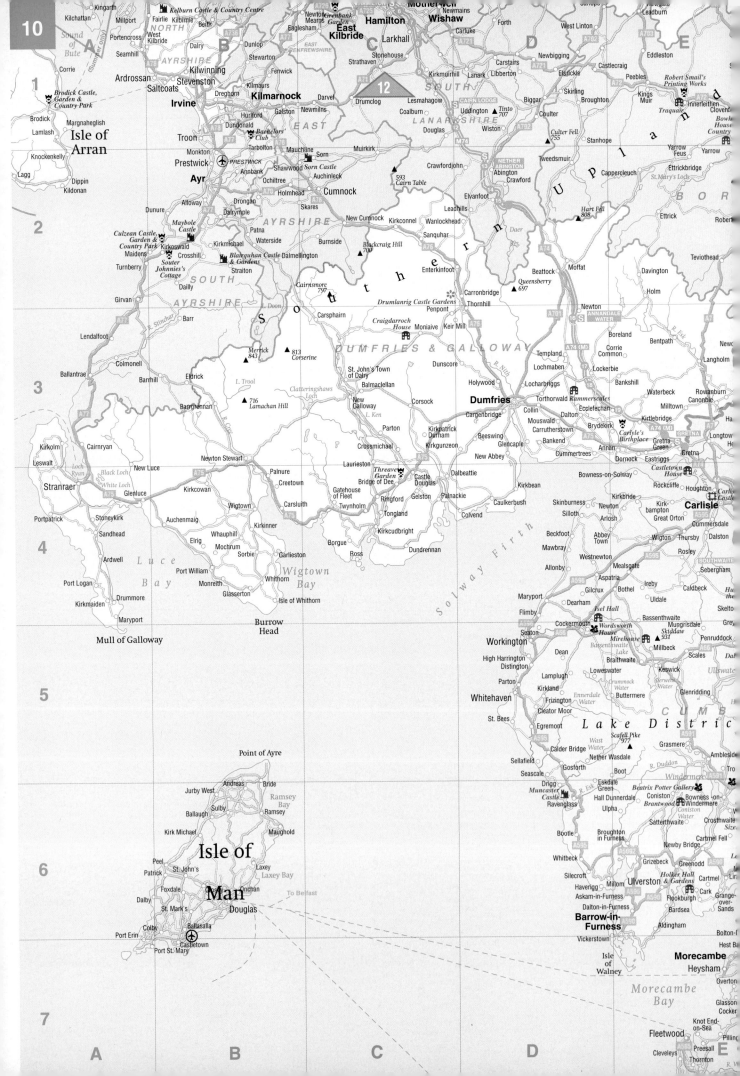

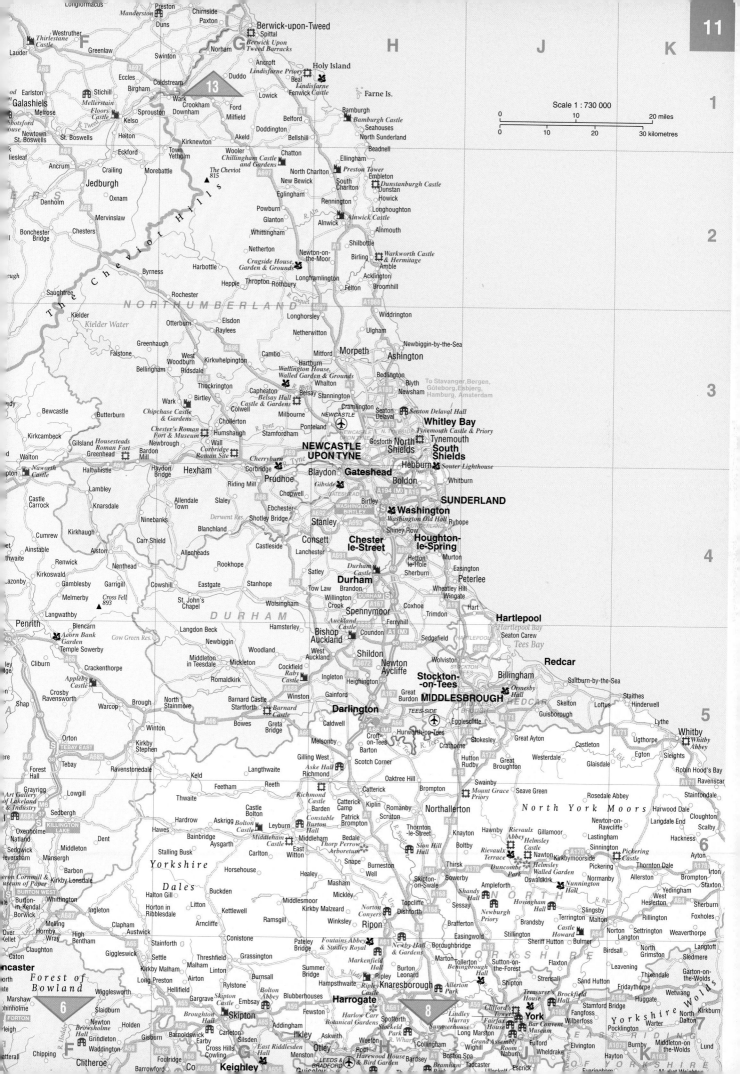

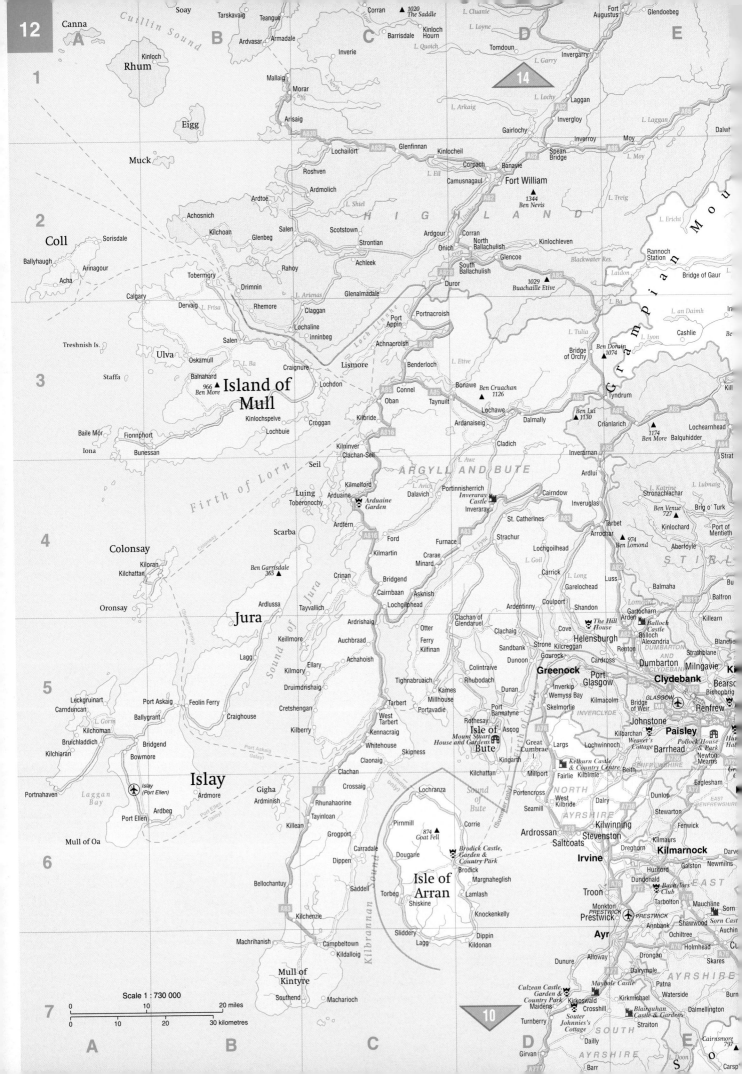

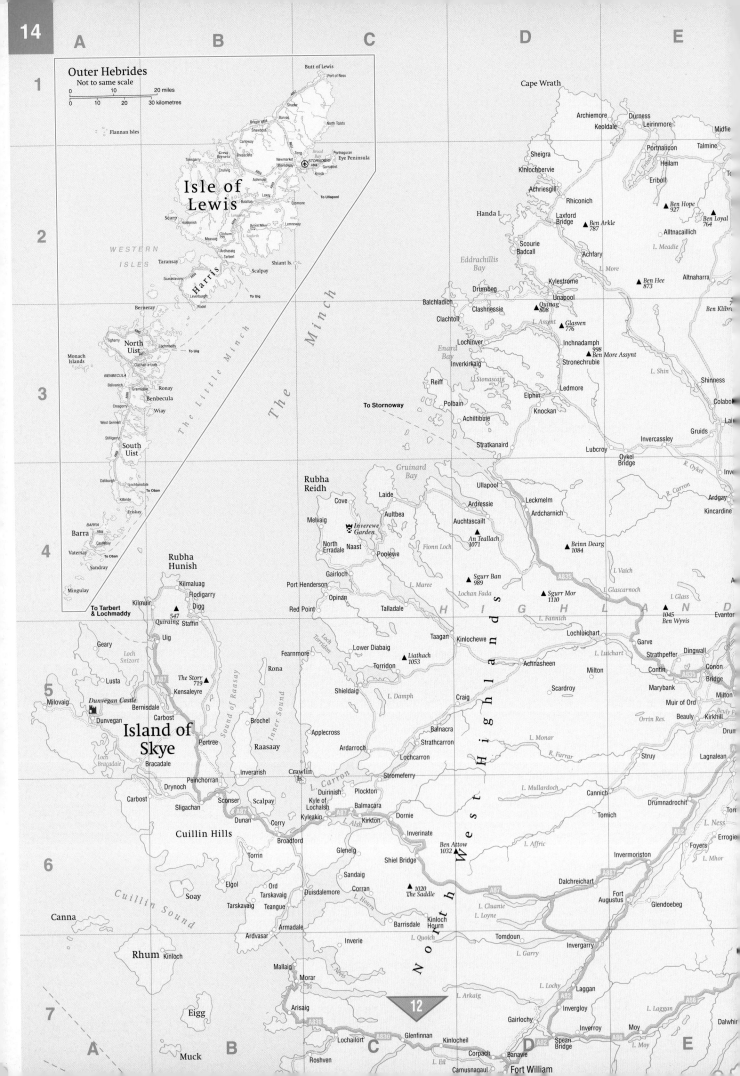

A   B   C   D   E

1

Outer Hebrides
Not to same scale

0   10   20 miles
0   10   20   30 kilometres

Flannan Isles

Butt of Lewis
Port of Ness
North Tolsta
Shader
Barvas
Bragar
Carloway
Shawbost
Newmarket
Stornoway   STORNOWAY
Tong   Broad   Portnaguran
Bay   Eye Peninsula
Garrabost
Knock

Tinsgarry
Great
Bernera
Breasclete
Achmore
Laxay
Balallan   Cromore
Isle of
Lewis
Scarp   Hushinish
Mealista   Benn Mhor
772   Clisham
799
Seaforth   Lemreway

2

WESTERN
ISLES
Taransay
Scalpay
Shiant Is.
Ardhasaig
Tarbert
Scaristavore   **Harris**
Leverburgh   Rodel
To Uig

To Ullapool

Cape Wrath

Archiemore   Durness
Keoldale   Leirinmore   Midfie
Sheigra   Portnancon   Heilam   Talmine
Kinlochbervie   Eriboll
Achriesgill   Rhiconich   ▲ Ben Hope   ▲ Ben Loyal
Handa I.   Laxford   927   764
Bridge   ▲ Ben Arkle   Alltnacaillich
787
Scourie   Achfary
Badcall   L. Meadie
*Eddrachillis   ▲ Ben Hee   Altnaharra
Bay*   Kylestrome   873
Drumbeg   Unapool   Ben Klibre
Balchladich   ▲ Quinag
Clashnessie   808   L. More
Clachtoll   ▲ Glasven   Ben Klibr
L. Assynt   776
Lochinver   Inchnadamph   Colabo
*Enard   998   L. Shin
Bay*   ▲ Ben More Assynt   Lai
Reiff   Inverkirkaig   Stronechrubie   Shinness
L. Sionascaig   Ledmore   Colabol
Polbain   Elphin   Invercassley   Lai
Achiltibuie   Knockan   Gruids
Stratkanaird   Lubcroy   Oykel   R. Oykel   Inve
Bridge

3

Monach
Islands
Tigharry
North   Lochmaddy
Uist   To Uig
Clachan-a-Luib
BENBECULA
Balivanich
Gramsdale   Ronay
Creagorry   Benbecula   Wiay
West Geirinish
Stilligarry
South
Uist
Daliburgh   Lochboisdale
Kilbride   To Oban
Eriskay

The Little Minch

The Minch

To Stornoway

To Uig

4

BARRA
Barra
Castlebay
Vatersay
Eriskay
Sandray

Mingulay

To Tarbert
& Lochmaddy

Rubha
Hunish

Rubha
Hunish
Kilmaluag
Flodigarry
Kilmuir   Digg
Kilmuir   547
Quiraing   Staffin

Rubha
Reidh
Cove
Melvaig   Laide
Aultbea
Inverewe
Garden
North   Naast   Poolewe
Erradale
Gairloch   Fionn Loch
Port Henderson   An Teallach   ▲ Beinn Dearg
Opinan   1071   1084
Red Point   Talladale   ▲ Sgurr Ban   ▲ Sgurr Mor
989   1110
Lochan Fada   L Glass
1045
HIGHL   Ben Wyvis   AND   Evantor

Gruinard
Bay
Ullapool
Ardressie   Leckmelm
Auchtascailt   Ardcharnich

5

Milovaig
Dunvegan Castle
Dunvegan   Bernisdale
Carbost
Portree

Lusta
Geary
Uig
The Storr   Kensaleyre
719
Loch
Snizort
Island of
Skye
Bracadale   Brochel
Loch   Carbost
Bracadale   Peinchorran   Inverarish
Drynoch   Crawlin
Carbost   Is.

Rona

Sound of Raasay

Inner Sound
Applecross

Fearnmore
Rona
Lower Diabaig   ▲ Liathach
Torridon   1053
Loch
Torridon   Taagan   Kinlochewe
Shieldaig   Craig
L. Damph   Scardroy
Balnacra
Strathcarron   L. Monar
Lochcarron   R. Farrar
Stromeferry   L. Mullardoch

Achnasheen   Lochluichart
Milton   L. Luichart
Garve   Strathpeffer   Dingwall
Contin   Conon
A835   Bridge
Marybank   Milton
Muir of Ord   Milton
Orrin Res.   Beauly   Kirkhill
Struy   Cannich   R. Beauly   Drum
Drumnadrochit
Tomich   L. Ness
Lagnalean

6

Cuillin
Sound
Soay
Elgol
Torrin
Ord
Tarskavaig
Teangue

Canna

Cuillin
Cuillin Hills

Sligachan
Dunan   Corry
Broadford
Sconser   Scalpay
Kyleakin

Duirinish   Plockton
Kyle of   Balmacara
Lochalsh   Kirkton   Dornie
Kyleakin   L. Alsh   Inverinate
L. Carron   Stromeferry
Glenelg   Ben Attow   L. Affric
1032
Shiel Bridge   ▲ 1020
The Saddle   L. Cluanie
Sandaig   L. Loyne
Corran
Duisdalemore   L. Hourn   Barrisdale   Kinloch
Hourn

West Highlands

North West Highlands

Invermoriston
Foyers   Errogie
L. Mhor
Dalchreichart
Fort   Glendoebeg
Augustus

7

Rhum   Kinloch

Eigg

Mallaig
Morar
Arisaig   L. Nevis

Ardvasar
Armadale
Inverie
Barrisdale

▼ 12

L. Quoich   Tomdoun   Invergarry   L. Garry
Gairlochy
Inverroy   Moy   Dalwhir
L. Lochy   Laggan   A86
Spean   Invergloy   L. Laggan
Bridge   A82   L. Moy

Muck
Roshven
Lochailort   Glenfinnan   Kinlocheil   Corpach   Banavie
A830   L. Eil   Camusnagaul   **Fort William**
Kinlochmoidart   L. Arkaig

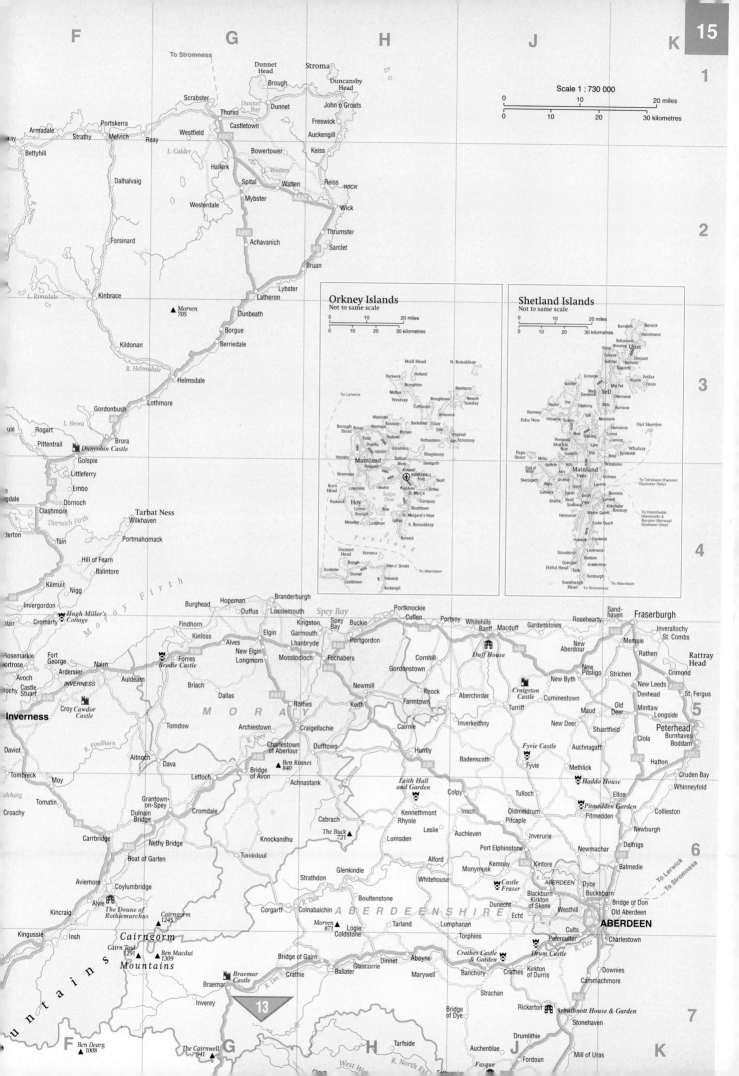

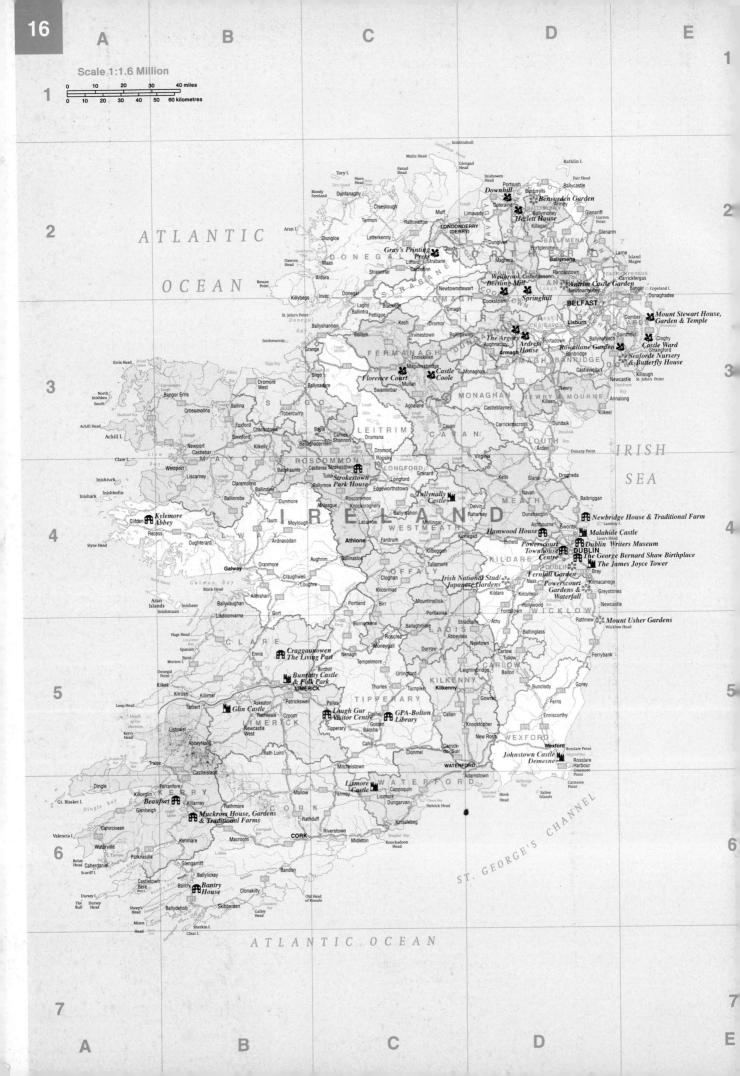